government of Francisco Franco. And when he composed or conducted he used his musical genius not simply to make sublime music but, as a self-proclaimed "militant of music," to further the cause of world peace and nuclear disarmament.

From the small Catalan village where Casals was born in 1876 to the Royal Palace of Madrid, the salons of Paris and London, perilous tours of the American West and South America, Casals' story is of a prodigious rise from total obscurity to worldwide fame. In the course of his lifetime, his friends included kings, queens, philosophers, and some of this century's most renowned composers and musicians—among them Saint-Saëns, Rachmaninoff, Ysaÿe, Paderewski, Fritz Kreisler, Rudolf Serkin, and many others.

The astoundingly long and successful life of Pablo Casals is set forth here in a definitive biography. Drawing upon Casals' own recollections—of his impoverished childhood, his musical and political activities, his personal life—and his own extensive research, H. L. Kirk paints a vivid and sensitive portrait of a magnificently talented and courageous human being.

H. L. Kirk met Pablo Casals in 1960 and six years later began work on his biography. Mr. Kirk has worked as an editor and writer in New York City. He and his wife divide their time between Manhattan and a two-hundred-year-old farmhouse in Vermont.

PABLO
CASALS

Pablo Carlos Salvador Casals y Defilló,
photographed in Japan, 1961

PABLO CASALS

A BIOGRAPHY BY

H. L. KIRK

HOLT, RINEHART AND WINSTON
NEW YORK   CHICAGO   SAN FRANCISCO

Library of Congress Cataloging in Publication Data
Kirk, H. L.
Pablo Casals.
Discography: p.
Bibliography: p.
1. Casals, Pablo, 1876–1973
ML418.C4K6   787'.3'0924 [B]   72-91569
ISBN 0-03-007616-1

First Edition
Designer: Betty Binns
Printed in the United States of America

Grateful acknowledgment is made to the following for permission to reprint material from their publications: *The
Boston Globe* for an excerpt from "The Magic of Pablo
Casals" by Herbert Kenny, which first appeared in the August
7, 1970, morning edition. Holt, Rinehart and Winston, Inc.
for an excerpt from *Rise to Follow* by Albert Spalding.
Copyright 1943 by Holt, Rinehart and Winston, Inc. Copyright © 1971 by Mary Pyle Spalding. *Music and Letters* for
an excerpt from "Casals as Conductor" by Sir Adrian Boult,
which first appeared in 1923.

See pp. 671–73, which are an extension of this page.

Contents

[v]

To Ruth Chapman Kirk

SIN QUIEN NO

Preface

FROM MY FIRST encounter with Pablo Casals, at his home in Puerto Rico in March 1960, I was charmed by the man, fascinated by the musician, and interested in the legend that surrounded him. I saw him often, in formal and informal circumstances, during the next few years, but only after an invitation from Columbia Records to make *Casals: A Living Portrait* did I begin systematically to study his life. By the time that album was issued at the end of 1966 for his ninetieth birthday, I was engrossed in tracing Casals' development, his associations with many of the important artistic figures of the late nineteenth and early twentieth centuries, and the changing world of his career as professional musician, which by 1966 had covered nearly eighty-five years.

I realized that the wealth of his extraordinary memory could easily be lost, yet he insisted that he would not write an autobiography. When he expressed willingness for me to undertake an extensive biography and offered his cooperation, I was naturally delighted and set to work at once, soon to find myself immersed in and intrigued by the world in which Casals was born and lived his formative years. Only gradually did I understand the full challenge of trying to report even the major events and the trends of a full life that has extended through nearly a century.

Clues and facts came from conversations and correspondence with people who have known or observed Casals—and there is a magnetism about him that draws forth admiration, affection, and a readiness to cooperate from many extremely disparate personalities. But outside Casals' immediate orbit, as well as within it, the most striking and heartening experience for me through many more years of investigation and writing than I had expected has been the willingness of people throughout the world to assist. Of the several hundred people approached, no more than half a dozen failed to answer, and a truly astonishing number generously shared their own special knowledge in many areas, often simply in response to a minor question or at a friend's suggestion. My debt and appreciation for the assistance of many is suggested in the acknowledgments that begin on page 667, and in some cases in the notes that begin on page 627.

The search for documentation led to libraries in Europe and in many parts of the Americas. It was rewarded, sometimes quite unexpectedly, with illuminating material such as the collection of letters written by Casals to Julius Röntgen, now in The Hague; letters from Casals, Tovey, and others in the Trevelyan Papers at Trinity College, Cambridge; and documents of interest in the Reid Music Library in Edinburgh, the British Museum, and the Royal College of Music, London.

A research trip during the autumn of 1970 to some of the places Casals knew in Spain gave me the gratifying opportunity to discover Catalonia for myself but, more important, it revealed Casals' undiminished impact on his homeland. In the country from which he had been in exile for thirty-one years, it was clear that neither he nor his stand had been forgotten. People who had known him or whose families had been associated with him before the Civil War were lavishly helpful in the search for clarification of facets of Casals' life there. One realized that, beyond courtesy and friendliness, the assistance was above all an act of devotion, but in Catalonia even those who had never seen him made unusual efforts to be helpful on hearing the name Pau Casals. At the ancient mountainside monastery of Montserrat, by tradition the site of the castle of the Holy Grail, the monks proudly showed manuscripts of compositions Casals wrote for the abbey and diary entries, sketches, photographs—souvenirs of his visits there in the 1930s. During the evening Angelus the boys of Montserrat's five-century-old choir school customarily sing a *Salve Regina* by Casals. On the day my wife and I stood to listen in the huge, dark apse with its age-blackened wooden image of the Virgin above the high

Preface

altar, they also sang the most haunting of Casals' devotional music, *Nigra sum,* so we might tell El Mestre we had heard it in the basilica he had not seen for so long.

The research uncovered many things Casals had not thought about for years and some he had not known, but I had the benefit of his reactions and his remarkable memory throughout. Occasionally that memory did not confirm the facts as I had found them, but it proved rich, well-informed, and amazingly precise. We consulted often, by letter and face to face; there were conversations after rehearsals and concerts, during relaxed hours in Vermont, in the Casals' homes in Puerto Rico, at airports, in hotels. Between 1966 and 1972 Maestro and Señora Casals opened their archives to me, and they saw many results of the research as the work progressed. For their help and that of so many others I am most appreciative, although responsibility for fact, interpretation, and content must remain mine.

As this biography goes into composition, Pablo Casals is energetically in his ninety-seventh year. He continues to seek perfection in music, to proclaim human dignity, and to crusade for peace in a time of violence. This book chronicles what has gone before.

Halifax, Vermont
August 1973

On Monday afternoon, October 22, 1973, less than an hour after marking final corrections of the page proof for this book, I learned that Pablo Casals had died just before two o'clock in the Auxilio Mutuo Hospital in San Juan. Less than two months earlier he had returned home to Puerto Rico, deeply satisfied with his participation in the festival celebrating the twenty-fifth anniversary of the State of Israel (where for him one high point was conducting the Festival Youth Orchestra in a Mozart symphony, which he did, critic Paul Moor wrote, with "almost slashing forcefulness"). Before he left the Middle East he promised he would return to celebrate his hundredth birthday in Jerusalem.

Actively and happily until mid-September he enjoyed guests and made music each day, continuing plans for the next San Juan festival and working on a composition. On the night of September 17, playing dominos at a friend's house, he was struck by a heart attack but recovered sufficiently in two weeks to return home to his piano and cello. Lung congestion soon forced him into the hospital, where further complications beset him. Even there, when he could, he communicated with Marta about music and the future.

On the night that followed his death, his bronze casket rested in his Rio Piedras home. Close friends and relatives came to be with the young widow during the night's vigil. Musical colleagues—Eugene Istomin, who had been in San Juan for several days, and Alexander Schneider and cellist Leslie Parnas, who arrived from the mainland during the evening—played slow movements of trios Schneider and Istomin had performed privately many times with Casals, including Schubert and the Beethoven "Archduke." There had been music in the house up to the time Casals had to go to the hospital—Istomin had been the last to play for him—and the day before his death a tape machine was brought to his room so Casals could hear the music of Bach through earphones. There had to be music in the house when he came back, and Marta Casals asked his friends to play. Later in the evening, after the trios and brief words from a priest and a Spanish friend, Marta handed Istomin a sheet of music from which to accompany Olga Iglesias as she sang Casals' setting of a Catalan prayer.

The following morning the casket, covered with the flags of Catalonia and of Puerto Rico, was brought to lie in state in the rotunda of the Capitolio, seat of the island's legislature in Puerta de Tierra. Thousands from the island and those who had been able to arrive in time from outside came to offer final tribute. During the first of the five hours the catafalque stood in the Capitol, the Puerto Rico Symphony Orchestra played the funeral-march second movement of Beethoven's "Eroica," then—with the University chorus and Olga Iglesias as soprano soloist—two sections from Casals' *El Pessebre*, the "Tears of the Infant Jesus" and the concluding "Gloria." Later a quintet of musicians who had performed many times with the Maestro—Schneider, Parnas, violinist Jaime Laredo, violist Walter Trampler, clarinetist Harold Wright—played Mozart and Schubert, beginning with the slow movement of Mozart's clarinet quintet in A Major, which Casals had wished to be played at his funeral. The orchestra played the "Eroica" funeral march once more, and the casket was carried down the imposing Capitol steps to the hearse for the slow procession to the Church of Nuestra Señora de la Piedad in Isla Verde, where Casals and Marta Montañez had been married in August 1957.

Preface

During the progress from the Capitol to the church, past United States and Puerto Rican flags at half staff, crowds lined many portions of the route. Automobiles stopped in the opposing lanes of the thoroughfares; drivers and passengers dismounted to stand silently as Don Pablo passed the last time. Policemen saluted, workmen raised their caps as the cortege went by. Governor Rafael Hernandez Colón had proclaimed three days of official mourning throughout the island; he and his wife accompanied Marta Casals, and he served as a pallbearer at the church. The four elected governors of Puerto Rico—Casals' great friend Luis Muñoz Marín, Roberto Sanchez Vilella, Luis Ferré, and Hernandez Colón—met publicly for the first time as honor guard at the bier.

At the Piedad chapel, Luis Cardinal Aponte Martínez, who in earlier years celebrated Casals' birthdays there, said a simple requiem. Then, suddenly, came the sound of Casals' cello, his recording of "The Song of the Birds," his arrangement of the ancient Catalan cradle song that had become so completely associated with his art and his endeavors. He had ended many festivals with it; for years he played no other work in public, a continuing determined plea for peace and understanding and love. At that moment, the noble voice of Pablo Casals' cello commanded pause in the ceremony of the day, a last salutation, eloquent, profound, overwhelming.

He was buried nearby in the white-walled, sun-flooded Puerto Rico Memorial cemetery, as he had requested, in a grave within sight and sound of the beach along which he had walked so many mornings.

When Casals was ninety-three, I heard him say he believed that death is as natural as birth, and he regretted that his friends might be sad at his going. But such matters did not occupy him too often, or too long. The Pablo Casals I knew was the man who said to a large crowd standing in the rain at a Central Park concert four months before he died: "I am an old man, but in many senses a young man. And this is what I want you to be, young, young all your life, and to say things to the world that are true."

HLK

New York
October 31, 1973

1876–1899

1

AT THE END OF June 1971, six months before his ninety-fifth birthday, Pablo Casals returned for a tenth summer to the tranquil green country of southern Vermont and at once started preparation for the first two public concerts of that year's Marlboro Music Festival. He planned to remain until mid-August—conducting the festival orchestra, giving master classes in cello, practicing every morning, courteously receiving a persistent stream of visitors, resting when he could. He was also working to complete the choral hymn he and W. H. Auden had been invited to write for the United Nations; the music was needed by the end of the summer. For months the task had challenged and worried Casals, usually a rapid composer; the intricate rhythmic changes and mechanistic imagery of Auden's free verse were not a congenial idiom to a man who had grown up during the last quarter of the nineteenth century and whose own artistic disposition was the ordered complexity found in the music of Johann Sebastian Bach.

In the two weeks before his arrival in Marlboro he completed the fifteenth annual Festival Casals in Puerto Rico, his home since 1956 (conducting Mozart and part of his peace oratorio *El Pessebre* in a performance broadcast by television satellite). He left

Casals conducting the first orchestral rehearsal
for the fifteenth Festival Casals de Puerto Rico,
May 1971. The concertmaster is
Alexander Schneider.

next morning with his beautiful sixty-year-younger wife Marta and two close friends for a week of concerts and almost uninterrupted festivities in his honor at Guadalajara, Mexico. Then he traveled to New York, sleeping little during the night flight because he was fascinated by the change of moonlight on clouds and the sea. Two days later Casals' party drove to Great Barrington, Massachusetts, for the dedication of the library of the Albert Schweitzer Friendship House. (In the morning, although surrounded as usual in public by a group that included reporters and a television crew, Casals saw a piano, went to it instantly and played eloquently a Bach prelude as a private consecration of the place. Afterward he smoked his pipe while he watched films of the life of Schweitzer and the work of his hospital at Lambaréné. In the afternoon Casals spoke gently to a large audience in tribute to the Alsatian humanitarian-musician, suggesting that the moral impact of the doctor's life had been all-important and recalling that he had told his friend Schweitzer "Jesus Christ never wrote any books.") Casals and his wife continued their journey in cloudless late-afternoon sunshine, north through the Berkshires and the southern reach of Vermont's Green Mountains to the comfortable onetime farmhouse in Marlboro in which they habitually stayed.

Rudolf Serkin's notable music colony was a good place to glimpse Casals in the summer of his ninety-fifth year, far though it is from his Mediterranean birthplace, and for Casals infinitely calm in comparison to half a century of the demanding yet glamorous life of one of the most celebrated of virtuosos. Casals reveled in the lovely countryside, except when the weather turned damp and rainy for days—high humidity sapped him of energy all his life. He thrived on the Marlboro idea—a summer gathering of dedicated expert musicians who would make music for themselves and for the sake of music—proclaiming the place unique and recalling that the only thing he had ever seen like it was a musicians' camp near Kiev in 1906 or 1907. The press referred to him as Marlboro's resident summer idol and since 1960 the festival management had billed him as Special Guest, but Pablo Casals was a participant: at the end of the season two summers earlier Serkin reported that—counting rehearsal and performance times and master-class hours only—Casals had logged more participant time than any other individual artist at the Marlboro School of Music.

No one kept a record of the hours Casals put into his personal

On his way to Marlboro Casals stopped in Great Barrington, Massachusetts, for the dedication of the Albert Schweitzer Friendship House and library June 27, 1971. When he entered the library building he saw a piano and, oblivious of a television crewman, played the first prelude from Bach's Well-Tempered Clavier *as a personal tribute to Schweitzer's memory. On his way to the public dedication ceremonies Casals paused with library founder Erica Anderson, pianist Lili Kraus, and his wife Marta.*

preparation in 1971. Every morning—even with an eleven-o'clock orchestral rehearsal or master class—after shaving, he played a Bach prelude and fugue on piano, had breakfast, then took his violoncello through a stern regimen of technical exercises and a few difficult passages from the instrument's literature, followed by a complete Bach solo cello suite—his first invariable daily duty. Often weary when he finished, he rebounded quickly.

Except for his own practicing each day Pablo Casals did not prepare himself specially for his master classes, but before orchestral performances he went back to the scores as though approaching them for the first time. All his conducting career, which began seriously in the first years of the twentieth century, Casals returned to the score in advance of the first rehearsal, no matter how many times he had led the piece. In his nineties, when he was certainly not obliged to restudy a work of the classical symphonic repertoire, he thought it perfectly natural to continue to seek new insights. In Marlboro in 1971 he spent days restudying the familiar scores, noting with a thick red-and-blue lead pencil instructions to be transferred to the players' parts before the first run-through.

There was an unusually good "student" orchestra at Marlboro that year; although all were musicians of professional caliber, a number of them had not played together before. In the week before the first concerts of the season, Casals took that orchestra through four intense two-hour morning rehearsals, communicating a considerable portion of his musical intention in the two works scheduled, Mozart's "Paris" symphony (number 31) and Bach's first suite for orchestra. On the opening Saturday night he led a fresh and vivid reading of the Mozart. That night he could not sleep at all, and the following afternoon Alexander Schneider directed the Bach—the only last-minute cancellation of an appearance by Casals as conductor in his years at Marlboro. (Monday morning Casals was once more practicing on the "Bergonzi-Goffriller" cello that had been his concert instrument for sixty years, and the following day he conducted an incisive and thoroughly energetic morning rehearsal of Mendelssohn's "Italian" symphony.)

In his late eighties and early nineties Casals could in fact be seen to best advantage as a conductor during his Marlboro summers. One notable description, by Boston *Globe* book editor Herbert Kenney, had appeared the preceding August:

When [Casals] comes from the wings, his short figure and bald head quite visible over the seated violinists, he walks with a quick step, without turning his head, directly to the conductor's stand. . . . He bows to the applause, but seats himself quickly . . . then at length raises the baton, and Haydn's Oxford Symphony is underway.

The whole is a phenomenon. This is not an old man conducting. Monteux in his 80's was less animated on the stand. Seated though he is for most of the performance, Casals stands briskly every so often, drawn from his seat by the music, and steps forward to encourage one deck of players or another. Obviously, he is in complete command, but beyond that, there breathes a rapport, an electric exchange, which conductors and musicians need for a superlative performance.

His mannerisms are unique. He frequently shifts the baton from his right hand to his left. This may be to raise minatory fingers for a pianissimo, or to free his hand for a violent gesture. Again, he will direct with the baton held in his left hand. The beat is clear, sure, and never listless.

The face is expressive, but the audience can catch only an occasional glimpse. The lower lip thrusts forward as in a man ready for a fight, indicating momentary dissatisfaction or perhaps mere determination. The smile can be wonderfully beneficent, a trifle impish, an accolade laid on a player or a section. At the close of one movement, he screwed his face up and thrust it forward at the strings. The reading was obvious: "We wrangled over that sequence in rehearsal, didn't we, and you thought it would never be done. But you did it. . . ."

Haydn is a composer who can be conducted with gaiety. Casals can also bring that element to his conducting. He exhorts the first violins to their best efforts by raising his left arm as if it held a violin, and then, his baton in his right hand, held as a bow, he saws above the imaginary instrument. The response was electrifying.

The splendid response of the orchestra, you know instinctively, comes from the realization of each member that he is playing at the direction of one of the immortals who has stepped out of time, and at 94, behaves with the impassioned youth of an Olympian dancing in golden shoes. The musicians know they are participating in a miracle, and the audience knows . . . also. That is an intoxicating sensation—to be immortal, if only for the duration of a symphony.

Except for slight difficulty in walking, Casals in 1971 seemed younger than he had when he first came to Marlboro eleven years earlier. Casual observers continued to be astounded by his vigor and precise creative alertness on the podium. Musicians, equipped to assess what was happening, jettisoned understandable initial skepticism and, usually, their cynicism.

At the beginning of the 1970s Pablo Casals had lived nearly a century. He enjoyed the special luxury of the beloved old, appearing to withdraw into himself whenever the proceedings did not interest him. He was distressed when he could not summon instantly the precise name of someone he had known casually perhaps sixty years before, although he had a pungent observation in response to the latest pronouncement from the governments of the United States or the Soviet Union or on political developments in Puerto Rico or in Spain. He was distinctly aware of the presence of a beautiful woman—or a plain one.

He had experienced a massive heart attack in 1957 and, being a creature of intense sentiment and quick anger, suffered numerous angina seizures in the years that followed. As he grew older in terms of the calendar, he had intestinal pain from diverticulitis. He had gone—protesting—to a hospital for a check-up for forty-eight hours the preceding May: tests showed that his heart was functioning beautifully. The arteries of the feet showed a bit of hardening; X rays revealed slight calcification in the bow hand, where arthritis would be least threat to a cellist, but none in the arm.

As the summer went on there were many nights he slept little, a result of his strenuous schedule and his preoccupation with completing the hymn in time for the United Nations Day concert. Those closest to him began to be increasingly concerned about the Maestro's resultant frequent sleepiness but also marveled at his sudden transformation in the act of music. Backstage, with his life-long paralyzing stage-fright before any concert, he may have looked exhausted and in obvious physical discomfort; once out of his deep chair, with a final anguished sigh Casals walked to the front of his orchestra and from the first note was unaware of pain and nervousness, unconscious of anything that did not bear on the re-creation of the music.

"My goodness, Maestro," observed a visiting physician after a Haydn symphony rehearsal (more vigorous than usual because

Vendrell

the orchestra seemed repeatedly unable to do what Casals demanded of it). "Your energy this morning was that of a man of forty." Casals' eyes widened for an instant. "Twenty!" he snapped. "I am old, but in music I am very young."

Casals' birth in Spanish Catalonia at the end of December 1876 came less than a year after the invention of the telephone. The span of his life witnessed such other innovations as travel by automobile, airplane, and spacecraft as well as wireless telegraphy and radio, illumination by electric energy, and exquisite refinement of man's ability to destroy himself. He grew up during the last quarter of the nineteenth century, a period his friend the French poet Charles Péguy contended had brought more change than all the preceding years since the birth of Christ. He survived as functioning artist and individual to become one of the twentieth century's symbols of the human spirit's living stubborn protest against tyranny. Because he lived so long he became a legend—like his contemporary Albert Schweitzer, with whose life Casals' had some parallels—and in later years there began a sort of bland canonization that in many respects Casals neither sought nor welcomed. The legend flourished and the myth enlarged; disciples gathered and detractors emerged discreetly, both groups focusing on the myth instead of the man, ignoring the facts and the continuing formidable accomplishment.

Pablo Casals was born in Vendrell, a town of four thousand just inland from the Tarragonese coast seventy kilometers southwest of Barcelona. In 1876 Vendrell was, as it still is, a typical small, provincial Catalan town situated agreeably in a section of coastal plain ringed on the landward sides by hills and dominated by the bell tower of its Renaissance church. Narrow streets meandered to join a few central tree-lined squares. Houses were lighted by candles if at all; wood, charcoal, and coal furnished fuel for cooking and warmth during the chill dampness of winter. Birth and infant mortality rates were high, income low. Most of the food was produced regionally, carried in from field to open market and tiny cluttered shops. Local transport was horse-drawn or ox-pulled vehicle, donkeyback, or foot. For most of the farmers, artisans, and shopkeepers of the Vendrell population the effective limits of the outside world were the circling hills and the Mediterranean shore four kilometers away. Although politics was a stimulus for violent discussion, most of the inhabitants were little affected by the unsettling ideas that were permeating Barcelona and the larger cities of Europe and America. Few Vendrelleños other than merchants, members of the handful of landowner families, and the town doctor traveled as far as Tarragona, the provincial capital thirty kilometers away, and fewer still to Barcelona, although Vendrell boasted a railway station on the coastal line that joined the two cities.

The outer world seemed one of stable, continuing institutions and optimistic development. The Spanish Borbón monarchy had been restored in Madrid two years before, when disgruntled gener-

Vendrell's winding narrow streets and town squares have changed little since Pablo Casals was born there in December 1876; the covered one-horse tartana *and small shops are still everyday sights.*

als put an end to the short-lived first Spanish republic and installed on the throne Alfonso XII, nineteen-year-old only son of the deposed Isabel II. Queen Victoria, plagued at fifty-seven by a weight problem, was happily preparing for the ceremony that on New Year's Day 1877 would proclaim her Empress of India; she had already sat on the throne of England for thirty-nine years.

The United States of America, caught once more in an economic recession, had seen in November the end of a costly exposition celebrating its hundredth year of independence, for the opening of which (and for five thousand dollars from the Women's Centennial Committee) Richard Wagner had written a mediocre ceremonial march. Jacques Offenbach, at that moment America's favorite foreign composer, had come to conduct open-air concerts at the exposition before making a financially and artistically successful United States tour punctuated by outraged newspaper editorials on the wickedness of the cancan and by personal entertainment so lavish that he suffered an attack of gout. During the year Sioux Indians under Sitting Bull had decimated an American cavalry detachment under Lt. Col. George Armstrong Custer in an encounter near the Little Bighorn River in Wyoming Territory. Ulysses S. Grant was within three months of the end of his second term as President.

Czar Alexander II's Russia was completing arrangements to go to war with Turkey. Ottoman Empire troops in 1876 had defeated Serbia, while Turkish irregulars put down uprisings in Bulgaria with a brutal six-month campaign Western statesmen labeled the Bulgarian Horrors. Japan had opened Korea to the outside world for the first time in two centuries by recognizing the peninsular kingdom's independence from China; and in her home islands Japan had declared the end of the samurai as a separate social class by prohibiting the wearing of two swords as part of social legislation abolishing feudalism. Pope Pius IX, hailed at his election thirty years earlier as "the pope of progress," had proclaimed the Roman Church at war against modern civilization, liberalism, and democratic government.

Insurrection against the corrupt and self-serving Spanish colonial administration had been going on in Cuba for eight years, watched with sympathy by the United States, which had already tried to purchase the island from the Madrid government. Puerto Rico, Spain's other important remaining possession in the West Indies, had obtained significant political gains as a province under the first Spanish republic. These were lost with Borbón restoration, and a reactionary colonial regime quelled any liberal expression in the island. In Mexico, Porfirio Díaz had recently overthrown Lerdo de Tejada, Benito Juárez' successor, to begin a thirty-five-year dictatorship.

A submarine cable between Australia and New Zealand was put into operation in 1876. Alexander Graham Bell, then twenty-nine, transmitted the first intelligible sentence to be sent across an electric wire on the tenth of March, three days after he had been awarded a patent for the telephone. That year a patent was also issued for barbed wire, an invention essential to completing the conquest of the great American plains. H. J. Lawson, an Englishman, in 1876 devised the rear-wheel-driven "safety" bicycle, supplanting after ten years Pierre Lallement's first crank-driven, two-wheeled velocipede (generally known as The Boneshaker), providing the vehicle for the spread of a craze through the Continent and overseas.

Another British Arctic expedition seeking a northwest passage from Atlantic to Pacific had returned home unsuccessful in 1876. Denmark established a committee to undertake the geologic investigation of Greenland. In Brussels, King Leopold II convened an international congress of geographers, explorers, and other scientists to found the International Association for the Exploration and Civilization of Central Africa, with suppression of the flourishing slave trade one of its primary purposes. About the same time Robert Hamil Nassau, an American missionary doctor, established a Protestant mission station on Lambaréné in the Ogooué River in Gabon, the northern province of the Congo Colony.

In Spanish Catalonia the *Renaxensa* had begun as a renaissance of Catalan literary works. Coupled with the growing but still disorganized unrest of industrial development, the *Renaxensa* made Catalan autonomy a serious political factor in Spain by the year of Pablo Casals' birth.

Uneven waves of republicanism had been buffeting Europe since midcentury; anarchism had erupted in the inquiet bloodstream of politics and had begun to flourish in Spain. Royalty still inhabited the palaces of the Continent, but with little assurance that the leasehold was really divine. And their tenures were scarcely directed by heaven: those few rulers who, like Alfonso XII, tried to move toward liberalized constitutional regimes soon discovered that, in fact, they ruled by dispensation of tenacious and self-perpetuating bureaucracies.

Charles Darwin's *The Origin of Species* had undermined established notions of biology as well as of theology in the seventeen years since its publication, and the scrutiny—predominantly by German scholars—of Holy Writ had further upset the comfortable Protestant scheme of things. The increased material concern that came with spreading industrialization added to impending social upheaval. The rights of man were coming to be couched in terms of the individual's place as one of a nation and of his responsibility toward the state and the ostensible will of the majority; less was said about the obverse of the coin.

Impressionism in painting was stirring among younger artists in Paris. The first piece of Art-Nouveau furniture, designed by Edward Godwin and James A. McNeill Whistler, was shown at the Great Exhibition in Paris in 1876. Popular literature was still shot through with sentimentalism, although the enormously popular works of Charles Dickens (who had died six years before) contained real concern for the dismal realities of the human lot in the English Victorian world, and in Russia Fëdor Dostoevski was traveling the path of exploration in the dark soul of man, finding a different play of shadow and light than did his contemporaries Ivan Turgenev and Count Leo Tolstoi. In 1876 Mark Twain published *The Adventures of Tom Sawyer*. Victor Hugo was very much alive and active and idolized at seventy-four; Émile Zola, half as old, was observing France with a caustic eye and skillful pen.

At the end of 1876 *avant-garde* was still a military term and anarchism had not yet begun to show in the techniques or subject matter of the major art forms. Evolution in serious music continued to take place within the mainstream, the traditional idiom, as it had since the time of Johann Sebastian Bach, who had been dead for 126 years. (Mozart's brief life had ended only eighty-five years earlier, and Beethoven had been dead forty-nine years.) Richard Wagner, sixty-three in 1876, opened his mammoth temple to music drama and himself at Bayreuth in mid-August with a performance of *Das Rheingold*. Franz Liszt, tonsured and quasi-retired at sixty-five, was noticeably frail. About six weeks before Pablo Casals was born, forty-three-year-old Johannes Brahms heard the first performance of his first symphony; French composer Edouard Lalo, ten years older, had just completed his D minor concerto for cello and orchestra. Hungarian Joseph Joachim, nine years old when Paganini died, was at forty-five the world's most influential violinist, although Pablo de Sarasate (then thirty-two) had been dazzling audiences throughout the world for seventeen years. Eugène Ysaÿe, an eighteen-year-old Belgian prodigy, was studying violin with the masters Henri Wieniawski and Henri Vieuxtemps after completing brilliant work at the Liège Conservatory. Fritz Kreisler was a toddler in Vienna.

Born sixteen years before Casals, Isaac Albéniz, who had entered the Madrid Conservatory at eight, run away, and earned his way by playing piano in Spain and the Americas, was studying piano at the Brussels Conservatory before heading for Leipzig. Enrique Granados was a musically talented schoolboy of nine. Manuel de Falla was five weeks old in December 1876.

In Paris, conductor-violinist Charles Lamoureux, forty-two, was championing contemporary French works as well as fighting the good and more difficult fight west of the Rhine for the music of Wagner. Camille Saint-Saëns, at forty-one famous as a composer-pianist and organist of the Madeleine for nearly twenty years, was finding production of his new opera *Samson et Dalila* impossible— too severe and too Wagnerian, said Paris' opera directors. Gabriel Fauré, a decade younger than his teacher and friend Saint-Saëns, was filling minor posts as an organist and composing diligently. Claude Debussy was fourteen; thirteen-year-old Gabriel Pierné was a student of Jules Massenet and César Franck at the Paris Conservatoire; Maurice Ravel was a year old.

Edvard Grieg, troubled by a damaged lung, was a busy pianist, conductor, teacher, and at thirty-three already acclaimed as Norway's greatest composer. In Finland, eleven-year-old Jean Sibelius was considering a career in law. Farther east, in St. Petersburg, Nikolai Rimsky-Korsakov, thirty-two, was an inspector for the Ministry of Navy Bands (a post that allowed him to work in music rather than to continue in naval uniform), professor at the St. Petersburg Conservatory, and a member of the influential nationalistic Russian "Mighty Five"—with Balakirev, Borodin, Moussorgsky, and César Cui. Sergei Rachmaninoff was a three-year-old living with his parents on a country estate. In Moscow, Alexander Scriabin was almost five. In the same city gentle, troubled Pëtr Ilich Tchaikovsky—thirty-six, a former law clerk, graduate of the St. Petersburg Conservatory, now professor of harmony at Nikolai Rubinstein's Moscow Conservatory and an established composer—was preparing to embark on a disastrous marriage.

Richard Strauss was twelve and living in Munich, where he had begun to study music and attempt composition. In Lucca, Italy, eighteen-year-old Giacomo Puccini was organist in two nearby churches and a celebrity in the region on the basis of two ambitious choral works performed before local audiences. A hundred kilometers to the north, in Parma, nine-year-old Arturo Toscanini was taking his first cello lessons. Maestro Giuseppi Verdi, musical idol of all Italy for more than thirty years, wealthy, an honorary senator by order of the King, had not written anything since his *Aïda*, commissioned to celebrate the opening of the Suez Canal, had been produced in Cairo five years earlier; he was quite certain that the new music dramas of Wagner, a man six months his senior, had made his own kind of opera old-fashioned and no longer of interest to the public.

Pablo Casals was not the son of an impoverished nobleman, as romantic publicity in the early 1930s had it, although the family had been paper manufacturers for at least two hundred years and *casals* is the Catalan word for small châteaus or substantial country houses. The name of a paper-maker Casals appears on a marriage document dated February 16, 1693, in Gerona; eight generations later Pablo's paternal great-uncle, Celedoni Casals, maintained a prosperous paper factory in the Catalonian town of Cardona from 1846 until 1879, when the church land on which it stood was taken over by the government.

Pablo's father, Carlos Casals, was born on August 29, 1852, in Sans, a working-class quarter of Barcelona, one of three children of Don Celedoni's brother Miguel Casals and his wife Eulàlia Ribas. A somewhat delicate child who had attacks of asthma from infancy, he displayed a natural talent for music and a strong early interest in mechanical work. He studied piano with two good teachers, one a faculty member of a Barcelona conservatory, and mastered the rudimentary technique of the organ. Opportunity to work in the family paper enterprise went to the first son, Carlos' older brother; his own combination of mechanical and musical aptitude made it natural for Carlos to find employment as an apprentice repairman in a piano factory. Carlos joined forces with a neighbor, a young barber named Peret who played guitar, to organize a small choral group in their section of Barcelona.

In the early 1870s Peret packed his razor and combs and went to settle in Vendrell. He soon urged Carlos to join him, proposing among other ventures to form another musical group. Carlos said he would be delighted if enough steady work could be assured. Peret discovered that the fine baroque organ in Vendrell's imposing Church of Santa Ana was not being used because it needed repair and convinced the priest that his friend Carlos Casals was the one man who could put it into working order without great cost. Carlos went to Vendrell, began repair of the instrument, and started to give private lessons in piano and voice. The organist

Carlos Casals (seated at the harmonium) and musical colleagues in Vendrell. The heavily bearded man with guitar is Peret the barber.

for nearly twenty years, Ferráu Rubío Pujol, died in 1872; Carlos was named successor, and by the time he was twenty was installed as the Vendrell parish organist and choirmaster.

Carlos and Peret did form a men's chorus, La Lira, which still exists in Vendrell. A photograph taken not long afterward shows six members of the original group fixed in various attitudes for the camera: the barber holding his guitar; Carlos magisterial in black suit and stiff hat, one arm resting on his *harmonium-flaute*, a foot-powered portable keyboard instrument; an unidentified accordionist arranged in a carefully careless sprawl. The group was available to supply music for weddings, funerals, the recurrent fiestas in Vendrell and nearby villages, and to serenade beneath young ladies' windows. Before long Carlos, sometimes alone and sometimes with his colleagues, began to furnish music in the evenings in the Café del Centro, the town's chief *local* and secular gathering place.

Carlos Casals found life in Vendrell congenial; as organist-choirmaster and professor of music he was soon one of the town leaders, with the doctor, the apothecary, the schoolmaster, a few landowners, and the rector of the church. Although he had very little money, he subscribed to French and Spanish scientific publications, which in the last quarter of the nineteenth century were full of discussions of intriguing and hopeful developments in technology and machinery. Throughout his years in Vendrell, he dabbled at invention, as many men of his generation did. Other than as a musician, his son's strongest memory of the father as a young man was of Carlos' fascination with physics and mechanisms. Some of his father's curiosity about the way machines work, but none of the practical aptitude, continued lifelong in Pablo.

Along with music and science, Carlos Casals had a passion for republicanism. He was a follower of Francisco Pi y Margall, one of the sanest nineteenth-century proponents of federal republic in Spain. Pi y Margall was a *progresista*, committed to the progressive reform of social institutions through such measures as separation of church and state, governmental rein on the power of the military, free compulsory education, and inclusion of workers on juries, as well as a single federal republic of several autonomous states in Spain to accommodate and focus the country's intense regional cultures. (Pi y Margall was actually president of the first Spanish republic for thirty-seven days in the summer of 1873.) Early in his life in Vendrell Carlos also became a Freemason, a loyalty that only strengthened his republican sentiments. Spanish Masonry at the time had no organized political thrust but it was actively anticlerical, and there is a certain irony in the picture of a Mason and avid republican as organist of the Catholic church in Vendrell. Carlos chose "Beethoven" for his name within the fraternal order.

A bit under average height and compactly built, in his twenties Carlos Casals was physically very strong and rather somberly good-looking. A photograph taken about the time of his marriage shows a high forehead beneath a head of dark hair that has begun to recede at the temples, eyes deep-set and widely spaced, slightly prominent small ears seeming to be set far back because the sideburns taper as they join the neat full-face beard. The ample dark mustache, groomed with care, is just to the modest side of flamboyant. The lean upper face is that of a youth; the entire visage

Carlos Casals y Ribas in his twenties

is that of a thoughtful man ten or fifteen years older who could be a teacher, an artist, perhaps a lawyer.

There was little actually somber about Carlos in his earlier years. He was gregarious and unaffected, with quick enthusiasms that were generous, consuming, and frequently contagious. He had a native kindness and a firm honesty that won liking and respect. Although he never made much money and did not have a great deal of formal education, he possessed a clear intelligence and an interested mind that embarked on whatever he did with persistent intensity.

Pilar Ursula Defilló y Amiguet, Pablo Casals' mother, arrived with her younger brother and widowed mother in Vendrell when she was eighteen, at the beginning of the 1870s, after a long voyage from the Spanish West Indian colony of Puerto Rico. Their arrival in the small town to stay with the mother's sister caused a mixture of curiosity and admiration.

Pilar's mother, Raimunda Amiguet de Defilló—Doña Mundeta —had emigrated from Barcelona to the Spanish Caribbean in the 1840s with her husband, José Defilló. Their move seems to have been made for political reasons as well as quest for fortune; the forties was one of the times in Spanish history in which it was dangerous to be either antimonarchist or an acknowledged liberal. The couple went first to Cuba, then to the neighboring smaller island of Puerto Rico. There they settled in the active port city of Mayagüez on the Caribbean face of the island. They set up a retail store that prospered quickly and in their good years José and Raimunda Defilló owned much land, a spacious town house in Mayagüez, and the customary labor force of African slaves. The family participated in local affairs: Ricardo Defilló was a member of a governmental assembly in Mayagüez by 1870, and Eliseo Defilló was elected Deputy Grand Master of the Grand Lodge of Freemasons on the island in 1885, at that period a position of considerable importance in Puerto Rican life.

Raimunda has been depicted in Spain as a sweet, docile wife, a gentle expatriate homesick for her Catalan birthplace, Vendrell, who suffered greatly on account of her husband's strictness. Family lore in Puerto Rico suggests, however, that Doña Mundeta was a woman of tremendous strength and decision who dominated the family. Her descendants say it was her habit every morning to march to the shop at the head of a single file of family members and slaves who worked there. José Defilló committed suicide in the course of time, family legend says; intimidated by his wife's Teutonic domination, he finally refused to eat and starved himself to death. In the meantime the couple had six sons and two daughters; Pilar was born on November 11, 1853.

By the time Raimunda and the two youngest children reached Vendrell, her eldest son was also dead by his own hand. Exactly what happened is no longer clear; one story has it that he fell in love with the most beautiful girl on the island, who was also admired by a colonial official and accustomed to great luxury. To maintain her in proper fashion this son embarked for Barcelona on a buying trip to expand the family business, leaving a will in her favor. When he had not returned in nearly half a year the lady assumed he had perished at sea. Defilló returned shortly afterward to discover she had gained control of his inheritance and found another man. He did away with himself. (Also according to family tradition, another son, José, a composer and a talented pianist, was accused of activities against the regime and arrested by colonial authorities in the 1880s. Well aware of the torture that would follow, he committed suicide by slicing the veins of his neck with a knife so sharp he was almost decapitated.)

Pilar, a pretty child, had a quick mind; by adolescence she was acting as bookkeeper for her parents' store. She nevertheless did not receive a great deal of elementary education, although as the daughter of a colonial family of means she obtained more than would have been the case had she lived her earlier years in Spain. Once in Catalonia she entered the school attended by her cousin Fidèlia, daughter of Raimunda's sister Francisca, a petite woman who had remained in Vendrell, married a man from nearby Reus, and become proprietor of a small tobacco shop. There is a credible report that on the first day less attention was paid to studies than to the fashionably turned-out new arrival whose speech had the soft accents of the Antilles.

Doña Mundeta died two years after her return to Vendrell and Francisca Felip accepted her sister's children as her own. Pilar's younger brother, a handsome youth who was never at ease among the Catalan provincials, soon went back to the Caribbean; Pilar never returned.

Compared to Mayagüez, Vendrell was a monotonous world for the orphaned girl who had reached marriageable age in living conditions far different from those of her childhood. Whatever had happened to the inheritance following the death of her father and oldest brother, by the time of her mother's last illness there was not much money left. A piano was nevertheless available, and with Carlos Casals the girl continued the music lessons begun in Puerto Rico—until Tía Francisca looked in one day to discover Carlos holding Pilar's hand during a discussion that appeared to have nothing to do with music. Thereafter, every day at the hour of the canceled lesson Carlos appeared outside the house with Peret the barber and other members of their musical combination to serenade his former student.

By the time Pilar was twenty there were those who considered her rather a strange girl, granting that she was extraordinarily at-

*Pilar Ursula Defilló y Amiguet about the time
of her marriage*

tractive and admitting that she was always prepared to respond
when help was needed. She was too much the lady for her circumstances, some thought: too unbending in her manner, somehow too
grand, too precise. Her reticence (she showed little inclination for
small talk and less for gossip) others considered more taciturnity
than shyness, and when she did enter a conversation her observations were both trenchant and unorthodox. There was something
about her too silent and implicitly elegant for comfort, and there

were those who felt that, like her brother, she put on airs in the presence of country cousins.

She was slim and well-proportioned, not tall; her eyes were large, their expression direct if sometimes enigmatic. Her extraordinarily smooth skin had kept the marble-white of the colonial Spanish woman, protected from the direct rays of the tropical sun, a fact emphasized by long dark hair. Her face had not yet lost its last hint of childhood plumpness and her mouth had full lips above a slightly cleft small chin. A certain tenderness and a suggestion of melancholy linger in Pilar Defilló's face, her small mouth capable of smiles that could have been warm and engaging.

There appears to have been deep and real affection between the couple whose backgrounds were so dissimilar and whose personalities differed in many ways, but no evidence that Pilar agreed to marry in the throes of overwhelming romantic passion. In any event, very much against her aunt's wishes, Pilar Defilló y Amiguet and Carlos Casals y Ribas were married in the Vendrell parish church on July 16, 1874. A civil marriage was performed three and a half months later, during the afternoon of the second of November.

If the civil wedding had taken place the preceding spring, the record would probably not have survived the sporadic fighting of the so-called Carlist wars, which touched Vendrell and in which Carlos Casals was directly if briefly involved. A Carlist contingent attacked and sacked the town, burning the municipal archives in the process.

The Carlist wars were a bloody effort by one branch of the overpopulated Borbón dynasty to wrest control of a diminished throne from another branch, a vendetta that began about halfway through the 230 years during which the Borbóns ruled much of Spain. (The last Hapsburg king of Spain, Carlos II, had bequeathed his empire to Louis XIV's grandson Philip of Bourbon in 1700; Philip became Felipe V to most of Spain, and the French Bourbons became the Spanish Borbóns.)

Fighting began at the death of Fernando VII—despotic, cruel, intolerant, a deadly anachronism in the vaguely liberal dawn of the nineteenth century—a ruler whose ineptness distinguished him even among his fellow occupants of the Lion Throne. The archreactionaries sniffed liberalism in Fernando's regime and decided that the throne should be occupied by his brother Carlos, who would champion the complete extermination of liberalism and such improvements as reestablishment of the Inquisition. Savage civil war continued during the turbulent quarter-century reign of Fernando's chubby daughter Isabel II, through the first Spanish republic, and was still being fought when the Borbón monarchy was restored at the end of 1874.

The last scenes of bloodshed in this dynastic civil war were played out in Catalonia in 1874. In March a Carlist force made a sortie into Vendrell in the course of a sweep to the sea; the village organist joined other local men in an attempt to protect the town. Carlos and other defenders had to flee on a Barcelona-bound train that was halted inland. From that point he was forced to make his way through farmland, hiding during the day and, it is said, returning home some days later through the mountains on foot. To his son, Carlos later dismissed his valor as a natural thing, but Pablo Casals referred to it with pride. At the time Pilar Defilló de Casals said nothing. She hated fighting in any form and for any reason.

After their church wedding Carlos and Pilar made their home in the two upper floors of a plain, dark narrow house, number 2 in the calle Santa Ana, a modest street not far from the church. Carlos gave music lessons on the first floor; living quarters were two small rooms on the second. Here their first son, named for the father, was born in June 1875 and died within a year of lockjaw. When Pilar became pregnant with her second child she had no older female friend to whom to turn for counsel (the estrangement from her aunt over her marriage had not healed), so she visited a *remeiera*, a peasant woman wise in female lore and nature's remedies, who prescribed long walks outside the village and specified that the new child's godfather not be a blood relative.

Pilar, just twenty-three, bore her second son at home late on the afternoon of Friday, December 29, 1876. The child emerged with the umbilical cord coiled around his neck, but the midwife (the coal merchant's wife) was experienced and he escaped visible damage. Carlos did not register his son's existence until Sunday, beyond the deadline for recording new births, so the time was entered officially as nine in the evening of December 30. Carlos showed a certain absentmindedness throughout his life, but at

Pablo Casals' birthplace, 2 calle Santa Ana,
Vendrell

Christmastime 1876 he was particularly busy, with his presence
as organist and choirmaster more in demand than usual during the
extended holiday season. And as the best musician in the locality
he was called upon to furnish music for noisier and more light-
hearted celebrations than those in church.

When the child was christened on the thirteenth of January
1877, with Pilar's cousin Fidèlia as godmother, his godfather was
Pablo Palau, a friend and pupil of Carlos but not a relative. He
was named Pablo for his godfather, Carlos for his father, and Salvador for the priest who baptized him.

2

THE FIRST AWARENESS that he was alive came to Pablo Carlos Salvador Casals y Defilló in the early autumn of 1877 at San Salvador, the small beach four kilometers south of Vendrell. He had been asleep in a room of a tiny secularized Romanesque hermitage, the Ermita, fronting the Mediterranean, which served as the municipality's inexpensive guest house. He woke to consciousness in the sound of the sea and to constantly shifting, surf-reflected light refracted through intact windowpanes and streaming through a broken one. As an adult he would delight in Corot rather than Cézanne and would consider the musical trend led by Debussy and Ravel to have decorative charm and harmonic interest but to be decadence in the path of great music, yet he always recalled his own earliest sentience impressionistically in poetic images.

The Playa San Salvador became the spot on earth Pablo Casals treasured most; for more than sixty years he came back at least once a year. Both before he could walk and as a young boy he spent hours here watching "the luminous tonalities and ceaseless flow of the sea" in endless movement but ever the same, and the gathering and processions of clouds. It was here particularly, almost from his first memories, that he began to feel a sense of exile in his mother's nostalgia for Puerto Rico, where nature had sown with an even more flamboyant hand and where the bordering sea can seem more intensely blue than the Mediterranean off the Costa Dorada.

Brief stays in San Salvador were the one minuscule luxury the family situation allowed, and Pilar went there whenever possible with Pablo and his brothers, who came in quick succession. She brought the third infant, Arturo, born in 1879, and three-year-old Pablo, recovering from mumps, to San Salvador for a longer stay than usual in 1880—the year her fourth child, named José for her father, was born and died. Arturo was robust; Pablo was a bright, normal infant, generally healthy in his first years except for a tendency to bronchitis and the fact that the top of his skull was so sensitive to touch that he cried out when his mother put her hand gently upon it. From the time of the 1880 visit the crippled ex-sailor caretaker of the Hermitage took the boys in hand, teaching them to swim, telling them stories of the sea and tales of Turkish pirate raids in the days before Vendrell had moved inland from that shore, when Catalonia was one of the greatest empires of the world. Like his young charge, the hermit was called Pau, the Catalan version of Pablo as well as the word for peace. Castilian was the official national language, imposed by the Madrid government, but as a language of life in the heartland of Catalonia it has never eclipsed Catalan, a tongue that shows roots earlier than the Roman conquest of Iberia. Pau, not Pablo, was the name Casals preferred for himself in later years.

The fact that he woke to human awareness in restless light from the sea and rhythm of surf on shore contributed to his strong lifelong response to nature, but the atmosphere of music cradled Casals' earliest fantasies; much later he spoke of being bathed in it all the time. His aural response was such that he could sing in tune before he could speak. Before he could walk, Doña Pilar brought him downstairs one day and interrupted her husband's singing class in the first-floor studio: the infant had been reproducing accurately a progression Carlos was demonstrating. The father played a scale, Pablo repeated his performance, and the young members of the class went home to report that Carlos Casals' baby already knew solfeggio. He himself remembered sitting rapturous on the floor at the age of two or three, head resting against the upright piano the better to absorb the resonances of the sound of his father's improvising.

While both were still quite young, Carlos began to test and teach Pablo and Arturo with a game in which the boys stood behind the piano and identified the notes of random musical phrases as they were played; Arturo's ear was the more acute. Pablo's digital control was sufficient by the age of four for Carlos seriously to begin teaching him piano—in 1881, the year the family's fifth child, Enrique, was born and died.

Then, nearly four months after his fifth birthday, Pablo Casals began his professional career, when he joined the Vendrell church choir as a second soprano on April 27, 1882, the feast of Our Lady of Montserrat—the patron of Catalonia. (The eighty-five centavos he received for each mass appears to have been a smaller sum from the choir fund supplemented by a few coins from Doña Pilar.) His mother had taken him to services occasionally while he was an infant; after he could walk he accompanied his father to the church. The Gregorian chant, the chorales and anthems, and Carlos' organ voluntaries became part of the boy's everyday experience and one basis of musical knowledge. The choirmaster's son paid close attention to everything that went on in the choir. A true musical instinct was apparently at work: he recognized and reacted to late entrances, poor dynamics, and faulty intonation. The impulse to conduct was also present; more than once in practice, choirmaster and singers were startled by a second-soprano voice informing the tenors they were singing off pitch.

The youngster found excitement and satisfaction in being an official participant, but he was enthralled by the vibrant closeness of the organ pipes. On occasion Carlos permitted Pablo to come along when he practiced and sometimes let him change registration of the stops, but said firmly there would be no actual organ-playing until he had grown enough to operate the pedals properly. The son's first actual organ work therefore consisted of pulling ropes in a room behind the organ loft to activate the stone-weighted double bellows furnishing air to the instrument's wind chamber.

One of the most vivid memories from Casals' early life was of the first Christmas in which he sang in the choir. Instead of a midnight mass, celebration of the Nativity began in Vendrell at five in the morning Christmas Day with the *misa del gall* (Mass of the Cock) and continued through *el día de los tres reyes* (the day of the visit of the Three Kings), the sixth of January. The twelve days of *Navidad* centered on the *pessebre*, the Bethlehem

Main portal of the Church of Santa Ana,
Vendrell

manger and its figures, its legends and their meanings. On Christmas Eve 1882, just before his sixth birthday, Pablo had been given an early supper and put to bed, but he could not sleep. He felt suffused in mystery, awaiting some extraordinary occurrence. Walking to the church with his mother next morning in the starlit dark, he noticed and was puzzled by the silence of the other people approaching the same destination. Suddenly through the open main portal of the sacred building he saw the bright altar and sensed celebration.

The choir made its procession past the figure of the Infant Jesus asleep in a manger before the high altar, young Pablo making a connection in his mind between the sleeping Babe and the three infant brothers his parents said had become angels when they died. He sang with jubilation.

For a child of six he played piano well. Musical prodigies demonstrate very young a muscular coordination, a sharpness of ear, and a mental capacity that enables them to master a musical instrument as naturally as they learn to walk. Pablo Casals also had in his father an excellent teacher from the beginning. By the time his son had been studying piano two years, in addition to exercises and simple tunes (some of which the father wrote) Carlos had introduced him to some of the simpler works of Chopin, Beethoven, and Mendelssohn. And, although Carlos felt no particular affinity himself for the work of Bach, he directed the boy into study of *The Well-Tempered Clavier.*

By six Pablo was also attending the community school in the calle Montserrat run by schoolmaster Calafell, a man so thin he is described as being more bones than meat. Pablo had already begun to read at home, and did well in his subjects. At this age he was active, gregarious although basically uncombative, and held his own among his peers. He also began making forays of exploration, alone or with his crony Jaime Nin, who shared a bench in Señor Calafell's classroom, into the fields and vineyards and olive groves that surround Vendrell. (His first independent foray of discovery had come at about four. For weeks he had seen a sturdy boy two or three years older than he trudging through the calle Santa Ana with heavy baskets of fertilizer; where he was taking them was a mystery Pablo had to solve. One day he followed the other boy to his destination—a vineyard outside town. Here Carlos found him some hours after his disappearance happily eating green grapes; a spanking was administered that his son remembered more than ninety years later. The only other spanking he recalled also came in early childhood, when his mother found him playing cards and said he had taken the first step on the road to gambling and wickedness.)

The youngster's curiosity was riveted by any sort of musical instrument, and he displayed a knack for playing any new one he could get his hands on. One of the most-repeated anecdotes of Casals' musical childhood tells of the day, when he was about six, that three peasant *grallers* appeared at the house to ask Carlos to teach them new dance tunes. The *gralla,* a reed instrument of

Moorish or Arabic origin that looks something like a primitive oboe, is difficult to play: stopping the finger holes in sequence allows the player to produce a whole-tone scale, but approximate half tones can be achieved only by very careful control of wind volume. While the visitors were waiting for his father the boy demanded to hear a tune, then asked if he could try. *Gralla* in hand, Paulito assayed a few tentative scales, reproduced the peasant's tune, and was playing an encore with great satisfaction when Carlos returned. (The *gralla* and its inseparable companion the *tabal or tamburí*, a tiny drum, figure distinctively in Catalan folk music, and the larger instrument's half-forlorn nasal summons woke village and rural Catalonia on days of fiesta. In his eighties, orchestrating his oratorio *El Pessebre*, Casals approximated the voice of the *gralla* in his scoring for oboes.)

Until he was seven his only formal musical training was in piano and singing, but for a short period while he was six the piccolo became young Pau's towering passion—even more than acting, a pressing ambition following his appearance in colonel's uniform at the head of the children's chorus in a local performance of a zarzuela called *La Marsellesa*. He found the small instrument in Carlos' studio (it was actually a *fluviol*, a diminutive five-holed pipe much closer in construction and technique to a tin whistle flageolet than to the side-blown little silver tube suggested by the name *piccolo*) and figured out how to play it. His career as flutist was brief: Carlos explained to him firmly that he was *not* to play the "piccolo"; the exertion of producing the wind was bad for his head. Whenever his father left the house Pau found the instrument—at the top of a closet, behind a cupboard, inside the piano—wherever Carlos had hidden it the last time he had surprised his son with it. The six-year-old reveled in the feel and the tone of the small high-pitched *fluviol* and at last he played it quite well, with a child's full happiness. One day when Carlos found the boy still playing the forbidden thing, he took the temptation from his son's hand and destroyed it. Pablo wept for hours, but Carlos' interdiction had not been capricious. On the first important saint's day after he found the flute and taught himself to play, the boy had turned up in his good sailor suit ready to march near the head of the procession through town to the church. March he did, piping away loudly, but he fainted before he reached the Plaza Nova, where his unsuspecting parents and Arturo were watching the parade with Pablo's godmother. Dr. Valls and the pharmacist both said the strain of blowing into the *fluviol* had been the cause.

Carlos had special reason to be concerned about any avoidable danger to his oldest surviving child. Within this year, 1883, his sixth son, Ricardo, had died a few days after birth and Pilar, now twenty-nine, had been gravely ill.

Pablo was already a mixture of charm and talent, ingenuousness and obstinacy. His and his father's great friend Matines, a winecask-maker and expert woodcarver who was the most popular character in Vendrell, made him a bicycle—a Catalan Boneshaker, a wooden machine with large front wheel, arching frame, and small back wheel. The delighted recipient, surrounded by a small invited audience, mounted at the top of the steepest available cobbled street and set off on his virgin ride. Part way down, the front wheel hit a loose paving stone and Paulito landed on his head. He remounted and, shakily but stubbornly triumphant, pedaled to the end of the street before he let himself be assisted home to have his lacerated skull bandaged. The speed of movement had not been what most delighted him about his first velocipede, Casals told a Spanish interviewer forty years later, but the expanded horizons it gave him.

By the age of seven, in 1884, Pablo could transpose any music before him into another key, and he began to study violin; Carlos knew enough of the technique to start his son's instruction. Within a year he appeared as soloist, playing an air with variations by the forgotten French composer Dancla and garnering his first press notice. This public display of violinistic prowess brought some hoots from his contemporaries. "What could you expect," he asked long afterward, "when the only violinists they had seen were blind beggars in cafés and the streets?"

The seventh Casals son was born in 1884 and christened Carlos. At almost the same time Arturo, the one brother who had lived long enough to be a companion to Pablo, became sick and then fatally ill from cerebral meningitis. He died on Three Kings' Day.

Pablo Casals began to compose music at the age of six or seven, a natural enough thing at the outset for a child who had seen his father writing melodies on lined paper for as long as he could remember. His first composition he recalled sometimes as a mazurka, for which his godfather rewarded him with ten reales and a plate of dried figs, and sometimes as a "rather good" song that had form and musical meaning. Casals' loveliest and most lyric compositions, about which he remained curiously modest after childhood, were works for voice. Carlos Casals apparently considered it perfectly natural that his son should have been putting musical signs meaningfully onto paper at seven, although identifiable creative talent so young is much more exceptional than mastery of an instrument. Carlos was the region's leading performing musician and teacher, but invention—the act of committing musical thought to paper—was his greatest satisfaction. His mastery of the techniques of composition was far from complete, but he was facile, melodic, and productive: hundreds of pieces, organ voluntaries, *canzonettas*, and dances went onto paper, although only a few short works have survived. His son maintained that, if he had had proper musical training, sheer talent would have put Carlos Casals in the front rank of Spanish composers.

One manuscript that still exists is the first musical collaboration between father and son, music for a Christmas pageant written in 1883 for the Catholic Center in Vendrell. The overworked father invited Pablo to contribute some melodies for a four-scene "Adoration of the Shepherds" in which, with suitable histrionics, the youngster played the role of a devil who attempts to thwart the shepherds' arrival in Bethlehem. The tableau was repeated during several Christmas seasons; seventy years later the co-composer was pleased and touched to receive from a Catalan émigré to Colombia a letter that enclosed some of the tunes from *Los Pastorcillos en Belen* the man still remembered.

If a band of itinerant musicians wandered into Vendrell to play in the streets or a café, Pablo would be found with them, as close as possible, oblivious of everything except their performance. One such troupe, dressed in clown costumes, materialized in a Vendrell plaza in 1885. This particular combination billed itself *Los Tres Bemoles* (The Three Flats). Their instruments included a washtub drum, cigar-box guitars and mandolins, bells, and such household utensils as teacups, drinking glasses, and spoons. What most intrigued the boy was a one-string implement made of a bent broomstick and cord played by a man standing.

Pablo described its delights to his father at length and in enthusiastic detail. Carlos chuckled, as he often did, but he and Peret the barber made and soon presented the most celebrated relic of the son's childhood—his first "cello." A long, narrow dried gourd served as body and sounding chamber, and there was a single string. Pablo tried it out with a few scales, then played Schubert's "Serenade." This primitive instrument enchanted the musical child and became for the man a souvenir glazed with tremendous sentiment. He wrote in 1930 for an English magazine that "on this homemade contrivance I learnt to play the many songs my father wrote, and the popular tunes which reached the village from the outside world." While it was still new he performed on it at nighttime in the ruined monastery of Santas Creus outside Vendrell on the evening of a saint's day. He revisited the site in the 1920s: "an innkeeper . . . remembered me as a boy of nine playing my queer instrument in one of the cloisters, in moonlight. And I remembered . . . the stillness of that night, and the music which echoed so strangely against the crumbling white walls of the monastery."

Although he characterized himself later as a high-spirited and rather mischievous youngster, Pablo Casals found no childhood pleasure in capturing insects or goading animals or bullying smaller or weaker contemporaries. His father's code of what is right and wrong and proper was strict; his mother abhorred violence. The tussles of his schoolmates did not particularly concern him (although he routed the local bully at least twice as a schoolboy), but the sight of armed pairs of the Guardia Civil on horseback or swaggering gendarmes struck terror in him even as a child.

His childhood was a period essentially of sunlight and happiness, the only carefree years of his existence. The family financial circumstances remained extremely modest, but respectable—he could have echoed the remark of his fellow cellist Gregor Piatigorsky, speaking of his own childhood in Russia, that he could not remember exactly how poor they had been—but he never went to bed hungry because there was no food.

The pipe organ Pablo longed so much to play is a handsome three-manual instrument of polished dark wood, shining façade pipes, and dark pearwood keys that has been called one of the four finest organs of its period in all of Spain. The parishioners of Vendrell voted in 1776 to have it built instead of putting the money into structural changes to the imposing rather than beautiful sixteenth-century church building that commands the town as a cathedral

(Left) Pablo Casals at six; (right) the eighteenth-century pipe organ of the Church of Santa Ana, which he learned to play at nine, was positioned on a side wall of the nave during Casals' childhood.

might a city. It was built by Luis Scherrer and installed on a side wall of the nave. When it was inaugurated in late April 1777 to the sound of the bank of little trumpets above the console, forty-eight pipes and fifteen stops had been added to the original design and the cost had risen from the 1776 estimate of 1570 livres to the 1777 bill of 2669 livres (seventy years later the 1000-livre rent the Casals paper factory paid the Church every year for its land in Cardona was considered a tremendous sum).

From the age of six until he was nine, Pablo tried everything he could think of to stretch himself to become tall enough to reach the pedal keyboard while seated on the organ bench (as an adult, absolutely erect in shoes, he stood five feet three inches). At nine he proved to Carlos that he could operate the pedals adequately, and his organ instruction began. With good piano technique to start, within a few months he was a competent substitute when his father was indisposed. The instrument was a new, wide musical horizon, against which it was possible to shape and command a complexity of textures and sounds impossible to attain alone with any other instrument except an orchestra.

Leaving the church one morning not long before he was ten, Pablo met the cobbler whose shop was across the small square from the church. The shoemaker had become an admirer of Carlos Casals' organ-playing. The man began to tell the boy, somewhat ecstatically, once more how much he enjoyed listening to the father. Pablo spontaneously set the record straight: he had been rehearsing; Carlos was ill. The aging music-lover called his wife to explain that they had been listening not to Carlets but to Paulito. The coupled embraced him, gave him some sweet wine and cookies, and the young artist departed not at all displeased with audience response. As he headed toward home, he glanced up at the Santa Ana's three-stage bell tower and the two objects that topped it. One was an eighteenth-century angel that had been damaged by French soldiers' fire in 1810 and by the 1880s had lost one arm and part of a leg. Next to it flourished a small wild olive tree that was a kind of totem to Vendrelleños, who spoke of (and sometimes to) it as *El Rabell* (the rebel).

The quality of music Carlos Casals (and, for a short time, his son) provided for religious observance in the edifice beneath the bell tower was of a high order for the times. Spanish church music had been notable from the sixteenth to the late seventeenth centuries, at least at court and in the major cathedrals, and early Spanish composers made important impact on the development of liturgical music in Rome. But by the later nineteenth century music for divine service in Spain was likely to be a sorry combination of slipshod plainsong and popular tunes, product of the demand or disinterest of the local priest and the limitations of the organist. "The señores canons do not care for music, neither do they understand it," says a character in Vicente Blasco Ibáñez' novel *The Shadow of the Cathedral.* "It is quite enough for them to walk in procession to some piece of Rossini's and . . . all they care about is that [the organ] must play slowly, very slowly. The slower

Beneath the bell tower of the Church of Santa Ana, stones still weight the bellropes, as they did when Pablo Casals joined his father's choir at the age of five.

it plays, the more religious they think it even though the organist may be playing an Habañera."

Carlos Casals' contribution to the organized services of worship in Vendrell had consistent musicianship and beauty. The strain of seriousness that from early years was part of Pablo's fabric also existed beneath the surface of Carlos Casals' cheerfulness. Carlos' organ improvisations, his great musical pleasure, were suitable to place and purpose. The solemnity and artistry of the Casals church music were such, in fact, that the Vendrell priest kept asking for something livelier, begging both father and son "Don't play such *sad* music!"

In 1887, while Pablo was ten, his parents' seventh son, Carlos, died at three of a heart deficiency complicated by diphtheria. On the sixth of May, Antonia, the first daughter, was born. She choked to death six days later. That spring Pablo ducked through a broken plank fence near the Vendrell railway station and cut his head deeply on a rusty spike in the course of a vigorous game of hide-and-seek. When he found he could not stanch the blood, his only thought was to go to the plaza and stretch out to let the hot sunlight dry the flow—a stoic ingeniousness as well as a certain impulse for the bright light of center stage. Here Carlos, walking home, found his son the focus of a gathering crowd.

The same year Pablo was bitten in the leg by a rabid dog whose bite had already caused the death of several animals. Dr. Valls knew that the Barcelona hospital was trying to save such victims with Louis Pasteur's hydrophobia serum, first put to wide practical trial the year before. There was little hope, but Carlos took his son to the city on the first train, a trip during which Pablo became aware for the first time of the presence of a girl—she laughed at him. He was put into a hospital ward where an old man in the next bed was dying, screaming in delirium. The treatment was a long series of painful, twice-daily injections of progressively stronger concentrations of the rabies virus in hot solution. The ten-year-old stuffed a handkerchief into his mouth as the doctors began. "Remember," Carlos had told him, "that men do not cry."

In 1888 a chamber-music trio traveled from Barcelona to perform in the Vendrell Catholic Center. The trio included José García, an accomplished cellist and a professor at the Municipal School of Music in Barcelona, and for the first time Pablo Casals saw and heard a real violoncello, played well. No previous moment in his life can be pinpointed as the realization of his true vocation. He had no summons to become a musician: he was born into music, and it was supremely natural to him that he should live in it as long as life continued. Nor had he a sudden call to play cello. What took place when he was eleven was a *coup de foudre*, stroke of lightning, love at first sight.

The legend has it that when he heard the first sounds of the cello Pablo whispered passionately, "Papá, *that* is the instrument I should like to play!" His earnestness persisted; he began to play violin upright between his knees as though it were the larger instrument. Repeatedly Carlos made him put it back on his shoulder; moments later the boy was continuing the other way. Carlos found a small cello and gave his son his first lessons.

One night the boy overheard his father and mother in a discussion that became an intense argument about his immediate future. Although neither voice was raised, he sensed a power struggle that focused on him, and he could not know that the bond between husband and wife can survive vehement disagreement. He had strong love and admiration for both parents, one so different from the other. From them he had absorbed a basic moral view and disinclination to compromise; now he saw himself as the cause of a rift between them and felt a terrible guilt. The greatest shock was that his father, who had roused in him the love for music, who had taught and inspired him, seemed to understand neither him nor the emerging sense that his life must cohere and take meaning in music.

Carlos Casals at thirty-six was a man of charm and contradictions who considered himself a nineteenth-century man of reason and practicality. Apparently cheerfully accepting his own place in life and the world, he had been giving serious thought to the practical aspect of his son's future. He granted that the boy showed real talent in music and considered it absolutely natural that this should be so, but he knew better than most that being a musician was not a satisfactory way to earn a good living. For proper livelihood his son needed to learn a trade. Manual labor had dignity; it also offered enough regular income to support a family. Carpentry was a good craft and steadily in demand; and the Vendrell carpenter, whose shop faced the calle Santa Ana house in which Pablo was born, was a family friend. (It was to this man's shop that Carlos went quietly for years to work on his inventions, since his wife disapproved his spending time on ventures that had no practical use.) Carlos had already agreed that Pablo would start his apprenticeship as a carpenter at the age of twelve.

Pilar countered that her one living son must and would be a musician, not a carpenter or a cobbler or anything else. He must now go to Barcelona to begin proper study, and she would take him there. He had become an excellent pianist and a good organist, his compositions showed a gift, and he had been wildly excited about the cello for months.

There was no money to settle the boy in Barcelona, even with relatives, and pay tuition in a music school. Further music study outside Vendrell was illogical, Carlos said, and pretentious—the result of his wife's inflated ideas, spawned in her luxurious colonial childhood. It was out of the question.

God had given the boy the talent, God alone, retorted Pilar; Carlos had taught him as well as he could, but it was a waste of time for him to stay longer in Vendrell. God, then—not the one of the church but *God*—would make it possible for their son to study in Barcelona and to go wherever else he needed to go later.

Carlos capitulated, as always. He loved and respected the intractable, soft-spoken, handsome woman who had married him; he was never able really to understand her, but in the end he always accepted her way. He wrote to the Municipal School of Music in Barcelona inquiring about the possibility of his son's enrollment. And, on a steaming day in the late summer of 1888, Pilar Defilló de Casals set her son's face toward Barcelona and the future as they boarded a third-class railway carriage in the train that chuffed slowly for two hours, flirting with the Spanish coast toward Barcelona. Carlos Casals would remain in Vendrell, working as before, while his wife went with their son. His presence had nonetheless been vital psychologically and musically to the childhood years, when the trends that governed his son's life had been set into effect, no matter how far away he was afterward. Pablo Casals believed the words he quoted of the mystic poet-journalist Charles Péguy, that "Everything is accomplished by the time we are twelve years old."

3

At eleven and a half years of age, Pablo was headed toward a manual apprenticeship more complicated than carpentry, although he showed no deftness in wielding tools or repairing broken objects at any time in his life. A stalwart youngster, he escorted his mother with deference and native gallantry. His black hair was cropped short; his jaw, set purposefully, seemed outthrust for reassurance against shyness almost pugnaciously. His right hand habitually formed a half-fist, as it had since infancy, as if in readiness to do battle against forces that could materialize unheralded. His eyes were his most arresting feature, startlingly blue, alert to the moment's impressions, and marked more by intelligence and wonder than by fear.

An observer might have given the greater attention to Doña Pilar during the two-hour journey to the Catalan capital on a late-summer day twelve years before the end of the nineteenth century. In her early thirties Pilar Casals' physical beauty had matured. She was leaner than at the time of her marriage; the suggestion of girlish fleshiness had gone from her face. She was pregnant with her ninth child but did not yet show the evidence of early aging that often marks Latin women, in spite of the children and having done all her own housework for fourteen years. The severe black in which she always dressed set off her almost translucent complexion, and she wore her long dark hair in two braids coiled about her head. From the time of her marriage few in Vendrell called her by a diminutive of her name, the practice to which Spanish lends itself so gracefully. Her unassailably proud bearing seemed so grave and resolute that it elicited from the first days of her marriage the honorific *doña* before her name, a form of address generally reserved for older women.

No other human being ever fully knew what occupied the mind of this undemonstrative but resourceful woman whose son remembered many years later never having seen laugh and who almost never embraced him. By the time she began this journey with her son, she had already displayed extraordinary strength of purpose: what had to be would be and therefore could be, and as soon as one perceived what was right and began to act on that basis, the means to realize the goal would be found. Mozart's mother lost four children and kept an unquenchable enthusiasm for living. Pilar Ursula Defilló de Casals had seen the death of seven of the eight she had borne, and with increasingly silent ferocity had devoted herself to the protection and direction of the life of the one son who had survived infancy. For her, Pablo was predestined to be a great musician, and the way would be found for him to study. She would make her choices and sacrifices solely to accomplish what she felt had to be done in his behalf until he could do for himself; she may already have been concerned that her son's apparent sturdiness of constitution belied a sensitivity of spirit. He was sometimes nervous and shy, alert to beautiful things and openly emotional; from earliest childhood he had been the victim of nightmares. Many boys his age in Spain were already completely on their own, but to Pilar her own son surely appeared terribly young and vulnerable on this first journey.

Pablo was accepted as one of the youngest of the four hundred students of the Escuela Municipal de Música after he had played for the director, members of the piano faculty, and the professor of cello. The school, already prestigious in Barcelona although it had only been in existence for two years, occupied part of the first floor of an old town palace at 7 calle Lladó in the ancient quarter of the city. The young Casals, talented and eager, was beginning five years of hard work and advanced study in harmony and counterpoint, musical theory, composition, piano and cello "to learn" (in the military figure he liked to use in later years) "to be a soldier so as to become in due time a general." He had learned well from his father, but on entering the Barcelona school he was at once in what seemed to him very deep waters.

He came home from the first day's instruction pale and at the point of tears, shaken by the new environment and the formidable authority of his teachers. He was so nervous that he simply did not understand what Maestro Rodoreda had explained to the new students, least of all the counterpoint assignment that was to be completed overnight. Doña Pilar calmed him as much as any parent can reassure a high-strung, serious child confronted by the first demanding and misunderstood homework assignment, reminding him that his expressed ambition was now to learn to be a composer and that he had already written songs and dances that were very good. Still desperate but eager to do well, Pablo decided the best thing would be to write something of his own on the foundation of figured bass the teacher had dictated to the class. Next day Rodoreda looked over what he had done, seemed to the nervous boy to laugh and weep simultaneously, and then embraced him. He had done a full-scale composition rather than an exercise. The neophyte composer determined to do his best in Rodoreda's subjects, counterpoint and harmony. Years afterward Casals remembered José Rodoreda, director both of the music school and of the Barcelona municipal band, as the fine teacher and excellent man who had introduced him to a larger musical world.

Pilar settled her son with Benet Boixados and his wife in the calle Nuevo de San Francisco in Old Barcelona, remaining for his first few days of school before returning to Vendrell to give birth to her ninth child. Pablo felt welcome from the first, and the Boixados couple were relatives of a sort: Benet was the brother of Gil Boixados, who had married Pilar's cousin Fidèlia, Pablo's godmother. He was too busy to be homesick, and one parent or the other visited fairly often.

Pablo's interest in the organ was diverted into other channels and he did not study the instrument in Barcelona, although he scored some of his compositions for it. He continued piano study with the famous Spanish pianist Joaquin Malats and, for a short time, Francisco Costa Llobera, both members of the Municipal

School faculty. His cello professor was José García, whose performance in Vendrell the year before had set in motion a lifetime of passionate, ambivalent thralldom to the violoncello. The cello classes continued through Casals' five student years in Barcelona and were, as it turned out, his only formal instruction on the instrument. (García was a member of the most notable dynasty of singers in the annals of music; its founder, Manuel del Popolo Vicente García, was the actor-composer-conductor for whom Rossini wrote the role of Count Almaviva in *The Barber of Seville* and who brought Italian opera to New York for the first time in 1825. Manuel García was the father of two of the dazzling stars in the grand-opera firmament—María Malibran and Pauline Viardot-García. It was one of Manuel's songs, "La Contrabandista," that in the early 1800's began worldwide excitement about the exotic color of the "Spanish idiom" in music. His son, Manuel García II, basso and voice teacher of Jenny Lind and Mathilde Marchesi, codified his father's teaching system into the famous "García method," invented the laryngoscope, and kept working to the age of 101. Casals, while a student at the Municipal School of Music, met him and heard him sing in Barcelona during a visit. He remembered him as a gentleman of great charm who still sang beautifully in his eighties.)

When Pablo Casals first became his student, José García was a man in his late thirties who wore an enormous mustache on a broad face so basically friendly and good-natured that the gruffness he affected toward his students was not always convincing. He produced a beautiful cello tone and handled the bow with skill; his hands were well formed for the instrument, with fingers that were neither too thick nor too fragile. He was a fine teacher and by the standards of the time an excellent cellist, although like the majority of musicians of the period he did not play absolutely in tune. (An acute ear and a certain musical fastidiousness did not allow Casals to be satisfied with approximate intonation in his own string playing, and he was never notably patient with imprecision in this particular on the part of others.)

Pablo in most respects took docilely enough to the laws and traditions of music, to a more sophisticated use of the techniques of his craft than Carlos could teach him, and to the existing cello repertoire. But he moved stubbornly if logically out of step with the ordinances of the musical establishment in matters of cello technique from the time of his first lessons with García. The largely unquestioned style of the epoch among string players was to play with the bow arm held relatively close to the body, forcing the elbow down and the wrist somewhat high. José García therefore instructed his cello students to practice with a book held tight in the armpit between the body and the right arm to assure the "proper" arm position. In fingering, the cellist's left hand was kept rather restricted, and the entire hand was moved to stop the strings at the desired point instead of extending the fingers.

These restrictions seemed artificial and silly to Pablo. He was attentive in class, but on his own he simply rejected the illogical, leaving the book on the reading table and the bow arm free to move as needed; he adjusted the prescribed fingering, opening up his hand to avoid unnecessary shifts when the result could be obtained equally well by extension of the fingers of the left hand. He began instinctively, in the stubborn assurance that what was natural had to be right—and easiest. Thus at the beginning of his study of the violoncello—before he reached his twelfth birthday—Pablo Casals was revolutionizing accepted cello technique and laying the foundation of his own manner of playing, which had much to do with bringing greater flexibility and grace to the instrument's artistry and making the cello the important solo instrument it had not been before.

There had been excellent and respected cellists from the end of the eighteenth century, and Casals did not invent the idea of stretching the fingers to touch a point on a string; by the time he began his musical studies in Barcelona a growing anti-Joachim school of violinists was proclaiming there was nothing wrong or inartistic about a string player's raising the elbow or moving the bow arm as freely as necessary, but he arrived at these things on his own. By and large, cellists continued to play in the old restricted way (and out of tune) until Casals began his wide-ranging concert career early in the twentieth century. In the years ahead, when instinct became rationale, Pablo Casals never himself used the terms *revolution* or *reform* about his impact on cello technique. He had made modifications, he admitted, and had applied them very young; they had come with the requirements of a moment, governed by freedom within order. "Perhaps I did introduce a more comfortable way of playing—but it is natural to give that great importance. It seemed to me easier, more natural. And in the left hand perhaps also I have had some influence in extension rather than the movement of the whole hand. In everything I tried to find what was physically more natural. . . . Cannot even a child observe, and have a true reaction to what may be wrong in the teaching?"

Freedom and naturalness were goals Casals sought through a lifetime, and he displayed courage very young. Convinced that beautiful sound could be produced from a large contrivance of pierced wood and taut gut more efficiently and easily without one arm strapped to the side and by extending a finger instead of moving a hand, Pablo continued his own way. Classmates began to notice and predicted that Garcían thunderbolts would fly when the Maestro saw what he was doing. Señor García watched and listened, frowned quizzically, then shrugged. Although he stalked about the room, hands clasped behind him, much of the time giving his back to the performing student, Pablo soon began to see pleasure and approval in his teacher's face as he played, when García thought he was not being observed.

Pablo was certain he would become a composer, but he spent regular hours of practice at piano and cello, already showing two lasting characteristics: a concentration when immersed in music that almost completely blocked out external stimuli and a dogged unwillingness to be interrupted until he had reached a logical stopping point—the end of a movement or the last note of a composition. He continued his education in general subjects with a university-student tutor. He began to explore the part of the city in which he lived with the Boixados—Old Barcelona, the *barrio gótico*, bounded by the harbor and ringed by streets that trace the irregular curve of ancient city walls, a quarter of twisting narrow streets and many medieval buildings. Hometown playmates were supplanted in Barcelona by companions and friends among fellow music-school students who were as ready to explore the city, wrestle, swim, or play tennis as to discuss music.

Life with Benet Boixados and his wife was without strain. Benet, a cabinetmaker and carpenter, was a gentle man with a sweet nature, a dedicated member of the Association for the Protection of Animals and Plants. His devoted wife María was the quieter of the two and a woman who seemed at times occupied with private worries.

Benet left the house alone nearly every evening after his meal and returned when Pablo was asleep, but the boy had no sense that his host caroused at night. The explanation came one day when the youngster noticed the scar of an old wound on Benet's arm and inquired about it. The man instructed him to open a large drawer in a cabinet. It was filled with revolvers, knives, blackjacks, and other implements of assault.

Boixados did go to taverns and cafés, but not to drink. Almost every night found him in the roughest waterfront hangouts, talking reform to ruffians and petty criminals. They were losing their lives, Benet told them, letting their own human value be dissipated by stealing and violence. "Give me your weapon," he demanded, and often grabbed knife or gun from the startled object of his attention. If the beneficiary was slow in surrendering the tool of his livelihood, he was likely to be speeded to action by a sharp blow from the stout ash-wood cane Benet always carried visibly but not prominently.

Benet Boixados' crusade as nocturnal missioner in the port's dives appears not to have been religious in the usual sense. He was not filled with Protestant zeal to be a vessel of salvation regardless of the cost, the logic, or the lasting effect; nor had inspiration from the Spanish Church set him to action. His curious apostolate was sustained by a personal vision of the dignity and worth of life so strong that it impelled this mild-seeming carpenter into the alleys of the night. Benet's wife, but not the neighborhood, knew his destinations in the darkness. And the denizens of Barcelona's late-nineteenth-century skid row began to know his reputation and frequently obeyed rather meekly his summons to give up knife or firearm. Sometimes, however, one of the thugs would be satisfied with his current mode of life and answer uninvited spiritual guidance with a blade: the scar that had roused Pablo's curiosity was a memento of such an occasion. Pablo Casals treasured and respected Boixados' solitary and quixotic behavior the rest of his life.

The ninth Casals child, named Pilar for her mother, was born during Pablo's first term at the Municipal School of Music; she died of tetanus within a week. When her strength returned, Doña Pilar came to Barcelona to be with her son and watch over him. She found third-floor rooms for them both in a house in the calle de Hospital, a street that curves through the heart of Old Barcelona to intersect the Ramblas halfway between the sea and the Plaza de Cataluña.

Pablo had already seen both the seafront and the plaza, although his mother's instructions had been to go directly to school and return by the shortest route; Barcelona was and remains one of the cities of the Western world that demand to be explored. The port of Barcelona, still in the age of sail when Pablo Casals first came to the city to live, was the most important in Spain as it had been for centuries, and the old seawall was still standing at the waterline. Thousands of cargo and passenger ships under many flags touched and departed its moles annually under the outward-pointing arm of a twenty-five-foot bronze statute of Christopher Columbus which that year had been placed atop a 195-foot iron pedestal guarded by eight bronze lions in the Plaza Puerta de la Paz. Inland a few hundred meters, in a building near the great cathedral, is the giant room in which Ferdinand and Isabella received Columbus in 1493 on the return from his first voyage to the New World. (Pablo Casals would become assured to his permanent satisfaction that Columbus was a Catalan Jew, not an Italian, delightedly pointing out when the subject arose in later years that the explorer signed his most important documents *Cristobal Colom*—a Catalan name—not *Colón*.)

When Pablo had come to Barcelona in 1887 for his injections of the Pasteur serum, building had been in progress for the Barcelona International Exposition of 1888—a fair emphasizing the technological progress of late-nineteenth-century Europe and North America that included a theater illuminated by electricity and the display of Gottlieb Daimler's first successful automobile powered by an internal-combustion engine. When Doña Pilar brought her son to study in Barcelona a year later, demolition of the exposition's nonpermanent buildings was still underway and could be seen from the cavernous Estacíon de Francia into which their train came. During his first year the Ramblas—running from the Columbus monument to the city's largest and busiest square, the Plaza de Cataluña, and one of the most fascinating avenues in the world—presented temptation to linger among mounds of fresh flowers surrounding shrill sellers in the mornings, or beside the cages of the bird market in the Rambla de los Estudios, or in the thronged promenade beneath the plane trees. The Tibidabo, the mountain to which the Devil is said to have transported Jesus to show him

*The Barcelona waterfront and seawall in
the 1870s*

the most appealing view of all the world, could be seen north of the city. And, some thirty kilometers northwest, the outline of the mighty massif of Montserrat rises in fantastic isolation from the west bank of the river Llobregat—*Montsagrat* in Catalan, the sacred mountain, the Monsalvat of the Middle Ages, place of the castle of the Holy Grail. Two-thirds up its face on a rocky spur is the Benedictine monastery of Montserrat, with its age-blackened wooden Madonna and the Escolanía, the school of sacred music that has continued uninterrupted since the fifteenth century, one of the centers of Catalan civilization.

Toward the end of his first year of study at the music school, in the spring of 1889, Pablo found his first full-fledged professional engagement—playing cello in a café trio seven nights a week from nine until midnight for four pesetas an appearance. The Café Tost was located on the chief street of the industrial suburb called Gracia, beyond the end of the broad Paseo de Gracia that led outward from the Plaza de Cataluña. It was well known for excellent coffee and chocolate; in those days as many as two hundred people could be accommodated, and the trio performed in the main room whose large windows gave onto the street. When the boy joined the group its repertoire was the usual one—popular songs, waltzes, marches, embroideries on operatic themes. The audience came to hear the music as much as to have a drink or meet friends; before phonograph records and radio, when hunger for music could be satisfied only by going to hear it performed, cafés famous for the music they offered grew up in every major city and in many smaller ones. The most celebrated drew top-flight musicians to perform and to listen; more than one important artist in the late nineteenth century and early in the twentieth was "discovered" as a café musician. The café audiences were often as discriminating and demanding of quality as those in the recital halls.

The four pesetas a night were some assistance to the family situation and three hours' playing a night was an important step in Pablo Casals' education. The youngster already exhibited a Capricornian seriousness in his musical attitude: even unpretentious café music ought to be done as well as could be, and for more than eighty years afterward Casals was constitutionally incapable of being uninterested in the music in which he participated, whatever the degree of sophistication involved.

At the boy's suggestion and with the cooperation of the trio's pianist and violinist some serious music began to appear "insidiously and occasionally" among the waltzes and zarzuela excerpts. The customers liked what they heard; the perpetrator considered it a coup brought off with a certain subtlety for one so young. Señor Tost was both a man of culture and a good businessman, and not much effort was required to persuade him and the other two musicians to try offering one evening a week of classical music, including instrumental solos. The experiment was a success except for a Brahms trio, which the public disliked loudly and immediately. Business boomed as word of the café began to spread and people began to come from central Barcelona to hear *El Niño del Tost* ("The Tost Kid").

When results of the music-school examinations were announced at the end of Pablo's first year, he had taken the prizes

*The Abbey of Montserrat has been a spiritual and
cultural force in Catalonia since the Middle Ages.
Pablo Casals wrote devotional works of beauty
and power for the Escolanía, its school of
sacred music.*

of his class and was one of the performers in the end-of-term recital. He had expected to remain in Barcelona because of his employment at the Café Tost, but Doña Pilar had discussed matters with Señor Tost and Pablo returned with his parents to Vendrell and went with his mother for a vacation at San Salvador. He appeared in a concert in Tarragona in late summer, and the newspaper *La Opinion* of that city noted in its issue of August 25, 1889: "In individual performance the boy Paulito Casals shone in the violoncello part . . . so much so that we do not hesitate assuring a brilliant future in the study of music if he continues to show today's application and native musical talent." (This was the first of the press cuttings Doña Pilar pasted into a small, clothbound blank book to which she continued to add notices until the day after her son's twenty-first birthday.)

When they returned to Barcelona for the beginning of the second year's study at the Municipal School of Music and Pablo resumed his job at the Café Tost, Doña Pilar found living quarters in the calle Valencia, within walking distance of the café. It was a logical move, but a distinct change of environment. The *barrio gótico* remained a complex of tiny streets and old buildings, the fascinating accumulation of centuries of unregulated growth; outside the semicircle of the ancient city walls the newer city had been laid out with wide, regular streets and plane-tree-lined avenues on which handsome houses fronted—a development plan influenced, like that of so many other growing cities in Europe and Latin America, by the spectacular rebuilding of Paris begun about thirty years before by Napoleon III and Baron Haussmann. It was much more sensible for Pablo to take the mule-drawn Gracia–Ramblas tramcar to school in the morning and return in the afternoon than for mother and son to travel together every night a long distance to and from the Café Tost. Although Pilar Casals seldom went to her son's recitals in later years, at this period she was to be seen nearly every night alone at her regular table with a cup of coffee while the trio played.

Señor Tost took his young star to concerts from time to time. Quite early during Pablo's employment at the café, they went to hear the celebrated Don Pablo of the age—Sarasate, whose showmanship was breathtaking. Later, after he knew Russian ballet, Casals said that Sarasate's impression on him had been the same as that made by a *premier danseur*, although he had found the program content rather insubstantial and Sarasate had not played in tune.

About this time Pablo started to know and appreciate the music of Brahms and, from scores, the operas and music dramas of Richard Wagner. By his early adolescence Casals could read a complex musical score as readily as the ordinary person reads a book, a faculty so natural to him that he never fully realized it is an ability many good musicians develop only through years of effort and some never attain at all. A typographer named Señor Fluviá, a Wagner enthusiast who was a member of the Orfeo Gracieno, the choral group that met weekly in rooms above the Café Tost, loaned Pablo copies of the *Parsifal, Tristan,* and *Ring* scores and went over favorite portions with him. Early in 1890 Señor Tost invited Pablo to join him for a concert conducted by Richard Strauss on his first trip to Barcelona. Strauss, in his mid-twenties already considered a revolutionary but substantial composer, directed a Mozart symphony and his own new tone poem *Don Juan*. The boy was impressed with Strauss' clear conducting and fascinated by his music.

While completing his second year at the Municipal School of Music and still employed at the Café Tost at night, Pablo earned extra money from time to time—usually six pesetas an appearance—playing with ensembles in churches for weddings, and sometimes for funerals in Barceloneta, the fisherman's *barrio* on a low spit of land that forms one boundary of Barcelona harbor. From the end of his second term definite summer employment was a necessity, although Doña Pilar ruled that there must also be some holiday time on the beach at San Salvador. That summer—and those following until he was sixteen—Pablo joined one of the traveling orchestras that furnished music for country fairs and dances throughout the provinces of Tarragona and Gerona. The pay was minimal and the work hard since the customers, sturdy and apparently tireless, were ready to dance through the night. Travel from one fiesta bandstand to another was in horse-drawn buses through fierce heat over dusty roads across the countryside of the North of Spain. These summer orchestras played some folk music and current popular songs, but what was most wanted was music to dance to: waltzes, mazurkas, meringues, paso dobles, schottisches. During the later demands of a major concert career, Casals could forget the discomfort of those hot journeys and long hours of playing, happily recalling his childhood summer jobs. During the one-night stands with such orchestras Pablo Casals' developing belief that music communicates to all people, regardless of station, education, or place, was reinforced. He had been conscious of Carlos Casals making the most beautiful music of which he was capable whether improvising during a mass or playing piano in the Café Centro. He realized that already he had a better formal training in music than his father and was giving himself without restraint in playing, as he said later, "from village to village in the summer trying my best to extract all the music there might have been out of waltzes and rigadoons." He felt a sympathy coursing between him and the listening rural dancers. He played solo voice in an "Americana," a popular slow Catalan step that was a great favorite with the summer audiences; often enough the dancers would stop

*(Top left) José Rodoreda, director of the
Municipal School of Music and the Barcelona
Municipal Band, Pablo Casals' first counterpoint
teacher; (bottom left) José García, the first
trained violoncellist Casals heard and his only
cello instructor; (right) Casals at eleven, about
the time he began to play at the Café Tost*

and crowd to the edge of the band platform, listening quietly until he finished, and he sometimes saw tears in listeners' eyes. There was understanding between him and them; he perceived in their shouts and applause homage to "the miraculous language of art."

Pablo was thirteen when he began his third year at the music school and resumed playing at the Café Tost, beginning an adolescence that was not financially or emotionally easy. Questions of the meaning of life, of his own identity, and of justice had begun to stir in him; at the café he began to observe the clientele more closely as he played, reacting to their expressions and, his sense of propriety already strong, finding in adult behavior more that was puzzling or distressing than was amusing.

Carlos Casals visited his wife and son in Barcelona whenever he could. With a delighted pride he showed Pablo's reports and talked about his son's progress to his friends in Vendrell, but in these years Pablo felt his father did not understand or support his ambitions and hopes. Actually, from the end of the first term, when Pablo carried home a full collection of first prizes, Carlos realized and admitted that the boy's natural musical aptitude was something well out of the ordinary and that it had been right for him to study in Barcelona. But, since the father continued to insist that a musician's life could not be economically profitable, it was easy for the sensitive son to feel at the time that Carlos did not understand him at all. As the boy became a better-educated and proficient musician, he was more aware of his father's considerable accomplishment as an autodidact, but the admiration further complicated Pablo's conflicting feelings about the man who had appeared in strong opposition to his advanced study and who clearly disagreed with Doña Pilar about a plan for the future.

His mother was again in the last months of pregnancy and Luis, her eighth son and tenth child, was born in Barcelona in October 1890. That night Pablo was late to work at the Café Tost for the first time. There had been times his mother had interrupted his reading or practicing to remind him it was time to go to work, and a balustrade overlooking gardens along the way invited daydreaming in the dusk, but in his months at the café he had always arrived no later than the other musicians.

The annoyed restaurateur was waiting at the entrance and, before the boy could explain, reached into his pocket and presented

Pablo Casals with the first timepiece he had owned, expressing the hope that "Señorito cellist" would learn to be on time. Naturally, after the circumstances were known, everyone congratulated him on his new state of brotherhood, but those who knew Casals well later in life can testify that his punctuality became formidable.

In November Pablo took part in a concert in Barcelona. The notice that appeared in *Ilustracion Musical* in December was the second his mother clipped and fixed in place in his first press book:

> The violoncello student, Don Pablo Casals, distinguished pupil of Señor García, demonstrated exceptional qualities in the performance of the *Allegro appassionato* of our lamented Tusquets, which won him an ovation quite as enthusiastic as deserved. Señor Casals, who is still a child in age, has proved in the Municipal School of Music, from the first year of solfeggio to his present participation in advanced courses of violoncello, piano, and composition, to be one of the students who most honor it through his application and indisputable talent.

4

THE YEAR he was still thirteen and still employed at the Café Tost, Pablo Casals became a Catalan and discovered Bach.

The old observation that every Spaniard's first loyalty is to his *patria chica*—the region of his birth—was true of Casals to some extent during the years of his virtuoso travels and inescapably so during the equally long period of his exile. From infancy he developed an almost mystic sense of place, of the Mediterranean shore at San Salvador and the environs of Vendrell, including the ruined twelfth-century cloister of Santas Creus in which he played his gourd "cello" in moonlight. His emotional identification with his homeland grew when he traveled as a summer musician in his early teens to include the ruined Cistercian monasteries of Poblet, where the kings of Aragon are buried; the sun-splashed fishing village of Sitges and the cotton-manufacturing and winemaking town of Reus; and Tarragona, the Roman city older and once more important than Barcelona, traditionally called the birthplace of Pontius Pilate.

Casals began young to wear the spiritual badge of his heritage. He studied Catalan history and that long chronicle, prodigal in noble deeds and names, inspired him. The Romans captured the

Catalan coast two hundred years before the birth of Christ when Scipio Africanus drove the Carthaginians out of Spain, and Roman colonies flourished on the site of Greek enclaves that had been Phoenician and Carthaginian landfalls. When Augustus Caesar made Tarragona the capital of Hispania Tarraconensis, the region from there to Barcelona became the economic center of the Iberian peninsula and of Roman Spain. The architect-emperor Hadrian was born in Spain, and the great epigrammatist Martial was a Catalan from Bilbilis.

But, as the boy learned, no force had been able to subjugate the North of Spain completely until his own century (in the ninth century Catalan peasants founded the republic of Andorra in an upper fastness of the Pyrenees so inaccessible that it was still sovereign eleven hundred years later). Neither the Romans nor the Vandals, the Germanic Franks from the north, the Moors from Africa, nor their successors ever really assimilated the Catalan people. Later in life Casals liked to point out that there had been a span of nearly three centuries in which the empire of Catalonia rivaled the greatest in history. After Wilfred the Shaggy threw off Teutonic control in 874 and established the *condado* (countship) of Barcelona, Catalonia spanned the Pyrenees, embraced the French littoral above flourishing Perpignan almost to Narbonne and inland to Carcassonne, encompassing Roussillon in a feudal complex that held together until the twelfth century and at one time reached as far as Greece. Casals liked to stress that Catalonia was ruled by its counts, not its kings; it possessed a form of constitution that reminded the king "Individually we are your equals; together we are greater than you." And, in the eleventh century, Catalan leaders met in solemn conclave in the ancient palace of the Majorcan kings in Perpignan to proclaim that warfare was an unsatisfactory way to settle differences between men and among kingdoms.

Sometime in 1890, well along in his employment at the Café Tost but before his fourteenth birthday, Pablo Casals discovered the six suites Johann Sebastian Bach wrote for unaccompanied cello. Carlos had come to Barcelona for a few hours' visit, a day already memorable to Pablo because his father had bought him his first full-sized cello. Then they had set out together in search of more scores for the Tost evenings. They went into a secondhand-music shop in the calle Ancha, a cramped street near the harbor. They found some Beethoven sonatas for cello and piano, then in a bundle of music the boy's attention was held by the Grützmacher edition of some suites by Bach for cello alone. It was the great discovery of his life.

> I forgot entirely the real reason of our visit to the shop, and could only stare at this music which nobody had told me about. Sometimes, even now [Casals wrote in 1930], when I look at the covers of that old music, I see again the interior of that old and musty shop with its faint smell of the sea. I took the suites home and read them and re-read them. They were to become my favorite music. For twelve years I studied and worked every day at them, and I was nearly twenty-five before I had the courage to play one of them in public.

Casals came to his early devotion to Bach, as to all the other important spiritual directions of his life, essentially by himself. Carlos had initially directed his son to *The Well-Tempered Clavier* in the terms in which Bach had written it, as a form of musical exercise; the father's romantic preferences tended to some of the Beethoven piano sonatas and the work of Chopin and Schumann and Mendelssohn, which he played with refinement. From early childhood Pablo began his day with a prelude or fugue from *The Well-Tempered Clavier* on his own impulse. Bach's work appeared in the curriculum of the Municipal School of Music, but he was not the most favored classical master of the time. García had never mentioned the Bach cello suites to his promising student—they had been as good as lost for a hundred years until Robert Schumann resurrected them by editing them and supplying piano accompaniments. But until Casals started including a full suite in his programs at the turn of the twentieth century neither cellists nor violinists played an entire Bach solo string suite in concert, although a secure performer might include one of the movements from time to time—prelude, allemande, courant, sarabande, minuet or bourrée or gavotte, gigue. A complete unaccompanied suite was deemed much too demanding for a paying audience.

Pablo Casals' second notable contribution to music thus began not long after he persisted in playing the cello in the way that seemed natural to him. That first step, important as its influence was, was restricted to musicians. When he began to offer the Bach suites in public (and much later to record them), his vision of that music became accessible to all who would listen. Even those wedded to the rigidly architectonic playing of Bach, outraged by the interpretation, had a more knowledgeable public to whom to complain of Casals' sins. But from the beginning Casals said, "How could anyone think of Bach as 'cold,' when these Suites seem to shine with the most glittering kind of poetry! As I got on with the study I discovered a new world of space and beauty . . . the feelings I experienced were among the purest and most intense of my artistic life." So from the age of thirteen his daily routine of cello practice included playing a Bach suite (with all repeats) after he finished the technical work.

Pablo made his first real Barcelona concert appearance February 23, 1891, less than two months after his fourteenth birthday, when he played two selections at the Teatro de Novedades as part of a benefit for the elderly comic actress Concepción Palá. Next day *La Renaixenta,* a Catalan-language newspaper, included six lines that praised his technique and the security, color, and sentiment of his playing, mentioned his accompanist, and reported an ovation. The *Diario de Barcelona* was longer and more florid in Castilian, devoting most of its notice to the boy's playing, including his intonation, and also reporting an ovation.

Beforehand had been terror. Even before playing solo at the Café Tost, Pablo had suffered a constricted stomach and clammy hands, but this always passed when he began to play. Just before he went on at the Novedades to play the Tusquets *Allegro Appassionato* (which he had been playing with flair and from memory for two years), he was struck by severe pain in his chest, as he would be the rest of his life when it was time to perform. And for the first time another monster gripped him: he was certain he could not remember the music. He told his father and Professor Sanchez, his pianist. Together they pushed him toward the stage.

Afterward three important Spanish musicians, who were in Barcelona performing as a trio—Isaac Albéniz, Enrique Fernández Arbós, and Augustín Rubio—came backstage. Albéniz, particularly, was exuberant. Short and stocky, wearing mustache and small beard and smoking a long cigar, he was a benign, totally musical whirlwind at thirty. A true infant wonder, he had given a public concert at four, taken the examination for the Paris Conservatoire at six, and entered the Madrid Conservatory at eight. He ran away

Isaac Albéniz

from his father's exploitation several times and at ten, having read Jules Verne, stowed away on the steamship *España* bound for Puerto Rico, only to be put ashore at Buenos Aires by the captain, although the passengers had taken a collection for the cost of his passage to San Juan. He made money playing piano in the Americas for three years before returning to serious study in Europe, including lessons with Liszt in Weimar and Rome. He began to tour as a mature piano virtuoso the year Pablo was four. Albéniz saluted the fourteen-year-old on the beginning of a great career and suggested at once that Pablo come to London, where Albéniz and Rubio were then living. Opportunities to perform would be better than in Spain and excellent cello teachers—including Rubio —were available.

Isaac Albéniz quickly found that in Pablo's mother he had met a clear-minded woman whose plans for her son were not to be diverted. Doña Pilar, appreciative and laconically gracious, said that the boy was not ready for anything of the sort. He would stay in Barcelona for the time being and continue his work at the Municipal School of Music. There would be time later for other things. Albéniz persisted. If London were not to be considered, she ought at least to take Pablo to Madrid, out of the provincialism of Catalonia and away from the cultural shortcomings of Barcelona. (Albéniz, born a Catalan, cared little for the region, saying the only place in Spain he felt at home was the Alhambra.) If Doña Pilar would consider sending or taking Pablo to Madrid, Albéniz offered a letter of introduction to the Count of Morphy, patron of music and musicians, enthusiast for Spanish opera, and now private secretary to the Queen Regent. The Count and Albéniz had met, the pianist recounted, when Albéniz was about Pablo's age. His money had run out and he hid under the seat in a compartment that, when the train started, turned out to be occupied by the Count. On discovering the stowaway, Morphy inquired somewhat formally who he was. With the boy's "*I* am a great artist. Who are you?" a friendship began and a royal scholarship was arranged for Albéniz to study at the Brussels Conservatory, where violinist Enrique Fernández Arbós was a fellow student. Rubio and Arbós agreed that the Count was a great and charming man who would be interested in Pablo and in helping his career. The letter of introduction was written and Doña Pilar put it away carefully.

Around this time Pablo left his job at the Café Tost to join an orchestra that was preparing for a season of eighteen performances of *Carmen* at the Teatro Tívoli. He enjoyed working in a full orchestra, and he adored the variegated, skillful score with its patches of fulsome lyricism and echoes of Wagner. Parisian critics, in fact, still damned the opera as a feeble imitation of Wagner, while Spanish pundits objected to what they called the pseudo-Spanish music written by one Frenchman to the melodramatic libretto of another. Barcelona audiences flocked to see the sixteen-year-old work—the sensual story and lurid characterization made distinctly up-to-date stage fare in the early 1890s.

If young Casals knew anything about the arguments among the musical journalists on the subject of *Carmen*, they concerned him as little as did similar parochial musical discussions later in his career. A neophyte composer fascinated by Wagner, he was interested in Bizet's use of the leitmotif; he reveled in the lushness of the sound and in the sentiment. He was buoyant leaving the stage entrance of the Tívoli after the season's final performance.

"What I like best about this opera is the end," proclaimed the contrabassist.

"Oh, yes indeed! Those notes that soar . . . the singing, the emotion, the finale of the work. . . ."

"No, no," said the longtime professional. "What I mean is that the damn thing's finally *over!*"

When their ways parted the youngster trudged home, shocked and dejected. Never in his life did he really understand how anyone could spend his working years making music and find it a chore.

Another café job became available with the opening in the Plaza de Cataluña of a fashionable new establishment called La Pajarera (The Birdcage), a large circular building with glass walls that did look something like a birdcage and was the first restaurant in Barcelona to be illuminated by electric light. Pablo began playing every night in a trio with two other musicians named Ibarguren and Armengol, and his personal following transferred from the Tost to the new place, which within a short time became the most popular musical *local* in town. Before long the trio was expanded to a seven-member group. The repertoire remained much what it had been at the Tost: waltzes by Waldteufel and Johann Strauss and dances by Catalan composers, operatic fantasies, popular melodies, an occasional bit of Schubert, Mendelssohn, or Schumann, although the formula of serious-music programs on scheduled evenings was also tried with some success.

At the end of the 1890–1891 term at the Municipal School of Music, Pablo walked away with first prizes in all his courses—he gave a notable interpretation of Saint-Saëns' showy *Allegro Appassionato* to a full, attentive concert room as part of his cello examination—and a special award was declared for a composition of his for mixed voices and organ. His private study in general subjects continued; history, botany, and the classics in literature interested him most.

By 1891 Pablo Casals and Enrique Granados had met in Barcelona, starting a close and happy friendship for both. Granados, born the son of an army officer in the Catalan city of Lérida late

*The Bar Torino fronted on the Paseo de Gracia
in Barcelona a few blocks from the Café Tost.*

in July 1867, was a tall young man with great dark eyes, wavy black hair, and the face and aura of a poet. He had made Barcelona his home in 1889 after a period of illness and sketchy musical study in Paris, and by the time he and Casals met was regularly giving piano recitals in Spain and Paris, establishing a reputation as a teacher, and composing assiduously. Pablo responded as to an older brother to the shy and childlike pianist, assuring Granados from the outset that in the restrained, aristocratic poetry of what he was composing he was giving form in music to the truest spirit of Spain. Too nervous to do it himself, Granados asked his fifteen-year-old friend to prepare the orchestra for an early performance of his opera *María del Carmen*, while the composer sat huddled in a corner of the auditorium during rehearsals.

If Doña Pilar had agreed to take the boy to London in 1891, her son's public career would have been launched nearly ten years earlier than it was. His talent was such that the Casals name would in all probability have been prominent in the roster of musical wunderkinder of the end of the nineteenth century. If his mother had allowed his exploitation, he would have been on display half as prodigy and half as sideshow attraction in a short-pants velvet suit and white sailor collar. Doña Pilar never explained her reasons, but she could not have had any firsthand knowledge of the psychic anguish suffered by many of the sensitive adolescents who did begin important musical careers very young. The decision of this remarkable and adamant woman seems to have been formed by her almost primordial concept that what must be will come in its proper time and in a natural way. Pablo Casals reflected the mind of his mother far more than he realized when he said long afterward that only the mediocre are impatient—"the great know how to wait."

In any event, Pablo's emotional readiness to function in a larger world must have been a matter of some concern to his mother, if not to both parents. There had been a time of particular strain and separation between husband and wife after Pilar first came to stay in Barcelona with their son. Carlos insisted that she return to live properly with him in Vendrell; she refused. She had lost eight children, and in a sense took refuge in the life of the one who remained. There was also an element of denial in this woman who soon would not attend her son's performances because she felt his stage fright too strongly. From the time of her marriage she dressed simply in black. "I am the wife of a poor man," she said; it was her explanation for refusing the jewelry offered long after her husband's death by the son who idolized her and was by then a wealthy man. Carlos had returned sadly and alone, preoccupied with his work in Vendrell and worried about money. Highly emotional, beginning to forge his identity and strongly drawn to both parents, Pablo still saw himself as the only cause of the disagreements between them.

A less highly tuned human instrument might have suffered less. In spite of his mother's presence, which was constant and strong and which Casals remembered as always supportive and sympathetic, his inescapable quest for his own identity and his battle to come to terms with the world was solitary and difficult.

He was working harder than a child should; he tended to be ruminative and serious; and the inwardness that characterized his mother scarcely communicated to the son a sense of the unfettered joys of living.

"Everybody has an epoch of distress. I had it very young," he said at eighty-nine to Louis Biancoli of the inner fight that cannot be articulated until long after peace has been made. "It lasted a long time. It made me physically ill. . . . It was terrible." Walking through the Catalan capital's restless thoroughfares, he began to search faces and was terribly aware of what seemed to him the flamboyant display of the wealthy and the sometimes equally ostentatious rags of the beggars, the braver cleanliness of the honestly poor as well as the self-satisfied swagger and selfish finery of the middle class. The faces in the anonymous street crowds seemed self-occupied and empty. He could not lose the thought of the children in his family who had died. Three quarters of a century afterward he remembered seeing the crowds smiling and chattering in the streets and thinking, don't they know they are going to die? Seeing a soldier in the streets, his only reaction was, that man's only function is to kill!

Returning through the calle Fernando from the Municipal School of Music, he went often through the main portal of the old church of Santo Jaime in search of a dark corner in which he could pray and meditate unnoticed; leaving, he sometimes hurried back inside, more anguished than ever. "I was religious, and I felt a pity for humanity that generally comes later. . . . I wandered about the streets by myself, and I discovered suffering. I saw people with nothing to eat. I saw the inequality of the rich and the poor. I saw people begging and in pain. I was overwhelmed by pity and grief. . . . I think more persons than we realize have such crises. How can they help it, if they have eyes to see?"

It was natural that his search should take him first to beg answers of the organized church. The sonorous and solemn words, the prescribed actions, the chants of priest and choir had been familiar and satisfying when he served as the smallest acolyte and youngest of choristers in the Church of Santa Ana in Vendrell. But "my religious fervor did no good . . . I went for a consolation I could not find." In hours of excited desperation he found in the Church much ritualism but nothing to appease his "ardor and exaltation." From childhood he had heard his mother say

"The real God can never be explained. The one of the church is another thing. . . . " But during the anguished introspection of Pablo's religious crisis Pilar Casals tried to console him and to turn his thoughts to God. He never again went through a formally religious phase; for the rest of his life he simply and quietly maintained "a sort of personal and intimate dialogue between [his] conscience and the Divinity." In the years of his greatest maturity and tranquility he further resolved the search and the answer: "If we truly have the awareness of *what* we are and *where* we are, we will find God."

Metaphysical questions alone were not what made the oversensitive adolescent wretched. He felt a mental revulsion in the face of a world that appeared to have neither charity nor justice nor meaning. From religion his search turned to political ideas. He explored socialist doctrines and read some of the works of Marx. Once more the answers gave no solace: "Marxist ideology foretold a world too good to be true. My critical mind could not accept this. I had only to look about me to see what men were like, and I sadly realized that nothing would change them—that they would never become 'brothers.' " There had been anarchist riots in Barcelona on the first of May, 1890, the spring of the year Luis was born (As soon as he was old enough, Doña Pilar took Luis to board with a family in Vendrell and returned to Pablo in Barcelona.) There were other flare-ups of violence in Spain during the next few years. It did not look as if the world was moving toward either good will or brotherhood, and the incidents raised in the youth's mind the lasting question how people could think they would improve the human lot by spilling blood.

His sixteenth birthday came at the end of 1892, almost halfway through Pablo's fifth and final year as a music student in Barcelona, when his interior crisis was most intense and he felt himself in a hopeless labyrinth, although he continued to go about the routine of life and learning. During the worst period he became obsessed with the thought of suicide, an uninvited idea that haunted him for months. Music was his only physician and confidant in the worst moments. His face showed some of the dark time of his mind, but when his mother asked what was wrong he answered that it was nothing, too fond of her to speak of the obsession, but he could not rid himself of it.

Pablo's last brother and his parents' eleventh child, Enrique,

*Pablo Casals at sixteen, as he was finishing five
years' study at the Barcelona Municipal School
of Music*

had been born toward the end of June 1892; that same year Carlos
Casals left his post as organist in the Church of Santa Ana after
twenty years, said farewell to his pupils, and rejoined his family
to live in Barcelona, where he immediately found music students.

The family was reunited, living in an apartment in the calle
de Paleyo near the Plaza de Cataluña, but the disagreement between the couple about their son's future continued. Carlos was
enormously proud of his son's accomplishment, still showing
Pablo's awards and press clippings to friends and repeating José

García's remark that his son had learned more than he had been able to teach him about the cello. Yet his ideas about Pablo's future still diverged widely, or seemed to, from the determination of his wife and son to seek greater musical opportunity someplace other than Barcelona. Carlos' stand was still that the life of a musician was not a practical aspiration and, even if it were, the necessary money was not available.

The continued rift he felt between his parents was possibly the strongest element in the boy's personal suffering at the end of his Barcelona student period. "My greatest wish was to get them to agree," he recalled. "But how could I do it? Fortunately, when I was sixteen and the crisis was at its height, my mother backed me up with incredible tact and understanding. But my father could not understand me and did not realize how near I was to a fatal crisis."

The inner force for survival, what he came to identify as Bergson's *élan vital*, was so strong that he came through the stage without being crippled emotionally. Without the presence of Doña Pilar—his guardian and moral guide, who never actually left him for long—he believed he would have foundered. Reflecting on his worst youthful despair, her son said: "She was an exceptional woman, a very strong character, a wonderful woman . . . her energy, her genuine understanding, and her deep humanity! I think she saved me."

In the spring of 1893, Pablo graduated with honors from the Municipal School of Music, having prepared the major cello concertos with critical guidance from García, and with a considerable repertoire of shorter pieces from his experience as a café musician. He was an expert pianist, and there was a respectable collection of his own student compositions. But whatever the specific path his musical career was to take, García and school director Rodoreda told Pablo and his parents, sights should be set on Paris and further study. The Barcelona City Council had announced a competition for a scholarship for advanced musical study abroad. Pablo should enter; if he won, the necessary funds would be available. The municipal prize went to another contestant, a hard shock and a surprise in the face of his sponsors' enthusiasm and Pablo's own hope. Further study seemed out of the question, and the honor graduate plunged once more into misery.

Albéniz had remained in touch through the years, as had

Arbós, now director of the Madrid Symphony. Doña Pilar wrote Albéniz to tell him the time had come to use the letter of introduction to the Count of Morphy. Her son had not been ready before, but if they did not go soon it might be too late.

Pablo returned briefly to Vendrell, where he was greeted with a mixture of nonchalance and honor for a hometown boy who has done well in the big city. Doña Pilar made preparations for the journey to Madrid for herself, Pablo, young Luis, and the infant Enrique. They left to Carlos' bewildered protests of impracticality as he himself made plans to return to Vendrell.

The eight-hundred-kilometer trip westward, inland from Barcelona and the coast to Madrid in the desolate central upland plain of the Iberian peninsula, took a day and a night in May 1893, and was more than ten times the distance of the trip the mother and the eldest son had taken in 1888 from Vendrell to Barcelona. Pablo, almost adult in years and physique, was attentive to the needs of the younger boys but spent much of his waking time during the trip quietly reading, watching the slowly passing terrain, thinking. He had with him in the cold, noisy, dirty third-class railway carriage his cello, a packet of scores, and his father's suitcase.

Doña Pilar, now thirty-nine, spoke little. She nursed Enrique when he woke and stirred with hunger on the wooden seat beside her, and from time to time she offered three-year-old Luis and Pablo food from a basket. The rest of the time, while there was enough light outside to see, she contemplated the austere landscape.

From the Estación del Norte in Madrid all four went directly to the town house of the Count of Morphy in the fashionable northwestern *barrio* of Argüelles.

5

LEGEND HAS IT that mother and sons traveled unannounced to Madrid and little more than an hour after reaching the spaciously monumental capital city were waiting, with luggage and cello, in the reception foyer of the town house belonging to the Count of Morphy, private secretary to the Queen Regent of Spain. It was characteristic of Pilar Defilló de Casals to go directly from the station, but it is unlikely she would have undertaken so long and expensive a journey without a tentative appointment.

The Count's majordomo Valentín showed the visitors into a handsome drawing room, where the master of the house greeted them. The carefully preserved letter from Albéniz recommending a talented fourteen-year-old café musician was presented. The Count read it carefully.

Pablo began to feel at ease as the Count of Morphy repeated the story of his first encounter with Albéniz—his version being that after he had discovered the youngster hidden under the seat in his railway compartment Isaac had indeed introduced himself as a great artist, adding conspiratorially "But I am traveling incognito!" The Count stressed that Albéniz had worked hard and studied well afterward in Leipzig and Brussels as well as with Liszt;

he had that very spring given up his concert career and was in process of settling with his wife and children in Paris. Among other things he was now writing operas—an excellent thing, Morphy said, except that the librettist was a wealthy English would-be poet and the results had so far been disastrous.

The Count of Morphy asked to see some compositions. Pablo gave him first the string quartet he had completed earlier in the year in Barcelona. The boy studied his host, who was short and somewhat heavy at fifty-six, with full mustache and a rather patriarchal beard. His clothing was impeccable. His manner, like his drawing room, was at once elegant and comfortable. His expression was open, his conversation that of a man of wide culture and personal refinement. He gave the impression of being a man who had maintained a position of influence at the highest level for a long time but who was also certain of his own identity; and he seemed interested. After a servant had fetched the cello the Count listened attentively as Pablo played, said he was indeed an artist, and returned to the subject of composition—he seemed particularly interested in the boy's potential as a composer. Pablo was to come back next day at three. A brief discussion between Doña Pilar and Valentín resulted in information about a nearby house with rooms to let.

Next day after siesta Pablo returned to the Count's home. Over coffee he met the Countess, Morphy's second wife, a gracious Hungarian who was a singer and onetime piano student of Franz Liszt, and was introduced to her daughter Crista, a striking girl not much older than he. Pablo played the cello again, the Count accompanying him on piano, before Morphy made a surprise announcement: Pablo was to play in the royal palace the following evening for the Infanta Isabel, eldest daughter of Isabel II and sister-in-law to the Queen Regent. Too startled and pleased to give his patron total attention, Pablo listened to the Count's explanation of the requirements of etiquette for performing in the presence of Spanish royalty.

Nervous enough at the prospect, Pablo was less than overjoyed to discover that his two sometimes noisy young brothers were also to be taken to the palace, although he had to admit his mother was correct when she pointed out briskly that there was nobody else to look after them.

Tense though he was the next evening, Pablo was conscious

of the mixture of charm and dignity for which the Infanta Isabel Francesca de Borbón had become known. In her early forties, not tall and already quite heavy, she looked somewhat like portraits of her mother at the same age. The young musician did not register physical details of the royal palace or of the Infanta's apartment on this occasion. He played both cello and piano, including some of his own compositions, for a small audience. While his brother was playing, eleven-month-old Enrique set up a competing wail. Pablo saw his mother's questioning look to the royal hostess and the Infanta's nod; Doña Pilar opened the bodice of her dress and began unconcernedly to nurse the hungry infant as the recital ended with a single soloist. That solo performance is reported not to have been the best of Casals' career. Afterward, however, he heard Her Highness say to Morphy "You were right. He is a marvel." She promised to organize a recital before the Queen.

The news did not take long to reach Vendrell, and *El Vendrellense* for the fourteenth of May 1893 expressed satisfaction in reporting that a son of the town, "the young and excellent *profesor de violoncello* D. Pablo Casals," had given a concert in the royal palace in Madrid, in the apartments of Her Highness the Infanta Doña Isabel, before a select audience that had given him an ovation, "acclaiming him not only for his vast knowledge and execution as a fine artist but also, and this is the most surprising part of the report [commented the hometown paper], for his talent and proper schooling as a composer. . . ."

It was logical for the Count of Morphy to have arranged for the older sister of the late Alfonso XII to be the first member of the royal family to hear Pablo Casals play. She liked music and also knew a good deal about it—not always a royal combination. Energetic, sensitive, generous, and with the means at her disposal to supplement the impulse, she encouraged young singers and other musicians, who were often trained at her expense, and for years no important concert was given in Madrid without her patronage and presence. Music, in fact, along with religion and the monarchy, filled the life of this intelligent, highly sentimental woman. She had been married at seventeen to the epileptic brother of the King of Naples, the morose Count de Girgenti, who shot himself three years later. She returned to Madrid when the monarchy was restored as hostess for her brother, a role she fulfilled gracefully until after Alfonso's second marriage four years later to María Cris-

*The Infanta Isabel Francesca de Borbón, oldest
daughter of Isabel II of Spain*

tina of Austria. The Infanta and Morphy were natural musical
allies, and they had both adored Alfonso XII. Even if protocol
had not suggested that Isabel be the first to hear the new discovery,
the Count knew that her enthusiasm would be a strong factor in
arousing Queen María Cristina's interest.

The Count of Morphy gave Pablo the news that he was to play
before the Queen that same week. Doña Pilar was not included

[75]

in the invitation. The son sat silent, watching the expression of the Count, as the mother spoke very quietly. She had been with her boy for five years in Barcelona, and she had brought him to Madrid. His first performance for Her Majesty would be one of the crucial moments of his life, and because it was of such importance to him, she must be there. Pablo saw surprise followed by respect in the man's face. "I apologize that you were not invited from the first," said the Count of Morphy. He rose and took Doña Pilar's hand. "Señora, I salute you."

The concert took place before about thirty guests, the royal entourage and leaders of musical life in Madrid, in the music room of Her Majesty's apartment, the sumptuous but not overwhelming room María Cristina favored for informal concerts. The music included Casals' string quartet, with the composer playing cello and Enrique Fernández Arbós first violin. On piano Pablo played a barcarole and another piece he had written the preceding year; the program ended with a cello solo.

Thus, Pablo Casals at sixteen met Her Majesty Doña María Cristina, Queen Regent of Spain, the beginning of a close filial affection for this intellectual Austrian woman—who was nevertheless very much the Queen of Spain—that continued, after one early lapse, for thirty-five years. The Count of Morphy announced the result of the concert the next day: Her Majesty had directed the award of a monthly allowance of 250 pesetas (about fifty dollars), enough to sustain the mother and three boys and to enable Pablo to continue his musical studies. Living quarters were found near the palace, and Pablo went to work.

He began private lessons in composition with Tomás Bretón, who had been among the guests at the audition for the Queen and was impressed by the talent the boy's string quartet indicated. Tomás Bretón y Hernandez had been famous for ten years on the basis of his zarzuela *La Verbena de la Paloma* (*The Feast of Our Lady of the Dove*), an amusing melodic one-act operetta about middle-class Madrid life which was destined to be one of the most popular examples ever written of that uniquely Spanish stage form. Now a handsome man in his early forties with a thin face and the beard and full mustache of the era, he had become one of the most articulate of those who were trying to free the Spanish musical stage from what he labeled the "stupid and disastrous" Italianism that had stifled it from the start (and, unlike his fellow zealots Felipe Pedrell and the Count of Morphy, even his first operas were successes). Of more interest to his student was that Bretón composed good chamber music—intricate and masterly in architecture and full of bold harmonies.

The Count of Morphy made the arrangements for lessons with Bretón; the completion of Pablo's academic education he undertook personally. The boy responded to the man who made him feel at ease and whom he soon addressed by invitation as Papá. Morphy, by disposition and a coincidence of material and intellectual circumstances, was able to give the youth the perceptions and opportunities Carlos Casals could not, and he worked at making the sometimes depressed and unnaturally serious adolescent smile. A man of strength who directed much of the boy's life for more than two years, the Count also was able to give him a sense that he was understood and that his aspiration was acceptable. "I have two sons," Morphy would say, "Alfonso the Twelfth and Pablo Casals!"

Much was still to be done; Pablo's academic education in Barcelona could scarcely be called intensive. The Count of Morphy believed that the true artist is knowledgeable about all fields. The world in which Pablo would move, when he became the important figure the Count expected him to be, called for grooming in advance if his place was to be taken gracefully. Courage, integrity, and sensitivity to the human experience have little to do with formal learning, but the course of action taken by a man who has knowledge of the world and has perspective may not be the same as that of one who does not. In the time he was with the Count of Morphy, Pablo Casals received what amounted to a court education in general subjects and considerable exposure to society. Without this influence his life would have had a much different intellectual texture, however great his musical accomplishment.

Pablo had acquired a remarkable mentor. For political reasons the grandparents of Guillermo Morphy y Férriz de Guzmán had left Ireland in Napoleonic times. Irish blood notwithstanding, the grandson had been born Castilian and was passionately a Spaniard. At twenty-eight, in 1864, he had finished his law degree (studying music simultaneously at the Colegio Masarnau in Madrid) and worked for a year at the Brussels Conservatory under its aged and formidably learned director, François Joseph Fétis. In 1864 he was

*Guillermo Morphy y Férriz de Guzmán, the
Count of Morphy, private secretary to the
Queen Regent of Spain*

named gentleman of the bedchamber and a tutor to the Prince of the Asturias, Isabel II's seven-year-old son the Infante Alfonso. After the forced departure of Isabel and her court for France in 1868 Morphy continued to serve as the Prince's tutor. When Alfonso's education was taken out of the hands of his mother and her dissolute circle (the only way he stood a chance of being called back to the throne) and he was sent for the last year of his education to the Theresianum College in Vienna, Morphy went along as his chief of studies. Alfonso styled him *conde* (count) in May 1875, and Morphy was his private secretary when Alfonso landed in Barcelona the preceding January to assume the throne. The Count remained a friend and close adviser until the King's death and had been private secretary to Alfonso's widow for nearly ten years when Pablo Casals became his protégé and hers.

Morphy still had the textbooks from which Alfonso XII had studied and in which the royal hand had scrawled marginal notes. These were used for Pablo's lessons; later the Count said that they and the rest of his important, beautifully bound library would come to Casals when he died. Doña Pilar also read from those few textbooks of Alfonso, and from her son's other books and his written exercises, to be able to discuss what concerned him at the moment. She also started to learn the languages he was studying.

Beginning soon after his arrival in Madrid in the spring of 1893, Pablo reported every morning at nine to the Count's house in Argüelles. The daily lessons were strong meat—ancient and modern literatures and history, geography, political theory, mathematics, the history of art—and lasted until noon. At luncheon he joined the Count, the Countess, and Crista for food and conversation; Crista also supervised his German assignments. Afterward he generally played piano for the Count—a composition he was working on, some Mozart or Bach, sometimes improvisation.

One of the Count's educational techniques was a happy consequence of place. Once a week he sent Pablo on a foray to the Prado, his assignment to choose and study a single picture, then write a report on the painting and his reactions to it. The whole history of Spain and of art is in this mammoth sandstone structure begun in 1875. The building was still being enlarged in the 1890s, but the collection (begun with treasures gathered by Carlos V) reached its present scope and richness three years before Casals was born, during the brief first Spanish republic, when Spanish and Flemish pictures from Spain's churches and monasteries were incorporated.

These assignments, to which he brought considerable enthusiasm, introduced Pablo to great pictorial art. He particularly liked the work of the Venetians, the French painters of the seventeenth and eighteenth centuries, and the Prado's two superb examples of fifteenth-century Italian painting—a Fra Angelico *Annunciation* and Mantegna's *Death of the Virgin*. But his first and lasting satisfaction was in the magnificent Spaniards: Velázquez, Zurburán, Murillo, Goya; he did not take immediately to the mystic linearity of El Greco, which seemed to him tortured and unnatural. These visits established the museum habit, and through the years of travel in his career as performer he would eagerly visit the great art collections of the world. He came first to know Renaissance art and that of the seventeenth through the nineteenth centuries, and in later years he felt a lack of form and discipline in the work of most of the experimental and exploratory figures who succeeded the Impressionists. For him even impressionism, in the graphic arts and literature as in music, showed clear evidence of the disintegration of the "true and lasting" art forms.

A parallel assignment was a weekly trip to the Cortes to sit in the gallery and listen to parliamentary debate and afterward write a résumé of what he had heard. Casals' late-adolescent years in Madrid were a time of fiery and sometimes elegant Spanish political oratory. The most famous figures of the Restoration were still present, in power or seeking it—Canovas del Castillo and Sagasta, and the opposition Republican leaders, including Castelar, Pi y Margall, Salmerón, Silvela, and Menéndez y Pelayo. Most of these men were deeply involved in their own political theories and many were eloquent. The visits sharpened his ear to precision and beauty in the Castilian language; they had little effect on the development of his political ideas beyond a lifelong skepticism of politicians.

From the imposing Palacio de las Cortes Españolas, Pablo returned through the heart of Madrid—so different in tempo, appearance, and climate from Barcelona—to his top-floor room across the park from the palace to write his essay and continue his music. Later he would read to the Count what he had written and sometimes attempt to translate the reports into German or French as a further exercise; then he and the Count would discuss the essay and ideas that rose out of it.

But the Count of Morphy's prime interest was not politics or rhetoric, Thucydides or scientific knowledge; it was music. He had composed a cantata, religious music that included a mass, and three operas and had written an important book on Spanish folk music as well as a monumental work dealing with sixteenth-century

Iberian music. He was a member of the Spanish Academy and was artistic director of the Madrid Ateneo. His zeal in fostering the cause of truly Spanish opera amused some important people and annoyed others. For years court and governmental functionaries called him *El Músico* with an intonation only bureaucrats can confer. His interests and words had weight with the sovereign, and many people at the top found more irritation than laughter in the fact that his concern was music and poetry and painting instead of politics and power.

Morphy's full influence in shaping the life of Pablo Casals in his late teens is incalculable. During the Madrid years, his musical guidance and pressure went toward making the boy a Spanish composer. Morphy's taste was refined, informed, and traditional. One incident made an indelible mark on the impressionable student whose ambition and self-confidence had begun to grow. One day after luncheon the Count instructed him to improvise on the piano and Pablo, as the Count appeared to drowse, started playing the unconventional harmonies and progressions that had begun to intrigue him. "No!" interrupted Morphy, wide awake. "*No*, Pablito! In the language of *everybody*."

When the 1893–1894 term of the royal Conservatorio de Música y Declamación began in the autumn following his arrival in Madrid, Pablo was enrolled in the chamber-music class taught by the director, Jesús de Monasterio. He did not study cello in Madrid; Monasterio decided there was no one equipped to teach him anything he did not already know or could not work through for himself. In any event, the young Catalan was being groomed to be a composer.

Monasterio's approach to music had been tested and refined for more than thirty years. A contemporary of Morphy and Saint-Saëns, his talent had been obvious enough at seven to elicit patronage from the royal house in the time of Isabel II. He toured for a while as a child prodigy, then settled down between the ages of thirteen and sixteen to study violin with Charles de Bériot and François Gevaërt at the Brussels Conservatory. By twenty-five he was touring central Europe, a thoroughly finished performer acclaimed as a virtuoso. He was invited to take the post of court kapellmeister in the Esterhazy establishment at Weimar but preferred to settle in his native land, where he was appointed violinist of the royal chapel and professor at the Madrid Conservatory. By the time Pablo reached the capital in 1893, Monasterio was head of the school and one of the most distinguished musicians in Spain.

Pablo Casals found a superlative teacher and, in the course of time, a friend in Jesús de Monasterio. Carlos Casals was the first important musical influence in his son's life; in an immeasurably more sophisticated way, Monasterio was the second. He did much to open the boy's mind to the inner significance of music, and he made him conscious of style. His personality was maturing, musically and psychologically; paralleling the general education he was obtaining under Morphy, his two years in Madrid completed the foundation of Casals' musicianship. Monasterio handled the talent and, almost always, the temperament of the Catalan adolescent with tact and authority.

Pablo was still unformed as an artist, still searching for direction and assurance. His tentative suggestions and embryonic aspirations, as he called them later, met agreement and reinforcement from the experienced musician. His personal tendencies often led him to question tradition in matters of interpretation as well as technique. He had developed what amounted to a mania for good intonation. And he had a strong but still inarticulate notion that music possesses an inherent and inescapable accentuation, difficult to explain but with analogies in breathing and in natural speech, in the ebb and flow of the sea, in the cycles of nature.

Casals received from Monasterio much more than reassurance that his ideas were sound and his instinct true. The younger musician's earnestness and dedication were buttressed by the words and the example of the older. To Monasterio music was an art of the greatest nobility and beauty, not a social amusement or a vehicle for showing off technical mastery. Discipline, refusal to compromise in taste or principle, a constant search for the inner meaning of the music were attributes Pablo Casals credited Monasterio for strengthening in him during his student years in Madrid.

The living quarters Doña Pilar found for herself and her sons after the monthly royal allowance was announced were garret rooms in a house at number 8 in the short, curved calle de San Quintín, which ends in the broad calle de Bailén across from the palace gardens. The house had been built around 1845 to house members of the palace staff, and in Casals' time the Queen's doctor lived in a spacious apartment on the ground floor. Accommodations became progressively less opulent on higher floors. The Casals ménage shared the top landing with women who worked in a cigar factory, a palace hall-porter fiercely proud of his livery and inordinately adored by his wife, and a shoemaker with two retarded children. It was like a set for one of the busier scenes of *La Verbena de la Paloma;* the neighbors were friendly but volatile, and the upper reaches of the house were noisy day and night. There was no interior garden, only a small central-hall court with a sixty-meter-deep artesian well that supplied good water, but the house looked out onto the Plaza de Oriente, the largest square in central Madrid, which contains beautiful gardens surrounded by forty-four statues of Visigothic and Spanish kings and is dominated by a great central equestrian statue of Felipe IV.

The palace across the way became a part of Casals' home life. The Palacio Real in Madrid is an unlikely place for the son of a Catalan village musician—or anyone else—to have found a second mother. Young Casals was nonetheless soon cutting through a corner of the Plaza de Oriente to enter the palace at the Queen's invitation to make music, talk with her, and sometimes occupy seven-year-old Alfonso XIII with a game or story.

As regent for her son, María Cristina was mistress of eight palaces of considerable impressiveness and various states of repair, but during his student years Casals visited her only in the giant Madrid establishment across from his garret bedroom. The Palacio de Oriente, more solemnly grand than beautiful, was served by a staff of about a hundred (there was also a roster of half that many ladies-in-waiting). There were more than two hundred horses and some forty especially bred carriage mules in the stables. The royal allowance was about four million dollars a year, an income from which María Cristina prudently saved a fortune. She was a woman of simple personal tastes and, unlike some of her predecessors, not avaricious.

When Pablo Casals first saw her, María Cristina of Spain was in her mid-thirties. There was too much Hapsburg in this second cousin of the Emperor Franz Josef for her face to be truly beautiful; she had the firm jaw and somewhat unyielding expression of that ancient house. Although she seemed plain beside her mother, the spectacularly beautiful Archduchess Elizabeth, she was actually quite good-looking—fashionably slender, with a tiny waist

(Top) During his Madrid student years Casals lived with his mother and two young brothers in rooms on the top floor of 8 calle de San Quintín, a short street that borders the Plaza de Oriente across from the royal palace; (bottom) the Plaza de Armas façade of the Palacio Real, Madrid

and an erect, regal bearing; she moved with a natural grace, dressed well, and wore her clothes with authority. "A very charming face and manner, brown eyes," reported Queen Victoria, and "a good nose." She had great dignity and enormous strength of spirit; in Casals' memory she remained every inch a queen. The Queen Regent was too regal for some of her subjects (to some of whom she was *La extranjera* or *doña Virtudes* [Madam Virtue]), too detached, too correct, too intellectual. She was far too conventional and controlled for the taste of the rebellious Infanta Eulalia, younger sister of the Infanta Isabel.

María Cristina and Alfonso XII had been married in 1879. At the beginning of 1878 Alfonso had married Mercèdes de Montpensier, with whom he was madly in love; their open and radiant happiness delighted their subjects and added to the luster of the people's nickname for the gallant, boyish king: *el rey romántico.* Mercèdes died within five months, two days after her eighteenth birthday. In María Cristina the government found an eminently suitable candidate for a second wife; she was a member of one of the oldest, most conservative, and most relentlessly Catholic royal families of Europe. Alfonso never really recovered from the shock of Mercèdes' death; the second wedding was arranged as an affair of state, but the twenty-one-year-old Austrian archduchess fell in love with her disinterested, tubercular husband. She bore Alfonso two daughters before his death in 1885, three days before his twenty-eighth birthday; his heir, Alfonso, was born six months later.

During his student years in Madrid, Casals saw the Queen Regent carry out enough of her ceremonial duties on state occasions to form a lasting admiration for a woman who did her job well—a job that included presiding over what was often termed the stiffest and most formal court in Europe other than the Vatican. But privately there was a sad, somewhat endearing look in the eyes of Maria Christina Désirée Henrietta Félicité Renier, and beneath the Austrian reserve a woman of great warmth. Casals remembered "his" Queen of Spain (he never liked her English daughter-in-law) as a person of strength, sentimentality, and motherliness. She was a dutiful parent to her children, a lady whose antidote for nausea at bullfights (which she loathed) was to eat a sandwich, and the first queen to make a balloon ascent. She had real interest in certain liberalizing measures for Spain but was frustrated because she did not have power to institute them nor was she able to persuade the parliamentary leaders to legislate her programs.

Her relationship with her sister-in-law Isabel was affectionate, to judge from Isabel's letters, but her personal life seems often to have been lonely. The uncomplicated hours of music and talk with the talented and diffident young Catalan were satisfying to her, and the boy's response to her friendliness gratifying. She was responsible for far more of the education and opportunities coming to him through Morphy and Monasterio than he knew at the time.

Generally the music-making took place in the Queen's private suite, often in her small library; very seldom during his student years in Madrid did he play for her guests. The Queen always wanted to hear how his education was progressing and to have news of his family. Sometimes Pablo played cello while the Queen did needlepoint or embroidered. Sometimes they played piano duets—Her Majesty played Mozart competently (even forty years after her death Casals would say only that María Cristina was a sensitive pianist and that, "like most Austrians," she had a real love for music).

During the student period María Cristina was aware of her protégé's republican views and his Catalanism, although not until years later did he try to press the latter point with her. Casals was never a monarchist—a fact for which some Spaniards have never forgiven him but one that never seemed to bother the royalty who enjoyed his music and were his friends. He went to the palace informally, as a friend, and enjoyed going. He played with the young Alfonso XIII as with one of his own younger brothers, although he always addressed him as "Your Majesty," and found that the little Prince's musical interest did not extend beyond military marches. Pablo took his quasi-adoption by the Queen and the Count of Morphy generally in stride, and at any signs of undue self-satisfaction Doña Pilar headed him back toward the path of humility with a few terse observations about the important things in life and a reminder that his musical ability was a gift. He saw enough of palace aides' behavior and learned enough of back-stairs hypocrisy and politics not to want any part of a court existence for himself; Morphy's cautionary anecdotes about the destructiveness of bigoted priests and venal royal favorites in the time of Isabel II reinforced his attitude.

At the end of the 1893–1894 conservatory term Casals joined a tenor called Roura, a pianist named Fresno, and the young violinist Francés for some concerts in the provinces. They appeared in Vigo and Bilbao in late September, where they received brief but highly complimentary notices, and in Santiago de Campostela they received reviews that would have raised the spirits of Orpheus on his way to Hades: the tenor was "splendid"; the playing of the notable violinist Señor Francés united "the bravura of Sarasate with the angelic sweetness of Monasterio"; but Señor Casals was "a violoncellist of such extraordinary merit that, hearing him play, one wants to examine his instrument to see if there exists inside some nest of spirits entrusted with producing such an outpouring of art."

The writer for *El Alcance* had more space than his competitors in the issue for September 25, 1894:

> Señor Casals deserves a separate paragraph; he is a true celebrity . . . young, so young he has barely passed the marker between childhood and adolescence, at barely eighteen years old he can proclaim himself *Maestro* and create true beauty with the violoncello. . . . His bow, sometimes sweet as a voice from heaven, at others vibrant and robust, produces such a sonorous combination of voices and tones that it seems that the body of his violoncello is the magic secret of sublime harmonies capriciously transformed by the contact of that hand, which so quickly nervously touches the strings . . . the most skillful and brilliant execution, the most inspired muse, the most artistic intuition . . . his violoncello appears to speak, to moan, to whisper, to exhale sighs and to sing . . . when he plays, one closes one's eyes and hears, more than a work of art made by human hands, music that seems the miracle of a spirit. . . .

The depression and uncertainty from which he had seemed unable to loose himself as an adolescent in Barcelona began to dissipate in Madrid. The passage of time had performed its cure.

Casals described himself as a youth of excessively emotional nature and overflowing sensitivity, and later his friend Emil Ludwig not unexpectedly identified a Wertherian sentimentality in the Catalan artist's adolescence. The personal ordeal did leave its mark; what

Casals called "a permanent sorrow" took lodging in him for the rest of his life, most evident in a particular seriousness and from time to time a slowness in admitting the full humor of situations.

His general lack of interest in bohemianism and in escapades was already discernable. Casals had friends his own age among fellow students, and sometimes went out with them, but was happiest when the association involved music. Most of the time he was not studying, however, his head was buried in a score or he was practicing or composing. One of his friends of that period, an Asturian violinist called Abelardo Corvino, remembered visiting Casals in Madrid. They discussed music—practice and theory—at great length and rehearsed together. Casals' exercise consisted of playing a single note, sustained perfectly in tune and losing nothing of its limpidly beautiful sound as it went from soft to loud, then decreased to the barest pianissimo. "What one of the Paganini studies are you going to do, Corvino?" he would ask. "The one in D." Casals would produce an immense D note, sustaining it as long as needed and varying the dynamics with absolute control, to serve as accompaniment while his companion executed the intricate Paganini. Corvino swore that Casals could play a full Bach cello sonata without lifting his bow from the strings—a musically impossible and artistically undesirable feat.

Jesús de Monasterio had announced by the start of the next conservatory term that his duties as director of the school made it impossible for him to organize and play in the concerts of the Sociedad de Cuartetos any longer. He had founded the society thirty years before as an association devoted exclusively to the performance of the masterpieces of the chamber-music literature, and through it he made an effort to raise the standard of performance and improve the appreciation of serious music in the Spanish capital. Early in the school year there was an announcement that a new, very youthful Quartet Society—string players Julio Francés, Rafael Gálvez, Casals, and Peralta, with pianist José Güervós—would offer a series of six chamber-music programs between the end of November and the beginning of February in the Salón Romero, where Monasterio's distinguished concerts had taken place.

Critics and aficionados were skeptical of the unknown group but, led by the Infanta Isabel, a contingent of society turned out for the first concert on the thirtieth of November 1894—according to *El Cardo*'s critic Señor Macdonald "a frightful night of black ice and cold that seemed to pierce the lungs like a sword." Monasterio and the Morphys were present, applauding enthusiastically. Eight Madrid newspapers recorded ovations and performances interrupted by bravos. Señor Macdonald wrote cheerfully that his own doubt had been unfounded and that the evening, except for the weather, had been a resounding success, "a real occasion."

After the second concert, early in December, Pablo fell seriously ill with double pneumonia. Child of the Mediterranean sun, he suffered always from cold. The cold of Madrid, although relatively dry, is so fierce that sentries have frozen at their posts, and it has been said for centuries that the winter winds that sweep down from the Guadarramas can kill a man without blowing out a candle. The Queen Regent sent food, messages of concern, and her personal physician—an Austrian doctor named Riedel—to examine the sick youth and treat him. The doctor did examine and prescribe, but Doña Pilar carried out few of the orders, although she did apply the cold compresses he specified. She tended to rely on natural remedies and treatment with little if any artificial medication. By the sixth day of the crisis stage the boy was not certain he was going to survive; then Herr Doktor Riedel was summoned to Vienna to treat a member of the Austrian royal family. Doña Pilar sought the advice of a Spanish doctor, who immediately began heat treatments. For the rest of his life Casals was certain that the change and his mother's care saved him; he passed the crisis successfully on the seventh day and left his bed on his eighteenth birthday.

The newspapers hailed Casals' recovery from his grave illness after the third Salón Romero concert on the eleventh of January, and the rest of the series received glowing reviews, as did an extra concert at the end of February of works by Enrique Granados.

Sixty years later Casals characterized Jesús de Monasterio as a most lovable man who "had a delightful way of doing nice things." During the unusually cold February of 1895 he circulated word that all students should be present the next day. When all were gathered, the director announced that Her Majesty had been pleased to confer an award on one of the students. After a suitable pause he called Pablo Casals forward and bestowed on him on behalf of the Throne of Spain the cross of the Order of Isabel la Católica.

The new Quartet Society garnered a heady success, and the young señores Francés, Peralta, Cuenca (who replaced Gálvez), and Casals doubtless made some money. On their own and without particular thought that it might be necessary to consult the academic authorities, they also made some arrangements. *El Noticiero Bilbaino* for the second of March announced a series of concerts, not naming the other artists but saying the writer could do no less than mention "the violoncello of the new quartet, Señor Casals . . . the first of the Spanish violoncellists, becoming unanimously recognized as a national glory."

Barely more than a week later the Count of Morphy sent a letter to Monasterio:

11 March 1895.

Excelentísimo Sr Don Jesús de Monasterio.

Dear Jesús:

. . . Casals has told me that you oppose his going to Bilbao, and since this trip has been approved by the Queen, because it has as its object augmenting the fund built up so that if Casals is called for military duty he can redeem himself without it being necessary for H. M. to make greater sacrifices; since it is consequently an act of charity, which a good Christian such as you could not oppose, I beg you to revise your decision, the result of a moment of ill humor. If not, I shall be obliged to speak to the Queen about this disagreeable incident, and since H. M. has charged me with directing the education of this young man, I should be forced to suggest to him that he leave the Conservatory, where he had gone mainly to seek your support and protection. . . .

He would not miss the class in which he is enrolled more than two Mondays.

Do not hold him responsible, however, for the unjustified animosity you have against me, and which would shame you if you knew what a good friend I have been to you on various occasions without your knowledge.

Answer clearly, then, on the Casals matter, because he cannot do less than fulfill his [Bilbao] contract.

Your most affectionate friend,

Guillermo.

"I suspect he hasn't given you the real reasons," Monasterio wrote back to Morphy the next day, using the same *tu* form of address the Count had. He would have given permission *"with*

the greatest pleasure if Casals had done what he should have."
Casals knew perfectly well, Monasterio said, that all the students
of the conservatory, "without exception (as is true in every
country), are absolutely prohibited to take part in concerts or
public performances without seeking *beforehand,* and obtaining,
the director's permission."

> Yet Casals only sought my authorization to play in the recent
> chamber-music programs, in the Salón Romero, after they
> were organized, and I nevertheless then gave it very gladly
> and without making the slightest comment about his tardiness
> in asking.
> And now, without having spoken one word *ahead of
> time* about his project of concerts in Bilbao, he has the im-
> pudence to ask permission to go there *to fulfill his contract.*

Morphy must now understand that "in the face of such lack
of discipline, consideration and gratitude" Monasterio's dignity as
director impelled him to reject Morphy's contention, and further
authorized Morphy, if he considered it pertinent, "so to indicate,
without either evasion or gilding the lily, to H. M. the Queen."
He would offer no obstruction to Casals' withdrawal from the Conservatory "if for any other reason . . . you judge it convenient."
And the next time he and Morphy were together, Monasterio
would give repeated instances of his own defense of his old and
dear friend against the attacks of which Morphy had been the
object.

The four Lenten concerts in Bilbao were given between the
seventeenth and the twenty-eighth of March to audiences of
señoras and señoritas in the aristocratic salons of the Bilbaina
Society.

Casals was caught up briefly in the movement, at its most fervent
in the mid-1890s, to free the Spanish lyric stage from Italian bondage. Morphy and Bretón were almost monomaniac on the subject
and the Count thought of his protégé as the young bright hope
who would lead the crusade to victory, a crusade Bretón called
after the Count's death Morphy's "constant longing, favorite idol,
golden dream."

Opera began in Italy at the end of the sixteenth century, and
Italianism had colored the development of the lyric stage through-

*The Queen Regent of Spain, María Cristina,
Pablo Casals' "second mother," patroness,
and friend*

out Europe thereafter. In post-Napoleonic Spain the operatic stage flourished under the interested eye of Isabel II's mother, María Cristina of Naples, who relished the *bel canto* of her homeland. When the Madrid Conservatory was organized in 1830, an Italian singer was imported to be the first director, and the language used in the singing and declamation classes was Italian, not Spanish. A

Madrid Conservatory voice professor, Baltasar Saldoni, appointed director of the Teatro del Príncipe in Madrid in 1848, rallied younger composers under a banner of musical nationalism and started the crusade to liberate Spanish opera by creating a body of works with a distinctly national character. By the time of Casals' student period in Madrid, Morphy, Bretón, and the distinguished scholar-composer Felipe Pedrell were striving to endow Spain with an indigenous grand opera, written by Spaniards to Spanish librettos, that would equal the most impressive lyric dramas of other countries. The cultural preoccupations of a man as highly placed as Guillermo Morphy drew only scorn from most of the politicians and the entire idealistic campaign stimulated little interest among the opera-going public. Spanish audiences, like those elsewhere, adored Italianate opera.

What really enchanted the audiences in the playhouses was Spanish vaudeville-operetta, the zarzuela, that unmistakably Iberian equivalent of Gilbert and Sullivan, Offenbach, and Johann Strauss. Most of the purists looked down on everything about the zarzuelas except the money they brought in, although there were a few efforts to expand them into grand operas. Pablo Casals went with Morphy to the opening night of one of the best of these in mid-March 1895—Tomás Bretón's regional opera *La Dolores*, about a seductive barmaid. The work had an impressive success—sixty-three consecutive performances in Madrid the first season and more than a hundred in Barcelona, as well as productions in Prague, Milan, and Latin America. But Casals was no longer stage-struck in the way he had been as a young child.

Doña Pilar would have had the tact not to quote to the Count of Morphy musical historian Antonio Peña y Goñi's observation in the 1880s that "Spanish opera does not exist; Spanish opera has never existed." She, nevertheless, spoke to the point when there was a suggestion in the spring of 1895 that Pablo be appointed a musician of the royal chapel. She believed true art to have no geographic boundaries—at least that of her son must not. The court post would bring prestige and a comfortable income, but it could wait, as could the composing. If Pablo had really great gifts as a composer, mastery of the cello and a concert career would not be an obstacle. Monasterio agreed with her stand that Pablo should first become known as a cellist. She discussed this with her

(*Left*) *Casals at eighteen, when he was halfway through his second year at the Madrid Conservatory;* (*right*) *Rosina Valls*

son, the Queen, and the Count of Morphy. The time had come for Pablo to go elsewhere, perhaps to Paris.

Morphy was not used to being thwarted, and his paternal feeling about the boy had become proprietary. María Cristina sided with her secretary. Discussion of the matter went on for weeks, punctuated by puzzled letters from Carlos, who had been able to visit Madrid only once during his son's years there. At eighteen Pablo was caught once more among strongly conflicting forces affecting his career. He suffered the crosscurrents, but now was able to come to terms with them. And he knew that at this juncture his mother was right.

Doña Pilar finally made clear that, other alternatives failing, she and her sons would return to Barcelona. The Count of Morphy capitulated: if Pablo would go to Belgium to study composition with Morphy's friend and onetime fellow student François

Gevaërt, now director of the Brussels Conservatory, he would give permission and have the monthly allowance continued.

The Count supplied a letter of introduction to Gevaërt and a somewhat disgruntled farewell; weeping, the Queen said adieu. Pablo, his mother, and his brothers left Madrid for Vendrell and San Salvador, the *Diario de Barcelona* noting on July 20, 1895: "Arrived from Madrid: Pablo Casals, nineteen-year-old violoncellist, who has been awarded a pension from the Queen Regent to travel to Brussels to perfect his art with professors at the Conservatory there."

There followed a short holiday by the sea in San Salvador and some time in Vendrell with Carlos Casals. Pablo sought news of Rosina Valls, the daughter of his childhood physician. The doctor had died during Casals' years at school in Barcelona; Pablo's first adolescent romantic interest had been Rosina who, he discovered just before he left for Madrid in the spring of 1893, had developed a haunting loveliness. His attentions had been strongly discouraged by the widow Valls on the basis that a musician would never have anything to offer her daughter and by Doña Pilar for other reasons. Now, just over two years later, he learned that she was married and had an infant son. It is still reported in Vendrell that in the summer of 1895 Rosina, then in an advanced stage of tuberculosis, left her bed when she heard Pablo was in town and sat for hours at her window in the hope of seeing him.

Casals played in Tarragona on the tenth of August with pianist Emilio Sabater. On the first of September he said farewell to the public of his native town in a concert he had organized for the benefit of the hospital and the poor of Vendrell; Carlos Casals accompanied his son's solos, and a local orchestra and the La Lira chorus also took part. Not long afterward Pablo Casals boarded a train in Barcelona with his mother and two younger brothers to begin another trip northward, this time toward Paris and Brussels.

6

NONE OF THE hundreds of enjoyable hours Pablo Casals was to
spend in Belgium's capital was part of his first visit, in early
autumn of 1895. The four travelers had spent a few days in Paris,
staying in the house of a hospitable Frenchwoman they had met
on the train. Then came the relatively short trip from the Gare
du Nord across the flatland of northern France into Belgium. Doña
Pilar settled the younger boys—Luis was nearly five and Enrique
three—into their room in a *pension* with an admonition to behave
and set out by tramcar with Pablo for the large ornate building
that housed the royal Conservatoire de Musique et de Déclamation
to see the director, Maître François August Gevaërt.

Gevaërt read the letter from the Count of Morphy, requested
recent news of his old friend, and asked to see Pablo's compositions.
This visit seems to have been made absolutely without advance
communication with Gevaërt. If either the Count or Pilar Casals
had written, the first international journey would not have been
taken, and the young musician's life would have followed some
other direction, at least temporarily. The problem was simply that
Gevaërt, in his late sixties, was no longer accepting composition
students, no matter how promising. His duties as head of the

conservatory took all his time and energy, and he was, he said, too old to take on anything more.

The compositions Gevaërt looked at included songs, short works for cello and piano, the string quartet, organ preludes, a mass for chorus and organ, and a cello concerto. They were very good indeed, said Gevaërt, showing talent of which a much older musician could be proud. He advised Casals to go to a major artistic center—ideally Paris—where he would have the opportunity to hear a great deal of good music and the scope for further study would be wider.

Doña Pilar pointed out that her son had been allowed to come to Brussels on a royal scholarship specifically to study composition with Gevaërt. Morphy had lengthened the tether, not removed it; he was still determined that Pablo Casals should become a composer of opera, *Spanish* opera, and few men at the musical summit of the time were better equipped to teach advanced composition than the Belgian.

The Count's letter had also praised Pablo as a cellist. The conservatory's cello department was considered the best in Europe; Gevaërt said he would make the necessary arrangements for a talk the next day with Edouard Jacobs who taught the advanced cello course. Brussels had some musical life outside the conservatory at the time—Gevaërt had himself conducted excellent orchestral concerts and cycles of historic music for years, there was good opera, notable musical artists came there to perform, and Eugène Ysaÿe had just started a symphonic series—but the director repeated that the wisest step would be to settle in Paris.

Pablo and his mother discussed the practical results of the setback but prepared to await the outcome of the conversation with Jacobs the following morning. Strangely apprehensive, Pablo traveled to the rococo conservatory building in the rue de la Régence, this time alone. Here the estimable Enrique Fernández Arbós had come twenty years earlier, under the patronage of the Infanta Isabel, to study violin with Henri Vieuxtemps. Albéniz had worked here, as had Rubio. Much earlier, in another building that housed the school when it was smaller, Guillermo Morphy had studied for a year, and Jesús de Monasterio had come to learn from Charles de Bériot, discovering in François Gevaërt an enthusiastic friend and protector. The Belgian virtuoso Eugène Ysaÿe, whose career and personality would impinge so happily on Casals' for thirty years, had been professor of violin here since 1886.

Pablo knew he was in the heart of the Belgian "school" of cello-playing—a style that by the later nineteenth century tended to be more sauce than meat, with display and sentimentality generally more evident than emotional or intellectual content. Adrien François Servais, who had been born during the reign of Napoleon Bonaparte, had settled in as cello professor at Brussels in the revolutionary year of 1848. He devoted almost his whole life to the instrument and became famous, but was remembered particularly for two things. He composed the dazzling series of pyrotechnics entitled "*Souvenir de Spa*" that became the showpiece of the Belgian school. His greatest fame, however, lies in that, having become tremendously fat late in life, he reportedly invented the base peg that supports the violoncello while it is being played. Adrien Servais was succeeded by his son Joseph, also a notable cellist, who was professor of cello at the conservatory until his death at thirty-five, in 1885. The current professor of the advanced course for cello was Edouard Jacobs, a rather flamboyant man in his late twenties who had gained local celebrity as a performer and was becoming known as a musicologist.

Pablo Casals sat down quietly in the back of Jacobs' classroom, unnoticed or at least unacknowledged. Some of the regular students took their turns playing. Most of the class seemed to Casals ultramodishly turned out; there was a scattering of velvet jackets, flowing silk neckerchiefs, shoulder-length hair. To the visitor the performers seemed unjustifiably self-assured; to his eye and ear the playing was not particularly good. The playing stance was traditionally stiff and mannerisms seemed affected. Even basic technique was often mediocre and no errors—blurred notes, dry tone, squeaks, slides that sometimes became yowls, imprecise intonation, bows meeting strings in attacks that produced rasping scratches—were pointed out by the teacher.

When the class was over the students remained in their places somewhat too expectantly. Jacobs appeared to see the interloper for the first time and wondered aloud if this noticeably unstylish person barely five feet tall, with short hair and a plain suit, who spoke halting French and lacked the air of the virtuoso, might be the phenomenon, the little Spaniard the director had instructed him to hear. Casals had not brought his cello to what he had thought would be an interview, but said he could try to play on one of the instruments there. As one of the students offered him a cello, Jacobs observed to the class that this was a remarkable boy indeed—presumably he could play anything on any instrument! *Le petit Espagnol* had begun to turn red. And what, demanded Jacobs, would the extraordinary young gentleman from Spain play for them?

> Without conceit or even thinking about my reply [Casals wrote years afterward] I said, "Anything you like." This was evidently the wrong thing to say, for the teacher smiled sarcastically at me and bitingly remarked, "Well, well, you must be remarkable!" The class tittered, the professor amused himself with further ironical remarks, and I began to feel more and more awkward. After all, it was only my second day in a strange country.
> Several standard concertos were mentioned, which every student would naturally study, and I was asked if I could play them. To every one he named I returned a laconic "Yes." It just happened that I *did* know them.

Casals also knew the Servais *père* virtuoso vehicle (it had been part of the Vendrell farewell concert); he could and would play the "*Souvenir de Spa.*" One version of what followed has it that Jacobs stopped Pablo as he began, to say that he should be using down bow instead of up bow. It was one of the times in his career Casals was so angry he did not have an attack of stage fright.

By the end of a few bars *le petit Espagnol* knew he was in control. So did his audience. He saw from the students' expressions that they were "a bit surprised." The grins had disappeared. Notwithstanding Pablo Casals' opinion of what he had heard earlier, this was a competitive class in a top-flight conservatory, and the students were musicians. They recognized superlative tone, and knew what was involved in producing and controlling it on an unfamiliar instrument. They understood the muscular control and technical finesse required simply to get through, much less inject freshness into, a composition that had already become a cliché of technique. The students could also appreciate the fluidity of the bowing, the extraordinary use of virtually the complete bow, and the unconventional extension of the fingers that gave astonishing speed and continuity.

There was silence when Casals finished. The professor beckoned him into a nearby office. If he would remain in the class for a full term, Casals remembered Jacobs telling him, quite against all the rules of the conservatory, he would receive top honors at the end of the year. Casals answered that he had been treated so shabbily he did not want to stay a second longer. He left, still furious. Professor Jacobs held the door for him.

Two days later the Casals were in a train on their way to Paris, the hub of the universe, which was on their arrival full of autumn sunshine. In modest rented rooms Pablo sat down to write a long letter to the Count of Morphy. He explained why Gevaërt would not oversee his further training in composition, a decision the Count could surely see was impossible to reverse. Then he described in detail the encounter with Jacobs, adding that any attempt to study in Brussels in such circumstances would be meaningless.

Morphy's reply was instant and angry. Pablo had disobeyed the royal wishes as well as his own. He could either return at once to Brussels and the conservatory or lose his allowance. The Count saw Doña Pilar's influence and interpreted Pablo's reaction to Jacobs' treatment as a stubborn if not arrogant refusal to face reality. Morphy wanted Pablo to compose and seemed unaware that the issue had been decided against him.

Affronted *pundonor* and wounded self-esteem on the youth's part contributed to his resolve, but the deeper reason was artistic. What Casals had seen and heard in Jacobs' classroom in Brussels did not fit his ideas of what music study must be. He tried to explain to the Count that any time spent at the Brussels Conservatory would be wasted. It had been his own reaction and decision, although his mother agreed. He could not—would not—return.

The Count canceled the allowance. Carlos Casals' response to word of the move to Paris and the end of the monthly income was further incredulity; naturally he would help financially so far as he could, but it would not amount to much. And were there not hundreds of young cellists of talent in Paris seeking to become known?

The City of Light in the *Belle Époque* was less than incandescent for Pablo Casals and his mother. Once the income from Madrid stopped, quarters were found in what Casals always afterward described as a hovel near the Porte St.-Denis. Not long after they moved there Casals met a fellow Catalan, a violin student he had known slightly in Barcelona, who told him there was an opening for a second cellist in the orchestra of the Folies-Marigny, one of the less chic of the Champs-Élysées music halls that offered a nightly fare of vaudeville turns, light popular music, and cancan. Casals applied for work. As an audition each candidate was somewhat incongruously required to play the first section of the Saint-Saëns cello concerto. When his turn came, Pablo was not stopped at the end of the first part, so he played through to the end of the work. He got the job, pay for which was four francs a day. (In his eighties and nineties Casals without the flicker of a disproving smile could be heard to tell an occasional visitor that when he was very young he had once played cello in the orchestra of the Folies-Bergère.)

This stay in Paris included little recreation and no frivolity. The Champs-Élysées is a considerable distance from the Porte St.-Denis quarter, and he made two round trips a day on foot, carrying his cello, to save the transport fare of fifteen centimes—enough to buy half a kilo of bread.

Winter began early in 1895, the start of one of the hardest in many years. Pablo contracted dysentery which became complicated by enteritis, and was too sick to work. Doña Pilar found sewing that brought in enough money to buy simple food and to purchase medicine. Carlos sent a small sum and a desperate message that his savings were gone. One afternoon Doña Pilar returned with her hair cut short: she had sold her magnificent long hair to a wigmaker for a few francs.

When Pablo had recovered slightly, Doña Pilar decided that he could no longer endure the cold. Their reserve fund for the return fare had been used, and she dispatched a telegram to Carlos to send money for the journey.

Pablo recuperated in the warmth and sunlight of Vendrell and San Salvador. Doña Pilar, her hair still very short, looked older and thinner. Although taciturn as always, she was clearly pleased to be back in Catalonia. Carlos was delighted to have his two younger sons with him, really for the first time.

As his strength returned, Pablo discussed the next step with his parents. His inclination was to see what could be found in

*Frasquita Vidal received her first cello lesson
from Pablo Casals in January 1896. The painting,
by her sister, is in the collection of the Villa
Casals at San Salvador.*

Barcelona. This time Carlos did not raise questions or interpose an objection; father and son were more relaxed with each other than they had been for nearly ten years.

Pablo celebrated his nineteenth birthday with his family. By the second of January 1896 he was in Barcelona. That was the day he first gave a cello lesson to Frasquita Vidal, a graceful and talented girl of seventeen who was the daughter of a wealthy and somewhat eccentric Barcelona furniture manufacturer who envisioned his four eldest daughters as a string quartet and contracted the best available teachers in Barcelona to instruct them.

In addition to teaching, by early March Casals had appeared as one of four soloists in a musical evening organized by a Señor

Morera at the Ateneo Barcelonès. By the middle of the month he was one of five artists in a program presented in the auditorium of the Ateneo Graciense to an audience of enthusiastic and, said the *Diario del Comercio,* lovely ladies. The featured pianist, Señorita María Luisa Ritter, had won first prize at the Madrid Conservatory, but Casals mesmerized the audience with his playing of the *"Souvenir de Spa."*

Casals was appointed provisionally to the faculty of the Municipal School of Music (he was not old enough to receive a full appointment) on May 12, 1896. His return to Barcelona at barely nineteen had coincided with the sudden emigration of José García to Argentina in the wake of a scandal that involved someone else's wife. All García's music commitments were open, and most of them were soon filled by his former pupil. He took over most of Señor García's private students and his chair in various concert orchestras and church ensembles. And, for the next opera season, he became principal cellist of the orchestra of the Gran Teatro del Liceo, at the time the largest opera house in Europe, an appointment García had never held.

The opera season brought a reunion with Isaac Albéniz, who had come to the city for the rehearsals and first performances of his new opera *Pepita Jiménez.* Albéniz was still caught in a contract he called "the pact of Faust" with English financier Francis Money-Coutts under the terms of which he could write operas only to the Briton's librettos, but he had finally persuaded Money-Coutts to abandon Arthurian legends for a Spanish subject. The result was a heavy-handed, complicated book without much drama (the Englishman was a mediocre poet and a worse playwright) and a score that showed German, Italian, and French influences (Albéniz composed superbly for piano but never mastered writing for orchestra). *Pepita Jiménez* was a poor opera and Albéniz was not happy, but it had a resounding success in Barcelona the first season. At least it had brought Albéniz back to Barcelona, where he and Casals got better acquainted; Arbós and Rubio were also in town, as was Enrique Granados, and Casals spent many hours with them talking and, of course, making music.

That Liceo season also included Puccini's *Manon Lescaut,* Verdi's *Falstaff, The Merry Wives of Windsor* by Otto Nikolai, and *La Prophéte* of Meyerbeer, among others. Casals came to respect the music of Verdi but he never cared for the perfervid lyricism of Puccini. His childhood passion for Wagner continued, but as the years passed he paid little attention to the development of opera after Richard Strauss; and, despite the hopes and urging of the Count of Morphy and Tomás Bretón, he never attempted to write an opera himself. He had a strong dramatic sense, and saw a fair amount of spoken theater, but he was so completely an instrumental musician that for him the sung portions of opera intruded disconcertingly into the orchestral music. The seasons in the pit of the Liceo were nevertheless a useful and fondly remembered phase of his musical education.

Casals' favorite memory of the Liceo concerned a *Lohengrin* rehearsal. The guest conductor was Leopoldo Mugnone, a onetime teacher of Toscanini who was equally at home in the Italian and Wagnerian repertories—"one of those Italians who seem to be born conductors, [but] who don't have much to do with the production," Casals recalled. During a pit rehearsal in front of the curtained stage Maestro Mugnone became conscious of a rhythmic whisking sound with an obbligato of non-Wagnerian human whistling. He stopped the orchestra, roaring for silence. The rehearsal continued. So did the competing sound, now identifiably from backstage. Mugnone ordered the curtain raised, to reveal an old man sweeping briskly and whistling cheerfully.

The conductor sprinted onstage, screeching. The old sweeper fended him off with the broom. Some agile members of the orchestra had followed the furious director and quickly separated the pair. Professor Mugnone was led fuming back to the orchestra pit, gesticulating and demanding that the stagehand be dismissed on the spot. Told that if the old man were sacked the entire orchestra would probably walk out, the conductor calmed down enough to turn his attention to Wagner. (It was the same Mugnone who, two years earlier, was in the pit when an anarchist set off a bomb in the Liceo auditorium. He and the chief tenor are given credit for having helped avert total panic, although twenty-four died and many more were injured.)

His economic situation greatly improved, Pablo established both parents, his two brothers, and himself in a house at number 6 on the Plaza de Cataluña in Barcelona. When he finally became subject to military service he paid the sum set by the authorities in lieu of active service, the equivalent then of about four hundred dollars.

One of the social events of the 1896 Barcelona winter season was the private concert given December 19 in the house of a Monsieur Jeanbernet in honor of Camille Saint-Saëns, culminating at midnight in what the *Diario Mercantil* next day termed a splendid "lunch." The cream of the Barcelona artistic, musical, and literary world had been invited. The well-known pianist Señor Calado played a minuet and waltz written by Saint-Saëns on themes from Gluck's *Alceste*. Then Saint-Saëns himself played. A formidable keyboard performer who had been hailed in Paris at eleven as a new Mozart, he had begun by sixty to complain irritably that all the pianists played his music too fast, but tore through his own works at a pace no one else would have dreamed of taking. The guest of honor performed his E minor trio, with violinist José Rocabruna and Casals. Then Casals, with the composer accompanying, played the Saint-Saëns cello concerto. Enrique Granados finished the musical part of the evening with some of his own Spanish dances for piano.

Casals had first seen the hawk-nosed Frenchman five years or so earlier when Saint-Saëns, in Barcelona to give an organ concert, was brought to the Café Tost to hear him. Later, in a meeting arranged in a private house, Saint-Saëns asked if the young gentleman could play his A minor cello concerto. Yes, he could, although he admitted he had studied it only on his own and had never heard it performed. Casals heard Saint-Saëns' high-pitched laugh for the first time as he remarked that this was the best possible way to learn a work. Saint-Saëns then went to the piano to play the accompaniment; afterward he announced to the listeners that this was the best performance of his concerto he had ever heard, embraced the young cellist paternally, and set Casals on his lap.

Saint-Saëns had a justified reputation for irritability and a waspish retort ("Do I send you *my* works to look at?" he wrote furiously to aspiring composers who had requested an opinion of their efforts), but Pablo Casals found him always kind and responsive, as did a number of others. Their friendship lasted until Saint-Saëns' death in Algiers in 1921, although there were long stretches during which they did not see each other: Saint-Saëns was a compulsive traveler and after 1900 Casals' career took him back and forth throughout the world. Their first meeting marked the beginning of Casals' mastery of the Saint-Saëns cello concerto, which he performed in public hundreds of times, and he treasured the composer's memory and his music the rest of his life. Casals performed with Saint-Saëns several times, at least twice in the Jeanbernet house.

One encounter, ten days before Casals' twentieth birthday, occurred during a trip Saint-Saëns made to Barcelona in connection with a staging at the Liceo of his *Samson et Dalila*. The biblical opera had become popular throughout the Continent, and the composer appeared in various parts of Europe to see it produced. During the Barcelona spring season the Samson, an Italian tenor, embellished an aria with a sustained high note the composer had not supplied but that brought cheers from the audience. Saint-Saëns heard this revision sitting in a stage box during a rehearsal for the Liceo winter season; he let out a shriek that rivaled the tenor's. Either the high note or the tenor must go, he insisted. The tenor stayed, and sang the opera as written, but no longer stopped the show.

In addition to teaching and performing, in the spring of 1897 Casals began to play chamber music regularly with Granados and Mathieu Crickboom, a fine violinist and former student of Ysaÿe who had moved from his native Belgium to Barcelona in the fall of 1895. Crickboom had played in a well-known quartet in Brussels in the late 1880s; now he was in process of forming another such group, which would include Gálvez and Rocabruna as well as Casals and Granados. In the meantime Crickboom, Casals, and Granados were booked as a trio in the Gran Casino in San Sebastián in August, giving performances at 6:15 P.M. and at least one "intimate concert" of trios and solos from three until five.

The local press praised all three artists lavishly, singling out Casals as being "without dispute the foremost Spanish cellist." Casals was described as being scarcely taller than his cello and rather slight; what was not reported was that he had grown a mustache that almost rivaled that of Granados, was wearing his hair somewhat long, and was dressing most fashionably.

Pablo de Sarasate was in San Sebastián and Casals saw him, but not at the trio concerts; during those Sarasate stalked back and forth on the terrace outside, wrapped in his long cloak. Casals had met the celebrated Pamplonan in Madrid earlier, when the Count of Morphy took him to Sarasate's hotel; then he had been struck by the violinist's eccentricity and his collection of walking-sticks, and put off by Sarasate's bluff, good-humored chaffing because Casals would not take a drink. Casals disapproved of Sarasate's tricks of showmanship, one of the most famous of which was to hold his Stradivarius at the juncture of the instrument's neck and body, then let it slip slowly through his fingers, catching it by the scroll just before it fell to the stage. He was also mildly scandalized by the fact that Sarasate did not practice. The great Don Pablo once told him "Oh, don't come to hear me until I get to Madrid. I'll be back in form by then." Casals emphasized the rest of his life that Sarasate did not play in tune. Casals admitted that Sarasate was a great violinist but would not call him a great artist.

San Sebastián was the northern Spanish seaside resort on the Atlantic to which much of Madrid society fled from the terrible August heat of the capital, and there was a royal residence nearby. Casals had written both the Count and the Queen since the break following the Brussels episode but received no answer. Now he wrote Tomás Bretón, asking him to sound out the situation in Madrid, since he would return to Barcelona through the capital. Bretón answered on the twentieth of August that he had spoken the day before with the Count—"too big a man to nurse a grudge"—adding that Casals' friends in Madrid would like to see him again, and urging him strongly to keep composing.

A splendidly emotional reconciliation took place in Morphy's house and the Queen Regent, resuming as though there had been no accusation of lese majesty, asked Casals to play a concert at the palace. When he had finished, she said she wanted him to have a tangible souvenir of her for the rest of his life and indicated a small sapphire in a bracelet on her left arm, which she suggested could be set into his bow.

Three months later Casals appeared with the Madrid Symphony, under Bretón's direction. It was Casals' first appearance as soloist with an orchestra. His performance of the Lalo D minor concerto was received coolly, since he refused to indulge in the gestures of showmanship the public liked. During the November visit, the Queen Regent asked Casals to give another palace recital, in the course of which she presented him the money to buy his first historic cello, a fine Gagliano, and named him Caballero of the Order of Carlos III.

Two days before Pablo Casals' twenty-first birthday, a Bar-

(Top left) Enrique Granados and Pablo Casals;
(top right) Casals about the time he first played
in Portugal and the Netherlands; (bottom) the
Crickboom Quartet with Casals as cellist

celona newspaper, noting recent performances given under the auspices of a newly formed philharmonic society in the Teatro Lírico, said that "Crickboom, Granados and Pablo Casals today form a trinity as agreeable as it is honorable," and devoted most of two columns to the young cellist: "How is it that Pablo Casals— . . . as always when he plays—can raise the enthusiasm of a public to a paroxysm? What a delicious manner of playing! . . . Short of stature, like that of a boy, he is transformed into a giant when he plays. . . . [And] we shall doubtless be having occasion to applaud him also as composer and orchestra conductor." The *Diario de Barcelona* had already observed "our compatriot the cellist Don Pablo Casals . . . figures today in the front rank of artists, not only of Catalonia and of all Spain, but of Europe."

Casals celebrated his twenty-first birthday with Granados and Crickboom in Bilbao on a free day between two concerts. *El Nervion* of Bilbao for the last day of 1897 speaks of Casals "of the incomparable violoncello" in the last clipping in the press book Doña Pilar began for her son in 1889. (There follows a clothing list in her handwriting that could be the inventory for a long trip and includes such items as swallowtail *frac*, *smoking*, and the business suit the Spaniards called *Americana*.) When he became twenty-one Doña Pilar told her son he no longer needed her to travel with him, no matter where his career led.

On the night of February 15, 1898, an explosion sank the American battleship *Maine* in Havana harbor. The United States and Spain joined battle late in April. The Spanish press continued optimistic propaganda as long as possible, but word of defeat of the ill-equipped Spanish land forces and ramshackle navy in the Caribbean and of destruction of the Spanish squadron by Adm. George Dewey at Manila became known and the truth finally was published. Casals saw army survivors from Cuba, emaciated and crippled by sickness and hunger, debarking like a procession of ghosts at the port of Barcelona.

Casals felt real distress for the personal anguish of María Cristina, who had continued until the last moment before the outbreak of war to enlist the aid of other monarchs, including the Emperor of Austria and Queen Victoria, in arranging a negotiated settlement. She had even approached the American minister in Madrid, but had to reject the offer of President Grover Cleveland to serve as mediator between the insurgents and the mother country, a solution that almost certainly would have caused revolution in Spain and the possible loss of the throne she held for her son. Although the peace treaty, in which Spain lost the last important vestiges of a once-tremendous empire, came months later at Paris, the Spanish-American War was over by August 1898. During this period Casals, who had been composing songs and instrumental pieces steadily, completed and dedicated to María Cristina an ambitious symphonic poem he called *La Vision de Frey Martín.*

Casals left Barcelona late in July for various performing engagements in Spain, then late in August made his farthest trip afield. He was invited to play in Holland at one of the gala concerts celebrating the "inauguration" of the young Queen Wilhelmina. She had acceded to the Dutch throne on the death of her father eight years earlier but did not assume it until the beginning of September 1898, when she turned eighteen. On this trip Pablo Casals had his first traumatic experience with international security personnel. At the Dutch border he was detained and questioned at great length by both customs officials and police. His identity documents and his explanation that his destination was Amsterdam to perform as part of the celebration of the coronation did not satisfy the police, who examined his cello case with special care. Eventually he was permitted to continue his journey, accompanied by a policeman as far as the desk of his hotel. It seems that Casals bore an uncanny resemblance to a young anarchist who had been making widespread assassination threats. (Fourteen years later, while Casals was dining at the house of Daniel de Lange, director of the Amsterdam Conservatory, the host was called away from table and returned laughing. A police official had arrived to inquire about his dinner guest. Nobody had countermanded the order that put Casals on the list of suspicious characters, and he was still under surveillance every time he set foot inside the Dutch border. Professor de Lange assured the inspector that Casals was a dangerous anarchist only in matters of Bach interpretation.)

He returned from the Netherlands to play in a sextet at the gaming casino in the fashionable resort of Espinho on the Portuguese coast just south of Porto. A village half again as large as Vendrell that was beginning to thrive as a fish cannery, Espinho was dominated by old fortress and the ultrafashionable casino, bounded by a splendid Atlantic beach and surrounded by sand

King Carlos I and Queen Amelia of Portugal,
for whom Casals gave his first command
performance outside Spain. Amelia was
considered the most beautiful queen in Europe.

dunes that supported groves of pine and stands of eucalyptus. The casino's purpose was gambling, not music, but like its competitors north along the French Atlantic coast and at San Sebastián, at the German and Austrian spas, and in the burgeoning playgrounds along the French Riviera it had a small musical group, often a good one.

The summer weeks by the sea were pleasant, even with a daily stint of practicing and the afternoon or evening performances, and the musicians attracted a certain amount of attention among agreeable people on holiday. There was diversion, although Pablo Casals already had shown himself the variety of Spaniard not likely to be found dancing on tables, and gambling did not interest him. His musical colleagues—all young Spaniards and all but one impressively mustachioed—were satisfactory, and the Espinho engagement resulted in an invitation to play in Lisbon for the King and Queen of Portugal. Casals arrived in the capital and presented himself at the castle on its ancient hill overlooking the city and the fine harbor formed by the mouth of the river Tagus. Inexplicably, he had left his cello in Espinho, nearly three hundred kilometers to the north, and the performance had to be postponed. Their Majesties appeared unperturbed and were prominent in the audience for whom Casals played the next night. King Carlos I of Portugal was a short, fat, outwardly jovial man who was monarch of a state that had gone bankrupt in 1892. His wife Amelia, the most beautiful queen in Europe, was tall and very coquettish. Seventy years later Casals recalled standing beside the King, both of them watching Her Majesty seated on a couch, very animated and rather coy, surrounded by people paying her court. The King had caught Casals' eye and given him a large wink.

Casals returned to Barcelona the first week of November 1898 after spending some time in Madrid. His family was well settled; the oldest son had established a financial base strong enough to support it. Carlos' time, in fact, was now partially taken up with handling his son's business affairs. The younger boys were growing up. Luis was not happy with schoolwork but displayed an eager interest in animals, agriculture, and mechanics. Enrique was beginning to show talent for music and at six was starting to study violin, an instrument he later said he took up only because his parents assured him it was a little cello.

After six weeks in Barcelona with his family, Pablo was on his way back to Madrid, early in the first month of the final year of the nineteenth century.

7

WHEN CASALS HAD BEEN in Madrid late in 1898, the Count of Morphy inscribed a photograph to him which was among the handful of pictures always displayed prominently wherever Casals lived. In failing health and, as the coronation of Alfonso XIII approached, a less powerful court figure, Morphy wrote on the picture of himself the gruffly sentimental quatrain

> *A Dios pongo por testigo*
> *porque Pablito me crea,*
> *que es esta cara tan fea*
> *la de su mejor amigo**
>
> G. MORPHY
> *noviembre 1898*

Then and during a ten-day stay in Madrid in January 1899 Casals discussed with the Count and with the Queen Regent—who still insisted on being brought up to date on his activities and plans each time she saw him—his decision to try the next venture of his career in Paris. He had made a considerable mark in Barcelona

* [roughly "I call God to witness for Pablito to believe this excessively ugly face is that of his best friend"]

for an instrumentalist just turned twenty-two and had been able to give up the post of first cellist of the Barcelona Opera after a couple of seasons, but there was a far wider world to be conquered. Morphy sent him off with his full blessing on a short exploratory trip to Paris at the end of January, followed by stops in Lisbon and Porto early in March and more time in Madrid in late April. Casals returned home to Barcelona from Madrid with a letter of introduction from the Count to Charles Lamoureux, the most important conductor in Paris. Four days later he left once more for the French capital, not to return to Spain until the end of the year. Pilar Casals, writing a niece in May, reported her son's widening travels and enclosed programs of concerts he had given in Madrid, but her focus was less on his successes than her constant worry for his safety and comfort. He "travels through Europe," she said, "and always I have my heart on a string."

In Paris Casals was a guest in the sumptuous Avenue Wagram house of American-born soprano Emma Nevada and her English husband Dr. Raymond Palmer. Casals had met them first at the Count of Morphy's house and had seen them in musical evenings at the palace. Mme Nevada adored Spain and sang there often after her engagement as the chief light soprano of the Madrid Opera for a season at the end of the 1880s. The evening she created the role of Lakmé in Spain under the baton of Luigi Mancinelli during the 1889–1890 season, the Queen rose in her box and was heard to say "She sings *absolutely* like a bird!" (The Queen and Nevada spent much of their private conversation comparing child-rearing notes on the royal youngsters and the Palmers' only daughter Mignon.)

When Casals saw the Palmers in Paris in May 1899, Mme Nevada's enthusiasm for Iberia had wavered. She was still furious about her treatment in Seville the month before. She had gone there, the first American operatic singer to visit Spain after the Spanish-American war, for a production of *Lucia di Lammermoor*. None of the calling cards the Palmers left at friends' houses was answered, an unusual reversal of Spanish courtesy, and the newspapers did not mention the diva. The house was sold out, but the first-night curtain rose to orchestra seats practically empty except for a few secret police posted in various places, although the gallery was full. The downstairs filled about ten o'clock, in time for the second act, but a large portion of the audience turned its backs to the stage and talked loudly, and at the end of the act there was silence except when a military officer came to the front of a stage box and said Bravo to the orchestra. A diplomatic functionary explained to the cast that the demonstration was against Mme Nevada's nationality. She was determined to finish the performance. In the first act she had been surprised, in the second disgusted: "Fear was the only sensation I did not feel." In the third act, she said, "I sang for my country." She was hurt most, she told the London press, because after years of near-idolatry, Spaniards were "turning their backs and making sounds anything but musical, all because I am a child of the Stars and Stripes." A spontaneous burst of applause for the artist at final curtain was drowned by hisses for the American. (She canceled the tour. The route back to France was through Madrid, where María Cristina invited Nevada to the palace to sing to an audience of royal family and government officials, then presented her a bracelet of uncut sapphires and diamonds set in gold.)

In May Casals left for England with the Palmers and Mme Nevada's young French piano accompanist, Léon Moreau. Mme Nevada had taken Lady Low's house in Kensington for the Season, and was scheduled to appear on the twentieth and the twenty-seventh in the famous Saturday Concerts that August Manns (then in his mid-nineties) had been conducting for more than forty years in the Crystal Palace, London's enormous pleasure dome that housed both industrial expositions and musical spectacles. In the concert on the twentieth Casals made his London début playing the Lalo cello concerto with the Crystal Palace Band. Casals thought the edifice less than an ideal environment for serious music, and at the concert it was Mme Nevada's trills and high notes that drew the ovations. Casals' performance elicited no more than polite applause.

The London Season ran from late May, when the wealthy and the aristocratic began highly competitive entertaining, until late August when, after the Cowes Regatta and a traditional ball, society returned to the country to unlimber fowling pieces and attempt wholesale slaughter of pheasant, grouse, woodcock, and snipe. One feature of the Season was the potentially interesting but often deadly institutions called Drawing Rooms and At Homes. Pablo Casals made a name for himself as a performer in this milieu. Some of the At Homes were equivalents of the salons of the Continent, and a few English society women (like a few of their sisters in Paris, New York, Vienna, and St. Petersburg) arranged formal seating for their musical entertainments, more or less compelling their guests to listen to what was being offered. But at most of the large London parties music was simply part of the decor, "a background for conversation and nobody listened to it, no matter who the performer was." An invitation from an important hostess was something of a summons; only a few independent spirits could reject one with some impunity—among them Bernard Shaw, who would scrawl "GBS likewise" across an engraved card announcing "Lady ——— will be At Home on Saturday from nine until eleven." For the young musician at the turn of the century, turning down an invitation to perform (usually without payment) was running a risk; hostesses able to pay as well as female minor royalty short on funds were able to convince many an ambitious musician that giving his services would doubtless "lead to something," although it seldom did. With few exceptions, musicians in England in 1899 still went in through the servants' entrance. Only a few internationally established stars of special glitter were sought as guests. Nellie Melba was one (she also named her own fee—500 guineas [$2500]—when she sang at a private party), and her friend Signor Francesco Paolo Tosti, composer of "Goodbye," "Forever," and similar tremendously popular songs, became a sort of unofficial master of the musical revels in Edwardian society.

Casals was spared the indignity, suffered more than once by other performers, of being pushed aside while performing by aristocratic gentlemen bearing down to greet the hostess. He played at entertainments during which the music was given full attention: half a century later he remembered a Rothschild house, a Member of Parliament's home, and the drawing room of Mrs. Constance Eliot in Kensington. The Nevada-Palmer introductions and the Crystal Palace début were helpful in drawing such invitations, and his talent and youth, his diffident charm, even his lack of English did no harm (his French was now fluent). Nor did the cachet of being a personal protégé of the Queen Regent of Spain.

Casals soon caught the attention of three sisters who were socially prominent—Constance Eliot, Enid Layard, and Blanche

Ponsonby—daughters of a Welsh iron magnate, Sir Josiah John Guest, and the vigorous and cultivated Lady Charlotte Guest. Constance, an accomplished pianist, was the wife of Col. the Hon. Charles G. C. Eliot, a Member of the Royal Household who bore the titles Gentleman Usher and Groom of the Privy Chamber. A framed photograph of her, signed "Constance R. Eliot" and showing a pleasant-looking, rather plain woman, hangs on the wall of a music room in Casals' villa at San Salvador. On the back is the notation in his hand "my English mother."

There is no comparable caption on the one nearby inscribed "Enid Layard 1899," which at first glance gives the impression of a poised and handsome swan-necked Englishwoman much younger than her fifty-seven years. Enid Layard (christened Mary Evelyn) had good taste and a genuine liking for diamonds, believed in the virtues of good breeding, held all the correct views, and was a bit patronizing. She was the widow of the great "Layard of Nineveh," the self-taught archeologist Henry Layard who had made the first important digs of Babylonian and Assyrian ruins in the Ottoman Empire during the 1840s. (He gave his wife antiquities instead of diamonds. For an engagement gift he had the jewelers Phillips of Bond Street make a bracelet of Esarhaddon's signet; for special evening occasions he had made up an elaborate necklace of cuneiform cylinders.) She had lived in Madrid from the end of 1869 until 1877, when her husband was the first British minister to Spain following the overthrow of Isabel II. She spoke fluent Spanish, refused to attend bullfights, could play the Spanish guitar, and knew the Count of Morphy. Casals saw the bracelet of sixteen enormous diamonds the Sultan of Turkey had given her as a little souvenir of his esteem at the end of her husband's subsequent ambassadorship in Constantinople, which she had kept over Sir Henry's objections but with Queen Victoria's approval.

In due course came the invitation commanding Pablo Casals to play for Victoria. There is a story that this summons started with a congratulatory note sent back to Casals after his Crystal Palace début by Edward, Prince of Wales. (Edward's wife Princess Alexandra, a celebrated beauty, was hard-of-hearing but extremely fond of music; her husband's esthetic tastes generally ranged elsewhere, although not too long before the Casals concert he and his brother Arthur, Duke of Connaught, had burst out in a spon-

(Left) Lady Enid Layard, one of Casals' first English patronesses. She and her sisters arranged to have him play for Queen Victoria in August 1899; (top right) Pablo Casals in the summer of 1899, the time of his first visit to London; (bottom right) Queen Victoria at eighty, photographed about the time Casals played for her at Osborne

taneous whistling duet of Gilbert and Sullivan tunes after a dinner at Sir Arthur Sullivan's house.) Actually, the arrangements had been made by Constance Eliot and Lady Layard's other sister Blanche, who was the wife of Edward Ponsonby, brother of Victoria's private secretary.

On Wednesday, August 2, 1899, Casals and Ernest Walker, the young English pianist who had accompanied him at Mrs. Eliot's Kensington house in July, traveled by train from London to Southampton, then took the ferry to Cowes on the Isle of Wight, where Queen Victoria was in residence at the royal country house called Osborne. They put up in a small riverside hotel, where they had time to get through a good dinner and cheerful talk in French before the royal carriage arrived for the drive to Osborne. Once inside the Italianate villa that had been Prince Albert's hobby and built under his supervision in the late 1840s, the musicians were led by footmen through long passages to a large room and told to wait until summoned by Lord Edward Pelham-Clinton. They sat for half an hour contemplating paintings of the Prince Consort in Scots hunting garb surrounded by dead prey. Pelham-Clinton appeared and led the artists through more long corridors, past more paintings of the Prince Consort, and stopped before the last of a series of gilt-handled doors. He opened that door and the three walked directly into the presence of Her Majesty, who was sitting by herself at a large table, with her musical daughter Princess Beatrice and the Duke of Connaught to her right. Casals' curiosity overcame any nervousness. This was the legendary Victoria Alexandrina, ruler of the British Empire since 1837, Empress of India, the Grandmother of Europe. She was in full evening dress, the low cut revealing her very white skin. A "very respectable lady" of nearly eighty, surrounded by silence and the most extreme reverence, with a turbaned Indian attendant who adjusted the footstool for her. A cultivated woman within the limits of her heritage and prejudices, she genuinely enjoyed the sounds of certain kinds of music and had herself once been something of a royal contralto. More than fifty years earlier Felix Mendelssohn played while she sang Gluck, "quite charmingly," he said, "in strict time and tune, and with very good execution."

Victoria finished her conversation with an admiral, then picked up a large hand-lettered program as the sign that the music was to begin. Her signal halted the whispering among the audience of about thirty, all of whom were in uniform or court dress. Casals and Walker played Fauré's *Élégie* in complete silence except for the pedal squeaks of the American Chickering piano. There was no applause during the half-hour program (Casals also played an old Italian sonata and the *allegro* of the Saint-Saëns cello concerto), and between numbers the Queen spoke German to Princess Beatrice. When the concert was finished, "two six-foot Indians came and grasped the Queen's arms, and helped her slowly, inch by inch . . . from her chair." Somewhat against custom, Victoria moved toward Walker and Casals to speak to them. She congratulated Casals in French, asking about the red ribbon of the Spanish decoration he wore on his jacket and saying that the Queen of Spain had spoken about him; she hoped his artistic career would repay the honor and trust that had been invested in it. Then, leaning on her Indians, the Queen of England withdrew. Before she slept she dictated a telegram in German to María Cristina and wrote in her journal: "Osborne, August 2nd 1899 . . . After dinner a young Spaniard Señor Casals played on the violoncello most beautifully. He is a very modest young man, whom the Queen of Spain has had educated, and from whom he received his fine instrument. He has a splendid tone and plays with much execution and feeling."

After the Queen left, Lord Edward Pelham-Clinton stepped forward to hand Walker a silver cigarette case (engraved "from V.R.I.") and Casals a case of gold cufflinks. (Casals later recalled receiving also a small pendant medallion with a cameo profile of Victoria that he gave to Doña Pilar, the only piece of jewelry she ever accepted from him.) The Duke of Connaught, who had an aquiline nose and a tremendous mustache, chatted with Casals for a moment in what purported to be Spanish, and the artists were conducted through passages to a small dining room with supper set for two. Casals insisted on saying good night to Lord Pelham-Clinton, and a footman led the musicians on a search that included a billiard room where a game was under way, but finally they had to leave without a farewell.

Early next morning, Alexander Grantham Yorke, the portly, dandified groom-in-waiting, appeared at the hotel with the royal birthday book for Casals and Walker to sign at the Queen's request. Afterward Casals went to send telegrams to Spain, and Walker had to summon his most insistent French to extricate his colleague from the post office in time to catch the boat for the mainland.

On Casals' return from England he was a houseguest of Emma Nevada and her husband at their country place, La Melun, at Pierrefonds near Compiègne. The Oise countryside and the Forest of Compiègne were lovely, the Palmer hospitality gracious, and there was music, but during the holiday news came of the Count of Morphy's death on August 28 in Baden-Argavia, Switzerland. Casals had known the Count was not well, but word of his sudden passing meant the loss of the friend who had guided his education, shown him new horizons, whom he had come to love as a second father. Shortly afterward Casals wrote a musical setting for a poem by François Coppée, "*Au Cimitière au Jour des Morts.*"

Once back in Paris he went to deliver Morphy's letter of introduction to Charles Lamoureux. In the envelope Casals carried was the Count's last gesture of assistance and patronage, one that could open the door to an international career if Lamoureux were disposed to give him the opportunity to appear in one of his orchestra's fashionable Sunday concerts.

Charles Lamoureux's short-fused irascibility was well known, and at the time he was occupied almost completely with the major undertaking of the first complete Paris production of *Tristan und Isolde*. When the office boy opened the conductor's workroom door at the Concerts Lamoureux headquarters to announce that a young man had come to deliver a letter, Lamoureux was furious. The short, round man, who had a bull neck and a head shaped like a cannonball, finally looked up from the score in front of him at Casals and said angrily that he was continually being interrupted to read letters of recommendation touting the unique talent of the bearer. Without losing his composure Casals answered quietly that he had come like a servant simply to deliver to Maître Lamoureux a letter that had been entrusted to him, and left. He was already in the lobby when Lamoureux, struck by the dignity with which Casals had replied, literally came running out of his studio to call him back. Lamoureux then read the Count of Morphy's letter and told Casals to return next day with his cello and an accompanist.

The following morning in the same room, in the company of a thoroughly nervous pianist, Casals again found Lamoureux at his desk grumbling audibly about being interrupted. With no taste for a repetition of the performance of the day before, Casals said respectfully but with a tinge of irritation that he did not wish to intrude and would withdraw at once.

"Young man," snapped Lamoureux, "I like you. Play!"

Le Maître went back to his papers and Casals began to play the Lalo cello concerto. "I could see that he was interested. He began to listen," Casals reported afterward. "To my astonishment [rheumatism made it difficult for Lamoureux to rise], he painfully and slowly got to his feet and remained standing until I had finished the concerto." Tears in his eyes, the prickly Frenchman embraced the slight Catalan: *"Mon petit, tu es predestiné!"*

The programs for the nineteenth season of the Concerts Lamoureux had already been set and soloists chosen, but Lamoureux said he would expand the opening one on November 12 to include Casals playing the first section of the Lalo. Casals asked if he might also play cello in the *Tristan* orchestra when rehearsals began. Of course he could, said Lamoureux.

The conductor introduced Casals to the *Tristan* orchestra at the first rehearsal as a fine young artist who had begged for the opportunity to play with them. His friends said that Lamoureux's bristling exterior masked kindliness and a big heart, but in earlier years there had been times during rehearsal that auditorium doors were closed to keep his abuse of the orchestra from being heard in the street, and at one point Lamoureux reportedly carried a pistol to protect himself against possible attack from orchestral players and soloists he had outraged.

Membership in Lamoureux's opera orchestra was Casals' first experience of working with a first-rate, internationally important conductor. Casals was willing to learn, and he could have had worse fortune than to have fallen in at twenty-two with Charles Lamoureux, a perfectionist whose loyalty to the composer was adamant. Born in Bordeaux in 1834, Lamoureux began as a violinist, became conductor of the Opéra-Comique for a short time the year of Casals' birth, and in 1877 became conductor of the Paris Opéra—a post he resigned within a year because the administration tried to dictate tempo to him in a portion of *Don Giovanni*. Having married a toothpaste heiress, he had a certain freedom from the tyranny of financial backers. For nearly twenty years he had cajoled and browbeaten his own orchestra until it was probably the finest in Paris. It played with matchless precision of attack but it had warmth and even passion of expression; only occasionally did a critic complain that Lamoureux sacrificed everything to lucidity.

By the time Casals joined the *Tristan* orchestra Lamoureux's conducting style was subdued so far as physical movement was concerned. He interrupted the orchestra often and talked a great deal, explaining, teaching, trying to get from individual players and sections the precision he demanded. In an era in which such influential artists as Joachim and Sarasate were not unduly concerned about playing exactly in tune, standards of orchestral playing were low. One of Lamoureux's accomplishments was to have developed an orchestra so precisely rehearsed that when it played there was "the entire absence of that murmur which one has come to regard as characteristic of the orchestra. If a wrong note was played, there was nothing to hide its nakedness. . . ."

During one of the *Tristan* rehearsals Lamoureux stopped the orchestra at the end of a solo passage for bass clarinet.

"It was out of tune, Brenoteau. Play it again."

The clarinetist played it again. "It is still out of tune," said Lamoureux evenly. "Once more, please."

After the fourth or fifth repetition Brenoteau said he thought he had now played the offending theme in tune.

"You think so?" asked the conductor, looking scornfully over his pince-nez toward the clarinets. "Let me tell you something that happened to me. I learned that a friend of mine was ill, so I went to see him. I was shown up to where he lay in a miserable little room with all the windows closed—they had not been opened for weeks. 'What an unpleasant odor,' I said. 'Why don't you open the windows to get rid of it?' 'What smell?' retorted my friend. Brenoteau, you know why my friend didn't notice the ghastly stench, do you not? *He was used to it!*"

Lamoureux also gave his attention to the singers. In one stage rehearsal Lamoureux put down his baton after trying several times to get something across to the Tristan. "*Monsieur!*" he shouted. "As a tenor, Monsieur, you have the native privilege to be stupid, but you are abusing it." And at one point he stopped a rehearsal to address Félia Litvinne, the Russian dramatic soprano who was singing Isolde. "This is not an Italian aria, Madame," he informed her acidly. "Put some force behind it."

During the period of the *Tristan* rehearsals Casals learned about the problems Wagner's music had had in Paris. In Barcelona, he had already seen the development of strong camps of Wagnerites and anti-Wagnerians who said their idol was Brahms; Casals was happy with the music of both. He discovered that for years Lamoureux and others in Paris had difficulty even when they tried to include excerpts of Wagner's works in their programs. (Lamoureux also encountered opposition when he introduced the works of contemporary French composers.) Jules Étienne Pasdeloup had mounted an unfortunately timed and disastrous *Rienzi* in April 1869. After France's glory had been tarnished and part of its territory wrenched away in the Franco-Prussian war, the frenzied patriots watched everything in public life for possible taints of Teutonism. Lamoureux was attacked for playing Brahms, Schumann, and Mendelssohn, and when he had the temerity to offer an all-Wagner program, members of Paul Déroulède's League of Patriots were stationed about the hall "with orders to boo, hiss and whistle from the opening bar to the last notes." The *melomanes*—"music lovers rash enough to enjoy Wagner"—answered noisily with cheers, standing ovations, and cries of "*Bis!*" (Uniformed police were finally stationed inside the hall and notices inserted into the programs begging the public neither to hiss nor to shout *encore*—"*Le public est prié de ne siffler ni bisser les auditions Wagnériennes!*")

After rehearsing for a year, Lamoureux mounted a single "perfect" *Lohengrin* at the Théâtre Eden in the beginning of May 1877, an evening that remains one of the notable shambles in French musical history. A phalanx of Left-Bank student adherents of the League of Patriots, shouting *revanche* against Germany, forced its way onto the stage and pelted the audience with balls of asafetida while mounted police charged a body of screaming demonstrators outside.

Things changed in the ensuing years, to the point where Bernard Shaw could write in 1890 about "the six old gentlemen who form the anti-Wagner party in Paris," and there was no disruption of the production of *Tristan und Isolde* for which Casals was in the cello section of the orchestra, before a gala audience in the Théâtre Nouveau on October 28, 1899. The political climate of Paris was calmer than it had been twenty-two years before,

*Charles Lamoureux, under whose baton
Pablo Casals made his first Paris appearances in
November and December 1899*

and the influence of Paul Déroulède was less in evidence. That war hero and author of a book of fairly appalling patriotic verses called *Songs of a Soldier* had headed an unsuccessful rightist coup d'etat early in the year.

The weekly concerts directed by Lamoureux and those of the Concerts du Châtelet organized by Édouard Colonne (who preferred to be called Édouard rather than Judas, his baptismal name) were immensely popular at the turn of the century among both music-lovers and middle-class Parisian women and the female members of Society. Both orchestras and conductors were good, but Society gave a slight edge to the Lamoureux concerts because of the romantic overtones of his name.

Two weeks after *Tristan* the poster at the Théâtre de la République, the old Château d'Eau theater in the rue de Malte, announced in large, bold type the participation of Mme F. Litvinne in the first concert of the 1899–1900 season. The names of Lamoureux, pianist Berthe Marx-Goldschmidt, and Casals appeared equal size in a slightly smaller display.

Early Sunday afternoon November 12, 1899, Pablo Casals was waiting backstage at the Théâtre de la République, hideously nervous, to make his solo début in Paris. The theater was full on that autumn afternoon; Casals played the first portion of the Lalo concerto, and Alfred Bruneau recorded in *Le Figaro* that "the public did not stint its bravos for M. Pablo Casals, a notable violoncellist."

In Paris it was still a time when the raised eyebrow or grimace of a leading musical critic could kill a career, but Casals no longer had to worry after he saw the papers. His interpretation was praised by Barbedette in *Le Ménestrel* as capturing the soul of the work and displaying "the always hoped-for, rarely attained coordination of technical virtuosity and artistic conception." Even the notoriously difficult-to-please Pierre Lalo, son of the composer, noted in *Le Temps* "Pablo Casals performed the *Concerto* for violoncello of Edouard Lalo with an enchanting sound and a beautiful virtuosity."

Lamoureux immediately engaged Casals to play again five weeks later, this time for an artist's fee. Casals' admiration for Lamoureux as a conductor was now almost boundless; he considered him a great director and a man whose first concern was music itself, not the effect he could produce with it. Lamoureux in turn had recognized in the little Spaniard a phenomenal talent and true musicianship. The long-experienced and hardheaded entrepreneur had also discerned a star quality, that indefinable temperament and style that is beyond technical and intellectual mastery.

If the first solo appearance with Lamoureux was a success, the second, on December 17, was a triumph. The audience went wild at the end of the Saint-Saëns cello concerto; Lamoureux embraced Casals and proclaimed him Knight of the Order of the Violoncello, "now and forever."

Casals wrote to Jesús de Monasterio the next day, regretting that there had been so few opportunities to see him during the last visits to Madrid. Casals was leaving Paris on the twenty-second and requested an appointment with Monasterio in Madrid the following morning. He told Monasterio he expected to make Paris

*Casals at twenty-two, photographed by
Gerschel in Paris at the time of his début
with the Concerts Lamoureux*

his winter base, for traveling convenience. He already had some engagements for February and March, among them three with Louis Diémer and Jules Boucherit in the Salle Pleyel. "Yesterday," he continued, "I played in the Concerts Lamoureux for the second time, with a lovely success; it appears, according to Lamoureux, that such great enthusiasm for a violoncellist has never been shown at any of his concerts."

Casals left Paris for Madrid and Barcelona on December 22, 1899, without knowing that Charles Lamoureux had died the day before, at sixty-five. In less than half a year he had lost two strong friends, older men whose generosity and interest had shaped his life indelibly. Their passing shocked and saddened him, but both had given him an opportunity at the right moment and encouraged the development of his own strength.

Casals observed Christmas and celebrated his twenty-third birthday with his family in Catalonia; with them and friends he greeted the first minutes of the twentieth century.

1900–1919

8

Casals' first home in Paris was a decrepit Montmartre hotel. Here, in the small *quartier* near the still-unfinished Sacré-Coeur basilica and not far from the famous and bizarre cabaret the Lapin Agile, one could live adequately on four francs or so a day. Some of the houses to which he was invited were illuminated by electricity; in his room Casals read and practiced by candlelight, although kerosene lamps were available and an energetic gas company was offering new subscribers a free gas ring for cooking, sparse warmth, and easy suicide.

Casals' bronchial tubes began to bother him in the damp January weather, and he took to his bed with a heavy cold that soon settled in his chest. He liked to tell years later of his rescue that, as he languished in bed, thoroughly miserable, a woman he did not recognize walked into his room. "Get dressed," she commanded in British-tinged French. "You are coming with me."

"*Mais non, Madame!* I believe you have the advantage. . . ." He pulled the bedcovers about him like a startled ingenue in one of the well-made farces of the day as she began gathering his belongings, saying that a shabby, unheated Montmartre room with a broken windowpane was no proper place to recover from influenza. Betina Ram, an unusually plain-looking woman with a half-Puckish expression, a British widow of means who was an excellent pianist and the friend of many musicians, had heard that Casals was ill. With the unassailable Englishwoman's determination that can paralyze strong men of any country, she announced that he was leaving with her at once. He did, and lived in her comfortable home for several months.

Mrs. Abel Ram's musical evenings in 1899 and 1900 were mentioned frequently in dispatches from Paris to the American *Musical Courier* and drew "notabilities" who included artists, writers, theater people, musicians, and visiting socialites from England and the United States. Emma Nevada was frequently present, and younger musicians who played at Mrs. Ram's receptions in late 1899 included pianists Harold Bauer, Léon Moreau, and Alfred Cortot, violinist Jules Boucherit, and a baritone named Viaud, cousin of writer Pierre Loti. Casals was performing there by the time of the *Tristan* production in late October 1899. One regular Casals got to know was a half-Basque a year older than Casals, Maurice Ravel, a composition student of Gabriel Fauré at the Conservatoire. He was an elegant, rather undersized young man with a large handsome head who moved in bohemian circles and among the culture-loving nobility. He liked to strike the pose of a bored esthete, as so many young artists of the time did, but he loved Mozart and Casals found him quite agreeable. One day Ravel played a piano piece he had written a few months earlier, a *"Pavane pour une Infante défunte"* ("Pavane for a Dead Infanta"), a title he chose because the assonance of the syllables pleased him. Casals thought it a masterful little work, and it turned out to be Ravel's first really successful composition when it was performed in April 1902 by Spanish pianist Ricardo Viñes.

The hospitality of Mrs. Ram afforded Pablo Casals at twenty-three a comfortable place to work uninterrupted at his daily musical routine. The social encounters and the recreation of this period were a satisfying and important part of his life, but his music always came first. Early in the day, immediately after breakfast or sometimes before, he played through some Bach on a piano if one was available. Then he worked with his cello for three or four hours in a fairly standard progression, first warming up both his hand and the instrument with scales and technical calisthenics, then working on a specific piece in his repertoire. If it was a new work he would already have gone through it many times without any instrument, rereading the score, and have worked it out at the piano to find the overall form of the composition and to fix in his mind the interplay of solo voice and accompaniment. Finally he turned to one of the six Bach suites for unaccompanied cello, as he had been doing every day since 1889.

This was intense, concentrated work, usually done alone, for Casals a natural and necessary part of daily existence as well as his profession. In spite of an ingrained courtesy and a self-control that were quite evident, Casals was likely to be irritable when interrupted at this solitary activity. He already showed a logical tendency to complete a full portion of one task at a time, with intensity, discipline, and concentration, a trait he had possessed in some measure since childhood. Then he was able to turn full attention to whatever was next on his agenda.

Nor did his artistic doubts and personal uncertainties obtrude when Pablo Casals was making music. The auguries were good in the late winter and early spring of 1900, but the bookings were not yet overwhelming, and he sometimes wondered if he had waited too late to start a career as a cellist. (Before his first tour with pianist Harold Bauer in the summer, Casals did his last brief stint as a café musician, appearing for a time at the Café Suez. It was a far cry from the Tost, and certainly no cause for embarrassment. Casals' fellow Catalan Joaquin Malats was performing in a nearby musical café. Jacques Thibaud played at the Café Rouge. Crickboom, Fritz Kreisler, and Eugène Ysaÿe at some point did the same thing in Brussels, Vienna, and Berlin.) The competition would have been much stiffer if Casals had been a violinist or pianist—in Paris the musical woods were full of them, many with the Conservatoire stamp. But the demand for solo cellists was slight and several respected violoncellists were on the scene at the time, among them Casals' friend Joseph Salmon, André Hekking, and the Dutchman Joseph Hollmann, who played well but grunted audibly in intense moments. The conflict among performing, the desire to compose, and the thought of becoming a conductor nagged Casals' mind from time to time.

There were moments of longing for the warmth and sunshine of Mediterranean Spain. He had a strong and nostalgic sense of family and at moments missed the Barcelona household of which he had become chief support, but he was too preoccupied with music and with forging his career yet to give more than passing thought to a family of his own.

But it is difficult to keep one's spirits from rising when spring comes to Paris and the chestnut trees bloom, the green returns to the trees in the Tuileries gardens and the Bois, flowers appear, and the clear days are warm. Work continued in the mornings, but the afternoons began to include sets of tennis with Léon Moreau, Harold Bauer, the Baron Conrad de Vietinghoff, and other athletic friends on the St.-Cloud courts. Paris was, as Gevaërt had said, the Mecca of all aspiring young artists. But even the hideously poor of Paris, of whom there were so many, and the inartistic would have told him readily that the capital of France was the hub of the universe in every respect. Paris had built an almost presumptuous International Exposition to vaunt itself and the new century, which began with optimistic pronouncements—especially after predictions that the world would end at midnight on the last day of 1899 proved unfounded. The municipal fathers had made one of their periodic official rediscoveries of the glamour of their city, promptly masking part of it with such things as the garish pseudo-Venetian façades built along the Seine for the Exposition of 1900.

Casals remembered central Paris as very noisy when he first lived there. Some streets were still paved with the sandstone blocks of the 1850s, which made rough going when they became worn; some of the streets in the busy center were surfaced by asphalt mixed with sand, an imperfect medium but one that could not be pulled up to make barricades; the main Champs-Élysées roadway was paved with creosoted wooden squares. The city had been served by public buses since 1828, with thirty lines by 1850 and many more by the turn of the century. The most impressive means of public transport was still the *impériale*, a double-deck omnibus drawn by three giant Percherons abreast from the Odéon to Clichy. Paris was still a city without automobiles, but the streets were crowded with thousands of smaller horsedrawn vehicles—landaus, victorias, buggies, fiacres, coupés, jump-seat phaetons, brakes, tandems, broughams, gigs—and traffic jams were frequent at intersections.

The bicycling craze had reached its peak in Paris in the 1890s, but those contraptions were mostly seen in the Bois de Boulogne, the favorite promenade of the leisured and fashionable (whom Parisians had started to call *le gratin*). In spite of distractions and the danger of being run down by an inexpert bicyclist, the Bois was a wonderful place for long walks, and Casals hiked when he had time and the weather was good.

Evening outings to a café with friends led through streets and avenues still illuminated by gas or arc lamps. Baron Haussmann, whose rebuilding of a half-medieval city a generation earlier had resulted in a Paris with grand avenues that gave long straight vistas to monumental buildings, rejected electricity for the lighting of streets as being injurious to the eyes.

The Paris theater was having one of its brilliant periods; theatrical personalities were even more popular than opera stars, and both the plays they were performing and their private escapades were subjects of lively interest. Casals saw Sarah Bernhardt on the stage in Paris during his early twenties and did not care for her; the acting and the golden voice were too unnatural for his palate. He saw the great Italian actress Eleanora Duse performing with Novelli. At Emma Nevada's house he met Yvette Guilbert and Sacha Guitry and became acquainted with the exotic American dancer Loie Fuller. He saw another American dancer, Isadora Duncan, half a dozen times at Mme Nevada's, but he did not consider her extraordinary on stage and did not care at all for her "original" style of dance.

He also went to occasional lectures at the Sorbonne and the Collège de France. Henri Bergson's writings had made psychology a subject of interest during the nineties; his lectures at the Collège de France (and those of Jules Lemaître on Rousseau), part of a subscription conference series, drew full audiences of serious listeners interspersed with society women who "took notes with tiny gold pencils in tiny ivory notebooks" and "wrinkled their blameless brows . . . in valiant attempts to understand." He also listened to the theosophist Annie Besant during this period and by 1914 had met an Indian adolescent named Jiddu Krishnamurti, her disciple at the time.

One of the concerts to which Casals went with Betina Ram was a recital by Ignace Jan Paderewski in the Salle Erard. In a front-row seat beside his hostess he was first puzzled and then disconcerted because Paderewski seemed to be looking directly at him; Casals told himself the pianist's attention was directed to Mrs.

Ram. Afterward in the artists' room Casals stayed back when Mrs. Ram began to greet the soloist, but Paderewski pointed a long finger directly at him and said "I already know this young man; tonight I played for him." Fixing him once more with what Casals remembered as a fiercely penetrating look, the Polish virtuoso announced "This youth is *predestiné*"—the same term Lamoureux had used, the word of Schubert for the young Brahms—"He is one of the elect." Paderewski did not hear Casals play for another ten years; after a performance by Casals in Montreux about 1910 the older man, then one of the most famous musicians alive, saluted Casals with the word "Master." They performed together in public only once, in 1916, and never met afterward.

When Emma Nevada presented him to her seventy-eight-year-old singing teacher, Mme Mathilde Marchesi, in the fall of 1899, that formidable lady told Casals he was a son of the house. She issued him a standing invitation, and he called often at 88 rue Jouffroy, the Marchesi home and studio located near the Parc Monceau, not far from the Palmers' house in the Avenue Wagram. Her own professor, Manuel García II, and Mathilde Marchesi were the two most influential teachers of vocal method of the second half of the nineteenth century; their pupils, with those of Francesco Lamperti and his son in Milan, dominated the world's *bel canto* operatic stages by 1899. Marchesi's students included, besides her daughter Blanche, Nellie Melba, Gabrielle Krauss, Marcella Sembrich, Etelka Gerstler, and the three great Emmas—Nevada, Eames, and Calvé. Her husband—Salvatore Marchesi, Cavaliere de Castrone, Marchese della Rajata—was a Sicilian baritone who had begun his own impressive career as singer and teacher in America after he was exiled from Italy because of his involvement in the 1848 revolution. He tended to remain slightly outside his wife's center-stage limelight, and for years had managed the practical aspects of their home and the singing school.

Both Marchesis were energetic links with a past that almost daily had fewer survivors. As a child Lisette Sophie Jeannette Mathilde Graumann, born in Frankfurt am Main in 1821, had lived for a time in Vienna with her aunt, Beethoven's friend and benefactress Baroness Dorothea von Ertmann, through whom she came to know and like Felix Mendelssohn. Mathilde Marchesi's close German friends included members of the wealthy Speyer banking family, who also had ties with Beethoven and Mendelssohn. Franz Liszt had been a musical admirer and friend of both Mathilde and Salvatore. Mathilde had studied voice with Otto Nicolai until Manuel García's sister Pauline convinced her she should study with García in Paris, which she did in García's studio dominated by a portrait of Jenny Lind. A friend of Rossini, Verdi, and Brahms, Mathilde Marchesi tried to convince Richard Wagner, during a long discussion following the first performance of an opera of his in Vienna, that the human voice cannot be treated as an orchestral instrument.

Mme Marchesi studied in Paris with García before the 1848 revolutions, but her teaching base for thirty years was Vienna. When she located her private École Marchesi in the rue Jouffroy in the 1880s, she had acquaintances of long standing with Ambroise Thomas, Charles Gounod, Jules Massenet, Camille Saint-Saëns, and Gabriel Fauré as well as a specially close, mutually admiring friendship with François Gevaërt in Brussels. By the turn of the century Casals could meet and be noticed by the best-established members of the Parisian musical world at Mme Marchesi's or when Emma Nevada entertained in her souvenir-filled house nearby.

All these were heady associations for a young musician, but for Casals the most glowing connection with the musical world of midcentury was Pauline Viardot-García, whom he saw in Mme Marchesi's salon. She had been a painter, a composer, the fabulous mezzo of her time although she was neither physically beautiful nor possessed of an enchanted voice like that of her older sister, María Malibran. She had been one of George Sand's few close women friends, studied piano with Liszt, and been the mistress of the Russian novelist Ivan Turgenev. Richard Wagner had played her portions of *Tristan und Isolde* in manuscript. Now she was nearly eighty and almost blind, but the magic of her personality and shimmering intelligence seemed undiminished. And, beyond Pauline Viardot-García's magnetism and charm, Casals was never unaware that he was in the presence of the last living member of the intimate circle of Frédéric Chopin in Paris.

Mme Marchesi became one of Casals' most active publicists and, in fact, was responsible for his second important public appearance in Paris. Exactly a month after his début with the Lamoureux orchestra there was a concert in the Salle des Fêtes in the Avenue Hoche celebrating Mathilde Marchesi's golden jubilee as a voice teacher, attended by four hundred, including a sprinkling of *le gratin* and the leaders of musical Paris. The gala's program was heavily vocal—opened by Madame's oldest living pupil, dramatic soprano Gabrielle Krauss, continuing through songs and arias sung by current students, and ending with four operatic scenes in costume, one of them a dramatic moment from Saint-Saëns' *Horace,* with the composer at the piano. Marchesi had insisted that Casals perform during the evening as the only instrumental soloist, a tribute to the caliber of his playing but also a fortunate opportunity. Casals, accompanied on piano by Mme Clothilde Kleeberg, played several cello solos before the operatic scenes. Emma Nevada did not take part in the evening; she had begun an American tour in the Metropolitan Opera House in New York the day Casals played at his first Lamoureux concert. But he did meet another American he would often see later in her Boston palace. Isabella Stewart Gardner had come to join the tribute to Mme Marchesi, and when the radiant old lady, standing very erect, entered the hall, Mrs. Jack Gardner pinned a lyre-shape diamond brooch to her corsage.

Early in his Paris years, Casals went to play cello for the deposed sovereign of his homeland, Isabel II of Spain, and her guests in the house she called the Palais de Castille, her home since 1868.

At seventy the former Queen of Spain was sentimental, old, and fat. Casals admitted that she was "rather large"; other less chivalrous observers had described her for twenty years as elephantine (especially when dancing, which she loved to do), almost as grotesquely fat as her gouty, apoplectic, dissolute father Fernando VII. Like everyone else who saw her, Casals was struck by how tiny her head seemed in relation to the rest of her.

Casals knew some of the facts and the gossip concerning the Spanish royal family. Fernando VII had opened the way for the Carlist wars when he assured the Spanish throne for his unborn heir by invoking what historians call pragmatic sanction, which in this instance effected a return to an old Castilian order of succession that allowed a king's daughter to inherit the kingdom. Despite Isabel's sovereign capriciousness as queen, thirty-five hundred miles of railway were laid in Spain and slight progress toward constitutional government was made in which some few rights for private citizens were guaranteed. There were hints of dark things at court: the Queen's confessor meddled in affairs of state and the notorious

Sor Patrocinio, the "bleeding nun" whose "stigmata" were widely considered self-inflicted, exerted a tremendous influence on both the King and the superstitious Isabel. Isabel's marriage at sixteen to her Carlist cousin Francisco de As s had been to the wrong man, unfortunately for her and for Spain. All Madrid knew about the progression of lovers that included soldiers, opera singers, and the composer Emilio Arrieta steadily more openly installed in the palaces, causing Isabel's subjects to call her *esa señora* ("that woman")—and contributing almost as much as republican sentiment to her forced abdication before she was forty. When Casals played for her in Paris at the beginning of the twentieth century, in spite of all the evidence of age and dissipation there still remained some of the charm that had always been undeniable in this good-hearted, emotionally infantile, Italian-Spanish woman who had once occupied the throne of Isabel the Catholic.

For three centuries the intellectual and artistic salon was one of the scintillating, productive facets of the French mind and civilization. Begun by intellectual Frenchwomen in the sixteenth century but shaped by Louis XIV's extraordinary first cousin, La Grande Mademoiselle, in the seventeenth, it was in its twilight when Casals settled in Paris. The decline was an indication that dusk had come for the kind of world in which the salon and many other graceful and extravagant and probably unnecessary things had been possible. But there were still a number of select, stimulating drawing rooms where journalists, fashionable artists, *littérateurs*, musicians, and politicians converged on schedule in the late afternoon or for the evening.

Casals was quickly introduced into the predominantly musical salon of Mme Ephrussi, the most important of its sort in Paris after Napoleon I's niece Princess Mathilde fell victim to sudden depressions and terrible rages and no longer entertained in her home in the rue de Berri, where the aging Charles Gounod once had come, and Louis Pasteur would arrive quietly for talk about matters other than science in the great house that seemed to many a Bonaparte museum and was dominated by the forceful Mathilde, who for many years had earned for herself the title *Notre Dame des Arts*. From the time he settled in Paris, Casals was also a frequent visitor in the house of Mme Lacroix, a delightful old woman who was a patroness of the arts and a close friend of the Morphys;

the Countess and Crista Morphy stayed with her for a time when they came to live in Paris after the Count's death.

The salon where Pablo Casals was adopted as a regular during his first extended stay in Paris was more political than musical. Its moving spirit and focus, Aline Ménard-Dorian, the daughter of a minister of transport in Napoleon III's government, was a very bright and notably handsome woman with a deceptively dreamy look in her eyes and an expression of great inner contentment. Mme Ménard-Dorian was the leading hostess of the political Left in Paris, and her elegant house in the rue de la Faisanderie became a Dreyfusard headquarters with the resurgence of the Dreyfus affair following the publication of Émile Zola's "J'accuse" in L'Aurore in January 1899. She had been a great friend of Victor Hugo, and her daughter Pauline was the first wife of Hugo's grandson. (Edmond de Goncourt noted in his journal forty-eight guests were at table in the Ménard-Dorian house for the wedding dinner.) Casals was soon on friendly terms with Paul Ménard-Dorian, an engineer in his fifties, as well as with his wife—a somewhat rare situation, because often the husband of the salon hostess had little common ground with or interest in his wife's collection of guests.

The Ménard-Dorians were interested in literature and art—an honored friend was the painter Eugène Carrière—but Madame's salon was political: "republican, favorable to free thought and to socialism," a place in which no opinions were barred so long as they were progressive or violent. At the time Casals began to go regularly to the rue de la Faisanderie, Léon Blum was Madame's secretary as well as literary critic for L'Humanité and a civil servant in the Conseil d'État; the elegant and witty Blum was four years older than Casals and seemed to the musician more esthetic than was absolutely necessary. Casals also met socialists Albert Thomas (then tutor to Pauline Hugo's children), René Viviani (later a premier of France), and Aristide Briand (premier eleven times between 1906 and 1932).

The journalist-doctor-politician Georges Clemenceau, an intimate Ménard-Dorian friend temporarily out of public life because of his pro-Dreyfus stand, was sometimes present. The future Tiger of France had discovered music in middle life and tolerated it if it did not come out of Germany, but the Catalan musician in his twenties and the imperious sixty-year-old political figure actually had little to say to each other. An ambitious young pianist named Alfred Cortot came to the house, and, "obsequious and eager, a young man called Marcel Proust."

After an evening in the rue de la Faisanderie in 1895 Goncourt wrote in his journal ". . . the Ménard women, who profess atheism, socialism—all the while stuffing themselves with carp roe [caviar] and sleeping in silk sheets," but the conversation there five years later did nothing to dampen Casals' social consciousness. He was young and fortunate, talented and sensitive; he practiced his art in surroundings of civilization, refinement, and ease, already lionized by the Establishment. Many of his audiences came from the fashionably idle or the well-off middle class. Now he was living in the comfortable *pension* of a Mme Rico in the rue Léon Cognet, but he never forgot the slum in which he and his mother and brothers had spent some weeks near the Porte St.-Denis; there were still hovels in the old fortifications and along the outer boulevards, with unbelievable filth and wretchedness in the St. Antoine quarter. The homeless huddled around trash fires under the bridge spans along the Seine; around the giant market pavilions of Les Halles beggars in rags slept in building corners and against the locked doors of churches; and after midnight vagabonds of both sexes could buy for a few sous a place at the wooden tables of the cheap eating places, where they buried their heads in their arms for a few hours' sleep. There was evidence for the eye and the heart that the *Belle Époque* was not beautiful for many of the more than two and a half million people of Paris. Not until Casals' first year in Paris had the workday of women and children been cut by law from twelve hours to ten, seven days a week. The winter rate for the embroidered dress trimmings made for the large fashion houses by needlewomen, who were often tubercular and who worked and lived in unheated garret rooms, was five centimes an hour. The clubmen and rich dandies, whose English clothes followed the dapper lead of the Prince of Wales, meanwhile sent their linen (especially the high stiff collars and starched shirtfronts) to London once a week to assure proper laundering.

Paris crowds could still be thrown into panic by the sound of an alarm clock ticking inside a box. There had been a series of bombings for which Anarchists took credit since Auguste Vaillant, an uneducated peasant with high ideals whose life had been one of unrelieved poverty and tragedy, set off a crude bomb filled

with nails in the Chamber of Deputies at the end of 1893. After
Vaillant was guillotined he became a popular martyr, and for a
while in Paris it was chic among some members of the artistic
and intellectual world to be parlor Anarchists. Anatole France and
Sarah Bernhardt were among those who contributed to the "Soup
Kitchen Meetings" and other proselytizing efforts, but Anarchist-
sympathizing became less fashionable as the bombings continued.

The Dreyfus affair had erupted while Casals was a student
in Madrid, when a rather colorless young Jewish captain on the
French General Staff, Alfred Dreyfus, was court-martialed on
charges of spying for Prussia; he was convicted and sentenced
to confinement in the penal colony on Devil's Island, off French
Guiana. Soon afterward Major Georges Picquart, head of the general staff counterespionage section, was directed by his superiors
to try to find the motives for Dreyfus' treason. He found no treason; what he did find was a web of spying, manufactured evidence,
and perjury at high level in the army. Ordered to suppress the
facts and posted to Tunisia, Picquart left the information with
a lawyer, in a sealed envelope. The country learned of the developments when Zola's open letter headlined "*J'accuse!*" was published
in the space usually occupied by Clemenceau's column in *L'Aurore*
at the beginning of 1899. The news threw the French Army and
government into chaos and tore France into two violent camps.

Casals met Picquart, by then a colonel, in 1900 at the Ménard-
Dorian house and they became friendly. Picquart, already a friend
of musicians Casals knew, was a man of educated artistic taste and
a good amateur musician. His stubborn honesty and courage made
him the hero of the Dreyfus affair, but when Casals first knew
him he was in disgrace and his career in jeopardy, although he
had kept his sense of humor and was able to sing each new anti-
Picquart ditty heard in the streets. Picquart told Casals and others
the whole behind-the-scenes story. He had never particularly cared
for Dreyfus personally (Picquart had been his superior before the
affair began) and observed that the concept of justice did not seem
to interest Dreyfus; all that really appeared to matter was his own
reinstatement in the army.

The Dreyfus case ravaged France for a total of twelve years
with intolerance, hatred, and ugliness and splintered the country:
families parted, careers were ruined; there were duels, suicides,
fallen governments, imprisonments. Picquart and the musicians

(*Top*) *Casals at the turn of the century, the
beginning of his Paris years;* (*bottom left*)
*Col. Georges Picquart, hero of the Dreyfus
affair;* (*bottom right*) *Aline Ménard-Dorian,
painted by Eugène Carrière*

were also concerned about the effect on musical life. Early in the affair, for example, Lamoureux engaged the pianist Fannie Bloomfield Zeisler, whose instrument was a Steinway, for one of his concerts. Here was a tinderbox: Fannie Bloomfield Zeisler had been taken to Chicago from her native Austria at four, but so far as Parisians were concerned she was a Prussian Jew, playing an American piano at a concert subsidized by the French government. As if this were not enough, she would be playing a concerto by Saint-Saëns, who was in disfavor with a large segment of the public because he had contemptuously declined to become president of the new musicians' union. On the Sunday of the concert the soloist was greeted with yells, catcalls, and whistles by a full house. She began to play, but the noise became so deafening she had to stop. After nearly ten minutes of pandemonium, Lamoureux turned to face the audience and said, as soon as there was enough quiet for his voice to carry: "You may as well stop shouting now, for we are going to play the concerto." The greatest American woman pianist of the day finished the concerto against laughter and loud derisive comments from parts of the audience. As the furor of the affair continued to tinge every level of French life, any artist considered a strong Dreyfusard could expect to have his performance disrupted, particularly in Paris.

Some people found Georges Picquart bland, others thought him stiff. Casals appreciated him as a musical amateur and considered him a man of heroic character; in time Picquart became a frequent guest in Casals' Paris home. The Dreyfus affair had a strong impact on the continuing development of Casals' social consciousness and conception of the inescapable demands of personal integrity. He had known few Jews and was not particularly conscious of the existence of anti-Semitism until he left Spain as an adult. He was horrified by the anti-Jewish incidents in France during the heat of the Dreyfus conflict—some as ugly as those in Germany during the first years of the Nazis. He was well aware of the threats to Picquart and other prominent Dreyfusards in the form both of anonymous letters and of angry crowds when they were recognized in public. The anti-Dreyfusards said that the guilt or innocence of a single individual did not matter when the honor of the French Army and the glory of France were in question, and the Franco-Prussian War veterans and the League of Patriots swore that anyone who demanded a fair trial for Dreyfus was a spy in the pay of Germany. Against this Casals balanced the cry of the young socialist poet Charles Péguy that there must be justice for Dreyfus in the name of national honor; the honor of a country must be based on truth, Péguy said, it is tarnished irrevocably by any lie. Casals knew that men in high places had tried to keep the truth hidden, but in Picquart he saw a man of authority willing to speak out for right despite the probable cost to himself, and felt he had done the only thing a man could do.

Casals and pianist Harold Bauer met in Paris in the autumn of 1899. Emma Nevada wrote Bauer about the young Spaniard and suggested that Bauer should meet him. Casals went to see Bauer and the two hit it off immediately. Bauer, English by birth and nearly four years older than Casals, had started out as a violinist; they reminisced about the great steel-and-glass hulk of the Crystal Palace, where Bauer had played several times under the direction of August Manns, remembering the place and the conductor, but not the country, fondly. Bauer had fled England for France in 1893, despairing of the chances for a native-born artist to make an important career at home and appalled by the quality both of what was being played and of British audiences in Edwardian London.

Bauer was impressed with Casals' playing, and Casals was delighted with Bauer's. After switching from violin to piano as primary instrument at about twenty, Bauer developed a repertoire that would have been remarkable if he had been concentrating on the keyboard since early childhood; it ranged from seventeenth-century harpsichord works to the newest compositions of Claude Debussy. Bauer and Casals compared notes about engagements. Casals had three Salle Pleyel bookings with violinist Jules Boucherit and pianist Louis Diémer in February and March 1900 as well as some others, but there was open time for both beginning in the summer. They agreed enthusiastically to try some recitals together. Casals would explore possibilities in Spain, Bauer those elsewhere in Europe. Harold Bauer's name was becoming reasonably well known in Western Europe. After what he described as rather a dismal tour to Russia with an American singer in 1894 and his first recitals in Spain in 1895 he had played in the Netherlands with such immediate success that appearances in Holland were his main source of income for the next few years.

They began to rehearse a repertoire that included Haydn, Mozart, Boccherini, Schumann, and Bach as well as David Popper's transcription for cello of the Chopin E-flat Nocturne and a few other light but eminently respectable offerings. Both remained in Paris through the 1900 *Grande Saison,* which began ten days after Easter and ended the day after the running of the Grand Prix in mid-June. Casals and Bauer spent a good deal of time together from the outset; their musical rapport was close, which was fortunate since both were already strong-minded men not at all unsure of their musical instincts. As they came to know each other better, they found they saw the world in very much the same way. Casals discovered that his colleague was a mixture of seriousness and boyish fun, with a sharp sense of irony, a good disposition, and a gloriously irreverent talent for mimicry. Their association began to include not only rehearsals but also tennis and joint visits to mutual musical friends across a spectrum that ranged from Picquart and Léon Moreau, Ravel and Fauré to Mrs. Ram, Mme Nevada, and Camille Saint-Saëns.

The first Casals–Bauer tour in Spain was a resounding success. Bauer was still startled and enchanted by the Spanish custom of tossing hats and bouquets onto the stage when the audience approved the performance, just as it would salute an expert matador in the bullring. He was almost speechless in his admiration for the responsiveness of unsophisticated Spanish audiences to serious music, which Casals accepted as a perfectly natural thing. In Spain Bauer sensed an untutored hunger for good music performed well. He proposed a theory to his colleague: this unusual enthusiasm was closely associated with an almost complete lack of musical education—nobody had ever told these audiences they could not enjoy so-called classical music until they had studied it! Music to them was "like painting, sculpture, and architecture—something beautiful which belonged to all the people." Casals tended to agree, adding his own contention that in every country the working people, particularly, would flock to listen to good music if it were offered in concerts exclusively for them, where they did not have to compete with the tiaraed crowd.

Casals and Bauer nevertheless played for an elegant crowd at the end of August in San Sebastián at the Gran Casino Easonense, which was familiar territory for Casals. It was here in 1897 that his solo performances had drawn so many patrons from the gaming rooms that one of his fellow musicians had observed "Casals can turn a gambling casino into a concert hall," a compliment to which a few years later a fervent admirer added "and a concert hall into a temple."

Bauer went on to Switzerland for solo recitals; Casals was to join him in Holland for programs together before Bauer left for his first performances in the United States. They had in hand a healthy schedule of firm bookings for joint recitals the following year. Casals stayed on in San Sebastián because of the expected arrival of the Queen. On the first of September 1900 he acknowledged an inscribed photograph and an affectionate letter from Jesús de Monasterio, reporting that he had no engagements until the twenty-eighth and was bored already. But while waiting for Her Majesty's return he had set into motion a scheme he hoped to see realized in a few days—a benefit concert for the San Sebastián orphans' home. He had already secured the backing of the casino, participation from a local conductor and his orchestra, and assistance from various local sources.

9

CASALS AND HAROLD BAUER gave a joint Saturday-afternoon recital at the Teatro de la Comedia in Madrid on October 26, 1901. One week later Casals was aboard the American steamship *St. Paul*, heading from Cherbourg into the stormy North Atlantic toward New York. Emma Nevada's American tour that opened the day Casals made his Paris début had been successful enough to encourage the soprano to plan another ambitious itinerary through the Western Hemisphere at the end of 1901, and she invited Casals to join the company as one of three assisting instrumental artists.

Emma Nevada's earliest memory was said to be of standing wrapped in an American flag on a table singing "The Star-Spangled Banner" in the mining town of Alpha near Nevada City, California, where she was born in February 1859. She never lost her strong pride in being American although she spent most of her life abroad, where the major triumphs of her career took place. Her father, a Scottish doctor named Wixom, left Wisconsin to make his fortune practicing medicine during the gold rushes into California Territory that began in 1849. Her mother, who was of Irish descent, died soon after Emma was born. She received most of her formal education in the Mills Seminary in Oakland,

California, and in 1877, at eighteen, embarked for Europe as one of a group of girls under the chaperonage of a Dr. Ebel, who maintained his own music school in Berlin. The doctor died on the trip, and Emma Wixom made her way to Vienna to study with Mathilde Marchesi and soon to become known as "the little American nightingale."

She studied acting, dance, and stage movement as well as voice with the autocratic voice teacher for three years and made her stage début at the Trieste Opera as Amina in Bellini's *La Sonnambula*. Mme Marchesi's interest in her students extended to matters of dress, the social graces, and sometimes diet; her concern for the motherless American girl not much older than her own daughter was the basis of a close lifetime friendship. Marchesi also paid attention to her students' names, changing some of those she considered unpronounceable or otherwise unsuitable for the stage, as when she persuaded Emma Boellmann to call herself Emma Calvé. Both Germans and French would find it almost impossible to pronounce Wixom, so Emma became Mlle Nevada, a name that gave Spanish admirers ample chance to make graceful puns about the melting qualities of its owner's voice. (Mme Marchesi had a geographic penchant: Florence Brimson from Canada became Florence Toronta; Helen Mitchell Armstrong from Melbourne, Australia, became Nellie Melba.)

Giuseppi Verdi, commissioned to find a prima donna for the new season at La Scala, heard Emma sing in Genoa; he stood up in his loge and applauded so enthusiastically that the attention of the house shifted from the stage to him. Afterward he telegraphed the Scala management one word: NEVADA. Her Milan début was also in the vapid but vocally spectacular role of Amina, which she sang twenty-two times more that season. Her first London appearance, under the management of Col. Henry Mapleson, lasted only one performance; after a disagreement about contract, star and manager parted company—an occurrence not at all unfamiliar to the colorful entrepreneur.

She was back under Mapleson's management in 1884, starring at twenty-four in the Colonel's United States-bound opera company with the flamboyant Spanish coloratura Adelina Patti and Italian mezzo-soprano Sofia Scalchi. Nevada made her American operatic debut (once again as Amina) on November 24, 1884, in the New York Academy of Music at the start of a transcontinental operatic tour that seems incredible almost a century later. Henry Mapleson had gathered together a good company with first-rate soloists, a chorus, sets, costumes, conductor and musicians for a six-month tour of works that included *Il Trovatore* and *Aïda*, Gounod's *Faust* and *Mireille*, Weber's *Der Freischütz* and Flotow's *Martha*, Donizetti's *La Favorita* and *Lucrezia Borgia* as well as his *Linda di Chamounix*, Rossini's *Semiramide*, and Bellini's *La Sonnambula*.

After New York, two weeks in Boston (where Nevada sang in *Mireille*), and a stop in Philadelphia, the Mapleson Opera Company opened in New Orleans (Nevada sang *La Sonnambula*), in 75-degree weather. The next appearance was in St. Louis (where it was thirty below zero), followed by Topeka, St. Joseph (Nevada again sang *La Sonnambula*), Omaha, Cheyenne, and Salt Lake City before an opening in San Francisco on the second of March 1885. In Cheyenne Emma Nevada caught a cold that almost developed into pneumonia and was out of the company four weeks. (She had close medical attention: her father was along on the trip, and her business manager, Raymond Palmer, was also a physician.)

Mapleson had announced two two-week seasons in San Francisco, featuring Patti and Nevada. First-night tickets were sold by speculators for as much as $150. Emma Nevada had been announced for the second night, but the impresario had to substitute Patti—to his great annoyance, because he had to deliver an extra fee before she would set foot onstage, and to the fury of a group of scalpers who took so great a loss they banded together to take Mapleson to court. By late in the season the iron shutters of the Opera House had to be ordered closed to stop the people who climbed ladders and got into the hall through the dress-circle windows. During the final performance of *Aïda* crowds wrenched off alleyway gratings and as many as could slid down on their stomachs into the theater cellars to hear Patti and Scalchi.

On Monday of the final week in March, Emma Nevada was able to sing again, in *La Sonnambula*, and drew the best San Francisco audience the company had—between three and four thousand people who "shouted and applauded a welcome as if they were all going mad." The enthusiasm of any other public would have spurred her on," Mapleson noted, "but she was here so much affected that, although she sustained herself splendidly . . . after the curtain fell she was unable to speak." The audience had listened attentively with "scarcely any interruptions," but when the final curtain fell the house went completely wild. "Nevada was called out . . . with shouts, cries, and every manner of wild demonstration." Flowers were thrown from the boxes and dress circle until the stage was covered. One of the floral set pieces (some were six feet high) carried down the aisle and handed up to the stage was a large seat built of roses, violets, and carnations on a wicker frame, "and Nevada, as the most natural thing to do, sat plumply down in it, whereat the house fairly howled with delight." On the back of the chair was emblazoned WELCOME HOME.

Emma Nevada was certainly the only girl from a mining town in the American West who made a notable mark in grand opera during its late-nineteenth-century heyday. She had an exceptionally clear, moderately powerful voice with a two-and-a-half-octave range up to F above high C. Mathilde Marchesi and many critics considered her a singer of the very first order, with brilliant execution, "a sentimental nightingale." She was not notably pretty, but she was a clever actress and had a winning personality. She excelled in and enjoyed most the bathetic, florid coloratura roles (Amina, Zora in Félicien David's *Perle du Brésil*; Mignon, Rosina, Lakmé), although she also liked to sing Carmen and both Susanna and Cherubino in *The Marriage of Figaro*. Casals did not consider her a true artist or her voice great. Very few singers inhabited his musical pantheon, a small band that included no exclusively operatic sopranos of any description.

From San Francisco Mapleson's company proceeded to Chicago for a two-week "Grand Opera Festival" during which thirteen different operas were played to 190,000 paid admissions. Nevada had recovered completely and she and Patti sang alternate nights to phenomenal audiences in the huge Opera House auditorium designed by Dankmar Adler and Louis Sullivan, which had seats for six thousand and room for almost that many standees. Nine thousand paid to hear Patti sing *Linda di Chamounix* (like *La Sonnambula* a silly, vaguely Alpine libretto in which the coloratura heroine goes mad on account of love); the program duly announced that she would interpolate her famous "Home, Sweet Home" into the finale. The next night Nevada triumphed as the mad Lucia. The following week Patti's Aïda attracted twelve thousand, Nevada's Amina eight thousand.

Emma Nevada remained with the Mapleson company for a

week's run in New York and a final week in Boston, returning in May to Europe, where in October she was married to Dr. Palmer in the Church of the Passionists in the Avenue Hoche. (Operatic composer Ambroise Thomas gave her away, and a chorus of Marchesi students sang.) The Palmers lived well while Emma continued her successful career in Europe over the next fifteen years. Little known in her homeland and practically forgotten in Europe after the first decade of the twentieth century, Emma Nevada became in her zenith one of the Queens of Song. Her one tangible bit of civic immortality is a medallion depicting her as Amina that was mounted (along with those of Giuditta Pasta and María Malibran) on the pedestal of the memorial to Vincenzo Bellini in Catania during the Bellini centennial in 1935.

Casals reached New York with Mme Nevada's troupe on Saturday, November 16, 1901. The group debarking from the *St. Paul* included the forty-two-year-old diva, her husband, and two of the European musicians—Casals and twenty-five-year-old French pianist Léon Moreau. Daniel Marquarre, gold-medalist in flute from the Paris Conservatoire and the third assisting instrumentalist, had already arrived. Raymond Duncan, Isadora's brother, who sometimes wore a flapping white toga, was listed as Madame's secretary.

If there were none of the massed bands and bunting Mapleson had arranged for Adelina Patti and other of his stars in the eighties, there were at least press and personal friends on hand when Emma Nevada, looking radiantly healthy, swept down the gangplank to greet her New York manager, Albert Sutherland. She touched almost all bases in a whirlwind interview that sounds, from the account in the next day's New York *Morning Herald*, as if she had no problems of breath control.

Greeting Sutherland, she remarked she had had a beastly trip, with storms nearly all the way, and was glad to get back. She had had a delightful time since her last appearance but this was her home. What had she been doing since she left? "Well, I sang in nearly every city of consequence in Europe and was accorded the best of treatment." She had had an invitation to sing before the Queen of Holland this winter, but turned it down because of her engagements in the United States. The current tour would be thirty weeks long and would cover the United States and parts of Canada and Mexico, with an opening in Boston, Tuesday, November 26.

"Pablo Casals," she continued, "who accompanies me on the tour, is a young violoncellist who is a protégé of the Queen of Spain. His performances won for him the decoration of the Order of the Cavaliers of Santiago, which was conferred on him by the Spanish Queen Regent. Moreau, the pianist, is also a splendid artist. His recitals in Paris have been accredited some of the best, if not the best, of all the young pianists of France."

Before she entered a carriage to go to her hotel, Mme Nevada deplored the movement, especially in the American Midwest, to suppress ragtime. "Ragtime," she said, "is popular, melodious and appeals to all classes of music lovers."

Some interesting things about Emma Nevada's 1901 company were its size, her plan to dress in the costume of the character she was singing in her operatic excerpts, and the scheduling of some morning performances. In Europe as well as America, solo tours even by instrumentalists were the exception save for a handful of top names. In addition to the pianist, who generally offered some numbers alone, a singer usually had an "assisting artist," frequently a violinist, who was featured in a solo portion of the program. Any self-respecting coloratura soprano who could had the services of a flutist to play obbligato in such showpieces as the Bell Song from *Lakmé* and the Mad Scene from *Lucia di Lammermoor*. For such a long and heavily booked tour it would have been suicidal for Nevada (and hard on the audiences) not to have had respite within the program. Although long afterward Casals remembered among the musicians only Mme Nevada, Moreau, and himself, other members of the group for the first portion of the tour included a promising young American basso, Heathe Gregory, and a Parisian accompanist named Garon.

The group's first appearance was in the Worcester Theatre, Worcester, Massachusetts, on Monday evening, November 25. Next day came the first advertised concert, a matinée in the Colonial Theatre in Boston, where Julia Marlowe was soon to follow with a run of *When Knighthood Was in Flower*. Bostonian composer Arthur Foote joined the program to accompany Heathe Gregory singing a group of Foote songs. The audience, like that in Providence, Rhode Island, three days later, was small but responsive.

[153]

The Boston and Providence programs were a fair sample of the company's offerings throughout the tour while Casals was a member of the group. With a grueling succession of single performances, there was no practical or artistic reason not to give essentially the same program over and over again. A local musician occasionally participated and the instrumentalists varied their numbers to avoid boredom themselves, but with the demands of travel and new houses almost every night there was little time to prepare new works.

Mme Nevada was given first billing, and her portions of the program—three groups to Casals' and Moreau's two—were tailored to display her technique to best advantage. It was a well-balanced program of considerable substance. Nevada sang three coloratura scenes and a group of art songs. As soloist, Moreau contributed works of Chopin, Schumann, Liszt, and a composition of his own. Casals' first group was the Fauré *Élégie* and Saint-Saëns' *Allegro Appassionato*, his second featured a Locatelli cello sonata. Of the assisting artists, Casals had the most prominent billing. In some of the advertisements his name is in larger type than those of the Frenchmen. His name was mentioned first in the news stories, and he is invariably called "Pablo Casals" while his colleagues are simply "Moreau, pianist" and "Marquarre, flutist." On this tour Marquarre, who later joined the Boston Symphony Orchestra, had a single solo, but he accompanied Mme Nevada in the Bell Song from Léo Délibes' *Lakmé*—an exercise not without challenge, because Nevada occasionally forgot the words and the flutist had to improvise sparkling variations until she remembered where she was.

Mme Nevada's encores were likely to include the perpetual favorite "Home, Sweet Home" and "Listen to the Mockingbird," which gave her chances to trill, soar, and exhibit extraordinary pianissimo control. (Nevada's art delighted many, but not everyone who heard her. When she sang for Queen Victoria at Osborne in July 1899, five days before Casals' recital there, Lady-in-Waiting Marie Mallet reported "Madame Nevada . . . is a sort of trick songstress and shakes [trills] and 'roulades' high staccato notes like a motor car in Bond Street.") She also had the tear (sob) in the voice so highly prized in those days. Casals could not recall her ever having sung ragtime even though she asserted she was going to do so. For himself, he experimented with several encore pieces, including the Popper transcription of the Chopin E-flat Nocturne that was proving increasingly popular on his European programs.

The concerts themselves ran two and a half hours, sometimes longer. Before Nevada appeared the assisting artists gave nearly an hour's recital—two piano solos by Moreau, a French song from Gregory, a piece for flute performed by Marquarre, and the Fauré *Élégie* played by Casals; then there was a pause. At the first matinée, in Boston, Léon Moreau sat down at the piano at just seven minutes to four (according to the *Transcript* reviewer in his critique published the next day), waited a moment, and then struck a chord. "Instantly the pair of red curtains across the Gothic door at the back of the stage were drawn aside, and there, in a Grecian robe of white and gold, a fillet of golden ivy leaves on her head, stood Madame Nevada. For a minute she remained motionless, then, amid hearty applause, she walked timidly down the stage and sang an aria from 'La Perle du Brèsil' and the Bell Song from 'Lakmé.' After the arias Madame Nevada ran lightly off . . . but returned to receive, with glad surprise, a pot of heather, and many beautiful bunches of roses. 'All these?' she exclaimed, under her breath, but still audibly . . . [she] laid the roses on the piano, but held the flower pot in her arms while she sang as an encore 'Shall I wear a white rose, shall I wear a red?' " The second half included a group of songs performed by Heathe Gregory, a group sung by Mme Nevada, two solos and an encore by Moreau, the Locatelli sonata performed by Casals, and Nevada ended the program with the Shadow Song from *Dinorah*. Few of the reviewers in other cities described the stage business, but most across the country awarded high marks to the work of all the performers.

From Rhode Island the company moved through upstate New York, including a one-night stand in Elmira, into the cities and mining country of Pennsylvania, then southward toward Baltimore, where the company had a matinée at the Academy Theater on the thirteenth of December. That night Casals saw his only prize fight—a bout at Germania Hall in East Baltimore between world's light-heavyweight boxing champion Joe Gans and a fighter named Bobby Dodds (he found the sport brutal). Four days later came an evening performance at the Academy of Music in Richmond, Virginia; the itinerary continued south as far as Florida, across the Gulf coast to New Orleans, and then into the warm, vast ranching country of the American Southwest. Precise dates

*Emma Nevada in a costume she wore during
the 1901–1902 American tour*

and exact programs and the curious names of strange small places
melted in Casals' memory into other data of other journeys, performances, and town names.

At the turn of the twentieth century every railway town of
inland America had its opera house, theater, or other structure
that could house performances, and a public hungry for entertainment. None of the audiences on this tour was so mammoth as the
thousands Nevada and Patti had sung for under Mapleson's management sixteen years earlier, but once away from the coastal cities

the Nevada ensemble had full houses. The schedule of performances was demanding, including morning concerts (which must
have been much harder on the singer than on the instrumentalists)
as well as the afternoon and evening appearances. The group gave
more than sixty concerts across some four thousand miles of country in the three months between debarking in New York and reaching San Francisco at the beginning of March 1902.

Casals formed an impression of North America on his first trip
to the United States that was sympathetic on the whole, and began
an association with America and Americans that had an enduring
ingredient of affection. The first thing that surprised and pleased
him was the marked absence of superficial class distinctions. He
was amazed to find libraries, museums, and even art galleries in
smaller towns; as the years passed he continued to articulate a half-
incredulous amazement at the amounts individual patrons could
and did give to subsidize musical organizations and to build and
maintain libraries and museums. He sensed in the country a dynamism, a young vigor, and a style of life that could be disconcerting to Europeans.

He passed his twenty-fifth birthday in America a little more
than a month after the tour started. Music came first for him, but
he was acutely interested in whatever was going on around him.
Léon Moreau was indefatigably curious; he wanted to go everywhere, to see everything. He and Casals explored widely. Wilkes-
Barre, Pennsylvania, for instance, had been cold when they reached
there in early December, but Moreau and Casals wanted to see
how coal was mined. American coalpits held a peculiar fascination
for European visitors; Sarah Bernhardt, on a visit to the States
in 1880, had wrapped herself in a cloak and descended to inspect
a mine, unconcerned by the superstition that the presence of a
woman in a mineshaft invites disaster. Once in the pits, Casals and
Moreau became so engrossed they forgot the time, arriving at the
theater looking, if not quite like Moors, like musical coal-miners.
Moreau, who played the first numbers, barely had time to change
and brought to his performance of Chopin and Schumann faint
wafts of coal dust.

When they reached Texas in January, the wild open country
and the cowboys constantly intrigued the two young Europeans.
Once the schedule took them into a small ranching center, where

during their free time the Spaniard and the Frenchman took a stroll around the heart of town in relaxed tourist fashion—two foreigners quite as picturesque to the natives as the locals to them. The two visitors ambled into a saloon in which the action appeared lively but safe and were soon engaged in a game with men wearing large hats and six-shooters attached to their ammunition belts, who seemed at least three feet taller than Casals.

Everything went well in the international exchange for a while. Then the atmosphere began to chill somewhat as the cellist continued to decline the offer of free drinks. Finally and forcefully one of the men at the table announced: "In Texas we gamble *and* drink, suh!" (Casals never particularly liked the taste of alcohol or its effect on him, but recalled: "Oh, yes, I drank. We *both* drank!")

At the same time silver dollars were beginning to pile up in front of Casals faster than in front of anybody else and he fancied that the poker faces of his new friends had begun to seem a shade menacing. The novelty of the encounter was fading quickly as far as Casals was concerned, and the romance of the American West was being supplanted by other reactions. Then Casals' luck fortunately changed and his pile of winnings began to dwindle. The faces of his fellow players started to brighten noticeably, and when the game broke up the participants went their ways after hearty handshakes and a certain amount of backslapping.

One excursion, somewhere in the New Mexico Territory, was made at Casals' instigation. A fellow passenger on the train had said that there was only one way to savor the great American desert; a long walk out into it would be an unforgettable experience. The endless, sun-baked miles of flatland that supported only low sagebrush, scrubby clumps of mesquite, and cactus certainly looked desertlike to Pablo Casals. He persuaded Moreau to join him for a long walk to sample the solitude and the grandeur. Before long Moreau had had enough of both, but Casals insisted on going farther. At last they saw a small house in the distance, and when they reached it the man and woman who had been sitting in the hot twilight offered the two explorers water to drink. The rancher's English was as heavily accented as the guests': he had been born, he said, in a country the two young men had probably never heard of—Catalonia.

*Casals at twenty-five, a portrait taken in New
York at the start of his first North
American tour*

After a performance at Myer's Opera House in El Paso on
February 4, the troupe traveled through the Arizona Territory
(where Casals saw the Grand Canyon, taking the muleback trip
down the steep path to the canyon bottom and the banks of the
Colorado River) on their way to southern California and a concert

in Los Angeles on February 11. The company continued up the Pacific coast to San Francisco, a city that delighted Casals at first sight. A wild frontier port fifty years before, San Francisco had grown into the American West's major city, with its own unabashed identity and its unique blend of formality and informality. Small dwellings, some with livestock in the gardens, scrabbled up the steep hills above the Embarcadero and the commercial center, and great houses of the affluent stood austere and pretentious on Nob Hill. San Francisco was as cosmopolitan as any city in the country, and everything was contained in a much smaller area than New York, which three months earlier had seemed to Casals busy, noisy, and rather muddy. At the hodgepodge San Francisco waterfront towered square-riggers, just returned from the Orient.

San Francisco had not forgotten the grand-opera star from Alpha, California. Stories with pictures began to appear in the San Francisco *Chronicle* in late February. The first of them picked up part of Nevada's manager's press release: "The diva is one of the native song birds, whose warbling has always brought credit to her State. Pablo Casals, court violoncellist of the Queen of Spain, will be one of the attractions. . . ." The story and the first advertisements appeared in the same papers that carried front-page stories of a reign of terror in Barcelona in the wake of Anarchist riots.

The musicians stayed at the Occidental Hotel rather than at San Francisco's nearby pre-earthquake showplace, the Palace, where Nevada's local manager J. S. Hirsh maintained his address. Casals and Moreau nevertheless soon saw the grandiose establishment where mining millionaires and their ladies drove in carriages into the hotel's great court, which was surrounded by seven tiers of galleries topped by a magnificent opaque glass dome. To European eyes there was some similarity both to the Crystal Palace in London and to the three-year-old hotel of César Ritz on the Place Vendôme in Paris.

Lillian Nordica, the American dramatic soprano from Massachusetts, had lived aboard her private railway car when she came to San Francisco for recitals two weeks before; Mme Nevada swept off a regularly scheduled train with her husband and one of the musicians the press mistook for their son, when the company arrived in the early evening of the first of March 1902. Before leaving for the Occidental, she talked to the waiting reporter for the San Francisco *Chronicle*, who recounted her immediate plans in detail in the next morning's issue. She would go to mass in the morning (she had converted to Catholicism about a year before her marriage; Mathilde Marchesi and Charles Gounod stood as godparents at her baptism). Weather permitting, she would then stroll about the city, and between five and six o'clock would receive friends. She would rest all day Monday before the concert, and early Tuesday the company would leave for Sacramento for a Wednesday-evening concert there. Mme Nevada planned to be back in London in time for the coronation of King Edward and then to sing for the first time in her mother's native Ireland. But while in California she was going to visit her own birthplace in Alpha, the forgotten suburb of Nevada City, for the first time since infancy; it was there that "Pet Wixom" had first sung in public at the age of three, and she had just received a petition signed by twelve hundred begging her to sing for them once more.

The Monday-night San Francisco concert at Metropolitan Hall, Fifth Street near Market, brought "Society . . . out in its best frocks and feathers" to honor the Californian singer who appeared on a stage massed with quantities of the "first brilliant flowers of spring. Encores followed encores, and Madame Nevada was most generous in singing all the ballads she thought her friends wanted to hear, ending with 'Home, Sweet Home.'" The *Chronicle* reviewer spent almost as much space on Casals' playing as on Nevada's singing: he was a "man whose art is of the highest order. Casals has genius back of his technical ability and rare intelligence. He gave four programme numbers and three encores." Another San Francisco concert was announced for the same hall on Saturday afternoon, March 8.

On Saturday, Nevada was at her best in the Mad Scene from *Lucia* and the Waltz Song from *Romeo et Juliette* and once more generous with encores, including "My Old Kentucky Home" and ending with "Listen to the Mockingbird," for which she played her own accompaniment. Casals' program numbers included Boëllmann's *Variations Symphoniques* and the adagio and minuet from the Locatelli sonata; his last encore was the Bach–Gounod "Ave Maria." The *Chronicle*'s notice was headed MADAME NEVADA'S LAST CONCERT, with the bank headline reading "Notable Success of Pablo

Casals, the Spanish Cellist." Emma Nevada would have had to be an unusually generous and unselfish artist to be overjoyed with the review, which began:

> With all due loyalty to Mme. Emma Nevada, one of California's singers, who has a world-wide reputation as a light soprano with much grace of style, it must be admitted that first honors of the just concluded engagement go to Pablo Casals, the cellist, one of the "assisting artists." This was virtually conceded the night of the first concert, and established beyond doubt yesterday at the second and last. Casals . . . is so unassuming in his appearance and address that his masterful playing comes as a surprise.

The company remained in the Bay area for another week, with concerts Tuesday in Oakland and Wednesday in Vallejo near the Mare Island Navy Yard. In the Vallejo performance Léon Moreau was seriously handicapped by a notably decrepit upright piano. Casals and Moreau immediately had a claque of young admirers in the hospitable city eager to show them the place and to entertain them. An outing was suggested for a free day, Sunday, March 16, across San Francisco Bay for a climb up Mount Tamalpais. The weather had been unusually harsh for a month. Storms had swept down from Puget Sound carrying snow, heavy rainfall that caused floods, and snowslides inland that killed twenty at a single mining site. In the Dakotas and the Canadian Northwest a great blizzard was raging, but the trip across the Bay for the climb was made in dazzling early sunlight on a palatial ferry that was the most luxurious vessel Casals had ever seen. Tamalpais, a gently sprawling outline the Indians said was the form of a sleeping maiden, commands Marin County north of the Golden Gate; on the lower slopes stood a two-thousand-year-old grove of giant California redwoods, a natural cathedral through which the party went on the way to begin its ascent through fields of early wildflowers.

Tamalpais is about two-thirds the height of Montserrat and much less formidable, but there are some steep slopes and narrow trails. Along one of these on the descent, Casals paused for a moment to look toward the Pacific. He had enough time to pivot his head and body out of the path of a plummeting, winter-loosened boulder, but he would have fallen if he had released his hold on an outcrop. The falling stone veered and went across his left hand, crushing it. When he looked at the bloody mass Casals thought instantly, "Thank God, I'll never have to play the cello again!"

It could have been true—he might not have had a choice. Injury to his right hand could have hampered him seriously, but lasting damage to the fingering hand would almost certainly have ended his career as a performing musician. The sudden thankfulness had been another stroke of lightning, but his ambivalence had returned long before the doctor spoke of the possibility of bone damage and nerve injury. Casals' artistic doubts and dissatisfactions flooded in. If there were no more concerts, he would be free of the paralyzing stage fright that made him ill every time he prepared to play in public. There would be time and energy to compose. A wounded hand would not stop him from becoming a conductor. But he was already enslaved by the cello. He expressed his art through that somewhat cumbersome instrument in a way that no other violoncellist had done before. He had experienced the rarest of communication with audiences—and he had tasted success.

By Monday, Dr. Oscar Mayer told the press that everything possible was being done to reduce the swelling and mend the bruises and said that Casals would surely be well enough to rejoin his colleagues at the end of the week. The company was reluctant to go on without him, but was obliged to do so. Dr. Mayer's prognosis was somewhat optimistic, and Casals spent two months while his hand healed at 3196 Washington Street, the home of Sarah Solomons Stein and her husband Michael. Michael Stein, a director of the Bay City street-railway system who preferred the violin to business routine, was a onetime childhood neighbor of Isadora and Raymond Duncan in Oakland. The Stein home was in many respects European—Stein had lived in Vienna and Paris as a youngster—and the congenial hospitality had a calming effect on Casals, who was at first in some shock as well as pain and very much aware that he was six thousand miles from home. Casals could not safely have returned at once to Europe (where, when word of the accident arrived, there was a flurry of concern in Paris that a European specialist should be sent to examine the hand). Dr. Mayer ordered almost constant massage of the injured hand during the early stages of healing, and Sarah Stein arranged for shifts of acquaintances to keep Casals company and help with the therapy.

Some spoke Spanish or French, but even those who could not were young and personable. In time Pablo Casals' spirits and English began to improve appreciably.

Whenever he felt like going out in San Francisco there was some competition among his companions to be Casals' guide to the new De Young art museum founded by the publisher of the *Chronicle*, for cable-car rides through the steep streets, and to points of interest in and around the city. The excursion Casals recalled most often in later years was a trip on which he accompanied Sarah Stein north of the city to call on what he described as a gypsy woman. This clairvoyant greeted Sarah, who had visited before, then turned her attention to Casals. He was, she informed him, from very far away, and began to describe details of his house in Barcelona. Then she said she saw a name very clearly; she spelled it—SCHUBERT. That was all.

Casals missed Mme Nevada's triumphal return to Nevada City at the beginning of April (thousands cheering and waving handkerchiefs, booming cannon, the Nevada City Band playing "Home, Sweet Home," and a specially decorated new carriage drawn by four cream-colored horses to take her to the hotel), and the chance to participate in her concert before old miners with tears rolling down their cheeks.

In the Stein home Casals heard about Michael's youngest brother Leo, who also played violin but was much more interested in art and was that spring in Florence, looking at pictures and spending a good deal of time with Bernard Berenson. There were also reports from the youngest sister, Gertrude, who was almost three years older than Casals, an adequate pianist, and who in fierce boredom was finishing her final year of medical studies at Johns Hopkins after studying psychology with William James at Radcliffe. Casals would soon meet them both in Paris, although a charming but apocryphal story tells that Gertrude stormed into his room while Casals was recuperating in San Francisco and told him that with his hand in a plaster cast he looked like El Greco's *Gentleman with a Hand on His Chest*.

Pablo Casals developed a warm feeling for San Francisco and a lasting friendship for his hosts. Late in May he gave a grateful and successful farewell recital and began the long, rough, noisy train journey across the North American continent to New York and embarkation in the late spring of 1902 for home.

10

CASALS' HAND WAS completely healed when he returned to Europe in June 1902. On the way to Spain he stopped a few days in Paris, where Mathilde Marchesi greeted him with an affectionate cry of "My son, my son!" as she embraced him. Hostess and guest gazed fondly at each other for a moment before Madame began to introduce him to the others in the room. Suddenly she embraced him once more, whispering "Quick! How is your name again?"

After a reunion with his family and a brief holiday in Spain, Casals was on his way to play again in Portugal. In Porto he gave a recital with Bernardo Valentim Moreira de Sá for the Orpheon Portuense, a subscription group of music-lovers of the sort that offered engagements to musicians in many parts of Europe during the early part of the century, which Moreira de Sá had organized in January 1881 and which called itself the oldest philharmonic society in Iberia.

Bernardo Moreira de Sá and Casals had known each other since Casals' first appearances at the Espinho Casino in the summer of 1898 and had given a concert together in Porto at the beginning of March 1899. An intense wiry man of nearly fifty in late 1902, Moreira de Sá was a man of indefatigable activity and the most influential musical personality in Portugal. A violinist (impressive concert début at eight, study with teachers in Porto and with Joseph Joachim in Germany) and pianist, he was also a director of orchestras and choruses, professor, lecturer, critic of music and art, permanent director of the Orpheon Portuense for more than forty years, and organizer and first director of the Conservatory of Music of Porto. At twenty-one he had founded a chamber-music society that was an important force in raising the standards of musical taste in Portugal—after his death in 1924, Casals hailed Moreira de Sá as the Monasterio of Portugal, a tribute more to his efforts to promote good music than to his violin-playing. Moreira de Sá was also a mathematician and an authority on educational methods whose textbooks were used in most of the elementary schools of Portugal, a classical scholar and linguist, whose important books included histories of music and a history of the plastic arts, and he owned the most important music store in the region. Casals, like many others, found him a man of refinement and charm. Moreira de Sá had already made a number of concert tours in South America, and he proposed that Casals and Harold Bauer join him for six weeks of recitals in Brazil in the summer of 1903.

Casals and Bauer embarked on another joint recital tour of Spain in the autumn of 1902. Casals had begun to play full Bach solo cello suites in public not long before his Paris début, and some of the programs during this tour included one. Bauer, sitting backstage with the stage crew, had further confirmation of the innate Spanish response to great music when he saw tears streaming down the face of the stagehand beside him listening to Casals play one of the unaccompanied Bach suites. "The composer of that music is Verdi," said the stagehand. "Of course it is," responded Bauer, "doesn't it say so on the program?" "I can't read. But I know it is Verdi's music, for that is the only music that always makes me weep."

When they reached Madrid they were invited to the palace to play informally. Visits of this sort were sentimental homecomings for Casals, who carried his Gagliano with him in its case. Bauer, however, knew that the royal grand piano was old and worn, and made arrangements for his own Erard concert instrument to be taken to the palace. The assurance from the manager of the piano store that he was not to worry sent him rushing to the theater, where he found his piano issuing from the stage door on the shoulders of about twenty porters, looking to him like an enormous coffin with legs and lyre attached. No regular piano movers had been available; police escorted the cortege through traffic, and the instrument was carried through the royal front door and up a grand staircase. The musicians went in by a back entrance.

The Queen wanted to hear the full program the two had played the preceding evening at the Teatro Comedia, and they invited her to select the order in which she would like to hear the numbers. First she asked that Casals play the cello transcription of the Chopin E-flat Nocturne. Next was the Beethoven "Appassionata" Sonata, which the Queen asked Bauer to play from the music so she could sit next to the piano and follow the performance with the notes. "And," said the Infanta Isabel, "I will turn the pages."

The two royalties, both near-sighted and holding lorgnettes to their eyes, crowded Bauer so closely that he scarcely had room to play. And they talked all the time.

"How like Wagner!" said María Cristina. "Yes, ma'am," Bauer said without stopping.

"This reminds me of Chopin," said the Infanta, turning a page at the wrong place. "Yes, ma'am," said Bauer, continuing to play.

By the end of the last movement both ladies were bent so far over the keyboard that Bauer had to play the last chords *tenuto* rather than with the customary short release.

Leo Stein, Michael's brother, settled in Paris late in 1902, although he continued to travel about a good deal. He and Casals were in touch soon (Leo inscribed a portrait of himself "To Pablo Casals in the assurance of permanent friendship" in January 1903). During a month that Stein was in town late in 1902 or early in 1903 he and Casals saw each other very frequently. They often dined together and went for walks during which Leo Stein was more likely than not to talk about his own particular concept of esthetics. Casals took this in stride gracefully enough, but Stein's musical tastes were a trial, as Leo himself realized: "I had a bad habit of half consciously whistling fragments of music, and whenever I noticed Pablo turning green and looking as though he wanted to jump into the Seine I knew that I had fallen upon something from the *Cavalleria Rusticana* or *Pagliacci*."

Casals' life had already developed the almost constant pattern of travel it would follow for another forty years as well as friendships throughout the world that would mean a great deal to him. By late 1902 Casals' acquaintance among the established in musical Paris alone was wide, and his contemporaries included, in addition to Bauer and his circle of friends, violinist Jacques Thibaud and pianist Alfred Cortot (who had just founded a concert association after three years as an assistant conductor at the Bayreuth Festival), cellist Joseph Salmon, young composers Jean Huré and Florent Schmitt, Italian pianist and neophyte composer Alfredo Casella, and Georges Enesco, a twenty-two-year-old Rumanian violinist whose compositions had been played by the Colonne orchestra in Paris and who had been named court violinist to the Queen of Rumania. About this time Casals again encountered contralto María Gay, a fellow Catalan and slight acquaintance who had been performing with Raoul Pugno and Eugène Ysaÿe in Belgium. She was three years Casals' junior and had worked at sculpture until she was sixteen, studied violin, and begun vocal study only after the quality of her own voice was discovered when she was imprisoned for singing a revolutionary song in a Barcelona street. María Gay soon afterward told pianist-conductor Alexander Siloti in St. Petersburg about Casals, and the two began corresponding.

Casals was already playing an annual benefit concert for the players' fund with the Lamoureux orchestra and with the Concerts Colonne orchestra. He formed a trio with pianist Camille Chevillard, Charles Lamoureux's son-in-law and successor, and Charles Herman, assistant concertmaster of the orchestra at the time of Casals' début. They made a number of trio appearances, and Casals and Herman gave joint recitals. Casals' reputation was quickly becoming what it remained thereafter, unique and perhaps timeless, but by the nature of his instrument and its repertoire he did not appear often alone on a stage. Among his early collaborators—and throughout his life his performing associates were among the greatest musicians alive—was Édouard Risler, Marcel Proust's favorite pianist, whose art Casals remembered and respected but whose mania for gambling seriously distressed him.

Casals heard many musicians in great private houses and in

*Portuguese violinist-impresario Bernardo Moreira
de Sá (seated), pianist Harold Bauer, and Casals
in São Paulo in the summer of 1903*

concert halls, and he went to hear what symphonic music was
being played whenever he could. He was appalled that Mozart
was considered a "filler" and usually played without rehearsal, and
puzzled that a work of Haydn almost never appeared on a program
of any of the four fine orchestras in Paris at the turn of the cen-

tury—the Lamoureux, the Colonne, the Opéra orchestra, and that of the Conservatoire.

Harold Bauer said of his collaboration with Casals that they were "comrades in the best and most complete sense of the term. Our tastes were similar in everything that pertained to daily life in the course of our numerous tours together, and there was never a dull moment." Their most ambitious tour to date began at the end of May 1903, when they and Moreira de Sá played four chamber-music recitals in Portugal—Braga, Porto, and Lisbon—before sailing for Brazil, where their first trio evening was given in the Teatro Lírico in Rio de Janeiro on June 18. Between then and the first day of August they played in Rio, Santos, Campinas, and São Paulo—eleven concerts with Moreira de Sá, although Casals dismissed him later as not a very good violinist, plus those in which only Bauer and Casals appeared.

The relatively brief tour was successful enough for Casals and Bauer to commit themselves to a more elaborate one the following year, despite at least one moment during the trip that had definitely not been pleasant. At the time they arrived in Rio a convention had preempted all the rooms in the city's better hotels, and Casals and Bauer ended up sharing a room in a place on the waterfront. Not long after they retired Casals was aware of a repeated, slightly metallic clacking sound. In this alien place he thought it could be anything, including someone unfriendly trying to open the door. "Harold," he called softly to his colleague in bed across the room, "do you hear that?"

Bauer heard. He also felt something at his feet. When a light was turned on the source of the sound was evident. The place was infested with *cucarachas*, the rapacious Latin American cockroach. There were hundreds on the floor and the walls. They had been at work on Bauer's toenails, since his feet had extended beyond the short covers of his bed. Both men put on their shoes and began a private extermination operation that proved instructive: smashed, the ugly creatures give out an exceedingly unpleasant odor. Next day they found another hotel.

The companionship of Bernardo Moreira de Sá was stimulating, and Bauer and Casals both remembered with admiration years afterward his conversation, his spirit, and his insatiable passion for knowledge. On the eve of the scheduled return to Europe, Moreira de Sá announced emotionally that he would be unable to accompany his two colleagues to Lisbon as planned. The realization of a lifetime ambition would keep him in Brazil for another two weeks: he had found a man who could teach him the classic technique of Japanese lacquer. Neither Casals nor Bauer ever saw him again.

Harold Bauer at thirty had a glorious mop of slightly unruly dark reddish hair. Casals had already gone quite bald. One bit of regular horseplay between the two consisted of Casals lifting Bauer from his seat by his hair with one hand. Once when he was quite young Bauer had played both violin and piano for Paderewski; after the piano piece Paderewski had pulled Bauer's hair playfully and told him in German that he had to become a pianist: he had the hair for it. "He ought to know," Bauer had thought, gazing with respectful awe at the Pole's celebrated blond mane. Casals and Bauer speculated on how much that hair, the flowing white-silk neckties and elegant manner had contributed to making Paderewski the romantic darling of female concertgoers on three continents and the highest-paid keyboard artist in history.

Transatlantic crossings, which took as long as two weeks, gave plenty of time for conversation, reading, relaxation, and practice: fellow passengers on Casals' and Bauer's early trips had the opportunity to hear a good deal of music in rehearsal, although Bauer fell victim to seasickness as soon as the sea became rough. Bauer and Casals played deck tennis and had wrestling matches in their cabin sufficiently vigorous to alarm their steward. They also had time to perfect a little parlor game they continued to perform for years. This game, which they proclaimed to be telepathic, involved correct identification by one of a playing card that had been shown to the other. Their sense of tempo meshed so completely that they were able to carry out the parlor trick successfully by silently counting the beats of an agreed-upon composition, stopping on a prearranged signal, and indicating suit with four slightly different foot positions.

Casals and Bauer both remembered their ensemble playing as almost effortless. They were collaborators, never soloist and accompanist. They also believed that the most natural and best way to play a cello and piano sonata was not to strive to give the impression of a single performer playing both instruments, the usual goal at the time. The Casals–Bauer "conversational" playing resulted in a kind of dialogue between two artists in complete agreement on tempo, dynamics, and rhythm, but differing with individual temperament in details of phrasing, preserving the validity of both personalities within the limits of a shared concept of the work as a whole. It was clearly understood that there would be no attempt to make piano passages sound like cello passages, or vice versa, but there were times Bauer longed for the power to reproduce on his less subtly flexible instrument "that inimitable tone" of Casals.

Only once in public during the more than twenty years Casals and Bauer played together was there a memorable shattering of the customary smooth interaction of their instruments' voices. The piano took a solo entrance in the first movement of the Brahms G minor quartet they were performing, and after only a few notes Bauer realized he had taken a tempo much faster than he should have. There was no immediate remedy and he could only pray that Casals would match the pace. Casals looked at him with an expression Bauer could not fathom and shook his head almost imperceptibly; at the cello entrance, Casals began at the usual, requisite tempo, throwing Bauer into temporary consternation. He recovered, the rest of the work went well, and the public applauded enthusiastically. Once in the artists' room, Casals threw his arms around Bauer. "Forgive me, Harold," he said, and there were tears in his eyes. "I tried to follow you, *but I could not. C'était plus fort que moi.* My fingers and my bow would not respond at that tempo." Like Martin Luther, Bauer thought, Casals could not compromise even when he tried to.

In Washington on the evening of January 15, 1904, early in his first solo tour of the United States, Pablo Casals, then just twenty-seven, played at one of Mrs. Theodore Roosevelt's musical evenings in the White House. The East Room Musicales were formal musical entertainments Mrs. Roosevelt instituted soon after her husband's inauguration in 1901, gala occasions held in the newly renovated Executive Mansion. The first of the famous "gold" Steinways was in place in the East Room, the largest salon in the White House. That piano, presented "to the American people" by the firm of Steinway & Sons in 1903, had a gilded case supported by golden eagles with wings outstretched on each of the three legs and was decorated by acanthus scrolls framing shields bearing the arms of the original thirteen states. Inside the cover was an elaborate allegorical painting of the nine Muses in a semicircle before the young Republic of America. The glare from the gold leaf was so fierce, reported pianist Adella Prentiss Hughes of Cleveland after she played on it a few years later, that she could scarcely see the music.

Invitations bearing the seal of the President of the United States in gold went out in Mrs. Roosevelt's name with the word *Music* in one corner. There was considerable prestige in being among the more than 400 people on the invitation list. "Those invited are the Four Hundred of Washington and the personal and political friends of the President," observed the New York *Herald* on January 9, six days before Casals played, noting also that there were to be four musicales in January. "At the first musical reception it was given out that the list was most carefully selected and it is observed that high rank, a long pocket or undoubted swelldom are essential in order to be bidden!"

The music began at ten and lasted without intermission for about an hour and a half. It was preceded by a dinner, not attended by the musicians, for as many as thirty couples who then joined those invited for the music.

These White House entertainments were the closest thing in America to the command performances of Europe; protocol and routine were detailed carefully for the White House staff:

> Guests will enter the house by the East entrance and will proceed to the main entrance hall where they will form in line to approach the north door of the Green Room. (Ambassadors will be taken out of line whenever they are seen and advanced to the head and at once presented.)
>
> At 10 o'clock an aide will notify Mrs. Roosevelt in the Blue Room and escort her into the Green Room. No one will be permitted to enter the East Room or come from the cloak rooms until Mrs. Roosevelt has taken her position. The people will enter the north door of the Green Room to [be] presented, passing before Mrs. Roosevelt into the East Room and aides on duty will seat them. Judgment should be used in reserving seats near the front for prominent people entitled

thereto who will probably not be the first to arrive. It is not necessary for the people to occupy the seats shown them if they prefer to sit elsewhere.

Two seats in front of the first row on the right will be reserved for the President and his Aide or anyone he wishes to sit with him. A large chair will be provided for Mrs. Roosevelt just inside the door at which she is receiving where she will remain during the concert.

Understand that no introductions can be made to Mrs. Roosevelt during the music. The doors between the Green Room and the East Room will be closed and guests arriving late will be requested to wait until the number is finished, when doors will be opened and the presentation made.

After the music, ushers will quickly move some of the chairs and servants will pass refreshments.

Upon conclusion, Mrs. Roosevelt will go directly to the Red Room to remain until the guests have departed. If a dinner has preceded the musicale, these guests will be shown to the Red Room to bid her goodbye. The other guests will be told it is not necessary to take leave of Mrs. Roosevelt and will depart as they have entered.

Uniforms will be full dress and officers on duty will report at 9:30.

All this was a far cry from Thomas Jefferson's informal evenings of chamber music there exactly a century earlier, but the music was of rather a more respectable caliber than that generally offered during the intervening administrations.

Casals never knew precisely how his White House invitation came about so early in his international career and so soon after the end of the Spanish-American War. Foreign embassies made known the availability of artists from their countries, but members of Congress frequently made urgent appeals that some prodigy from their constituency be included. The supply of musicians had become so much greater than the demand by 1903 that Steinway & Sons attached a member of the firm to serve as adviser and to screen the artists, a relationship still in existence in the 1970s. Steinway's policy was to use young American artists whenever possible.

Mrs. Roosevelt liked to present two or three musicians during an evening; on January 15, 1904, the bass and the pianist were American, but Casals was given top billing:

MR. PABLO CASALS, Violoncellist.
MR. MYRON W. WHITNEY, Jr., Basso.
MR. WARD STEPHENS, Pianist.

PIANO SOLOS

Barcarolle	*Liszt*
Danse Orientals	*Gartz*
Moto Perpetuo	*Gottschalk*

SONGS

Three Gypsy Songs	*Brahms*
Widmung	*Schumann*

CELLO SOLO

Sonata	*Boccherini*

SONGS

L'invito *Nissun lo sa*	*Vannuccini*
Couplets de Vulcain	*Gounod*

CELLO SOLOS

Le Cygne	*Saint-Saëns*
Spanish Dance	*Popper*

SONGS

Finland Love Song	*M. V. White*
Little Irish Song	Traditional
Bedouin Love Song	*Chadwick*

Theodore Roosevelt was an outdoorsman and politician who knew very little about music and was not particularly interested in it, but according to his daughter the cello was probably his favorite instrument. In January 1904, then barely nineteen, Alice Roosevelt herself was more interested in dancing, beaux, and Alice-blue gowns than in her stepmother's musicales, but she was present at this one and said in the late 1960s of Casals "I can't remember what he played that first time, but through all the years I have never forgotten the sound of that cello." The atmosphere of the East Room and of the Executive Mansion was impressive and dignified, and the President was accorded the respect of a powerful head of state, but Casals, sensing an indefinably republican classlessness and informality he had never felt in any European palace, realized once more that the American style was distinctly its own. After the music the Roosevelts chatted briefly with the musicians, who were given autographed photographs of the couple. Casals came away with the impression of Teddy Roosevelt as a healthy and tremendously vigorous man.

Casals' first American tour on his own, from early January until the first part of May 1904, took him as far inland as St. Louis, but most of his concerts were in the East. His first appearance had been as featured soloist with Sam Franko's American Symphony at the New Lyceum Theatre in New York on January 12, when he played the Haydn D major cello concerto in Gevaërt's arrangement for modern performance. *New York Times* music critic Richard Aldrich reported about Casals' "charming artistic capacity and exquisitely finished technique"; the other reviewers agreed that Casals took the artistic honors of the evening. He was applauded enthusiastically and finally returned to play two movements from Bach's third solo-cello suite as an encore. Engagements in Baltimore and Pittsburgh followed.

Casals was announced as one of the artists to appear in Carnegie Hall on February 14 in an evening of instrumental solos, chamber music, and song—with American baritone David Bispham, Jacques Thibaud (his own first American tour), Dalmatian conductor-composer Felix Weingartner, and soprano Susan Metcalfe, a twenty-four-year-old New York socialite who had been giving local recitals for three or four years. Casals withdrew at the last moment, for reasons that were not announced, and an American cellist performed instead. He did appear in the same hall on March 9, however, as soloist in the first American performance under the composer's baton of Richard Strauss' tone poem *Don Quixote*, in which the voice of the solo violoncello is the rich personification of Cervantes' hero. Strauss, by 1904 musical director of the Berlin State Opera, had become an important composer and an eminent conductor, respected for his interpretations of Mozart, Wagner, and his own works and, among orchestral players, for the clarity of his conducting beat.

As usual, Casals arrived at the theater well in advance of the concert and began to warm up in the artists' room; Strauss and his wife arrived not long before performance time. Pauline Strauss-De Ahna was also to appear, singing four of her husband's

Susan Metcalfe about 1904

songs with the Wetzlar orchestra and three more with him at the piano. Casals was eager to check last-minute points of interpretation and tempo of his own solo with the composer, but Frau Strauss, a handsome but imperious Hungarian noblewoman, interrupted. "Richard," she said, "I'm cold. Go back to the hotel and fetch my boa!" Strauss, authoritarian to almost everyone but his wife, left meekly. "I could have killed her," Casals remarked later.

The evening before, Casals had appeared in a recital at Mendelssohn Hall, New York, in a program that included the full C major solo-cello suite by Bach as well as featured groups of art songs performed by Susan Metcalfe, accompanied by Mrs. David Mannes.

Casals' American bookings were handled at this time by an energetic New York manager (whose artists also included Josef Hofmann and Fritz Kreisler) who suggested that Casals did not project enough of a virtuoso image and said he could assure him better fees if he would agree to wear a hairpiece. This approach was totally unsuccessful with Casals, so the manager sent out publicity releases explaining that Señor Casals was bald so young because he had given countless locks of hair to breathless female admirers.

From the beginning of his career Casals had both a genuine distaste for actually handling money and a sharp eye for the account ledgers. The agents arranged contracts that Casals approved, and they deposited the income in one or another of Casals' accounts. During the 1904 tour Casals began to suspect that his New York representative was collecting higher fees than he reported and was pocketing the difference, two or three hundred dollars a concert. Casals said nothing, but continued to watch. When the tour had ended, he summoned the manager to a conference in the lobby of his hotel with the promise the conversation would not take much time.

Casals was waiting in one of two chairs he had placed beside a small table near the entrance. When the manager arrived, the only pleasantry was his question how the tour had been. Casals replied quietly that it had gone well enough except that he had been robbed blind by his management. He told the manager that he knew precisely how much had been taken dishonestly. As the other man rose, pale and stuttering, Casals pushed him into the revolving door between the lobby and the street—exactly as he had planned—and began to spin it as fast as he could. The door broke; for a moment Casals watched his former manager running away down the street, before he returned to the lobby to pay for the damage.

Casals and Harold Bauer left New York on the fifth of May on the *Byron* for their second South American tour, one they both considered interesting, uneventful, and on the whole unprofitable. In Buenos Aires the concerts were artistically successful and attracted good houses of the musically sophisticated, but the general public showed less interest in them or their variety of music than did the mosquitos that plagued them almost constantly. Buenos Aires was one of the world's great cities, but to Casals and Bauer its musical culture seemed slight and superficial; probably, they agreed, a result of the way music was taught there. In 1904 the city had fifty or more so-called music conservatories. Bauer and Casals visited at least twenty of them, all noticeably prosperous, but found no trace of fundamental musical training. The teaching went no further than a few easy pieces for piano, violin, guitar, or mandolin, and vocal study involved little more than learning a few Italian arias and some popular songs in Spanish.

The editor of an English-language periodical invited Bauer to write an article giving his musical impressions of the city. He called the piece "Conservatropolis," was more ironic than courteous, and was never invited back to Argentina. Casals avoided this sort of pitfall during the early years by not writing for publication and giving as few interviews as possible.

Casals and Bauer enjoyed Montevideo more than they had Buenos Aires, and while there Casals had the pleasant opportunity to startle an old friend. Many musicians are addicted to practical jokes; in Casals this penchant took the form of liking to surprise people—in the case of friends, with an unexpected gift or a graceful gesture. In Montevideo he learned that a ship on which Camille Saint-Saëns was traveling would make port the night of one of Casals' concerts.

Casals knew Saint-Saëns' invariable routine and that at one in the morning he would find the Frenchman composing at a table in a corner of the dining saloon. After his recital Casals took a hired launch out to Saint-Saëns' ship, anchored well offshore because of the shallowness of the Montevideo harbor. He came up behind the composer quietly, then announced loudly in French "I am here!" Irritation changed to pleasure when Saint-Saëns recognized him and they sat and talked animatedly until dawn. The friendship between the ironically articulate older Frenchman who deliberately avoided all display of feeling and the openly emotional Spaniard had become one of mutual regard through the years, close enough for Saint-Saëns to speak to Casals about tragedies he seldom mentioned: Saint-Saëns' adored first son fell to his death from a second-floor window in Paris at the age of two, and a younger boy died of a fever barely a month later. Saint-Saëns would come to be remembered more for music he wrote as a private joke, *The Carnival of the Animals*, than for his ambitious symphonies, twelve operas, and chamber music, but Casals never forgot and never stopped reminding younger fellow musicians of the large body of important and worthy compositions that Saint-Saëns had written. Casals loved the man, and as a cellist he knew his debt to the composer, for Camille Saint-Saëns was one of the few ever to write a violoncello concerto that is really successful in matching the special qualities of the cello with those of the orchestra.

In Rio de Janeiro Casals and Bauer found New Jersey-born pianist Ernest Schelling stranded. He had come to South America on tour with Loie Fuller, the Paris neighbor of Emma Nevada who had for some years been attracting a fair amount of mystified notice by fluttering diaphanous scarves and waving Chinese-silk butterfly wings in her brand of interpretive dance. The tour had collapsed, and Schelling was arranging such solo performances as he could. After Casals and Bauer came to town the local music critics divided into two pianistic camps, one side trumpeting the supremacy of Lechititzky-trained Schelling, the other proclaiming the excellence of Bauer. Casals, Bauer, and Schelling found the situation ridiculous, but had to admit that the squabble drew audiences to hear both pianists.

They all decided to use the silly feud to mutual advantage and the benefit of art. Casals, Bauer, Schelling, and a famous older Brazilian pianist, Arthur Napoleão, announced a monster concert to be given in the huge Rio de Janeiro Opera House that would settle the question. The musician-impresarios engaged the full Opera orchestra; they played and conducted interchangeably, using every possible combination in the course of the evening. Every ticket was sold, and Bauer maintained that it was "in a word, one of the greatest shows ever witnessed in the Brazilian musical world."

While Casals was playing the Saint-Saëns cello concerto with Bauer on the podium, there was an outburst of angry voices and scuffling backstage loud enough to cause puzzled glances between conductor and soloist. Casals and Bauer went off at the end to find Schelling stretched out on a couch, clothes disarranged, his nose bleeding vigorously into a basin held by a stagehand. He had interposed himself between two disagreeing gentlemen of the

*Casals (at top of the pole) during a youthful
outing with friends*

press—one a Schellingite, the other a Bauerian—and had naturally
sustained the only injury. He recovered enough to join Bauer and
Napoleão in the final work of the evening, a Bach triple-keyboard
concerto with Casals conducting the Opera orchestra.

The participants and some friends adjourned to a grand supper.
Casals and Bauer returned to their hotel near dawn, Bauer carrying

the concert receipts, quite a large sum in very dirty banknotes of small denomination, crammed into a small valise. No one could be found at that hour to put the money into a vault, and Bauer and Casals decided wearily it would be safe enough through the remainder of the night in the room they were sharing. They went to bed and slept heavily until almost noon.

Casals roused Bauer by asking the time; Casals could not find his watch. When they got out of bed they saw their door open and the room in disorder. The suitcase of money was still there, untouched with a shirt still draped over it. But watches and billfolds were gone, studs and cufflinks had been taken from shirts, and the cello case stood open with the undamaged instrument on the floor. The manager summoned the police; two suspects were detained, one a distinguished-looking man with Casals' visiting-card case in his possession.

Both musicians felt ill all day. Casals' theory held that the burglar had stupefied them with a chemical or gas as part of his elaborate plan to make off with what he expected to be a large sum of money. Bauer pointed out that they had consumed not inconsiderable quantities of the local wine at the supper following the concert. (Several years later in Paris Casals read in the newspapers about the capture of an elusive and famous robber the press called "The King of the Pickpockets"; the accompanying picture was of the dapper gentleman who had had Casals' card case in Rio. Casals pointed out thereafter that he had been robbed not by some petty amateur but by the profession's top artist.)

The commercial return had actually been satisfactory this time, but Casals remained distressed that the general public had not responded. On his tour with the Nevada company, once outside the large cities of the northeastern United States, people had crowded the theaters and concert halls. There had been as many workmen and miners and their families, it had seemed to him, as people of larger means and higher social position. And in Spain and Holland ordinary people came readily enough to their recitals. Casals felt that great music fulfills so native a hunger in the human being that the mass of the population would come eagerly to hear it if it were available at prices they could afford. In South America there were even greater contrasts than in Europe between the few rich and the many poor. Perhaps the reason the laboring class in South America had not come to hear them was more a matter of psychology than of ticket cost. The Rio, São Paulo, and Buenos Aires audiences had been well-dressed when not actually elegant. Workers would have been acutely uncomfortable seated with the splendidly dressed society women and wealthy businessmen. Perhaps, Casals told Bauer, as he had before, the only solution was to offer concerts exclusively for workingmen and their families.

When their French ship, infested with Brazilian insects, reached Lisbon in August, Casals and Bauer received a message from the palace—Her Majesty requested them to come to tea and give an informal concert for her guests. The Palacio dos Necesidades had deteriorated noticeably in the few years since Pablo Casals first arrived there from Espinho absentmindedly without his cello. To Bauer, seeing it for the first time, it seemed downright shabby, with carelessly indolent guards and an overall impression of formal untidiness. The two musicians sat talking with the Major-Domo until a woman's voice came from the adjoining room: "If you gentlemen have finished your cigarettes you might come and have a cup of tea!"

The speaker was the Queen, "the lovely Amelia of Portugal." Bauer decided there might be something good in monarchy if queens were as beautiful as they had been in fairy tales, but Queen Amelia turned out to be the only good-looking queen he ever saw. Nor did he think her too tall—no more than six foot three, he guessed. He found her pleasant, friendly, and witty as well as beautiful, and she handed the tea-cakes around herself.

The musicians played specific requests of the Queen. It was all very cozy and enjoyable for everyone except Bauer. The palace piano was an Erard, "the case covered with paintings and bas-relief carvings brightly gilded in every possible way." It was seriously out of tune and so much in need of regulation that Bauer had to use all the agility he could summon to lift up keys that stuck to prepare them for the next attack.

After the music Queen Amelia decorated the deserving Bauer with the Portuguese Order of Christ (Casals already had one), saying that she wanted him to remember his visit to the court of Portugal. Bauer did not think he was likely to forget.

11

THERE HAD BEEN little opportunity for Casals, still a bachelor in
his twenties, to establish a home for himself in Paris in the first
two or three years of his international career. But by 1904 he had
found and rented number 20 in the Villa Molitor, a cluster of
some twenty-five dwellings in the reasonably fashionable suburban
Auteuil district. Number 20 is a small house with its own tiny
garden at the end of a private street that gives into the rue Molitor.
To the right of a small entrance foyer a stairway led up to two
bedrooms and a bath. On the ground floor, to the left, were a
dining room and Casals' studio-office. Downstairs was a kitchen.
All the rooms looked onto the small garden, behind which the
land fell away, giving a vista of trees and other gardens. It was
very calm and pleasant. This house, easy to reach from central
Paris, became Casals' haven between journeys, the place his books
and music were kept, where paintings and souvenirs began to accu-
mulate. From here he went to the St.-Cloud courts to play tennis,
and often during the first years to the nearby airfield to watch
the flying experiments of Blériot and his fellow aviators.

Casals had a favorite restaurant in Paris, to which he went
frequently with friends. He continued to call on people as well

as to receive—Mme Marchesi and Emma Nevada until both moved to London; the Ménard-Dorians; the Countess of Morphy, who had settled in Paris and resumed her singing career, and Crista. He went out, particularly often to Jacques Thibaud's house, to play chamber music with friends. But 20 Villa Molitor was his home and the place of his *tertulia*, that quintessentially Spanish conversational gathering that often focuses on one personality but draws together people who have a community of interest and are sometimes interesting themselves. Already on the virtuoso's treadmill, where his habitation was a hotel room, railway compartment, or stateroom more often than his own house, Casals really preferred to stay home.

The Villa Molitor was a comfortable place to continue interrupted friendships. Even as a young man Casals came to feel rapport with a new person quickly or not at all, and his interest in his friends was already a great element of his charm. The established relationships were resumed when opportunity arose almost as if there had been no interruption, or no more than a day or a week instead of months or years. When he wished, he had the capacity to respond intensely during a short visit with a friend or even a stranger able to reciprocate his enthusiasm and interest. The important friendships developed with time and association, as such things must, but his own sense of identity kept Casals from distrusting his closest associates even when concert schedules made meetings impossible for long periods.

There were guests at the Villa Molitor every evening Casals was in Paris, the majority of them musicians. Number 20 "bubbled with conversations and rehearsals" and music for pleasure. Casals was always at the center of the discussions of "philosophy, religion, music, interrelation of the arts, style, inspiration, technique" in an ambience "so dense," according to Casals' poet friend Juan Alavedra, "that many artists found it hard to take. It was like a small secular convent," although Hungarian composer Emanuel Moór considered even that tone too frivolous. Others recalled lighter moments among the prevailing solemnity, and the presence of at least one of the regulars, the violinist Larapidie, introduced a degree of the bizarre. Larapidie, a sometime member of the Boston Symphony Orchestra, designed and made his own unorthodox clothing and refused to take a cab, always walking to Auteuil, brandishing his heavy walking-stick at the laughing children who followed him in the street. The day after he visited the Villa Molitor in the throes of a severe toothache he had all his teeth pulled, returning to announce that he would never suffer toothache again. The three Chaigneau sisters, attractive and talented musicians who toured successfully as a chamber-music trio throughout Europe, were also often among the guests. The young host's younger students and colleagues with a certain awe discovered themselves in the same room or even performing with famous musicians and afforded a chance to listen, if not always to talk, to celebrated personages of the day. When the Polish prodigy Mieczyslaw Horszowski settled in Paris to study at eighteen he became part of Casals' closest circle; his friendship and musical collaboration with Casals remained strong in the 1970s. Horszowski remembered Larapidie at the Villa Molitor, among many others, as well as the regular visits of a distinguished, conventionally dressed violinist named Lambert and his wife; there he also saw Manuel de Falla, Enrique and Amparo Granados, Casals' close friend Georges Enesco, and the young violinist Adolf Busch. Dutch composer Julius Röntgen, in Paris for a few days early in 1910, wrote his wife about being entertained in the afternoon at the Villa Molitor by the singing of Mme Piazza-Chaigneau; there had been many other people, but the one who interested Röntgen most was General Picquart, then Minister of War in a government headed by Clemenceau.

It was perfectly natural to Casals to receive visitors both expected and unexpected every evening he was free. Such was the custom of the city and the time; people were drawn to Pablo Casals, and throughout his life he responded.

One day Dr. Sandoz, a gentle Swiss doctor of philosophy, brought Henri Bergson to the Villa Molitor, an encounter that led to one of the most treasured associations of Casals' life. Casals afterward called on the philosopher-psychologist many times, finding a warm welcome and a continuation of their last conversation as though it had been broken off in midsentence. In the course of one of their later visits Bergson, who was nearly twenty years older than Casals, paid the younger man one of the compliments he appreciated all his life. Casals had wondered aloud how on earth an important savant could find pleasure in talking with a man such as he, who really knew very little. "My dear boy," Bergson retorted, "you have taught *me* a great deal!"

They discussed religion; both had a real but not traditionally prescribed spiritual inclination and had similar views on the subject (it was a shock to Casals to learn that Bergson was on the point of turning to institutionalized religion at the time of his death in 1941).

For Casals, Bergson's theory of an *élan vital*—the impulse and the strength to live, a creative urge throughout all nature, an intuitive vital force beyond reason governing human existence—was appealing and convincing. For his part, Henri Bergson was interested in Casals' subjective reactions to music—what did he *feel* when he was playing the music of Bach or Beethoven? Casals tried to explain that if he was satisfied after a good performance (relative terms that had nothing to do with the attainment of perfection), he had a special feeling, an almost physical sensation that could be likened to carrying inside himself a weight of gold.

Bergson wanted to know if this weight was the same thing one ought to feel after doing a good action. Casals said it was quite different. The feeling Casals knew after a good action was disembodied, outside himself. For him, the good action and his reaction were immediately followed by a desire to forget because savoring a good gesture or recalling it would lead to dangerous self-admiration. The feeling that comes from artistic creation and re-creation is within the inner self, "as if one's participation had been deeper and more definite." A successful performance seemed a part of him; it evoked self-recognition rather than hazardous self-adulation. The feeling, at any rate, was almost physical, that sensation of bearing a tangible weight of something inestimably precious within. It did not occur to Casals to tell Bergson that after even a good performance he sometimes walked the street for hours or lay sleepless in bed going through in his mind what he had just played before an audience.

Bergson asked about the role of intuition in the performance of great music and the balance among the physical, the intellectual, and the intuitive factors. Casals told him flatly that in the end musical instinct both creates and directs the performance. He never believed in momentary inspiration during a performance. Everything must have been worked out before. The artist must use the physical mastery but must go beyond it: the technical side is what brings fluency and control and drives the artist to deep study—it is the necessary and natural groundwork. But in the musical creation or re-creation (and an interpretation can be better than the work) another part of the artist's being comes into play: the mature intuition. Intuition is the decisive factor, although intelligence is its potent ally. Intelligence assists the unfolding of development and the assimilation of the musical forms as they are perceived, but intelligence must be nourished and shown the way by intuition; both elements must be present and must blend. The highly intelligent people—in music at least, Casals told Bergson—who continue to think feverishly and cannot stop thinking and questioning and reexamining from different angles, who cannot let intuition take ultimate control, end in absolute confusion.

Of course, complete understanding of a work of music does not come altogether intuitively or at once, Casals continued. One must perceive the complete architecture, discern the principal directions, and sort out among the different elements the relationships that make up the structure—the difficult different shape of the notes, their connection with each other and with the whole. The true artist has to look for the meaning of the music; and he can begin to find it only if he sets about his task honestly, persistently, and with humility. The artist has full responsibility for the music he plays: he must experience it and create it anew. The first musical commandment is total respect for the music. After everything else exists, as it must, instinct controls. Casals told Bergson that every time he played a good or a great composition he found something new in it, no matter how many times he had played it before, but he never improvised in a public performance.

There were chances to improvise if momentary inspiration came, however, while playing chamber music privately. During Casals' first Villa Molitor years Paris was full of musicians arriving from America, Russia, and various points on the Continent, particularly at the end of the spring tours, all eager to make music together. At Number 20 and the two or three larger houses at which they gathered (including Thibaud's and that of the instrument collector Reifenberg), the regulars included pianists Ferruccio Busoni, Raoul Pugno, Alfred Cortot; violinists Eugène Ysaÿe, Fritz Kreisler, Georges Enesco, Jacques Thibaud; and violist Pierre Monteux.

Their ages ranged from the early twenties to the early fifties. All had established reputations; most appeared for the public chiefly as soloists, and all were insatiable about playing chamber music for their own pleasure. They led frenetic lives of travel and public performance, playing together informally far into the night if they felt like it, the only audience a few fortunate friends. They played whatever music was suitable for the combinations of instruments present, sometimes shifting instruments, sometimes changing personnel between movements. Ysaÿe enjoyed playing viola in some of these sessions even though he was one of the supreme violinists of his generation and at the top of his powers; when he played first violin in a quartet with Kreisler as second violin, Casals remembered, the magnificent Kreisler sounded like a talented child alongside the master. The gods were at sport, and the result was often performances of the sort that usually exist only in the dreams of connoisseurs of chamber music and the minds of ambitious managers. An impresario was once present, and he made an immediate euphoric proposal to handle a spectacular tour, a suggestion he withdrew next day, after he estimated the fees he would have to arrange for the artists.

The most famous chamber-music trio of the twentieth century was formed during one of these sessions in late 1904 or early 1905. Alfred Cortot, Jacques Thibaud, and Pablo Casals were friends and had appeared together in public; members of the same social and musical circles, they played together privately for mutual satisfaction. One informal evening—when, according to Alavedra's recounting, Alberto Casella, Dr. Sandoz, cellist Diran Alexanian, Enesco, Harold Bauer, and Casals' student Guilhermina Suggia had gathered at the Villa Molitor—they decided to play together in public, and thus began the Casals–Cortot–Thibaud trio, which toured about a month each year, except during the First World War, until the 1930s.

Casals, who turned twenty-eight at the end of 1904, was the oldest and the best established of the three. Alfred Cortot, a Swiss by birth and eleven months younger than the cellist, had studied piano with Louis Diémer at the Paris Conservatoire. He was an incurable Wagnerian who had not only worked as an assistant conductor at Bayreuth but had also memorized Wagner's operas and could play them all through on the piano; in 1902 he conducted the first Paris performance of *Die Götterdämmerung*. He also had

Casals, Jacques Thibaud, and Alfred Cortot

an enthusiasm for the works of the new French composers that Casals did not share. His playing had much more emotional and physical force than was usual in French pianism, and his art combined intellectual authority, aristocracy, and masculinity with poetry, severe elegance, and logic. He became professor of the most prestigious piano class at the Conservatoire; he wrote books and treatises, edited scores, gave concerts, and in time made hundreds of records. He did so many other things, in fact, that he did not always keep his technique at prime, and Casals and Thibaud were occasionally disconcerted by wrong notes and memory lapses.

Jacques Thibaud, the trio's violinist, was the youngest of the three (he was born in Bordeaux in September 1880), but was already very successful, particularly in France. He too had graduated from the Conservatoire. Édouard Colonne had "discovered" him in 1898 playing in the *café-concert* called the Café Rouge at eighteen and launched his career by presenting him as soloist with the Colonne Concerts orchestra, a début that resulted in fifty-four solo bookings in Paris the same season. Casals would speak of him as "a star from Heaven" and "a natural product of the French school" of violin-playing, although Thibaud was later influenced by Ysaÿe and Kreisler. He was a supremely elegant stylist although he considered practicing drudgery and therefore avoided it when he could. Thibaud was witty, charming, and full of pranks.

The trio was founded on friendship and the love of music. The members had three strong and differing temperaments, and strains of various kinds came to the surface through their years together; as musicians a special chemistry subordinated everything else to the music they produced together. The trio made an interesting appearance. The two beautifully tailored Frenchmen, both rather tall and emanating an indefinable Paris Conservatoire aura, towered physically above their colleague. He also dressed well and with taste, but his whole style was outwardly less flamboyant. Yet, of the three, attention ultimately focused on Pablo Casals. What was it so compelling in the presence of "this unobtrusive little man"? asked one observer. "He stole quietly into the room. Unimpressive physically, he gave you a sense of power and authority almost as if by inversion—the sensation you sometimes have in a museum when, as you face walls crowded with brilliant canvases, a single picture (it may actually be the lowest in key) suddenly claims all your attention. The claim grows in strength, in intensity, and you feel yourself drawn more and more to it."

Casals consciously lent his prestige to the formation of the Casals–Cortot–Thibaud trio, and early in its history advanced a considerable sum of money to underwrite expenses. Not yet thirty, he was in Horszowski's words "already the famous Pablo Casals" and had played in all the countries of Western Europe except in Scandinavia and Austria. Casals' earliest success in Paris—the two solo appearances in Charles Lamoureux's concert series in 1899—was exceptional, the kind of thing that happened, rarely, late in the nineteenth century and very early in the twentieth but never thereafter in similar circumstances. The only comparable explosion into success in Paris at a début was Eugène Ysaÿe's in 1885, when Colonne, at the urging of Saint-Saëns, had reluctantly scheduled the Belgian violinist as soloist.

Ysaÿe was a great musician; tall, temperamental, and quite handsome, he easily fitted the stereotype of the virtuoso. Casals, who was not a conventionally romantic figure, made no overt attempt to woo the public with his manner. When he played he nevertheless communicated a sense of controlled passion and produced from the violoncello a tone that seemed richer and more profound than anyone else could elicit. "It was a revelation," recalled Charles Kiesgen, Casals' student and later his French manager for years. The French school of cello-playing had produced nothing like this, nor had any other so-called national style of playing. Whatever the reasons, the violoncello simply was not an important solo instrument to the public until Casals entered the concert arena.

Within five years following his début, Casals became thoroughly established and indeed famous. Kiesgen said the fees he could command were at the highest level being paid any musician. The response from fellow artists was on the whole distinctly cordial (Harold Bauer spoke of Casals even in the early years as beloved and admired equally by his colleagues and the public), although there were a few dissenters. César Thomson, for instance, a violin colleague of Edouard Jacobs at the Brussels Conservatory, began a prolonged barrage of criticism of Casals' cello technique, and the eminent German violoncellist Hugo Becker was outraged at Casals' interpretation of Bach.

Students came to the Villa Molitor for lessons, for rehearsal, and occasionally to stay for a time when Casals was in Paris. Early in the century Casals' concert schedule allowed him little sustained opportunity to teach, and requests for lessons came from many more prospective students than he could possibly accommodate (although through the years the list of excellent twentieth-century cellists who worked with Casals at least briefly came to include a startling proportion of the best-known names). Charles Kiesgen began to study with Casals in 1903, after a year's military service, and continued until 1909, when diagnosis of a heart condition forced him from a performing career into more than sixty years of artistic management. A second regular student by 1906 was a Barcelona child named Gaspar Cassadó, who had begun to study cello at seven; a public concert at nine won him a scholarship to study abroad. The third long-term student of the Villa Molitor years was a talented and temperamental Portuguese, Guilhermina Suggia.

Casals' strong impulse to teach, one facet of a personality disposed to giving, contributed to the development of some important artists, but not all students were destined for greatness. One came to Casals at the Villa Molitor for only a short time, but the teacher never forgot him and as a result forever afterward disliked the term *personality*. Ysaÿe had sent the young man, with praise for his gifts, and a warning that Casals would have some difficulty bringing order out of uncontrolled chaos. The boy did have some good qualities, but his mannerisms distorted them and he showed no musical discipline at all. He had tremendous self-confidence— "not a bad trait," according to Casals, "though in his case a little premature." "Maître," he told his teacher, "I have come to learn the secret of some of your tricks!" Casals masked an amused irritation, nodding gravely; yes, he would try to teach the young man such tricks as there were.

They started work from the ground up. With talent and application the boy made good progress in a short period but, Casals realized, without any sense of where he was going. And everything remained a trick instead of the foundation stone of a real structure. "When I would show him how, by the elimination or substitution of a needless or unidiomatic shift of position, a phrase could be restored to its natural modesty, he would pause and give me a sly wink as if to say, 'So that is the way it's done!' " Casals was dismayed, but he was not dissatisfied with the general progress. He therefore gave consent for the student to perform a concerto in public, and went to the concert with no forebodings.

"It was imprudent of me. Rarely have I passed so uncomfortable a half-hour. Such, I reflected bitterly, are the results of my teaching. What kind of teacher are you after all, I asked myself. The boy played with all his old, arrogant self-confidence. Rhythm, discretion, control were thrown to the winds, and what came forth was an impudent array of vulgarity. Not one cheap effect did he miss. It was a caricature of the music—and worse than a caricature!"

Casals did not trust himself to go backstage, having decided to have his say next day at the Villa Molitor. He asked what had caused the disaster, almost eager to hear and accept the excuse of extreme nervousness. "Maître," the young scoundrel explained, "this was my first chance at a public appearance. I realized that I must forget for the moment everything you had taught me.

*The Four Cats café in Barcelona was famous as
the artists'* local, *but writers and musicians,
including Casals, also found it congenial. A 1900
drawing by Ricardo Opissa shows a gathering of
painters that included Santiago Rusiñol, Ramón
Casas, and (in armchair at end of table)
Pablo Picasso.*

Otherwise people would think that here was another Casals playing. I must let my own personality speak!"

"Get out of here," Casals roared, "and never let me see your
face again. *Personality! I* have not taught you anything of *my*
personality. Nor could I. It would be easier to graft my fingertips
onto yours. . . . What I *have* tried to teach you, imbecile that
you are, is a true, simple, and reverent regard for music. But you
have not the character to see it. The shabby costume you falsely

call 'personality' will neither cover nor disguise the vacuum that lies beneath."

Among Casals' acquaintances in Spain and in Paris were a few painters and writers, but most of them worked and lived in a world quite removed from the musician's. He did visit Leo and Gertrude Stein in their home at 27 rue de Fleurus, behind the Luxembourg Gardens, always finding them, he remembered, in the same positions: Leo painting, Gertrude always reading in the same chair. The sensitive, melancholy, red-bearded Leo pressed on Casals, as he did on everyone, his appreciation of the work of Cézanne, Matisse, and Picasso, but the paintings and drawings were not to Casals' taste. He had known Pablo Picasso slightly in Barcelona in the 1890s, when the young painter was living there and was one of the group of graphic artists who gathered in the Four Cats café, but their paths seldom crossed in Paris and no personal warmth developed between the two.

A close friendship did develop between Casals and the painter Eugène Carrière after they had been brought together by Aline Ménard-Dorian. Carrière completed an evocative, muted portrait of Casals on Christmas Day 1903, four days before his twenty-eighth birthday. A certain spirituality and sentiment set the work of Carrière apart from that of most of the symbolists; in the shadow that always eclipsed part of his representation of a live subject he sought "to discern the second reality," to capture the shadow of thought. This man who said he never painted a person he did not esteem said that Casals' likeness and his 1891 painting of Paul Verlaine were the two he liked best. In the portrait of Casals, Carrière set forth an ageless, provocative face. In a letter to Mme Ménard-Dorian in late May 1903, just after he had first seen Casals, Eugène Carrière also set down one of the few surviving descriptions of the young man: "I am happy . . . to be able to agree with you about the face of that likable M. Cazals [*sic*]. He is extremely *sympathique*, of a youthfulness he would, I think, have people ignore, perhaps because of the [concert] posters, who, in fact, without realizing it has a charming personality that recalls the diligence of Heinrich Heine, a fine and candid spirit with an illusion of great sophistication; all this is charming in the young, because it is youth itself. . . ."

The Casals portrait was one of Carrière's last—he was suffering from cancer of the larynx. His favorite aphorism was "We must consent to life"; a year and a half after his first major throat operation he wrote Mme Ménard "Have confidence, dear Madame, in life." Shortly after a second operation, in November 1905, Carrière suffered a stroke that paralyzed his left side and deprived him completely of speech. For four months he continued to receive his friends, writing his part of the conversation, reading Marcus Aurelius when the pain became intense. Toward the end he indicated that he would like Casals to play for him, and Casals came to the artist's house in the rue Hégésippe-Moreau in winter twilight that filled the bedroom with the mysterious colors of which Carrière was so fond. A few friends were seated in the shadows; Casals sat near the bed and played some of the quiet sections of the Bach cello suites. "We all sat there in gloom and silence," wrote Camille Mauclair, "listening only to the glorious instrument that seemed to pray for Carrière and also to carry our inner thoughts, which words could not have expressed. . . . Shadows, waves of sound, the ghostly knowledge of an agony relieved by the comfort of the music, all contributed to make us realize that these minutes would be remembered as a kind of extraordinary perfection given us by Carrière. Not until we left the place did we dare weep."

Carrière's Spanish student Zuloaga and Casals became friendly, and Casals knew other Iberian artists who were working or had lived in Paris—among them his childhood neighbor in Barcelona Ramón Casas, Santiago Rusiñol, and Maurice Utrillo. He admired their work, but much of their style of life, which in Paris had centered around the Moulin de la Galette, was as uncongenial to Casals as their joy in the music of Erik Satie. The writers who roused the most interest among the Spanish artistic colony in Paris were Baudelaire and Verlaine, both dead, and Maurice Maeterlinck, then in his forties. Casals and Maeterlinck never became acquainted; Casals appreciated his lyricism but was more comfortable with Romain Rolland. Pablo Casals was not interested in deliberate eccentricity. It was prefectly natural to him that music and the other art forms should be approached seriously (as should life) and with complete devotion. For him music held fantasy and lyricism, passion and fulfillment, but it had always to exist within absolute order; the artist must create and re-create music with flawless discipline, always conscious and in control.

Casals seldom found obscure subjective jokes amusing and he was skeptical of a great deal of experimentation. He believed in his twenties as in his nineties that music is governed by certain general laws and that, while the mainstream of the art is in constant change, true evolution takes place within the limits of those laws. Egocentrism in creation, and abstruse irony, seemed neither natural to him nor "the language of everybody." Harold Bauer, who helped introduce the music of Debussy, was as horrified as Casals to hear Beethoven called "the old deaf one" in the Debussy–Ravel circle; there was a time in the Paris years that it was impossible to try to talk of Brahms to Debussy or Ravel, or even to Fauré. Casals watched the development of impressionism in music, especially in the work of Debussy and Ravel; he found interest and charm and suggestiveness in it, but declined to call it more than decoration. Debussy's melodic line he did not find notable; only considerable inventiveness of harmony supplied charm and furnished interest. Fauré, Ravel's composition teacher and a strong influence on the younger men (Florent Schmitt and Georges Enesco, among others), contributed to the impressionist climate by the delicacy of his own work, his capacity for harmonic inventiveness, and his open-mindedness to the experimental questings of his students. But for Casals, Fauré continued to work and create in the mainstream, with both personal and artistic refinement. Some of Fauré's songs, he contended, were the greatest since Schubert's.

Casals was as skeptical about the development of Maurice Ravel's career as of the trend it represented. By 1904 some Parisian musicians considered Ravel an important composer; others thought the Conservatoire's fourth refusal to grant him the Prix de Rome just. When they met in Mrs. Ram's house in 1900, Casals and Ravel had some rapport; they could certainly agree about Mozart even if they approached from different vantages. For Casals, Mozart was one of the giants in the grand sweep of civilized music. To Ravel, Mozart was the last classic pinnacle; his revulsion against the sentimental excesses of romanticism was so strong that he would not tolerate or honor anyone between Mozart and his own time. When Ravel helped create the *Société des apaches,* the transient school of French music that preached the impressionist gospel, called continually for experiment, and granted toleration of any style that called itself creative, his position had become about as far removed as possible from Casals'. By 1907 the Paris musical

*Guilhermina Suggia at thirteen, a member
of Bernardo Moreira de Sá's string quartet
in Porto (1901)*

world was divided over Ravel in two hostile factions. One set of enthusiasts claimed Ravel had plagiarized Debussy and was going inexcusably far afield with exotic scales and modes (and in the titles for his works), while the apologists contended that any similarity between the works of Ravel and those of the older man were both superficial and coincidental.

Casals observed these tempests with some distaste; so far as he was concerned, they had nothing to do with real music. He continued to go his own way.

By Casals' thirtieth year, friends who came to the Villa Molitor when Casals was in Paris expected to see Guilhermina Suggia. At eighteen she was his most promising student, toward whom Casals displayed a certain protective gallantry. His attention had been called to the talented Portuguese-Italian child in Porto as early as his recital there in 1899, when she was eleven, but he was told about and listened to talented children almost everywhere he went, and she made no lasting impression at the time. A student of her cellist father, Augusto Suggia, Guilhermina had begun to play in public at seven and was leader of the cello section of the Porto City Symphony by the time she was twelve. The following year she became cellist in Bernardo Moreira de Sá's quartet, playing in fifty recitals with it before the farewell concert in her honor in November 1901 that preceded her departure to study in Leipzig on a royal grant. At the beginning of 1902, nearly fourteen years old, she began to study violoncello with Julius Klengel, one of the most respected cellists of his generation. She became a member of the distinguished Gewandhaus orchestra and at seventeen made her solo début in a Gewandhaus concert under the direction of the renowned and electrifying Arthur Nikisch. While in Leipzig she came under both the notice and the influence of Casals, who was friendly with Klengel and who performed there frequently. When, about 1906, Casals learned she was in Paris, he sent word that she should come to play for him. Her father had died, and Casals discovered that the Suggia financial backing was not great. He agreed to give her lessons, and after Guilhermina's mother asked Casals to keep a protective eye on the girl she was invited to stay in the Villa Molitor house, under the scrutiny of Casals' housekeeper Mme Coderq, while Casals was on tour.

Guilhermina Suggia was still an unformed artist, but she was altogether musical and already produced from the cello the rather small, marvelously beautiful tone that was notable in her mature art. Tall and well formed, with olive skin and very dark hair, she had an explosively gay laugh and an instinct for center stage. Exuberant and attractive although not beautiful, she had an independent mind and spirit as well as bohemian tastes her teacher did not approve. From the beginning she was unpredictable and temperamental, but people realized that when Casals played cello she sat quietly, her eyes never leaving him.

Casals' concert contracts, mostly solo appearances with orchestra or an accompanist, had begun to number 250 a year. The respites in Paris were brief, some merely overnight, but every return made the Villa Molitor seem increasingly a haven. The more the demands of his career pressed on him, the more Casals wished a domestic life of his own. Nearly all his close colleagues had married—most recently, and obviously happily, Harold Bauer in 1906. With Guilhermina Suggia a new element entered Casals' life when he was nearly thirty, an element he later bitterly regretted. Enchanted by his quicksilver student and her musicality, Casals proposed marriage. Unwilling to relinquish professional ambition for a domestic role, Guilhermina Suggia temporized, remaining on the scene and continuing to study cello.

By late March 1907 Casals was including greetings from Mlle Suggia in a letter to Julius Röntgen in Amsterdam—a natural mention, since by then the Dutch musician was conscious of her as Casals' favorite pupil and had heard about her during the period of study with Klengel, a relative of Röntgen's mother. Less than a year later, when Casals made his first formal Paris appearances as symphonic conductor, Suggia appeared as a soloist and was identified on the face of the programs as Mme P. Casals-Suggia; for the next five years she was so known in much of Europe, on concert programs when she and Casals performed together and in the correspondence of musicians from Rachmaninoff in Russia to Röntgen in Holland, although in Spain she was billed under her own name.

The association of these two high-strung Iberian artists was tempestuous. Much later Casals admitted that there had been people who suggested he possessed a fierce temper during the Villa Molitor years; virtually everyone knew Suggia as a creature of grand temperament, and musical folklore continues to tell of confrontations as violent as those between Teresa Carreño and Eugène d'Albert during their stormy three-year marriage in the 1890s. Suggia's high spirits may well have sometimes made her restless in the rarefied atmosphere of the Villa Molitor evenings and during the days of rural peacefulness at San Salvador—except, of course, when there was music. Her apparent flirtatiousness certainly distressed her serious-minded protector, heir to centuries of the Spanish code of honor and chivalry as well as a man with distinct ideas about propriety, although some considered privately that much of it was a thoroughly successful campaign to make him jealous. Sixty years later Casals' friend and confidant Juan Alavedra suggested that Suggia's disruptive presence made Casals' personal life during most of the Villa Molitor years an almost continual state of nervousness which unsettled his study and disrupted concentration on his work, and that he suffered greatly from an influence that tended to distract him from his art or make him neglect it. Even so, during that time Casals continued to forge

(Left) Eugène Carrière's portrait of Pablo Casals dated Christmas Day 1903; (right) Casals in the garden of 20 Villa Molitor, Paris

for himself one of the formidable virtuoso careers in musical history.

And, although few glimpses are to be had of Casals relaxed at home in his Villa Molitor days, there were moments of calm. Two eyewitness accounts happily exist in letters written to his wife by Julius Röntgen, among the most truly admiring and least complicated of Casals' close friends at the time. Röntgen appeared at the house in June 1908 with a new composition:

> I found Casals stretched out on the sofa in dressing gown and Suggia playing cello nearby. [After warm embraces] he threw himself at once on my new cello sonata, made a short sight-reading first, and then we played, and perfectly indeed. Everything sounded as I had thought of it. . . . And how he played! The second part we just repeated: *épatant!*

We could play it in a concert today with no change necessary. A more beautiful first performance could not be possible, and Suggia nearby, so musical, understanding everything so well. And this warm inspiration of Casals!

After playing we went into the garden, Casals turned on the fountain, Suggia brought out Spanish wine, the blackbirds were singing, [it was] the most beautiful summer afternoon. Then Casals disappeared to dress; now and then we saw him . . . at the window, talking with us. Then I played the first part once more with Suggia, who also read the music splendidly, and then we went together into town to Casals' beloved restaurant *Boeuf à la mode*. . . . This evening I am once more a guest in his "villa Molitor" . . . we will again make hearty music.

And from a visit in April 1910 Röntgen wrote his wife, at home in Amsterdam with their children, that he had "such a pleasant, cordial impression of the Villa Molitor—so quiet and green and peaceful—and both its inhabitants that I am quite bubbling over with it":

I had to tell immediately about my new composition and Casals was quite excited that it was a cello concerto and had to hear it immediately. Thus directly to the piano—and you know how he is at such new works, how he catches everything immediately and takes pleasure and says so. We played it several times, then he played the piano part and sang the cello part. *Épatant*, etc! . . .

At table it was very gay: Pablo drank Catalan fashion from a bottle with a long pointed spout [a *purrón*] out of which the wine runs in a stream and, held far away, is caught in the mouth. . . .

12

AFTER FIRST MEETING Casals in 1905, Emanuel Moór, a Hungarian-born composer and naturalized British citizen living in Switzerland, became a regular visitor to the Villa Molitor. He came from Lausanne at least once a month to play his new works for Casals, who did his best to fend off other visitors on those occasions. For one such visit Moór arrived quite early in the morning and began to play through works he had completed since his last trip. Repeating nothing, Moór played through until dinnertime, when there was still a one-act opera to go. Just then a knock at the door announced the arrival of Tivador Szántó, a distinguished Hungarian pianist well known for his piano transcriptions of works Bach had written for other instruments. Moór was noticeably put out by the interruption. In the course of conversation the Hungarian asked the former Hungarian, possibly a bit smugly, if he knew the Szántó Bach transcriptions. From Moór's response Casals knew trouble was unavoidable.

Szántó sat down at the piano to repair the lapse in Moór's knowledge. He played through one transcription and was greeted with silence. He played a second: glowering silence. "Well," asked Szántó, "what do you think of them, Monsieur Moór?"

"I think," shouted Moór, on his feet, "*du bist ein Esel*—a bloody jackass!"

Casals took Szántó aside, explained that Moór became upset rather easily, recommended a return visit another time, and saw Szántó out. When Casals returned to the studio he suggested to Moór what he thought of his behavior. Moór lowered his head for a moment like a scolded child, then looked up and asked "Well, you agree with me, don't you? So———" That was one of the problems; Moór had no consideration for others and a genuine talent for offending people, but his critical faculty in music was deadly accurate.

Casals and Moór had met in the spring or summer of 1905 in a Lausanne café, when the Russian cellist Anatol Brandoukov pointed out to Casals a tall man with penetrating eyes and mobile sensitive hands as an "amateur composer." Something in the brusque intensity and the expression of the older man interested Casals at once, and he invited Moór to come to see him in Paris. Moór appeared the first time at the Villa Molitor with a great sheaf of compositions under his arm. Casals was prepared to find things to appreciate but not for the strength of his reaction. The way Moór dealt with the piano, his Magyar aura of melancholy unfulfillment and brooding, and the first music he played told Casals he was in the presence of a remarkable man, and he responded to the thread of sadness in the music. Moór was playing his first cello concerto, written the same year and dedicated to the French violoncellist Marguerite Caponsacchi. When Moór paused, Casals, greatly moved, remained silent until Moór could stand it no longer and asked an opinion. Casals looked straight at him and said, "I think you are a genius!"

Moór threw his arms about the younger man and began to weep. He sobbed out a recital of a life of tragedy and disappointment. Nobody but his wife appreciated his music; he had been rebuffed and told his work was inconsequential so often that he had come to believe it and had not composed for ten years.

From that moment Emanuel Moór did not remain unrecognized or unaccepted through any lack of effort on Pablo Casals' part. For ten years he mounted a propaganda effort on behalf of Moór's work with an unblinking persistence he showed for no other musical creator except Bach. Moór was the most strident voice in what Casals sometimes called his trio of great friendships, and with Julius Röntgen and Donald Francis Tovey he was one of the three modern "unknown masters" whose lack of recognition as composers continued to puzzle him. Casals often pointed out that the music of the great composers of his youth—among them Saint-Saëns, Fauré, and Franck—was not being played anymore, but he remained mystified that his three friends had never really been recognized at all and was both saddened and shocked that younger musicians later in the twentieth century did not even know their names. He often said that a fourth great unknown, the Catalan watchmaker and composer Juli Garreta, was the finest composer Spain had produced, but he always referred to him in a separate tone of admiration and affection.

Emanuel Moór was a relatively obscure musician when Casals met him, but hardly the complete unknown his tearful account in the Villa Molitor suggested. Moór was an extraordinary pianist, although he expressed early and loud dissatisfaction with the limitations of the instrument. Casals praised his artistry in exalted terms and said Moór had the ability to transcend the mere notes so that the complete design was always apparent. Even Alfred Cortot, not Moór's staunchest admirer, spoke of the Hungarian's playing as orchestral, the painting of tonal frescoes and grand decorations. But Moór really wanted to compose.

Moór was born in the village of Kecskemet, Hungary, in February 1863, the son of Raphael Moór, a tenor who, rebelling against his pious father's demands to join the family fur business, began an opera and concert career, then returned to Kecskemet to become cantor of the synagogue and give singing lessons. By six, encouraged and helped by Raphael, Emanuel was a wunderkind pianist. At thirteen—the year Casals was born—he was in Prague, where he had made friends with the family of Thomas Masaryk and received the gold medal of the organ school. He had informal lessons with Franz Liszt at the Esterhazy estate in Eisenstadt; he also studied in Budapest with Robert Volkmann and in Vienna.

The fame of Raphael Moór's voice had spread through central Europe and to America; a group of immigrants invited him to become cantor of a New York congregation in 1885. So, at the age of twenty-two, about the time Pablo Casals was proving to Carlos he was tall enough to reach the pedals of the Vendrell church organ, Emanuel Moór sailed with his father to the United States. He soon captured the attention of the piano manufacturers, then the chief arbiters of the American concert scene; Steinway, Chickering, and Sohmer each placed instruments at his disposal. Moór was booked for recitals in New York and the Northeast, and made an eastern tour as assisting artist to the German dramatic soprano Lilli Lehmann, who was being hailed at the Metropolitan Opera for her Brünnhilde and Isolde.

Moór loathed his short musical career in America. He was impatient with the conventional repertoire the managers demanded, and more and more frequently his audiences heard elaborate improvisations in place of the standard works indicated on the program. In fairness, some of the engagements may not have been overwhelmingly stimulating for a young artist with an unconventional attitude and limitless personal ambition. Moór's first known New York appearance, for example, in Steinway Hall on the first of November 1885, was a Sunday-evening Musical and Literary Entertainment given by the Livingston Association for the benefit of the Sir Moses Montefiore Fund. Participants in addition to Moór were the Beethoven Männerchor, the New York Zither Verein, a female singer, a bass, a violinist, and two elocutionists.

Through American friends of the Masaryks in America Moór met Anita Burke, daughter of an Irishman who had made a fortune importing malt liquors into the United States, and fell in love with her. Like Moór, she adored animals; she was a good horsewoman, fond of dancing and good at cards. She had gone to schools in New Jersey and England, studied singing in New York and philosophy with the French philosopher Joseph Antoine Milsand in Dijon, and been on two trips around the world aboard her uncle's yacht. Her father and brother approved the match, but the rest of the clan reacted as to a major earthquake. The couple was married in London in February 1888; at the same time Moór's father Raphael left the United States to become a landowner at Perchtoldsdorf near Vienna, where he lived quietly and gave singing lessons.

The couple settled in England, where Moór became a British citizen, performed a few times in London, and began a lava-flow of composition, the ideas sometimes coming faster than they could be written down. The first seven or eight years of their marriage saw an almost uninterrupted flood of composition from Moór's worktable. Anita Moór's reactions to her husband's compositions were invariably favorable. And, since Moór liked company while he composed, she sat with him while he worked. Her energy and resources were devoted to furthering his career the rest of her life.

George Henschel, who founded the London Symphony Orchestra in 1886 and led it for a decade, included Moór works in his programs. Moór was hailed in his native land when he went to Budapest in 1895 to conduct performances of his second symphony. A burst of writing between 1900 and 1902 resulted in several operas. One, which never reached the stage, had a libretto adapted from Bret Harte's "Alkali Dick" and was the romantic saga of a cowboy from Buffalo Bill's Wild West show who ends up as a French aristocrat. Two others were produced in 1902 at the important Cologne Stadt-Theater—a tragic Napoleonic music-drama, *Andreas Hofer*, and *La Mouche*, from Musset's story with a libretto by Anita Moór and Fräulein Lolo von Ferro, an Austrian member of the Moór household.

Instrumental compositions by Moór had been played or were scheduled for performance in Berlin, Warsaw, Vienna, Wiesbaden, Frankfurt, and elsewhere on the Continent by the end of 1905. Emanuel Moór was thus not quite the victim of unmerited neglect he painted himself the first time he called on Casals in Paris, although nothing would or could satisfy him. Moór had too many interests, abilities, and drives to be content with the recognition that came to him, no matter how real. Emanuel Moór reached voraciously for the unattainable. Dissatisfied with the limitations of the piano, he invented an instrument with two keyboards that could be coupled with a lever, thus facilitating the playing of octaves, tenths, and chromatic glissandos. He made an instrument intended to replace all the strings of the orchestra; it looked like an enormous beetle and had six strings ranging from the violin E to the cello C. He was an architect, painter, and teacher. He invented a new kind of dog leash, an improved hairpin, an automotive bolt that would not come loose, more efficient surgical instruments— and never followed through far enough for commercial development of any of them.

But there were no shades of gray for Casals. In Moór he sensed genius and saw work that deserved to be known; he would do everything in his power to aid the cause, and Moór's was a banner he flourished the rest of his life. Casals' enthusiasm swept everything before it; no fellow musician could have wished for a better propagandist or more loyal friend. And no composer, with the possible exception of Wagner, made friendship or promotion more difficult.

Casals played a Moór cello sonata during his first tour of Russia late in 1905, then with Swiss pianist Marie Panthès in Geneva and Lausanne early in December, and with Cortot in Paris later in the month. He wrote Moór: "I will truly rejoice to see you again and hear more of your music, which touches me so profoundly," and he began to include works by Moór in his 1906 programs. After performances of his own in Amsterdam in January 1906, Casals remained to hear Henri Marteau play Moór's violin concerto—an extraordinary work, he wrote Julius Röntgen, "but to my mind . . . not performed as it should be—which bothered me. But this music still has to ripen in the minds of artists before the public can get an impression of its real meaning." Moór had been in Leipzig at the same time, listening to Marguerite Caponsacchi perform his first cello concerto. Casals had put Röntgen in touch with Moór and had fired the interest of Willem Mengelberg, who conducted the Concertgebouw orchestra for Marteau and with whom Casals had been appearing for several years. In February Mme Panthès gave the first of many performances of a new Moór piano concerto. Mlle Caponsacchi was playing the first cello concerto in Germany and Switzerland.

Moór was becoming known gratifyingly fast, but the nurture of his insatiable psyche was another matter. Moór was furious that Mlle Caponsacchi had not included his work in her programs in Denmark and Sweden. Casals wrote from the Villa Molitor early in March that he could not believe Caponsacchi had behaved ungratefully toward Moór; he was sure the exclusion was not her fault. "My dear friend [Casals went on], I wish you could relax, you who have so many reasons to be happy—Nature has given you what she gives so rarely, *genius*—You have friends who love you and understand you. Work without upset—think not just about your health but about your creation that is suffering—Relax and be happy! I repeat."

Moór was composing volcanically, as he had since his first visit to Casals in Paris: orchestral improvisations on an original theme; a second cello concerto, for Casals; a sixth symphony. He began promising new works that were barely finished in time for performance. The more exposure his work was given, the greater his hunger for acclaim. During the summer of 1906 Moór works were played in Bad Nauheim, Montreux, and elsewhere. Conductors such as Schneevoigt, Fiedler, Steinbach as well as Mengelberg, were becoming interested in his music, and Moór traveled frequently to be present for rehearsals and performances. And he was composing other new works—a violin concerto for Carl Flesch and his seventh symphony, dedicated to Mengelberg and the Concertgebouw orchestra.

Casals and Moór traveled together to Amsterdam for the rehearsals of the first performance of Moór's second cello concerto—the first of several such journeys on which composer and cellist were companions. The concerto had its première on October 24, 1906, under Mengelberg, a second performance in Amsterdam the next day, and was played in The Hague on the twenty-seventh. Moór was present at all the performances. There was little response from the public except to a brilliant performance.

Moór's second cello concerto is one of his most significant works. It has long, almost improvisatory melodic lines, a looseness of structure that gives it a rhapsodic quality, and what some identified as a combination of gypsy spirit and Hungarian-Jewish flavor—passionate lyricism and melancholic severity. It is nevertheless a tightly integrated whole, with areas of skillful contrapuntal writing; Moór knew musical structure well—he was steeped in Bach—and was capable of genuine craftsmanship when he applied himself long enough and with enough discipline to exercise it. Moór wrote the work for its ideal performer. His composition was extremely difficult, a vehicle for major technical virtuosity that also required deep musical understanding.

Nearly two months after the Amsterdam première, Casals played the concerto in St. Petersburg without telling Moór. He wrote the composer afterward that he had wanted to spare his friend the long journey he would have wanted to make and the anguish of an orchestral accompaniment Casals had feared might be less than satisfactory—but everything had been fine. The explanation was graceful: Casals knew perfectly well that if all had not gone to his liking Moór would have created a thoroughly unpleasant situation. Casals and Moór had been together during a

Casals and Emanuel Moór playing chess as Jacques Thibaud watches. Casals, an expert player, preferred dominos because it permitted faster moves.

concert in Cologne at which Fritz Steinbach conducted Moór's sixth symphony. The audience's response was cool. When a lesser composition received an ovation, Moór leaped to his feet and delivered a harangue on the stupidity of the public at large and the specific idiocy of the Cologne public. An embarrassed Casals managed to quiet him, but the reverberations continued through the Rhineland for years. Seated next to a distinguished German critic during a festival performance of *Die Götterdämmerung* at Bayreuth, Moór turned to his neighbor during a protracted narration and asked loudly "Can you tell me who wrote this long-winded opera?"

During the winter of 1906–1907 Emanuel Moór wrote a triple concerto for piano, violin, cello, and orchestra for the Casals–Cortot–Thibaud trio. It was to be included, at the cellist's insistence, in the group's autumn 1907 tour, along with trios by Schumann and Franck. Moór was late, finishing at breakneck speed in early July. The first run-throughs took place in Paris in an atmosphere of considerable restraint, although neither Cortot nor Thibaud made any comment. Rehearsals of the full repertoire continued at Cortot's summer place in Switzerland. The strained atmosphere worried Casals so much that after one session he finally asked his colleagues outright if it was advisable to continue preparing the Moór work. Cortot said he could not play the thing unless he revised the piano part; Moór's score was unpianistic. Casals answered briskly that the composer would have to be consulted about any changes. Cortot wrote Moór, who accepted the emendations, to Casals' astonishment and rather to his annoyance at what seemed compromise on Moór's part. (The work was published exactly as Moór first wrote it.)

In due course Moór came from Lausanne to hear advanced rehearsals, and agreed to everything, although relations between Moór and Cortot were still not altogether cordial. While he was at Cortot's, a storm came up. The station was a considerable distance from the house, but Clothilde Cortot (the former wife of Romain Rolland) declined to invite Moór to stay the night, and his colleagues had to hold Casals back physically to keep him from walking to the station with Moór. (Thibaud and his wife Marguerite, who looked and spoke like a smaller Sarah Bernhardt, were better disposed toward Moór and his family, and Thibaud was preparing a Moór violin concerto to play later in the year with Arthur Nikisch in Leipzig and in Berlin and Geneva.)

At the first Swiss concert, the program was a success—including the Moór triple concerto. It was well enough received by the public as the tour went on, and Cortot and Thibaud seemed less hostile to the work each time they played it. After the final concert of the series they knocked on the door of his hotel room after Casals had retired. Confessing a certain lack of pleasure in the concerto during rehearsals, they said they wanted Casals to know that in the course of the four concert performances their interest had grown to the point that they could now share his admiration for the composition.

Eugène Ysaÿe had been more difficult to convince, but he likewise succumbed eventually. Casals had introduced Ysaÿe to

Moór at the end of 1906, but the violinist's interest in Moór's first violin concerto was not great. Some time later Casals and Ysaÿe met unexpectedly on a cross-Channel steamer bound for the Continent. Ysaÿe said he had something important to report, and they retired to a quiet corner of one of the public rooms. Ysaÿe asked if Casals remembered urging him in Berlin to take up Moór's concerto, but it had left him cold. Casals remembered very well, and also that he had brought up the subject another time but dropped it in the face of Ysaÿe's continued lack of interest. Well, the giant Belgian announced, he had become a convert; as time passed he had come to admire Moór's work a great deal. He had just performed a Moór concerto nine times during a tour of England and the night before, playing it in Plymouth, had begun to think it as fine as the Beethoven concerto. (Not long afterward Moór finished his fourth violin concerto—dedicated to Ysaÿe.)

The peak of Emanuel Moór's success as a composer came between 1908—when Casals and Guilhermina Suggia began to perform the concerto for two cellos Moór had written for them—and 1910, when Casals played Moór's second cello concerto at his Vienna début. By then other important artists were also playing Moór pieces—Ysaÿe, Thibaud, Harold Bauer, Marie Panthès, and the young pianist Maurice Dumesnil.

The double cello concerto is a comparatively short four-movement work that is notably lyric and contains virtuoso passages for both soloists within a clearly defined musical outline. The first performance was given in January 1908 in Brussels under Ysaÿe's direction; thereafter Casals and Suggia included it in joint programs they played in France, Germany, Switzerland, and Russia. Several times during those tours a movement had to be repeated by audience demand, a most unusual accolade to an unfamiliar work, although how much was a response to the playing rather than to the work is unknown.

Casals used the three 1908 Paris concerts in which he made his first appearances as *chef d'orchestre* as a showcase for Moór. Some six weeks after his thirty-first birthday Casals hired the Lamoureux orchestra for a series of what were "without doubt the most important concerts of the year" in the Salle Gaveau.

The manner in which Pablo Casals is conducting these concerts is extremely characteristic of him [reported Louise

Llewellyn, Paris correspondent for *Musical America*] . . . so little advertised that the critics of some of the largest musical papers were ignorant of them the night before the first one took place. . . . Casals is the one living musician to whom any sort of réclame is sincerely distasteful and [he] would prefer a thousand times to play to an audience of half a dozen appreciating musicians than to have the rest of the chairs . . . filled by an indiscriminate public . . . even though it might mean an empty purse. The fact that on the evening of the first concert, February 7, the Salle Gaveau was filled almost to seating capacity, attested to the confident and interested admiration in which he is held.

The focus of the first evening, as Casals arranged it, was Moór's concerto for two cellos, played by himself and Suggia. It drew "storms of intelligent applause from floor to ceiling" and it could "surely be said that the music of Moór is at least strong and human and vital and that there is nothing in it of the 'passion-less sensuality' . . . that permeates so much of the modern French stuff." A long unsigned criticism in *Le Monde Musical* welcomed "the admirable improvisations of M. Moór" as infinitely preferable to "those dry painful productions without inner continuity of ideas . . . loudly acclaimed as being fully correct in form." But, the reviewer suggested, M. Moór might give a bit more thought to construction, perhaps reconsider his speed of composition.

Casals had begun the evening by conducting the Lamoureux orchestra in Beethoven's fifth symphony. The *Courier Musical* found that the orchestra, having recently been in the hands of a number of conductors because Lamoureux's successor Chevillard was ill, did not always follow Casals or grasp his ideas, "though his intentions throughout were excellent, and he succeeded in attaining, upon occasions, effects of the rarest beauty." After the Moór concerto, Georges Enesco conducted the first hearing of two Rumanian rhapsodies he had composed. Louise Llewellyn thought them "amusing . . . well put together and orchestrated, but the sort of music that one scarcely thinks of taking seriously."

In the second concert of the Salle Gaveau series, on February 28, Cortot, Thibaud, and Casals played the Moór triple concerto; Casals conducted Brahms' third symphony and led the orchestral accompaniment for Suggia playing the Dvořák cello concerto. The final program, on the sixteenth of March, saw Casals on the podium

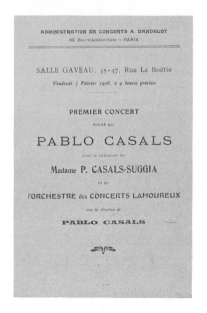

---

*The program of Casals' first appearance as a
conductor in Paris, February 7, 1908. The
concert included a work by Emanuel Moór and
the first public hearing of two Rumanian
rhapsodies by Georges Enesco.*

---

to conduct Moór's sixth symphony, a ballade for orchestra by
Julius Röntgen, and the Beethoven "Emperor" concerto, with his
Vendrell contemporary, Bienvenido Socias, as piano soloist.

A year later, February 7, 1909, Casals and Suggia once again
played Moór's double concerto in Paris. This time anti-Moór vol-
leys were fired, the tersest *L'Eclair*'s "Why the devil must M. and
Mme Casals play such ordinary music?" Moór was always temporarily pleased by kind words, but even the mildest and friendliest
adverse criticism sent him into an abysmal Hungarian despondence.

From this point on, Moór seldom went to public performances of his own music, often waiting huddled in bed until the reports about a performance and its reception reached him.

Moór's friends were distressed, but Casals saw a challenge—to show the Parisian music critics that Emanuel Moór was no lone reed to be buffeted by their wind. He instigated and partially underwrote a Moór Festival set for the fifteenth of June in the Salle Pleyel under the nominal sponsorship of Gustave Lyon, head of the Pleyel piano manufacturers. This gala affair set musical Paris talking, and the house was so full that members of the audience filled even the stairs leading to the artists' room. There was a full evening of Moór works—a string trio played by Cortot, Thibaud, and Casals; preludes for the Pleyel chromatic harp performed by Hélène Zielinska, a Polish harpist; six sketches for piano played by Maurice Dumesnil; and a new quartet for four cellos, with Casals, Joseph Salmon, André Hekking, and Diran Alexanian. At the end Moór received the most enthusiastic ovation of his life, and the Paris critics temporarily softened their attacks.

For the time being Moór's musical productivity remained at torrent force, including work on an eighth symphony, many smaller pieces, and songs; it was almost as if he sensed his musical progress was to be interrupted. Opus numbers on his works had reached 150, with many more unnumbered in manuscript. He dashed about Europe—playing, conducting, once more attending programs of his own music. The regulars continued to play his works faithfully, and the ranks had been swelled by Mieczyslaw Horszowski and by the gifted young Brazilian pianist Guiomar Novaes, who made her Paris début at sixteen in 1911.

Moór and his wife were strongly pacifist and pro-British, and he possessed a mimetic gift that enabled him to produce at will a scathing impersonation of friend or foe—present or absent. During his trips to Germany, especially as war was approaching, Moór derided militarism and burlesqued its supporters with blissful tactlessness on every possible occasion. He could not understand why the German press—especially in Munich—blasted away at him.

The glue that held the battered structure of friendship together for Casals and Moór was, above all else, their agreement on Johann Sebastian Bach. Moór's musical outlook stemmed from a devotion to and deep knowledge of the works of Bach, although most of his composition showed other influences more clearly. He played Bach extremely well.

Casals had few doubts about his own musical instinct and was willing to stand against the world on matters of principle, but he had been shaken and puzzled by the storm that erupted about his playing of the Bach solo cello suites, particularly in Germany. He had started to include a full suite in some of his programs by 1899, after working at them every day for the years since he found them in the musty shop in the calle Ancha in Barcelona. Except to use a single movement occasionally for an encore, he played them complete: the prelude and five dance movements, with all repeats to maintain the coherence and internal structure of each movement within the architecture of the whole. At first the managers complained: an entire unaccompanied suite was too much for a paying audience—an understandable judgment in a period in which Bach was usually played mechanically. Bach's is the most "classical" of serious music and Casals brought it to audiences in extenso and without apology. By the time he began to do so, although he was still very young, his imagination and musicianship enabled him to make Bach relevant and illuminating to the human condition. By then Bach had become for Pablo Casals everything in music; Bach was the Shakespeare, the Rembrandt, the god of music, and in his works Casals found expressed the meaning of life, every nuance of beauty and joy and sadness of the human experience, the most shimmering of poetry. Bach was for everybody, he insisted, and accessible to everyone. Startled audiences responded jubilantly to his "free," revolutionary interpretation, and so did some of the critics. When he first played the suites in Germany, the academics cried sacrilege (as some continued to do in succeeding generations), with the voice of German cellist Hugo Becker among the loudest; for Becker, the more severe didactic approach to Bach's music was the only possible one. The other opinion, which held that it had taken a Spaniard to reveal Bach to his homeland, was represented by Julius Klengel at Leipzig, whose stature as a cellist was at least equal to Becker's.

The journalistic critics did not really concern Casals; he paid little attention to them, and they tended to cancel one another out. And the public who came to hear music did respond joyfully to the way he read Bach. He had refined his interpretation of these masterpieces faithfully for nearly half his life with intelligence and devotion and perception; he felt his approach was natural, and therefore could not be wrong. Yet some musicologists and some musicians who had earned credentials worthy of respect said vehemently that he was very much wrong.

Moór agreed with Casals that the work of Bach must be played in such a way that the poetry and inner life of the music would show through. When the nineteenth-century revival of Bach's music took place, most musicians had a misconception of the nature of polyphonic music and particularly of the style of Bach, in which that tradition had culminated. Performers generally did not consider anything other than the cantatas and such overwhelming religious works as the Passions to be concert music; most conceived of the solo music for strings as exercises and played it literally as written, strictly, with little artistic value and no sense at all of its dance quality. The public shied away from Bach; the academic label and stylistic ignorance had stultified the playing of his music. The usual "filagree" interpreters shackled the essential vitality of the music and made realization of its scope impossible, as did the *ein, zwei, drei, vier* Prussian tradition. Emanuel Moór reinforced Pablo Casals' convictions at a time and in a way that were very important to Casals, who said later that more than any other musician Moór had reassured him his understanding of Bach was right.

Some of the best and most demanding of Moór's own music was written for Casals or in the glow of his encouragement. Moór deliberately chose classical forms; within them his vocabulary and his lyric gift ignored the accepted nineteenth-century "four-measure phrase" in rhapsodic passages of intentionally loose construction. At the same time, he was not in sympathy with those for whom expression of emotion and individualism was more important than form and style. Critic Philip Hale of the Boston *Herald* found Moór almost as much of an enigma as Frederick Delius, each with "his idiom that is peculiar and . . . not . . . influenced by predecessors or contemporaries. Of the two, Moór is the more emotional, yet in his music there is often a certain sobriety that is not far removed from austerity." Showing no clear debt to the past but also less experimentation than, for instance, his younger fellow Hungarians Bartók and Kodály, Moór was embraced neither by the publicists for the strict traditionalism of the nineteenth century nor by the avant-garde of the early twentieth.

Moór, "a musician who has written not only very much but who has written it very earnestly," produced music like an unregulated fountain. Driven by his own demon, too impatient to linger for polishing and revision, Moór produced some works that had architectural flaws and others that were skillfully constructed but threadbare in invention. For some, Moór's music was old wine of fairly good vintage served in bottles that were not new. For them, the music did not soar.

The reasons the public did not take to the music of Emanuel Móor in his lifetime are various; the fact remains that it did not. Why Pablo Casals was Moór's champion for the greater part of a century is of more interest. Moór loved the beauty of nature, was tender with animals and children, and hated war. He was a difficult human being, his own worst enemy. He was capable of much warmth and great charm, and called forth from the younger man sympathy and protective aid as for a self-defeating older brother. Also, in Casals' consciousness and affection there was another human being who had been inventor as well as composer, his father, a man of charm and force and frustration who had had no one to help him gain public recognition.

All such speculations Casals answered with a shrug. He granted that Emanuel Moór was an impossible person, that he had no real thought for others. "Of course he looked slovenly and was without manners," Casals would admit. "But he was a genius!"

13

THE CIRCUMSTANCES of Casals' first musical foray into Russia, in November 1905, were dramatic but—like many travelers to that country—he had or expected difficulties at the border on each of his nine annual trips there before 1914. Russia was at the time the only European nation that demanded passports, and visas were required for both entry and exit. (The practical folklore of travel said about Russia "Lose your pocketbook or your head, but never your passport.") The sometimes illiterate officials were notoriously suspicious, and travelers were advised not to wrap parcels in newspaper or anything else that bore the written word. The country both fascinated and depressed Casals; although he quickly came to like the people he got to know, he always felt a sense of suffocation when he entered Russia. The Russian customs officers, bearded brutes with enormous hands, looking down at him suspiciously, always made him feel he was entering a prison.

It is curious that a man so small and on first glance so unprepossessing should have drawn the attention of security police—perhaps it was the cello—but Casals was repeatedly the object of their special notice at many national boundaries. Once when he crossed the border from Finland, czarist police began

Casals about the time of his first trip to Russia

to question him in Russian in what seemed rude language, then forced him to strip and submit to an intensive search. Casals, who could speak German but did not understand Russian, refused to sign a document without knowing its content. He was finally allowed to continue the short distance to St. Petersburg, where, still furious, he told his friend Alexander Siloti what had happened. Siloti took the matter up with a highly placed friend, and the issue was discussed on the floor of the Duma. A few days later Casals was offered an official apology.

Casals had recitals scheduled in Berlin on his way to Moscow. He set out in October 1905 for the capital of Wilhelm II, Emperor of Germany and King of Prussia, who—along with preparing the German military apparatus to subjugate Europe—was interested in music and enjoyed conducting rehearsals himself. The Kaiser liked Bach (in the Prussian interpretation), Handel, Gluck, and Weber; Wagner was too noisy and Richard Strauss too unmelodious for his taste.

Casals' Berlin manager was Frau Louise Wolff, widow of impresario Hermann Wolff and head of Konzertdirektion Wolff & Sachs, German impresarios for almost every famous European musician before 1914. "Queen Louise" dictated matters with an imperious air, sharp tongue, and crisp business mind. Bruno Walter remembered her as both temperamental and radiantly smiling; awaiting an audition in the early days, he watched her flip through a stack of rave reviews handed her by another young hopeful, then snap "Now let me see the bad ones!" A later client, Gregor Piatigorsky, first saw her in the 1920s sitting majestically at her disordered desk, "her massive torso wrapped in what appeared to be numerous blouses, scarves, and shawls." He thought her knowledge of music not above the level of other managers, but her judgment carried great weight and her influence was international. (Casals later shifted to other management for his German concerts. He never found dictatorship tolerable and was less amused than most by Frau Wolff's tyranny.)

The Berlin–St. Petersburg segment of the trip to Moscow normally took thirty hours, but Casals' train was stopped at Vilna, halfway between Warsaw and St. Petersburg, and all passengers were ordered off the train. A Russian general who was a railway director and had heard Casals play in Berlin introduced himself and explained that a general strike had halted all regular trains but invited Casals to share his compartment on a special official train that would move on as far as St. Petersburg. Moscow was out of the question this trip, but at least Casals would not be stranded indefinitely in Vilna, nearly fifteen hundred kilometers from Paris. Casals joined the general and his lady in their luxurious but overheated compartment for the rest of the way to St. Petersburg.

By 1905 in Russia dissatisfaction and potential violence were close to eruption due in a large degree to the growth of industry since the 1880s and the emergence of an industrial proletariat living in hopeless misery. Unrest spread from the cities to the rural peasants with the devastating famine of 1891–1892. On the twenty-second of January 1905—Bloody Sunday—two hundred thousand workers led by a woolly-minded priest, Father Gapon, moving across the square in front of the Winter Palace to petition the Czar for minor improvements in their working conditions, were fired upon by troops; seventy died and more than two hundred were wounded. An epidemic of strikes followed. There were many student demonstrations—the St. Petersburg Conservatory was closed as a result of one series—and the workers emerged for the first time as a real element in the movement for civil liberties and the demand for parliamentary government. Russia had been at war with Japan since February 1904, Port Arthur fell in January 1905, and the war was finally lost in a disastrous battle off Tsushima at the end of May. From June through August there were more strikes, peasant outbreaks, separatist uprisings in the provinces, and mutinies in the army and navy. Just after the middle of August Czar Nicholas II, intelligent but weak-willed, announced creation of the Imperial Duma—a parliament with powers so limited as not even to satisfy the moderate liberals, much less the revolutionaries. Nicholas had finally proclaimed a constitution for Russia on the thirtieth of October, as a general strike was spreading through the country. The situation had begun to improve, but Casals was to find some disruption still in effect, including the rail strike that made it impossible for him to continue on to Moscow.

Casals' first move in St. Petersburg was to telephone Alexander Siloti, who was told by a servant that some sort of maniac was on the wire—all he could say was *"Monsieur* Siloti. *Monsieur* Siloti, *s'il vous plaît!"* As soon as Siloti learned who the French-speaking madman was, he told Casals to remain where he was until he could send transport for him.

Siloti had been living through the impresario-conductor's nightmare. The rail strike that stranded Pablo Casals in St. Petersburg had also detained Eugène Ysaÿe—scheduled for two concerto appearances with Siloti's orchestra—in Warsaw. Alexander Siloti organized an annual series of symphonic concerts, devoted to the classics and the works of living Russian composers, in which he and guest conductors directed the excellent Maryinski Theater orchestra; he also engaged top soloists from Russia and Europe. The Siloti Concerts, begun in 1903, were the first continuous effort of such quality in St. Petersburg and when Casals reached the city were perhaps the best in Russia. Born in October 1863 into an

Alexander Siloti in St. Petersburg

aristocratic family of landed proprietors, Siloti had been a favorite Liszt pupil at twenty and bore an uncanny physical resemblance to the Master. He had firmly established first-quality chamber music in turn-of-the-century St. Petersburg; his personality and his abilities as conductor and pianist endowed him with a glamour in the eyes of social and musical St. Petersburg that—according to his cousin Sergei Rachmaninoff—"shone undiminished up to the catastrophe."

Casals and Siloti had corresponded; when they met Casals found the Russian an engaging man and gracious host who welcomed him fraternally. Casals pressed Siloti for recollections of Nicholas Rubinstein and Tchaikovsky, and particularly for memories of Franz Liszt. Of the resemblance, Siloti would say "coincidence—or affinity," but when he spoke of Liszt Siloti was like someone hypnotized and Casals got little more than a description of Liszt as "sort of a Franciscan gypsy." He did demonstrate Liszt's daily warm-up exercise of dazzling, ingenious arpeggios, "which he did . . . half an hour for each hand, very mechanically, with a newspaper propped up before him." Siloti had very large hands and played piano with a mixture of vigor and refinement based in a superb technique, like his speaking style in both Russian and French a mixture of educated speech and the colloquial. He was certain he was still in communication with his teacher; even during Casals' first visit he informed his guest matter-of-factly that Liszt had just told him how to play a passage that had been giving him problems the day before, and toward the end of his life Siloti could be found of an evening revising Liszt scores on fresh instructions from the composer. ("What is this?" Casals asked Siloti's wife the first time it happened. "You are a man who should be able to understand these things," she said. Liszt had died in July 1886.)

The first concert at which Casals played in Russia was on Saturday, November 5, 1905 (by the Julian calendar, which remained in effect in Russia until 1917—the eighteenth in western Europe). There was a rehearsal that morning in the auditorium of the Salle de la Noblesse (the Hall of the Nobility), an eighteenth-century structure on the Nevsky Prospekt that accommodated more than two thousand people. In the audience were Nikolai Rimsky-Korsakov, Alexander Glazunov (works by whom were receiving first performances that night), and Anatol Liadov, conductor Felix Blumenfeld, and other members of the St. Petersburg musical community. Kyriena, the tomboy daughter who became the only musician among Siloti's children, was backstage that morning and saw the look that passed between the conductor and the Maryinski orchestra when Casals began to rehearse the Saint-Saëns concerto. At the end of the concerto the orchestra members broke into spontaneous applause.

The power plants were still inoperative that Saturday night, and Casals always remembered the flicker of hundreds of candle flames reflected in mirrored sconces around the austerely elegant great hall. Even the giant seated statue of Catherine the Great in the center of the room was softened. (Siloti's youngest son would listen at the concerts as long as he could, slip over to the statue, climb the pedestal and then Catherine's knee, which was higher than his head, and contentedly go to sleep in the Empress' lap.)

Despite the disturbance and the strike, the concert drew a large house. Women with jewels and furs and Paris gowns and men in formal suits or dress uniforms filled the prominent seats. Siloti was concerned about the reaction of the highly critical audience who had come expecting to hear Ysaÿe, not an unknown Spaniard not yet twenty-nine. The murmur that swept the hall on announcement of the change became helpless laughter as Casals and the conductor made their way through the orchestra to the front of the stage—a sight that must indeed have been irresistibly funny. Casals was dressed in a business suit, since his luggage was still in Vilna. By protocol he entered first, a minuscule, slightly stooped young man already quite bald, carrying the Bergonzi cello he now played and that was nearly as tall as he. Siloti followed, appearing even taller and more Mefistofelian than usual.

Casals sat, retuned the cello—his usual paroxysm of stage fright had gone with the sound of the public's laughter—lifted his bow, and nodded to Siloti. A powerful astringent A-major chord resounded from the Maryinski orchestra. After the first imperious entrance of the cello the silence in the auditorium was complete. At the end of the opening *Allegro non troppo* of the Saint-Saëns concerto the audience was on its feet, shouting and applauding.

One member of the 1905 audience was a university student named A. A. Borisiak who was studying cello at the St. Petersburg Conservatory with J. C. Rosenthal, a disciple of Carl Davidov. Borisiak was thunderstruck:

> An unforgettable impression was made by this concert at which, instead of Ysaÿe whom we expected, an unknown cellist appeared on the stage, a short man with a childlike smile. His face subsequently took on the expression of a powerful concentration that at once riveted the attention of the audience. The interpretation that then came forth was so convincing that at every phrase one had to think: "Yes, indeed, this is how this should be played!" This impression became characteristic . . . of all the future Casals performances. . . .
>
> We did not hear either Casals or the cello; we were not interested in the technique, or the intonation, or the touch: we only heard music as such.

Borisiak was a fellow musician rather than a journalist, and his tribute supreme: *We only heard music . . .*

One major attraction of that evening was the first performance of Nikolai Rimsky-Korsakov's new symphony, based on the revolutionary song "Dubinushka." The dismissal of Rimsky that spring from the directorship of the conservatory had become a cause célèbre. He had written a strong protest of the expulsion of conservatory students who took part in demonstrations following Bloody Sunday; he had been fired and his works banned from public performance for a time. Rimsky's liberal views were well known, and at sixty, after thirty-five years on its faculty, his love and concern for the St. Petersburg Conservatory and generations of its students had become clear. Other features of the long program were the first hearing of an orchestral fantasy on "The Song of the Volga Boatmen" by Rimsky-Korsakov's friend and successor as conservatory director, Alexander Glazunov, and Anatol Liadov's "Russian Songs" for orchestra.

In 1905 Casals entered what had until then been the domain of the respected and beloved Carl Davidov, who had died sixteen years before. The Russian cello school was still dominated by his memory and manner. Like so many other Russian musicians, Davidov began as a mathematician; he began to study cello seriously only after he took his mathematical degree at twenty. He became a notable performer with an expressive tone, sure intonation, extraordinary technique, and great stylistic individuality, and his book of cello exercises became the fundamental guidebook for the study of the instrument in Russia. He also wrote music of "elegaic grace and melancholy and occasionally . . . glowing passion"; Casals learned and played one of Davidov's four cello concertos—his first encore group in St. Petersburg included pieces by Davidov and Glazunov.

But Casals' first encore in Russia was the prelude of Bach's D minor suite for cello. Borisiak's recollection of Casals' first impact on Russian audiences touches with wonder on one of Pablo Casals' great musical contributions—the inclusion in his programs of complete unaccompanied Bach cello suites. Following his second St. Petersburg performance, four days after the first, critic A. P. Kontiaiev chuckled in the *Petersburgskie wiedomosti:* "The ladies expected some Spanish dances à la Sarasate, but he played

Bach . . . and Bach again as an encore!" Within six years, when a competition was established for young cellists from all parts of Russia, the playing of a complete Bach suite for solo cello was one requirement for entry.

There had of course been cellists before Casals, musicians of importance, but he revolutionized the concert life of the instrument, changing the attitude of the public toward it as well as its repertoire and technique. "The forgotten repertoire found again—and often for the first time—an able performer," observed Borisiak. Casals was neither the first nor the only cellist, but he was in his time the greatest, a fact that was not always comfortable for those—including Russians—who came after him chronologically. No cellist before had done what he did to make the public hungry for the sound of the solo cello; no cellist afterward needed to. Casals' musical career began at a confluence of time and civilization at which a vacuum existed; with a combination of genius, astuteness, dedication, and opportunity he filled it.

Before Casals was twenty-nine years old, Russian observers were writing about him in specific terms as a truly extraordinary musician. Kontiaiev, reviewing Casals' second Russian concert, would not agree that the new cellist was better than the late Davidov although many others seemed to think so, but he found Casals to have full technical equipment and definite opinions about art, "a complete, a remarkable artist." His technique is "without a doubt phenomenal. His basic manner of keeping to *mezzo voce* against which his *forte* stands out in unusual relief is interesting. The large tone, the purity of the sound, the intelligent phrasing and the vivacity—all have been united in this artist for our wonderment."

One portrait of Casals through the eyes of others during his earliest Russian tours appeared in the intriguing newspaper notice by A. N. Ossovski in the Moscow *Slovo* for November 22, 1906:

> On the stage appeared a tiny, skinny little man carrying an instrument almost as big as himself. . . . Not a man, but a personification of an idea, the exterior shape reduced to a minimum so as only to contain the mere idea of life. . . . He walks carefully, as if afraid of spilling the pent-up emotions. Now he sits down and, not having tuned his cello [he tuned it backstage], he gets ready to join his tone to the

harmonious web of the orchestra. The first stroke of the bow—and a nervous tremor resounds in the depth of thousands of hearts. The eyes of the virtuoso are closed. The world of reality disappears for him, transforms itself into visions, into immaterial images. . . . Certainly, I had in front of me Johann Kreisler [in E. T. A. Hoffman's tale *"Kreisler-Fragmente"*] himself, and his instrument was the same . . . the one into which the living soul . . . has moved. How otherwise would it be possible for a mechanical instrument to sing with such a profound passion, to reveal such important secrets, to be so angry and so caressing?

And wasn't it a living spirit that this Kreisler was communicating with? He would lovingly bend his head toward the instrument as if listening to its whisper. . . . Then at once he would proudly turn his head—all the time without opening his eyes—as if he commanded a crowd of spirits, and these would rush to all the corners of the concert hall to dispatch the orders of their ruler. And the orchestra wasn't an orchestra to him any more, but a single living being. Now he carried on a dialogue with it, now he joined it to sing hymns in one voice. . . .

Being himself a romantic, he played the romantic Schumann—and there, where others had seen only unnecessary technical difficulties, only the form, he got through it and discovered behind it a living substance.

Comfortably established in Siloti's large apartment when he was in St. Petersburg, Casals met everybody of consequence in the musical circles of the city, and such nonmusicians as theatrical designer Léon Bakst and the Czar's doctor, each married to a Siloti sister-in-law. And there was talk—wild, long conversations (in French more often than Russian; many upper-class St. Petersburg children learned to speak French before they learned Russian; almost all also spoke German, and many knew English as well) about music, gossip, and politics. The apartment, comfortable but not unduly ostentatious, was a perpetual open house, and Siloti was a relaxed host.

Casals talked with Rachmaninoff, Rimsky-Korsakov, César Cui, and Glazunov, but there were many others, like the composer Anatol Konstantinovitch Liadov—a taciturn man, secretive about his domestic life (he never received at home and nobody ever saw his wife), with a catlike walk and myopia. Violinist Leopold Auer called, as did the cellists Alexei Davidov and Alexander Wierzbielovich, who looked like Rasputin and drank—if he hadn't, Carl Davidov had said, he would have been one of the world's great cellists. It had been Wierzbielovich, according to the story Casals heard, who had planted drunken kisses on the mouth of the corpse of Tchaikovsky, dead of cholera. Alexei Davidov also drank, as did the diminutive, bespectacled César Cui. Casals came to the rapid conclusion that all Russians drank. "Since *I* do not drink," Rimsky-Korsakov would announce when he arrived, "I can have a glass of vodka."

Casals thought Russia and its people a world very much its own, both fascinating and depressing. He first began to know it through St. Petersburg, Peter the Great's fortress "Window on the West" in the far northwestern corner of the Russian empire, built on salt marsh on either side of the broad Neva River where it debouches into the Gulf of Finland. St. Petersburg was a modern city in comparison with Moscow—the hub of Russia, the "Third Rome," city of the Orthodox church, focus of the reactionary landed aristocracy and home of the long-established business fortunes. A difference of style and values in almost every sphere, including the musical, fueled the traditional antagonism between the two places. Conservative Moscow accepted Tchaikovsky but withheld admiration from Rimsky-Korsakov and Borodin and laughed at Moussorgsky. St. Petersburg—from the beginning, according to Muscovite opinion, tainted with Enlightenment, too fancy, too much concerned with baubles and appearances—flirted with the new French music and scorned Tchaikovsky.

In this strange city, Casals felt himself in the mainstream of Russian music among an assortment of musicians more eccentric than any he had met in Europe—except Emanuel Moór. There was, for example, Alexander Konstantinovitch Glazunov. Glazunov's musical abilities were astonishing. Everything about the art seemed easy for him; he had a phenomenal inner pitch and "the ability to read music and see everything." He was a beautiful pianist—and a very bad conductor, who so loved to conduct he accepted every invitation offered him (both students and professionals liked him so much that when he directed the student orchestras at the conservatory the players did their best to give a good performance in spite of their leader).

Glazunov was forty in 1905—huge, fat, clumsy, slow, a man who usually spoke very softly and deliberately. He was seldom seen to smile—probably because of bad teeth—and was the kind of pedagogue who cannot really teach but from whom it is possible to learn. Named director of the St. Petersburg Conservatory when it was permitted to reopen in the fall of 1905, he was not a very good administrator, but he took the students' problems very much to heart. It was not unusual for Glazunov to make a personal call on a Grand Duke, a rich merchant, or a member of the wealthy aristocracy to plead for scholarship money for a deserving student, and in dozens of cases he cosigned the note of a student who was buying a piano.

Until he left Russia forever in 1928, Glazunov lived in the house—sleeping in the same bed, in the same room—in which he had been born. He had an omnipresent mother who, even when he was in his fifties, would veto a proposed conducting stint in a distant city such as Odessa with "No! You'll catch cold." He had what was spoken of as an "unfortunate illness"—drinking. The bouts were unpredictable, and at first would last a week at a time, until the first signs of delirium tremens sobered him. After he began psychiatric treatment his binges started lasting two weeks.

Glazunov became animated when he talked about national character and folklore in music. Mikhail Glinka, the effective founder of modern Russian music, had been intrigued by Spanish themes (he lived his last years in France and Spain) and—Glazunov contended—had realized the possibilities of Spanish music in his own Russian compositions. Casals concluded that the Russians were passionately attracted by color; he saw that country only in late autumn or winter, and developed the theory that Russians were attracted to the sun-washed southern themes because everything outside was so cold and dismal. The Slavs had an instinctive thirst and need for color that drove them to develop the marvelous spectacle of ballet and to seek relief from the chill in music inspired by the Mediterranean lands. Casals admired Rimsky-Korsakov's *Capriccio Espagnol* which, although basically Russian in approach, he thought a remarkable intepretation of the Spanish spirit "through the eyes of the Slav." Even if Glinka had exploited the potential of Spanish music, Casals was not certain Glazunov had. When he played Alexander Konstantinovitch's

"Spanish Serenade" in his Russian programs and elsewhere Casals made some discreet changes in the melodic line.

Casals could derive a slight wry amusement from the Russians' idea that one of their composers had been able to realize the possibilities in music of the spirit of a country so unlike theirs as Spain, but in nonmusical conversations he felt the disturbing undertone of a Russian conception that the country's destiny was to dominate the world in every way.

Literary talk at Siloti's included the name of Pauline Viardot-García's friend Ivan Turgenev, and mention of Gogol, Pushkin, Dostoevski, Anton Chekhov (who died the year before Casals' first trip), Leo Tolstoi, and two much younger writers, Ivan Bunin and Maxim Gorki. There was little disagreement about the importance of Glinka in Russian music, but there were arguments about the work and worth of others, bearers of such melodious names as Stassov and Dargomizhsky.

César Cui and Nikolai Rimsky-Korsakov were the two survivors still active of The Mighty Five who had brought Russian nationalism into existence in music during the sixties. Of the other three, Alexander Borodin and Modest Moussorgsky were dead, and Mily Balakirev had withdrawn in 1895 into religious obsession (a state, Rachmaninoff called it, of gloomy bigotry and misanthropic introspection).

Cui was seventy when Casals met him at Siloti's, a small man dapper in his uniform. He was professor of military fortification at the Military Academy and had also been Nicholas II's music teacher. Rachmaninoff and others considered Cui no longer to be taken seriously, and it may have been in Siloti's drawing room that Casals heard Glazunov's comment on hearing Cui's children's opera *The Snow Knight:* "He should be in the conservatory . . . on scholarship."

Cui appeared to many a kind old gentleman who enjoyed the company of young women and never missed a performance of any of his own works, "even if it was one song of two minutes' duration. He would usually sit in a box, resplendent in his General's uniform—dark green, with bright red lapels and lining—and medals, with some attractive young female at his side, and acknowledge the applause, trying to warm it up into an ovation, which he often succeeded in doing." Cui's Russian nationalism comes through best in his operas, none of which survived him (he died in 1918, ten years after Rimsky), and he is best remembered for a single piece of fluff, an "Orientale" from a group of twenty-four violin and piano pieces he called *Kaleidoscope*.

Casals found him quite delightful.

Casals remembered Nikolai Rimsky-Korsakov most for a flattering gesture he considered enormously modest on the part of a famous composer. On one of his early trips to Russia, Casals accompanied Siloti to the white-blue-and-gold auditorium of the Maryinski Theater to hear Chaliapin sing in Rimsky's new opera *Le coq d'or*. During the first intermission Glazunov appeared in Siloti's box to say that the composer had been nervous to learn of Casals' presence, fearful he might not like the music. Casals thought Rimsky's attitude very friendly and sent back a message that he was enjoying everything thoroughly.

Casals discovered other things he admired in the tall naval architect-turned-composer who when unhappy had a habit of frowning and plucking at his full beard. Rimsky-Korsakov was diligent and efficient, and tried to foster those qualities in his students. His ethical influence was tremendous, and he would not tolerate signs of laziness among his pupils. He was friendly to and conscientious about all his students, including those who did not have much talent. When he was removed from the directorship and the St. Petersburg Conservatory closed in the spring of 1905, Rimsky continued to give lessons in his home, free of charge. He was always punctual and seldom missed a class; he shared his experience, his ideas, and his prejudices with conservatory students for more than three decades.

As appealing as anything to Casals was the fact that Rimsky-Korsakov loved music. "You do not *love* music enough," he once reproached a class. "Amateurs *love* music. They play chamber music until all hours of the night!" Rimsky attended rehearsals and performances because he felt he needed it, not because it was a duty, and listened attentively, usually with score in hand.

The preferences, not to say prejudices, of the leading figures in any given musical community tend to affect what is heard there and Rimsky-Korsakov had strong opinions. He was antagonistic to Tchaikovsky both because he was irritated by what he considered technical shortcomings and because he was annoyed by Tchaikovsky's success. He was disdainful of Rachmaninoff and Arensky, hated Richard Strauss, and Richard Wagner was anathema. Russian professional musicians of the time did not appreciate Verdi and abhorred Puccini; Rimsky's attitude toward both has been called utter contempt. He was also often unhappy on the subject of the public: "The audience, each of them separately, is right. But together, it is just an overgrown fool." In the St. Petersburg Conservatory during Rimsky-Korsakov's administration the exclusive outside influences were Schumann, Berlioz, and Liszt, so that at the turn of the century the students "never received the impression that a reverent attitude toward Haydn or Mozart, not to speak of Bach, even existed," according to conductor Nikolai Malko, who had been one of them. Rimsky exploded at compositional irregularities in Beethoven: "How could he do it? It must have been his illness—the deafness." And once César Cui reported: "Just imagine! N. A. insists that whether it is Ysaÿe or just some other violinist playing in tune, it is all the same to him!"

The Russia Casals found himself in was hardly a semibarbaric milieu, although there were many disturbing undertones. Every student he met seemed to him straight out of Dostoevski; some of them—committed to changing the bad things of their time, longing to work for the people and to open new horizons—frustrated, furious, and realizing their impotence against the system, turned for refuge and comfort to music. The country's conservatories, good and influential for fifty years, were now superlative. Russia was mad for Italian opera to an extent Spain had never been. Kiev, Odessa, Moscow, and Tiflis each had an opera company with an annual season of up to eight or nine months. The better Russian companies drew the great European stars (Caruso sang his first Russian *Aïda* in December 1898), and success in Italian roles in Odessa was often as important to an international career as in the crucial houses of Italy. Such artists as Josef Hofmann and Eugène Ysaÿe, and soon Casals, could fill the three-thousand-seat houses in St. Petersburg and Moscow any time they played. People would stand in line on the street all night despite snowstorms or subzero weather to buy inexpensive tickets.

The burgeoning recording industry realized some of its biggest early profits in Russia (the Deutsche Gramophon Company erected a separate pressing plant to provide disks solely for the Russian market), and there were gramophone shops in every large Russian city by 1900. The especially lordly establishment on the Nevsky Prospekt in St. Petersburg, run by an astute merchant named Rappaport, had soft carpets and potted palms and was even more overwhelming than that of the brothers Pathé in Paris. (Rappaport was responsible for a recording development that had no small effect on Casals' own later career. It was he who convinced Deutsche Gramophon by 1901 to begin recording leading singers of the Imperial Russian Opera—including Chaliapin—in serious music and to sell the product in deluxe, expensive editions called Red Label Records, to distinguish them from the routine black-labeled productions of gypsy singers, comedians, tinny dance orchestras, and elocutionists.)

St. Petersburg's theaters made more than one European manager pale with envy, and there were four active opera houses. One of these, in the People's Palace—a complex that included theaters, concert halls, and restaurants—had been built by Nicholas II in 1901 so the ordinary people could hear music and see drama for as little as twenty kopeks. The intellectual and cultural achievements of the first years after Nicholas came to the Romanov throne in 1894 were so glittering that the period has been called both the Silver Age of Russia and the Russian Renaissance.

The dynastic royal family was receptive to music of a sort. Nicholas' father, the autocratic Czar Alexander III, had frequently summoned small chamber-music groups and dominated them with his bassoon-playing. Russia's last Czarina, Alexandra, Nicholas' wife and Queen Victoria's favorite granddaughter, played the piano "almost brilliantly." Casals never saw her.

Although he never performed in the imperial residences in Russia, Casals was invited to visit or play in some of the magnificent palaces and residences of the princes and Grand Dukes, the aristocracy, and the prosperous bourgeoisie in St. Petersburg located both on islands in the Neva and on the mainland. The hereditary wealth of the Russian nobility and the fortunes gathered rapidly by some businessmen were phenomenal. The private palaces, which had their own ballrooms, were kept very hot at the time of year Casals visited Russia and were often filled with palms and foliage plants from the Crimea or flowers sent by special train from the South of France. Private owners had fantastic collections of objets d'art, paintings, and sculpture, but none could match the royal collection housed in the Hermitage Museum in an annex of the Winter Palace, a treasure of jewels and art amassed by virtually limitless wealth for more than three centuries.

Much of the life Pablo Casals observed in Russia after he became famous was lavish and extravagant. But distress was obvious to him everywhere underneath the opulence: he felt the poor were totally controlled by the bureaucracy and under the yoke of the aristocrats, who flaunted their luxury provocatively and scandalously. Nor did all the demonstrators realize the issues completely, he found. Casals persuaded an unwilling Siloti to drive with him to one of the bridges across the Neva, within sight and sound of the action, in November 1905. Casals heard shots in the distance and saw smoke drifting toward them, the wide river still unfrozen and dark gray-green, and a man running past shouting wildly. Siloti translated into French. The man was yelling "Long live the republic of the Czar!"

Pablo Casals' most horrified memory of prewar Russia was of leaving a palace one night after having played for a Russian prince and his guests. He encountered a double line of servants who threw themselves onto the floor ahead of him. Casals was aghast; there was no way to get through the corridor without stepping on them. "Walk over them," the prince said. "That is why they are there."

Casals remained in St. Petersburg nearly three weeks in November 1905, then gave concerts in Vilna and Warsaw on his way back to Paris. His Russian tours generally lasted three weeks to a month and covered much more territory but he never missed recitals in St. Petersburg and a visit with Alexander Siloti. Lev Ginsburg of the Moscow Conservatory lists St. Petersburg, Moscow, Warsaw, Kiev, Riga, Lodz, and Lvov as the most important Russian cities in which Casals played between 1905 and the 1913–1914 season. (Professor Ginsburg has also tabulated part of Casals' repertoire in Russia during those years: He played the Bach suites—always. He offered concertos by Haydn, Tartini, Schumann, Davidov, Dvořák, Lalo, Saint-Saëns, and Emanuel Moór. Sonatas included those of Boccherini, Locatelli, Valentini, Beethoven, Chopin, Rubinstein, Grieg, Strauss, Julius Röntgen, and Rachmaninoff. He performed pieces by, among others, Boëllmann, Davidov and Glazunov, Saint-Saëns and Fauré.) For these tours Casals normally appeared alone, as soloist with orchestra or in recital with piano accompanist, although he did play chamber music with Siloti and others, and Guilhermina Suggia performed the Moór two-cello concerto with him in St. Petersburg and Moscow in the 1908–1909 season. (The Moór double was not a great success, although the lyric intermezzo had to be repeated and the finale—a burst of fireworks—was dazzling always.)

During his fifth and sixth Russian tours, in 1909 and 1910, Casals began a musical collaboration with Sergei Rachmaninoff that resulted in performances together later in Western Europe and in the United States. In Moscow he met Siloti's unusual and wildly talented relative Alexander Scriabin, then in his late thirties, a handsome man with waxed mustaches and a small beard. Scriabin's composition had progressed from beautifully constructed Chopinesque works through Wagnerism to a nebulous, musically rambling and tonally free mysticism that was at once strange and powerful. When he and Casals met, Scriabin had just completed his last orchestral work, *Prometheus: The Poem of Fire*, which was to be performed not only with piano and orchestra but also with a special "keyboard of light" that projected colors on a screen as an integral part of the composition. Casals was more interested in the harmonies put together by this slender, nervous man, who was at the time also giving piano lessons to young Boris Pasternak, than in his light-keyboard. Discussing those harmonies, Casals sat down at a piano and played a long Arabic melody, the sort of thing that had had influence on native Spanish music. Scriabin contended that such historic threads had nothing to do with his own work, nor would he agree that his harmony had anything in common with the language of either Debussy or Rimsky. He was already seeking to compose a new metaphysical pronouncement, a summation of the history of man from the dawn of time to final destruction; it would consist not only of music but also of drama, poetry, dance, colors, perfumes, and a new verbal language of exclamations and would be performed in a great temple constructed for the purpose in India. Scriabin died in the spring of 1915 after he had completed only the text and fragmentary sketches of the music for this colossal *chef d'oeuvre*.

Some of his Russian acquaintances asked Casals about the

United States when they learned he had been there, especially about its customs—Scriabin had gone to America in 1906, where he had performed his piano concerto and begun a tour that was suddenly broken off. Scriabin returned home immediately when faced with the choice between voluntary departure and deportation on a charge of moral turpitude after it was discovered that the woman traveling as Mme Scriabin was his common-law wife.

Casals also met Serge Koussevitzky who, then in his middle thirties, was devoting himself to orchestral conducting after a distinguished career as Europe's premier double-bass virtuoso. (Since the solo literature for the double bass is even more limited than that for the cello, he often performed cello concertos on his own splendid but cumbersome instrument.) In 1905 Koussevitzky married Natalie Ushkova, the very intelligent daughter of a tea millionaire. Thereafter he led the life of a gentleman and art patron as well as of a dedicated musician, with sumptuous houses in Moscow and Berlin. Alfredo Casella, who was a Moscow guest in December 1909, remembered that Koussevitzky "kept in his home a symphonic orchestra [a wedding present from his father-in-law] on which he 'practiced' every day, as if it had been a piano." Koussevitzky made his first appearance as a conductor in Berlin in 1908, and the same year founded in Russia the Editions Russes de Musique, a house devoted to publication of new Russian music. Early the next year he instituted a distinguished concert series in Moscow, in which Casals played, that began to rival Siloti's in St. Petersburg.

Since Casals was never in Russia in spring or summer he could not accept Koussevitzky's invitation to join one of his summer musical cruises down the Volga, although the idea and purpose appealed to him. The first of these month-long trips, in 1910, took the Koussevitzkys, a number of excellent musicians from Europe and America, the full orchestra, and service personnel by steamer twelve hundred miles along the great river, making music on board and debarking every night to play for village and rural audiences who had never before heard a concert, "agitating the peasantry with Beethoven and Scriabin."

Casals had been pleased to learn that Siloti also took his music into the countryside, although on a more modest scale. Whenever he could he traveled to provincial villages to perform, always including something by Bach. "What an eccentric, silly thing to do, playing Bach for peasants!" observed a city relative. "Not a bit," retorted Siloti. "It is so great that those with any openness to music will understand it."

During Casals' seventh annual Russian tour, in Moscow in January 1912 at a benefit concert for the Friends of Music, Casals, Ysaÿe, and Siloti joined forces to play trios by Beethoven, Mendelssohn, Brahms, and Tchaikovsky. The critics said they found it difficult to speak of ensemble in the case of three such strong personalities. Ysaÿe proposed that he and Casals also play the Brahms double concerto together. Their paths had crossed since the turn of the century in Paris; they had played chamber music together for fun there and, after 1908, in the summer at Ysaÿe's country place in Belgium, but they had never before appeared as joint soloists with orchestra. They played the Brahms with Siloti in Moscow, then in St. Petersburg under the direction of Albert Coates, a young St. Petersburg-born, German-trained conductor who had been assistant to the hypnotic Arthur Nikisch at the Leipzig Opera. After the Moscow performance Ysaÿe wrote his wife Louise: "Casals is really a sensitive, profound artist, musical in the broadest sense of the word. No detail escapes him, everything is focused with tact, wisdom, and discernment and always without 'pose,' without head movements. His body moves well; the action is the movement of the thought behind it and is right, alive, full of emotion to the very depth of the soul. . . ."

Others who wrote about Casals' appearances in Russia at the time stressed several things again and again: the tone, the "singing"; the precision of intonation; the controlled freedom of the playing; the staggering technical mastery. On one point there was unanimity: with Casals everything was subordinate to the music. Intellect and emotion were certainly present; the control, the gorgeous sound, the blinding virtuosity, the fresh nuance were all there, but the essence of the music was supreme.

Searching for the ultimate Russian superlative, public and critics began calling Casals "the Chaliapin of the cello." A strangely persistent comparison; sixty years after Casals' first trip to Russia, the individualist British publisher Victor Gollancz tried unsuccessfully to find a single image that could evoke Chaliapin's voice. "The smell of burning logs in the distance; of wood violets; of earth after an April shower," he wrote, "and something too of the look of a flame rising high and steady but with a little smoke about it . . . think of autumn at its gravest and most beautiful; of words deep with compassion; of Casals' cello—that above everything: for Chaliapin had all the qualities of a great singer and something . . . I have found . . . in Chaliapin's singing and Casals' playing almost alone. . . . Some unanalysable residue. . . ."

As soloist with the Moscow Philharmonic directed by Rachmaninoff, Casals played the Saint-Saëns cello concerto on December 14, 1913, his last concert in Russia.

When Pablo Casals stepped into the snowy street outside the Hall of the Nobility, St. Petersburg, after his first concert in Russia, he saw the ranks of sleighs with their wretched, noisy coachmen and members of the elegantly dressed audience making their way to one or another, sidestepping beggars. Everything spawns fear in Russia, he thought, the luxury quite as much as the misery.

He was not surprised when news of full-scale revolution in Russia came in 1917. He was concerned for friends there, most of all for Alexander Siloti and his family, but there was nothing he could do immediately. There was no word until a letter reached Casals in Barcelona in 1919 telling him the Silotis had reached Antwerp. Casals traveled at once to Belgium. His friends looked to him like ghosts, and their story horrified and infuriated him. Siloti's piano and fine library had been confiscated; for two years he, his wife, and five children lived in the kitchen and one adjoining room of their former spacious quarters—the rest was occupied by young members of the new revolutionary establishment. The only item of value they had been able to salvage was a necklace. (Casals always believed that money from its sale enabled the family to escape from Russia; actually British Intelligence got them out to Finland.) Casals quietly gave Siloti some money for immediate needs and set about contacting friends to help him find a permanent position. Siloti gave well-received concerts in England in 1920 and 1921, performed on the Continent, and in 1922 accepted an appointment to the faculty of the Juilliard School of Music in New York, where he taught until 1944. In the late 1930s, after the revolution in Spain, when Casals broadcast an appeal for funds to help child victims, one of Siloti's daughters who had been working in New York sent back the amount Casals had given her father in Antwerp, with interest.

From the day he saw the Siloti family again in Belgium after their escape Pablo Casals never wanted to go back to Russia. Of course there are excesses when there is revolution, he said, but what gives the leaders of revolution the right to think that under the pretext of establishing a new and better social order they can persecute blindly precisely those people who have practiced fraternity with the workers and the people? A theoretically good end does not justify evil means, in music or in life. "I have protested against inhuman means," Casals said slowly and distinctly when he was ninety-five years old. "I shall always protest."

14

TEN CONCERTS in Holland with Julius Röntgen in January 1906 followed Casals' return from his first trip to Russia. Friendship with Röntgen and his family was inseparable from the thought of Holland for Casals from 1903 until late 1914, when war intervened. The relationship emerges as one of the warmest and most gratifying of Casals' life. His letters to Röntgen between 1903 and 1914 survive as the most important group written to a single correspondent during his early performing career; a sense of close and admiring friendship and professional association runs through them all. They also give an idea of the constant movement from place to place during Casals' late twenties and thirties.

Julius Röntgen was a little more than twenty years older than Casals—born in Leipzig in May 1855 to the former Paulina Klengel, a member of the musically distinguished family, and Engelbert Röntgen, leader of the Gewandhaus orchestra and a cousin of the physicist who discovered the X ray. The Klengels "could raise a piano quintet among themselves, and together with their Röntgen cousins a small orchestra." Julius started to compose when he was eight; he learned to play the organ on an old instrument that had once belonged to Johann Sebastian Bach. By fifteen he had begun to develop into a fine performer of chamber music. Ethel Smyth, who was a student in Leipzig in the 1870s, spoke of him in her memoirs as "composer, viola-player, pianist, and all the rest of it." That vigorous but not unduly sentimental English woman composer recalled the natural *Gemütlichkeit*, the aura of comfortable warmth and ready friendliness, as well as the musicality of the family home. And, she added: "There was one more belonging to that household, a dear Swedish girl called Amanda Meyer [Maier], violinist and composer, who afterwards married Julius; and then for the first time I saw a charming blend of art and courtship very common in those days. Thus it must have been in Bach's time, thus with the old Röntgens, but I don't see how it can come off quite in the same way under modern conditions."

Julius Röntgen and Amanda Maier were married in 1873; in 1877, Julius assumed his father's Dutch citizenship and they settled in Amsterdam, where for fifty-five years he worked as pianist, conductor, and professor at the Amsterdam Conservatory. He also made frequent concert appearances in Scandinavia, England, and throughout the Continent. He came to be known as one of the great chamber-music players of a period that included Joseph Joachim (a close friend) and his colleagues, Brahms, Clara Schumann, Arnold Josef Rosé in Vienna, the Flonzaley Quartet. Röntgen was also a gifted and prolific composer, essentially a romantic. He was much interested in old Dutch music, and his arrangements and editions of early Netherlands songs and dances are important. His production was considerable—twelve symphonies, three piano concertos, three operas, music for cinema, songs, and a large body of chamber works.

When Casals met him, Röntgen was not yet fifty and was well established in an influential and productive stratum of the musical life of the time. He had a charming home on the Vondels Park in Amsterdam. His first wife had died in 1894, leaving two sons who were schoolboys when Casals first came onto the scene— Julius, a violist, and Engelbert, a talented cellist who soon became Casals' student and friend (and whose instrumental preference filled out the Röntgen Trio a few years later). Röntgen's second wife was Amorie van der Hoeven, sister of the wife of British poet Robert Trevelyan. The names of the couple's three musical sons were mementos of parental friendships with musicians:

Johannes, who was born in 1899 and became a pianist-composer; Edvard, also a cellist, born 1902; and Joachim, born in 1906, a violist.

On the second of December 1904, Röntgen wrote to Edvard Grieg in Norway: ". . . beautiful days with Bauer and Casals, two of the best artists I know, not only virtuosos but also musicians of the first order. For me the cellist surpasses all I know. To hear him play one of the solo suites of Bach is an indescribable delight. . . ."

A Casals letter to Röntgen, dated July 9, 1905, from 20 Villa Molitor in Paris, carries the salutation to a dear elder brother (*"Mon cher frère aîné"*) and closes *"votre sincere frère cadet"* but is couched in the formal second-person *vous*. The short letter concerned confusion of arrangements between an Amsterdam concert manager named Stumpff and Casals' agent Strakosch. (Things seemed arranged to Röntgen, who wrote Grieg in late September that he was to have a tour of ten concerts with Casals in January, but Casals wrote on the tenth of October that he was still waiting: Stumpff "promised me a final decision last Saturday, and I am still without news."

Close and dependable scheduling was becoming distinctly necessary. Casals had already played on three continents in the first half of the preceding year. During the concert seasons, particularly in the first fifteen years of his career, Casals was seldom able to be in one place for long—an occupational fact of life for most musical virtuosos, as for their troubador predecessors. A life of friends not often seen, of admirers and adulation and—depending on the artist's requirements of himself—of high art; but also one of drudgery, nervousness, discomfort, and loneliness. At a conservative estimate, Pablo Casals gave more than five thousand public performances from the time of his Paris début until he was closed in at Prades by World War II.

Usually he returned to Spain every year for three weeks or a month in August or September. Carlos' chronic bronchial condition had become worse as he reached his late forties. Pablo bought a pleasant small house and farm called Del Moliner (The Windmill) for him at the village of Bonastre in the mountains between Vendrell and Barcelona. Carlos was happy there, living quietly and teaching music to the children of the area. The rest of the

Casals in the studio of Dutch artist
Charles Gruppe, 1907

family divided its time among Barcelona, Vendrell–San Salvador, and Bonastre. Doña Pilar supervised the development and activity of her two younger sons—Luis was fifteen in October 1905 and Enrique thirteen in June. Enrique was studying violin and building a collection of the post cards his oldest brother sent from faraway places. Doña Pilar began to tell Pablo that he should find a place for a permanent home for himself in Catalonia.

After his holiday in Spain in 1905—in his October tenth letter to Röntgen—Casals thanked his dear friend for his "lovely work," a sonata in G minor for cello and piano: "I received it the day before yesterday and played it yesterday with Mademoiselle Thérèse Chaigneau, who read very well. I am very proud to have been to some degree the cause of your idea of composing it. I like it tremendously, you know, and hardly dare tell you because I identify with it so completely that I come to believe I have composed it myself.

"I shall work at it with love and await the moment I can play it with you—hoping that we can include it in some of our programs in Holland."

The January 1906 commitments included an appearance by Casals as soloist in the Schumann cello concerto in the Concertgebouw on the third under Mengelberg's baton. The program ranged from Wagner and the Tchaikovsky "Pathétique" to Dr. Ludwig Wüllner from Berlin in Max Schillings' declamation with orchestra *Das Hexenlied*. By the ninth Röntgen was reporting happily to Grieg that he had already had seven concerts with Casals—so far as he is concerned, more than ever absolutely the best of all cellists. Casals, starting his thirtieth year of life, was also radiant:

Paris 11 January 1906

My very dear older brother

I have thought of you constantly since my departure from Amsterdam—I am still under the spell of my sojourn with you and those performances of that superb music with you and Mme Röntgen—it was pure art and much more, made with devotion and religious exaltation!

You have given me much joy, dear friend, because I treasure your spirit, and on our marvelous journeys along the path of beauty I have felt you to reflect the same divine sensation. Alas, it happens so seldom.

[He has stayed in Amsterdam to hear Marteau play Moór's violin concerto.] Moore has written me from Leipzig, where his first cello concerto was performed (by Mlle Caponsacchi) to say he received your letter and what great pleasure it gave him.

À bientôt, dear friend. I send everyone my deep affection

your younger brother
Pablo Casals
20 Villa Molitor
Paris XVIᵉ

Oh! When I passed through The Hague Boogaard told me he sent the orchestra material of the Schumann concerto to you—is that right? If so, would you be good enough to mail it to me, because I need it. Thanks and forgive!

Röntgen wrote Casals that Edvard Grieg and his wife were coming to Holland; he was eager that they should meet. He also brought up the subject of Casals' appearances in Vienna, where Röntgen had been giving recitals for years. Röntgen had written in German, which Casals said in his answer toward the end of January he had understood well. He would be happy to play the sonata of "your great friend Grieg—and we will have to arrange the question of dates." Then he turned to the proposed Austrian performances:

> I am much obliged to you for proposing to give some concerts with you in Vienna; but I consider it unfair that I should profit from the name you have in a country in which I am absolutely unknown. Here is my thought: I should like to begin by being engaged for some large orchestral concerts; after that—we could start our own concerts because the public and the press will already know me a bit better. Tell me if I am wrong. . . .

A fortnight later Casals' name appeared for the first time on two programs of the Società del Quartetto di Milano, a concert society founded in 1864; Lucien Wurmser was the pianist. Their first program, at 3:00 P.M. on February 11, 1906, listed:

Beethoven:	*Sonata in G minor*
Valentini:	*Sonata* for violoncello
Handel:	*Gavotte in G* for piano
Schumann:	*Novelletta in F* for piano
Mendelssohn:	*Scherzo* (opus 16)
Saint-Saëns:	*Study in form of a waltz* for piano
Grieg:	*Sonata in A minor* for piano and cello

The announced program two days later was:

Beethoven:	*Sonata in A major*
Mozart:	*Variations in F* for piano
Chopin:	*Berceuse, Waltz, and Polonaise* (piano)
Fauré:	*Élégie—Siciliana* for cello and piano
Saint-Saëns:	*Allegro appassionato* for cello and piano
Boëllmann:	*Sonata* for piano and cello

It was after the second concert that Pablo Casals met Mieczyslaw Horszowski. Doña Pilar and Enrique had already met Miecio and his mother in Barcelona, where at thirteen Horszowski had given several solo recitals. The two mothers had liked each other, and the boys had gotten along well—Horszowski was only days older than Enrique and much farther along in a musical career. He had studied at the conservatory in his Polish birthplace, Lemberg, and at seven became a prize pupil of Theodor Leschetizky in Vienna. (Leschetizky was nearly seventy and most of his students received an occasional lesson with the master but were supervised the rest of the time by one of Leschetizky's assistants; the Professor always taught young Horszowski personally.) The boy made an impressive début in Vienna before he was nine; when he played for Casals between the end of his concert and the departure of his train on the thirteenth of February 1906, Horszowski and his mother were on their way to London, South America, and Horszowski's first appearance in New York. Twenty-one years later, as Mussolini was coming to power, Horszowski was Casals' piano collaborator when he played the last time for the Società Quartetto di Milano.

Toward the end of February 1906 the Röntgens, the Griegs, and Casals were together in the Röntgen home. To Casals the Norwegian composer seemed quite old, a tiny man who looked smaller because he had a slightly bent back. His white-haired head seemed disproportionately large for the rest of him; he reminded Casals of a better-looking Albert Einstein, with alert, unusually blue eyes and a gentle expression. In a photograph taken at the time Grieg, rather dapper, looks like a refined Mark Twain; his wife, even tinier, has an irrepressibly elfin expression.

Röntgen and Casals played the cello sonata Röntgen had written for Casals, and Casals played the Bach C minor cello suite. Grieg found the performance dramatic and that night wrote to his Norwegian publisher "This man does not *perform*, he resurrects!" After the Bach, Grieg went to the piano and accompanied his wife in the song cycle he had written for her during their engagement. When these two tiny people were not making music, they reminded Ethel Smyth of wooden figures from a Noah's Ark; when they performed, audiences went mad. Nina Grieg sang in Norwegian and a listener often had only a vague idea of the meaning, but a "transfiguration" took place—"one wept, laughed, and thrilled with excitement or horror without knowing why. The song over, she again became Noah's wife." Her singing was, Casals remembered, delicious, her voice flutelike.

There was talk of Liszt, whom Röntgen had called on with his mother at fifteen, in 1870; he had been staggered by the music in the house but was scathingly funny about the idolatry, the fuss and incense, flattery and hand-kissing that surrounded the old eagle. Grieg remembered his own first meeting with Liszt, when he had brought along one of his violin sonatas. The Master took a score he had never seen, a sonata for two instruments. "He was literally all over the whole piano at once, without missing a note, and how he played! With grandeur, beauty, genius, unique comprehension. I think I laughed—" Grieg said, "laughed like a child." There was also reverent talk of Bach, about which Casals had some private reservations. Grieg, like so many nineteenth-century musicians, had done some "improvement" of certain works of Bach by cutting and rewriting. It was still the period of tinkering with composers' music—Liszt rewrote Schubert, for example, and Siloti adjusted Liszt, and almost everybody turned a hand to revising Bach. (Grieg nonetheless was thoroughly annoyed when the tempestuous Venezuelan pianist Teresa Carreño, who had splendid octaves, decided to end his piano concerto with them rather than the arpeggios he had written.)

Grieg was a skillful pianist, but he never pretended to be a concert artist. Casals found him cultivated and thoroughly *simpático*, with a simplicity and purity of spirit that success had not tarnished. A day or so following the afternoon at the Röntgens, the composer was in Rotterdam when Casals and Röntgen performed Grieg's cello sonata, a graceful work that continued to appear on Casals' recital programs for years. Casals could not remember later whether Grieg had conducted: he was not a very good conductor, and knew it. Once he was invited for an enormous fee to conduct an entire program, not merely the portion that was his own work. He refused, saying he was too bad a director. "The public won't mind," persisted the manager. "They'll be there to *see* you conduct. Furthermore, since you conduct your own music surely you can get along well enough with the others'." Grieg had shaken his head angrily: "Any fool can conduct his own music, but that is no reason for murdering other people's!"

Harold Bauer also met Grieg at Röntgen's this visit—he and Casals were giving recitals together—and hoped to see him again in Paris, where Grieg was to conduct a Colonne concert. (Grieg canceled at the last moment, incensed by the Dreyfus affair, explaining his refusal to visit a country "where such injustice is possible.")

Casals and Bauer rejoined forces in Spain in late summer, where they encountered one of the most bizarre hazards of their careers. Both artists had had nerves shattered by the totally unexpected explosion of a photographer's flash light during a performance; both had been attacked by mosquitos while playing in South America. A piano collapsed during a Bauer recital and, he said, he had been arrested in a small city outside Moscow for playing rather than dancing the Hungarian dance on the program. Casals would soon have to try to play his cello on which the varnish had gone tacky because a servant had leaned it against a radiator in a private house on a winter night. He had already ripped the skirt off Blanche Marchesi as she strode onto the stage of the Salle Gaveau in Paris by inadvertently stepping on her long train. And both Bauer and Casals had more than once used scowls and even words to silence noisy audiences. But when Bauer reproved a man who persisted in talking loudly during his and Casals' recital in La Coruña in August 1906, the gentleman—Señor Jaime Quiroga, son of the Marquesa Pardo Bazan—sent two military officers backstage as his seconds with a challenge. A special cable to the *Musical Age* datelined August 23 from San Sebastián reported that both Herr Bauer and Señor Casals had in turn appointed seconds and come to San Sebastián to await developments: "As far as can be seen, there is all probability that a duel will be fought."

Casals passed his thirtieth birthday on December 29, 1906, and Julius Röntgen was never again saluted in his letters as an older brother by a *frère cadet*. The affectionate tone and phrases continue, subtly quieter and stronger; the polite *vous* persists. (Letters from Röntgen to Casals are not to be found. When Casals gave up his Villa Molitor house in 1914 he stored packing cases of books, documents, letters, and souvenirs in a place that appeared secure. After the war he discovered there had been a police search; all the boxes had been opened, papers were strewn about, and files of letters from Röntgen, Saint-Saëns, Fauré, Richard Strauss, and Emanuel Moór, among others, had disappeared. Inquiries to the French police and government agencies during the next fifty years went unanswered.)

Casals and Bauer made a tour in Holland—eight concerts in ten days—in January 1907; Casals' next letters to Röntgen concern musical matters and scheduling to a great extent. A hint of the ceaseless pace of performing and travel, often for a considerable distance, is in a letter from Casals to Röntgen confirming approaching dates. The preceding May Casals had asked Röntgen to shift a proposed engagement for February 16 because he was to play in Dresden on the nineteenth, and before the sixteenth he was also to be a long way from Amsterdam.

Paris 13 February 1907
My dear friend!
The 22 – 24 – 25 are understood—but I do not know if I shall be able to do anything about Viotta [director of the Conservatory of The Hague from 1896 until 1917]—I play the twenty-seventh in The Hague. Would you let me know? It would give me great pleasure if you will send me the cello part of your sonata to Leipzig, Hotel Furstenhof, where I arrive the evening of the seventeenth. I leave Paris the evening of the sixteenth. If you think you have time to send it to Paris I should prefer that.

Even the handwriting in this letter seems hurried, but Casals added:

I was happy to meet your sister. By lineage she has everything it takes to be a musician, and I liked her.
A thousand affectionate regards for all of you—also for our dear friend Madame Tieventhal.
I am in agreement with the programs you have proposed.

By the third week in March 1907 much of the fall and winter season was booked, but Casals was pleased at the prospect of recitals with Röntgen in Denmark:

I am happy about your good trip to the North [Casals wrote Röntgen on March 21] and congratulate you on the decoration . . . it surely has never been better conferred! You flatter me, and I thank you for having thought of me to give concerts with you in Copenhagen. I accept with the greatest pleasure. I am going to give you an idea of my occupied time in October and November to arrange Copenhagen. . . .

From 24 Oct to 12 Nov   Spanish tour

From 15 Nov to 15 Dec   Dutch tour

I will therefore be free before Spain and after Holland—for you to choose. As to terms, I do not really know what to say . . . I want only not to make obstacles and I shrink from doing that by letting you fix the guarantees. Arrange that yourself and I know that you will do it for the best.

Casals had hoped to arrange some evenings of modern piano and cello sonatas in Paris in October 1906, but they did not take place until April 1907. After plans were firm, he wrote Röntgen on March 24, 1907, confirming his idea of giving two concerts, on the eighteenth and twenty-second of April, and asking if Röntgen still has "the amiable intention of coming to Paris for one of these sessions and to take the piano part of your *two* sonatas, the second and third."

. . . These two performances will be quite special. To avoid a mixture of public I have decided to invite artists and people sensitive to the manifestations of art. There will be no paying places at all. This will therefore be completely artistic, and I should be so happy to be able to play your two works.

I have been looking at home for your G minor sonata and cannot find it. Is it by chance possible for you to bring it?

How would you like to play the 2 sonatas—together (I mean one after the other), with rehearsal or without; or separated by the sonatas of other authors—?

I am so happy to be giving this festival myself—it will be first of all a homage offered to Masters—— What day do you prefer, 18 or 22—?

Röntgen chose one appearance on each program. The eight sonatas were modern; work by Julius Röntgen, Emanuel Moór, Max Reger, Alfredo Casella, Ernst von Dohnányi, Georges Enesco, and Jean Huré. Röntgen, Enesco, Huré, and Casella played the piano part of their works. The two concerts also introduced to Paris a young Spanish pianist named Bienvenido Socías, who played the Dohnányi and Moór sonatas with Casals; Casals had actually invited Socías to Paris with the thought that his fellow Vendrelleño would work with him as an accompanist, but Socías preferred to try for a solo career. Casals' Paris manager at the time, Arthur Dandelot, arranged the "Homage to Masters" for the Salle Berlioz, 55 rue de Clichy. Casals performed the cello part of each sonata and underwrote the expenses.

Röntgen wrote Grieg a week later, telling him about the evenings:

> Both concerts were very fine, a distinguished, completely artistic public, and the success of the enterprise was extraordinarily great. Only, eight sonatas were too much and I often had the feeling that one composer was killing another. Casals played admirably and with indefatigable perseverence to the end. All eight sonatas were first hearings in Paris. One agreeable work is the sonata by the Rumanian Enesco, composed in his seventeenth year. Enesco is one of the best violinists and he played the piano part of his sonata perfectly.

Back in Paris in early June to show Casals a new cello sonata he had completed, Röntgen sent a further report to Grieg in Norway. His son Engelbert is highly enthusiastic about Casals' teaching, he says, adding that it is quite wonderful how Casals "develops all technique from a purely musical point of view. The musical phrase fixes the fingering. Thus all virtuosity stands in service of the work of art. For us this sounds natural, but how few do it that way now."

After Casals' Danish and Spanish tours, he was back in the Netherlands for a month beginning November 15. Röntgen reported on the eighteenth to Nina Grieg (Edvard Grieg had died on September 7, 1907) that Casals and Suggia were staying with them for some days and that they had given a first performance of one of Grieg's quartets: "It was a singular feeling for me to think that the quartet now sounded for the first time and that Edvard never heard it. . . . Now you must hear who played: Harold Bauer, the great pianist, had first violin and played really very well. Casals played second violin and held the violin like a cello between his legs, I viola, and [Suggia] excellent cello, all four with greatest enthusiasm, with my wife as the only public!"

Casals wrote to the Röntgens on the ninth of December from the Hotel de Klomp in Enschede, Holland (electric light—the stationery proclaims—public telephone, and omnibus to the stations), as soon as he had freshened up and eaten something after a long trip inland from Amsterdam. He was feeling tired, depressed, and somewhat alone and said he was writing to weary his friends with an explanation he felt he should make. Casals' letters occasionally touch on the fatigue of his career; few reflect such low spirits.

Casals reported that he had played indifferently, unable to interest himself in the music in spite of all his efforts to do so. He was preoccupied and sad—"what unhappiness to have to present oneself to the public in such circumstances." He had been upset all through the current tour—there was either something wrong with his cello or he was going through a wretched phase; he hoped there would be a change for the better so far as his playing was concerned. His explanation centered on being unable to forget that Guilhermina Suggia had been so nervous at their departure the day before that she had not spoken either to the children or to the servants. It had been an oversight, and she had been desolate when she realized her absentmindedness.

Casals was genuinely preoccupied and dispirited. The schedule was relentless. Fatigue, loneliness, and a species of self-pity descended, understandable but difficult to throw off. Suggia's lack of graciousness on leaving the Röntgens added to the distress; all his life Casals was aware of the reactions of other human beings, but he was acutely conscious of the sensibilities of children and serving people. (On his trips to Holland he always brought toys for the young Röntgen children and took great pleasure in seeing the youngsters playing with them.) He was also displaying the delicacy that was a lifetime characteristic—actually, Suggia had gone back to Paris after an argument. Casals returned from his tour of Holland to discover that she was in a medical clinic awaiting surgery. Despite their clashing temperaments and their disagreements, Casals was deeply concerned and, as he reported to Röntgen, terrified that she seemed to take so long to return to consciousness after anesthesia. Directed by the doctor to leave after "a tiny half-hour" so as not to tire the patient, Casals returned to the Villa Molitor where, "without any heart for it," he practiced for a concert he had to give in Lyon.

By the summer of 1908 Eugène Ysaÿe had found for himself and his family a country place he called La Chanterelle at Godinne on the Meuse River below Namur, and from then until 1914 Casals and the friends who made chamber music together for pleasure in Paris made short visits to Belgium. Casals especially enjoyed his memories of Ysaÿe relaxed at Godinne. He described the friendship, extending back to Casals' first days in Paris at the beginning of 1900, as fraternal—a small brother and a big brother. Ysaÿe, twenty years the elder, was more than six feet tall, with a great shock of black hair that he wore long, eyes the color of blue sky, features that were handsome although fleshy. Violist Lionel Tertis described him as a huge man who smoked a correspondingly huge pipe. "Even his match-boxes were outsize. Only his violin was of standard dimensions, and in his hands it looked a toy." Casals thought of him as leonine and graceful: in spite of his size and weight he was an expert swimmer, fine fencer, and good tennis-player. Without much opportunity in his youth for formal education, he became a connoisseur of painting, read widely and discerningly in French and English literature, and was a "really aristocratic *gourmet.*" Ysaÿe also became a summertime fisherman at La Chanterelle—a sport Casals had disliked from childhood because of his distress at seeing the hooked fish being pulled wriggling from the water. (Ysaÿe's practice of the sport was possibly less brutal than Casals assumed. Fritz Kreisler found him on the riverbank one day, half asleep with a huge sombrero over his face; he stirred occasionally to pull in his fishing line and retrieve one of the bottles of beer attached to the end.) In the evening, twenty or more relatives and friends would sit down to a tremendous Belgian dinner, then play whist or poker (with a twenty-five-centime limit) until Ysaÿe said casually "What about some music?" More than once the players were Kreisler (first violin), Thibaud (second violin), Ysaÿe (viola), Casals, and Ferruccio Busoni—although the pianist was sometimes Cortot, or Ysaÿe's frequent recital colleague Raoul Pugno, another huge man but short, a bear to Ysaÿe's lion. Outside in the gathering darkness people from the nearby villas, local inhabitants, and even passing motorists would crowd the garden to listen. The music continued for hours, usually brought to an end by Ysaÿe playing a solo chaconne.

Casals played occasionally with the Concerts Ysaÿe orchestra in Brussels from early in the century until after Ysaÿe's death in the 1930s. It was in Brussels also that Casals made one of his earliest public protests for the human and professional rights of musicians, well before World War I. He was engaged to play a concerto with the orchestra of the Brussels Conservatory and in the second half to perform a Bach suite. Casals knew that in Brussels, as in Paris and elsewhere in Europe, there was a long-established custom of admitting a paying audience to the final rehearsal, although soloists and orchestra players received a fee only for the announced performance. Virtuosos since the days of Paganini had submitted to the tradition; Casals felt his career had reached a point at which he had the authority to do something about it. He therefore treated the rehearsal as such, purposely interrupting to clarify points of interpretation with the conductor, congratulating the orchestra with a *Bravo!* for well-played passages. The puzzled audience became restless. When the concerto was finished Casals prepared to put his cello into its case. The director asked him to continue with the Bach suite. Quite unnecessary, said Casals; he had already rehearsed it that morning. The audience became noisy at the delay, but Casals made no move to play again until the director offered to pay the fee for two concerts instead of one. After the concert Casals kept one check and gave the other to the orchestra's benefit fund, explaining clearly to all concerned—including the press—his stand and the reasons for his protest. The conservatory discontinued admitting paid audiences to rehearsals.

About this time Casals also appeared as soloist with an orchestra in the fashionable seaside resort of Ostend; at the first rehearsal he noticed that Edouard Jacobs was in the cello section. The two did not speak. During the luncheon break a number of musicians, including Jacobs, were at Casals' table in a café. The guest artist recalled his first visit to Brussels a decade or so before as an unknown nineteen-year-old, telling in flawless French and considerable pantomime about his fruitless interview with Maître Gevaërt and the reception of *le petit Espagnol* in the classroom of a cello professor whose name Casals remembered as something like Jacob. A fellow musician in Brussels, Casals was told later, was so irritated with Jacobs that he hit him over the head with an umbrella.

In autumn of 1908 Casals went to Basel to take part in a performance of Bach's *St. John Passion*. One of the soloists was Julius Röntgen's close friend the Dutch baritone Johannes Messchaert, with whom Röntgen had made many tours as accompanist. Casals often said later that Messchaert was the greatest singer he had heard in his life. In the course of the 1908 rehearsals in Basel Casals dispatched a telegram to Röntgen that said "If only I could play like Messchaert sings. . . ." Röntgen told him next time they met that at approximately the same time Messchaert had sent a wire the burden of which was "If only I could sing like Casals plays. . . ."

During the performance of the *Passion* in the Basel cathedral, while Casals was playing the viola di gamba obbligato to the great aria *"Es ist vollbracht"* ("It is finished"), he suddenly felt an overwhelming certainty that his father was dying. Directly after the performance he canceled his immediate engagements and began the journey to Vendrell. When he arrived he discovered that Carlos Casals had in fact died in Bonastre at the time of the Bach performance in Switzerland. He had already been buried in the cemetery in Vendrell, from which there is a long view of the bell tower of the Church of Santa Ana. Returning to Paris, Casals had another of his bizarre experiences with the police. He had barely settled into his seat in an international train when he was approached by a member of the civil police who intended to arrest him. Casals produced identification and demanded to know the charge—which he never learned. People nearby began with amusement to confirm that Casals was indeed who he said he was, and a famous Spanish musician in the bargain, as the gendarme grew more flustered. A solution was effected when Casals agreed to sign a hastily prepared statement that he had been confronted with arrest but had identified himself as Pablo Casals, which was not the name of the person the police were seeking, and he continued his journey.

For a short while after Carlos Casals' death Doña Pilar lived in the Bonastre house, then she returned to Barcelona, to an apartment in the calle de San Francisco. She again told her oldest son that he should have a home of his own in Catalonia, near the sea, where he could rest completely when he was not on tour. Soon after, Casals bought a small plot of land at the farthest end of the empty beach at San Salvador, later purchasing adjoining land until the property totaled five hectares (fourteen acres). Doña Pilar began to design a house and plan its construction and the planting of gardens.

15

By 1909, when Casals was thirty-two years old, the year his fame was widely and permanently established in England, he could command fees in most of Europe equal to or better than those of any other instrumental performer. The only real pattern that had emerged was one of almost constant professional travel. No year passed now without performances in Switzerland, Germany, Russia, Spain, Holland, and Italy—although that country, he found, was still essentially operatic. (His delight was Venice—he thought nothing of traveling eighteen hours to be able to spend a day there.) Paris was his base, a logical and agreeable one, although his home in spirit and mind was never other than Catalonia. He worked hard; once, exhausted, he fainted during a Berlin recital, revived, and finished the program. He had been ill in Spain during his vacation in 1908 and grew a beard, which he wore for a short while, giving him the look of a self-conscious apprentice smuggler. Frequently preoccupied with the demands of his career, Casals nevertheless had in his life something of what he had in his playing—the ability to relax instantly, if only for a brief span, between the times of tension and absorption his art required.

In the month of March 1909 alone, Casals played the Dvořák

Casals in Vendrell at thirty-one. He had grown
the beard during an illness.

concerto with the Hallé Orchestra in Manchester under Hans
Richter on the fourth, then hurried to Spain. There he participated
as soloist and conductor in several of eight rather spectacular concerts during the second-centennial Lenten season of the Musical
Association of Barcelona (which also included Gabriel Fauré conducting his *Requiem* and *Calígula* and Wagner's son-in-law Franz
Beidler leading 450 performers in Beethoven's ninth symphony).
In one concert Casals was joined by Suggia to play Moór's double
cello concerto (the newspaper *La Actualidad* ran front-page pictures of the two artists under the headline THE CELEBRATED
CONCERT ARTIST PABLO CASALS AND WIFE. Casals was furious). Two
days after the end of the Barcelona festival Casals was in Utrecht,
playing Saint-Saëns and Boccherini with the local symphony
orchestra.

In spite of uninvited newspaper stories and the ordinary hazards of the life of a traveling musician, the tone of Casals' letters to Röntgen—even the handwriting—in early 1909 have a lightness and joy seldom evident before. Röntgen had presumably attempted writing in Spanish; Casals' answer, dated Paris, March 30, salutes Röntgen as "Friend who is making progress" and continues for a few lines in Spanish before it goes into the usual French:

> Bravo for your forthcoming trip to Paris (*première audition!*) or if you will *prima vista*. It is good of Madame Röntgen to accompany you; I rejoice.
>
> It is therefore understood one sonata each concert; I want to play the other sonata in my third concert—[Casals gives a musical phrase followed by four heavy exclamation points.] It seems to me that I will always be so transported as to commit that enormity whenever I play that part—whenever I think about it I have goosebumps!
>
> Have you thought about the Denmark business—do you think you can propose dates to me soon—?
>
> I await the cello score of the G minor sonata—I must rework it drastically!

Röntgen brought the score; he and his wife stayed several days—a marvelous visit for all concerned. As the time approached for the guests to leave, the two couples sat in April sunshine in the garden. Röntgen got up without a word, went into the house, and to say *au revoir* played—magnificently—the haunting first movement of Beethoven's piano sonata number 26, which the composer himself had titled "*Les Adieux*."

A surprise visit later in the spring was Röntgen's way of delivering the cello concerto he had written for Casals. On June 4, 1909, using *tu* in his letters for the first time, Casals said, "Your hurried passage left ineffable memories—they will endure always." He wanted to get to work on the concerto: "It is not difficult to play approximately, it will be difficult to play well—I will apply myself and I rejoice in this work and above all the performances that come later." Would Röntgen make a copy of the *Fantasia* when he had a moment? "It is always good that I look at it from time to time. I received the Irish songs yesterday . . . they are exquisite. . . ."

A letter from English banker Edward Speyer, founder of the Clas-

Part of a letter from Casals to Julius Röntgen

sical Concert Society in London, asked if Casals would help the society by appearing as a soloist in the fall. In 1902 Speyer had founded the Joachim Quartet Concert Society, which had fallen upon lean times by 1906, when Joachim, too crippled to play very well any longer, had become a favorite target of the anti-Brahms claque in England. When the Joachim Society disintegrated, Speyer and his associates organized the Classical Concert Society on the same rather stuffy classical tradition of its predecessor (nothing later than Brahms). Within two or three seasons, in the Edwardian musical climate, prospects were once more dismal. Speyer had not heard Casals play, but he had read splendid reports in the Continental papers.

Casals responded with a letter the seventy-year-old Speyer found charming, saying that he felt honored to assist an organization that reflected the art of Joachim. Casals never met Joseph Joachim, a man of ambassadorial presence and wide culture, as—with vastly more regret—he never met Brahms. He had heard Joachim in London on his first visit in 1899, and recalled having been present for the Diamond Jubilee concert in Joachim's honor at the King's Hall in 1904. His presence had a certain propriety, because Joachim (who made his first London appearance at thirteen playing the "thankless, rather trivial" Beethoven violin concerto with Felix Mendelssohn conducting) had attained colossal respect as a musician similar to that accorded Casals fifty years later. There were many differences, even in musicianship, and Joachim accumulated more vehement detractors in England in the last years of his life than Casals did throughout his career, but in searching for the most complimentary comparison musical commentators for years wrote of Casals as the greatest musician since Joachim.

Joachim's name today is that of a gray eminence towering over half of serious nineteenth-century music; early in the twentieth century, when he was in his seventies, his presence and influence were considerable. As a child prodigy studying in Leipzig he became intimately associated with Mendelssohn and Schumann; at eighteen he became concertmaster of the Weimar orchestra, then conducted by Liszt. His prestige as a teacher helped make Berlin, where he settled in 1868, a major center of violin study for half a century. He helped many young musicians, particularly violinists. It was Joachim who "discovered" Eugène Ysaÿe playing in a Berlin musical café, urged him to leave to make an international career, and saw to it he had the assistance to do so. Joachim's interpretations of the violin concertos of Bach, Beethoven, Mendelssohn, and Brahms became the criterion against which all others were measured. He wrote a number of works for orchestra and for solo instrument and orchestra (the best-known a Hungarian Concerto in A major for violin and orchestra); his cadenzas for the violin concertos of Mozart, Beethoven, and Brahms are still used. His string quartet, created in 1869 with Joachim as first violin, was for thirty years the most distinguished chamber-music group in Europe; Casals heard and respected it before illness forced its founder to withdraw in 1907, the year of his death. But Casals found the most influential violinist in the generation before Ysaÿe not conspicuously original. He aimed so much at being "classical" that he was afraid to let himself go, with the result that the performances were cold. In spite of an impressive career and playing that nearly always commanded respect and sometimes reached great heights, Casals felt the famous Joachim did not go to the heart of the music.

In October 1909 Casals went to stay and rehearse at Ridgehurst, the Speyers' spacious country house in Surrey. The cellist and the banker (a distinguished musical amateur whose father had been a friend both of Beethoven and of Mozart's oldest son) quickly became great friends. Ridgehurst offered both the amenities of a cultured wealthy man's country seat and one of the finest collections of musical manuscripts in Britain. Speyer remembered having been taken to a Mendelssohn concert at the age of five; his family had been friendly with Clara Schumann and Johannes Brahms, and his own friendship with Joachim was intimate. Lady Speyer, an accomplished violinist, would sometimes hire the London Symphony Orchestra for an evening to play for twenty guests in her house. Speyer was an excellent host as well; during the next twenty-five years Casals was a frequent and welcome houseguest. One could always count on music at Ridgehurst, and when he was a guest Casals was always the first to suggest making music and usually the last to want to stop. "I remember his arriving," Speyer wrote of a subsequent visit, "in a white flannel suit with a tennis racquet under his arm one lovely summer morning and announcing: 'Now, six sets of tennis first and then the two Brahms Sextets.' . . . So in the afternoon there was a triumphant performance of the Sextets. Casals always used to say that this was the kind of music-making which he really enjoyed." Some years later Casals played the Brahms double concerto with Speyer's son Ferdinand at Ridgehurst, with Fanny Davies at the piano. Afterward

Miss Davies began sketching phrases from the Brahms cello sonata in F. "Casals, with his 'cello still between his legs, took up the challenge, and they then played the first three movements of the work from memory! For Casals . . . this was perhaps no great feat . . . but . . . it was some years since [Fanny Davies] had last played the work. The two had never done music together before, and Casals was so highly impressed by the incident and her musicianship that he immediately engaged her to play at one of his own concerts in Barcelona. . . . On one occasion, when she was playing Brahms' Concerto in B flat, Casals surrendered the baton to a deputy in the Andante and himself played the lovely violoncello solo." Fanny Davies reciprocated by presenting Casals a lock of Mendelssohn's hair.

Installed at the Hotel Dieudonné in London before his first Classical Concert Society performance on October 20, 1909, Casals discovered he had forgotten his *frac*. A telephone call to Speyer resulted in the appearance of twenty-year-old Mischa Elman, his swallowtail suit, and his violin. The suit fitted Casals splendidly. Elman was delighted—and insistent that Casals stay to hear him play some Mozart. Casals reached Bechstein Hall barely in time to avoid an infraction of British punctuality.

That evening Casals played a Brahms trio and a Schubert trio with Leonard Borwick and violinist Marie Soldat. Between the trios Casals played the complete Bach C major cello suite. Speyer wrote:

> From the moment when Casals started the Bach Suite, beginning with that stupendous downward scale of C major, the audience followed him with rapt attention. The excitement grew from movement to movement, until at the end there was a demonstration the like of which can seldom have been heard in a London concert-room. Casals had for the first time obtained the ear of an English audience. The Bach Suite carried away his hearers, because it was Bach played with the strictest regard for classical form and yet with complete spontaneity of feeling, instead of the dry unimpulsive manner which the pundits had tried to persuade us was the right way to play Bach.

On his first visit to Ridgehurst Casals met Speyer's associate and adviser Donald Francis Tovey, a tall, loosely built, boyishly attractive pianist-composer a bare year and a half his senior. There was an immediate spark of musical and personal interest between the two. Before long Tovey began to proclaim that in Casals he had met the greatest musician since Joachim, whom he had idolized. For Casals it was the beginning of a mutual regard that, although interrupted, endured; Tovey was one of the three composers of his time, Casals maintained, whose music never received the recognition it merits.

Their first association was rather brief, but intense. When they met they began to rehearse for a first performance Tovey's *Elegaic Variations*, written in memory of Robert Hausmann, cellist of the Joachim Quartet. The stimulation and admiration grew on both sides when they talked and played Bach. They agreed completely on the approach to interpreting the Leipzig master's music—the "purist" dry, passionless, exercise-precise playing of any of Bach's music was unthinkable to either of them, and for both Bach was the foundation of all music. (Tovey, whose disposition was analytical, is said to have known familiarly if not by heart every note of Bach's keyboard writing, including the organ works, and played them eloquently.) The musicians gave two concerts together before Casals' Classical Concert series appearance and the collaboration was so agreeable that they scheduled concerts together for the next season.

Donald Francis Tovey was a phenomenon. His father was a clergyman—a classical scholar and authority on the poet Thomas Gray—who was quite unwilling to accept his son's musical gifts as important, although Donald was writing large compositions in full sonata form by eight, reading musical scores fluently at twelve, and had mastered a huge piano repertoire at fifteen. Young Tovey's education was taken over in early childhood by Miss Sophie Weisse, who ran a fashionable school called Northlands at Englefield Green, thirty-five miles west along the Thames from London. Miss Weisse, a friend of Joachim, brought the seven-year-old to the violinist's attention. Through the years, despite Joachim's encouragement, his family's reluctance to consider him special saved Tovey from the precarious and sometimes tragic career of a prodigy.

Tovey graduated from Balliol College at Oxford with classical honors, one of the most brilliant students in the history of the college. He appeared in a joint recital with Joachim in London as early as 1894, when he was nineteen; he made his début as a solo pianist in November 1900 at St. James's Hall, startling Hans Richter among others by coupling two demanding sets of variations on a theme—Bach's thirty *Goldberg Variations* and Beethoven's last work for piano, thirty-three variations on a little waltz by Anton Diabelli. Tovey composed fiercely from early adolescence until his late twenties—string quartets, trios, sonatas, pieces for piano, a piano quartet, the beginning of a symphony—when some of his energy went for a time into arranging concerts and his own performances. From the time of his early concerts, Tovey furnished analytic program notes so comprehensive and profound that they gained for him an academic label he was never able to shake. His brilliant, pungent writing, collected in the 1930s into six volumes titled *Essays in Musical Analysis*, set a high standard for the writing of program notes thereafter and are a lasting contribution to the literature about serious music. When he and Casals met in England in 1909 he had been working for four years on his article "Music" for the *Encyclopaedia Britannica*, but Tovey's great hunger was to be recognized as a composer and pianist.

Their mutual friendship with Julius Röntgen and his lively family was an additional common ground for Casals and Tovey. Röntgen had met Tovey when, at fourteen, Joachim had him play for the Dutch musician at an evening party, and Röntgen and Tovey had performed together in Vienna in 1901. Tovey had spent two weeks in Holland at Easter in 1909, and R. C. Trevelyan, the brother-in-law of Röntgen's wife, had started work on a libretto for Tovey's projected opera *The Bride of Dionysus*.

Casals played two programs with Tovey—as they had planned the year before—on June 2 and 9, 1910, in Aeolian Hall in London: Brahms, Bach, sonatas by Tovey and Julius Röntgen, and Tovey's *Elegaic Variations* for cello and piano. *The Times* of London duly recorded the first of two recitals "by Mr. D. Tovey and Señor Pablo Casals, the violoncellist who made so deep an impression when he played before at the Classical Society's concerts." Tovey's sonata, an early one in F, "is very much under the influence of Beethoven and Brahms, and except in the first movement is very restrained . . . but even the dull parts were infused with life by Señor Casals' wonderful playing." Between a Brahms sonata and the Tovey piece Casals played the Bach solo cello-suite in G. "It was indeed difficult to know what to admire most," according to

The Times' reviewer "—the player's control of rich and varied tone, the strength and flexibility of his bowing, or his beautiful phrasing. In response to loud and prolonged applause he played the first movement of the unaccompanied Sonata in C major."

Casals' initial interest in Tovey was reinforced during this second association. Joachim had been quoted as saying that he was willing to discuss music with the Schumanns and with Brahms, but not with Tovey—"after an hour with Donald Tovey I feel as if my head were on fire," Joachim told Edward Speyer. "I have never seen his equal for knowledge and memory." Casals himself was awed both by the Englishman's knowledge and by his musical memory. "It is not too much to say that he knew the whole of music from Palestrina to Brahms thoroughly and completely and much of it by heart," recalled Fritz Busch, another Tovey admirer. "For instance, if one sang him the second violin part of a rarely played Haydn quartet, a few bars were enough for him to name the place they came from and to drop some trenchant remarks on the peculiarities of the work." Tovey also had a sense of musical fun of a sort not always found among classicists, and Casals remembered his imitations of current work and hilarious parodies of Handel—but never of Bach.

The two June concerts were so successful that a third evening of Bach and Beethoven sonatas was arranged in Aeolian Hall for the first of July. A reviewer thought "nothing could exceed the beauty of the violoncello's soft cantabile tone in the first movement" of the Bach G minor sonata, and Mr. Tovey's treatment of the piano part "was remarkably sympathetic." The reviewer considered Casals' playing of Bach's unaccompanied music ideal, and said that his performance of the C major suite "has now become famous." When Tovey attacked a Beethoven sonata alone "he indulged in a number of crude contrasts of loud and soft tone, which gave the impression that in his close study of the letter he had forgotten that the pianist's main task is to convey the spirit of the music to his audience." Tovey had very small hands, but Fritz Busch among others considered him an excellent pianist; Casals more than once said that anybody who doubted Tovey's personality as a great pianist either would not—or could not—understand him.

The committee of the Classical Concert Society took note of the success of the Casals–Tovey recitals in Aeolian Hall and booked both artists for the first of the ten concerts of the society's autumn 1910 series. Casals returned to Paris, then took a holiday in Barcelona and San Salvador, where construction of his beach-front house was progressing under the supervision of Doña Pilar. Casals had paid the required money so that Luis, who was now nineteen, did not have to serve in the army. He was at San Salvador helping with the plantings of gardens beside the house and the vineyards behind it.

In October Casals returned to Manchester for his third solo appearance with the Hallé Orchestra, currently under the stormy leadership of Hans Richter. (Casals played with this organization fairly regularly through a period of thirty-seven years, spanning directorial tenures from Richter's to that of his mercurial but de-voted friend John Barbirolli.) "Did the old bear growl at you?" Joachim had asked violinist Albert Spalding. "He generally does. . . . Richter is not famed for kindness." Casals had no such problems with him, and liked to remember that before a concert together Richter always said, "Remember, we have a long talk afterward!"—in a mixture of French and German. Hungarian-born Richter's English was terrible, and Casals still had difficulties with the language. Richter would take Casals by the arm and they would walk to a favorite pub and talk over beer into the small hours about conducting and music in general, but particularly about Liszt and Wagner. Pubs were obliged by law to close rela-tively early; the long-suffering or music-loving proprietor would lock up at closing time without disturbing Richter and his com-panion, then wait patiently until they decided to leave.

Hans Richter, described in youth as "a big, blond, stolid giant, slow-moving and perhaps not very brilliant," was a natural musi-cian who could play every instrument in the orchestra, an expert pianist and organist, and a singer good enough to appear in concert in Vienna. Some found Richter's conducting ponderous (Brahms fled from his box during a Richter performance of one of his sym-phonies) and Thomas Beecham proclaimed that Richter was able to conduct a maximum of five works. He nevertheless moved audi-ences, impressed musicians, and was hailed by many of the knowl-edgeable as the finest conductor of his time. He had admirers in men as articulate, irritable, and different as Debussy and George Bernard Shaw. Shaw considered him a conductor of genius and praised the directness and economy of his conducting: "He did not pose and gesticulate like a savage at a war dance"—something that also made a lasting impression on Casals. Casals, in fact, was disposed to say that his three conducting teachers had been his father, Lamoureux, and Richter. As both man and musician Richter was direct, dependable, honest. Once, having miscued badly and thrown the orchestra into momentary confusion near the coda of Brahms' "Academic Festival" Overture, he repeated the work, then turned to the audience to explain the fault had been his, not the players'. He was a technician, an unashamed craftsman. In the music he knew and loved, he was powerful. And Casals admired most of all that he went directly to the heart of the matter—to the music.

Richter was nearly thirty-five years older than Casals. His hair, red-gold in the early Bayreuth days, was gone and his beard was grizzled. His face had the effect of unfinished masonry, but "behind his gold spectacles his eyes still flash magnificently . . . the eyes of a prophet," said Debussy. "If Richter looks like a prophet, when he conducts the orchestra he is Almighty God; and you may be sure that God Himself would have asked Richter for some hints before embarking on such an enterprise."

Richter talked intoxicatingly and with the enthusiasm of a man certainly no older than Casals' thirty-three years. But the great days of Wagner, in which Richter had participated, had been two generations earlier; Wagner died of a heart attack at nearly seventy in Venice in February 1883, when Pablo Casals was six. Casals hung on all of Richter's words about Wagner, trying to learn Wagner's own ideas about the interpretation of his music. Wagner and Richter had been close, although, as for everyone associated with the composer, there had been rough moments. In 1866, at twenty-three, Richter had gone to live with Wagner in Lausanne as his musical assistant. He conducted the first Brussels performance of *Lohengrin* in 1870; the summer of the year Casals was born Wagner invited Richter to conduct the first complete *Der Ring Des Nibelungen* at the inaugural festival in Bayreuth. He continued as principal conductor of that Teutonic event until his retirement in 1912 and lived in the pleasant Bavarian city with its hideous Festspielhaus until his death in 1916. In the meantime Richter mounted the cultural barricades for Wagner in England as early as 1877, conducting alternately with (and considerably more effectively than) the composer in a London festival that triggered the Wagner craze.

Casals and Richter discussed the productions at Bayreuth; Casals had visited there in 1907 and thought the singers not very good. But he thought that few musicians of his generation had not fallen under the spell of *Tristan*, remembering his time in Lamoureux's orchestra preparing for the first Paris presentation and the story of Ysaÿe's reaction to the work. Ysaÿe, on arriving home after hearing *Tristan* the first time, pulled off his shoes and threw them into the fire, muttering that it was an imperfect state of life when one had to interrupt ecstasy for something so dull as unlacing boots.

The first appearance in Casals' second round of Classical Concert Society recitals included three cello sonatas and a solo group of piano pieces played by Tovey. It was an immense success with a crowded audience, noted the possessive Sophie Weisse in her diary. *The Times'* man thought the concert long, the cello too constantly the leader where force and energy were needed, with too much contrast between Casals' vitality of phrasing and "Mr. Tovey's rather limp treatment. . . . One also missed variety and beauty of tone in Mr Tovey's playing. . . ."

Casals had not accepted an engagement in Vienna until November 1910. The reasons he had given Julius Röntgen at the beginning of 1906 for not going then were characteristic and reasonable: he was unwilling to trade on another's established name, and a pattern of exposure beginning with solo appearances with orchestra was a sensible one. But he had said nothing about the emotion that deterred him. For Casals Vienna was the Holy of Holies of music, and for him Mozart, Haydn, and those who came after were still very much alive; he would half expect to see Beethoven come striding around a corner or Schubert emerging from a *Weinstube*. The fact that good notices in Vienna were very important was not a vital concern.

For his Viennese début, in fact, Casals decided to play a work that definitely would not automatically call forth good reviews—the second cello concerto of Emanuel Moór. Onstage in the gilt-pilastered Great Hall of the Vienna Musikverein, with Franz Schalk conducting the Vienna Philharmonic Orchestra,

Casals felt his bow slipping. By instinct he began a twirling motion he had perfected as a child's trick, but in his nervousness the bow flipped out of his hand and landed nine rows into the audience. He watched in fascination as it was handed carefully back row by row in absolute silence. His nervousness gone, he played very well indeed.

His second concert, organized on short notice at the insistence of piano professor Theodor Leschetizky, was a sonata recital in the Bösendorfersaal in the Herrengasse, once a riding academy, a room with some of the finest acoustics for music in the world. The accompanist was Bruno Walter, who for nearly ten years had been Gustav Mahler's assistant at the Vienna State Opera. In his student days he had earned some money playing for Mathilde Marchesi's voice classes.

Casals accepted an invitation to luncheon next day at the house of one of the important musical hostesses in Vienna, who became concerned when he had not arrived half an hour after the appointed time. When he did reach the house, profuse with apologies, he charmed everybody, including the cook whose meal had been delayed. He was preoccupied: the violinist with whom Casals was scheduled to play had been taken ill, and he did not know of anybody else available on such short notice. Further, the Vienna impresario had replaced the announced work with a Casals performance of a Bach suite without consulting him; Casals was quietly furious. A young woman in the party said Vienna possessed a first-rate violinist in the person of Arnold Rosé, founder of his own quartet and since 1881 concertmaster of the Vienna Opera and the Vienna Philharmonic. She telephoned Rosé, who had a performance the same time as Casals, but with a certain amount of juggling (Casals agreed to play the Bach after all and the Philharmonic arranged an interval ten minutes longer than usual) Rosé agreed to join Casals in playing the Brahms double concerto. Casals had an enjoyable luncheon, and he and Anka Bernstein Landau, who had done the telephoning, became lifelong friends.

"Excuse my delay," Casals wrote Röntgen from Paris on January 7, 1911. "I am distracted by a mass of things to put in order and everything goes as the good Lord wishes but not as I should like. . . . I am nervous because I do not have your concerto more under my fingers!"

Casals had another reason to be nervous. He was taking Emanuel Moór with him to England. In another of his triumphs of persistence, Casals had prevailed upon the Classical Concert Society to relax its nobody-since-Brahms policy and let him play a Moór cello sonata along with Beethoven and Bach. Moór overcame his almost irrational dislike of sea travel to make the Channel crossing to play it with him. Rehearsals of the non-Moór sonatas, which Casals was to play with Leonard Borwick, a distinguished British pianist, were to take place in Borwick's home. Casals invited Moór. Things went well enough during the Beethoven, although Casals saw Moór becoming restless and tried by gesture and grimace to calm him. When Borwick and Casals began the Bach, Moór jumped from his chair and pushed Borwick off the piano bench, saying he would show how the work should *really* be played. Borwick listened with every outward show of composure; when Moór finished he bowed almost imperceptibly. "Thank you, sir. I shall do my best." (Paderewski, recipient of similar treatment from Moór on the subject of composition, successfully avoided later encounters. He also announced that the notices on Lausanne tramway structures should not warn of possible injury or death but should caution populace and visitors they were "*en danger de Moór.*")

Moór stayed on in London after the Classical Concert Society performance for the production of a double bill of his operas during Marie Brema's Opera Season at the Savoy Theatre. Each opera (*Wedding Bells* and *La Pompadour*) was to be sung five times in English, with Brema singing the lead and producing. Mme Brema was a versatile singer who had sung Wagnerian villainesses at Bayreuth and the first Lola in *Cavalleria Rusticana* heard in England. She was also a tyrant in her theater and completely overrode Moór's objections, demanding (and getting) new translations and winning every argument. In the process Moór lost a suitcase containing the manuscripts of a mass and two solo cello suites.

Moór's *La Pompadour* tells how Mme Pompadour befriended a pair of young lovers. *Wedding Bells* (*Höchheitsglocken*, as Moór wrote it) is a short two-act operatic tale of love and death in an alpine village: a Swiss peasant, Gottfried, loves and is loved by the older of two sisters but is going to marry the younger because she has saved his life. In the second act a rejected suitor of the younger sister sets her house on fire. The press said very little about these works one way or the other. *The Times'* review observed that the worst part of performing two operas by one composer the same evening is that someone is going to quote Rossini on such an occasion: "I prefer the other one." Such was not the case with Moór's pieces; both "deserve high praise, both are musical in a remarkable degree, and in each the beginning is better than the end."

Casals had gone from London to Budapest for a solo recital and a trio concert with Ysaÿe and Raoul Pugno; in mid-March he was back to play for the first time at one of the popular Promenade concerts. Their director, Sir Henry Wood, remembered the evening well:

> On March 18 Casals made his acquaintance with the Queen's Hall Orchestra and myself. His is an interesting if somewhat curious personality. There is no outward show of virtuosity to attract the public, yet his technique, tone, and musicianship positively command riveted attention with the first stroke of his bow.
>
> At this concert he played what is to my mind the finest of all 'cello concertos—Dvořák's in B minor. As usual, I used my own band-parts and whenever the solo 'cello entered I reduced the accompaniments to a double quartet of strings and two basses, only allowing the full strings to play the *tuttis*. I found this worked admirably because there was no danger of swamping the soloist—so easily done owing to the depth of the 'cello's register. Any conductor who has accompanied Casals knows how fidgety he can be over a concerto. He has a habit at rehearsals of turning round to the orchestra and hissing them down if they dare to make too strong a *crescendo*, but I flatter myself I have always given Casals entire satisfaction. Before he arrives I always make a little speech to the orchestra.
>
> "Now Gentlemen! Casals will be with us in a few minutes. You know what an intensely light orchestral accompaniment he demands—no colour at all. So I beg of you Strings to try to play on one hair of your bow; perhaps two—sometimes three—but never more. Thus you will save endless stoppages and many scowlings and hisses." This always has the right effect and I think I am pretty safe in saying that I am the only conductor in the world with whom Casals has risked playing the Boccherini concerto *without a rehearsal*. . . .

(Conductors almost unanimously respected Casals' musicianship, but more than one found him difficult to accompany. Casals'

In the music room of Miss Sophie Weisse's
finishing school in England, May 1911. Standing,
from left: poet Robert Trevelyan, Donald
Francis Tovey, Jelly d'Aranyi, Casals. Seated,
Mrs. Robert Trevelyan, Miss Weisse, Adila
Fachiri (on floor), Julius Röntgen, Mrs. Röntgen
(Mrs. Trevelyan's sister)

habit of swiftly changing bow—"playing up to the heel of the bow, then, quicker than the movement of a chameleon or an ant-eater's tongue, restarting at the point"—caused some orchestral problems for Sir Adrian Boult during a 1945 recording session in England. Boult, who respected Casals greatly both as an artist and as a teacher, finally exclaimed with mixed admiration and frustration: "There is no known conducting technique for keeping an orchestra together with this man! The only useful practice would be fly-swatting.")

An April solo appearance in Budapest with the Leipzig Phil-harmonic was followed late in the month by a brief visit to Holland, what seemed only a moment in Paris, and a return to London to play in the two Chelsea Concerts presented that year by Donald Francis Tovey. The first, on Wednesday evening the tenth of May, coincided with the opening of the London Season and featured Casals, Röntgen, and Tovey playing Bach, Brahms, and a Röntgen cello sonata. The houseguests at Miss Weisse's Northlands school afterward included Casals, Professor and Mrs. Röntgen, Mr. and Mrs. Robert Trevelyan, and Adila Fachiri and Jelly d'Aranyi (violinist great-nieces of Joseph Joachim who, with their older pianist sister Hortense, had settled in London after Joachim's death). A group picture taken in the music room at Northlands shows some of them, frozen patiently for the photographer, Casals in high starched collar, cigar in hand.

The second Chelsea Concert, in which only Tovey and Casals performed, was on May 17. Casals had written Röntgen the night before from Paris "I continue to feel tired—and these several trips and concerts that remain to finish my season are very painful for me—." Casals then answers his friend about proposals for the next season:

> . . . I have reflected and in spite of the artistic fulfillment I experience in making music with you—and the pleasure that being with you means to me—I really *shouldn't* accept the engagements for Haarlem and Rotterdam. The fees they offer are absolutely insufficient either for you or for me—and for myself I must leave this kind of fee for artists beginning their careers or those who cannot aspire to the top honoraria—Last year I accepted but did it as an exception— the rest of Holland is a great disappointment for me and I have much pain each time we give a concert there—and I have now completely decided to abandon that country ex- cept for the organizations that accept *my* terms—they are agreed to in every country—why not in Holland?
>
> You understand my reasons and in any case you will forgive me—believe that I am sad to write you so harshly.
>
> Affectionate thoughts to you all.
Your
Pablo

After about seven years a phase in Casals' life was ending. More invitations, musical stimulation, and satisfactory fees would come from England than from the Netherlands, until war ended an epoch of history. The friendship of Pablo Casals and Julius Röntgen survived more than another twenty years, and after the older man was gone Casals honored the memory of the person who served as an older brother. Independent of mind and sincere, Röntgen was a human being who refused to be involved in either jealousy or intrigue and who had always been open, considerate, and unselfish to Casals. Of both the man and his music Donald Tovey said that "to those who have come into Röntgen's sphere of influence, he will remain rather as an inspiration for the future than as a link with the past." Neither Julius Röntgen's performing artistry nor his tremendous body of composition has won a prize in the unpredictable competition of musical history, but Pablo Casals judged him one of the few great modern contenders.

In the meantime Casals' wandering life in art continued strenuously, and after May he did not write again to Röntgen until Christmas Day:

> at *Villa Casals*
> *San Salvador*
> *25 December 1911*

My dear Julius,
Here such a long time has passed without writing you! *Mon Dieu*, always the same thing; the rush of my trips—not even time for the things that are most urgent! This is no way to live! After a round of 60 concerts I decided to come to spend a few days at San Salvador near my mother and my brothers—I think I could not have done better—indeed, I have all the calm possible, we are alone on this beach and rejoice undisturbed in the beauty. I am also happy to be able to report that all my loved ones are well and that I am gathering the strength and the fortitude to continue my vagabond life.
You have heard that your sonata has been played at the Classical Concerts—and after that in Prague and then in Regensburg—always to enthusiastic acclaim.—I expect to play it shortly in Budapest, where I have already made the acquaintance of some musicians. . . .
We wish you the best for the new year—I hope to be with you a little more than has been the case. . . .
Pablo

16

THE CALENDAR YEAR 1912 began routinely enough after the end
of what Casals remembered as one of the most musically outstanding of his Russian tours, his seventh. Then, at the beginning of
the second week in January, he joined two other celebrated artists
to appear in the Zeneakadéma in Budapest as the ABC Trio, still
sometimes spoken of as the world's worst trio. Eugène d'Albert,
like Pablo Casals, diminutive physically, was a fiery, completely
individualistic Scots-born pianist and composer. He was the pupil
of whom Liszt had been proudest, and during his twenty-year public career many considered him the greatest piano virtuoso of the
age. His approach to the piano was heroic and not amenable to
work with other performers. Willy Burmester, who rebelled early
against Joachim's teaching to become a "virtuoso" and later ripened
into one of the great violinists, suffered for his art—he wore his
index finger down to the nerve playing his instrument. Remarkable
players they were, but the critic of the official Budapest music
magazine *Zeneközlöny* wrote that they "united in an ugly dishar-
mony at their trio concert. . . ."

> This could have been predicted because they had never
> played together before. Burmester does not care a hoot about

chamber music since he has started peddling his knick-knacks, d'Albert has forgotten to play the piano amid the thrills of Tiefland, while Casals made music for himself superbly and divinely. One cannot talk of artistic standards, nor even of an art ensemble—there was constant fluctuation and sometimes they were not together for . . . several measures [although] to be quite truthful . . . the slow movement of the Beethoven trio in B flat major worked out very beautifully. The audience applauded a great deal and sympathetically. If it is all right for [Casals], everything is all right.

In Hungary, where Casals played more than fifty concerts between December 1910 and December 1937, he performed in major towns—Debrecen, Györ, Székesfehérvár, Miskolc—as well as the capital. In no country, in fact, did he play exclusively in the great halls of the chief cities, which resulted on occasion in his appearances before somewhat rustic audiences in primitive rooms in distant places on snowy nights. Some of these audiences Casals remembered as among the most responsive of his career, unwilling to have his music end even after midnight had passed. In Budapest the demand for tickets was such that his concerts were arranged for the sixteen-hundred-seat Vigadó because the Academy of Music had only eleven hundred; his appearances with orchestra took place in the Városi Szinház, which holds twenty-six hundred and was filled when Casals played there.

In Hungary, too, Casals encountered and was fascinated by the music of gypsies. He was always interested in genuine folk music and in the valid musical expression of national spirit or personality, no matter how unsophisticated it might seem to others. In Budapest there were cafés in which gypsy ensembles furnished musical entertainment. The music of most such groups was as commercial and synthetic as the so-called native dances advertised for foreign tourists in Spanish cities, but in one place the real thing was offered and Casals never missed a chance to go there. The sometimes wild Romany coloration and musical flavor intrigued him, and he thought the intuitive musicality of the gypsies close to miraculous. One gypsy-group leader, a cellist whose tone sounded "like that of four cellists playing together," used the same fingering by extension that Casals arrived at himself early in his own formal cello study. The leader was so big he is said to have been able to play the cello as though it were a violin. Casals admitted it is an exaggeration to think of a man quite big enough to hold a cello under his chin, but insisted this gypsy's hand was so large that he used violin fingering even in the first playing position.

Early 1912 was a vintage period for Ysaÿe–Casals Brahms. After playing the double concerto in Moscow and St. Petersburg in January, they presented it again to their own great delight and much public acclaim on February 20 in the Great Hall of the Vienna Musikverein. Ysaÿe was at the very top of his ability and gave the violin concerto by Viotti before he and Casals played the Brahms with the Vienna Tonkünstler orchestra; then he performed the Mendelssohn concerto. A photograph of the two artists captioned *Souvenir of the Concert of 20 February 1912* could be seen in Viennese shop windows for several years afterward. The photograph satisfied both the Viennese idolatry of great musicians and the natives' streak of special humor: Casals had reached his full height of five feet three inches with shoes, lost most of his hair, and become one of the celebrated musicians of the world. Ysaÿe, who had kept a great mane of hair and was likewise famous and loved, stood well over six feet and weighed in at more than 250 pounds.

On February 26, Casals wrote Julius Röntgen from the Hotel Bristol in Warsaw, thanking him first of all for his letter and a sample of some pills, presumably a variety of tranquilizer Röntgen thought would help Casals through his devastating stage fright: "Please send me a whole box with instructions for use."

> I have not seen you for a long time [he continues], which cannot go on—on one hand Holland has let me go and on the other all the other countries invite me back, making it so that if I want to come to Holland I can't—it is very sad for me. What are you doing in April? I don't know if I will go to Italy for a long tour—but if that falls through I will be in Paris and then you can come with your Mina [Röntgen's wife] to Villa Molitor. . . . I am lonesome for you—but it is the fault of circumstances—you know how much time I have given to my career, which once more in these last years has taken a completely unexpected turn—it absorbs me, I tell you, to the point of consuming me. . . .

Casals wrote Röntgen again on March 21, 1912, this time from the Dieudonné Hotel in London, touching on a mixture of subjects.

Röntgen's letter had been brought by M. Jean de Ponthière, "a charming young man to whom I shall arrange to give some lessons, probably in June." Casals had "swallowed your pills the other day in Paris between two trains—I like them and will say more on a day I do not have a concert." He proposes to arrive in Amsterdam on the fifth of April:

> —we will hear the Matthew passion together at the Concert Gebow and afterward we and Mengelberg can remain a few days. . . . I will receive (this afternoon) the Beethoven Gold Medal of the Philharmonic Society of London—it will be a simple and touching ceremony—I am humble to find myself beside Brahms, Joachim, and [Anton] Rubinstein; *que Dieu soit loué!*
>
> Yesterday I played the *Stücke im Volkston* of Schumann with the Classical [Concert Society], this afternoon with the Philharmonic the C minor suite of Bach.

The Gold Medal of the Philharmonic Society (it became the Royal Philharmonic in November 1912) bears a profile of Beethoven; the date of award and the recipient's name are engraved on the edge. Recipients were also given a replica of the bust of Beethoven by the Viennese sculptor Schaller, one copy of which had been placed in front of the platform at every Philharmonic concert since 1871. The Society had been friendly and helpful to Beethoven during his lifetime (one of his symphonies was included on its first concert in 1813), and this association added to the emotional impact for Casals.

The program on March 21, 1912, featured Casals, playing the Bach suite, and Ferruccio Busoni, who played Liszt; the conductor was Sir Alexander Mackenzie, Scots composer and educator who had written one of the solo parts of his oratorio *Rose of Sharon* for Emma Nevada in the 1880s.

Casals considered Busoni a great artist, very much worthy also of the Philharmonic honor, and made his opinion known. He was, in fact, somewhat embarrassed that the Italian, older by ten years and one of the most penetrating musical minds of his generation, had not been similarly honored, but the pianist gave no indication of irritation or jealousy. The paths of Casals and Busoni had crossed a number of times, and they had played chamber music together in Ysaÿe's house and elsewhere. Casals had so high a regard for Busoni that he respected the Italian's ideas even when he disagreed with them (a feeling he did not have about Paderewski). Like so many other musicians of his time, Busoni was not shy about "touching up" other composers' music, a tendency that appalled Casals in principle as much as in practice. Casals remembered with special horror that Busoni rewrote portions of César Franck's noble, mystical "Prelude, Chorale and Fugue," explaining cheerfully that Franck had sometimes not known how to obtain the effects he desired. But Busoni also considered Bach the foundation of pianism, and like Casals could not sleep after a recital. After a triumphant concert Busoni was known to sit all night at the piano, replaying critically the program he had just finished.

The two other recipients of the Beethoven medal in 1912 were Harold Bauer and Luisa Tetrazzini. Casals made strong representations to Philharmonic Society officials concerning the appropriateness of honoring Busoni, to the point of threatening not to appear again. The medal was never given to Busoni, and Casals' name does not reappear on the programs of the Royal Philharmonic for nearly ten years, three years before Busoni's death.

The beloved private chamber-music orgies of earlier in the century in Paris and Belgium had become less frequent, but whenever Casals was in London between 1911 and early 1914, he often took part in sessions in "Mrs. Draper's cellar," a place Ysaÿe called "la Cave." Muriel Draper, American wife of singer Paul Draper, had made of an attached outbuilding behind her house at 19 and 19A Edith Grove in London a room for music "big enough," at Thibaud's request, "for the Mendelssohn octet," and there many of the Continental regulars continued to gather irregularly. Mrs. Draper, an energetic organizer and music-lover in her twenties, was a friend of Casals' English manager, Montague Vert Chester, who loved music and pink food, was "astute, asthmatic, benevolent, bald-headed" and invariably wore immaculate white gloves. Casals and Thibaud were invited to play trios for pleasure with Arthur Rubinstein at the Draper house soon after Rubinstein's London début (for which Casals had been responsible) in 1911. In succeeding seasons, musicians—Casals among them—would converge on the Draper house when they were in town, still at high pitch from a concert, and the music would go on from midnight until near daybreak, when one or other of the players had to catch a boat train. (One neighbor wrote a grateful letter for the magnificent music when he moved away; others protested, and on one occasion staged a demonstration outside.)

The onetime cellar-stable had been converted into a room that Rubinstein remembered as giving the impression of the interior of a Florentine palace—a Gothic tapestry over the fireplace, Renaissance tables, giant candles—with a Bechstein concert grand. There were also plenty of easy chairs, cushions gigantic enough for Thibaud to stretch out on strewn about the floor, and excellent food and drink generally sent in from the Savoy. Regular non-musical visitors, of whom there were few, included John Singer Sargent and author Norman Douglas (Muriel Draper tended to try to banish even the wives or female companions of the musicians to an upstairs room, where they could talk). The focus and the welcome guests were the musicians, including Ysaÿe, Casals, Thibaud, Harold Bauer and his sister Gertrude, Cortot, Polish violinist Paul Kochanski, composer Karol Szymanowski, Rubinstein, violinist Albert Sammons, Lionel Tertis (the English violist who shared Casals' birthdate and longevity), Enrique Fernández Arbós, and Augustín Rubio. Rubio was a special favorite of Muriel Draper, who said that to be a friend of Casals and a good cellist to boot was enough to have endeared him, but he was so lovable in himself that he won enduring affection from everyone who came in contact with him. Just before the First World War, the man who had come with Albéniz and Arbós to hear Casals nearly a quarter-century earlier "looked like a seventeenth-century Spanish painter's idea of a gentle God with a flowing beard, reclining . . . on billowy clouds in a very solid heaven . . . skin like gold-and-brown parchment, eyes of deeper brown velvet that would trust a murderer." Rubio spoke a mixture of Spanish, French, Italian, and English with emphatic gestures, and with a beaming smile always introduced Casals as *Pablísimo*.

The music ranged from solos and duets to octets. Muriel Draper said that the greatest performance of her life of the Schubert "Trout" quintet was one in her house by Thibaud, Tertis, Casals, Felix Salmond, and Rubinstein. The performance Tertis remembered above all others was Brahms' C minor piano quartet, played by Ysaÿe, Casals, Rubinstein, and himself. "Prodigious, the lusciousness and wealth of sound! Ysaÿe with his great volume of tone and glorious phrasing, Casals playing in the slow movement with divinely pure expression, Rubinstein with his demoniac command of the keyboard (his ferocity in the second movement was frightening)—what an experience. . . ."

On a night in 1912, when Casals, Thibaud, Rubinstein, Kochanski, and Szymanowski were to be the nucleus of an evening at Edith Grove, Muriel Draper wrote Henry James—whom she already knew—inviting him to come. The novelist sat quietly beside her as the Brahms B minor piano trio began. "As the music progressed and the incomparable tone of Casals' cello was heard in the short solo passage of the first movement, [James'] solemnly searching eyes fastened on Casals' face, and he seemed to listen by seeing. When Thibaud began the brilliant passage for violin in the second movement, his eyes left Casals, as if he had drunk him all in through his organs of sight—music, hands, bowing and all—and centred on Thibaud . . . with meticulous care during the whole second movement." When Rubinstein "was burning the music out of the piano with an accumulating speed that left even those great artists somewhat breathless," James turned his eyes toward Rubinstein, where they remained until the end of the performance. Only then did James begin to speak.

Casals asked for the Schubert octet—his favorite; "one drank fresh milk" hearing it, and he asked if he could listen rather than play. He sat on one side of Muriel Draper, smoking a long cigar. Henry James sat on the other, his hostess aware he was "watching, absorbing, recording every gesture and expression of each man or woman in the room," including the fragile blonde delicacy of Mme Thibaud sitting in an enormous armchair under a vase of pink and white camellias, and Suggia, "who sat in swarthy gold, white, and black of dress and skin and hair on a small upright Chinese Chippendale chair in the spectral shadow of paling almond flowers."

Muriel Draper's second son was born in December 1913, and three days later some of her musical friends came to Edith Grove to salute him, among them Casals and Rubinstein. Mother and child were brought downstairs to the "cellar" and installed in a big sofa. The friends played a Brahms sextet, Mrs. Draper's beloved Schubert quintet; Casals played a Bach suite, and Rubinstein played Chopin and Scriabin. Mrs. Draper had tucked the infant under her arm in a corner of the sofa, where he alternately slept and awakened. When he was hungry she nursed him, which outraged the proper English nurse but, Muriel Draper noted, particularly pleased Casals, "whose reverence for birth and children mounted to a passion almost tribal in its intensity."

Casals reported to Röntgen from Paris on April 4, 1912; he was traveling and playing as always. Tovey had come the day before to hear Casals' program with orchestra at the Société des danses Chaigneau, left that afternoon for Frankfurt, and was planning shortly to come to Amsterdam. Casals appeared in two of Tovey's five 1912 Chelsea Concerts at the Aeolian Hall in London, in April and May.

Tovey's music was being taken up, not just by Casals, but by the Klingler Quartet, Adolf Busch, and Julius Röntgen, who were playing Tovey compositions all over the Continent. His work was creating considerable interest in Germany, as was Joachim's statement that "of all musicians now alive Tovey is without doubt the one who would have interested Brahms the most." Before the First World War Casals' voice was not totally a solitary one proclaiming Tovey, Moór, or Röntgen.

During this period Casals was also a propagandist for new compositions by such other living composers as Georges Enesco, Jean Huré, Alfredo Casella, Ernst von Dohnányi, and—less predictably—Florent Schmitt, Béla Bartók, and Zoltán Kodály. Each of these men was at least an acquaintance; Enesco was a close friend until his death in the 1950s. Casals did not, however, mount the kind of campaign on their behalf that he sustained for Moór, or even for Tovey and Röntgen. The work of the other composers began to draw some early recognition on its own, and most of them began to experiment with unconventional forms and to introduce various degrees of dissonance with results that were most uncongenial to Casals. Further, Moór and Tovey and Röntgen began to write a considerable amount of music for the cello after friendship with Casals developed, giving him new and acceptable vehicles for performance. Since Casals was the single most powerful force in the popularization of serious music played on the violoncello during the first two decades of the twentieth century, the question remains how much more extensive this century's cello repertoire would have become if he had had more interest in and sympathy for the idiom in which Debussy, Ravel, and Stravinsky were working; the result would surely have been a larger body of cello works by these composers and their followers.

He crusaded for his friends, but the work of Bach, Beethoven, and Brahms made up a greater part of Casals' recitals. And a considerable proportion of his appearances was as concerto soloist with orchestra—the virtuoso's obligatory high-wire act that has satisfactions as well as hazards but that Casals enjoyed less than playing the Bach solo suites or chamber music. Although he included Moór concertos and later those by Elgar and Tovey, conductors and managers for more than forty years asked for the staples—Saint-Saëns, Lalo, Schumann, Boccherini, Haydn, Dvořák.

Shortly before the First World War a contretemps arose in Paris over a Casals performance of the Dvořák cello concerto, an incident that reveals much about Pablo Casals at that time. He arrived in Paris after a long tour with only enough time to go from the railway station to the Théâtre du Châtelet for a morning rehearsal (with paying public) on the day of his annual benefit performance with the Concerts Colonne orchestra. The Dvořák concerto had been agreed on some time before. Gabriel Pierné was a French composer and conductor nearly fourteen years older than Casals. He had studied with César Franck and Jules Massenet at the Paris Conservatoire, won the Prix de Rome at nineteen, and succeeded Franck as organist of the church of Sainte Clotilde in Paris. After a long apprenticeship as the assistant conductor, he became principal conductor of the Colonne orchestra at Edouard Colonne's death in March 1910. He quickly began to make a reputation both for the authority and the distinction of his directing and for his dedication to the new French music.

When Pierné came into the artists' room at the Châtelet, Casals—himself tired from his tour and from the preceding night's train journey—had the impression that the conductor was flustered. Casals thought Pierné was preoccupied with other matters, as well as the waiting audience. Pierné answered Casals' questions about tempos and some performance details in a disinterested fashion, then suddenly threw the score onto a table, saying that this was not music, it was *cochonnerie*—something out of a pigsty. Casals knew that some of the French, especially those who had lived through the war of 1870, treated Dvořák's work as German music and considered him the butcher's apprentice he had been as a youth rather than as a fine composer. But Pierné had suggested the concerto for the benefit program. Casals thought at first the man was making a joke in very bad taste, then realized he was serious. Perhaps the wild-eyed Frenchman had suddenly gone mad.

Casals loved the Dvořák concerto. He reminded the conductor that Brahms had called it a masterpiece. "Well, Brahms was another one," said Pierné, adding that if Casals were any sort of musician he would realize just how bad a piece of music it was. The discussion grew more heated as word came that members of the audience, angry at the delay, had begun to come up onto the stage. Pierné told Casals there was no choice: he would have to play. Casals said that to play a work with a conductor who felt about it the way Pierné did would be a desecration. He not only could not play, he would not. Trembling with anger, Casals asked to be allowed to speak to the audience before he went home. Instead, Pierné stormed onto the stage—Casals remembered seeing him, hair disarranged and beard disheveled, raise his arms for silence. He announced that Pablo Casals had refused to play.

As the commotion grew and more angry members of the audience came toward the stage, Casals saw Claude Debussy standing nearby, turned to him, and quickly explained the situation. Then he asked the composer's support in assuring Pierné that no artist could perform in the circumstances. Debussy shrugged and said "Oh, if you really wanted to, you could play."

Not he, the cellist assured Debussy; he now did not have the slightest intention of playing with a man who had either gone crazy or was blind to real music. Casals was detained at the Châtelet until a *hussier* arrived to take statements.

Next day Casals was formally served notice of action against him for breach of contract, although the appearance was to have been in a benefit for the orchestra. There was a flurry of published comment and talk in musical circles about Casals' temperament. The technicalities of the law went on for months. Casals was represented by his lawyer when the case finally came to trial. The opposition attorney, Casals was told, conceded in court that the cellist had artistic justification for his behavior, but the judge pronounced against Casals and directed that he pay damages of three thousand francs and court costs.

No one knows the basis for what were, at the least, ill-advised and undiplomatic words on Pierné's part. Later Casals speculated that things may have gone badly with the orchestra before his arrival. The question remains whether the incident had been planned. The musical community knew about Casals' bringing to issue in Brussels the presence of paid audiences at final rehearsal without additional compensation to the performers—a protest that did not go down well with managements or all resident conductors. Casals would quite possibly have ignored a personal affront, but it would have been safe to predict that he would react as he did to an insult to music he respected. The administration of the Concerts Colonne may possibly have thought the resulting publicity would help fill its houses.

In any event, Casals and Pierné did not meet again, although Gabriel Pierné continued to conduct distinguished concerts in Paris until the 1930s. He once asked Alfred Cortot how Casals would receive him if he went to apologize. Cortot answered that he would find a ready acceptance once he explained, but Pierné never attempted to find out.

Casals took his 1912 summer holiday in September, and Donald Francis Tovey came to Spain to spend a month at the seaside house on the Playa San Salvador. The villa, recently finished under the supervision of Doña Pilar, was pleasant but not yet palatial. A two-story portion with three large windows upstairs and a triple-arch veranda at ground level faced the narrow sandy beach and the Mediterranean surf; a single story of the main house extended inland. On the west side were the beginnings of the gardens on which Casals would expend great care and attention; on the east a good tennis court had been constructed. There were comfortable accommodations for several guests and family. Other guests in September 1912 were Mieczyslaw Horszowski and Enrique and Amparo Granados.

Casals was a good, stimulating, and considerate host. In normal circumstances, life could be leisurely for guests if they wished. But even in the warm September languor of the Costa Dorada, Casals on holiday was seldom idle. He rose early, swam and walked, then worked in the morning—practicing and attending to correspondence. At other times there was tennis or music. Casals was now a major international celebrity, and when he was in Spain people called in the late afternoon—neighbors, doctors, writers, artists, businessmen, an archeologist, and always musicians. But his

*(Top) The original main house of the Villa
Casals at San Salvador, built under the supervision
of Doña Pilar; (bottom) a group on the Villa
Casals terrace in September 1912 included
Amparo Granados (standing), Guilhermina
Suggia, Enrique Granados, Mieczyslaw
Horszowski, and Casals.*

life was in many respects complete within him, and in many ways he was a man who existed very much alone all his adult life, surrounded though he was so often by others.

With Tovey as a guest, San Salvador took on a special texture. Tovey, friends remembered, never entered a group without dominating it by his intellect and force of personality, in spite of his unusual appearance. Tovey was very tall; his features were aristocratic. He would have been handsome except for the fact that he stooped badly, moved clumsily, and displayed savage neglect of his clothing, which was always of the best English material. Like Max Reger, Tovey had an unorthodox technique of dressing and undressing. "It was his habit," Fritz Busch remembered, "without heeding the money and other things that fell out of his pockets, to strip off his clothes and let them lie on the floor so that in the morning he had only to slip back into them." Tovey's apparently effortless brilliance was dazzling, no matter what subject he took up—he was the only person, Fritz Busch recalled, who had ever been able to explain Einstein's theory of relativity clearly enough for him to understand it as long as three hours.

Casals, who like other of Tovey's close friends felt a tremendous sincerity in the man, also reveled in the musical give and take when Tovey was among the company—from fresh insights into Bach to Tovey's identification in the music of the Catalan sardana the full embryo of the symphonic form. (Early in his visit to San Salvador Tovey wrote one of his most ingratiating string works, a sonata for two cellos, the second movement of which is a variation on a Catalan folk song.)

Tovey's domination extended to planning the daily activities for everybody in sight at San Salvador—including the host. Every morning he would appear with an inflexible agenda that made problems for every one but the compiler, although the one who suffered most was the shy young Horszowski. As for Tovey, he was having a marvelous time. "In spite of the heat," he reported back to England, "I have never felt better in my life. Exercise consists of disturbing the waters of the Mediterranean. The piano is marvellously out of tune." Actually, there were three pianos at San Salvador. They were all out of tune.

Then word came of the serious illness of Tovey's father. The relationship between the musical youngest son and the Reverend Duncan Crookes Tovey had always been complex, but this devel-

*A sardana being danced on the beach front of the
San Salvador villa for Casals and his guests on a
day of fiesta*

opment was a shock. Casals was able to write Miss Weisse on the
sixteenth of September: "Donald is calmer; the first news about
his father upset him—but the later reports reassure him more and
more. There is much to do—for a holiday perhaps a bit too much,
but it goes well."

There was an unworldly quality about Tovey, and he was quite
shy. He tended to take others on their own valuation or on his
own not necessarily sophisticated assessment. Much of the time
he was full of his own thoughts. He had a furious intolerance
of what he considered—realistically or not—musical humbug or
false values of any kind. His violent and sometimes quite unexpected reactions made him enemies, and throughout his life he was
liable to explosions of rage that could be formidable. An incident
in London the preceding fall should perhaps have been a danger

signal to Casals. The faltering Classical Concert Society series had been put under the management of a concert agent whose concern was to make the programs pay. Some of his methods annoyed Tovey. When he discovered that, for better box office, the agent had ordered posters that carried the name CASALS in large bold type but did not mention the other artists, Tovey had stormed, threatened, and broken with his good friend Speyer—to the real distress of Casals, who knew nothing about the advance publicity.

There was an exceptionally delicate emotional balance among three unusually sensitive people in September 1912 at the Villa Casals, San Salvador. A bitter quarrel followed a misunderstanding between Casals and Tovey, breaching their friendship for more than a decade and ending forever Casals' affection for Guilhermina Suggia. Tovey lost his sense of proportion and left precipitately for home. Suggia traveled to England by way of Portugal. The facts of the near tragedy that brought pain to the lives of three extraordinary people are not likely ever to be known. Tovey's biographer, noting that at twenty-four Suggia was at the height of her attractiveness but not yet her artistic maturity, suggests that once more she had toyed with fire, disastrously. The rest of her life, discussing the art of her instrument, Guilhermina Suggia paid tribute to Pablo Casals as the greatest cellist in history. Casals, citing his rigid conception of honor, seldom ever again spoke of Suggia except as a violoncellist.

Within days Casals was himself on the way to Britain for the first engagements of the heavily booked 1912–1913 season. His concert artist's life did not allow time for withdrawal to let private sorrows heal. In early October in a Birmingham festival he played the solo cello part in Richard Strauss' *Don Quixote*. Sir Henry Wood, who conducted, noted of that performance that Casals gave "to the part of the Chivalrous Knight quite a new interpretation and an added value. . . ." Casals also had a Liverpool engagement in October 1912. Tovey, driven by a wish to clear up the misunderstanding between them, dashed there—but instead of trying to see Casals spent the evening in his hotel room drafting a long, elaborate letter in which he tried to make clear his side. Things that could have sounded natural and genuine if spoken became stiff on paper. The only answer possible was Casals' short, formal reply. Tovey also communicated with Röntgen, who attempted to mediate.

For the first time in more than a year, Casals wrote Julius Röntgen, from St. Petersburg on December 8, 1913, with dignity and pain:

Dear Julius,
I thank you for your amicable letter and suffer because I cannot accept without reservation the hand you offer.
A friendship such as I feel must have spontaneity. . . .
There is so much you do not understand. . . . My feeling of affection for you is such that I would not risk a fresh contact with you unless I were to feel on your part more comprehension of what has happened or, better, until time and new developments in my life have come to efface the memories that do not cease to torment—I pray that this moment will not be too far distant, dear Julius, because I assure you that you do not desire more strongly than I the rapprochement that must come about to end the most cruely unhappy episode of my life. Believe as you wait my unfaltering affection

your
Pablo

17

Most of Casals' thirty-seventh birthday was spent on an express train between St. Petersburg and Berlin. After New Year's Day 1914 in London and performances elsewhere in England he made an Italian tour. He played in Bucharest in mid-February and afterward at the Academy of Music in Budapest. In March he sailed to the United States for the first time in ten years, and on the fourth of April was married in New Rochelle, New York, to Susan Scott Metcalfe. An exclusive story in the issue of the weekly *Musical America* that appeared the day of the wedding cleared up the "mystery surrounding the sudden visit of Pablo Casals to America" by announcing the marriage, a fact verified by Miss Metcalfe to a reporter who called on her in her New Rochelle home.

Susan Metcalfe was a daughter of Frank J. Metcalfe, the son of a well-established New York physician, who had recognized the opportunities for an American medical man in Florence (where most of the foreign doctors were British) and established his own practice there after the American Civil War. Frank Metcalfe married Helene Rochat, member of an Italian-Swiss family that for generations supplied the secretaries to the Grand Dukes of Tuscany. Their children—Louis, Lily, Susan, and Marie—were born

*The portrait inscribed to Casals by Queen
Elisabeth of Rumania (Carmen Sylva) in
Bucharest, February 1914*

in Italy. After Dr. Metcalfe's death the family lived at 105 Neptune
Avenue in New Rochelle, in a house designed by Louis, who had
studied architecture at Yale before setting up his office in New
York City. Susan made a private début as a singer in New York
at about eighteen, in 1897. She and Casals could very well have
met in Paris at the beginning of the century, as was often reported
in newspaper stories; in any event, they appeared on the same program in New York in March 1904.

Through the end of 1907 Susan Metcalfe gave two or three solo recitals a year in New York and appeared as soloist with groups in such auditoriums as Cooper Union Hall and the Grand Central Palace (two concerts in honor of Mozart's 150th birthday; afterward she wrote a cousin in Italy about the excitement she had felt singing for an audience of workingmen). She had a good small voice that reviewers frequently called beautiful and naturally appealing, but in trying to make it bigger she developed disagreeable mannerisms and a strident tone. The six New York reviews of a recital she gave in Mendelssohn Hall on February 11, 1907, for example, were typical, but hardly the sorts of messages a sensitive, aspiring, obviously hard-working young artist could have been hoping for at the Valentine season, although the *Telegram* found her singing marked throughout by "a return to the smooth tone production that characterized this singer earlier in her career." The *Sun* thought her undeniable intelligence and unmistakable interpretive purposes "somewhat obscured by the monotony of her tone." "Her phrasing is always delightful" and her breath control admirable, reported the *Post,* but the recital as a whole was rather monotonous and uninteresting.

The *Telegraph,* under the headline A GOOD VOICE AND A BAD METHOD, observed: "Miss Metcalfe has individuality, pronouncement. There emanates something from her unusual and emphatic. Her voice, while sledge-hammered and ultra-decisive, is a remarkably good one, while her method is a remarkably bad one. She sacrifices everything to a good single note. . . . Let her strengthen her medium tones and resist the attempt to be a vocal dynamitard, and she will wake up one morning a very clever and a very satisfactory artist. She was very quaintly garbed and Hepnered."

After a New York recital in March 1908—except for the brief notice of a song recital in the Stockbridge (Massachusetts) Casino in September and appearances in Pittsburgh and New York in the spring of 1912—Susan Metcalfe concentrated on making a new name in Europe (although she had sung in Berlin as early as January 1905, under the same management as Casals at the time, Wolff & Sachs). She made her London début in Bechstein Hall in 1908, and appeared as soloist with the Concertgebouw orchestra in Amsterdam the same season. She joined the list of artists who appeared in concerts of the Classical Concert Society in London. She was invited to sing before British royalty, and essayed further recitals in the English capital. ("An American singer has excited the London critics with her program models," burbled the final March 1909 issue of *Musical America*. "It is none other than Susan Metcalfe, who, as one of fortune's favorites, can be indifferent to financial compensation, prefers to spend the larger fraction of the year abroad. She confirmed her title as a mistress of the art of program-making at the first of the two recitals she gave in London's Bechstein Hall. . . .")

Late in 1913 Susan Metcalfe appeared backstage to greet Pablo Casals after a concert in Berlin. Very petite, a bit shorter and some two years younger than Casals, she then had a piquant attractiveness that suggests itself in photographs but was captured specially well in a sketch made two years before by John Singer Sargent. Some found her a bit cool, but others felt great élan in her manner; she had both temperament and temper, culture, and—although born and educated abroad—the point of view of an American woman. She and Casals talked a long while; Casals offered to coach her in some Spanish songs she was preparing and (according to Juan Alavedra many years later) before they parted that night they had decided to marry. The word spread fast among Casals' friends (Muriel Draper recounted that she had seen Casals in London at the beginning of 1914 and found him changed—glowing over what Mrs. Draper termed his "recaptured romance," making brave attempts to keep it secret and revealing it in every gesture, word, and expression. She twitted him, saying she knew everything but the name. "Everything about what?" he asked, with an unsuccessful attempt to seem bewildered. "Why, the state you're in!" She then reminded him he had spoken to her about Susan Metcalfe a year before and that he had let his cigar burn his finger while he talked, which she had considered intense absorption indeed for a performer.) A few expressed reservations—to others—one of the most outspoken being the harpsichordist Wanda Landowska. When one female acquaintance attempted to counsel Casals to move cautiously, he told her crisply he had known his fiancée for years.

The morning following the wedding the New York *Telegraph* reported the event in a full-tremolo story of which the first two headlines read WOOED AND WON BY 'CELLO'S NOTES/However, It Takes Ten Years for 'Cellist to Complete Life's Symphony. This was a prime example of the society reporting of the period, and,

Sketches of Susan Metcalfe by John Singer
Sargent and of Pablo Casals by Ramón Casas

except for the names of the principals, was almost completely inaccurate. The civil ceremony took place in the small courthouse on the grounds of the New Rochelle estate of State Supreme Court Justice Martin J. Keogh, a neighbor and friend whose wife was a descendant of the Irish patriot Robert Emmet. It was the first marriage Judge Keogh had solemnized; the certificate was afterward approved by the Spanish consul in New York City. "The ceremony was conducted in front of a big open fireplace in the Justice's courtroom," chronicled *Musical America* the following week. "No attendants were present nor was the place decorated. Only a few immediate relatives witnessed the marriage. . . . The reception was a quiet affair."

The newlyweds began a short wedding trip in Washington. They were back in Europe by late April: Casals had a spring tour of trio recitals with Cortot and Thibaud that took them to Italy

(Top) Engraved announcement of the Metcalfe-Casals wedding, sent out jointly by their mothers; (bottom left) Casals on a tennis court about 1914; (bottom right) a few hours after arrival in New York from Spain on November 11, 1918

at the end of the month. The major personal chore was moving from 20 Villa Molitor; the small house would have been unsatisfactory in the new circumstances even if international conditions had not been unsettled. They decided to take a house in London and establish their winter base there. Things from the Villa Molitor house were packed, some sent to Spain, some to London; many souvenirs, documents, and letters were packed in boxes and put into temporary storage in Paris.

Granados and his wife sent congratulations, which Casals answered from the Dieudonné Hotel in Ryder Street, London, on May 25, 1914: "I cannot tell you how joyously my life moves . . . all is changed for me and already I can see it in my face. I know and count on your affection and friendship—this word is to tell you that your friend is happy."

The engraved wedding announcements had been sent out widely, parallel notices in the names of the two mothers. Julius Röntgen responded to the news with an affectionate note, to which Casals replied from 48 Oakley Street, Chelsea, London, on July 10, 1914, twelve days after the assassination of the Austrian Archduke Franz Ferdinand at Sarajevo. There is in Casals' letters written in the spring and summer of 1914 a sudden hopefulness and a sense of personal joy that had not sounded before:

> A new life begins indeed for me, and one that will bring happiness—. . . . This happiness that has invaded me has helped every trace of past sufferings to disappear and has given me the calm to repair so many of the important things of my life—
>
> If you will give me the news of you of which I have been so long deprived it will do me so much good—
>
> My wishes of good health, dear Julius—and it is very sweet to be able to send you anew my invariable affection.
>
> Your
> *Pablo*

Casals' knowledgeable friends, most of all the bankers, warned him that war was both inevitable and imminent; like many liberals and most men of good will, Casals hoped until the actual declarations of war that fighting could be averted. At any rate he disregarded advice to shift his considerable deposits in the Bank of

France to the safety of Swiss banks. This was money he had earned in France, he replied; as a matter of honor and principle it would remain in the vaults of that country.

Although war had begun, the annual musicians' tennis tournament was held in August at the St.-Cloud courts in Paris; Casals entered the competition as usual: "his skill with the racquet again commanded attention." He and his wife spent September and October in Spain, which had remained neutral. Their plans for establishing a home in London became less feasible.

The situation of many of his friends as a result of the war preyed steadily on Casals' mind. He was specially concerned about Emanuel Moór, although Moór and his wife were physically safe in Switzerland and at no time suffered the hardship of those who lived in the combatant lands. But even in Switzerland life and attitude required adjustments, and Emanuel Moór was not adaptable. A curtain had fallen for Moór; the effect of all Casals' propaganda efforts for nearly a decade, like those of Moór's other devoted and resourceful friends, had been wiped away. Germany and Austria were blocked to him, and neither France nor Belgium had musical performances any longer. The first shock of war shattered the Moórs' strong pacifism. Anita Moór became actively pro-Allies and anti-German. Moór himself went into a heavy depression colored only by a feeling of cataclysm and futility, stopped composing, and withdrew into himself. He remained the center of his own universe, but the fact of a suffering Continent distressed him deeply. "We are here in safety," he wrote his nephew, "but it feels as if there would be an eclipse of the sun." Soon, feeling himself completely alone in the farmhouse his wife had bought high on Mont Pèlerin above Lausanne and in their apartment in the city, he began to give free lessons to local singers.

Casals continued his efforts to encourage Moór, writing from Barcelona on October 22, 1914: "I hope that, in spite of the sad conditions, you are not too dispirited and that in any case you find consolation in your admirable art. Socías has just this moment come; we have spoken of you, and my wife has sung a number of your songs. I have been working at the Ballade and it commences to move."

As the German army swept toward a Belgium that would not barter its neutrality at the beginning of August 1914, Casals was much worried about the safety of Ysaÿe and his family and the well-being of such other friends as the Socialist leader Emil Vandervelde, who had married Edward Speyer's daughter Lalla. Over the next two weeks came news of the doggedly heroic stand of six ragged, poorly equipped Belgian divisions with the King of the Belgians at their head against thirty-four divisions of the strongest and most efficient military machine in the world. Europe was amazed by the resolution and bravery with which the little country defended its violated neutrality, alone. Casals thought often of the tall, awkward Albert of the Belgians and his birdlike music-amateur queen, Elisabeth, who was as much interested in better nutrition for her subjects as in chamber music and who had already become a faithful member of the audience whenever Casals played in Brussels. Ysaÿe later told Casals of the only measure he had been able to take to protect his country home before fleeing to England via Dunkerque in August 1914 at the last possible moment, as German troops were actually marching into Belgium. He nailed a large sign to the front door: *"This house is the property of an artist who has lived and worked in the cult of Bach, Beethoven, and Wagner. Treat it with respect."* When he returned four and a half years later, everything was intact.

Aboard the RMS *Adriatic* on the nineteenth of November, on the way to the United States for the winter, Casals wrote Röntgen:

> I have wanted for a long time to write to you, but we have been in the most terrible depression during all this unhappy time— We are so dispirited that we can neither think nor do anything—I know you would report the same thing. Dear Julius, God grant that we shall be able to see you soon and that all these horrors will end— Your country and mine have so far been spared. We must thank the good Lord and hope that no more complications come to trouble this peace—although we suffer the consequences all the same. . . .
>
> We will pass the winter in America and think of returning in March if it is possible.
>
> Where is Engelbert? I suppose he is with you because I suppose that after the start of the war there was nothing for him to do where he was. If your Conservatory continues to operate [Röntgen became director of the Amsterdam Conservatory in 1914] it will be a good thing because you can channel into it much of your time and interest.

My affectionate regard to all. I wish you all the strength.
to endure the emotions of these unhappy days—write me
when you can—
    I embrace you

                                                              your
                                                              Pablo

When he and his wife sailed from Europe, Casals' professional life
took another unexpected direction. He had been scheduled for
a major tour of Russia that was no longer possible. Paris was dark,
Belgium overrun since August; Germany and Austria-Hungary
were closed to Western artists and, in effect, to neutrals. Casals
saw England again during the war and returned at least once each
year to Spain, but his major sphere of operation became the United
States.

The preceding fifteen years had been ones of largely unrelieved performing for Casals; once he had begun playing his average of more than two hundred concerts a year in Europe, he maintained that pace until the start of the 1914 war. (Although there
had been moments at the very first, he admitted considerably later,
when he was still an unknown artist in spite of the first successes
with Lamoureux, that "offers of contracts not only did not pour
in, they did not even trickle.")

Some fifty appearances were scheduled for the three and a
half months Casals expected to be in the United States at the end
of 1914 and the beginning of 1915. Many people on both sides
thought the war would be over within months; in any event Casals
held to his plan to return with his wife to Europe in the spring.

One of his first American appearances was to play the Saint-
Saëns cello concerto and the Bruch *Kol Nidrei* at a Sunday-night
Metropolitan Opera House concert on December 13, 1914. The
Opera orchestra was conducted by the Dutch opera conductor
(and later composer of motion-picture music) Richard Hageman;
the program also included solos by Casals' countrywoman Lucrezia
Bori. These Sunday-night concerts were often gala vocal and instrumental music with orchestra, entertainment offered in place
of the more secular theatricality of the operas given there on other
nights and Saturday afternoons. (Arturo Toscanini conducted at
the Metropolitan through the 1914–1915 season, including some
Sunday evenings, but he and Casals never appeared together on
the same stage.)

Some of the things that were occupying Pablo Casals at the time emerge in a letter he wrote Granados on December 28, 1914. Two weeks before he had talked with G. Schirmer, the New York music publisher, concerning the publication of Granados' compositions: ". . . this gentleman is very well disposed toward you and has the greatest confidence in the success of your piano works, and this is to say that you should make money with them in this country." Casals advised Granados that the publisher, in fact, had an arrangement much more important for himself than the benefits that came to Granados through it. Granados need not be satisfied with the present contract; at expiration "impose *your* conditions without allowing any wheedling." Schirmer promised to look at his books and Casals would bring payment for the royalties that had accumulated since October with him when he left for Barcelona.

"I want you to handle this next with *much* delicacy. My brother-in-law Mr. Louis Metcalfe, a most clever young man—an architect and writer familiar with our literature and our language [and] a great admirer of Blasco Ibañez—wants to translate some of this author's works into English." With that in mind Metcalfe had written Blasco Ibañez the preceding summer, at his publisher in Valencia, but never received an answer. Casals didn't know if Granados was personally acquainted with Blasco Ibañez and supposed he would not know where to write him but thought sometime he could drop by the publisher to find out how one could communicate with him. Granados would understand the extent of his interest in this matter, and Casals would "count on [his] characteristic energy (!!!)"

> I hope that all of you are well [the letter continued] *and* that you are not suffering from this ignominious war. Here we run into all the artists whose arrangements for the next season have fallen through and more are coming, disillusioned and miserable. —Little word about the friends trapped in France and Belgium— No word of Crickboom. The three children of Ysaÿe are all right— Thibaud is an automobile-driver— [Florent] Schmitt a bicycle-messenger and telephone-operator. Ravel a driver—Monteux is in Toul— Gaveau and [Auguste] Mangeot in the forces defending Paris— Cortot employed in the Ministry of Fine Arts— Ysaÿe in London with his family— Kreisler here after being

wounded. He is playing very well and gives concerts to excellent houses.

The shift of focus to the Western Hemisphere during the years of the Great War was both natural and practical; the situation and moral climate for musicians was far different in 1914 than it would be twenty-five years later. At the beginning of the earlier conflict there were few neutral havens and fewer opportunities for artists. Many of the Belgians and some of the French were obliged to flee to England; a number, including Ysaÿe, later came to the United States. Many, among them Leopold Stokowski, Thibaud, and Harold Bauer, settled in America, living in Eastern cities and gathering in the summers on the Maine coast or in the Berkshires, irrepressible high spirits coming unavoidably to the surface although—for those with close European connections—consciousness of the war hung over every group and gathering. Fritz Kreisler, after being conscripted into the Austrian army, made his way to England and then to America, as Casals had reported to Granados. Their friends in Allied countries were distressed for such of their colleagues as Adolf Busch and Bruno Walter, obliged by nationality and circumstances to remain behind the barrier of battle for the duration, with infrequent information arriving only through indirect channels.

Casals was not widely known by the North American public—essentially because he had been too busy performing in Europe during the preceding ten years to make tours in the United States—but now he would set the deep and permanent foundation of his American reputation as a cellist. His new management was the Metropolitan Musical Bureau (which became Coppicus and Schang, Inc., in 1917); F. C. Coppicus handled Casals' arrangements personally, a relationship that was more pleasant and much more honest than the experience with his manager during the 1903–1904 trip.

Casals played a memorable recital with Harold Bauer in Symphony Hall, Boston, on February 28, his first trip to that city since he had played there with Emma Nevada's company at the Colonial Theater in November 1901. A week later he played the Lalo concerto for the first time with the Boston Symphony Orchestra, then under the direction of Dr. Karl Muck.

In Boston Casals faced a knowledgeable and demanding audience and some of the sharpest musical critics in the United States, to whom little was sacred unless it met their standards. Although he had played solo and ensemble with Bauer the preceding Sunday, the concerto appearance was work in a different milieu, and the first hearing of a "newcomer" by an audience that readily characterized itself quite as discriminating as any in Budapest, Vienna, Paris, St. Petersburg, or—assuredly—New York. The *Transcript's* Henry T. Parker, crustiest of the Bostonian professional reviewers, observed that once or twice a Symphony season the assisting artist and his music "are more interesting than the orchestra, its pieces and even the conductor himself." This had been the case when Fritz Kreisler and Dr. Muck had played the Beethoven violin concerto; "it has been so once and again when Mr. Paderewski recalled his prime; and it was so yesterday afternoon when Mr. Casals appeared for the first time at the Symphony Concerts." At each pause in the concerto the applause of the audience "warmly and spontaneously" called Casals to his feet and, "contrary to their usual habit, the men of the orchestra laid by their instruments to swell the plaudits. At the end, Dr. Muck himself, first shaking Mr. Casals by the hand, joined in the clapping with which the hall now rang. Not a few of the players in the band were standing and turning eagerly toward the virtuoso and musician who had so impressed them. . . ." The outburst was marvelous for a matinée, noted Louis C. Elson in the *Globe*. "Señor Casals began a walking match from the green-room to the platform, then back again, then to the front again, and so on. . . ." The concerto had been the third portion of the program, just preceding the intermission. The audience knew perfectly well that there was an inflexible tradition of no encores, but the applause continued through the interval and until the first bell that signaled resumption of the concert.

Elson had entered one reservation. Pablo Casals, he said, "is the Paganini of the violoncello. This is a statement which is not wholly praise. Paganini was king of every technical point of violin playing. Casals is equally monarch of his own instrument. But Paganini never was moved in his own heart by his music, nor appealed deeply to the hearts of his auditors. It may have been the fault of the composition, but we were never thrilled to the core. . . . Everything was finished, perfect, wonderful, but it was not a soul's voice appealing to other souls." (Another reviewer also thought Casals began the first movement, the noisy and empty orchestration of which this critic felt "might have been written for a brass band," in "a commonplace manner, as though sensible of the music's limitation.") After that quibble, Elson continued, "we may go into ecstasies, as the audience did. Señor Casals has a beautiful tone, a technique beyond anything that we have heard, and an absolute purity of intonation. . . . Everything was perfect."

Another music critic of stature recorded reactions to Pablo Casals' first Boston Symphony appearance. Olin Downes, only twenty-nine but music critic of the Boston *Post* since 1906, considered the first and second movements of the Lalo concerto entertaining music as well as stuff for a virtuoso's holiday. "And how incomparably did Mr. Casals play this music!" Downes had written a long piece for the preceding Monday about Casals' style. It was not necessary to go over that ground again, he said,

> . . . save to remark that the tone which was so wonderful in solo and ensemble performances last Sunday seemed, if anything, richer, more beautiful, more wonderfully controlled yesterday. There was again annihilation, oblivion of technical difficulties, and the superb balance of head and hand and heart that only the great of the great artists achieve.
>
> Mr. Casals is a virtuoso among virtuosos, but how many virtuosos are such musicians as he? . . . Mr. Casals does indeed feel with his head and thinks with his heart; and is not the man who does that greater in deed than he who takes a city? . . . For once a great artist received merited recognition. Mr. Casals—clean-shaven, entirely unassuming, of rather serious mien, a little bent, as through [from] a life spent over his instrument—came and went from the stage with only a trace of a smile at the ovation accorded him by orchestra as well as audience. He is surely a man to whom words mean little and accomplishment a great deal. The applause continued half through the intermission.

Downes' older *Transcript* colleague, Henry T. Parker, was likewise struck with the artist's personal manner: "Needless, almost, to say, Mr. Casals bore himself as quietly and modestly as is his wont. While he was playing, he was intent upon his work with his usual tranquil air of absorbed abstraction. When his hearers were lavishing their plaudits upon him he received them with as tranquil but clearly courteous content. Yet the applause of the orchestra and the warmth of Dr. Muck toward him plainly touched him."

Unlike most cello virtuosos, Parker noted, Casals played the concerto "without the excision of a single measure." The technique was so great as almost to be imperceptible, but for Parker too it was Casals' tone that was overwhelming:

[throughout] exquisitely edgeless and undulating almost beyond idealized imagining of the voice of an instrument of wood and strings. . . . In the higher register [it] never loses full body and suave texture; in the lower it never loses its limpidity and its fineness. . . . The spirit of Mr. Casals answers to what the imaginative believe is the spirit that dwells in the finger stringed instruments.

Always, too, it is the characteristic voice of the violoncello—deep, grave and rich when it seeks songful intensity of warm and ample utterance, and fine, clear, bright and soft when it is speaking as in running and figured pattern upon the yielding air. As Mr. Kreisler's tone seems the perfectly attuned voice of the violin, or Mr. Bauer's or Mr. Hofmann's . . . of the piano, so does Mr. Casals's seem the perfectly attuned voice of the violoncello. . . . No virtuoso unless he were [an] unusually sensitive and imaginative musician and no man unless he were of poised, discerning, refined and susceptible mind and temper, could produce and sustain such a tone and infuse into it, as Mr. Casals does, the very accent and color of his personality. . . .

Nearer his ideal than is the lot of most mortal men does Mr. Casals seem to come.

During the spring of 1915 Casals appeared for a first time before audiences in Cleveland, Ohio, among other places—in a postseason concert of Adella Prentiss Hughes' Musical Mornings, begun in 1912 in the new Statler Hotel, following a successful pattern established by Alfred Morris Bagby at the Waldorf in New York City. The number of matinée and even morning performances Casals gave is startling, but such was the custom of the time, one to which musicians had to adapt themselves whenever possible. (At least as an instrumentalist Pablo Casals could tune his cello at any hour, and he was used to playing early in the day; he did not have the problem of Chaliapin, who refused an 11:00 A.M. engagement to sing at a very good fee, saying "Madame, at that hour I cannot even spit!")

Casals began to make recordings for the Columbia Graphophone Company during this trip to North America.* On January 15, 1915, he recorded the Rubinstein "Melody in F," Elgar's "Salut d'Amour," the *Largo* from Handel's *Xerxes*, and the second movement of a Tartini cello concerto—some of them, transferred to long-playing records, still available nearly sixty years later. During sessions later in the month he recorded the Bruch *Kol Nidrei*, a Popper Spanish dance, Saint-Saëns' *Le Cygne*, and a Campagnoli romance. He made further recordings in March, and in April made his first records of portions of the Bach suites. Columbia began to advertise the disks widely.

As Casals and his wife sailed for Liverpool and London on their way to Spain on May 29, 1915, three weeks after the sinking of the *Lusitania, Musical America* announced that Casals' first North American season since 1904 had been remarkably successful. When they returned in the autumn for the beginning of the 1915–1916 music season, Casals' concert bookings took him farther west than he had been since the 1901 tour with Emma Nevada and included an appearance in Chicago. In that city, a magazine called *The Violinist* published in its February 1916 issue a short piece about Casals that sounds like the work of a reporter who had been completely unsuccessful in gaining information directly from his subject. Casals, a "man of set convictions," had a deep aversion to publicity, the story said, with his strongest distaste reserved for photographers; he did not even keep press clippings. It is said, noted *The Violinist*, that he never plays an encore, "no matter what pressure is brought." He was described as a "small man with a smooth face and a strictly limited growth of hair, with a gentle smile and a manner so modest it seems at times almost apologetic." Casals still did not have the air of a virtuoso: the Chicago *Journal* observed "He looks neither Spanish nor like a musician, and in outline, costume and demeanor, is strongly suggestive of the English solicitor."

Mid-December 1915 and January 1916 had brought a reunion with Enrique and Amparo Granados in New York, an unlikely place.

* See the Discography beginning on page 568.

Granados did not share any of Albéniz' wanderlust, and his dislike of sea travel was almost morbid; even the few hours' trip from Barcelona to Majorca was a torture, and when a friend once asked what would happen if he had to give a concert in America he said with finality he absolutely would not go. Yet he had agreed to sail from Barcelona to New York on the *Montevideo*, through winter Atlantic waters haunted by German submarines, to be present for the world première of his opera *Goyescas* at the Metropolitan Opera. At almost the last moment it had been decided that his wife, rather than their oldest daughter, would make the trip with him. Traveling with them was Granados' librettist, a journalist named Fernando Periquet who had fashioned a book to fit the music.

Granados had caused a sensation in Paris in 1914 playing his two books of piano pieces (written in 1909 and 1910) inspired by his fascination for eighteenth-century Madrid life and the work of the painter Francisco Goya. The Paris Opéra commissioned him to adapt them into an opera; when war came the Metropolitan took the project over, a shift in which Ernest Schelling, who had been influential in popularizing Granados' music in the United States, played a role.

Granados, who spoke French and Spanish but not English and was shy with people he did not know, got off to an unfortunate start when he was quoted by the press as having said his opera would show America *real* Spanish color—a remark that the Met's general manager Giulio Gatti-Casazza and others interpreted as Granados' pronouncement that he thought he had written a better opera than *Carmen.*

Problems erupted in the opera house at once, first with the conductor, Gaetano Bavagnoli (who had come to the house to direct Italian repertoire) and with the orchestra. According to the New York *Press* the day after the opening "the extraordinary number of errors in the instrumental parts published by G. Schirmer" had been the reason for "fully a dozen" orchestral rehearsals alone. Casals, who was in and out of New York at the time, did his best to help in the preparation and was able to attend the *Goyescas* rehearsals. Granados, almost speechless with nervousness, sat in a corner like a frightened child while Pablo Casals found himself in the role of devil's advocate as well as interpreter. The fault had not been all Schirmer's: Granados was to a great degree self-taught in orchestration techniques. This was not in itself crippling, but Granados was also in many ways as innocent in musical as in human situations. He felt the music he wrote so completely that he really believed the way it should be played would emerge naturally and unmistakably from the score. He had therefore indicated few marks of expression in the orchestral score of his opera, and when conductor or individual players asked precisely how certain passages should be played, Granados invariably answered that they should play it in the way that seemed right to them.

Casals did what he could to help clarify the scoring, but the situation was tenuous (and even the reviewers found the orchestration a conspicuously weak element of the production). The conductor was temperamental, impatient, and threatened to walk out. Casals finally went to see Gatti-Casazza, who was not particularly sympathetic; so far as a Spanish opera was concerned he much preferred Manuel de Falla's *La vida breve*, and he still considered Granados presumptuous.

Gatti and Bavagnoli agreed to continue with the production if Granados would write an entr'acte à la *Cavalleria Rusticana* to keep the audience interested during a scene change. Granados wrote the required addition in his hotel room in a single night. Casals called the next morning and found his friend depressed and close to tears. What he had written was unworthy, pandering to the public, he said, capitulation to unreasonable demands from the directors of the theater. Casals listened to the natural poetry of the strikingly beautiful melody, and, as he had for twenty years, reassured Enrique Granados of the value of what he had composed. The "Intermezzo" transcribed for solo instrument became a popular concert piece (Casals recorded it and included it in his recital programs for years) and is the best-remembered part of the opera.

The Metropolitan's press releases began to appear in the New York papers about two weeks before the opening. No expense had been spared for this first grand opera to be sung in Spanish in the United States. Gatti, although he continued to call the work "a sort of symphonic poem with vocal parts set to a poor libretto," had sent Milanese scenic artist Antonio Rovescalli to Madrid for inspiration in designing the sets. The chorus, "which has the most difficult music to sing," was being trained by Giulio Setti. The dress rehearsal drew the largest audience in several years, one that applauded like a first-night house. The *Evening Telegram* on the day of the opening carried a large advertisement for La Galerie Wanamaker displaying new fashions showing the Spanish influence—Poiret's "Infante" evening gown, the "Goya" gown of rose satin and tulle by Worth, and from Lanvin the "Velasquez" evening gown of black silk tulle, beaded in crystals.

The *Goyescas* world première was Friday, January 28, 1916, sung to a Caruso house. There were only two empty orchestra seats; the Golden Horseshoe boxes were full and the standees were five rows deep. Lucrezia Bori had originally been scheduled to sing the star soprano role, but removal of a growth in her throat forced her to leave the stage temporarily in 1915. The role of the beautiful *madrileña* Rosario was therefore sung by Anna Fitziu in her Metropolitan début. The other three leads were Giovanni Martinelli, Giuseppi de Luca, and Flora Perini. The opera's action is set in and near Madrid about 1800. The episodes Periquet wove around Granados' piano suite hang together somewhat loosely in a conventional libretto that is not particularly dramatic but is not so bad as Gatti liked to think. The curtain opens on a tableau inspired by Goya's famous tapestry cartoon *El Pelele*, which shows four *majas* tossing a dummy in a blanket. The plot concerns interacting jealousy among Rosario's guard-captain suitor Fernando, the bullfighter Paquiro (with whom Rosario is flirting) and his sweetheart Pepa; the end is tragic.

The first-night audience was emotional and appreciative. Most of the Spanish community attended; Casals remembered never having seen so many of an audience in tears. The New York *Herald* called the audience brilliant and the evening one of the important social events of the winter. There were, the *Telegraph* reported, "ecstatic bravos over Signor Granados's music and biscuit-colored waistcoat." The Spanish ambassador and Señora Riaño and the Schellings were guests of Mr. and Mrs. Otto H. Kahn in Box 29. Belmonts, Vanderbilts, Mrs. J. P. Morgan, and Astors were present. Gatti waived one of his restrictions and allowed presentation of wreaths of laurel in silver to composer and librettist. Mr. and Mrs. Gustav White gave a supper for the composer and his wife in Sherry's restaurant off the Metropolitan's Grand Tier.

But between *Goyescas* and the gala supper another opera was performed—*Pagliacci*, with Enrico Caruso and Ida Cajatti heading the cast. *Goyescas* received a total of five Metropolitan performances, between January 28 and March 6, 1916. After the first night it was always the second offering of the evening, coupled with Mascagni's *Cavalleria Rusticana* except on February 26, when it followed *Hansel and Gretel*.

Two days before Enrique and Amparo Granados were scheduled to return to Barcelona on a Spanish ship, an invitation came for Granados to play for President Woodrow Wilson at the White House. The change in plans gave Casals an opportunity for further visits with his close friend—long talks in Catalan about music and Spain, about times spent together, about future plans, including Casals' idea of establishing a permanent symphony orchestra in Catalonia. Casals was in New York when Enrique and his wife sailed for England on the *Rotterdam* on the eleventh of March. Granados, pale and drawn, said as he and Casals embraced farewell that he had a strong presentiment that he would not see his children again. Casals reassured him, but could not sleep that night.

Casals learned from newspapers that Granados and his wife had been killed. The trip to England had been safe; they reembarked at Folkestone on the *Sussex* to cross the English Channel to Dieppe. The *Sussex* was torpedoed by a German submarine on the twenty-fourth of March, and the Granados were among the eighty who died. One survivor said that Enrique had been in a lifeboat when he saw his wife in the water and jumped in to save her. Amparo was a strong swimmer. Her husband had never learned to swim.

The poet, the "wildflower," the unsure genius who was for Casals the embodiment of what Chopin must have been, was gone except for the memory and the music. The wasteful idiocy of war was brought terribly and intimately home. Enrique Granados was in life always lost in dreams and fantasies, a native genius who worked hard to articulate his gift, and who had possessed a physical and spiritual beauty and an almost total unpredictability. Enrique Granados y Campiño was a child and the most lovable of men, whom Harold Bauer had once seen attempt to lighten the atmosphere of a restaurant meal with stuffy friends by trying successfully to balance a fried sardine on the tip of his nose.

The music that flowed from him so naturally that Granados could not believe it of value left one of the two real monuments of Spanish piano music, exquisite songs, dances, and the operas, all "full of the kind of scent—there is no other word—of Spanish rhythms, Spanish melody, Spanish life that nobody but a native-born composer could bring." At the time of his death at forty-eight, he was just finding the true direction of his genius. Casals asserted that Granados' was the purest musical expression of the Spanish soul.

For all his unworldliness, Granados had insisted on being paid by the Metropolitan in gold, which was lost with the *Sussex*. Casals organized a benefit concert for the six Granados children, one of whom was his godchild. Paderewski and Kreisler agreed to take part. This concert, the only consolation Casals could find in the disaster and one he sometimes remembered as the most moving he ever participated in, was given in a jammed Metropolitan Opera House on Sunday night, May 7, 1916. Arriving at the red-brick house in the rain, Casals saw crowds still hoping for tickets. The participants were Paderewski, Kreisler, Casals, the Irish tenor John McCormack, María Barrientos (the Barcelonan who had made her Metropolitan début as Lucia two nights after the *Goyescas* pre-mière), and the Dutch contralto Julia Culp, who had been the other solo artist at the White House when Granados played there on the seventh of March. Casals, Kreisler, and Paderewski played the Beethoven "Archduke" trio—the only time Casals and Paderewski performed together in public and the last time either saw the other. Casals played piano accompaniments to solos by Kreisler and María Barrientos. Kreisler played piano when Casals performed solo works and violin obbligato to songs by John McCormack; Coenraad van Bos played for Julia Culp. During in-termission Mesdames Kreisler, Paderewski, and Casals sold dolls made by Polish refugees and souvenir programs at five dollars each to add to the benefit, which realized more than eleven thousand dollars for the Granados orphans. At the end of the concert, with the Metropolitan Opera House dark except for a single candle on the piano, Paderewski played the funeral march from Chopin's B-flat minor sonata.

By 1916 Donald Francis Tovey was able to report to the Trevel-yans that Julius Röntgen had been writing "some most beautiful unaccompanied choral music: Psalms against war, beginning . . . 'Put not your trust in princes' " as well as having formed the Röntgen String Trio with his two eldest sons; and that Fritz and

Adolf Busch were safely out of the fighting lines. Horszowski, just beginning his mature pianistic career after a period of study in Paris, was in Switzerland when war began and could not return to France because he carried an Austro-Hungarian passport, even though he was born in Poland, but he was able to live out the period of conflict in Italy. Although his sponsors there included Arrigo Boïto, he had to behave with circumspection and report to the police once a week. Emanuel Moór wrote Horszowski regularly from Switzerland; the letters were opened by the censor but fortunately did not contain anything inflammatory, only pleas that Horszowski play Moór works always and learn new ones for future recitals.

Moór's nephew Laurence Burke, who had lived most of his life with his aunt and uncle and had taken the place of their two sons who died at birth in the 1880s, was killed in action at Vimy Ridge at the end of April 1916. Anita Burke Moór never fully recovered from the shock of his death; the requiem Emanuel Moór wrote in his memory was, with two string works, his only composition after the beginning of World War I. Casals wrote after the sad news had reached him, from Stockbridge, Massachusetts, in July 1916:

> . . . It is difficult to try to tell how often I think of you, because you are always in my thought. I would have written many times if I had known where you were. I suppose you are living on the mountain; through these times it is only in harmony with nature that we can survive as men this cataclysm, the inevitable result of our basenesses, egoisms, and all the rest— May God give you many years of life to compose and contribute to the betterment of our poor humankind. Your music has been a great comfort to me and my wife. She often sings your songs, a dozen at the least; I always play the piano part and can give you my word as a musician that your works have had good interpretations. Also the public is beginning to accord them some enthusiasm—the same people who used not to be able to understand you. How I would like to know everything you have composed since the last time I saw you! You know that, in spite of distance and silence I am always the same toward you and your music, and you must know that one of the goals of my life is to be the standard-bearer for your music with honor over all the rest of my career as a musician. . . .

Casals sailed alone aboard the *Touraine* in August 1916, making a brief stop in London on his way to see family and friends in Spain. Susan Metcalfe-Casals spent the rest of the summer at Stockbridge preparing for her next-season concert appearances, a few of which were to be joint recitals with Casals—they had given one, at Aeolian Hall in New York, in April.

Pablo Casals had been writing, accompanying, and listening to songs since childhood, and at forty was learning the genre even better than he might otherwise have. On the afternoon of January 11, 1917, he attended part of a song recital at the Princess Theater in New York; next day he wrote an eloquent salutation to the artist and to the universality of music on two sides of a small correspondence card from the Blackstone Hotel, East 58th Street. Although his conversation was full of his feelings about art, his correspondence seldom touched on them:

> Dear Madame,
> We went to the Princess Theatre yesterday and heard the entire last part of your recital. It was a feast for me to hear this music that for most listeners must seem strange and far-away but that I feel very close to my soul, because to me all the peoples of the world express the same sentiments and emotions. The multitude of languages that exist may divide humanity, but music and its song is the essence of the soul and a universal spiritual language and brings people close whether they realize it or not. This is to tell you that I understood the intervals and the nuances in your songs—and your remarkable interpretation. I felt them as you felt them yourself. How you have been able, a foreigner in the music you interpret, to identify to such a degree, giving the same inflections to your voice, the same gesture and line, is really extraordinary. With my warmest regards and felicitations and a thousand thanks I remain extraordinarily admiring of what is a remarkable talent.
>
> *Pablo Casals*

The recital had indeed been off the beaten track. The singer was an Englishwoman, Mrs. Anada Coomaraswamy, who used Ratan Devi as her stage name and whose art the Indian poet Tagore had praised. What Casals had heard was part of a program of East Indian *ragas* and Kashmiri folksongs, performed in costume and with incense.

The treadmill showed no sign of slowing. Almost everywhere Casals played he received an invitation to return the following season, a pattern that became as strong as it had been in Europe. When the United States entered the war in early 1918, like other important artists he contributed his art to benefits for the Red Cross and other humanitarian organizations. Commitments for the spring of 1918 included a tour as soloist with the New York Phil- harmonic (New York, Brooklyn, Cleveland), a tour with Harold Bauer, and what was becoming an annual set of concerts in Boston. With Bauer, Kreisler, and John McCormack, he founded the Bee- thoven Association in New York in an effort to combat the grow- ing wartime boycott of German music.

Led by the *Musical Courier*, the American press was starting to find Pablo Casals good copy. Margarita Spinoza's piece "Pablo Casals—an Artist's Life" in the *Musical Courier* for May 28, 1918 appears to be the first American solidification of the Casals legend in print. Casals is from "Spain, that romantic land of the past, rich in tradition and poetic beauty" that also produced Cervantes, Velásquez, and Lope de Vega, "among whom he holds a high place." The facts of his early life—teaching by his father, making his way to Barcelona "at eleven or twelve . . . already a finished musician capable of making his own way in the world by his musi- cal genius," discovery by important musicians, translation to Ma- drid and patronage by the Queen, disaster in Brussels and a spec- tacular début in Paris that opened the door to fame. There was something about Casals, even in early middle age, that drove journalists of the time to romantic superlatives in the attempt to explain the fact that so unpretentious a man should produce art so great.

A serious epidemic of what both French and Germans called Spanish influenza had swept Europe in the spring, but Susan Met- calfe accompanied her husband to Spain in the summer. (The Sum- mer Supplement to *The New York Social Register* indicated that her address would be Casals' house at 440 Diagonal, Barcelona. Casals had become officially a member of New York Society when he and Susan Metcalfe married; they were listed under the entry for her mother.) The sea air at San Salvador was detrimental to Susan's throat and voice. Some were distracted by her vocalizing. Many of Casals' Spanish friends observed her unfavorably. It was noted that Casals' accent when speaking English was American, his wife's British. The couple arrived back in New York on the eleventh of November 1918, Armistice Day.

Casals opened a four-week, fourteen-concert season in Mexico City on January 10, 1919. He and his wife found themselves in a country that had been in upheaval almost continuously for eight years and in which travel outside the Federal District was not possible, so all performances took place in the capital. Porfirio Díaz, who had taken dictatorial control of the country the year Casals was born, had (except for a short period in the eighties) kept power until 1911. Rival political forces had been competing for position ever since. During his stay Casals prevailed upon unwilling friends to drive him out toward the forest of the Sierra Leone, where forces loyal to Zapata were bivouacked. Nearing the mountains they were stopped by a heavily armed Zapatista sentinel on horseback and ordered away; Casals remembered the ferocity of the young guerrilla's scrutiny for many years. Even in the heart of the city there was a certain amount of danger. The manager of Casals' hotel was so horrified when he learned of the cellist's penchant for strolling alone after dark in Alameda Park that he detailed a bodyguard to keep him in sight when he went out in the evening.

The director of the Mexico City Symphony was José Rocabruna, violinist with the Crickboom Quartet when Casals had been its cellist twenty-five years earlier, now professor in the Conservatory and head of the chamber-music institute. Casals performed in concert halls and, with his wife, in private houses. When he learned that the nine-year-old Philharmonic Union was in serious financial trouble he declined to play a benefit concert for it but did suggest that he appear with the Symphony, he and the musicians to be paid normal fees in proportion to their participation. The giant concert, with Casals participating as both performer and conductor, was given in the Mexico City Plaza de Toros and was a fantastic success artistically, financially, and emotionally. It was, among other things, a substitute for the bullfights the beleaguered government authorities had banned and, Casals sometimes said, the most colorful concert in which he was ever involved. Afterward, admirers unhitched the horses and drew his carriage by hand from bullring to hotel. Casals' fee was delivered to him as specified. A few days later the secretary of the musicians' union was handed an envelope that contained a check for the exact sum and a card that read *"From Pablo Casals for the hospital fund of the Unión Filarmonica de México. Fraternally. . . . "* Casals very often gave his total fee to a worthy cause, but he seldom waived it—a matter of delicacy, principle, and assurance the money would go where he intended.

Casals learned from the newspapers that Anna Pavlova was bringing a ballet company to Mexico City. Her season opened to near-failure attributed to the high ticket prices in the first weeks (the company started out in the Teatro Arbeu with seats costing eight pesos each, moved to the Teatro Principal at six pesos, gave four or five Sunday performances in the bullring at three pesos a place, and finally played the Cine Granat for peso-and-a-half admission. It was still in Mexico on the fifteenth of April, presumably attempting to recoup expenses, although final performances had been announced for the end of March). When he heard that Pavlova would dance in a benefit for herself in February, Casals went to see Alexander Smallens, conductor of the ballet orchestra, and arranged the kind of surprise Casals enjoyed. Mexico might have been in troubled times, but the upper classes turned out in jewels and full dress—as some of it had for Casals—on the night Pavlova was to dance her gala on the flower-bordered stage of the Teatro Arbeu. When she came onstage to dance her most famous single number, "The Dying Swan," the cello solo of the accompaniment—Saint-Saëns' *Le Cygne*—came from the wings at stage right rather than the pit. Casals saw the ballerina send a startled glance in his direction, but she danced superbly. When she finished, Pavlova rushed offstage to embrace Casals, smearing him liberally with makeup, then returned to take a call and stood center stage facing and applauding Casals. The audience's cheers continued when she brought him on.

The war over, Casals was able to resume tours in Europe after his return from Mexico by way of the United States. He made some U.S. appearances at the end of the 1918–1919 season, including a joint one with Rachmaninoff in New York and a Sunday-night performance at the Metropolitan Opera House. Paris was alight again; Casals returned there on his first trip to Europe after the

Armistice to look after his affairs and possessions. The boxes he had left in storage had been rifled thoroughly; most of the correspondence had disappeared. His bank deposits were unavailable.

Some of the human loss of the war had come terribly home to him with the drowning of Granados; now he saw the material waste of ruined towns and the remains of combat trenches. He performed with Siloti in Budapest, and was more and more appalled as he began to understand what the revolutionaries had done to this Russian and his family. What he learned of the sufferings of Belgium during military occupation for four years was beyond immediate belief. He saw expanses of desolate fields and burned woodland, and the burial grounds with thousands of uniform markers of the deaths of young men of many nations.

1919–1945

18

For the twenty years following the end of the First World War Pablo Casals was in great demand throughout Europe and was still being urged to settle permanently in America. He was acclaimed a consummate artist wherever he played by the time he was in his early forties. In many respects his was a pleasant life; three hours or so of work at piano and cello in the morning was for him natural activity rather than burdensome exercise. He was able to take a holiday of a month or more a year. Personal dissatisfactions were real but intermittent even in the twenties and coalesced only later into private regret. He had security and authority in the knowledge of what he had done and could do in the art of the violoncello, and he would never loosen his grip on that mastery. But he was still seeking a greater world to master.

The cello never completely satisfied Casals the musician, according to his repeated testimony. It had given him fame and a fortune, but he spoke of it as a tyrannical companion more often than (as once in his seventies) "a beautiful woman that has not grown older . . . but younger with time, more slender, more supple and more graceful." He had written Julius Röntgen early in their friendship "If I have been happy scratching away at a cello, how shall I feel when I can possess the greatest of all instruments—the orchestra?"

In the autumn of 1919 Casals came home to Spain with the intention of making Barcelona and San Salvador his base for the rest of his life. He had resolved to have a hand in developing a permanent symphony orchestra worthy of the Catalan capital, a scheme he had begun to discuss with Enrique Granados nearly ten years earlier. Catalonia was materially prosperous as a result of business and industrial growth during four war years as a neutral and Casals was certain that the important city of Barcelona should and could support such an organization. Barcelona had changed in the quarter-century since Pablo Casals had been a provisional member of the Municipal School of Music faculty. A city clustered around the ancient Gothic quarter and port in the 1890s, it was now the major industrial center of the Iberian peninsula, with a population of a million and a half.

His first intention was to work through one of the existing organizations in Barcelona. The nearest thing to permanent orchestral groups were the government-subsidized symphonic Municipal Band of Barcelona, established during Casals' childhood by Rodoreda, and the orchestra of the Gran Teatro del Liceo; but the musicians who played in these groups had to play elsewhere or take jobs outside music to earn a living. The Orfeó Català (which Amadeo Vives and Luis Millet had founded in 1891) was essentially a choral group and was for Casals, along with Montserrat, one of the two cultural pillars of Catalonia. At the time there were two other symphonic groups, established by able Catalan musicians—Francisco Pujol and Lamotte de Grignon—but neither played regular seasons or rehearsed together frequently; certainly they were not permanent in comparison to the major orchestras in other European cities. Casals approached the various directors and offered his cooperation in making one of the orchestras first-class and permanent. He was willing to appear as soloist and conductor if they wished; he would see that funds were raised. They were not interested. The arguments ran that there was not enough musical talent in Catalonia to shape a better orchestra and, even if there were, the prospects for survival would be poor. Luis Millet, who had put much effort into his excellent Orfeó Català, was particularly unreceptive to the idea. But what finally and unequivocally impelled Casals to establish his own orchestra was the chance remark that after all he had become an international figure and so did not know the possibilities in Barcelona.

He went to the leaders of the musicians' union, talked over his scheme with them, and asked what their membership was earning. He was appalled to learn how low standard fees were; he announced impulsively that he would guarantee *his* players double the going wage for two seasons each year. With the assistance of his brother Enrique, who was twenty-seven in June 1919, Casals set about forming his orchestra. (Enrique had become an excellent violinist. After his first lessons from Carlos Casals he studied with Rafael Gálvez in Barcelona; in 1908, at fifteen, he went to study in the Brussels Conservatory with Crickboom and Joseph Jongen, then had a further period of study in Prague. At nineteen he served as first violinist of Lamotte de Grignon's symphonic group in Barcelona, and at twenty was a concertmaster of the Imperial symphony orchestra in St. Petersburg. By the time Enrique became subject to military service Spain had universal conscription and immunity could no longer be purchased. Doña Pilar put the choice straightforwardly to her youngest son, for whom she showed an increasing tenderness, in a discussion in 1913 at which Pablo was also present. The law in Spain demanded universal military service but she said that did not mean he had either to learn to kill or prepare himself to be killed; he could leave Spain. Enrique sailed for Argentina and lived there, working as a musician, until he was twenty-five and the Spanish government declared an amnesty for those who had avoided conscription.)

Enrique had opened an academy called the Instituto Musical Casals in a house Casals owned in the Rambla de Cataluña, and auditions of prospective orchestra members commenced there. Many were Enrique's students and their friends. Eighty-eight *profesores* were engaged for a first season, projected for the spring of 1920. Most of them were Catalan, few had any real orchestral experience, some had not played professionally at all; a sense of potential had weighed heavily in many choices. Enrique Casals was assistant director and first violinist; he had married a Vendrell girl, and their daughter Pilar (called Pilareta) later became the orchestra's mascot. The assistant concertmaster was Enrique Ainaud, the music student who had met Casals on a Paris street in 1894 and told him about an opening in the cancan orchestra of the Folies-Marigny. First cello was Casals' long-time friend

Bonaventura Dini, whose seventeen-year-old nephew Pau joined the second-violin section. The new orchestra's offices, social hall, and focal point were Pablo Casals' house at 440 Diagonal—a handsome broad avenue many Barcelonans continued to call by that name although it became officially the Avenida General Goded after 1939.

Pablo Casals' primary reason for establishing an orchestra in Barcelona was homage to Catalonia. When he began his efforts he was prepared to serve in almost any role necessary to accomplish the goal. Only after he began to encounter general apathy, active opposition, and even scorn did he decide to make the venture in his own name and on his terms. Once his mind was fixed on doing the thing himself, Casals set about creating a sound organization with adequate support. He knew that his name carried real prestige in Spain, and while he was prepared to devote some of his own funds if necessary at the beginning, he did not expect real difficulty in finding adequate financial backing.

There were more problems than he anticipated. One wealthy aristocrat told Casals he did not care for the *toros* but was much more interested in the bullring than in anything that could happen in a concert hall. Other potential contributors said that they had no funds to spare. There was some highly opinionated comment in the Catalan press against the project. Casals was genuinely surprised to learn of antagonism in Barcelona musical circles toward him and the idea. He worked all the harder as his frustration grew. For a time solid support came only from his mother, Enrique, and a small collection of close friends. The first contributor was Carlos Vidal Quadres, once a man of great wealth, in whose house Casals had played his first string quartet in the Café Tost days, now quite an old man and generally considered eccentric if not senile. He was no longer able to be a full-scale Maecenas, but he said, "I am giving you the little I can for your orchestra." Casals, tears in his eyes, responded that in manner and spirit he was giving everything.

Concurrently with the selection of the orchestra members, a committee of directors of the Orquestra Pau Casals was incorporated and a drive begun for membership, especially for members of the *patronat*, sustaining members able and willing to pay a double fee. The governing board of the *patronat* (their names always listed in the Catalan form, as all programs and program notes were in Catalan) had as president Josep Soldevila. The vice-president was the Count de Lavern, and members were Carlos Vidal Quadres, Francesc Cambó, Claudi Sabadell, Jerón de Moragues, and Lluís Guarro, one of the most important paper manufacturers in Spain. The secretary was Joaquim Pena i Costa, who later wrote notes for the orchestra's programs, a good friend and a confirmed pessimist who had already invested a considerable amount of his own money in musical activities in Catalonia. He had been a chief founder of the Barcelona Wagnerian Society and had translated into Catalan the texts of all the Wagner operas, Schiller's "Ode to Joy" used in Beethoven's ninth symphony, and works by Schubert and Grieg.

Queen Mother María Cristina offered her patronage for the formation by Casals of an orchestra in Madrid. But not only was the Madrid Symphony well established, Madrid was also not Catalan.

One thing did reveal that Casals had been away from Catalonia for some time. He was disconcerted to find his board of directors more interested in talking politics than in discussing music or completing plans for the orchestra's first season. Strong republicanism as well as the traditional Catalan desire for freedom from Madrid's control were in the air. The demand for iron and war matériel by the belligerents in the 1914 war had brought tremendous industrial development for neutral Spain, particularly in Catalonia, but the prewar political structure of the country remained. The rapid growth of industry merely increased the long-standing tension between the entrenched Army–Church–landowner upper classes and the growing body of socialists and anarchists. The resurgent demand for Catalan autonomy resulted in general unrest that some called a compelling reason against the sort of artistic innovation Casals was proposing. But Casals visited the leadership of all the local political factions and argued that music, the universal language, was a unifying medium for the good of all and had nothing to do with sectarian divisions.

On his return from his January–February 1920 North American tour, Casals went to work on the first season of his new orchestra. Contracts had been given the musicians for six weeks of rehearsals and ten concerts in both the spring and the fall. Concerts were to be given in the colorful auditorium of the Palau (Palacio) de la Música Catalana in Barcelona, a heavily decorated building designed in 1905 by the Catalan architect Doménech Montaner for the Orfeó Català. There were to be two rehearsals a day, one at nine in the morning, the other at 5:00 P.M. sharp. The scores and orchestral parts were mostly from the library of Hans Richter, which Casals had bought from his widow in Bayreuth at war's end.

First rehearsal of the Orquestra Pau Casals was set for the first week of June. On the night of the second of June Casals took part in the second annual Sardana Festival at the Teatro del Bosc in Gracia, by then a part of the city of Barcelona. Always distressed by stage lights as by bright sunshine, Casals found the illumination while he played more painful than ever. That night he collapsed. The doctors said it was exhaustion, brought on by months of anxiety, frustration, and lack of rest during the organization of the orchestra. The condition was complicated by a severe inflammation of the irises of his eyes, which had caused him acute pain at the Teatro Bosc.

The specialists who were called in prescribed and administered an injection of milk—the standard treatment at the time for this condition. Casals' reaction was drastic—his head fell to one side and he was unable to lift it; he began to sweat violently. A few hours later a nurse, unaware an injection had been given, came in and gave him another. After that Casals could not move at all and could speak only with the greatest difficulty. The family sent for its regular physician, who announced with some admiration that the dosage had been enough to kill a horse. Casals suffered violent headaches for many years afterward.

Pablo Casals knew that cancellation of the new orchestra's first rehearsal would be disastrous psychologically and as a practical matter, but he could not leave his bed. He sent Enrique with word of his illness and the instruction that the players were to meet regularly and punctually at the scheduled times until he had recovered sufficiently to join them. They were to discuss compositions and practice individual parts. Casals saw to it that they were paid at the end of each week. After the second week a deputation came to the sickroom, protesting that the arrangements could not continue; they were draining away what they knew to be Casals' own money. It was not right to accept payment when they were meeting to rehearse and there were no concerts. Casals thanked them for their concern and reminded them of their contract. They must continue to meet and rehearse; he would be with them as soon as it was physically possible. In the meantime they must play, *play!* Toward the end of July, with the traditional vacation time approaching, Casals was well enough to go to the Palau (against his doctor's wishes) to address the orchestra at the last session before autumn. He spoke of his faith in them and thanked them for their confidence in him. He looked forward with pleasure to working together in the fall. Casals now felt that the musicians knew he was serious and that the project would continue.

He had time to reflect during his convalescence, much more than he welcomed, being a man of quick decision. During his forced inactivity his own feeling about Catalonia and its "renaissance" reinforced his conviction that his patriotic and artistic duty lay in the development of a Barcelona orchestra. Every conversation about the future of the organization seemed to merge inescapably into discussion of the future of Catalonia as well. Unable for weeks to carry on his lifelong musical routine, for the first time he had the uninvited opportunity to think about politics—with a sharp awareness of the gulf between rich and poor, the governing and the governed, that had driven him toward darkness in adolescence. Every day strengthened his knowledge that what he must do was the thing he was best able to do, make fine music available to the people of Catalonia. He felt waves of regret that he had composed virtually nothing since 1902.

Orchestral work started in earnest after the late-summer holiday. Pablo Casals set about molding a motley combination of musicians into a cohesive ensemble. Every one of them had something to learn—those with some experience perhaps more than the neophytes, because they had to overcome sloppy habits the others had not had a chance to form. There were a few basic rules: promptness at rehearsals, attention to the work at hand, no deputies. There was a still-prevalent practice in much of Europe whereby a regular player would send a substitute to rehearsals or even to the concert if he had found a better-paying engagement, resulting in the conductor's facing an orchestra some of whose members he had never seen before.

Casals addressed the orchestra before the first autumn rehearsal, stressing their community in music, the great privilege they

*Casals rehearsing his Barcelona orchestra in
the 1920s*

had of making music together and their sacred responsibility to
the true meaning of the music, the duty of absolute integrity. First,
they must all be musicians and must master their parts as though
each was a soloist, yet each must be a leaf on the same tree. They
began to rehearse the "Ride of the Valkyries" from Wagner's *Die
Walküre*, a flashy workhorse that most of the players with any
orchestral experience knew well but were used to playing carelessly and out of tune. After a run-through Casals began to work
on the familiar piece note by note. Later he would beseech members of orchestras he led not to play only notes, but initially he

worked on the first step in an effort to make each player conscious of the importance of every note and to produce it with precision. Except for the opening address, Casals did not talk a great deal to the orchestra. But from the first he taught. He illustrated his wishes by singing or by demonstrating on a borrowed violin or cello. His gestures were clear. He inspired. He was patient, never sarcastic or bullying. The orchestra became tired during a demanding rehearsal, one player remembered; some began to talk, others started rolling cigarettes. No angry shouts from the conductor, few scowls. Casals merely put down his baton and said very quietly "*Pero señores*" ("But, gentlemen"). All conversation stopped, there was full silence for a moment, and work continued with full concentration.

After a week's rehearsal the first of the five concerts of the Orquestra Pau Casals' opening series was presented in Barcelona's Palace of Music at 9:45 P.M., October 13, 1920. The program was the Bach orchestral suite in D, Beethoven's seventh symphony, the Ravel "Mother Goose" suite, and Franz Liszt's tone poem *Ideals*. Although certain influential people had circulated word to their friends and debtors to stay away, the house was a good one. Casals' illness earlier in the year was general knowledge, and the ovations were loud and emotional.

Subsequent concerts that season included one for the Barcelona Chamber Music Association (Associació de Música de Camera), a long-established and fashionable series for which Casals had played benefit concerts in lean times years before and which, now a successful operation, engaged Casals' orchestra for one or two concerts each year. Programs during the first season included Beethoven (*Coriolan* Overture and the "Eroica"), Mozart (symphony number 40), Mendelssohn ("Fingal's Cave"), Weber (Overture to *Der Freischütz*), Schubert (symphony in B minor), Richard Strauss (*Ein Heldenleben*, Enrique Casals violin soloist), Fauré (*Masques et Bergamasques*), Debussy (*Rondes de Printemps*), and Enesco (*Rumanian Rhapsody* number 1). Also performed were a "Hymn to Justice" by Magnard, Emanuel Moór's *Improvisations for Orchestra*, and two sardanas by Juli Garreta, the watchmaker-composer whom Casals considered the greatest native talent in the history of modern Spanish music.

The people of Catalonia's capital recognized the importance of the orchestra. But the public, especially in Barcelona, idolized

Casals as a cellist and felt strongly possessive of him in that role. The announcement that he would give a recital assured a sold-out house anywhere in Spain, and there was some feeling in Catalonia even before 1920 that he played in his own country too seldom. When he established his orchestra the public still preferred the bow to the baton—fellow musicians engaged in making their own livings observed that as a conductor Casals was a first-rate cellist— and the press reflected the public's reaction: Why does this man feel he has to branch out into other areas of music? So far as he was concerned, Casals was patriotically working to make Barcelona an important center in the world of international music, and he was endeavoring to do this with the most complete of musical instruments, a symphony orchestra. Popular interest grew; Casals would note few empty seats during the orchestra's existence, and it soon became clear to Barcelona music-lovers that virtually the only chance they would have to hear Casals publicly was as an infrequent soloist with his orchestra. He did not give a recital in Barcelona between 1920 and 1929, drawing from one local musician the remark that a well-known Catalan woman pianist hadn't played there for five years and Casals not for ten, so he wouldn't have to give a hometown recital himself for twenty. A small annual contribution was eventually received from the city government after it was obvious the Concerts Casals would survive, but Casals personally made up a deficit that averaged nearly half a million pesetas a year for the first eight years, a final total of between three million and four million hard-currency pesetas (close to half a million dollars). Casals was a wealthy man and seemed to some in those days to live like a prince, but his winter concert tours through the 1920s were a necessity to maintain himself, his family, and the Orquestra Pau Casals.

Casals often termed the seventeen years he was artistic director and permanent conductor of his own orchestra the most fruitful of his life. They spanned what for most men would have been the "mature" years, from late in his forty-third year until he was sixty-one. He did not reject his career as a virtuoso solo performer until he was seventy, and he would not have stopped then except for a moral position that allowed him no other course. But when he started his orchestra in Barcelona in 1920 he had embarked on a second musical career, the break quite clear in his own mind.

The contention that the Barcelona public wanted only café

music and zarzuela tunes was quickly disproved by the demand for tickets and a *patronat* membership that soon was more than a thousand. Finding enough Catalan musical talent to staff a good symphony orchestra was more of a problem. There were string players in plenty, and enough woodwinds, but some brass had to be imported. The original first horn, a Frenchman named Lambert, was a good musician but no longer had the requisite endurance: he brought along an assistant to play the *tuttis* while he saved his strength for the solo passages. By the second spring, Casals had been able to obtain the participation of Willem Valkenier, the first-horn player of the Berlin State Opera. Casals remembered his work as first-chair horn of the Vienna Konzertverein orchestra, with which Casals had appeared frequently just before the war. Valkenier, who was given unusual leave from Berlin as a courtesy to Casals during the Barcelona seasons from 1921 until 1923, recalled an additional small but important operational problem: Casals gave all his instructions in Catalan, which Valkenier fortunately knew; he had to translate them for his second horn, an Andalusian who, like most of the musicians who were not from the North of Spain, did not understand a word of Catalan.

Each instrumental section had a leader who was at least a competent musician and who worked with his component of the orchestra to bring it somewhere close to the conductor's standard, but more than one experienced musician wondered after each season's first rehearsal how it would be possible to play adequately, much less well, after only a week's preparation. They were always amazed by what had been accomplished by the end of that week and at the orchestra's improvement at the end of the season.

What Casals accomplished with his orchestra—and the orchestra with him—was the result of Casals' persistence and his rehearsal work as much as of his genius. Casals always knew exactly what he was doing—or trying to do, when the execution involved others—in music. His manner and technique in rehearsing the Orquestra Pau Casals was watched in action carefully and critically in 1923 by a fellow conductor who described the experience in some detail. Adrian Boult, an English director who had just turned thirty-three but had been leading orchestras in his own country for eight years, came to Barcelona to spend three weeks attending rehearsals of the Orquestra Pau Casals and to conduct two British works during the concert on the twenty-sixth of May. Boult found

Program covers of the Orquestra Pau Casals—
for the inaugural concert in 1920 and an
autumn concert in 1935, six months before
the outbreak of civil war

himself in fascinating but alien territory. He had gone to the trouble to learn Spanish, only to find Casals habitually speaking Catalan. Rehearsal hours were unusual—every day at 2:30 and 9:45 P.M., but it was not unusual to see orchestra members strolling away from the rehearsal after midnight to sit on benches along the Ramblas while the less acclimatized foreigner was hurrying off to bed. Sessions lasted two and a half hours, with a fifteen-minute break.

Rehearsals always began with meticulous tuning of the instruments, Boult recalled. Casals listened to the A of each wind instrument, then of each member of the string sections. What would be rehearsed was not announced beforehand, so every member of the orchestra was present at every rehearsal. Boult noted that Casals took the works in cycles,

> . . . though not necessarily beginning with the most diffi-
> cult. Starting with a run through without a stop, he would
> then immediately rehearse the work in close detail, and this
> was, of course, the most interesting time, for he would some-
> times spend ten minutes on two or three bars with one instru-
> ment or group alone . . . the Spanish temperament makes
> it possible for the rest of the orchestra to sit in perfect silence
> without even a surreptitious puff at a cigarette during an
> interval of this kind. I actually counted 19 repetitions of the
> chromatic scale in the middle of the Scherzo of the *Midsum-*
> *mer Night's Dream* music, where each division of the string
> department has two bars of the scale as it runs through four
> octaves. When he had finished the details of one work, he
> would carry on with this process with the rest of the
> programme.
>   Then began a second repetition of the whole cycle; start-
> ing sometimes with a few special passages, but usually going
> straight through with stops whenever necessary. This would
> go on until the concert. No work was ever perfect, and there
> always seemed fresh details to attend to.

The absence of letters in the individual players' parts, a precise guide to where the conductor wished to start after he had halted the orchestra ("two measures before B"), did not seem to present problems. Casals, Boult discovered, "would go back 40 or 50 bars after a stoppage, [which] would have the double advantage of con-firming some previous point and allowing . . . forgetfulness to creep in before the passage under discussion was again approached, thereby ensuring its permanent improvement."

Boult felt that the members were musicians perfectly compe-tent to take their place in any symphony orchestra in Europe. Nine rehearsals of such an orchestra would result in performances "of the most uncommon perfection of ensemble and dullness" unless managed with great skill. He came to the conclusion that the Bar-celona rehearsals were really lessons, "and Casals the teacher is no less eminent than Casals the player."

Long study preceded the rehearsal of any work Casals planned to direct. Musically, he was more demanding of himself all his career than of any of his colleagues or students. Days, weeks, or longer went into the study and marking of the score of a work scheduled for one of his concerts, labor as unsparing as any he ever put into mastering a new work for his solo repertoire. The conductor must know every technical facet of the music, then he must work toward the meaning of the music within the composition as a whole; it must be his before he can convince his players to join him in approaching "the ultimate in beauty."

"Casals had to teach," said one of his musicians, "and he is a great teacher. He does not talk at length about style . . . he sings, he inspires. He is not a conductor who shadowboxes. All his gestures are for the orchestra. . . . His sole concern is the music and the interpretation of the composer's intentions so far as one can decipher them from our rather primitive system of notation. . . . At times he would ask, let us say, the first viola (an excellent musician) 'Please give me your viola,' and he would play and say 'Play it this way.'" The player, no matter how highly esteemed, who countered with the suggestion of a variant articulation or bowing received so curt a dismissal that he understood instantly how unwise it would be to press the matter. Casals maintained complete artistic control and determined the programs. Although the Orquestra appears never to have been treated to outbursts, batons thrown or broken in fury or frustration, said one player, "One can well sense it when a thunderstorm is brewing."

Boult set down some technical observations of Casals the conductor at work:

> EXECUTION. On the slightest want of clearness, whether in an inner part or a more obvious passage, Casals would stop and often ask the orchestra to find their own way through by means of separate practice for a few minutes. He would then take the passage together, and it was remarkable how the development of the passage from a rough scramble to a finished performance was always based on the need, not only for correctness of intonation, rhythm and so on, but on the style of the work as a whole. The same rhythmic figure occurring in a work by Schubert and in a work by Tchaikovsky would be handled in a totally different manner. Modern works were given a certain freedom, but a mathematical exactness of rhythm would put glowing life into the classics. It was a thrilling experience to hear how a simple figure like the first subject of the Schubert C major Symphony, or the minim-followed-by-crotchet [half note fol-

lowed by quarter] so often found in classical scherzos, played in *absolutely* strict time, gained in character and point.

Boult felt the full benefit of this when he began to rehearse the orchestra himself, in a contemporary British composer's work—Butterworth's *Folk Song Idyll*—when "the absolute regularity of the playing at once brought the right things to the surface, although no pains were spared in working out details when necessary. Matters of bowing, and sometimes, too, of fingering, were often discussed, and in all important passages the strings bowed together [still not a universal practice in the 1920s]. This was arranged by the fine leader of the orchestra, Mr. Casals' younger brother."

> EXPRESSION. Here, again, as one followed the rehearsals it was continually obvious that Casals' attitude towards every detail was built up on the style of the work as a whole. Quality of tone, attack and release, chording (. . . whether the notes of the chord were of equal force, or whether one was made more prominent)—the management of all these things was dictated, not by any arbitrary rule, but by the expression of the particular work in hand. Everything was explained, every member of the orchestra was made to feel the passage himself in its inevitable relation to the expression of the moment and the style of the whole work.

Casals used a heavy stick, making no pretense of "the modern type of virtuoso conducting with all the expression shown with the point of the stick, as we must do in England where rehearsals are so few." Modern work of the more brilliant type, Boult allowed, calls for a light stick held by a loose wrist and fingers to obtain certain effects.

> But what is brilliance in modern work compared to performances of the classics which convince all hearers that they are inevitably right? Classical music has stood the test of time, and we *know*, therefore, that it is good, and when a work like the C major Symphony can be made so moving that the whole audience is spellbound, and a rather jumpy executive musician even forgets throughout its performance that he has got to go and take charge of the next number on the programme, it is surely an achievement worth far more than mere clever stick work of a modern conductor. Out of every dozen musicians who excel in modern work,

it would be rare to find more than one who can do equal justice to the classics. We all know Casals' playing of the classics. Casals, the conductor, is no less great an artist.

Some cuts were made in the Schubert symphony, but the entire work was rehearsed thoroughly, cuts being made only during the final rehearsal. Musicians not needed in a particular piece (contrabassoonist and harpist, for example) sat as attentive listeners in the front of the house until the rehearsal was finished.

Boult kept a record of time spent on rehearsals of three programs:

1st Concert (15 May)		Hrs	Mins
Beethoven. 5th Symphony		6	55
Saint-Saëns. *Le Rouet d'Omphale*		2	10
Enesco. Roumanian Rhapsody in A		3	15
Debussy. Gigues		4	45
Bach. Overture in D		2	30
	9 rehearsals	19	35
2nd Concert (20 May)			
Berlioz. Fantastic Symphony I		2	00
II			30
III		1	35
IV			35
V		1	05
Beethoven. Leonore No. 2		2	50
Korngold. Overture to a Drama		4	50
Morera. Two Sardanas		2	00
Tchaikovsky. *Hamlet*		3	35
	9 rehearsals	19	00
3d Concert (26 May)			
Schubert. C major Symphony I		3	20
II		2	10
III		2	10
IV		2	10
Butterworth. Folk Song Idyll		1	05
Holst. *Perfect Fool* ballet		4	10
Mendelssohn. *Midsummer Night's Dream*			
Overture		3	30
Scherzo		2	20
Nocturne			40
Berlioz. Rakoczy March			40
	11 rehearsals	22	15

Boult was guest conductor for the Butterworth and Holst compositions, while Casals conducted all others.

The programs of the Orquestra Pau Casals were predominantly classical and romantic, ranging from Vivaldi and the Bachs to Reger and Saint-Saëns. They also included works by Catalan and Spanish composers, and compositions by men working actively in a variety of styles—among them Arnold Bax, Ernest Bloch, Casella, Dohnány, Enesco, Percy Grainger, Honneger, Zoltán Kodály, Charles Loeffler, Luigi Malipiero, Darius Milhaud, Prokofiev, Respighi, Arnold Schönberg, Igor Stravinsky, Anton Webern, and Felix Weingartner. Ravel was represented in the first concert, Debussy's clarinet rhapsody appeared early in the second series. The program content was well-balanced and substantial. Missing—as from the repertoires of most symphony orchestras—was the experimental music of the first quarter of the twentieth century. Members of the orchestra felt that their director was not particularly interested in much of the newer music, but maintained stoutly that in the classics he was the equal of any conductor anywhere.

The nearly sixty guest conductors during seventeen years were a mixed, frequently distinguished, and somewhat unpredictable assortment. Among those of international interest were Ernest Ansermet, Arbós, Boult, Fritz Busch, Emil Cooper, Alfred Cortot, Vincent d'Indy, Manuel de Falla, Otto Klemperer, Koussevitzky, Clemens Kraus, Pierre Monteux, Ildebrando Pizzetti, Franz Schalk, Hermann Scherchen, Arnold Schönberg, Richard Strauss, Igor Stravinsky, Donald Francis Tovey, Anton Webern, Felix Weingartner, and Ysaÿe.

Violinists included some of the great names of the age—Kreisler, Thibaud, Ysaÿe—as well as Joachim's grandnieces Adila and Jelly d'Arany, Mathieu Crickboom, and Casals' brother Enrique. About a hundred pianists, international stars and a great many Spanish artists, figured as soloists. Wanda Landowska's name appears on the programs as harpsichordist in November 1921 and November 1926, in a concert devoted entirely to the works of Manuel de Falla, with Casals conducting and Falla appearing as piano soloist. The singers were primarily Catalan (one exception: Elisabeth Schumann), headed by Conchita Badia, one of the remarkable Spanish singers of the twentieth century and among the greatest interpreters of Granados' vocal music. Susan Metcalfe-Casals is listed three times as soprano soloist with the orchestra: October 1923, singing *Phidyle* by Duparc and arias from Handel's *Acis and Galatea;* November 1924, in the Mahler fourth symphony; and April 1927, when she sang six Beethoven songs accompanied on the piano by Casals, during the Beethoven-year celebration.

Compositions by Pablo Casals appear only twice on the programs of seventeen years—his *Sardana* for cellos was played in May 1929, and on the third of November 1935 Concepció Badia sang six of his songs for soprano. Sardanas by Enrique Casals were performed much more frequently. Pablo Casals purposely did not give cello concerts in Barcelona from 1920 until 1929, when the Orquestra Pau Casals had become self-supporting. The public still wanted to hear him as cellist: after the announcement that Casals would give a solo recital for orchestra patrons only, in the fall of 1926, membership doubled.

He invited and accompanied other cellists—including Diran Alexanian, Horace Britt, Gaspar Cassadó, Bonaventura Dini, Maurice Eisenberg, Pierre Fournier, Raya Garbusova, and Gregor Piatigorski—but his own appearances averaged one a calendar year.

The Orquestra Pau Casals often brought music to other cities in Catalonia, but its only trip abroad, a major undertaking, was to Paris in 1926 to take part in a festival of international orchestras in the Théâtre des Champs-Élysées. Taking music to smaller cities of Catalonia was part of what Casals saw as a sacred duty—trips outside Spain were not—and such short journeys were feasible early in the organization's existence.

The existence of the Orquestra made possible another project— concerts for workers—that Casals had discussed with Harold Bauer and other friends since the beginning of the century; for practical reasons its realization had to be postponed until the organization had become almost self-supporting. It was Casals' unswerving belief that the receptiveness to great music is as large and immediate on the part of those who work with their hands as from those whose economic and social advantages make daily life more comfortable. The workers, Casals' argument ran, in fact deserve to have first-rate music available to them more than the privileged, because they have many fewer pleasures. In this he was influenced by his father's attitude, although a more obvious example was the life of José Anselmo Clavé, a remarkable self-taught musician and

Catalan patriot, a weaver by trade who had died two years before Casals was born. Clavé formed choral groups among factory workers and craftsmen, first in Barcelona and then in other parts of Catalonia. The Catalans seem instinctively musical, and traditional songs and Clavé's own simple, sentimental tunes were not difficult to master. Literally hundreds of town choruses grew up— and hundreds of village groups continued to sing together regularly. Clavé's movement for choral singing among the workers was intended to bring some beauty into their bleak lives.

Casals discussed the idea with his orchestra board. "Popular" concerts even at lower prices were not the solution. The workman could afford only the cheapest balcony seat; looking down on the well-dressed middle-class people in the boxes and orchestra, his mind would be on things other than the enjoyment of music. (Prices listed for the autumn series of six concerts in 1922 ranged from 300 pesetas [about $48] for a loge box to 20 pesetas [just over 50¢ per concert]. Average wage for a worker was no more than 10 pesetas a day [about $1.60 in pre-1929 U.S. currency].) Nor were charity concerts the proper answer; Casals knew that the Catalan sense of honor and dignity would make a manual worker reject the appearance of accepting charity, artistic or material, as quickly as would an aristocrat. The board took a dim view of the project, but afterward one member put Casals in touch with some union leaders who had shown an interest in cultural affairs, "intelligent people who did things for their men."

Casals called on these labor-syndicate men at the Ateneu Politecnicum, a night school for workers that had made a few ventures into amateur dramatics, scholarly lectures, and art exhibitions. Casals proposed an organization under whose auspices his orchestra would offer six concerts a year; he would play for them and assure the appearance of famous soloists. The organization would elect its own governing committee and set its own rules, including criteria for membership. It would not be charity; members would have to pay something within their means. He wanted to create the need to hear good music in the families of workers.

The representatives of labor listened courteously and said they would think the offer over. A few days later a deputation who had come in work clothes directly from their places of employment waited upon Casals in his Diagonal house. They had some hard questions for the Maestro; they were still skeptical. Casals was offering so much for so little (a peseta per seat per concert). Here were men used to receiving nothing they had not worked for; there had been speculation that this might be a camouflaged scheme for promotion of the Orquestra Pau Casals and its director. Discussions went on for several months; finally "they understood that I had no other interest than their need—*their* need—of music."

Word was circulated—top income limit for admission to membership would be 500 pesetas a month, the salary of a Barcelona university professor and 40 percent more than an expert workman could expect to earn. Casals had been particularly strong in stressing that by paying a peseta a concert the audiences would in effect be paying proportionally more than a rich man did for his 20-peseta single ticket to a concert at the Liceo. A test concert was given one Sunday noon in the two-thousand-seat Teatro Olimpico. The house was packed; looking out at the plainly dressed men and women in place for the beginning of the program, Casals felt an indescribable elation. The ovation at the end changed to a unison chant of Casals' name, a salutation he said many years later meant more to him than any other applause he ever received.

The Workingmen's Concert Association (*Associació Obrera de Concerts*) was launched, spectacularly. Beginning in May 1926 Casals gave the workmen, in a concert hall full of their peers where they could develop their appreciation "without the interference of class consciousness," strong Sunday-morning musical nourishment. Bach, of course; in later years Casals asserted that the canvass at the end of the season always revealed that the membership liked the Bach best of all. Beethoven, nearly all the symphonies (on one program, both the first and the ninth), overtures. Mozart, Haydn, Brahms, Mendelssohn, Borodin, the other Russians, plenty of Wagner, Berlioz, Schubert, Richard Strauss, Humperdinck, an all-Schönberg program conducted by Schönberg, Liszt, Grieg, Reger conducted by Fritz Busch, Roussel. Music of many Catalan composers, and of Albéniz, Granados, and Falla. Jelly d'Aranyi, Horszowski, and Maurice Eisenberg as well as Spanish artists and Casals himself were among the soloists. Pianist Blanche Selva's reaction after playing was one of those Casals recalled longest. Savoring tumultuous applause after she had performed a concerto, she turned to Casals and said, "One can hear it—those are workers' hands!"

Pablo and Enrique Casals donated volumes to the association's music library and helped found its music school, to which a number of local musicians donated instruction. A very respectable amateur orchestra was formed by members, as well as a choral group, and both performed in prisons and hospitals. From an original membership of about twenty-five hundred in Barcelona in 1926, the *Associació* and its branches in cities throughout Catalonia had grown to a membership of three hundred thousand by the Spanish Civil War—a fine backing, Casals remarked later, if he had wanted to make a revolution.

The Workingmen's Concert Association, proportionally a small part of the Orquestra's life, and its flowering were the accomplishment of which Casals many times said he was proudest. A similar venture was started in England, and observers came from Germany, the United States, and elsewhere to Catalonia to study its work. This, more than his international fame, was the basis for the proliferation of streets and squares named for Pau Casals in Catalonia during the late 1920s and the early 1930s.

Perhaps its zenith was reached by the Orquestra Pau Casals during the spring season in 1927. The orchestra itself had developed a cohesiveness through thirteen spring-and-fall concert seasons. Even if it dispersed after each six-week *temporada*, a considerable stability had been attained. The musicians were joined by a bond of loyalty to the organization, a real devotion to Casals, and assurance of the best musical wages in the country for at least three months a year. Now, when the critics carped, players came instantly to the defense of the orchestra and its leader, and critics as well as public had come to respect the new career of Pablo Casals.

The programs for the 1927 seasons honored Beethoven, who had died a hundred years before. Casals fixed on the dream of bringing the great Ysaÿe out of retirement to conduct in Barcelona and to play at least once more. The great violinist, now in his seventies, was weak and ill, and his full life had taken a toll. He had severed an artery in one wrist as a child breaking a window to escape from a room into which he had been locked; from time to time during even the height of his career the hand simply would not work. Diabetes and rheumatism had set in by the end of the First World War. After a disastrous last solo performance he had withdrawn to work on an opera, although he continued to direct the Cincinnati Orchestra until 1922 and his orchestra in Brussels, where he had begun the Concerts Ysaÿe in 1895.

Casals went to see Ysaÿe late in 1926 and insisted that he come to Barcelona to take part in the Beethoven celebration. Ysaÿe protested that he had not played the violin concerto since before the war, and behind the words Casals knew his friend's grief and embarrassment about that attempt. Casals convinced Ysaÿe the miracle was possible; Ysaÿe agreed to try.

Shortly afterward Casals received a letter from Ysaÿe's son Antoine that upset him considerably. Antoine questioned the wisdom of raising Ysaÿe's hopes that he would ever be able to play in public again and reported that his father was spending hours in his room laboriously practicing scales, learning to play all over again, working so valiantly that the family was in tears when they heard him.

In Barcelona on the nineteenth of April, Eugène Ysaÿe conducted the Orquestra Pau Casals as Casals, Cortot, and Thibaud ("The Holy Trinity," he called them) played the Beethoven triple concerto, then led the third symphony, the "Eroica." On the April 23 program the symphonies were the second and the fifth; Ysaÿe played the violin concerto between the two. The rehearsals had been careful, and Casals had seen to it that the audience had been somewhat prepared. Ysaÿe was terribly nervous. So was Casals, who made every effort to appear calm and reassuring. With the first entrance of the solo violin Casals knew he had not done his old friend the disservice he had feared. Ysaÿe's nervousness continued and at moments he seemed about to falter, but there were flashes of the glorious earlier mastery. At the end the audience began a frenzied series of ovations. Casals fled the stage in tears and went into a small backstage room to try to regain his composure. Here Ysaÿe found him, went to his knees, and took Casals' hands, murmuring "Resurrection!"

Within three months the Casals–Cortot–Thibaud trio was in Belgium during its summer tour. The evening after their second Brussels performance they went to dinner in Ysaÿe's house at 48 Avenue Brugmann. Also present, as usual, were members of Ysaÿe's family, a Conservatory professor, and a few other friends. After dinner Ysaÿe, remembering a trio made up of Anton Rubinstein, Vieuxtemps, and Servais, rose to toast the present trio and expressed

*One of the emotional peaks in the sixteen-year
history of the Orquestra Pau Casals. Casals
and Eugène Ysaÿe stand before the orchestra
in the Palau de la Música on the night of
Ysaÿe's last important public performance,
April 23, 1927.*

the hope that Casals and his colleagues would continue united to
perpetuate a tradition of beauty. Casals was the first to respond:
"The name of Eugène Ysaÿe will always remain the symbol of
all that is highest and best in music!" Thibaud and Cortot also
spoke. A rather solemn silence followed, broken by Ysaÿe: "Don't
let's become too serious—we're here to enjoy ourselves!" Thibaud
rushed to the piano in the other room and dashed off a brilliant
polka. The host then gave imitations of assorted famous violinists
that dissolved the company in laughter. Casals had brought his
cello and wanted to play something with Ysaÿe. In no time, Ysaÿe
and Thibaud had their violins out of the cases; Eugène's son Gabriel and one of the guests took turns on viola; Cortot was at the

piano, the Conservatory professor at his side to turn pages. Then Ysaÿe, "his eyes shining, all of him brimming with vitality, for music stimulates him as a drug might stimulate other men," asked someone to bring him the Beethoven quartets. Very soon he, Casals, Cortot, and Thibaud were hard at it. There was no stopping them until they were reminded that it was after two in the morning. Casals, Cortot, and Thibaud had played in Paris two days before and in Brussels the preceding night and that afternoon. They should have been tired; at least it was time they got back to their hotel. But Ysaÿe had to play for them once more, a solo sonata. He smiled—"I may not get through it." He played brilliantly, was not satisfied, did it all the way through a second time.

Henry Wood said that when Ysaÿe first appeared as a conductor in London his reputation as a violinist plummeted by half. Casals faced a different handicap. His fame as a cellist was so complete that for years reviewers and public alike seemed to have to be convinced anew each time he appeared as conductor. The handful of legendary orchestral conductors of the late nineteenth century and the first half of the twentieth were directors almost exclusively. The cluster of great and well-established European orchestras also had personnel more likely than not products of the same music schools, whose technical education resulted in similar phrasing, kindred interpretive approach, and the habit of playing together. These were the orchestras on which the celebrated individualistic full-time conductors were able to show the imprint of their own musical personalities and urge to command, and even the visiting leaders had to do relatively little basic repair work in the rehearsal time available. The established conductors were not unduly eager to welcome into their club a competitor who had so formidable a reputation as an instrumental virtuoso, but Casals continued unperturbed to conduct, often superbly, for more than sixty years.

Casals had directed chamber music for the Beethoven Society, but his full-scale New York début as an orchestral conductor took place Friday evening, April 7, 1922, at Carnegie Hall. The papers began announcing the event nearly a month beforehand; Casals, "who has been conducting since he was twenty," was to direct a ninety-man orchestra recruited from among musicians of the symphony orchestras of the city in a program of Beethoven's

Coriolan overture and "Pastoral" symphony, Brahms' first symphony, and the Prelude and Love Death from *Tristan*. He put forward, *The New York Times* reported, and promptly justified a new claim to distinction as symphonic conductor: "An eager public saw no Quixotic tilt with windmills in such adventure by the man whom Kreisler called 'the best that draws a bow.' Though the music lay open Casals had the score in his head, not his head in the score; he led eagerly, with persuasive force, clear upward beat and colorful variety." There were many recalls at the pause and at the end, with the stageful of players heartily joining in the demonstration.

Queen's Hall in London was filled "with an audience the majority of whom . . . had never heard Casals conduct and came wondering whether he could be as great with the baton as with the bow," reported *The Times* after Casals' first conducting stint with the London Symphony Orchestra, on the fourth of December 1925.

> Curiosity was soon allayed. Brahms's "Tragic" overture at the beginning of the programme told all there is to be told about Casals as conductor. A complete knowledge of the music, a sure instinct as to the sort of phrasing which will give the utmost significance to every part, a single-minded determination to secure it from every player, and that intense absorption in the task which makes him shut his eyes and turn his head away when he plays the violoncello but crouch and peer earnestly through his spectacles when he conducts, secured his authority. He is a great conductor because he is a great artist, and under him the orchestra carves out every phrase as if with his bow on the strings. . . . [In] Schubert's Unfinished Symphony . . . Casals's absorption so dominated the players that they forgot their vain repetitions of it as the most hackneyed symphony in existence and discovered its loveliness anew.

Dissenting votes were difficult to find, but one was registered by "F. B.," in *The Musical Times* for January 1928:

> The London Symphony Orchestra in engaging Pablo Casals to conduct one of its concerts made sure of a good audience. It is a natural thing to wish a man who distinguished himself in one capacity should attempt something new. It is the next best thing to doing something unusual ourselves. Moreover,

conducting, like 'cello playing, is music, and there was a reasonable hope that Casals should make a good job of it. . . . Casals . . . tried—and tried vainly—to get from the orchestra something like the sweetness of tone, the clearness of execution, which characterises his own performances. Had he used the time at his disposal in testing different tempi his good taste would have told him that his own were hopelessly wrong. His misreadings of Brahms's "St. Anthony" variations can only be explained by . . . the fact that soloists in the green room do not know what is happening on the platform.

Casals pretended never to pay attention to musical critics. He did discount, although he did not dislike, the reviews of fulsome praise, and he recognized the special penchant of London journalists to resounding pronouncements and parochial quibbles. Nevertheless, this attack on the tempo at which he directed Brahms' Haydn variations (along with the London critics' reactions to his first performance there of the Elgar cello concerto not long afterward) was one to which he was still sensitive forty-five years later. "F. B." had made a frontal attack on Casals' musical sensibility and instinct and pictured him as existing in a soloists' vacuum. The tempest bubbled along in the London teapot for a week or so, until Arthur Henry Fox-Strangways, onetime musical critic of *The Times* and the *Observer* and founder of the journal *Music and Letters*, published a counter pronouncement. Fox-Strangways had known Brahms, and he said Casals' tempos had been the true Brahms tempos for the work in question. Casals was radiant with vindication.

Another *Musical Times* writer the year before had set down reactions of more pertinence after Casals led the London Symphony Orchestra in a Bach orchestral suite, Brahms' first symphony, and Beethoven's sixth:

> As other great instrumental virtuosos have done, [Casals] seems to resent the limitations of the art that has earned him his triumphs. . . . Liszt, Beethoven . . . composed. Casals has taken to conducting. . . . It was all uncommonly good to hear. Casals was full of enthusiasm and carefulness. He communicated his zeal to the orchestra and audience, and after the exciting end of the Brahms, everyone felt flushed and self-congratulatory as after a common effort. He . . . worked

indefatigably at details, and when victory was achieved he probably enjoyed a pleasure such as 'cello playing had not yielded him for years . . . and we all felt we had spent a good evening.

Casals' zeal and carefulness did not weaken with passing time. He continued to conduct, and in the later years as in the twenties many who came with curiosity and misgivings left having forgotten the phenomenon but remembering the music. For Pablo Casals the orchestra remained the supreme medium of expression "for the man who feels music profoundly and wishes to express the form and texture of his deepest and most intimate thoughts and emotions. And what appeals to me equally in it," he said, "is the idea of cooperation. I am enchanted by the experience of many gathered together to make music."

19

From his early forties until he was nearly sixty, Casals spent more of each year in Spain than he had since he left Barcelona for Paris in 1899. He cut down his schedule of solo tours to concentrate on his orchestra although he continued to give concerts until after the start of World War II; during much of the 1920s the international appearances were a practical necessity to replace the capital Casals was funneling into support of his Barcelona group.

Throughout the war he had maintained contact with friends still in Europe with whom it had been possible to communicate, although there was a silence between him and Julius Röntgen. He remained constant toward Emanuel Moór, with a special concern after the death of Anita Moór. Casals included Moór compositions in his wartime programs in America, and Susan Metcalfe sang his songs in public. He conducted Moór's orchestral improvisations in the third concert of his orchestra's first Barcelona season, in November 1920, having written Moór a month earlier "I think of you more than you realize—compose! compose!" But Moór no longer appeared particularly interested in the performance of his music or in creating more, even though Leopold Stokowski had temporarily become one of his enthusiasts; he was not even specially incensed by "those brutes of critics." Moór had taken up painting, plunging into the new medium ferociously and soon had made hundreds of drawings and watercolors. Many had little artistic value and the color sense was often questionable, but there are flashes of brilliance; Casals was particularly struck by a self-portrait that reminded him of Van Gogh's. Moór remained unaffected by his friends' urging that he begin writing music again. In the winter of 1919–1920, with the help of a village carpenter, he had built the all-purpose stringed instrument he envisioned as the replacement for all the strings of the orchestra. At the beginning of 1920, after a vivid early-morning dream of playing Bach, Moór began to develop his Duplex-Coupler Pianoforte, the project that consumed most of his energy the last eleven years of his life.

After the war Casals resumed his solo performances. In England—where his reputation was tremendous—he made tours every year, appearing in London and other cities; he returned five times between 1921 and 1926 to perform concertos with the Hallé Orchestra in Manchester. One memorable evening in London was December 2 of the latter year, when Enrique Fernández Arbós conducted the London Philharmonic in Respighi's *The Fountains of Rome*, Albéniz' *Iberia*, a Ravel work, and two dances from *The Firebird* of Stravinsky. On the same program Casals played the most popular of Luigi Boccherini's cello concertos, the B-flat, using the cadenzas he had written himself. Postwar economic conditions were bad, and the Philharmonic's future was in jeopardy. Casals returned his hundred-guinea fee ($264, equivalent in purchasing power to a thousand dollars twenty years later) as a donation and indicated he would be willing to sign a suitably worded appeal and would persuade other famous artists to do the same.

Guilhermina Suggia had settled in England after she left Spain in the autumn of 1912 and made an impressive concert career there until 1923, when she returned to live permanently in Portugal; in 1927 she married Jozé Mena, a radiologist. From 1917 she was a frequent visitor to the Edward Speyers at Ridgehurst; she had met them before 1912 with Casals and had also been a soloist with the Classical Concert Society. She appeared in concert, accompanied by Tovey, at Miss Sophie Weisse's Northlands School in the autumn of 1919 and was soloist with Tovey's Reid Orchestra in Scotland during the 1919–1920 season. She too continued to include work by Emanuel Moór in her recital programs.

*Guilhermina Suggia playing Bach, painted
in England by Augustus John in the early 1920s*

Her talent had ripened during the years she studied with Casals, and she had already showed determination in working with a supposedly "masculine" instrument at a period few women in her own country sought a career of any kind. In the years she lived and worked in England her musicianship grew toward the stature that earned her the title of the greatest woman cellist of her time and that, for a period, led critics to rank her among concert cellists as second only to the great Casals. In her playing there were echoes, which she acknowledged, of the phrasing, clarity, and logic of his readings. Most of all, as an English cellist friend of both artists wrote after Suggia's death, from Casals she had imbibed "a sense of style . . . previously associated solely with his name. To this she added a temperament that was entirely personal."

Suggia and Casals appeared on different programs with the Hallé Orchestra during three seasons in the 1920s but saw each other only by chance, in a London rail station in 1923. Suggia, who was to play a Haydn cello concerto at a Leicester festival under Malcolm Sargent, and English composer Herbert Howells encountered Casals as he was buying a ticket. He was traveling to Manchester by the same train; the three shared a compartment, Casals and Suggia saying little. Howells remembered that Suggia was radiant when she turned to him in the taxi on the way to De Montfort Hall, saying "Tonight I shall play like a goddess." She did, and looked like one as well, wearing the geranium-red gown in which Augustus John had recently painted her.

America saw an annual Casals tour from 1920 until 1928, usually at the beginning of the calendar year and seldom running later than the beginning of April to avoid conflict with preparation for the spring season of the Orquestra Pau Casals. None of these tours was restricted to the large Eastern-seaboard cities, nor were all the recitals uneventful. Women still carried fans and fluttered them even during recitals—which Casals (like Kreisler and others) found badly distracting and invariably antirhythmic to whatever he was trying to play. During one performance a woman with a vigorous fan technique was directly in his line of vision. He stopped playing and, most politely, asked her to desist. She fainted. In Walla-Walla, Washington, he continued playing to allay panic in an audience forced to leave the hall because the building was burning.

Casals and Harold Bauer maintained their long friendship, and continued to give some joint recitals in the United States in the 1920s. They arrived at Princeton, New Jersey, late one afternoon in 1922 for a recital that evening at the University and were met at the station when the train arrived from New York by Francis Roudebush, an architecture student and the college's official student greeter of visiting artists. Roudebush noted that Casals carried a suitcase and his cello; Bauer's only luggage was a bundle wrapped in newspaper. The trio went to the Nassau Inn, where rooms had been engaged for the musicians. Casals came downstairs immaculate in evening clothes—white tie, tail suit. Bauer reappeared dressed as he had been when he left the train—dark trousers, blue shirt, brown coat. At the end of a light meal in the University dining hall Casals got his cello, Bauer his newspaper bundle, and their student escort walked with them across the campus to the concert hall and into the artists' room.

Casals, preparing to warm up, asked Roudebush what he could play for him, then went through a complete Bach sonata while

Pablo Casals

Casals in the 1920s, a portrait taken by George Kossuth in Wheeling, West Virginia

Bauer dressed for the recital. He unwrapped his bundle, which contained a dress coat, cardboard shirt front, white tie, and two cuffs. He removed his brown jacket, turned the collar of his blue shirt inward, put on his cardboard shirt front with a fresh collar and the white tie, pinned the cuffs into his dress coat, put it on, and was ready for the stage.

Musicians have long found Princeton a good place to play, and the house was full, but not all of the American houses were sold out when Casals appeared. He had a Sunday-afternoon concert scheduled in Chicago during one of his first postwar tours. Jacques Thibaud and Albert Spalding had played nearby and were able to stay through the weekend to hear him. The violinists and their accompanists, Charles Hart and André Benoist, joined Casals on Saturday evening; he was "as naively pleased as a child" to learn they would be in the house next day. Tickets would be waiting for them, and with such colleagues present he would not notice the vacant places. But empty seats at a Casals concert were an impossibility, protested the others. Wait and see, Casals warned.

A very popular tenor was singing in the civic auditorium at the same time, and how could a mere cello compete against that?

Casals had been right. The house was so sparse that Thibaud took one look and whispered to Spalding that it was sacrilege to be there on invitation. Casals' guests trooped out to the box office to pay for their tickets. "Mr. Casals wouldn't like it," said the box-office manager uncertainly. "He is not to know anything about it, nor is anybody else," the musicians told him. "It's a matter of conscience."

Spalding was then in his early thirties, an American violinist who had come to mature if not spectacular artistry after easy celebrity in his teens. He and Casals had a mutual friend in Camille Saint-Saëns, and Spalding had spent time during the war in Spain on a secret mission with Capt. Fiorello La Guardia. He had not heard Casals play for some time. Casals had offered unforgettable experiences in the past, and as he waited for the recital to begin he wondered if memory had magnified them.

Spalding knew "with the first commanding phrases of a Handel sonata" that memory had played no tricks:

> This, then, was Casals. As he played, a kind of renascent beauty flooded the dingy, all but empty theater. It was achieved by an extraordinary absence of display, a baffling simplicity to be appreciated only by those who think and feel deeply. His pulsating rhythm is a miracle in itself. It has none of the mechanical beat of the metronome; it has the elasticity of nature, and its inevitability. And Casals' technique—rarely spoken of because how he says a thing is so easily forgotten in the significance of what he has to say. All the facilities of a craft developed over a thousand years seem to have been brought to a point of effortless ease.

Thibaud leaned over to whisper that it was abominable of Casals to disguise difficulty with such unconcern. Then Casals played a Boccherini concerto in the slow movement of which the solo phrase opens with a long note played half-voice "but with incredible and increasing intensity." There is a little passage, a turn articulated almost as if spoken, as the bow, drawn slowly from hilt to tip, nears its end. "With a hardly perceptible movement of the wrist, Casals played this turn in the same bow-stroke, as a kind of parenthetical addition. Here again was the picture—low in key, and compelling in power."

A Bach cello suite followed. For Spalding, Casals' art reached its greatest heights in these works; for him Casals spoke "with the voice of a prophet imparting some of the wonders and mysteries of an unreachable universe. The present-day level of solo cello-playing owes its eminence to this master's influence; the great virtuosos . . . are the first to admit this truth. . . . It was an imperishable memory."

The American tours—all tours, in fact—began to seem more and more onerous to Casals, although postwar travel showed some improvement in speed, and even before the 1914 war first-class transatlantic-liner accommodations offered many comforts. At the same time, Casals felt and was resisting much pressure from the Metcalfe connections and from many others to settle permanently in the United States or at least to accept an offer to conduct six months a year in America. To do so would have been exile from his own family and his homeland, and neither logic nor necessity forced him in that direction.

Casals' own demand for areas of privacy as well as his standard of civilized behavior kept his own unhappiness quite well camouflaged. Soon after the wedding Casals realized that the marriage to Susan Metcalfe had been a mistake for him, but not until the 1920s did casual acquaintances begin to sense the estrangement. There is often an undercurrent of potential conflict between musical couples when both have public careers, even if their personal relationship is stable, and the chemistry of the star performer is seldom such as to allow him to be bland behind the scenes. For several years after his marriage to her, Casals devoted time and energy to accompanying Susan Metcalfe in public and otherwise assisting her career, and in time they gave joint recitals in the United States, Vienna, Paris, Barcelona, Budapest, England, Mexico, and Cuba. His collaboration, however, simply increased the strain when it became evident that even as pianist Casals drew more public enthusiasm than did his wife as singer. Vigorous and outspoken Wanda Landowska, one of the most articulate critics of the Metcalfe-Casals marriage, was heard to say "She's not the one for him. When he plays for her he doesn't even sound like himself!"

Neither Susan Metcalfe nor her husband was temperamentally a shrinking violet. Susan was known to explode with anger from time to time; the volcano inside Casals seldom erupted completely, but occasional rumblings and minor earthquakes were reminders of its presence. A nephew of Susan Metcalfe, who developed in early childhood a lifelong admiration and affection for his uncle, remembered the fiery discussions that came unexpectedly but passed as quickly as summer thunderstorms. After fourteen difficult years of a marriage that had not worked, Casals and Susan Metcalfe parted permanently, although she refused the divorce he offered.

Casals often returned to Paris in the 1920s, usually arriving there after the spring Orquestra season in Barcelona. He maintained a particular interest in the École Normale de Musique in the French capital, to the founding of which he had contributed both his prestige and about twenty thousand dollars. He never taught as a resident faculty member, but he took seriously his job as one of the artistic directors. He had seen to the appointment of Diran Alexanian, an excellent cellist and teacher, as resident head of cello instruction. Casals, Cortot, and Thibaud—all associated with the founding of the school—each gave a series of courses in the interpretation of the important repertoire during the summers. Casals' master classes for 1921 (six sessions between June 20 and July 1) included the Bach solo cello suites, concertos by Haydn, Boccherini, and Schumann, and Beethoven sonatas. The 1921 classes carried a fee of 100 francs for participants, 60 for auditors of the entire series, 15 for a single session. (Others teaching there that summer were Landowska, Marguerite Long, Blanche Selva, Marcel Dupré, Reynaldo Hahn, André Hekking, and Isidore Philipp.) During its regular months the school offered a complete musical education "to all degrees, without consideration of . . . age limit" in composition, piano, organ, violin, violoncello, voice, solfeggio, chamber music, history of music, and so on, taught by professors of the Conservatoire National and winners of the Grand Prix de Rome.

Casals was diplomatic in handling master-class participants, although there were a few memorable exceptions in fifty years. He never exercised control of the participants' choice of work to be played, and one student scraped his way through a Beethoven cello sonata considerably beyond his power. When he finished, Casals said equably that the choice of so splendid a work indicated excellent taste. "And now, let us work through the first part together."

Such consideration led to misunderstanding by those who did not know the man and his style. Those who took what Casals said on a single occasion in literal terms, outside the context and without taking into account what he left unsaid, could be surprised, disconcerted, or permanently alienated. Something of the sort happened in his first meeting with Gregor Piatigorsky, the first cellist of international importance to find himself competing in a world Pablo Casals had shaped, in the late 1920s in Berlin. Francesco von Mendelssohn, himself a cellist and a son of the banking family to which the composer had also belonged, summoned Piatigorsky to meet a houseguest who wanted to hear him. In a great Berlin house "filled with El Grecos, Rembrandts, and Stradivaris," the tall Russian was introduced to a small bald man with a pipe and to Rudolf Serkin, who had already played. Casals wanted to hear them together, saying he was always pleased to meet young musicians of such talent. Serkin, less than a month older than Piatigorsky (they were in their mid-twenties, Casals twice that), was particularly shy; they stood stiffly together, fighting their diffidence. Nervous and barely acquainted, Serkin and Piatigorsky played the Beethoven D major sonata, "a poor performance that terminated somewhere in the middle." "Bravo!" said Casals, applauding.

They then played the Schumann cello concerto and some Bach, both very badly. Casals embraced the younger cellist: "Splendid! *Magnifique!*" Piatigorsky left, knowing how badly he had played and knowing that Casals knew, puzzled by the whole encounter and saddened by the celebrated artist's insincerity.

Several years later Piatigorsky dined with Casals in Paris; afterward they played cello duets long into the night. Relaxed and elated, the younger musician reminded his host of his praise for the mediocre playing in Berlin. Casals responded with anger, picking up his cello. "Listen!" he said, playing a phrase from the Beethoven sonata. "Didn't you play this fingering? Ah, you did! It was novel to me . . . it was good . . . and here, didn't you attack that passage with up-bow, like this?" Then he went through the Schumann and the Bach, emphasizing what he had liked in Piatigorsky's playing that first night in Berlin.

"And for the rest," Piatigorsky remembered Casals saying passionately, "leave it to the ignorant and stupid who judge by counting only the faults. I can be grateful, and so must you be, for even one note, one wonderful phrase."

In free time between the interpretation courses at the École Normale de Musique in the early 1920s Casals, Cortot, and Thibaud gave afternoon and evening concerts together and separately. There were no names more luminous in chamber music at the time. A photograph taken outside the École Normale and published on the front cover of *Le Monde Musical* for August 1922 shows the three celebrated artists standing like three undertakers watching the approach of a hearse.

Few paid much attention to appearances, however, once the trio began to play. Victor Gollancz remembered as one of the great annual events of his London boyhood the appearances of Cortot–Thibaud–Casals, and "an emanation of Casals that allowed him to play trios without loss of his identity, and without loss to the identity, either, of Cortot and Thibaud, partners that came near him in greatness." Their recording of the beautiful Schubert B-flat piano trio in 1926, among the first of the important records made through the electric microphone, is one of the artistic and commercial successes in the history of classical-music recording. They also collaborated in a recording, made in Barcelona, of the Brahms double concerto with Casals and Thibaud as soloists and Cortot conducting the Orquestra Pau Casals.

Donald Francis Tovey played two well-received New York recitals crammed with "the greatest piano works in existence" in 1925; Casals was among the audience. Casals' name appears on the programs of Tovey's Reid Orchestra in Edinburgh the same year, and Casals performed with Tovey many times during the next fifteen years. The renewed friendship of the two men was warm and lasting, and especially poignant during Tovey's later years. The Englishman was appointed to the Reid Professorship of Music at the University of Edinburgh in July 1914 and held the post with distinction until his death in July 1940. He married in 1916 an Englishwoman from whom he was divorced in 1922 and then an American, a former student at Northlands.

Soon after his appointment at Edinburgh, Tovey succeeded in establishing a symphony orchestra in the Scots capital in the face of various difficulties (not least his own personality) and the competition of other musical groups. The annual series of Reid Concerts began in the 1916–1917 season. The orchestra had some fine instrumentalists and some run-of-the-mill professional players.

Tovey lacked the polish and surface brilliance of a "born" conductor, but Casals felt that he was one of the great ones. The important thing, Casals maintained, was his interpretations; they reflected the depth of penetration of the man's mind into the music as well as a burning sensitivity. "The Reid Orchestra has the courage of its conductor's convictions," observed a London *Times* writer. "It can give music that is real without asking first whether it is in the fashion of the moment." Casals conducted the Reid Orchestra only once. Tovey had included on one concert program a *Pastoral* by Juli Garreta. During rehearsal Tovey said he felt he was not getting at the real character of the work and asked Casals to conduct it, which he did to a great response from the northern audience.

There was further contact between Tovey and Emanuel Moór after the 1914 war. In 1921 Moór sent Tovey a copy of his pamphlet "The Reformation of the Piano," describing his Duplex-Coupler Pianoforte. The interesting machine had a second keyboard behind and above the first, tuned an octave higher, so positioned that it was possible to play on both keyboards with one hand at the same time; a pedal allowed for the coupling of the keyboards. Tovey's imagination grasped the possibilities even before he saw the prototype instrument; after a visit to Moór in Switzerland he wrote an almost ecstatic piece about it for *Music and Letters*. Tovey embraced it as a great expansion of the potential of the piano and began to envision the possibility of a triplex-coupler pianoforte, with a third keyboard and various linkage possibilities. Tovey was less excited about Moór's cembalo stop, which lowered a metal plate and produced a harpsichord sound. Tovey's favorite way of demonstrating Moór's invention was by playing duets with himself on it, an intellectual feat not many others were equipped to try. He did give some public performances on the piano in England and Scotland, although the manufacturer did not always get an instrument to the proper destination in time. Tovey's interest flagged, and his energy went into other ventures. After the renewal of relations between Englishman and Catalan, Tovey returned to Spain to play with and conduct the Orquestra Pau Casals. He was there in October 1927 as piano soloist in the orchestra's first performance of the Beethoven Choral Fantasy.

In 1928 Tovey accepted an invitation Casals had declined—to join a jury formed by Columbia Graphophone in a ludicrous record-promoting scheme. The jury would award ten thousand dollars for the best completion of Schubert's "Unfinished" Symphony. It was for the meetings of this body that the authorities allowed Alexander Glazunov to leave the Soviet Union; he never went back. "Have you heard that the Unfinished Symphony is to be finished for the hundredth anniversary of Schubert's death?" Julius Röntgen had written Tovey. "A real American idea! At least it will not be necessary to write in atonal or pluritonal style, although that to be sure would be easier than writing in Schubert's." The reaction from other reputable musicians was so fast and stunning that Columbia changed the ground rules: a smaller award would go to the best composition written "in the style of Schubert."

Casals' appearances with orchestras in England were highlights of the musical season from the end of World War I until the early 1930s. One of the concertos he was most often asked to play was Robert Schumann's; he performed it under the direction of Albert Coates in December 1921 on his first appearance with the Royal Philharmonic since he had been awarded the Philharmonic Society's Beethoven Gold Medal in 1912, and he played it with Hamilton Harty and another orchestra in 1920. The performance with Harty was memorable and recalled to the mind of the Manchester *Guardian*'s longtime critic Samuel Langford a reading of the work by Casals with Hans Richter and the Hallé Orchestra in Manchester ten years earlier—a performance Casals spoke of even half a century later as one of those that had most satisfied him. "We remember to have heard Casals himself play Schumann's cello concerto at the Hallé Concerts under conditions when it was so ineffectual that we felt ready to curse not only this but every other cello concerto . . . as monstrosities perpetuated to administer only to human vanity. But that was when Richter . . . was contending for the last ounce of Schumannesque style, weighed in terms of fullness and dignity." No longer: "To feel music as a net of air, a noose flung to entrap the spirit . . . that is the refinement . . . Casals had in store for us."

It was for the Schumann too that Casals and Bruno Walter joined forces in London. What stayed in Walter's memory was "not only . . . his glorious playing but also . . . his fantastic immersion in the technical problems of his instrument." The conductor arrived at Queen's Hall for rehearsal on the morning of the concert to discover Casals practicing in an adjoining soloists' room. Walter apologized; he had asked the management to inform Casals his presence would be needed only for the second half of the program; Casals replied that it was quite all right and continued playing. He appeared on the platform at the appointed time and "played . . . with all his saintly seriousness and perfection," to the orchestra's delight and Walter's. Changing clothes after the rehearsal, Walter heard Casals practicing again. The conductor's customary preconcert afternoon walk took him by Queen's Hall to inquire for mail. The "well-known, noble sound of Casals' playing floated once more from the artists' room," affording Bruno Walter "an impressive insight into the man's thorough absorption in his music and instrument. I listened to his intensive practicing for fully fifteen minutes," Walter recounted. After the concert he twitted Casals for not starting to practice again immediately.

One of the few times Casals was seriously incapacitated during a concert was in London late in 1926. He had begun to play the Haydn concerto under the direction of Felix Weingartner; halfway into the first movement he stopped. A conference between soloist and conductor, then Weingartner faced the audience to announce in his special variety of English: "Mr. Casals has the cramp. We shall play the symphony now, and Mr. Casals shall play the concerto at the end from the evening." Casals had developed a serious cramp in one hand. (Guilhermina Suggia was sitting in a front row, but Casals asserted he had not seen her and there could therefore have been no connection.)

Casals' professional association with Sir John Barbirolli, which lasted more than half a century of mutually admiring friendship, began in London in 1927. John's father, Lorenzo, a very good violinist (he and *his* father had both been in the orchestra of La Scala at the time Toscanini had been in the cello section) who had his own small orchestra and a trio at a London hotel, had been in the Crystal Palace audience when Casals first played there in May 1899. Casals and the younger Barbirolli first met about 1911, in connection with young people's concerts given in the Royal Academy concert room by a Miss Gwynne Timptin, an elderly lady who conducted her own orchestra. John, aged eleven and a cello-student soloist at the last concert of this particular series, was introduced to

Casals (then thirty-five) following his appearance as soloist at the first concert. The boy was already in awe of the older musician; his father had said of Casals' earlier performance of the Lalo concerto at the Crystal Palace "I'd never heard a cellist like him, and I don't suppose I ever will again."

John Barbirolli went on to become quite a good cellist himself and made some recital tours as Giovanni Barbirolli. Then he began his long conducting career, starting as a director of opera performances. In 1927, when he had been conducting seriously for about a year, Barbirolli was given the opportunity to conduct one of the famous London Symphony Orchestra Monday-evening concerts, replacing Sir Thomas Beecham on short notice. The program on December 12 was Haydn's "London" symphony (number 104), the Haydn cello concerto in D with Casals as soloist, and the Elgar second symphony. Barbirolli knew the Haydn well; the nearly hour-long Elgar he had learned in forty-eight hours.

At the concerto rehearsal Barbirolli took a great deal of trouble over the phrasing of the opening *tutti*. The members of the self-governing orchestra had voted to give the young leader a chance in an important concert, but they began to mutter when he took such pains with a passage they had played many times, although there was no open rebellion. Casals watched the entire procedure—in those days the soloist rehearsed facing the orchestra—and when Barbirolli finished said to the members, "Gentlemen, listen to him. He *knows!*" The younger man's appreciation and admiration for Casals' qualities of mind and heart never faltered after that moment. "Only a great man would have uttered these words for a very young boy." The concert itself went off vigorously, ending in "enthusiasm and cordial noise," Casals having given the only serene moments of the evening in the concerto, according to *The Musical Times'* postmortem. Casals' support of Barbirolli's musical insight during rehearsal may have given way to second thoughts during the performance; *The Times* said "Of the concerto we prefer to say no more than that the conductor had evidently not had the opportunity of absorbing the soloist's view of the work and that Mr. Casals attempted to conduct it by proxy."

In June 1969 Barbirolli, who at nearly seventy seemed much more fragile than his older colleague, came to Puerto Rico to conduct Jean Sibelius' fifth symphony and Gustav Mahler's fourth during the thirteenth Festival Casals in San Juan, where he and Casals met for the first time in many years. Casals' *abrazzo* was so powerful that a lens of Barbirolli's reading spectacles, suspended on a cord around his neck, was shattered. "I'll never have them fixed," he said delightedly.

Sir John had heard all the great violoncellists of his time, including Casals' Bach-antagonist Hugo Becker, whom Barbirolli considered the finest before Casals and "perhaps the first creator of modern cello-playing. But then, then came the Master. . . ." Barbirolli spoke of the particular quality of Casals that "is not only cellistic but musical. People say that he is a very great artist, but they forget that he was and *is* technically the greatest cellist. . . . That is what enabled him to be such a great artist: such a command of the instrument that he could do what he liked. He could phrase like he did because he completely revolutionized the fingering of the cello, but he revolutionized it so that he could make the musical phrases—you know the cello is a big instrument, so we have fingers shorter than the violin—and he created a technique so that he could make all the phrases as they should be made, as if he had another finger, even. Therein lies his greatness."

"I can remember even now," Barbirolli continued, "certain phrases in the recording of the Schubert trio with Cortot and Thibaud, when he plays his phrase in the slow movement . . . something unique . . . a magician." As for instinct, "it begins in the heart but as you grow older perhaps the mind plays a little part . . . the [Casals] mind is sensitive, beautiful; this technical mastery made him able to fulfill all his thoughts and ideas about music. A most inspiring figure, an adorable person . . . with a volcano inside, the fires of the devil—under absolute control."

Barbirolli's greatest memory of Casals was of the Catalan's last solo appearance with the Royal Philharmonic in London, on the thirteenth of March 1930. Barbirolli had conducted; Casals played the Schumann concerto and a new work by Ralph Vaughan Williams. Barbirolli remembered it in 1969 as though the performance had been the night before: "He was in the most wonderful form that night. He was a very nervous man in those days. Ooh! He told me of his sufferings. He used to grunt out of sheer nerves, trying to control them, and yet he played with all his emotions—marvelous! But that night he was in complete form and . . . it sounded as if he'd improvised it, not that he was playing a piece that is great. . . . The orchestra was completely transfixed."

The other violoncello feature of that evening was a fantasia on Sussex folksong themes Ralph Vaughan Williams had written specifically for Casals. The composer's first-night reaction puzzled Casals for forty years, although he knew him fairly well, and Vaughan Williams and Casals had a number of mutual friends, including Tovey, the Robert Trevelyans, and Henry Wood, who was doing so much in making new works by British composers heard.

Backstage after the performance, the composer shook the soloist's hand as he voiced merely a gruff "Thank you" and walked away; Casals was normally far more demonstrative in such circumstances. Vaughan Williams, very shy in any event and averse to what he considered fuss (in the course of the concert he had been given the Beethoven Gold Medal), was remembered by others than Casals to have been particularly "English" that night.

Vaughan Williams had written an all-purpose *Six Studies in English Folk Song* in 1927 for cellist May Mukle—it was published "for cello (or violin, or viola, or clarinet) and piano." The next year he wrote the *Fantasia on Sussex Folk-Songs* for Casals, and the cellist worked on it carefully for a full year, although the composer was still refining it two and a half months before the first performance. Vaughan Williams wrote from Dorking, Surrey, on Casals' fifty-third birthday:

December 29

Dear Sir

In preparing my "Fantasia" I have made a few slight alterations which I am sending you herewith.

Also I am not quite sure about the final cadenza. Perhaps it has not enough technical display. Would you feel inclined to be so very kind as to help me with this?

The fantasia is a pleasant but not a major work, and neither Casals nor Vaughan Williams was fully happy with it. The composer, feeling the cello part did not fit well enough, withdrew the work after a few years but did not destroy the manuscript; the rest of his life he intended to do something with it. Any reservations on the composer's part focused on the composition, not on the performance; in later years Vaughan Williams, four years Casals' senior, wrote sketches of a cello concerto intended for Casals. He also made an arrangement for cello solo and orchestra of Bach's choral prelude *Schmücke Dich* for a London concert given in honor of Casals' eightieth birthday.

Pablo Casals gave his last solo recital in the United States at Town Hall, New York, Sunday afternoon February 26, 1928; his accompanist was Nicolai Mednikoff, and the set program:

1. Sonata in D major (cello and piano)	Bach
2. a. Piéces en concert	Couperin
b. Adagio and Allegro	Boccherini
3. a. Kol Nidrei	Bruch
b. Neapolitan Serenade	Sgambati
c. Mazurka ⎫	
d. Vito ⎬	Popper
4. Sonata in D major	Rubinstein

Had the concert been announced as a farewell—which no one at the time actually knew it to be—Town Hall would have been jammed. In the absence of such notice the house was rather a sparse one. That Casals did not return to the United States on tour as a solo cellist after the spring of 1928 was the result more of circumstances than of any firm decision. The demand for his appearances in Europe was tremendous, and Casals was in a position to be selective. And by the late twenties the Orquestra Pau Casals was a self-sustaining organization that no longer required the financial support Casals had given it at the beginning of the decade. Planning and realizing its concerts, however, consumed a large segment of each fall and spring and, after the American stock-market crash in 1929, the economic situation was not conducive to U.S. concert tours.

Trips to Belgium during the 1920s saw the development of one of the most interesting of Casals' associations—the friendship offered by Elisabeth, Queen of the Belgians, that was gallantly reciprocated for fifty years. This slight, rather birdlike woman of sharp intelligence and apparently boundless energy was the unconventional, courageous queen of her brave small country for twenty-five years and became one of the controversial public figures of her time. Born the same year as Casals, she had met him casually by the time her husband came to the throne in 1910.

Elisabeth was a member of the extraordinary, thousand-year-old Wittelsbach family. Her father, Charles Theodore, Duke in Bavaria (the Dukes *of* Bavaria belonged to the reigning royal family), was a brother of the beautiful Empress Elizabeth of Austria and a cousin of the bizarre King Ludwig II, Wagner's patron. Duke Charles Theodore insisted on studying medicine in Munich and Vienna and, after receiving his degree, on practicing ophthalmology. He founded three hospitals, the primary one situated in the family's Schloss Tegernsee. In her teens the Princess Elisabeth assisted her father in hospital and accompanied him on his rounds to peasant homes. She was raised simply in an intelligent, compassionate family that had no time for "the busy trivialities which made up the lives of so many royalties." She also went with her father and brothers on mountain-climbing expeditions.

From her mother, Marie-José, princess of the Portuguese branch of the reactionary House of Braganza, Elisabeth inherited some of her strong character and tenacity, but her personality showed more of the traits of the somewhat eccentric, liberal Wittelsbachs with their strong but unpatronizing sense of duty toward the underprivileged. Second of the Duke's five children, Elisabeth was particularly close to her father, who supervised her education personally and encouraged her strong musical interest; she played piano and violin with some skill. (Autocratic old King Leopold II of Belgum, who loathed music but had been required to sit through his wife's musical soirées early in his reign, warned his nephew Albert, who persisted in becoming engaged to Elisabeth: "Well, if she insists on playing to you, remember that you insisted on marrying her.")

Elisabeth and the tall, shy Prince Albert met in the Bavarian alps in the summer of 1900 and were married in Munich in October. It had been very close to love at first sight—there was a strong affinity based on tastes, ideals, and mutual interests. The couple settled down after their marriage into a house in the Place de l'Industrie in Brussels, where they began to do something real about social reform, the problems of disease and poverty, and the intellectual life of their country. The old Leopold, occupied with imperalism in Africa and amour at home, might not be seen by the public for a month or more at a time, but it was a rare day "the little Princess" Elisabeth was not to be observed tramping through the poorest quarters of Brussels, bringing practical aid to the sick and

Queen Elisabeth of the Belgians, Casals' friend and admirer for more than half a century. In this picture, taken about 1910, Elisabeth (a longtime violin student of Ysaÿe) is shown coaching her son Leopold. King Albert is seated, holding a score.

the needy and acquainting herself with such matters as wages and living conditions. With Albert's accession to the Belgian throne she began to put to work what she had learned. With the help of some of Belgium's most prominent doctors, she established various medical organizations; it was estimated at the end of her life that Elisabeth had founded or assisted 175 charitable, scientific, and artistic foundations. Her husband was once heard to remark that he would not be able to capture her full attention until he broke a bone or came down with a fatal disease.

For everything that interested her Elisabeth showed an unflagging enthusiasm and intelligence. She brought a professionalism, a complete absence of royal dilettantism, to everything she touched, except possibly music. And music was really her first love. She took violin lessons from Eugène Ysaÿe for many years, studying with the same enthusiasm she brought to her charitable works. From time to time she even included herself among the performers at the private concerts she organized.

Playing frequently in Belgium in the years preceding the 1914 war as he did, Casals came increasingly to admire the straightforward charm of his royal contemporary and to like her diffident husband. He was pleased by her presence at his recitals and concerts, although at least once discomfited by her disregard for protocol. At one event Elisabeth motioned Casals to sit in the empty chair next to her, becoming insistent when he hesitated and started to protest that it was on her right, the side of honor, and therefore the King's chair. He finally sat and they talked, Casals still recalling long afterward that it had caused "quite a scandal." The Queen was a good conversationalist and loved to talk to people who interested her. A private conversation that intrigued her was likely to be a very long one; the King had to resort to leading her out of the room to get her to retire. "You see," she once said over her shoulder as Albert marched her out of the room, "the cow is being taken to its stable."

King Albert, so tall he towered over any company, with very bad eyesight and unruly hair, seemed in public more an absent-minded professor than a king. In later years he appeared happiest when he could travel incognito and dress shabbily ("Pick the worst-dressed fellow of the bunch," he told an official unsure how to recognize him) as he shambled down the streets of a foreign city headed for a museum or, quite as likely, a cinema—he and Elisabeth were both film devotees. Casals remembered an early occasion in Albert's reign during which the King was to decorate him. They both stood awkwardly before the guests, the King nearly two feet taller than Casals, unable to put either himself or his guest at ease. At last, still distracted and shy, Albert stammered, "May I present you with the Star of the Order of Leopold?"

Elisabeth followed her curiosity in many directions—to the horror of her suite she demanded to be taken up in an airplane and to go down in a submarine. She continued to study music, sculpture, painting, and photography, and took courses in physiology, psychology, and yoga. She swam and played golf. At the summer palace of Laeken outside Brussels she lavished attention and care on her magnificent rose garden.

Not until after the First World War did Casals hear the stories of Elisabeth's valor. German troops, delayed by the brave and initially effective resistance of Belgian forces, swept into her adopted country, ravaging land and people at the very beginning of the war. Elisabeth and Albert looked on in impotent horror. The Queen took their children to safety at Hackwood, Lord Curzon's country home in England, and returned to the side of her husband in the twenty-square-mile enclave of Belgian soil at the mouth of the Yser River that was the only unoccupied portion of the little nation for three years. Settled in a stolid red-brick villa at the far end of the desolate resort town of La Panne eight miles from the front and just over the French border, she assisted in setting up field hospitals. It was chiefly her idea to organize a three-stage system of base hospitals, intermediate medical centers, and first-aid posts near the front lines. The Queen visited the hospitals each day—comforting the wounded, assisting doctors and nurses. Dying soldiers, it is said, would call for her, and the face of the fragile Queen was the last seen by many a Belgian soldier. The Germans had streamed into the country so quickly that most of the inland medical installations and supplies had to be abandoned. The main field hospital, l'Hôpital de l'Ocean at La Panne, lacked even the most elementary facilities. The Queen characteristically solved the problem by telephoning Harrods, the London department store, to order what was needed. Harrods equally characteristically delivered the order safely to Belgium within days.

During one heavy wave of delivery of wounded to a field hospital Elisabeth was visiting near the front, a soldier with a perforated lung was brought in, a case that required an immediate operation. In the absence of an available nurse the Queen offered to assist the surgeon in the complicated procedure. She rolled up her sleeves, put on an overall and gauze mask, and took her place beside the operating table. "She knew exactly what to do. I did not have to tell her anything," the doctor reported. Her early training was put efficiently and unostentatiously to use. She refused, sometimes testily, to be hustled off to safety from a dangerous situation or a sudden raid. "I have never experienced any sensations of fear," she once said. "I do not know what it means to feel afraid. The people I admire are those who are afraid and don't show it." It is said that only once was she seen publicly to have lost her composure. One day early in the German invasion of August 1914, at a town on the road to Ostend she was observed wandering alone in a rose garden, sobbing heartbrokenly.

As time passed, the monotony and the relentless despair of the Queen's days were occasionally relieved by visits of British allies who slipped across the Channel, foreign statesmen and personal friends who had access to the enclave from France. Pierre Loti, the exotic French novelist, was granted an interview, a conversation confined almost exclusively to the religions of the East. Painters, writers, sculptors came to La Panne when they could, and among the brightest moments for Elisabeth were the visits of such musical friends as Ysaÿe and Saint-Saëns. In the summer of 1916 the King and Queen asked Ysaÿe to come to their bit of free Belgium to play for them and the troops. Ysaÿe invited Lionel Tertis to join him. Tertis went for a seven-day stay that included making music for soldiers literally in the front line and a tour of the trenches that faced the German forces. The sightseeing engendered paroxysms of nervousness on the part of those charged with the visitors' safety: Tertis was a small man, but hiding or camouflaging Ysaÿe was nearly impossible.

After the war, when Casals began to see her often again, Queen Elisabeth had plunged into work for the lasting betterment of Belgium. At the same time she became steadily more chic—by the late twenties she had become, with the exception of Marie of Rumania and Queen Victoria Eugènie in Spain, the best-dressed queen in Europe. She resumed her violin lessons with Ysaÿe, continuing them as long as he was able to teach. "Today Her Majesty . . . came for her lesson," Ysaÿe wrote his wife in December 1929, "bringing with her a bunch of flowers and a pot of caviar, both of which gave me great pleasure." Of her musicianship Ysaÿe had reported for years "She plays badly divinely." Their mutual friend Casals, when asked, always responded, "She plays like a queen."

It would have been impossible for Pablo Casals to have remained totally unconcerned about the political developments in Europe during the 1920s, especially in Spain, even though professionally occupied, as he had been all his mature life, with making music. He came back to Catalonia intending to make the texture of life better and more beautiful in that region of earth he loved most. For him life and music were now inseparable. The founding of the Orquestra Pau Casals was to Casals a patriotic duty. By his fifties Pablo Casals was aware of the authority he had attained; he also had a very strong sense of the responsibility he felt inseparable from accomplishment and fame. To him it was something not to be questioned that his musicians in Barcelona should be paid double the miserable existing wage. The sensibility that made him a great musical artist led him in maturity to his concern for the rights of all other human beings, each of whom he thought of as a related but unique leaf on the tree of humanity.

Soon after Alfonso XIII came of age and succeeded to the Spanish throne in 1902, Pablo Casals had a short visit with him in Madrid. The brotherly cordiality had begun in Casals' student days, when he was sixteen and Alfonso an active seven. Now his onetime playmate was a man; Casals felt obliged to state clearly to His Majesty that, although his personal friendship was unchanging, he was unalterably a Republican. "That," said Alfonso XIII with a smile, "is your privilege." It is possible that for an instant the King of Spain remembered the time years earlier when, locked into an upstairs room for some misbehavior, he had startled his mother's lawn-party guests by leaning well out the window, shouting as loud as his young falsetto permitted *"Viva la Republica! Viva la* Republica!"

Spain declared neutrality in World War I within days after German forces overran Belgium, although Alfonso XIII assured France it would be safe to withdraw border troops from the Pyrenees for commitment to the western front. On his trips back to Spain between 1914 and the end of the war Casals found a country divided from the top down. The family of the Queen Mother was fighting on one side, that of her daughter-in-law on the other. Alfonso's actual sympathies were never revealed—his enemies called him "the Kaiser's understudy" and he had an admitted admiration for German military efficiency, but he also had a real affection for England and France. The Conservative aristocracy favored Catholic Austria, the Liberals and Socialists were pro-Allies; the middle class had been anti-French since the Napoleonic occupation of Spain early in the nineteenth century.

Barcelona was full of agents for both sides. Casals found the situation very distressing.

In 1922 Mussolini overthrew parliamentary government and became dictator in Italy. The following September the Captain-General of Barcelona, Miguel Primo de Rivera, using a riot in the Catalan capital as pretext, declared martial law and signaled other military commanders to do the same. When the Madrid government demanded Primo's dismissal, the General called on Alfonso (who was on holiday in San Sebastián and presumably did not know in advance of the coup) to dismiss the government and rule the country "with the help of the Army." Within days Spain was once more a dictatorship, ruled in fact by a military directorate headed by Primo de Rivera. Martial law was proclaimed throughout the country, the Cortes was dissolved, jury trial suspended, and rigid press censorship imposed. Well-known liberal opponents were either imprisoned or left the country (among those who went abroad were the poet-philosopher Miguel de Unamuno and novelist Vicente Blasco Ibañez).

Although horrified, Pablo Casals was personally not immediately threatened by these developments. Nevertheless he was soon embroiled, unexpectedly and unwillingly. Fairly early in the period of Primo de Rivera's nearly six and a half years in power Alfonso XIII made an ill-advised speech in Barcelona during which he spoke of himself as the successor of Felipe V. The name of the first Spanish Borbón was, more than any other, a flag waved before the Catalan bull: in 1714 Felipe had besieged and captured Barcelona, imposing an iron rule and negating in a single proclamation many of the ancient *fueros*, the rights under which Catalonia had been able to keep many aspects of its government in its own hands for centuries. No comparison could have been calculated to make Alfonso less popular in Catalonia at a very serious time.

Casals foresaw serious reactions to the speech and determined to speak to the Queen Mother about the anger in Barcelona and to suggest that she urge her son to make some effort toward calming the troubled waters. When Casals arrived at the palace he was shown in to see Alfonso, although he insisted that his appointment was with Doña María Cristina. The King's greeting was cordial; he said he knew an audience was scheduled with his mother, but he also wanted to see Casals. They chatted about general matters; Casals did not refer to the Catalan problem, thinking a more effective route was through the mother, one of the few people to whom Alfonso XIII listened attentively.

The Queen was irritated at having been kept waiting twenty minutes; Casals explained what had happened, and they began to chat. Casals had made up his mind to use María Cristina's first silence to broach the subject of the Barcelona speech and the outrage the Catalans felt; the Queen had always told Casals she was particularly fond of Catalonia. The first time he said something about the situation she acted as though she had not heard and went back to a discussion of Casals' orchestral concerts, tours, and family news. After a second attempt, he gave up. Casals left the palace dejected and apprehensive. He had been talking with a woman who had shown him affection and friendship for nearly thirty years, in the course of which they had discussed a very wide range of subjects. Now he was trying to bring to her attention a situation that contained real dangers to her position and her son's reign, and she refused to listen. Thus it is, Casals said long afterward, the great and powerful prepare the way for their own downfall.

It was one of the last visits Casals had with María Cristina. She died in the palace in Madrid on the last day of February 1929 at seventy-one, the first Queen of Spain not to die in exile in more than a century. Casals had lost a friend and the person he called a second mother, perhaps the highest praise he was able to give. He would acknowledge his debt and affection in public in Spain when it was not a popular thing to do, and of all those he knew she alone would always be "my Queen."

Casals' representation to the Queen Mother may have had more effect than he realized. Alfonso and the entire royal family were in Barcelona in connection with the grandiose International Exhibition of 1929, and Casals received a message that they wished to attend a concert of the Orquestra Pau Casals with Casals as soloist. He replied that he would of course be pleased. Alfonso's presence at a Casals concert of classical music was more of a gesture of conciliation than it might have seemed, for Alfonso XIII never displayed the serious-mindedness and gravity the Spanish so love in their leaders. In his mid-thirties, he appeared to many to be less interested in the intellectual or artistic life of his country than in playing polo, driving his sports cars as fast as possible, and dancing through the night.

The royal party arrived customarily late at the filled Barcelona opera house just before Casals was to play the Schumann cello concerto. The reception of the King and Queen was noticeably chilly and reaction to the Royal March indifferent. Then Casals came onto the stage to a standing ovation. Men applauded and shouted, women waved fans and handerchiefs. The demonstration continued so long that the royal entourage rose and joined the applause. Police removed some of the noisiest of the audience from the hall, and Casals realized the concert had become a political protest. After his performance there was an equally vigorous outburst. Casals was not invited to the royal box, as he customarily was. He was certain it was the end of his relations with the palace and regretted the break, but he also felt deeply the affront of Alfonso's speech to Catalonia and on principle could not himself initiate an apology. Some Catalan writers assert that that concert signaled the end of the monarchy in Spain.

In Paris not long afterward, Casals received a royal request through the Spanish ambassador to perform in Madrid during a forthcoming state visit of Victor Emmanuel and Queen Elena of Italy. The concert was given in the magnificent Armería of the Palacio de Oriente, a sumptuously tapestried, candlelit room with excellent acoustics. At the conclusion of the music King Alfonso rose, walked to Casals, and began to talk to him. He asked about Doña Pilar and about Casals' brothers. He reminisced about how Casals had amused him with games and tried to interest him in music when he was a child and Casals had come to play piano duets with María Cristina. He talked on and on. All had risen when the King stood; they remained standing—the Spanish Borbóns, the Savoys of Italy, Madrid society, diplomats, everyone. After what seemed forever to Casals and had in fact been nearly ten minutes, Alfonso XIII smiled and said, "Well, Pablo, I'm happy to see how well the Catalans like you." The King had made his gesture, and newspapers reported the incident widely, especially in the North of Spain.

Doña María Cristina had awarded Pablo Casals the decoration of Isabel la Católica while he was still a conservatory student in Madrid more than thirty years earlier. Awards and honors had continued steadily. As he grew older Casals accepted them—pleased and often touched—as recognition of a certain quality of life for which he strove and even more as acknowledgment of his service to the cause of music, but the recognition from fellow Catalans pleased him the most. In 1927 he was proclaimed a favorite son of Vendrell; a bronze plaque with an inscription in Catalan was unveiled on the house in which he had been born and he was given a volume that contained twenty thousand signatures. Casals' response was to conduct his orchestra in a program in the main Vendrell square, give a cello recital in the afternoon, and—after the unveiling of the plaque and a procession to the town hall a few streets away—deliver from a balcony a graceful address of thanks before he watched the traditional human pyramids called *castells* that had been rehearsed in his honor. Two years later there was another Vendrell ceremony marking the restoration of the organ in the Church of Santa Ana, for which Casals had given the funds in memory of Carlos Casals. At the same time the eighteenth-century angel that tops the bell tower had been restored, at Casals' urging. In the process the rebel wild olive tree that had kept the angel company had to be taken away. Local officials suggested making a baton or a music stand for Casals from its wood but he asked that instead he be allowed to take it for planting in his garden at San Salvador, where it still grows. One of the squares in Vendrell was rechristened the Plaza Pau Casals, and Barcelona named an avenue for him when he was made an honorary citizen of that city in 1934.

20

THE VILLA CASALS on the San Salvador beach had begun to take on a new aspect of spaciousness and elegance by the beginning of the 1930s. Casals himself gave much closer attention to the planning of the expansion than he had been able to do when the main house was built. Doña Pilar lived more of the year in Barcelona than she did at San Salvador, but kept a close eye on what was happening when the renovation began in the late 1920s. She was now in her middle seventies, but her presence remained formidable and quietly authoritative. She had retained the laconic quality of earlier years and still startled people with terse observations that cut directly to the core of an issue. She disliked using the telephone and had absolutely no patience with the noise of radio broadcasts. Yet those who knew her best found her sweet, affectionate, and greatly concerned for the good of others. Paula Eisenberg, who began in 1928 to come with her cellist husband Maurice to spend the summers in one of the villa's guest cottages, said that the two older women who had had the most important influence on her life were Doña Pilar Casals and the Russian princess who was the mother of Nadia Boulanger.

Luis Casals, his wife Teresina, and their children lived at San

Salvador. Luis, who had both aptitude for and interest in agriculture, was closer to the land in a practical way than either of his musical brothers. He managed the San Salvador property for his older brother for years, among other duties supervising Casals' excellent vineyards, which produced grapes that found a ready market among French winemakers. Luis Casals was overshadowed by the local celebrity of Enrique and the international prestige of Pablo, but in these years he went about his own life with a steady attention to crops and buildings. (During the terrible cholera epidemic of 1911, Luis Casals had gone out night after night with a cart to remove the bodies of the victims for burial, the only person in the region willing to do so.)

Casals commissioned a statue of Apollo from a leading Catalan sculptor and Rodin pupil, José Clará, for the expanded Italianate formal gardens to the west of the main house. Clará told Casals that this was a passé subject for a modern sculptor but finally undertook the project. After a time Casals went to Clará's studio to see how the work was coming along. He complimented the sculptor on excellent sketches of athletic young men but said that the studies lacked both the beauty and the dignity of his own conception of the god of music and poetry. He spoke of Apollo as the god of harmony, the ideal embodiment of the human form, and a sort of Hellenic St. Christopher—the protector of travelers, who gave them calm seas and safe returns. Clará's real interest was at last engaged, and in the end he produced a statue that satisfied both him and Casals. It was exhibited at the Barcelona International Exposition in 1929, where it was awarded first prize by a unanimous jury.

On the ground occupied by the tennis court on the east side of the main house, construction began of a wing containing two music rooms that together would accommodate several hundred people for concerts. In the smaller Casals had installed an eighteenth-century room he bought from a Catalan country château belonging to a count of the historic Güell family, with painted wall and ceiling panels of allegorical and pastoral scenes by Vigotà, fine crystal chandeliers, and tiled floor. The adjoining larger room Casals planned as his Hall of Remembrance—a gallery of photographs, paintings, books, his father's piano, a stone from the windowsill of the room in which Beethoven died, hundreds of souvenirs of his career and of friends. Throughout the house was displayed Casals' accumulation of paintings, which included a small Zurburán, an excellent oil by Ramón Casas, and many works of Catalan artists. Through the years Casals bought or was given a great number of paintings; the quality ranged widely, but to the owner the sentiment was often more important than the object. From a distinguished gallery in Barcelona he bought a number of works, some first-rate, others that appealed to him. The collection also included many representations of Casals himself—paintings, sketches, and portrait busts.

At San Salvador Casals, in his early fifties, swam nearly every morning, took a walk every day, and rode his horse Florian. He nevertheless fell ill in December 1928—a recurrence of the enteritis with complications he had suffered in Paris so many years before. The illness kept him from making concert appearances for more than four months—another factor that broke the fifteen-year pattern of North American tours. Reports circulated in musical circles that Casals was paralyzed and would never play again. Once more Casals had an enforced period of idleness and he found himself taking stock, thinking much more than he welcomed. He was depressed, concerned about conditions in Spain and in the world, and tired from thirty years of a full career.

He had recovered sufficiently by April 1929 to lead the rehearsals and direct the concerts of the Orquestra Pau Casals' spring *temporada*. These programs were still generally in the classic-romantic mold that had characterized the offerings of the Orquestra during its first decade—well-balanced, substantial mainstream programs that led to a certain amount of muttering among some

Pablo Casals

At San Salvador

younger and more impatient musicians that Casals was not interested in what was going on in modern music. But the spring 1929
programs presented a first hearing of Zoltán Kodály's *Psalmus
Hungaricus*, the *Sinfonietta* by the young Madrid-born composer
Ernesto Halffter-Escriche, as well as a full evening of compositions
by avant-garde French composer Arthur Honegger under the auspices of the Barcelona Chamber Music Association. The Honegger
session included the concert version of his sometimes-atonal
oratorio *King David*, the tone poem *Pastorale d'Été*, and his *Pacific
231*—a piece, startling for the 1920s, in which abrupt rhythms
and building dissonance imitate the noises of a locomotive. (The

season also included the first official performance of one of Pablo Casals' own instrumental compositions, the *Sardana* written in 1927 for a double quartet of cellos and played during the May 9, 1929, concert by thirty-three violoncellists.)

The pattern of travel began once more, and Casals performed in Budapest for the first time since the 1914 war on December 1, 1929, accompanied by Otto Schulhof, his usual European accompanist between the world wars. He also reappeared in Prague and Bucharest as well as in France, England, Switzerland, and Spain.

In Italy Casals stayed at Fiesole near Florence in the home of Alberto Passigli, the cultured and successful businessman (married to a cousin of Susan Metcalfe) who in 1919 established the still-active *Amici della Musica* concert organization in the Tuscan capital and, with others, the Florence Symphony in 1924 and the Maggio Musicale in 1931. Their friendship began just after World War I, when Casals first played in Florence, and they remained close as long as Passigli lived.

On successive visits to Italy Casals watched with mounting distrust the effects of government by Mussolini's Fascist bureaucracy. He saw evidence of diminishing individual rights in Italy as in Spain and read as evil omens the exchanges of visits between high Spanish and Italian officials culminating in a treaty of friendship between Mussolini and Primo de Rivera. Like others who had traveled in pre-Mussolini Italy, he and Horszowski—who spent more time there than Casals did—were wryly amused that one of the chief reports the Roman publicists put about as an example of the new government's excellence was that Mussolini had made the trains run on time and brought order to the postal service. They had found trains quite as punctual before Mussolini as after and the mails as unreliable at the beginning of the thirties as ten years earlier. Both were appalled when Arturo Toscanini was manhandled by a gang of young Fascisti because he refused to conduct the Fascist hymn during a Bologna concert.

To be able to return to San Salvador, rest and enjoy the company of his family and neighbors, immerse himself in the gradual progress of work on the villa was to find a welcome tranquility. But even in Catalonia there were strong political currents to which Casals could not be insensitive. By the mid-1920s radicalization and the movement for Catalan autonomy were spreading through the worker population, intensified by repression from Madrid. Opinion was strong on both sides: composer Jaime Pahissa told German publisher-diplomat Count Harry Kessler in Barcelona that the military directorate of Primo de Rivera had saved Spain from the communism that had threatened to overwhelm it. In a time of spreading tension Pablo Casals found his home beside the Mediterranean a special haven and a place of light among the shadows that had begun to gather.

In November 1930 Casals went to Brussels to play Lalo—the cello concerto and a *Meditation* for cello and orchestra—as part of the last concert Eugène Ysaÿe was to conduct. Ysaÿe, seventy-two, ravaged by diabetes and rheumatism, walked on an artificial leg—part of his right leg had been amputated to save his life from gangrene. The concert was in celebration of the hundredth anniversary of Belgian independence; in the grand manner that characterized so much he did, with the King and Queen of the Belgians and a gala audience in attendance, Ysaÿe conducted five hundred musicians.

    The old man was in great spirits, full of reminiscence and thoughts for the future. A few days after the mammoth patriotic concert Ysaÿe was forced to take to his bed. He was carried on a stretcher in late April 1931 to the Théâtre de La Monnaie for a performance of his opera *Peter the Miner* and was able to sit up to receive the applause of the crowd, supremely happy. Back in his home in the Avenue Brugmann, Ysaÿe lay in his room, listening to May birdsong and was heard to whisper *"Quelle symphonie!"* He thought, it seemed, more of the future than of the past. "We must not forget Wieniawski's centenary in 1935," he told his son. "I should like to take part in it. Write to Paderewski and ask him what they are doing about it in Warsaw. He and I might do something together." On the eleventh of May 1931 a young British violinist named Philip Newman appeared at Ysaÿe's house. Newman, a friend of Ysaÿe's son Antoine, had an uncanny resemblance to Ysaÿe himself. He had rushed up to kiss Ysaÿe's hand the night of the performance at La Monnaie, and Ysaÿe had invited him to come to the house to play. Now Antoine told Newman that it was only a matter of hours until the end, but on impulse said to come upstairs to the landing outside Ysaÿe's bedroom with his violin tuned. Finding his father conscious, Antoine Ysaÿe signaled

Newman, who began to play Eugène Ysaÿe's fourth violin sonata, dedicated to Fritz Kreisler. Ysaÿe opened his eyes when he heard the violin; listening intently, he tried to beat time and whispered "Very fine!" at the end of the first movement. Newman played the finale brilliantly. When it was finished Ysaÿe said "Splendid . . . a little too fast"—his last words.

Eugène Ysaÿe had lived well and had been generous to others in money as well as friendship. To provide for his family, he had invested income from his American recordings and a portion of his fees in a lumbering enterprise that went bankrupt in the 1929 stock-market crash. Quietly Casals set about seeing that there was adequate provision for his friend's young widow.

Nineteen thirty-one was a year brushed several times by death. After a concert in Geneva Casals was handed the telegram that contained word of the death of Pilar Defilló de Casals on March 11, 1931, at the age of seventy-seven, in the arms of her son Luis, at the Villa Casals in San Salvador. She had asked for news of Pablo some days before she died, and then afterward spoke no more. She was buried near her husband in the Vendrell graveyard.

At almost the same moment Casals received the telegram, his Florentine friend Alberto Passigli came backstage and was with him during the first hours of shock and grief. Casals afterward believed that Passigli had felt so intensely that he was needed he had left Italy to find Casals. He had in fact been in Geneva only accidentally, but Passigli did not discount the operation of something beyond simple chance that had placed him at Casals' side. It is said that in the first days after the passing of Doña Pilar her son seemed like a child lost in a crowd.

The other sons expressed real affection for their mother, and she lived with one or other of them and their families during her later years, but her oldest son idolized her. When all three boys had been quite young, Pilar Defilló de Casals predicted with startling accuracy how the life of each would turn out, and for Pablo she had foretold almost limitless accomplishment. During his years of development she had directed the course of his life in virtually every respect, and after he began to travel alone her presence was strong in her son's awareness no matter where he was, as long as she lived. After her death his consciousness of who and what she had been never left him. He acknowledged that all the good

Pilar Casals in her seventies

he spoke and practiced was only what she would have wished and done.

On April 12, 1931, the day after the first spring concert of Casals' orchestra, municipal and provincial elections were held throughout Spain. Primo de Rivera, discredited and ill, had resigned in January 1930, to be followed by another general, Damaso Berenguer, whose government restored some civil rights and promised parliamentary elections. When censorship was removed in September, Republican leaders, intellectuals, and university students openly blamed Alfonso and his circle for supporting dictatorship and leading the country to disaster. By early February 1931 the King had been obliged to announce the restoration of the constitution and to set a date for elections. The result was an overwhelming victory for Republican candidates. Alfonso XIII left Spain without abdicating on April 14, and on the fifteenth a republic was proclaimed.

In Catalonia the Republicans were led by an honorable and delightful old colonel named Francisco Macía, who had resigned from the Army to devote himself to the Catalanist cause and who had spent the years of the Primo dictatorship plotting in France. When the Republic was announced in Barcelona (by Macía's lieutenant, the able and dapper young lawyer Luis Companys) to the playing of both the *Marseillaise* and the Catalan national song *Els Segadors*, it was proclaimed as "the Catalan Republic," although Macía and his Esquerra party were persuaded to await passage of a Catalan home-rule statute by the new parliament. That first week of the second Spanish Republic Pablo Casals led his symphony orchestra and the Orfeó Gracienc in a concert of celebration in the great palace on the Montjuich that overlooks Barcelona; an audience of some seven thousand people came to hear Beethoven's ninth symphony. Colonel Macía said that the Republic had come to Catalonia on the sound of a hymn of brotherhood, the Schiller "Ode to Joy" that ends the Beethoven work.

Casals was enchanted by Francisco Macía, who was called affectionately "the grandfather of Catalonia," a man so courtly he would never precede Casals through a doorway. Casals had never been a member of a political party but now, at fifty-four, he voted in an election for the first time. His conscience, he said, did not allow him to stay aloof from crucial political issues in his homeland. The idealistic Republicans represented to him Spain's hope for freedom and justice for all the people.

As the slates of candidates for parliamentary elections began to be formulated, a deputation from the Workingmen's Concert Association came to call on Casals. Its membership, already in the thousands with local groups throughout Catalonia, was a force of considerable potential. Casals had a good idea what his visitors had in mind, but waited through the polite conversation about the Association's progress and various other matters until they made their proposal. The subject came around to the cultural influence of the Association and the thought that it should be extended by participating in village and town councils and even seeking representation in the national legislature, with the hesitant suggestion that Casals agree to let himself be proposed as their candidate.

Casals told them sharply that they had fallen into a dangerous trap. Their contribution to the life of Catalonia had been important and could continue to be *if* they did not dabble in politics. If they did, he said, they would find that all the cooperation they had built would evaporate, and that there would be enemies everywhere.

As one of his nation's best-known international figures, Pablo Casals was offered various positions and declined them all. Later, after the Catalan charter of autonomy was drawn up and adopted by plebiscite, he did accept the presidency of the Council of Music of Catalonia, a cultural division of the provincial Generalitat. The Minister of Culture in Luis Companys' Catalan government was Ventura Gassol Rovira, one of Casals' closest friends in Spanish political life during the Republic—a small, intensely patriotic poet who always wore a long bow tie and whose unruly forelock made him look to some like an early-nineteenth-century violinist. One of the things that appealed to Casals, in fact, about many of the Republican governmental leaders was the quality that most later historians believe led to their downfall: They were men of intense social consciousness and high ideals, not routine politicians and bureaucrats; they were liberals, humanists, men who loved their country passionately but not always practically. Among those Casals admired especially were two of the prime ministers of the Madrid Republican government, brilliant writer Manuel Azaña and Juan Negrín, a physician; Fernando de los Ríos, a philosopher and Minister of Education; and the noted Catalan historian Luis Nicoláu d'Olwer, a member of the first Republican cabinet.

A small and unimportant thing, an unrequired courtesy, defined for Casals a subtle difference between the period of the monarchy and that of the Republic. The royal family's friendship for Casals was warm, affectionate, and frequently thoughtful but did not necessarily represent the State's position. In the nearly thirty years of his concert career and wide travels during the reign of Alfonso XIII, Casals was never met by a Spanish representative on arrival in a foreign place. From 1931 until the revolution in

1936, whenever he reached a city abroad in which there was a Spanish consulate or embassy he was invariably met by a representative who generally offered to put a car at his disposal and otherwise tried to be of assistance. It was not, Casals said, treatment of a visiting dignitary: "I was made to feel like a member of the family." Meanwhile, the family of close friends was still being reduced: word came during the fall Orquestra season of Emanuel Moór's death in Switzerland on October 21.

On November 27, 1931, Casals wrote Julius Röntgen—the first letter in seventeen years—from the Amstel Hotel in Amsterdam to say he was glad to have had good news of Röntgen from his son Joachim in Zürich a few days earlier and the day before from mutual friends in Holland. "I spend most of the time in Spain, because since I have had my orchestra in Barcelona I am cutting down my trips more and more. If you write me I shall be very happy."

The tour in progress ranged as far as Budapest on the ninth of December. A second letter to Röntgen, written from Spain on the eighteenth, as Casals was approaching his fifty-fifth birthday, has much of the tone of those of twenty or twenty-five years before:

Dear Julius,

I finally arrived in Barcelona following my fatiguing concert tour, happy to return to my own and to have a good rest before the festivities of Christmas and the New Year— Your letter gave me much pleasure—you are always the same, so energetic and full of ideas and zest—your voice on the telephone, your handwriting, absolutely the same and always so young— Will you accept the warmest sentiments from the friend you have not seen for so long? This I regret so much and it is I who have lost—

Your title of Doctor honoris causa delights me. Holland has not conferred one on you before Edinburgh?!? I want so much to bring myself up to date on all your compositions since the Van Eeghenstraat days — I hope I shall have the occasion — It is my great sorrow not to be able to dedicate myself to composition—life has pushed me onto other paths— I know that the world would be neither better nor worse but the musical ideal of all my life has been to make up this loss—

And now I will rest and await the month of May to see you, dear Julius— A thousand greetings to your wife with the longtime faithful friendship of

your
Pablo

Happy holidays!

Casals visited the Röntgens in May 1932, after the Barcelona spring season, for a short but highly emotional visit. Host and guest were photographed in Bilthoven on a brick terrace of the house Röntgen called Gaudeamus. Casals, squinting a bit in the light, stands grinning on a step above Röntgen, which makes him seem the taller, a flower in his right hand, his left arm over his friend's shoulder. They discussed a trip to Barcelona for Röntgen to participate in one of the October concerts. A letter from Casals on the nineteenth of June said:

> Our Secretary will send you on behalf of the Committee a word of invitation and of appreciation for your cooperation in one of the concerts of my orchestra next season— Your offer to come to Barcelona has given me a special joy because I had almost given up the hope of seeing you here to participate in what I consider the most important undertaking of my life. I had never thought I could ask you to make so long a trip for my pleasure— Your offer is therefore most gratifying and I thank you with all my heart—
> I am at San Salvador surrounded by my dear brother and sister[-in-law] and the three little ones—I am happy and aware of their affection and I am working in the calm that I love and that is necessary to me. . . .

(Casals' communication with children, and their response to him, was remarkable. He lavished thoughtful attention and affection on his seven young nieces and nephews, on the growing battalion of his godchildren, and on the children of friends. The children most often at San Salvador were Luis and Teresina's three; one of their uncle's pleasures was to untether a favorite burro, one of the numerous animals at the villa, and lead it in to say good morning to the youngsters.)

Casals wrote Röntgen again on the first of September 1932, expressing concern for the older man's health. Röntgen, seventy-seven, had been in a clinic for several weeks but was brought home in September, very weak. His wife wrote Casals, who came from Barcelona to visit him at mid-month. Röntgen's strength appeared to return with Casals' arrival; they spent most of a day making music and reminiscing. The following day Röntgen went into a coma. He died on the nineteenth of September 1932.

Casals continued to perform in Germany from the end of the First World War through the first part of the 1932–1933 season. In January 1933 Adolf Hitler came to power in Berlin; street attacks against Jews reminded Casals of what had happened in France during the Dreyfus affair. A staged Nazi "unpleasantness" for one of Casals' last appearances in Berlin had been threatened. It had been canceled by pressure applied at the right bureaucratic point by friends. The incident did not necessarily perturb Casals for himself, but the implications worried him very much. He began to hear of incidents and threats to such men as Albert Einstein, Bruno Walter, and Fritz Busch. Wilhelm Furtwängler, whom Casals still liked as a man and respected as a musician, believed he had the stature and the support to protect his musicians, no matter what their background or political stand. He also thought he could safeguard the circumstances of German musicians in general if he could get prominent artists from outside to continue to play in Berlin and elsewhere in Germany. As he began to plan the 1934 season of the Berlin Philharmonic, Furtwängler wrote personal invitations to Casals, Cortot, Josef Hofmann, Huberman, Kreisler, young Yehudi Menuhin, Piatigorsky, Thibaud, and Schnabel. All declined, although Alfred Cortot later changed his mind and accepted. Art and politics were separate things, Furtwängler had written. From San Salvador, Casals drafted a long letter of great dignity that expressed strong personal friendship and understanding for the struggle in which Furtwängler was engaged, but said that he could not and would not enter Germany until its musical life was free again; the letter made clear Casals' personal surprise that Furtwängler would care to stay and work under such conditions. Even so, for Casals Germany remained the native land of Bach, Beethoven, and Brahms, and he had many happy memories of his performances there over thirty years—one of the most treasured was the evening in the palace of Sans Souci at Potsdam when he and Frederick Lamond had given a recital in the room in which Johann Sebastian Bach had played for Frederick the

Great. Casals neither had nor professed true foresight of what was, in fact, developing in Germany, but he said that every man had a duty to speak out against injustice—more so "the privileged people who have won the esteem of the world"—and that protests of affronts to human dignity must be made as a matter of conscience. He refused any longer to play there.

Austria for a time was a different situation, and Casals accepted an invitation to take part in the 1933 Brahms Festival in Vienna directed by Furtwängler, with Bronislaw Huberman and Artur Schnabel. (Hitler's favorite pianist at the time was Wilhelm Backhaus, and official Berlin was furious that he had not been invited instead of Schnabel.)

Donald Tovey had long wanted to write a major violoncello concerto for Casals; he had mentioned the idea to Casals and discussed the project with Julius Röntgen before the Dutch musician's death. He had composed little for some time and had been ill for nearly a year when he wrote his Edinburgh assistant in March 1933: "Did I tell you that the first movement of my 'cello concerto is now finished and fully scored? It's the biggest single movement I've ever written (or ever want to write) and very much the juiciest. The 'cello dominates a trombone-orchestra quite easily, and the whole thing is as dramatic as I can manage to be." Tovey had already sent the solo part of the movement to Casals, who acknowledged receipt on the twelfth of March:

> Dear Donald,
> The day of the arrival of your concerto is marked on the calendar of my life—I have a great joy and appreciate the sentiments that emerge from your words of dedication, which I hope I can honor.
> The bowings seem all right—if after I work at it I find any necessity for alterations I'll submit them for your approval. . . .

After it was fully sketched Tovey described the concerto in a letter:

> The slow movement turns out to be a very gloomy affair in F minor, which has been in my head for about six years without my being able to find out what it was to be. . . . A recklessly sentimental Intermezzo acts as buffer between the

solemn slow movement and a big grotesque finale. . . . I'm putting down all the bad jokes in my sketches for the finale; there's such a lot of material that the good ones are sure to crowd the bad ones out. . . .

Casals expressed a desire to give the first performance of the concerto with Tovey in Edinburgh in the fall of 1934. The concerto plays for exactly an hour and is laid out in three elaborate movements, with a three-minute Intermezzo between the second movement and the finale. (The twenty-five-minute first movement, with long ruminating cello passages over a dark-toned orchestration, anesthetized some listeners, but Casals said nobody but Tovey "could even plan, let alone carry out a first movement on such a grand architectural scale.") To Tovey directly Casals was enthusiastic:

> . . . there is nothing technically impossible about your concerto—that you know as well as I. All that is required is to assimilate your violoncello technique which is, thank God, as good in you as those of Beethoven and Brahms were to them. To correct your work would be to ameliorate it, but you do not have to change anything to make my task easier—it excites me and I am going at it, believe me, with the greatest pleasure and interest.

The dates of the Reid concerts in Edinburgh were set, and Casals' appearance in the first performance of the Tovey cello concerto scheduled. "The twenty-second of November will be the most important date of my musical life," he wrote Tovey. "Joachim must have felt the same joy and honor the day he first played the Beethoven violin concerto and that of the first hearing of the Brahms." Casals had played with the BBC Orchestra and also conducted one of its concerts the preceding week, so the British Broadcasting Corporation decided not to broadcast the Tovey première from Edinburgh. Music-lovers and critics traveled from London and elsewhere for the concert, which was considered a success. ("The whole concerto grows out of the genius of the violoncello," observed *The Times* of London, "and it takes all Casals's genius to display its qualities. That in itself is worth going to Edinburgh to hear.") Tovey and Casals left the concert hall in the same vehicle. Tovey, deeply moved, told his friend that at last he had been given what had for nearly sixty years been denied him—recognition as a composer. Tentative plans were made for London performances of the concerto and for recording it.

None of the public knew that the soloist was far from well that night. He had a painful infection of his left thumb, a condition that soon became so serious he was unable to play for nearly two months. The pain of the thumb became acute, and Casals consulted specialists in England and on the Continent. The problem was finally solved by Dr. Ernest Vila in Figueras, a small Catalan city between Gerona and the French border, who took tweezers and removed a nailbrush bristle.

The day after the first performance of the Tovey cello concerto the composer sent out a call for "someone who could photograph Casals, Schweitzer and me in our spangles and tights" the following morning. Albert Schweitzer, like Casals awarded an honorary doctorate of music in absentia at the graduation of the preceding summer term of the University of Edinburgh, had come with his wife for a stay of several weeks with the Toveys while he delivered the Gifford Lectures in theology. Casals knew Schweitzer's writings, especially *The Poet Musician*, his book about Johann Sebastian Bach; they found their "poetic vision" on the subject parallel. Their paths had not crossed directly before, although both had been in Paris (which Schweitzer had disliked vehemently) at the same time just before the turn of the century. Neither had been decked out in full academic finery before and both were enormously pleased by the proceedings. Tovey's search for a cameraman was successful; the resulting photographs are among the most unflattering ever taken of Casals.

In response to his degree Casals gave a recital and Schweitzer urged him to remain longer in Edinburgh so they could play still more Bach together; but there were firm commitments and Casals had to leave. As he was departing for the station Schweitzer caught up with him, out of breath. Since Casals must leave, Schweitzer said, they must address each other as *tu*—put their relationship on a first-name basis—before Casals left. The two men embraced and parted emotionally, not to meet again for seventeen years.

Barcelona, too, honored Casals in 1934. He was proclaimed an honorary citizen and awarded the gold medal of the city in addition to having his name given to a major avenue. Two hundred academic and artistic societies were represented at the ceremonies, which culminated in a concert by the Orquestra Pau Casals, the

Madrid Philharmonic, and the Madrid Symphony under Enrique Fernández Arbós in the Palace of Montjuich. The city struck an additional medal in Casals' honor, and an exhibition of his souvenirs and memorabilia was opened in the Museum of Art of Catalonia.

By 1934 the Republic was in serious trouble. From its beginning Casals had been in sympathy with many of the purposes of the new regime—universal suffrage to elect a parliament to which the government was responsible; rights to jury trial and other individual civil liberties; universal education. There were also things he had not liked, because he feared they would lead to the extremist reaction that in fact came quickly. Not only were state and church separated, but the Republican government also enacted stringently anticlerical legislation and made both churchmen and the military ineligible for most governmental posts. These conservative elements, which had wielded power in Spain for so many centuries, predictably resisted and a serious military uprising had taken place in Seville when the Republic was little more than a year old. On the other side, there was serious disaffection among workers and the poor, unhappy with the speed of social reform. A great radical rising spread from Barcelona to other large cities in January 1933; there was ten days of fighting in Barcelona during a syndicalist-anarchist revolt in December, and a great Socialist-led strike in Barcelona in April 1934. The uprisings and strikes were put down, often with difficulty, by the national government in Madrid. Municipal elections, in which an increasing number of candidates of the Right were victorious, reflected middle-class reaction to the labor unrest. When President Luis Companys declared Catalonia independent in October 1934 the move was suppressed by government troops and the statute of Catalan home rule was suspended.

Throughout all this chaotic period Casals kept up the regular orchestra seasons and a still-substantial schedule of international solo appearances. When free, he was to be found at San Salvador, composing a little, enjoying guests, watching progress of the formal Italian garden he called "my mother's garden," and explaining to the architect his own structural and artistic ideas to be carried out in the complex of villa buildings.

Late in 1935 the Tovey concerto once again took center stage. The first London performances, November 11 and 12, under the auspices of the Courtauld–Sargent Concert Club, were disastrous in spite of Casals' devotion. There had not been enough rehearsal time for the long, complicated work. The competent but routine-hardened orchestra players, used to Malcolm Sargent's briskness, became impatient and then irritated with Tovey and his rambling explanations, and they found the concerto itself too long and somewhat dull. The audience was slightly more appreciative than the press; Fox-Strangways said in the *Observer* that "the composer conducted, and proved himself the enemy of Casals and of his own music." Tovey, like Moór, had a lifelong sensitivity to criticism, and was furious. His pain was not much assuaged by Casals' letter afterward: "What enormous pleasure for me to do your concerto in London! All that counts is whether you are satisfied—the rest is of no moment."

Tovey was eager to have Casals record the concerto. After several false starts, it was finally put onto disks two years later, November 17, 1937, during a broadcast concert by Casals and the BBC Orchestra, with Sir Adrian Boult conducting. Observed *The Times*:

> Señor Casals, to whom the [concerto] is dedicated and who now played it for the third time in London, has been its persistent advocate, sometimes perhaps to the point of indiscretion, for people do not want to be lectured into the appreciation of genius. His best advocacy is . . . his own performance, for when a great virtuoso insists on repeating such a work as this in face of public apathy . . . simply because he believes in it, he is certain to make converts.

Fritz Busch wrote from Copenhagen that the transmission had been heard well there and that the work had made a great impression on him. Guilhermina Suggia, writing Tovey from Portugal, said "I heard your concerto through the wireless and it sounded beautiful. I wondered how ever it was possible to master it in such a way and I am convinced that there is only one 'cellist in the world who could have done it." Practically no other cellist since has tried.

There can be no greater evidence of Casals' musical respect for Donald Francis Tovey than the fact that (along with Röntgen's) he used Tovey's edition of *The Well-Tempered Clavier*, dedicated to Albert Schweitzer, and that he played the Beethoven cello sonatas in Tovey's edition. At the time of his last appearance in Edinburgh, just after the end of World War II and five

years after his friend's death, Casals went to the apartment in Buc-
cleuch Place where Tovey had lived, then kept as a museum. He
sat down at the beautiful old Bösendorfer piano and, weeping,
played the opening of Tovey's cello concerto.

There were those who said that Pablo Casals' great heart and
stubborn loyalty had taken precedence over his head in the cases
of Emanuel Moór, Julius Röntgen, and Donald Francis Tovey.
But Casals' genius was music and his instinct seldom failed him
or went long astray. It is possible that Pablo Casals found in the
creation of these men, and in them, durable treasure that others
were unable to recognize or too impatient to seek.

The capital of Spain honored Pablo Casals in December 1935. In
a week of celebrations during which there were concerts, speeches,
and receptions, Casals was named an adopted son of Madrid,
awarded a gold medal, and inducted into the Academia de Bellas
Artes de San Fernando of the Spanish Academy. The Republican
government pressed Casals to accept as his own the Stradivarius
cello from the palace collection. He refused, insisting that the collection be kept intact and safeguarded. (During the monarchy,
it was kept among the treasures of the royal chapel, but in his
student years in Madrid, although a protégé of the Queen Regent,
Casals was never invited either to see or to play any of the historic
instruments.) On the day after Christmas, three days before Casals'
fifty-ninth birthday, there was a gala concert in the Cine Monumental that netted eighty-five hundred pesetas for distribution to
the city's poor. An *homenaje* attended by the leaders of government, society, and the arts was held in the seventeenth-century
City Hall on the Plaza de la Villa. When the end of the evening
came and with it the prescribed time to respond to the eulogies,
Casals rose and spoke about his parents, his childhood in Vendrell,
his early years in Barcelona. He recalled his student days in Madrid,
the Count of Morphy, Monasterio, Bretón, and the noisy top landing of the house in the calle de San Quintín. Then he began to
speak of the royal palace that stood no more than five minutes'
walk distant, of the hours he had spent there, and of its former
inhabitants. A shock that was almost physical went through the
Republican audience at the mention of the monarchy. Casals said,
as tears came to his eyes, that he would never forget or disclaim
his personal gratitude for the affection and help of "that wonderful

and unforgettable woman, Queen Doña María Cristina." The audience came to its feet, cheering.

Seven months later, when the Spanish Civil War began, Casals was in Barcelona. The last season in the life of the Orquestra Pau Casals had ended on the twenty-eighth of June, but the organization was intact on July 18 for rehearsal of the Beethoven ninth symphony. It was to be performed in the same Montjuich auditorium in which it had helped celebrate the beginning of the Republic five years earlier. The occasion was in connection with the Barcelona Olympiad, which had been arranged in competition as well as opposition to the Berlin Olympic Games. The rehearsal was being held in Barcelona proper, in the Orfeó Català's Palace of Music. Casals had worked through the first three movements of the Beethoven and the chorus was on stage to sing the final chorale when a messenger brought him an urgent note from Minister of Culture Ventura Gassol. A military revolt was expected in the city any minute. The following day's concert had been canceled; the rehearsal should be broken off so that the musicians could go home immediately. The messenger added that insurrection had already begun in the Madrid garrison and very possibly had started in Barcelona. Casals read Gassol's note to the orchestra and chorus. Then he asked if they wished to leave at once or to say farewell by completing the work together. They would finish.

Casals could not see the score for his tears as he led the orchestra in Beethoven's music, the chorus singing in Catalan Schiller's words ". . . all mankind are brothers." At the end he promised they would one day perform the ninth symphony again, when there was peace once more. Casals and the musicians went home through streets already barricaded.

The rebellion, which began among the army chiefs in Morocco and was led by generals Francisco Franco and Emilio Mola, soon spread to many of the garrison towns of Spain, including Cadiz, Seville, Saragossa, and Burgos. In Madrid and Barcelona, government forces were able to remain in control. Germany and Italy soon began to supply the Insurgents with great quantities of matériel and men. France, briefly, and the Soviet Union were the only powers that gave substantial material aid to the legitimate government—although public opinion, insofar as it was concerned at all, in France, Britain, and the United States was strongly on the Republican side. Spain became the focal point of rival ideologies.

In San Salvador Casals was anguished and, for the time being, uncertain what he must do. He felt his place was among the Catalan people, yet he had contracted to perform elsewhere in Europe during the next autumn and winter. In September, before he left San Salvador for his winter concerts in central Europe, he played the Haydn concerto with personnel of the Orquestra Pau Casals at the Liceo in Barcelona in a benefit for war victims.

In the course of his travel a visit with an old friend buoyed Casals' spirits temporarily. Queen Elisabeth of the Belgians, now the Queen Mother, had found her way back into some of her former activity. Following her long depression and seclusion after her husband's death in February 1934, her interest in life began to return during a visit to her daughter Marie-José, who had married the Crown Prince of Italy. Near the sea in a Savoy villa between Naples and Sorrento Elisabeth's physical health improved in three months of sunshine and some of her former curiosity and enthusiasm began to return. (She loved sea and sun—she had once had herself lashed to the mast of a boat to enjoy a storm, and would stretch out in sunshine in the park of Laeken long before sunbathing became fashionable.) She was now in her late fifties, but she learned both to dive and to drive a motorcar. Music, she told Casals, finally brought her truly back into the world. One of her attendants coaxed her into taking up the violin again, and eventually this brought her back into the world of composers and performers. By the time Casals saw her in late 1936, she was completing plans for the cultural project for which she was best known internationally. First called the Concours Ysaÿe and later the Concours Reine Elisabeth, this is a major competition for performers and composers. She had become the last great royal patron of music, and was constantly in evidence during the competitions from the inaugural contest in 1937 until her death in 1966.

The *anarquistas* dominated Barcelona and much of the territory that remained in the hands of the Republic after war broke out in Spain. The country was bathed in blood; it is estimated that some seventy-five thousand people were killed in other than military engagements in Republican territory in the six weeks between

July 18 and September 1, 1936, and the number of murdered grew as Insurgent forces moved inland from the northwest coast and up the Tagus valley toward Toledo and Madrid. Political theory and labels meant little to Casals, but what he saw to be moral and human issues meant a great deal. The anarchist ideal of absolute freedom he could not accept because he could not conceive of liberty without order; the Anarchists further set about destroying what they determined were institutions and examples of upper- and middle-class mores—always violence in the name of a utopian goal. Word came of the death of a man known to Casals and his brother Enrique, executed by a shower of scalding water. Monks of the order of San Juan de Dios were shot within a few hundred meters of Casals. During the first days of the Civil War many personal scores were settled, but the great surge of uncontrolled vengeance was against the symbols of repression—the Church and the prosperous. Even here chance sometimes played a hand, but so did past action. The priest who was known to have worn a clean collar for a rich man's funeral but not for a pauper's stood an excellent chance of being shot; the doctor who had treated his poor patients fairly and carefully was likely to be safe.

There is a legend that Casals was arrested in his house in Barcelona by an Anarchist gang that intended to shoot him. They refused to believe either that he was a friend of the people or that he was who he said he was; it was inconceivable to them that so famous a man would have a house in a bourgeois district. To prove his identity he picked up his instrument and played. The Anarchists listened with tears running down their cheeks, both because they found the music unbearably moving and because they realized how nearly fatal their mistake had been. Actually, Casals was not arrested by the Anarchists, but there were brushes with them. One day armed men appeared at the Villa Casals. Casals was playing; they waited until he finished. They were looking for Señor Renom, a prosperous Barcelona businessman and friend of Casals who had a neighboring summer home, and had not found him or his wife in their house. Casals knew what was happening: the Anarchist village councils met daily, and at night or early in the morning the knock could come at the door. Casals acknowledged Renom was a friend but said he was not in his house. The men left after stationing one of their number at the front of the house and one at the back.

*(Left) Casals giving a solo recital in the convent
of Valldemosa on Majorca (May 1931);
(right) Casals practicing at San Salvador*

Renom and his wife appeared in the villa a few minutes later, somehow having entered without being seen by the guards. They were desperate. Casals was playing his cello again when the Anarchists returned an hour later. This time their spokesman said he knew the people they were looking for were in Casals' house. Casals said that, yes, they were there now. His friend was a good man, he continued, and nobody would seize him in the home of Pau Casals. Casals telephoned the Anarchist mayor of Vendrell, saying furiously that he would not permit an injustice to a good man. The local politician hedged at once, explaining everything away as a mistake; the men had come to the wrong house. . . .

Casals' big house and gardens at San Salvador, nearly completed when the revolution came, seemed tremendously luxurious to most of the local people. Every time the Vendrell extermination council met to decide who was to be shot next, Casals was told, his name and that of his brother Luis always figured on the list, but invariably one or other of the group would say "No, not them;

not yet. We have to think their case through very carefully."
Others in the neighborhood, however, disappeared forever. Casals
spoke to officials of the Barcelona Generalitat and urged them to
take the necessary measures, even if that meant sending troops to
restore order: too many innocent people were suffering. They,
as well as union leaders and members of the national government,
had broadcast repeated appeals for restraint, but they admitted they
were powerless to do more. "Then you ought to resign," Casals
said. There were no other cases of intervention on behalf of individuals so dramatic as that for his friend Renom, but he spoke
out for people he knew to be good human beings whenever there
was opportunity. When the *anarquistas* came to San Salvador to
burn the Hermitage, Casals was able to persuade them to spare
the building in which he had had his first conscious memory: a
bonfire of broken furniture and religious objects of no artistic value
outside the structure saved the relics within and saved face for
the local activists. Casals had occasion to talk with a number of
Anarchists at this time, especially in the Vendrell region. They
listened respectfully, but he had the feeling they understood little
of what he was saying.

One of Doña Pilar's most startling pronouncements had been
"In general I do not respect law," certainly on its surface anarchis-
tic-sounding and an implicit approval of civil disobedience. As a
child Casals had overheard her explaining her reasoning to his godmother, her cousin Fidèlia. Every individual on earth is unique,
Pilar Casals had said; there is no possible way that a law governing
any subject or action could be written that would be right or fair
for all. Casals found the *anarquistas* equally opposed to authority
and without respect for law, but with a far different emphasis.
His mother's aversion had been strongest to legislation that con-
doned the deepest moral wrong and denied human beings the opportunity to refuse to fight and to kill. The Anarchists in Spain
in 1936 were men of violence. "The people," they told Casals,
"are the only law." To him they seemed like children who had
suddenly gained control of the world.

A few days after the Renom incident Casals had to leave for
Paris. The Anarchists required anyone who left the area to carry
travel documents issued by them. Casals went to the regional *anar-
quista* headquarters in nearby San Salvador de Comarruga, where
the chief of the district greeted him cordially. They had a long

The Hermitage and the small interior chapel at San Salvador as they appeared in 1926. When the Anarchists were in control of the Vendrell region at the beginning of the Spanish Civil War, Casals persuaded them not to burn the building.

talk, in which the leader told Casals that in the eyes of the Anarchists he was a good man, a friend of the people; he made good use of his property and therefore deserved to have his home and gardens. He might come and go as he pleased.

Casals was at home in San Salvador most of the short period of the summer of 1936 that the Anarchists had control, and Luis and Teresina Casals were with him. Soon after he left to fulfill his concert contracts abroad, the local *comunistas* wrested that control away. Casals felt that his property was in greater danger, as he personally would have been, under the new authority. Casals had read Karl Marx first when he was an adolescent; Marx's theories had opened up a vast new area of thought to him, he said, but he had not found in them answers he felt would work for him or for the world. In late 1936 he was well aware of, and grateful for, the material help the Soviet government gave to the Spanish Republic. Yet he remembered what had happened to the Siloti family and others he had known in Russia during the Communist revolution in 1917, and the situation for Casals was one not of ideologies but of human values, even in rural Vendrell and San Salvador. Luis and his family fled the Villa Casals. (The villa and its contents were generally respected. The Communists damaged books and broke records, but the house suffered its only slight physical damage during the war in an artillery action when the Nationalists overran the area early in 1939.) Casals had taken precautions to safeguard some of the objects that meant most to him; he instructed that other things, including a number of documents, should be wrapped carefully and buried. Whatever the reason, perhaps a wave of fright that had a realistic basis, instead of being buried the photographs inscribed to Casals by María Cristina, Alfonso XIII, the Infanta Isabel, and other Spanish and foreign royalty as well as all correspondence that could have been considered monarchist was burned while Casals was out of Spain. (The climate of terror was one impossible to grasp years afterward by those who had not experienced it, and explains why so few letters written by Casals exist in Spain. The widow of Juli Garreta, to whom Casals' bankers sent a monthly check during the twenty years between her husband's death and her own, was arrested during the Civil War because a letter from Casals was found in her possession.)

Pablo Casals stubbornly maintained that his place was in Catalonia, among the people of his homeland. His friends in government, particularly Ventura Gassol, finally convinced him that he could be of greater help to his country by continuing his concert career, taking every possible occasion to tell the rest of the world what was actually going on in Spain. He had a home when he wished to use it in the Paris apartment of Maurice and Paula Eisenberg. He stayed there for a time in September 1936, greatly depressed, but winter weather in Paris can be harsh and it is far both from the sea and from Catalonia. The season was over and many coastal hotels had closed, but Casals made a trip to the South of France in search of a place to live between his tours. His friend Luis Guarro had told him in Paris about the French-Catalan village of Prades— where Guarro had taken his own family—a few kilometers across the Pyrenean border from Spanish Catalonia. Casals decided to settle there until conditions improved and moved into the village's Grand Hotel. With him was Frasquita Vidal de Capdevila, the widow of the treasurer of the Orquestra Pau Casals. Señor Capdevila had died in the 1920s and on his deathbed had sought Casals' promise to care for his widow. Señora Capdevila had helped with the Orquestra administration, and at San Salvador in the late 1920s she occupied one of the guest cottages at the villa. When Casals was persuaded he could best serve Spain outside its borders he offered his friend's widow the choice of remaining with Luis and his family or of coming away with him.

Through 1936 the Barcelona region remained an oasis in the ground fighting between Republican and Nationalist forces, although German and Italian planes had begun aerial bombardment of the city and other centers. Casals continued to go back and forth to Spain, still arguing that his place was there and still suspecting that he was being urged to stay away for his own protection. Spring concerts in 1937 ranged from Prague at the end of April to Paris in mid-May. On July 12 he played the Haydn concerto at the Liceo in Barcelona, a benefit concert for war victims and the last concert of the Orquestra Pau Casals as an entity. Five days later he sailed from Boulogne for a two-month South American tour, his first in thirty-three years. In the six weeks preceding his sixty-first birthday he played in various cities in England, conducted in London, played in Amsterdam and The Hague, Prague,

Vienna, Budapest, Bucharest, Zürich, and Paris, then gave a solo recital in Amsterdam.

He went from alien city to alien city, a choking pain inside. Every newspaper brought fresh news of death and horror in Spain. The reports of friends and of governmental officials he met in Paris, London, or Geneva only increased his personal anguish. He accepted honorary chairmanship of the U.S.-based Musicians' Committee to Aid Spanish Democracy. It became daily more a matter of conscience to him to support the legally constituted government of Spain. He lost his last vestige of respect for the League of Nations as a result of its handling of the Spanish question.

Casals made his first and only North African tour in February 1938, playing for Les Amis de Musique in Rabat, Casablanca, Oran, Algiers, and Tunis within two weeks. On his return he was greeted by the widely circulated newspaper report that identified him as "president of the Catalan National Committee of the Friends of the USSR." It was one of the first of many spurious reports that appeared in the press during the Spanish Civil War, in some cases planted by Republicans to lend his prestige to their cause and in others by opponents to discredit him. Casals was not hesitant in making known on which side he stood, but most often his plea was for the child victims of the war; their plight haunted him. His last concert in Spain was a benefit for the Children's Aid Society given on October 19, 1938, as Francisco Franco's Nationalist forces moved steadily closer to Catalonia. The orchestra, which included many of the personnel of the Orquestra Pau Casals, played overtures by Gluck and Weber under Casals' direction, then accompanied Casals in the Haydn and Dvořák cello concertos. During rehearsal there was a bombing raid; and when there were hits nearby the orchestra musicians dispersed into the auditorium. Casals picked up a cello, sat down alone, and began to play a Bach solo suite. The orchestra soon returned to its places and the rehearsal continued. During the intermission of the concert Casals went before microphones with an eloquent and clear plea for the children's cause; the message, repeated in English and French and containing a warning that Spain's freedom was in gravest danger, was retransmitted internationally. In Free Spain, work was stopped for two hours on a Monday afternoon so that workers could hear the music.

Later in October Casals had concerts in Belgium; in November he played concertos with orchestras in Prague and Zagreb, then concertos and recitals in Bucharest, Istanbul, and Athens; and during the first week in December he performed in Cairo and Alexandria. He decided against a projected tour to Japan in 1939.

Returning to Spain, Casals found his villa filled with refugees. With most of the rest of the country in their control, the Nationalist forces began a campaign in Catalonia that gradually drove the Loyalist forces back. Franco's troops, with Italian aid, took Barcelona on January 26, 1939. Forty-eight hours earlier Casals had been summoned to a hasty convocation of remaining faculty and officers of the University and presented an honorary doctorate, handwritten because there had not been facilities to have the customary calligraphy and illumination done. Many at that meeting left almost immediately to go into exile. A few days later Casals himself left San Salvador for Prades, and within two weeks the Nationalists had overrun all Catalonia, forcing some two hundred thousand Loyalist troops across the French border, where they were disarmed.

On March 28, 1939, Casals played the Elgar, Dvořák, and Haydn concertos with Albert Coates and the London Symphony Orchestra in a benefit concert to aid Spanish children. There was an almost unbearable tension in the Royal Albert Hall: the last Republican stronghold, Madrid, had fallen to the Franco forces a few hours earlier.

At the beginning of the war Casals had answered a Barcelona journalist's questioning: "If the Revolution is justice and equality, if it is not a simple changing of coats, if it is not a conflict of egotisms and the satisfaction of hates and personal scores and will flower tomorrow in human happiness, I accept and identify myself with it. I am an artist and with my art seek only Peace and Harmony among men." But as time passed he had become increasingly outspoken in his public pleas that the rest of the world awake to the plight of his country; reaction from the Nationalist side was strong. Casals was now a sufficient irritant to the Falangists to be singled out for notice by the Nationalists' chief propagandist, Gen. Gonzalo Quiepo de Llano, in the course of one of his rambling nightly ten-o'clock broadcasts. To the laughter of his claque in the broadcasting studio in Seville, Quiepo declared that he would end Casals' agitation when he caught him by cutting off both arms at the elbow. Casals could not return to Spain. He was told un-

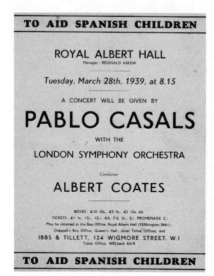

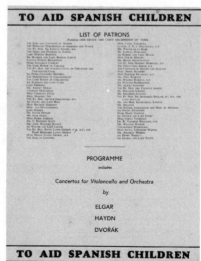

First two pages of the announcement of Casals'
London concert for the benefit of Spanish
children March 28, 1939, the day Madrid fell
to the Nationalists. The list of sponsors contains
names of unusual interest even more than three
decades later.

equivocally that if he did he would be executed. Luis and his family remained safe but terrified in Vendrell; Enrique and his family had stayed in Barcelona. Word came eventually that the San Salvador villa was unharmed; the Nationalist commander of the Vendrell region let it be known quietly that the house and its treasures were to be respected. Casals went to Paris, where he stayed at the Maurice Eisenbergs' home, prostrate and inconsolable in a darkened room for days, unable to bear light. He had sent telegrams to the new mayor of Barcelona and the civil governor of Catalonia offering his continued help in behalf of widows and orphans; there was no reply. A friend who came to Paris found Casals aged and defeated, passing his hand carefully over his head and his reddened eyes as though in pain.

Casals fulfilled a contract for a recital in Cannes on the twelfth of April 1939, then returned to Prades. The hotel management began to complain that the noise of Casals' cello was disturbing the other guests.

As the Insurgent generals' attack in July 1936 became civil war the stream of Spaniards traveling into exile began, but the deluge of Republican refugees—especially from Catalonia, the last major geographic region to fall—did not start until the end of 1938. Toward the end of the war there were a million adult refugees in Barcelona, as well as six hundred thousand children. France opened its border for the flow of war material into Republican Spain, but until January 1939 refused to open its Pyrenean frontier to refugees. The French proposed a neutral zone just inside Spain, with financial support coming from other nations; the victorious Nationalists would not consider such a solution. Not until midnight on January 27–28, 1939, were the fleeing thousands allowed to cross into France in the snow and rain. Entrance at first was granted only to the wounded and to civilians. During the first week ten thousand wounded, one hundred seventy thousand women and children, and sixty thousand male civilians left Catalonia by this route. Between the fifth and the tenth of February another two hundred fifty thousand defeated and disarmed soldiers joined them. The frontier was a scene of ceaseless tragedy, but many who saw the human stream never forgot how few complaints were heard or the dignity with which these people left their crushed homeland.

A large processing camp without shelter was opened at Le Boulou, on the French side of the border. Other large camps were established at Argelès, St. Cyprien, Septfonds—fifteen in all, guarded by Senegalese troops and members of the French *Garde Mobile*. The smaller camps were simply sand-dune areas near the sea, enclosed by barbed wire. Here men dug into the sand like animals for shelter, making deeper holes to find water to drink. For ten days there was neither adequate water nor a minimal supply of food; many wounded died from neglect rather than from their injuries. At Le Boulou during the first days, bread was thrown into the pushing crowds from a truck driven through the camp. Food supplies improved later, but not the sanitation or shelter—it was a very harsh winter—and there were almost no medical facilities. The authorities' problems in trying to provide for nearly half a million refugees were overwhelming, but it is certain that the French government hoped the conditions would make a great many of those who had fled decide to return and throw themselves on the mercy of the victors. (In response to French pleas, Belgium agreed to allow two or three thousand Spanish children to come there. The British and Soviet governments would not at first admit any Spanish refugees, although England later admitted certain of the leaders.)

Friends had known for years that he disliked writing letters, but from Prades Casals answered in his own hand the hundreds that began to reach him asking help. Usually when money had been requested he enclosed a few hundred francs. He also rented a truck, stocking it with bread, water, and whatever other food he could purchase. With a driver, and often with such friends who had come to Prades as the journalist-poet Juan Alavedra, he drove to the nearest refugee enclosures to help distribute the stores and talk with the people there. He was still a man of wealth, and drew on his French and English accounts to continue the refugee aid. The correspondence also brought contributions for the cause—most of them token, but gratifying to the man who had already begun to proclaim "Someone must remember!" and to whom the good gesture meant a great deal. A friend of those days recalls a wide range of contributions from those who wrote: twenty francs from a newsboy, a hundred dollars from a young American, money from hospital patients and from a monk. There were also steady contract offers to Casals for appearances either as cellist or as conductor from Europe, Central and South America, Australia. A New York manager sent a contract with all terms left for Casals to fill in and a personal message that any fee he named would be met. Casals replied that, while he continued to study every day, he was too dispirited and too preoccupied with the Catalan exiles to play in such a time.

On the first day of September 1939 German forces invaded Poland; Britain and France declared war on Germany on the third. Poland was defeated within a month and German armies moved to the borders of France. On November 12, Casals played the Lalo and the Saint-Saëns concertos with the Lamoureux orchestra in Paris, marking the fortieth anniversary of his Paris début. As the autumn continued, several friends who were leaving for the Western Hemisphere came to Prades to bid Casals farewell and to urge him to leave. There were offers of air transport for Casals and Señora Capdevila to England and the United States. He turned them down, believing he could be of use where he was. That most of the important musicians—almost all who could—were leaving Europe was not of real concern to him. They did what was right for them, and he would do what seemed right to him. The only actions he really could not understand at that point were those of such musicians as Furtwängler, who had continued to conduct in Germany.

Insatiable for news, he began to follow the BBC broadcasts faithfully. England was fighting valiantly through the "phony war"; someone advised Casals not in any circumstances to agree to play in London—it was being bombed every day. Nothing would please him more, retorted Casals, than to be there; to see his friends, reassure them and play "in case a concert of mine could be of service." A companion of that time in Prades remembered Casals saying that "what I most enjoy is standing up for something."

Casals had performed with the Concertgebouw orchestra in Amsterdam and The Hague in February 1940; without warning German forces invaded Belgium, the Netherlands, and Luxembourg in a lightning thrust on the tenth of May. The Queen Mother of the Belgians, like her friend Casals in her early sixties, found herself in what must have seemed the repetition of a nightmare: a hurried flight from Laeken, refugee-clogged roads toward the same villa on the La Panne shore, the same word of defeat. Unable after a day or two to endure the old villa without her husband, she moved next door. She sent her grandchildren off in a convoy of cars to haven first into France, then Spain. Once more she turned her attention to hospitals and refugees. In less than three weeks Elisabeth's son, Leopold III, had capitulated. The Queen had refused to leave her land and subjects: "How can we leave?" she burst out. "Our people are being killed all around us!" When she left for the palace of Laeken, where she would be a prisoner until after D-Day in June 1944, resting carefully in the back of her automobile were four of her most treasured possessions—an Amati, a Ruffini, a Guarnerius, and a Stradivarius violin—that had been packed there for the preceding eighteen days.

In his room at the Grand Hotel in Prades Casals kept a framed photograph of Eugène Ysaÿe playing his violin on a sand dune. "La Panne 1916, Élisabeth" reads the inscription. A souvenir of the First World War, it was an encouragement to Casals throughout the Second. It had come to him unexpectedly in Prades after the war had begun.

Late in 1939, a tall, athletic Briton dashed into the Grand Hotel and inquired for Maître Pablo Casals. His unusual style and somewhat eccentric appearance attracted the immediate attention of the local police, who questioned him. He produced a revolver and explained that since he was English and thus an ally he had a perfect right to carry a firearm. He also told them they and he were *cochons*, but "here in Prades you have a total genius, a demigod—Casals!" After a session at the Prades subprefecture Philip Newman, who had played at Ysaÿe's deathbed, was allowed to call on Casals, who had a sharp flood of nostalgia when the Englishman came into the room. There was considerable resemblance to the young Tovey as well as to Ysaÿe. Casals and Newman became firm friends and spent several days making music together—Newman was an excellent violinist and a tremendously warm if somewhat unconventional human being. When the time came to say goodbye Newman tried to press a roll of bank notes on Casals. When Casals refused adamantly, Newman said that instead, then, he would give the master his most treasured possession, and left with him the photograph Queen Elisabeth had taken of Ysaÿe.

Friends continued to urge Casals to come to England or to the security and freedom of America, but he continued to refuse to leave France. He had made a stand against totalitarianism that had forced him from his homeland; he would not leave France. "But if France is lost?" Alavedra asked him. "For that very reason I do not choose to abandon her." At the age of sixty-three, Pablo Casals showed a kinship to Cervantes' hero. For Don Quixote, and in many respects for Casals, there was no such thing as practical idealism: "If it was practical, it was not idealism to him . . . [the essence of living] meant precisely engaging in a death struggle against the stronger forces of injustice and evil, no matter the odds or consequences . . . a man committed his whole soul without thought of compromise, retreat, or appeasement."

Yet in the days that followed the German occupation of Paris

Eugène Ysaÿe at La Panne early in World War I,
photographed by Elisabeth of the Belgians

on June 13, 1940, and the fall of France nine days later, Casals had to reexamine his position. A number of people had urged Casals to come back to Spain, particularly as France became endangered; he did not consider it seriously. His moral stand that he would not return while Franco was in power forbade his going. Hundreds did go back, believing the chances and conditions of life in Spain, whatever they were, would be better than concentration camps and labor battalions in France. Many were imprisoned at once; there were nearly half a million people in Spanish prisons in 1940. The victors showed little mercy and no charity to defeated Republicans. Nevertheless the Prades police chief advised Casals that he and the people closest to him must leave France. With the fall of France there was strong belief that the Nazi forces would move down into the rest of the country. The Italians waited to move into Provence from the east, and it was generally thought that Franco was preparing to throw Spain's lot in with the dictatorships so that Nationalist forces could sweep across the unprotected Pyrenean border. This would amount to a potential death sentence not only for Casals but also for Frasquita Capdevila, the Alavedra family, and Enrique's daughter Pilar, who was also in Prades.

The French passenger ship *Champlain* was to sail for the Western Hemisphere from Bordeaux before the end of the month; passage could be arranged if Casals and his friends could get to Bordeaux. The necessary travel documents were made out, and Casals found two taxi drivers who for the incredible demand of a quarter-million francs (five thousand dollars) would transport the group the five hundred kilometers from Prades to the Atlantic port. Letters from Spanish refugees that might be compromising to their senders were burned, as were other documents, including Tovey's letters. With Casals, Frasquita Capdevila, and Casals' niece in one taxi and the Alavedras with two children and the luggage in the other, the little caravan set out on a difficult and circuitous route, east to Perpignan—where they began to travel against the stream of refugees from farther north in France; then north to Narbonne, west to the medieval fortress city of Carcassonne, and on west and north through Toulouse toward Bordeaux. The trip took more than two days; they spent one night in the white-wine country of Sauternes, where they had incongruously luxurious accommodations in the Château Yquem. Casals, nearly sixty-six, burdened with a sense of responsibility for the people with him, was often near tears at the sight of fields full of refugees resting or trying to sleep as the taxis moved against the tide.

The Prefecture in Bordeaux was a crowded madhouse, and Casals had a spell of faintness on the way up a flight of stairs. After he assisted Casals to a seat, Alavedra continued to search for the necessary travel authorizations and Nansen passports. He encountered the former secretary of French president Albert Seurrat, M. Dubois, whom Alavedra had met as a secretary to the last president of the Spanish Republic. Dubois helped cut through some red tape and the colonel in charge of the document office moved expeditiously. The required papers were in hand by the end of the day. Alavedra reported that during his search for the proper office he had met Alfred Cortot; on being told Casals was in the building and ill, he had said "Poor Pablo! . . . Forgive me, I am expected. Embrace him for me." As the two Catalans walked back to the parked taxis and the waiting women and children, Alavedra pointed out a building emblazoned with the name of one of Bordeaux's notable sons, Charles Lamoureux.

No open café could be found, but Casals and his companions held to the prospect of food aboard ship. In asking directions to the port they learned that the *Champlain* had gone to the bottom off La Pallice the night before after striking a mine dropped by enemy planes. There were no other ships leaving.

Casals directed a return to Prades; there was no choice. Two days later the exhausted travelers arrived at the locked and barred door of the Grand Hotel in the early hours of the morning. Enough noise was made to rouse the proprietor of the little hostelry (and the inhabitants of nearby shops and houses), who conducted his part of the discussion from an upstairs window.

The hotel manager maintained there was no room for the Casals party—they had left his establishment to embark for the Western Hemisphere. Furthermore, the proprietor suggested heatedly, he would put himself in jeopardy by harboring so prickly an antifascist symbol as Casals should the Germans extend the occupation. Alavedra countered that the Germans would not be there before morning. The proprietress of Le Café Grand, who had not only been awakened but had also joined the conversation, invited Casals and his companions to stay the rest of the night with her. Friends gave them shelter the next day, until they were able to find a tiny house in the Route Nationale, where they lived for about a year.

In the months that followed the German occupation of the northern three-fifths of France Casals played a series of benefit concerts for the Red Cross in the unoccupied zone—Perpignan, Beziers, Montauban, Montpellier, Toulouse, Lyon, Cannes, Bordeaux. Except for fees to the accompanist and assisting artists, income from these consistently sold-out performances went to the Red Cross for its work in aiding wounded, prisoners, and other victims of war. Early in 1941 Casals received a letter of thanks and an inscribed photograph from Marshal Henri-Philippe Pétain, head of the French government at Vichy, expressing appreciation for Casals' humanitarian work. These survived, but Casals rejected them angrily when they were brought to his attention thirty years later. (At the time, Pétain was still a hero and a hope to many, not the discredited figure he became at the end.) From Prades Casals and his friends continued to answer the requests for help that still flooded in from Spanish and other refugees. He also continued to visit some of the Spanish refugee camps, which had not yet been abolished, occasionally playing for the people there and, always, talking with them. His ability to help materially, like his freedom of movement, was becoming constricted. The packages of food and clothing and the contributions of money from Allied countries or even from Occupied France no longer reached him. No longer did he have access to large deposits in Paris; any income from stocks or bonds and record royalties there, or in England or the United States, were frozen. So, through 1941, to earn money to live as well as to make benefit appearances for the Red Cross, Casals traveled back and forth from Prades to Switzerland. In the seven weeks from July 21 to September 15, 1941, for example, he played concerts and recitals in Gstaad, Zürich, Lucerne, Basel, and Geneva, fees totaling 35,000 Swiss francs (some $8200).

Charles Kiesgen, Casals' onetime student and his Paris manager since 1920, forwarded repeated requests that Casals travel to Paris to play, either alone or with Cortot and Thibaud, hinting that Pierre Fournier was being considered to play trio engagements if Casals were unwilling to come. The tone rather than the words of Kiesgen's letters suggests an understanding of and respect for his client's stand and indicates that he told all who inquired only that he would present the invitations to Maître Casals for his consideration. Kiesgen remained in Paris; Casals' engagements were handled in Unoccupied France through 1942 by a cooperating manager in Marseilles. The trio had broken up in 1937, due to growing minor irritations and Casals' feeling that his personal reputation was sustaining the success of the ensemble to an unnecessary degree; in any circumstances he would have been unlikely to be interested in resuming the association musically. After the beginning of the war Jacques Thibaud, less political than either of his former colleagues, continued to give concerts in Vichy France, Spain, and Switzerland, but not for the Germans; one of his sons was killed in action and another taken prisoner by the Nazis. Al-

*The Villa Colette at Prades in French Catalonia,
Casals' home for nine years during and
following World War II*

fred Cortot accepted a position in the Ministry of Cultural Affairs
in the Pétain–Laval government and continued to perform frequently—his audiences in Paris and elsewhere included Germans.
Despite his admitted collaboration with the conquerors, a substantial body of testimony emerged later that he used his position and
connections to save the life or assist the escape of people who might
otherwise have perished during the war. Cortot also played in neutral Spain, at least once with an orchestra in Barcelona under the
direction of Enrique Casals, who continued his teaching and other
musical activities in the Catalan capital.

From the small house in the Route Nationale, Casals and the
Alavedra family and Señora Capdevila—who had lived elsewhere

in Prades after the return from Bordeaux—moved into a modest two-floor house called the Villa Colette, Casals' home for nearly the next nine years. Casals had two rooms that were little more than cubicles on the second level; his bedroom-studio was so small that when he was awake the only place his cello was not in danger of being tripped over was on the bed. Both comfort and privacy were minimal, but the window gave a view of the peak of the Canigou, the magic mountain in the legends of eastern Catalonia and of Roussillon, and through it in the springtime came the delicate scent of acacia in bloom and the song of nightingales.

The Allies invaded North Africa on November 8, 1942; three days later the Germans took control of Unoccupied France. Prades was controlled by the Gestapo and the Vichy-French militia. Casals, his associates, and his house were under surveillance from that point on. Casals discovered that townspeople who had at the least exchanged friendly greetings with him in the street now seemed not to see him, even those he supposed to be members of the Resistance. Before long, security agents arrived to search the house. Casals watched as they looked through every book, every piece of paper and music. They found nothing that could be termed incriminating, but one of the men told him that if anything turned up to confirm their suspicions he would be arrested. Particular attention was paid to Casals simply because he was both avowedly antifascist and internationally famous. The most serious accusation, initiated by his detractors during the Spanish Civil War and one that was pronounced as fact from time to time for the next thirty years and more, was that he was a Communist.

One day Casals looked up from the worktable at which he was writing to see the approach of a German official car that stopped at the gate to the Villa Colette. Three officers got out; Casals had a fleeting sense that the end had come. The Germans were young and impeccably groomed; they seemed gigantic to Casals when they entered the small room and gave the Nazi salute. The first words, he recalled, were to the effect that they had come not as foreign enemies but as musical admirers who had known his name from their parents and grandparents. Casals asked the real purpose of the visit. They seemed disposed to make admiring conversation; they inquired if Casals and his household had enough food and fuel. He answered stiffly that nothing was required, repelled by their courtesy.

Casals thought he saw the purpose of their visit when the ranking German asked equably why he did not return to Spain. "Because Franco and his regime are things that I cannot approve for my country," he answered, "and if I would go there I surely would be shot because I wouldn't accept things as they are; I would talk, and in Spain today no one can talk without permission or prison." To their response that Franco was an honorable man he retorted, "That is your interpretation." The full purpose of the conversation was clear when they broached the subject of his coming to play once more in Germany. Casals said no at once, "rather unamiably"; his reasons were the same as for not going to Spain. The Germans exchanged glances Casals interpreted as menacing, but after a moment the spokesman began to explain that their host was mistaken, that *Der Führer* was a man of great culture, a connoisseur especially of the music of Wagner, a patron of artists. Casals remonstrated that he was an old man; travel of any sort was almost impossible for him. The German officer said a *wagon-lit* would be sent to Prades for him and that the journey to Berlin could be made without transfer.

The visitors asked to see the cello. Casals took it from the case and placed it on the bed, watching almost nauseated as men he considered barbarians touched its wood. He declined to play anything for them—rheumatism that had attacked his shoulder during the winter made it impossible, he said. He had tried many times; he could no longer play as before, for anyone. Casals' lower jaw was thrust out farther than usual and his expression was even colder in the silence that followed; he had not invited the Germans to sit during the more than two hours they had been in his room. At last one requested a memento of their visit. Casals found photographs of himself, asked the name of each officer, and added in French on each print "in souvenir of your visit in my house in Prades." He did not show them to the outside door and stood watching through the window as they left the yard and entered their car. They did not drive away immediately, and when they got out once more Casals came downstairs and went out onto the entrance terrace to see what more they wanted. The Germans asked him to remain outdoors while they took photographs—further proof, Casals was convinced, for their superiors that they had seen him.

Casals had told his unwelcome visitors that the household had everything necessary for food and warmth, which was far from the truth. Food was hard to come by even in a region in which vegetables grew through longer seasons than in the North; coffee, which Casals liked very much, and sugar became treasures beyond luxury. Remembering the hardest days of the war and recalling the relative comfort of his former trio colleagues at the time, Casals said to a friend that Cortot or Thibaud "never once sent food or inquired about me, although they knew very well where I was. I would have refused, of course, but they should have tried." (On his side Thibaud was quoted after the war in *Time* and *Newsweek* magazines as having been unlucky with his friends' politics: "Cortot very bad, Casals a little *dérangé*.") A few years later Alfred Cortot came to play in Casals' Prades Festival; with tears he admitted his wartime collaboration, asking and receiving Casals' forgiveness. Thibaud never sought pardon, and Casals ordered him out of his sight the last time they met.

Casals' friends in other parts of the world, cut off from news of him, did not forget. Representations were made through neutral channels in the names of a group of prominent musicians in America to arrange safe conduct for Casals to Portuguese territory; the request was refused. In January 1943 Casals received a confidential letter from the Argentine ambassador in Vichy indicating that his name was among those of eminent Spaniards the Minister of Foreign Affairs in Buenos Aires had directed him to offer help in leaving France "in a practicable and discreet manner."

His name was on other lists as well. A young Vichy militiaman, engaged to the daughter of a family Casals knew in Perpignan, reported that both Casals and Alavedra were among those to be arrested in Prades. Casals was deeply touched to have been warned by this boy, and was convinced that the youth had saved his life when he discovered that the soldier had also gone to his superiors to say that he knew Pablo Casals to be a good man, greatly loved, and in no way a politician. Soon after, German troops were pulled back for defense of the Fatherland. Following the Nazi withdrawal French and Allied tribunals began to try accused collaborators. When Casals learned that the young soldier who had befriended him had been arrested, he wrote the president of the Perpignan court asking to testify for the defense. The boy was on trial with four other French militiamen. Four were shot; Casals' friend was sentenced to thirty years' imprisonment, but his life was saved.

Casals threw himself back into efforts for needy Spanish refugees, whose cause was further submerged in the tidal wave of suffering and want among all the victims of war. In December 1944 he gave concerts in Perpignan and Montauban for the benefit of prisoners and the homeless, and in Montpellier, where profits went to the University. Each was given to packed, near-hysterical houses where the Catalan flag was displayed, and Casals played consummately well. He now ended each program with his arrangement of *El Cant dels Ocells* ("The Song of the Birds"), an exquisitely simple old Catalan folk melody that tells how the birds came with their song to salute the Child in the manger at the Nativity.

During the war Juan Alavedra had asked Casals why he practiced so faithfully every morning. Among other reasons Casals had replied, "to be ready to go to give concerts when the fighting is over." Now, where to agree to play next became a problem. The requests had begun again from America and England as well as from Paris. The Paris deluge, in fact, amounted to a diplomatic challenge better ignored for the moment: a tally showed invitations from fifty-six separate organizations to sponsor Casals' first postwar appearance in the French capital.

For nearly four years Casals had listened hungrily to the BBC Foreign Service broadcasts, during half that time with a blanket over his head and the receiver to muffle the sound against discovery by informers. They had been his only real source of news from outside—it had been Britain alone, Casals told his English friend Milly Stanfield, that gave him hope when all the other European nations had fallen. He decided on England for his first tour after peace had come to Europe. And so in July 1945 Pablo Casals at sixty-eight set out to perform in London again, forty-six years after he had first done so.

1945–1973

21

WHEN CASALS WROTE reassuringly to Eugène Ysaÿe, "Age is the glory of the great, don't you think?" Ysaÿe was nearly seventy, long after the finish of his great career and near the end of his life. In June 1945, Casals was almost the same age, but still possessed mastery of his instrument. He set out to play the June and July dates in England with a sense of freedom and great hope after nearly four years of forced inactivity. The British and the Americans competed to fly him from Paris to London. The English won: "To England one should fly in an English plane," Casals had said. British European Airways refused payment for the passage, and Casals was escorted through Customs with deferential smiles and no inspection. Seeing the London bomb damage for the first time, Casals was appalled and reminded of the destruction in Barcelona in 1939.

On June 27, 1945, he played with an orchestra for the first time in nearly three years, the BBC orchestra under Sir Adrian Boult, in the Albert Hall in London. He performed the Schumann and Elgar concertos, with the Sarabande from the unaccompanied Bach cello suite in C minor as an encore. The crowd in and around the hall was estimated at between ten and twelve thousand. Each seat was occupied, and standees filled every possible location. Augustín Rubio, wrapped in his usual flowing cape, his enormous eyes characteristically opened very wide, was waiting at the stage door. "Remember, Pablísimo," he said, "I told you when I first heard you that you would make good someday." One of the first backstage visitors was violist Lionel Tertis; Casals' instant question: "Have you played for the soldiers?"

The crush outside was so great that police had to clear a path to the car for Casals and his cello. While a passage was being cleared for the car, Casals rolled down the window and gestured to the crowd, murmuring "God bless you!" The German writer Emil Ludwig described the reception given Casals in London as matching those for Churchill. Of the ovations in the Albert Hall and the salutations of the crowd around his automobile, Casals said he "could sense very distinctly . . . an admiration for the artist, affection for me as a person, and support of my attitude."

Casals and his companions drove to Broadcasting House, where they heard portions of the tapes of the concert (broadcast throughout the British Isles four nights later) and where Casals spoke in Catalan over the still-operative network that had beamed messages to resistance forces on the Continent during the German occupation.

One of Casals' first acts on reaching England had been to address a tribute to British musicians and the English people through the medium of the *London Philharmonic Post* in which he wrote of his happiness to be able to tell them "of the solicitude with which I have followed all that had befallen them during these six terrible years," preoccupied in his little Pyrenean refuge "from hour to hour [by] all the experiences through which your great country has passed." He attached as much importance to the travels of the Philharmonic and its soloists through air-raid danger from town to town in England "to keep alive the cause of great music" and create "millions of new listeners to the works of the great masters" as to "the many inspiring calls to action of your political and military leaders."

> I am sure that history will always preserve the memory of how the British people kept alive the flame of civilisation in wartime, and I am glad that I have lived to see that such things are possible. I was old enough when this war started and I am older still today, but let me say that I have lived

fully during these years: I have survived all these great changes throughout the world.

I have seen the collapse of the two most hateful forms of dictatorship, and having lived through them has given me renewed strength.

Casals had reached an age at which it is phenomenal for a string player to be able to play with untarnished control. "When Casals played . . . after six years' absence from London few could have gone with any doubts, though many may have brought questions. In string playing above all things finesse of style depends on fine control of mind over muscle; and Casals will be 70 next year. Soon after Schumann's concerto began the answer came clearly: technique can be superb at 70 and the rest follows . . . ," *The Musical Times'* critic reported, although he considered the Schumann an uninspired work. Another London journal set the general tone of the British press during Casals' first postwar tour:

> In his seventieth year the great artist is ready to embark again on a virtuoso career with the energy and idealism of youth. As the familiar figure, unassuming, completely bald, not much taller it seemed than the cello he was carrying, picked his way through the violin desks of the B.B.C. Symphony, the vast audience . . . rose to its feet to proclaim a tumultuous welcome for the artist whose name will live not only as an artist but as a great humanist, and as a foe of tyranny. Again there was that noble simplicity which marks the perfection of his art and which has given him a place apart among the world's virtuosi. From the first notes it was clear that none of the magic of his playing had been lost. . . . He has come to symbolize the spirit of resistance among musicians. The greatness of the artist is indeed matched only by the humanity of the man.

The reception of his performance of the Elgar concerto righted a balance for Casals. He had given two performances of the work in London in the late 1930s, one at the benefit concert for Spanish refugee children a few hours after the fall of Madrid. The critics across the board had lambasted the Spaniard's interpretation of what they termed a quintessentially English work. Now, although *The Musical Times* disagreed with the Casals–Boult tempos, other professional observers were full of praise. *The Times* considered that Casals played "rhapsodically, extracting the last drop of autumn sweetness from it, and with the way that Elgar's melodic line demands. The mastery and maturity of the playing reached the ripeness and the fullness of Elgar's last great work." Elgar would gladly have entrusted the work, for all its "Englishness," to Pablo Casals, speculated a writer for another paper, "knowing that even its most subtle native qualities would be fully comprehended and conveyed. . . . Casals brought to strenuous passages full eloquence and a golden tone, yet it was in the deeply meditative sections where his playing was most touching, for it reached to an Elgarian mood of wistfulness that few artists now understand."

The recording of the Elgar concerto made at this performance became one of the most successful of Casals' phonograph discs. Sir Adrian Boult was asked what the differences had been between Casals' 1945 reading and the earlier one the critics had damned. "None," said Boult.

Gerald Moore was the Canadian-born pianist who had earned respect as one of the finest accompanists of the time, a witty and urbane gentleman who had performed with a wide range of important artists in the 1920s and 1930s (including a number of recitals with Suggia after World War I and a 1936 song recital with Susan Metcalfe at Wigmore Hall in London). In the spring of 1945 he received word that Casals wanted him as partner for the English tours: "After six years of existing in a blackout came this blinding light; I was to play for the world's greatest living musician . . . the biggest assignment I had ever had." Moore and Casals met for the first time on an afternoon at the beginning of July 1945. Casals greeted the Englishman warmly, lighted his pipe, and they began to play—Beethoven's sonata in D major (opus 102, No. 2), "third-period Beethoven . . . a hard nut to crack in that it demands perfect accord and sensitive reaction between the players."

The sonata contains a fiery first movement, a deceptively simple slow movement, and a hair-raising fugue. Casals indicated the second movement for a start; this *Adagio con molto sentimento d'affetto* has "a slow noble theme with the most delicate dynamic inflections rising and falling within the phrase which each player observes in like degree. If one player augments or decreases more than the other, the music is thrown out of proportion and becomes meaningless." Casals "sang on his 'cello, and I crouched over my

keyboard with every nerve alert and my very soul in my fingertips." They played away together without exchanging a word for
about two dozen measures. Then Casals stopped abruptly, placed
the cello gently on its side, looked very straight at Gerald Moore,
and said, "I am very happy."

Moore was enchanted by Casals—his simplicity, his warm-
heartedness, his quality of intense attention to other people. He
also never forgot that Casals chose the slow, apparently simple
chorale tune of the Beethoven sonata, "whose notes, at least for
the first twenty bars, could have been read at sight by the veriest
amateur," instead of the dramatic movements, to see whether their
musical chemistry blended.

Speaking directly of the experience of listening to Casals in
the autobiography he called *Am I Too Loud?*, Moore confessed
the same problem that has faced both musicians and others who
have tried to communicate the aural and emotional experience of
the actual musical performance of a supreme virtuoso. "Of the
man's music," wrote the articulate Moore, "it is fairly obvious that
words fail me." He did nevertheless try to explain, more than
twenty-five years after he first accompanied Casals, something of
Casals' unique qualities. "Many a good musician of modesty uncon-
sciously thrusts himself between the composer and the listener
through his concern over his fourth finger, through technical inse-
curity, or through fright. . . . Casals has no such problems."
Moore knew that Casals was nervous before playing—never after
he began—and he recognized in the Catalan artist a true humility
in relation to music, speculating that possibly Casals' concept of
the performer as the servant of his art furnishes a key to the man
himself. Casals "began where lesser mortals left off: supremely sure
of himself technically. . . . He thought only of the music—of the
message of the composer and that he was the bringer of that
message. I know this sounds trite," said Moore, "but with Pablo
Casals it is literally true . . . an attitude of mind or spirit."

During the 1945 trips to England Gerald Moore observed a
large portion of Pablo Casals' postwar life—the visitors. His hotel
room became another Spanish Embassy, a Republican one; such
a constant stream of Spaniards and Catalans came to see him that
Casals remarked to Moore he had become a statesman rather than
a musician. Moore responded with Georges Clemenceau's remark
on seeing Paderewski at the Versailles Peace Conference and being

told the pianist had become prime minister of Poland: "What a comedown!"

The steady parade of exiled Spaniards that descended on Casals wherever he was had begun to appear when he came out of Spain toward the end of 1936. The Eisenbergs' spacious Paris apartment overlooking the Place de La Porte Champerret, Casals' home when he was in Paris, became a seat for councils of the Republican government during the Spanish Civil War. After former Catalan President Luis Companys was handed over to General Franco by the Vichy government in 1940 and assassinated, Casals was formally asked by the council of the government in exile to become its president. He refused; more than thirty years later exiled Spaniards still believed that Pablo Casals was the one man who could have held the dissident elements together and that, had he accepted, his authority and the stand he maintained would have had enough impact on other governments to change their pragmatic accommodation of the Falangist regime in Spain in the decades after World War II.

Casals' sense of the moral issues in the battle against political tyranny and for freedom in Spain, which was first of all an emotional rather than political response, strong from the beginning of the Civil War, had further clarified during World War II. But Casals had not traveled to perform in the Soviet Union since 1917 as a protest against a repressive government and the unwarranted injustice friends had suffered. This was clear in his own mind and known to others even if, in his refusal of Russian contracts, he did not necessarily go into detail. He had made public his reasons for not playing in Germany after 1933 and in Italy after 1935. By the time the Second World War began Casals was a symbol of moral and ethical protest. His actions between 1945 and 1947 were therefore part of a long and characteristic pattern. He was also consistent in private judgments on matters of principle concerning individuals. In early 1945 Casals saw Wilhelm Furtwängler, then a refugee in Switzerland, for the first time since 1934. The German conductor came to see Casals; he brought with him copies of letters from Jewish musicians and others he had helped in Germany and Austria, where he had become Director of Musical Life in Vienna after the *Anschluss*. Casals believed that Furtwängler had come to enlist his colleague's good word in the inquiry into his wartime activity more than to make personal amends or seek Casals' forgiveness. (Furtwängler was officially absolved of pro-Nazi activities in 1946.) Casals told Furtwängler that it was not necessary to explain, adding that in any event he was powerless to influence the outcome. When Furtwängler repeated that he was above all a musician and wanted to continue actively to make music Casals told him to be patient, adding "and consider yourself fortunate that Switzerland has given you a welcome!" Casals admitted that Wilhelm Furtwängler was one of the great musical interpreters, a man of deep insight and immense scholarship. But Casals believed that such stature as an artist only adds to a man's responsibility for all his actions, and that Furtwängler's association with Nazi party members tarnished his life and his art beyond restoration.

During the same period Casals accepted an invitation to a dinner given in his honor at the French Ministry of Education in Paris. As soon as he arrived he wished he had not come; in the reception salon he saw "certain musicians who . . . had not behaved with any dignity or patriotism during the German occupation." At dessert Casals, seeing a lectern being moved into place, asked the government minister seated next to him if he intended to make a speech. "Naturally." Casals asked him not to, explaining levelly but emphatically that if he did speak Casals would have to respond and would be bound by conscience to say "certain things which would be very disagreeable."

War continued meanwhile in the Pacific, but it would only be a matter of time before the victorious forces that had destroyed the totalitarianism of Hitler and Mussolini won. When they had defeated Japan, Casals maintained, they would take up the remaining logical and moral duty—the removal of Francisco Franco and his clique from control in Spain. Then he would be able to direct the Orquestra Pau Casals and a great chorus performing Beethoven's ninth symphony in celebration. Following a large reception at the Spanish Institute arranged by the Spanish-exile community in London on the eleventh of July 1945—very emotional, very Latin, characteristic of Casals' public appearances for another twenty-five years, with speeches, music, reporters and photographers—Casals went to Broadcasting House, where before an invited studio audience he played and broadcast a message carried by the BBC International Service "with some words of salutation to my faraway friends." It was the first broadcast since 1938 that large numbers of Catalans could have been expected to hear. As he began, at first in an indistinct voice, his eyes brimming with tears (he had tried on several pairs of glasses before he found the reading set), he choked with emotion. Picking up his pipe, he pulled furiously on it a few seconds while he regained control.

> I have come to England from my retirement in the shadow of Canigou, the other side of the Pyrenees [he commenced], and first want to convey my gratitude to the English people for the cordial and enthusiastic way in which I have been received, these British people who have shown such civic conscience and heroism in meeting the sufferings of the war, even during those difficult hours when they were alone in the fight. They merit the admiration and love of all men who care for liberty and justice, and we continue to expect from them the consolidation of the peace and the moral reconstruction of Europe.
>
> In addressing to you these words from the heart of London my thoughts go to all those Catalans who have heard us here, and to those in our own good land of Catalonia. I would like to think that when, by the miracle of the waves, our ancient melody—*Cant dels Ocells*—reaches you these sounds may be like a gentle echo of the nostalgia we all feel for Catalonia. The sentiment which holds us together, and makes us proud of being native sons, must make us work together—even those who in a moment of uncertainty and vacillation perhaps have had doubts—like brothers united in the same faith, and with the same hope for a tomorrow of peace, when Catalonia will again be Catalonia.

Pablo Casals was convinced that he was approaching the end of his own exile from Spain; Churchill had promised that Fascism would be uprooted, wherever it existed, and to Casals that meant the end of the Franco regime. Since he was in England, he addressed himself directly to Great Britain, to reporters, intellectual leaders, and politicians from both parties. His arguments were directed to France and the United States as well, but his plea was that the country which had struggled so valiantly alone in the past now accomplish its moral duty to free Spain, alone if necessary. Implicit was Casals' feeling that Britain bore the greatest ethical responsibility to do what had to be done about Spain; the nonintervention policy of the British government during the

Civil War had caused France to cut off aid to the legal Spanish government at the beginning of the fighting and had heavily influenced the American government's policy of neutrality.

Before Casals' return to the British Isles for five orchestral appearances and six recitals between October 17 and November 8 Japan had capitulated after the atom-bombing of Hiroshima and Nagasaki, attacks that horrified Casals. His first engagements were in London and Edinburgh; disillusion set in within a few days. From the reports of Spanish friends, the tone of the press, and conversations both with English members of government and with musicians Casals began to realize that neither Britain alone nor the Allies together were going to remove General Franco. Before a week of the tour had been completed Casals had reached a decision. He dropped the bombshell among his companions in the car traveling down for a recital with Gerald Moore in the Reading Town Hall on the twenty-fourth of October: "I am not going to play after this." He became preoccupied with the form of his protest. He canceled all discussions of a proposed tour for the spring of 1946 and rejected elaborate plans for recording the Brandenburg concertos and other works for His Master's Voice. He debated breaking off the tour at once and publishing his reasons, but decided to fulfill the contracts for the remaining two weeks.

The first public indication of his decision was the message that Casals would not attend the luncheon scheduled in his honor on October 30 at the Apothecaries Hall in Blackfriars Lane by the Worshipful Company of Musicians, which had made him an honorary member and given him its gold medal in 1937. Oxford University had been about to award Casals an honorary doctorate of music when World War II began; now Casals' distinguished scholar friend José Trueta (a Republican refugee teaching at Oxford whose 1947 book *The Spirit of Catalonia* was dedicated to Pablo Casals as the embodiment of that spirit) came to ascertain an open date for the ceremony. Casals asked Trueta to "tell the directors of the university that in the present circumstances I find it, to my profound regret, an impossibility to accept the honor." When composer Roberto Gerhard, another Catalan, came to offer an equivalent doctorate from Cambridge University, Casals' reply was "that I will have to defer this intention until the position of England in respect to Spain be changed." Neither institution ever again proposed an honor to Casals.

The scheduled tour continued—recitals with Gerald Moore in Brighton, with Kathleen Long in Nottingham and at Guildhall in Cambridge. Dame Myra Hess and Casals gave a memorable recital together at the Cambridge Theatre in London on Sunday afternoon, November 4, 1945. There had been a contretemps when Dame Myra telephoned Casals' London agent, Ibbs and Tillett, announcing she would like to play with Casals; by this time there were very few recitals left, and all arrangements had been made. But it was difficult to say no to one of the most respected pianists in the world. She was a national heroine as a result of nearly seventeen hundred wartime concerts she had arranged at the National Gallery, featuring more than a thousand artists. Her own series of noontime recitals there through the period of severest daytime bombing had been a great factor in maintaining civilian morale. An adjustment was made, and Dame Myra was at the piano for Pablo Casals' last sonata recital in England.

Myra Hess was also instrumental in arranging introductions to members of Parliament; Casals went to the House of Commons for private conferences in which he tried to convince influential politicians of the injustice of British policy toward Spain. (He dismissed an invitation to talk with Sir Stafford Cripps at home, however: "We would not understand one another. He would be speaking about politics and I about morality.") Shortly before Casals left England, Dame Myra arranged an appointment for him with Sir Alan Lascelles, private secretary to King George VI, at Buckingham Palace. Casals set out his view of the Spanish case as clearly as he knew how and stressed that he considered it the moral duty of England and the United Nations "to reestablish a regime of freedom and tolerance in Spain." The democratic nations had to bear responsibility for the "fatal policy" of so-called non-intervention, which had crippled only the Loyalist side in the Spanish Civil War. The Spanish people would not understand why, since other dictatorships had been vanquished, they were not once more to be given the chance to be masters of their own destiny. The next day, after Lascelles had reported the conversation, a palace car was sent to the Piccadilly Hotel to bring Casals back to talk with the King and Queen Elizabeth, but Casals had already left for Prades. Six weeks later, still trying to explain the position Casals could not accept, Myra Hess wrote him: "You spoke so much of our democratic ideals . . . in helping to reconstruct this bewildered world on democratic lines, this country is pledged as a matter of honor not to act independently of its Allies, and again not independently of the United Nations Organization which we are working so hard to set up. Although this may appear on the surface to be a slow process, please believe me when I tell you that a great deal is happening. Here you are looked upon as the most important Ambassador of your beloved country."

Casals had not talked with Winston Churchill; his second 1945 tour coincided with the first postwar election period, in which Churchill's government fell. Churchill was scheduled to pass the Royal Academy of Music while a reception was being given in Casals' honor and it was thought that arrangements had been made for the two famous men to shake hands. At the appointed time Casals and Academy dignitaries went outside to wait at the street entrance. Churchill lifted his arm, gave the victory sign, and waved, but his motorcade did not stop.

Once he had made up his mind on the action he would take, Casals drafted a long letter to the London *News Chronicle*. He protested the damage done by Britain to the victorious cause of democracy by refusing to deal straightforwardly with the Spanish problem. Spanish democrats were disillusioned, he said, and Britain's "incomprehensible" attitude held the danger of driving them to "extremist solutions," including formation of guerrilla units. Britain was allowing "the continued existence of a system which preserves intact beneath temporary disguises not only the germ but all of the aggressive and intolerant mentality of fascism against which we Spaniards, and millions of young people of all lands, have fought to the death." The free world was ignoring the sufferings of the Spanish people, who felt "cruelly let down— we who believed implicitly in Britain's historic and moral mission in the world."

After his last concert in England (playing the Elgar and Dvořák concertos with the Liverpool Philharmonic under Sir Malcolm Sargent), Casals played in Paris for the first time since World War II on November 13, 1945. The concert was a benefit for the Lamoureux Orchestra Pension Fund and the Spanish orphanage in Neuilly, and marked the forty-sixth anniversary of Casals' Paris début. The Grande Salle Pleyel was completely filled; the house manager, escorting Casals to the waiting car after the concert, said that never in his memory had there been such a demonstration in response to a musical event as he had seen that night. Casals slept in a simple room in the Spanish orphanage in the Avenue Bineau. It was here that young French cellist Paul Tortelier came to play for and be encouraged by him, finding Casals surrounded by orphan children who addressed him as *Papá*. In Paris Casals sensed as little concern about the Spanish question as he had found in England, perhaps less. He still had some hope that the situation would change, and that his cancellation of his next year's activities in England as protest would have some effect in shifting the British position, but he nevertheless returned to Prades dispirited.

In 1946 he played only a few previously scheduled charity concerts for Spanish refugee relief, the Red Cross, and similar causes. He continued his own work with cello every morning but for a time refused to take any students. He had also returned to composing—songs, work on a violin sonata, the transcription into sardana form of an old folk song honoring St. Martin of Canigou, daily work toward completion of an oratorio he called *El Pessebre* (*The Manger*), which he had begun in 1943. Most of his other time was devoted to the work of Spanish refugee aid. Packages and contributions were once more arriving in Prades from many parts of the world. The French refugee camps were disbanded in 1946, but the lot of thousands of orphans and adults was little improved. Casals could not forget the plight of non-Communist Spanish refugees, whom he knew to be the least remembered of all the victims of nearly ten years of war (the Communist refugees who got out of Spain received some aid from the party organizations in other countries). And he was haunted by the thought of the tens of thousands of men and women who were political prisoners in Spain, perhaps the most forgotten victims of all.

Many tokens of honor came to Casals following the end of fighting in France. A list Casals set down in minute handwriting in 1949 includes more than fifty awards in the five years following his being named honorary member of the *Casal Català* (Catalan Center) of Montauban on December 11, 1944. The list includes honorary presidency of or membership in a number of such organizations and in associations of artists and intellectuals in France and England—ranging from honorary vice-presidency of The International Arts Guild to vice-presidency of the Workers' Music

Association, Ltd., of London. In the years immediately following the war Casals was declared an honorary citizen of Montauban, Perpignan, Béziers, Prades, Foix, Narbonne, and Castres and given the medal of the city of Toulouse. In 1946 he received word that he had been elected an honorary member of the Spanish Bullfighting Club of Béziers, and on April 6 of the same year was awarded an honorary doctorate of music by the University of Montpellier (he already held degrees from the universities of Edinburgh, Prague, and Barcelona, received before the war).

On November 7, 1946, Pablo Casals was named a Grand Officer of the French Legion of Honor. Two weeks later the president of the provisional government, Georges Bidault, wrote former premier Albert Sarraut that he had gladly signed the decree of promotion. "This artist, I know," wrote Bidault, "joins to his musical genius generosity of heart and force of character. He is a conscience of our time. . . ."

Casals had been in correspondence from 1938 with Alfonso XIII, in exile at the Grand Hotel in Rome, asking help in the relief efforts for the child victims of the conflict and, in later letters, for all the refugees. The deposed King of Spain replied in affectionate terms but could do little—he was ill with the angina pectoris that had killed his mother. He died at the end of February 1941, having renounced his rights in favor of his twenty-eight-year-old son Juan. Don Juan and Casals had a long talk in Gstaad, Switzerland, not long after the end of the war. Casals thought Alfonso's son very sincere and full of goodwill; he had greeted with tempered enthusiasm Don Juan's call in March 1945 for the resignation of Franco and restoration of the monarchy. Now Casals gained the impression that Don Juan agreed there should be a plebiscite in which the people of Spain would choose the form of government they wished. He said he did not intend to accommodate himself to any direct offer from General Franco. (The Pretender changed his stand in several respects afterward, losing Casals' respect completely.) They spoke of Catalonia, of course; Don Juan said that he was specially happy to include among his hereditary titles that of Count of Barcelona and that his ideal would be to settle Catalan affairs as the excellent people of that region wished. Casals spoke most frankly when Don Juan asked what he thought about the situation in Spain, saying that he would not personally be a party to either a republic or a restored monarchy but would accept any regime freely chosen by his country's people, remaining loyal to it on the basis of performance rather than label. The Pretender said that the only other person who had spoken to him with equal sincerity recently had been another Catalan, a refugee priest in Switzerland, and that he liked such people. Casals then proceeded on a tack that was less well-received: Don Juan would have to justify himself to the people of Spain, Casals warned, for having offered in his early twenties to support the military insurrection that began the Civil War. Alfonso's son answered that it had seemed to him the only thing he could do at the time.

A long letter from Casals was published in London's *News Chronicle* on July 18, 1946, on the tenth anniversary of the beginning of the Spanish Civil War under the headline WHY FRANCO MUST GO. It concluded:

> I say again to the British people, whom I respect and admire so much, that we feel cruelly let down . . . by this policy of turning a deaf ear to our just protests, by this method of ignoring our sufferings, of damping down any magnanimous impulse to help us, and of systematically postponing the solution of a problem which troubles the conscience of millions of democrats.
>
> As you are aware, the exiles hounded out of Spain by Franco's rebellion and nazi and fascist forces represent the best elements in our country. Do not forget that it was these men who peacefully introduced the democratic republic in Spain. And it is more than likely that, in spite of the adverse circumstances of today, there will be found among them the men of Spain's tomorrow, for there are not only politicians, but artists, university teachers, writers, poets, journalists, lawyers and magistrates among them. It is bitter for us all to think that one of the chief obstacles to our return is Britain's present policy of reticence and procrastination.

It was only natural, Casals thought, that Spain under Franco should be excluded by the San Francisco Conference from membership in the United Nations Organization. On March 4, 1946, the United States, Britain, and France addressed an appeal to the Spanish people to oust the Franco regime and prepare the way for democratic elections. Every Spanish refugee leader had been trying to make the politicians of those same countries realize that those who opposed Franco within Spain could not accomplish this themselves or with merely clandestine help, but that only a little pressure from them would force Franco and his chief officers to step down, with free elections to follow. There was momentarily renewed hope when the United Nations General Assembly voted in December 1946 to bar Spain from all UN activities and urged its members to break diplomatic relations with the Falangist government, but nothing really had changed.

Casals made a trip of homage to the tomb of Frédéric Mistral in Millane, not far from Montpellier. Mistral, the Provençal poet who had celebrated "the wonderful race of peasant princes" and was a Nobel laureate in 1904, had been friendly to Casals early in the century. Casals and his group were greeted at the entrance to the ancient village by children in local costume, the girls carrying flowering branches, the boys sounding flutes and tambourines. The townspeople watched the procession with curiosity, joining it as it moved toward the magnificently kept garden of a cemetery bounded by four walls of cypress trees. Mistral's tomb within a larger| pantheon is a small colonnaded temple, a replica of the pavilion of a medieval queen that the poet had much admired. |Casals| went close to Mistral's burial place and loudly spoke the poet's name. Cello in hand, he leaned down and called again "Mistral!" in a voice that resounded through the pantheon. "We Catalans have come to pay you homage!" Then he played a Bach suite and "The Song of the Birds" while the people stood silent in the solemn twilight. He rose and left, followed by the still-silent crowd. Later, in the car, Casals said to Juan Alavedra "Someone must show the way."

Eleven months later Casals set up another guidepost: he said that hereafter he would not perform publicly in any country that recognized the government of Francisco Franco. He had expected that his cancellation of British and then French appearances would have had enough general impact to produce the result he desired. When nothing had changed after more than a year he took the final step of protest in the renunciation (his own word) of further formal cello concerts.

He had begun to speak of the cello as his only weapon and the silencing of it as his strongest protest against the compromise, expediency, and moral insensitivity of the world's governments.

He thought of himself as "the militant of music," and having become once again a sought-after and powerful musician, his withdrawal into silence was the strongest action he felt he could make. "Everybody had already forgotten what happened," he would say. "But someone has to remember, and my attitude will be a reminder."

Pablo Casals knew better than anyone else that he was at full power mentally and physically so far as music was concerned. He had had no thought of retirement. Yet in the spring of 1947 Casals cut off his chief means of communication to the widest possible public. "My build is more that of Sancho Panza," he said to a French friend, pointing to a sketch of Cervantes' characters hanging on a wall of his little workroom in Prades, "but my outlook is Quixote's." Asked if it were not a terrible sacrifice to renounce his career, Casals answered that it was the greatest sacrifice any artist could make voluntarily, and the greatest of his life. But it was one he had to make, whatever others did. Casals did not judge the actions of others who did what they must; his brothers, for example, who had families to support, had remained in Spain after the Civil War. When Alavedra and his family went back after ten years of exile Casals explained that it had been because Alavedra had to make a living. Casals had no children himself; he did what he had to and could do.

In other parts of the world, those who were concerned about such things reacted quickly. By letter, cable, and visits to Prades, friends and strangers urged Casals to change his mind. Entrepreneurs kept up the barrage of contract offers, directly and through acquaintances. They offered him excellent, sometimes astounding, fees, places to live, personal benefits, contributions to refugee enterprises, everything very much on his own terms. At the time Casals would consider no offer. Those propositions Casals considered essentially commercial were dismissed briefly, politely, and with an expression of regret. To the arguments of friends and admirers that Casals was depriving the world of sublime music, which it much needed, he would say "I cannot do it." He was invariably fond of the country in question and of its people, but said "I cannot go back to the countries where I should have to reproach their governments for injustice." He could not entertain the argument that his protest should take a different form and could in fact be stronger if he continued to appear throughout the world.

He was certain that Doña Pilar would have approved of his decision; "At least now I can sleep with a clear conscience since I know I have done my duty," he said. A message from Spanish Refugee Aid urging him to come to the United States to further the cause of Spain and of music, signed by Albert Einstein and others of accomplishment and fame, saddened Casals by its lack of understanding. Of the intimate group in Prades, Juan Alavedra particularly appears to have reinforced Casals' thought that nobody in the outside world understood him or the extent of his sacrifice. Casals' feeling of responsibility to the people of Spain had become overwhelming. In rejecting the degrees from Oxford and Cambridge in the autumn of 1945, he had said that "if in these moments I should accept honors in England it would appear to my compatriots that I was indifferent to their unhappiness." A year and a half later he felt even more strongly that if he were to play again the public would believe only that he had succumbed to the lure of fame and wealth. So he withdrew to the mountains and to silence. The world would have to come to him.

As soon as the war was over, inquiries began to come to Casals about teaching. There was no question of anything of the sort during 1945; Casals was fully involved with refugee work and with concerts. He continued to rebuff such overtures into 1946, pleading that too much of his time and energy was going into the refugee efforts to take on anything else. At last, late in 1946, a talented American cellist named Bernard Greenhouse, armed with persistence and impressive recommendations from Diran Alexanian and Maurice Eisenberg, persuaded Casals to hear him. Greenhouse could play for him, Casals told the younger man on a postcard, if he would come down to Prades from Fontainebleau (where Greenhouse had enrolled in music classes) and would donate a hundred dollars to Spanish refugee assistance. Greenhouse left immediately for southern France. After some negotiation he was able to get a room in the Grand Hotel in Prades at double the normal rate because a cello was prominent among his luggage, and settled in to practice and await the audition.

Casals greeted Bernard Greenhouse on his arrival at the little Villa Colette at ten o'clock on the appointed morning. He had not yet shaved and was wearing what appeared to be a pajama top. Asking to be excused while he finished his toilette, Casals told

Greenhouse to warm up and practice until he returned. Half an hour passed, and Greenhouse played on but became puzzled. Finally his eye caught a slight movement reflected in a mirror and he saw Casals' bald head through a crack in the doorway. Casals reentered the room, still unshaved and still wearing his pajama top. He had of course been listening all the time, but said "I did not want to hear you first when you were nervous." Greenhouse continued to play, and then the two men talked for a long time. The result was Casals' agreement to give Greenhouse lessons if the younger man would undertake to stay and work in Prades. Lessons would be twice a week, the charge twenty dollars a session.

Greenhouse went to the Villa Colette for the lessons promptly at four in the afternoon. He and Casals would work at the cello for two hours, then talk for two more. The student would leave in time to get back to the Grand Hotel by eight—the latest he could get dinner from a menu that still depended heavily on turnips and potatoes. Greenhouse found his teacher a man of great warmth and strong decision concerning both music and other matters. They worked through a great deal of the cello solo repertoire, much of which Greenhouse already had well in hand and memory from his own exploration and a period of study with Diran Alexanian, who had left the École Normale de Musique in Paris late in the 1920s to teach in the United States. Alexanian as a teacher was directive and frequently less than gentle. Casals' technique was quite opposite, Greenhouse found. Maurice Eisenberg, Alexanian's successor at the École Normale, had told him of one of his own early student experiences. Casals had heard Eisenberg play the Schumann concerto; the next time they were together Eisenberg picked up his bow to go through the same composition. Casals told him to put it down. "Sing for me that opening A." Eisenberg sang a *la*. "Now direct it. . . . Now pantomime the bowing." Eisenberg did as he was told, in some bewilderment. "You do it very well so; why is it you then do *this* when you play?" Casals drew his bow across the strings of his cello, producing a good tone but waggling his elbow exaggeratedly. Eisenberg did not fully understand until, practicing in front of a mirror, he suddenly realized he had been producing the note with an unnatural and unnecessary arm movement. Casals never mentioned the subject again. Greenhouse similarly found in his own work with Casals that the Catalan's purpose was to make his student's mind and musical instinct do their own work, without goading and most of the time without an explicit demonstration from the teacher.

There was, however, a period of a few weeks during which Greenhouse began to think Casals had turned into another Alexanian. They started work exclusively on the most demanding of the Bach suites. At lesson after lesson Casals insisted on an exact copy of his own playing from Greenhouse in interpretation and technique—every bowing and fingering, each shading of nuance and every subtle variation of emphasis. Greenhouse followed instructions, although with growing rebelliousness, and in due time was able to reproduce a close facsimile of Casals' performance—but no valid artist wishes simply to offer a mirror image of another's interpretation of a great work. The day Greenhouse had almost made up his mind to protest he played through the suite in quite acceptable and faithful Casals style. "Very well," said the teacher. "Now listen." He began to play the suite, only this time everything was different. Greenhouse watched and listened, fascinated and close to awe. Casals, playing beautifully, had changed the bowings and fingerings he had made Greenhouse learn; there was changed light and contrast. The same work had been given a subtly but absolutely different re-creation. Bernard Greenhouse understood what Casals had been doing and knew at the same moment that the older artist had freed him. Casals had forced Greenhouse to assimilate the structure and style of the suite until they were second nature. Then he demonstrated that there is no one absolute or inflexible approach to the music, that within the order of the polyphonic framework almost limitless variety is possible and interpretation can be both intensely personal and different with each new playing.

Greenhouse in time began to worry about money. He had sold his car for a thousand dollars, which had enabled him to come to Prades to study. The double rate at the Grand Hotel amounted to about two dollars a day and, although what Casals asked for lessons was certainly reasonable, Greenhouse's reserve began to get smaller. He paid Casals at the end of each lesson. One day Casals refused to take the money. "You have played so well today there is no charge," he said. At the next lesson the American did not play so well, and Casals took the money. At the finish of the following session Casals once more declined payment, saying that he knew Greenhouse did not have a great deal of money at the moment; they would not talk about money again, and when his career was successful Greenhouse could send him something for the Spanish relief work, which he was able to do with a four-figure check within a few years.

Teacher and student played together during the lessons, Casals always contending that he learned a great deal each time himself. The wide-ranging discussion that followed covered the responsibilities and characteristics of the artist—what Gerald Moore called the gospel according to Casals: one must always be humble; remember that one is a servant of Music, not the other way around; and not forget that the talent was a gift from God. (The stronger the evidence of talent, the more intensely Casals seemed to stress these points. Dietrich Fischer-Dieskau, accompanied by Gerald Moore, sang at Prades and Casals was moved by a singer as he had been only once before, by Julius Messchaert. Afterward, sitting with the baritone and the pianist, Casals spoke so long about humility that Fischer-Dieskau asked Moore "Does he feel that I am conceited?") "The true respect for music is the one that makes it *live*," Casals insisted. That was why he had never had any use for what he called the purists—those who tried to ascertain and adhere to the way Bach played his own music or insisted it be played only on the instruments available in the composer's time, or who felt themselves bound absolutely by traditional editions and established fashions of playing. "An infantile game," he called it. "There is no single interpretation, there are three dozen: what a pity that the [usual] thirty-seventh should be the bad one. Listen to what the music is trying to tell you, then play it with all the power you have!"

The respect and the courage to flout tradition must be joined by persistence, Casals told his students. For years he had been saying that no one should hope to be able to find the solution to musical problems at the last moment. "I have no faith in sudden flashes of illumination and, personally, I never improvise."

In addition to the sophisticated mastery of a musical instrument, Casals' genius brought him directly to the essence and the beauty of the music, cutting through without concern or apology the superficial and the tangential. And there continued unabated the inner drive that had made Pablo Casals the greatest of cellists and among the most exceptional of musicians. It had been clear from childhood that Casals played to win, as in later years his fellow participants at tennis, chess, dominos, and music discovered.

Music was his profession and his passion. The need both to love and to be loved was unusually strong in Casals, but in the service of Music the impulse to excel was the deciding factor. "It is not so important to be considered nice," he told Bernard Greenhouse toward the end of his first period of study in Prades. "It is more important to play well."

Casals' life as the Hermit of Prades—a title European journalists liked to use as a parallel with that of the Hermit of Lambaréné, Albert Schweitzer—was the existence of an anchorite only in the sense that for a time he refused to go great distances from his home. It was retirement into a life of intensive activity in a dusty provincial French town. Still in the tiny house called the Villa Colette, living conditions for the Casals–Alavedra household were both cramped and extremely modest. Casals continued to work, to sleep and dream, in his eight-square-meter upstairs room. Relatively few people were invited into this hermit's cell, Pablo Casals' single refuge of privacy. The room had on the right against the wall a daybed with a worn gray cover, on which were some books—Emil Ludwig's *Beethoven*, *Silence de la mer* by Vercors, a volume of Baudelaire, Federico Garcia Lorca's *Blood Wedding*—and a faded garnet-red pillow at the head with the embroidered initials *PC*. Above the bed hung a small crucifix. Cello and bow were propped up against an undistinguished armchair upholstered in a frightful mauve fabric. A collection of pipes was aligned between two tobacco boxes and letters and folders were piled on the little dining table, facing the window, that served as worktable. On the back wall, dominated by a bust of Casals, were shelves of thick folders (some formed by folded newspaper sections) containing correspondence, press clippings, refugee accounts. To the left of the table, to the full height of the window, were shelves full of an assortment of books; one visitor noted particularly books about Casals in English and German (Emil Ludwig completed a profile of Casals soon after World War II and included it in his *Gallery of Portraits* alongside sketches of Leonardo and Carl Maria von Weber), Ludwig's *Stalin*, an illustrated album of the châteaus of the Loire, a biography of Churchill, a history of music, some of the works of Henri Bergson, a *Richard Wagner*, lives of Ysaÿe, Victor Hugo, Lamartine, Goethe, and Plato. (Others also noted volumes of Seneca, Maeterlinck, Dante,

Cervantes, and Montaigne.) In the corner opposite the daybed was a bulky piano with no bric-à-brac on it except a small wood carving of one of Columbus' caravels.

"The walls," Casals said; "they say walls have ears. I prefer to say that they speak, and if you listen well they will tell you better than I can what you want to know. They are neither discreet nor honest." Casals' visitor Artur Conte, a member of the Chamber of Deputies, had not dared say that the furnishings had already spoken to him in a cruelly moving way as no book could of the man who lived here and suggested "all Spain, in its apparent disorder, its contradictions, and caprices that do not hide the passions: the faith that dwells with the crucifix, the folly of the adventure with that caravel, the multiple and vagabond taste with all these books scattered about, the passion of eloquence with all those letters, the passion for music with this violoncello. . . . All that seemed to be missing was a story of Durruti the Anarchist and a portrait of Don Juan." Casals said the Ysaÿe photograph would do well enough for the Don Juan.

A sketch of Don Quixote and Sancho Panza was prominent on one wall, with an old photograph of the Joachim Quartet signed by all four members, a portrait of Brahms in profile with a grave and gentle expression. Another group included Casals' family—parents, brothers, nieces, godchildren—pictures of Vendrell and its church, the Arch of Bara at Tarragona, a photograph of the Catalan nuns who ran the Spanish orphanage in Paris, one of Casals' horse Florian (living at San Salvador), a postcard gray and dulled by time from which smiled Frédéric Mistral.

Another wall held a descent from the Cross executed in a style influenced by the German expressionists, a photo of Casals playing at Chester Cathedral, his English godson at his side, the photograph of the Count of Morphy, crayon sketches and watercolors of Catalan subjects, some quite good, others mediocre, all of them offerings of the artists—"all they can give. These pictures are perhaps not beautiful," said Casals. "But they are a love. And, so long as I live, they will not go into the cellar. They remain beside Brahms and Quixote. . . . I cherish the homage of my lost country as much as the loveliest symphony of Beethoven."

Casals paused a moment. Gesturing toward the window: "The final picture." Beyond the houses and gardens of Prades, toward Spanish Catalonia, could be seen the ridgeline of the Albères range

Casals plays in solitude at Prades

violet in the evening light. "Poor as we are, there is nothing we lack. . . ."

In the first years of his seventies Pablo Casals arrived at a mature and intimate sense of nature, its wonder, and its kinship that sustained him in the most private area of his life and thought. He had been aware of a special wonder in sea and sunlight from his first remembered consciousness and was responsive all his life to the beauty of flowers, trees, and mountains. He felt that he had come completely to the sense of his own identity by the time he was thirty—who and where he was, with the concomitant realization of the miraculous uniqueness of every other human being.

[447]

A morning salutation to the Canigou

He had not found fulfilling answers for himself in the forms of institutional religion, but acknowledged readily the existence of a power greater than men; his life, he stressed, he considered a constant dialogue of his conscience with the divine.

The ritual beginning of each day in Prades for Casals was the playing of Bach and a walk. Early in the morning, accompanied by a part-shepherd dog called Follet, Casals' short figure was a familiar sight to those who were about at that hour, striding along the route to Cerdagne, then the Codalet highway leading out of the village into the fertile fields of the plain of the river Conflent, past vineyards and laurel copses and old peasant *bastides*. Invariably he greeted the snow peak of the Canigou standing sentinel at the frontier of Spain by raising his hat. The natives of the region seemed hardly to notice the peak; anyone less notable than Pablo Casals who paid it such faithful attention would have been considered at least a little mad.

Many a morning during the warmer months Casals would stop near bushes and trees in which the nightingales nested. He would begin to whistle, softly at first—a bit of Schubert, some Bach—and the birds would start to answer, building to a cacophony that pleased him as much as the sound of any orchestra and also reminded him of the cages of canaries in his villa at San Salvador. It was among the song of the titmice and the nightingales of Provence, Casals liked to say during those days in Prades, "that I understand better than I ever have the purity of nature, all the magnificent miracle of the first moments of Creation. . . ."

After his first months of study with Casals in 1946, Bernard Greenhouse returned to the United States to continue his career. Lunching not long afterward at Dumbarton Oaks in Washington with Alexanian, Alexander Schneider, and Igor Stravinsky, he was still understandably full of the experience. For Schneider, who was still in his thirties, the conversation touched a spark. He had been second violin of the distinguished Budapest String Quartet from 1933 until 1944, following eight years with the Frankfurt Symphony, of which he had become a concertmaster at seventeen. He was on his way to Europe and as a result of the luncheon he went to Prades to visit Casals.

The two men, thirty years apart in age and dissimilar in almost everything except unwavering devotion to music and generosity of spirit, were immediately in rapport. Casals was delighted and slightly overwhelmed by Schneider's whirlwind enthusiasms and unquenchable sense of humor, which from the start was able to pull Casals out of his deep preoccupations at least momentarily. It was not long before they were making music together and Schneider was proposing projects. A friendship had begun that Casals would later call precious to him as well as a working relationship as productive as any in Pablo Casals' career.

[449]

Schneider had found the answer to what he would do next; he had wanted to take time out from trio and quartet playing to work intensively on Bach's solo violin compositions. Casals agreed to work with him for six weeks in the summer of 1947.

Sasha Schneider had brought with him a firm offer to Casals for a series of North American concerts at what Casals considered an astronomical fee. "It is not a matter of money," Casals said, "it is a question of morality." When Schneider returned to Prades to work at Bach with Casals, he continued to urge Casals not to sentence his art to silence. Most of the time Casals merely said it was out of the question, or changed the subject, or nodded gravely without saying anything, as he did when Yehudi Menuhin arrived with the exuberant proposal that they play the Brahms double concerto and make some new records together.

After Schneider returned once more to the States there arrived in Prades forty-five volumes of the photo-offset edition of the complete works of Bach, duplicating the original Bach-Gesellschaft edition, a further reminder of the approach of the two-hundredth anniversary of the composer's death. The presentation note included a breathtaking galaxy of signatures, among them those of Toscanini, Bruno Walter, Koussevitzky, Dmitri Mitropoulos, Stokowski, Paul Hindemith, Ernest Bloch, Heifetz, Arthur Rubinstein, Wanda Landowska, Artur Schnabel, Rudolf Serkin, Gregor Piatigorsky, and Schneider. Casals received a further stream of invitations to play, conduct, or both in connection with the Bach anniversary. Elizabeth Sprague Coolidge suggested a Bach Festival and an honorary doctorate at Harvard; others asked him to appear in New York, in London, in Paris, in Geneva.

Schneider wrote to Casals from New York in October 1948 that he had sent photostatic copies of the Maître's letter of thanks to those who had signed the Bach edition. He had recently had dinner with Mieczyslaw Horszowski, he added, and there had naturally been talk about Casals. In the course of the evening Horszowski had had an excellent idea: "A Bach Festival next summer, in June or July, in Prades or Perpignan, under your direction." Schneider suggested the cathedral in Prades for the concerts, since there was no other auditorium in the town, unless Casals had a better place in mind in Perpignan, the much larger city forty kilometers away. All proceeds could go to the hospital at Perpignan (which had helped Catalan refugees) or to anything Casals considered equally important. The best available players could be chosen to play the Brandenburg concertos and to record them. Casals should decide what else was to be played to complete six concerts in the course of the festival, and of course he should play the six solo cello suites. Schneider also wondered if Albert Schweitzer would consider taking part if Casals invited him personally. Thus, from Horszowski's suggestion and Schneider's readiness to see to details, once Casals agreed to the idea, began a legendary series of summer music festivals.

Casals did not agree immediately, and a festival in honor of Johann Sebastian Bach did not take place in Prades, as Sasha Schneider had proposed, in June or July 1949. Through 1949 Casals continued his work much as he had during the two preceding years. He was putting a great deal of effort and energy into new work on his oratorio *El Pessebre*, hoping that by the time it was complete he would be able to conduct the first performance in Barcelona. There were more students—among them Zara Nelsova, who came to Prades from England, and Madeline Foley from the United States. Casals was named a member of the consultative committee of the International Musical Fund of UNESCO. His correspondence continued to take hours every day, and Casals' concern for Catalan exiles, so many of whom were still living in the region, was unabated. The stream of visitors continued.

In the spring of 1949 Casals moved from the Villa Colette to another small home, the gardener's cottage on the grounds of the Château Valroc. The modest surroundings did not concern Casals; not until he was in his mid-nineties did he live in surroundings at all comparable to those at San Salvador. The childhood poverty and the tight economic conditions in which Casals lived even during the years he was a protégé of the Spanish court did not build in him any discernible urge to live ostentatiously when he became a wealthy man. The Spartan influence of Doña Pilar, continuing as it did strongly in her son's life until he was in his mid-fifties, had some effect, but more telling was the fact that Casals lived so richly within himself and his personal art that he was many times quite oblivious of his immediate environment. For Casals, as French critic Bernard Gavoty said of him, "when once a man has possessed fame and fortune he desires no more than to love what surrounds him."

The gardener's house was named *El Cant dels Ocells* with

the words in ceramic near the entrance. The Alavedra family returned to Barcelona in 1949, but Señora Capdevila stayed to supervise the household, and one or other of Casals' brothers' children was generally in Prades. People who visited in those days remember Frasquita Capdevila well, and those who came to know her developed real affection for the still-handsome, cultured woman who saw to the details of daily living and schedules with efficiency and the devotion to the Master she had shown for half a century.

The rent for the small house was reasonable, which was fortunate as Casals' funds remaining in the Bank of France were low. When he said he was now poor, Casals was simply reporting a current fact of life. Some record royalties and income from investments had gone into American and English accounts, but they were unavailable to Casals as a result of agreements among the Allied governments at the end of the war.

The Bach Festival, as Schneider projected it, was not a money-making proposition for anyone. Still Casals hesitated, although Schneider was asking Mohammed's permission for the mountain to move. If Casals would not come to the United States to play, would he agree to make music at Prades with a group of international musicians? Casals was concerned that some people would misconstrue his taking part in a festival, but at last admitted that he could participate at home—Prades—and for friends in a homage to Bach without obscuring his protest, and possibly strengthening it by the attention the event would attract. Once Casals agreed, Schneider began to arrange for soloists and orchestra, festival committees were formed in Europe and the United States, and the world was informed that Pablo Casals would play once more, in honor of Bach, in June 1950.

Casals was elated, and began preparing himself for the festival "with the fervor of a youngster about to make his professional début."

22

PABLO CASALS was seventy-three years old in the spring of 1950, and through mass communication the nineteenth-century man became a twentieth-century symbol. One of the first major stories was a feature in *Life* magazine, written by Lael Wertenbaker with photographs by Gjon Mili, published in May 1950: "Pablo Casals: At last he is preparing to play in public again." The colorful piece, with excellent photographs of Casals in Prades, reported that the announced festival would be in honor of the two-hundredth anniversary of the death of Bach, "perhaps the greatest composer of all time," but what made the Prades celebration unique was "the reappearance in public, after three years of silence, of the musical world's great voluntary exile, Pablo Casals." Casals made better copy than Bach.

Members of the thirty-piece orchestra, about half of them Americans, arrived nearly a month before the first concert to begin rehearsals. They found an "agreeable, dusty, vivacious, fly-ridden mountain village" that had one hotel (twenty-seven rooms and a bath), a few hundred more than four thousand inhabitants, and Pablo Casals. Fares to Prades were paid for most of the participants, who received a fee that barely covered living expenses for two months in Prades. All were excellent musicians, "professionals from major symphonic and movie-studio orchestras; a tougher type of musician does not exist." Most of them were quite young; for many, Casals was simply a legend, since he had actually played little in public for ten years and not in the United States for twenty-two. Part of Alexander Schneider's argument to persuade him to reenter a wider world had been a reminder that by his premature silence Casals was withholding his unique inspiration and example from young musicians who had never heard him.

Rehearsals were held in the dining hall of the local girls' school. Casals' brief greeting at the first one was emotional: They were there because of Bach, would give pleasure to those who later came to hear them, and in making music together would also please themselves. "I thank you for coming. I love you. And now, let us begin."

The musicians responded. Even those who arrived in Prades with an unconcealed air of skepticism, according to Paul Moor, who wrote about the Bach Festival for *Theatre Arts*, "were almost pathetically thankful for what they got from their daily association with Casals." These were musicians curious about and interested in working with a living legend and "the world's greatest interpreter of Bach," but most would not have made allowances for faded grandeur, no matter how great the luster once had been. But it turned out to be Casals who had to make most of the allowances. A letter the orchestra addressed to Casals at the end of the festival said,

> When we first played together people from different nations, languages, beliefs, religions, personalities and styles of playing . . . we had much spirit but little ensemble. Patiently, you explained a phrase. We listened, and played what we understood you to mean, if not what you meant. As the weeks went by, each gave up a little of his individuality, a little of his ego, listened more to his neighbor, understood your meaning a little better and blended his style to the ensemble. The results were obvious. With the common aim of trying to understand and interpret Bach under your guidance, we finally really began to play together and each had the tremendous pride of being a part of the beautiful collective work.

[454]

What a lesson this has been. . . . We are convinced, that we of all nations can live together in this world peacefully, respect each other's culture, way of life and character, and work together for the common good of humanity and the dignity of man.

An idealism and a willingness to work together suffused the 1950 festival in Prades to an extraordinary degree. Casals represented an integrity that had become rare in "the commercialized rat-race" music had become by midcentury, and the manner in which that integrity showed through his music and his everyday viewpoint made a profound and lasting impression on musicians who had been born and grown up in a world very much different from that of Casals' youth.

Patiently, carefully—singing more often than speaking his explanations—Casals molded the orchestra into a remarkable entity during the three weeks before the first concert, preparing it for the series of six "orchestral evenings" (there was an additional interspersed series of six "chamber-music evenings"). The morning rehearsals in the dining hall of the Collège Moderne des Jeunes Filles were, like Casals' orchestral rehearsals for the next twenty years, quite as rewarding as the public performances, because here it was possible to witness Casals shaping the group closer to his musical desire. As the festival approached, an ever-larger crowd gathered to listen to the rehearsals, finally so intimidating the local gendarme assigned to guard the door that he admitted everybody.

The soloists began to arrive, the first the twenty-four-year-old, round-faced pianist Eugene Istomin. Mieczyslaw Horszowski, Casals' friend and colleague of so many years, and Clara Haskil, whom Casals had also known and respected before the war, reached Prades, as did Rudolf Serkin, who had known Casals slightly since the 1920s but whose path had crossed that of the older man only infrequently in the intervening years. The violinists who came to the 1950 festival included Joseph Szigeti and Isaac Stern as well as Schneider, whom Casals asked to be concertmaster; Enrique Casals came to Prades from Barcelona in May and was installed as leader of the orchestra's second violins. Soloists who came to Casals' house for run-throughs were dismayed to find the piano out of tune and below standard pitch. Casals' venerable Goffriller cello had not been worked on for years—a folded paper beneath the bridge under the A string gave the necessary support; on top, a matchstick had been inserted in the deep groove to allow the string's free vibration. (For the festival itself one of the best European piano-tuners came down from Berne without charge to care for all the pianos, his contribution to the noble event. A Buffalo, New York, admirer had sent Casals a splendid Pleyel piano for his own daily use after he heard a description of the instrument Casals had used in Prades for so long.)

Even after the orchestra arrived and the date for the opening of the festival drew close, a good many of the citizens of Prades were not certain of what was happening, although it was clear that something considerable was afoot. The publicity was more intense farther afield, with assorted results. It was announced in Spain that the Pyrenean border into France would be closed to Spanish nationals between the second and the twentieth of June, since there were reports that Casals, with Schneider as his chief of staff, was organizing a guerrilla force in Prades as part of a grand plan to mount a Communist overthrow of the Spanish government.

By the first of June 1950, Prades was convinced it had become the musical capital of the world, and appeared generally to like the idea. Streamers of welcome stretched across the narrow streets. Every available lodging place was full. The shops displayed Catalan flags and photographs of Casals as well as an adequate supply of Casals phonograph records and such books and pamphlets as were then available about Prades' most venerated citizen: Lillian Little-hales' 1929 biography in English, updated in 1948; Arthur Conte's charming new poetic evocation called *La Légende de Pablo Casals*, published in time for the festival in various limited editions by a Perpignan firm with six photographs by Gjon Mili; Rudolf von Tobel's slight but scholarly 1945 study in German; a 1947 Spanish reissue of a 1929 interview with Casals, available both in paper and leather binding and called *Pablo Casals: La Vida del Gran Musico*. In the days just before the concerts began the Pradeans gathered dazed and incredulous to observe the outlandish travelers arriving on the morning train from Perpignan and to examine and discuss the big automobiles in which others had come.

Few of the visitors would have chosen Prades for a summer holiday; it is situated too far inland to offer any of the attractions of the shore but is too low for the good climbing and skiing of the High Pyrenees. It does not even possess any of the thermal springs that made nearby Vernet-les-Bains and Molitg-les-Bains popular prewar watering resorts, places for which many who came to the festival were grateful even if the hotels were "all ivy and colonels and melancholy angloid cooking." Many of the visitors found the people of Prades sweet-tempered and hospitable; one visitor explained it as a general feeling that anyone who voluntarily underwent the ordeal of a trip to Prades out of love for *le Maître* was automatically a member of the family. The experienced traveler was also astonished and delighted to find, that first year, prices for everything had not trebled for the period of the festival.

Like all twelve of the 1950 Bach Festival programs in Prades, the opening concert was given in the Church of St. Peter in the center of the town. By eight-thirty in the evening of Friday, June 2, 1950, the audience had moved through the Catalan-flag-hung floodlit plaza and packed the nave of the church—including the local schoolchildren Casals had invited personally who were allowed to sit on the floor to the left of the small platform that had been installed before the altar. Also present were such American patronesses of music as Mrs. Elizabeth Sprague Coolidge and Mrs. Rosalie Levintritt; the former President of the Spanish Republic, Juan Negrín, incognito; and the wife of the President of France. Casals had interrupted his rest period following the final rehearsal to talk with a contingent of Catalans who had slipped across the border without exit permits and come down the Pyrenean slopes on foot to hear him again. Some were old friends, and the group ranged from a bishop to an aged shepherd.

The Bishop of St. Fleur delivered an interminable address of welcome that ended with the request there be no applause within the sacred precinct, and gestured to Casals. Pablo Casals emerged from the clerestory and walked diffidently to the small wooden platform in front of the ornate reredos dominated by St. Peter; the crowd, obedient to but frustrated by the bishop's proscription of applause, could only stand in silent acclaim. Casals bowed soberly a single time, "with something of the air of the stage-manager in a Chinese theatre," and gestured almost brusquely with his bow for the audience to be seated. When he finished the final gigue of the first Bach suite for solo cello the audience rose once more in the silent ritual, although "many hands ached to disregard the ecclesiastical calm," Paul Moor noted—"a miserably unsatisfactory expression of the exaltation that vibrated through the audience with the tautness of a string."

A month before, early arrivals had found Casals living alone "with his housekeeper and his dog, playing only for them and for Catalan friends who came to his house every Saturday night to listen to music and revile Franco in the exquisitely contumelious vocabulary of the Catalan language." At that point there were still rumors that Casals had stopped playing in public because of muscles that no longer responded rather than an adamant moral stand, and there were unspoken questions in the minds of many who came to Prades, both those who had not heard him for years and a new generation of musicians and listeners who had never heard him. After the first phrases of the Bach suite there were no more doubts:

> . . . certainly he played as no other string player on earth can play. He opened each of the six larger concerts with one of the unaccompanied Suites, and these performances were an unalloyed miracle. His art lies in that limpid quintessence of simplicity which is the end result of only the most intense and artful musical sophistication. He has so absorbed and assimilated the notes themselves that what emerges, filtered and distilled through a phenomenal but unobtrusive technique, is as noble and fair a music as any of us is likely to hear in our time. He plays with such freedom that at certain moments, during lyrical passages, he seems almost to be improvising; his lips, moving slightly, seem to be singing to himself; his head moves in sympathy, his face turned straight towards the audience, but his eyes are closed and he clearly might just as well be entirely alone in his room with his pipe in his mouth and his dog at his feet, instead of before a pulsating audience occupying every square inch of standing-room.

It was only natural that Casals be heard again after long silence with Bach, and first of all with one of the solo cello suites. Pablo Casals had retrieved these works from virtual oblivion, so far as a general audience was concerned, when he began to play them in public nearly fifty years earlier. His most revolutionary contribution—some feel the accomplishment for which he will be remembered longest—was his interpretation of Bach. He displayed the Leipzig master as a fully human creator whose art had poetry and passion, accessible to people of all stations. Casals' recordings of the suites, the last completed in Paris a few months before World War II, stand among the superb accomplishments of phonographic recording; these and Casals' other records still in print were all of him that were available during his years of intentional silence, but in no way could they communicate the impact of Casals' actual presence in performance.

From that first Prades Festival onward, the experience of participating in a Casals festival drew forth strong individual reactions from members of the audience as well as from the musicians directly involved. The proximity to Casals seemed to bring out the best qualities in everybody, with the orchestra and most of the soloists playing as if specially inspired. There was an inexplicable chemistry among the musicians. Some sophisticated visitors arriving from Paris and New York recoiled from the worshipful atmosphere they found both generated and nourished by the orchestra members. But on closer observation what seemed an unexpected, even fanatic discipleship was an absolutely genuine and moving veneration. Whatever the Bach Festival at Prades in 1950 became for the listeners and the observers, for the musicians—both the great names and the artists then less well known—it was an experience none was ever able adequately to communicate to an outsider, and none was quite the same when he left Prades.

It may have been a love feast among the musicians, with both large and small concerts of superlative music, but the festival proper was a very busy time for most of the musicians. Rehearsals continued, and two days after the first concert recording sessions began (Columbia had made a twenty-five-thousand-dollar grant in return for exclusive record rights). These took place in the girls' school dining hall, which had been hung with red brocade draperies to improve acoustics. Incidental noise could be controlled to some extent in the makeshift studio, but the narrow-gauge Perpignan–to–Vernet-les-Bains railway was close by; the train schedule fluctuated from one day to the next, driving Columbia Masterworks' British recording engineers frantic.

Following the solo cello suite that opened each of the six orchestral evenings in 1950 Casals conducted various Bach works for orchestra and soloists. The last work of the final evening of the 1950 festival was a Bach cantata, conducted by Casals, with

[459]

Hélène Fahrni and Doda Conrad as soloists. At the finish, Casals' whole body sagged as he lowered his baton. The Archbishop of Perpignan jumped to his feet and began to applaud; cheers and applause exploded from the rest of the audience and lasted through many recalls and repeated presentation of flowers (some tied with ribbon in the colors of the Catalan flag). After twenty minutes of this Casals brought out his cello again, to play "The Song of the Birds" in his arrangement for solo cello and orchestra. The first of the music festivals at Prades had ended.

By comparison to the established music festivals, the one in Prades was organized on a modest scale, but it turned out to be one of the influential musical events of the mid-twentieth century. For everyone there it was a time of discovery or rediscovery; for a new generation it was a revelation of the prowess and art of Pablo Casals and his free, noble conception of Bach. Some of the enthusiasts called Prades the new Bayreuth—a dated and somewhat unhappy label with overtones of weighty humorlessness and the cult of a powerful if unappealing personality. Pablo Casals had consistently said the event must be called a commemoration of Bach, not a Casals festival, although the publicists did not much follow his instruction and to most of the nonmusicians it was at least a pilgrimage to a double shrine. The atmosphere of Prades 1950, like the landscape, differed much from that of Bayreuth in any year. The *esprit* of the smaller group of participating musicians in Provence was incomparably warmer than could be found in Bavaria: to leave a tangible souvenir for Casals, the orchestra applied the fees from a special Radiodiffusion Française broadcast concert to the purchase of an electric refrigerator for his house. Some of the string players of the first year's orchestra asked to stay for a while to study with Casals. Others began to rearrange their concert schedules for 1951 to be able to participate in the projected second festival. Eugene Istomin, who already had an international reputation as a pianist, was asked about his immediate plans as the participants and the spectators began to depart. He said he could not be certain until things had become quieter and he could talk with the Master. "Do you know," he said, "he's been living down here without anyone even to play the piano for him, and you just can't let things like that happen to him. If he wants me to, I'll stay on just as long as I can."

There was a final reception in the garden of the Prades Subprefecture, with champagne and speeches and an aura like that at the end of an especially happy year at school, when the crowd breaks up for far-away places. Casals, wearing his hat, sat wrapped in his overcoat in the June weather, smiling rather abstractedly and wiping his eyes from time to time. The festival had originally been thought of as a gathering of Pablo Casals' friends and family, said the Maître's physician and friend Dr. René Puig, "only we did not know then how big the family would turn out to be." And none of that family, or even his oldest friends, could remember hearing comparable performances by Casals of the six cello suites.

Casals responded first in French, then—to the American contingent of patrons and friends—in English. He seemed to speak barely above a whisper, with many pauses, but the only other sound was the call of the nightingales. "I am not able to say what it means, at my age, to know this great happiness. To Dr. Puig, these dear friends, it remains only—— It is so beautiful, this joining together of so many hearts."

Gaining composure, Casals turned to the orchestra: "It is very hard for me to tell you goodbye. It would be an honor to me for you to come again, to another festival. If you were to come again, I would not receive you as members of an orchestra, but as individual friends—real friends, for you have all proved that you are my friends. Tomorrow we will make the last recording, and meet for the last time. We must part then as if we would see one another the day after, just as we have done these two months. But I will tell you goodbye now, so that tomorrow you will not let me show too much my emotion, something which comes from the bottom of my heart. Thank you. It was wonderful, wonderful. Thank you. It was wonderful, wonderful. Thank you. Thank you."

Very few have the experience of knowing a day—much less a period of weeks—when a considerable number of colleagues and admirers travel thousands of miles to pay them tribute. For Pablo Casals the summer of 1950 was simply the first of more than twenty years during which he was the focus of at least one important international musical event a year. The closest counterpart, perhaps, was the admiring court that gravitated to Franz Liszt at Weimar.

The 1950 Bach Festival stands supreme in the Prades annals, although succeeding years included notable performances and Casals participated in sixteen seasons (early on he had said he would continue to take part until he was ninety). The idealism, the overpowering affection for Casals, and the uncritical enthusiasm did not sustain themselves in precisely the same way after the first year, although the aura remained.

The second festival was held in Perpignan; the success and euphoria of the first led the steering committee to press for Casals' agreement, since Perpignan was much easier to reach from the outside world, and had a number of hotels and *pensions* available for visitors. There were many superlative moments during this festival and several first-rate records were made, but there were also some problems. The orchestra did not always match the 1950 one. Acoustics were poor in the courtyard of the ancient palace of the Kings of Majorca, where outdoor concerts were given, and almost all the musicians—including Casals—had problems playing in gusts of chilly wind. The year before, all Prades had displayed a proprietary interest in the event and everything associated with it; the citizens of Perpignan showed a different attitude. The committee decided to move the festival back to Prades for 1952. That and the 1953 concerts were given in the ruin of the eleven-hundred-year-old abbey of St. Michel de Cuxa, two kilometers south of Prades. Much of the fine medieval building was gutted (twenty-seven columns had been saved when they were removed to form part of The Cloisters of the Metropolitan Museum of Art in New York), but the committee estimated that the reconstructed pink marble basilica would accommodate twelve hundred. (Close to two thousand actually fitted themselves in.) In 1954 the concerts were moved back to their first location, the Church of St. Peter in Prades, where they were held thereafter.

The spiritual impact of the Prades summer gatherings continued, as did the high quality of performances. A group of regulars among musicians and listeners evolved, although there were new faces each year. Behind the scenes, some problems did arise. Enrique Casals had taken a considerable hand in the festival adminstration; neither he nor the dedicated members of the steering committee were experienced in this area, and as success and popularity increased, strains emerged. Pablo Casals himself was unaware of this kind of problem at first—he was occupied with rehearsals and preparation of his own performances, and with the stream of visitors who wanted to see him; he was not, for example, confronted personally with the need to resolve the conflict among festival visitors who discovered they had purchased the same seat for a concert or with kindred problems. By the end of the 1952 festival, Alexander Schneider, who had organized the first Prades seasons in high idealism and charitable purpose, withdrew. Frustrated by the informal record-keeping and saddened by personality conflicts, he found no other path open to him. (Certain improvements and his affectionate loyalty to Casals led him to reconsider later, and in time he returned to the festivals.) The French tax investigators, accustomed to slapdash accounting practices, finally gave up in despair and irritation trying to audit the festival's books. Casals was very unhappy when he became conscious of the state of affairs, and things were sorted out sufficiently for the later festivals to be carried through on a more conventional administrative basis.

That the Prades Festivals were a continuing plea for the world to remember the plight of Spain was never in doubt in the mind of Pablo Casals. Moreover, the number of Catalans in the audiences and at the fringes, as well as the display of the Catalan colors and mention of the subject in almost every conversation in the groups around Casals, kept it alive in the minds of the summer visitors to Prades. Casals was encouraged by some of the American soloists who had friendships and contacts in the Washington establishment to begin writing letters to (and, later, having conversations with) successive American chiefs of state, primarily concerning the Spanish situation but occasionally about other matters he felt to be overwhelming moral issues. His first letter of this kind went to President Harry Truman some six weeks after the Bach Festival. In each letter, Casals addressed himself to a specific point: a later letter to Eisenhower was a plea for commutation of execution for Julius and Ethel Rosenberg; letters to John F. Kennedy concerned continued American aid to Spain and nuclear disarmament; a letter to Richard Nixon concerning United States military support in Spain was acknowledged by an aide, although Nixon did sign a letter sent to Casals in the early summer of 1972, congratulating him on his ninety-fifth birthday. When Casals wrote to Truman at the end of August 1950, the United States Congress was debating the grant of a $62.5-million loan of Marshall Plan funds to the Spanish government.

Dear Mr. President,

I take the liberty of addressing you from this little town of Prades on the French side of the Pyrenees frontier which my dignity, personal and ideological, prevents me from crossing.

I am, Mr. President, an old artist who has travelled many times around the world and am not concerned with politics as such, not belonging and never having belonged to any political party. Rather, I feel, so to speak, a citizen in every country where public life is inspired by the true spirit of democracy. So I feel toward your great Nation which, in the course of many visits I learned to love and admire. I am simply a man who believes in democracy and who loves the soil of his native Catalonia and Spain in which Catalonia is included. These feelings of patriotism I have never considered incompatible with that larger faith in liberty which is the common good of mankind.

You can well understand, then, Mr. President, how painfully disappointed I was at seeing the manner in which the great democracies left the Spanish Republic to its fate as it was fighting the three-fold menace of Nazism, Fascism and Falangism. . . . How the Democracies, after their victory, could permit to flourish in Spain a regime of Tyranny which stands morally condemned by all free men, is beyond my comprehension.

An exile from my own country since 1939, I was forced to become an exile from the democratic world in 1945. With grief I watched the Democracies ignore France's generous initiative in severing relations with the present Spanish regime. Alone, of course, France could not succeed, but success would have been a certainty had the other nations followed her example. Under these conditions, I was obliged to renounce my life of touring and concertizing because I felt that I had no right to acknowledge tributes of appreciation from audiences in countries whose governments, through what seems to me neglect of duty, were doing nothing to put an end to the regime that keeps my land in bondage.

In . . . despondency I settled down in this peaceful town where I have been living in silence for many years. This silence was broken for the first time just a few weeks ago when the time came to commemorate the bi-centennial of Johann Sebastian Bach in a fitting manner. . . . Mr. President, I address you now without any political credentials. A life devoted to the service of art and a faith in the dignity of man are my only credentials. It is with these that I appeal to you and hope and believe that my appeal will not go unheard.

At the Capitol in Washington it has been proposed to give financial aid to Franco Spain. . . . The sacred principle of Democracy would, thus, suffer a grave reverse. Would it be possible to retain faith after such a negation of liberty? I fear that my belief would be shaken as well as the faith of millions of men all over the world who look to the stars and stripes as a symbol of liberty. No totalitarian regime should find protection under the flags of freedom. They are all enemies of human dignity.

It is your constitutional right . . . to veto this bill which would encourage the Spanish dictatorship but would in no way diminish the suffering . . . of the Spanish people. In the name of one million Spaniards who died in the fight for liberty against Hitler, Mussolini and Franco; in the name of thousands of Spaniards who voluntarily enlisted and gave their lives on the battlefields of Europe and Africa; in the name of thousands of Spaniards who died in German concentration camps . . . I appeal to you to use your right and veto this bill.

It would be too bitter and ironic to find that their sacrifice has been thus rewarded. Your gesture, and only this gesture, is worthy of your country—to which all the world looks desperately for comfort and confidence.

On the sixth of September Congress recommended the loan, with a few restrictions on the use of the money. Just under two months later the United Nations voted to rescind the December 1946 exclusion of Spain from UN activities, opening the way for her admission into the Western anti-Communist alignment of nations. The move, sponsored by several Latin American states, was supported by the United States delegation.

With the Bach Festival of 1950 Casals entered what was personally a vastly fulfilling time, a period that he then felt summarized his life. He told many people who came to Prades that summer that the festival had given him a second youth. He was able to keep in as close contact with the rising generations of musicians as he had with his own contemporaries in his youth and middle years, and in circumstances that were more relaxed for him. And he had found a way to resume communication with a large public through music without compromising his postwar stand. For this he justly gave credit to the affectionate persistence of Alexander Schneider, *"qui avait pitié de moi, et de mon silence."* Although he had been a celebrity for more than fifty years, when he broke that silence in the mass-communications environment of midcentury Casals became a world figure.

At the end of the first Prades Festival he was a bit fatigued from the two months' intensive activity, but his energy and vitality were extraordinary; he thrived in the activity and challenge of the rehearsal-performance milieu. He had become quite stocky, but his health was good, although he suffered occasional severe nervous headaches, felt chill when most others did not, and had complained for years of attacks of intestinal discomfort from still-undiagnosed diverticulitis.

Photographer Gjon Mili, who discovered Casals to be "the most unalone alone man" he had ever seen, captured a glimpse of Casals about 1948 startlingly unlike almost any other photograph taken of him from the late 1940s to the beginning of the 1970s. Casals sits with his cello in his house in Prades, right hand holding the bow upright, left wrist resting on the body of the instrument, his hand formed loosely into a fist. Casals waits for the camera to do its work; the expression is one of rather taut patience, as if the artist is indulging an artist in another medium with courtesy but without full attention. The angle of light shows a face that seems almost lean, with nothing flabby, a man of the traditional Catalan compactness; the effect is of strength and total assurance. The face in Mili's sharp focus could easily be twenty years younger; it is in many respects as ageless as the face recorded in the swirling mistiness of Carrière's technique more than forty years earlier. The clenched hand likewise communicates strength and impatience—the left hand that had been damaged by a falling rock, that sometimes had had blood around the fingernails at the end of a concert but that had never done any sort of manual labor. "My hands exist in ignorance of everything that is not music," Casals had told Emil Ludwig.

Having breached his silence, Casals clearly felt freer to think about a wider world. He accepted a doctorate in 1950 from the

Philadelphia Academy of Music and a Chopin medal from Poland, but for nearly a year he did not travel far from Prades. After the first festival the pattern of Casals' life continued much as it had for years before: the early rising and a walk in the warm months, then practicing followed by correspondence or composition and an occasional business conference; rest, correspondence, teaching in the afternoons. Diversion in the evenings included a great deal of Parcheesi, although it was a game Casals enjoyed less than dominos.

Early in August 1950, after the festival, came news of the death of Guilhermina Suggia. She had obtained tickets for the concerts in Prades but became ill; her doctors ordered an operation, which was performed in a clinic in London, and she died in Porto barely a month after her sixty-second birthday. Casals asserted he had not thought of her for years.

In September 1951 Casals increased his scope by traveling to Zürich to direct two of his own works: the "The Three Kings" section of his oratorio *El Pessebre* and, with an ensemble of 120 cellists from all parts of the Western world, his *Sardana* for four cello voices. Proceeds of the concert were earmarked for the Spanish Pavilion of the Pestalozzi Institute of Switzerland. Afterward Casals discovered that Albert Schweitzer was present, and the two met for the first time in seventeen years. During this conversation an exchange took place which, Casals believed, planted a seed that later flowered in Schweitzer's public stand against the threat of nuclear war. Schweitzer, who had just been awarded a ten-thousand-mark prize in Frankfurt by West German publishers and booksellers in recognition of his efforts for world peace, took Casals somewhat to task for his public pronouncements on social and political matters, saying that it was better to create than to protest. "No," said Casals, "it is necessary both to create and to protest . . . there are times the only creative thing we can do is protest; we must refuse to accept . . . what is evil or wicked."

When he returned to Prades after six weeks' absence Casals found stacks of correspondence that had arrived while he was away; someone had counted a total of 665 letters. Friends enjoyed quoting the bewildered but admiring announcement of the local postman that Casals received more mail than the police chief. By far the greatest number were from Spanish refugees or concerned the efforts to aid them, and Casals had always answered every

With Albert Schweitzer in Zürich

such letter and card in his own hand. In Switzerland just after the war he had shown a trembling hand to Mme Emil Vandervelde, Edward Speyer's daughter and widow of the Socialist premier of Belgium in the late 1920s; she thought the unsteadiness was a result of uncontrollable emotion, but he explained that it came from the constant writing. Just as the task became too great for a single person to handle, an offer of assistance came from a young Catalan writer and teacher named José María Corredor, who had been coming from Perpignan to Prades every Sunday afternoon with various friends to visit the Maestro. Casals received the callers "with his habitual warmth and friendliness, sitting in a patriarchal armchair in front of a table covered with books and papers—and, of course, pipes and tobacco." As time passed, Corredor observed more and more papers on the worktable and on the piano, sometimes also on chairs and the bed. Corredor finally convinced Casals that not to accept help in dealing with routine matters was to waste time and energy that could better be spent in other ways.

Thereafter Corredor spent several hours once or twice a week with Casals, attending to correspondence and talking to the accompaniment of birdsong in summer from the neighboring gardens or the violent battering at window-shutters of the winter *tramontana* pouring downward from the Pyrenees. Corredor had studied at the universities of Barcelona and Madrid, later earning a doctorate at Montpellier; he was a poet himself, and an admirer of the fine Catalan writer Juan Maragall, for whom Casals also had great affection and respect; he was a linguist and sometime United Nations translator, a qualification that was of special help in handling Casals' international correspondence. Given Corredor's inquisitive mind and Casals' readiness to talk, the younger man was soon taking down answers to questions he put about Casals' memories and opinions as well as the responses to letters. After a time Corredor began to arrange the notes according to general subject, with the thought of making them into a book. Casals was amenable to the idea, and continued through many months to respond to a wide range of Corredor's questions. The result was a volume of *Conversations with Casals*, published first in Catalan in 1955, verbatim transcriptions of Casals' observations on many facets of music and the events of his career—sometimes elliptical, but suggestive and stimulating, views of a genius on life and his art. Although Casals implied some reservations about the book in a letter published as a preface and tended later to point out that Corredor was not a musician, the volume was circulated widely and translated into eleven languages.

Casals lived in Prades until the autumn of 1955, although he began to conduct a three-week annual master class in cello and chamber music at the Summer Academy of Music in Zermatt, Switzerland, in the late summer of 1952. The festivals, which developed into essentially chamber-music series rather than orchestral ones, and Casals' presence continued to draw to Prades some of the most luminous names in the musical world, and much of the earliest concerts was put on tape and records by Columbia. "It is good for one's soul to make a pilgrimage to this sage," Gerald Moore said, "and it is good that one should have to take time and trouble to

Pablo Casals

(Left) Yehudi Menuhin, Karl Engel, and Pablo
Casals play a trio in the Église de St. Pierre
during the July 1958 Prades Festival; (right)
Russian violinist David Oistrakh, the Dowager
Queen of the Belgians, and Casals in Casals'
house at Molitg-les-Bains in the summer of 1961

do so." A Catholic Spanish-language newspaper noted that among
living men only the Pope drew more pilgrims. To some it seemed
the celebration of a secular musical creed: "There is no Bach but
Bach, and Casals is his Prophet." Few who traveled to the shrine
came with a basic disagreement about the Bach canon as preached
there; few who had even slight personal contact with Casals left
without a feeling of benediction.

Bernard Gavoty, musical critic for the Paris newspaper *Le
Figaro*, did not go to Prades until 1955. All but one of his cellist
friends in Paris had warned him to stay away because he would
be disappointed; Casals was finished, any cellist seventy-nine years
old had to be finished. How right they had been to try to keep
him away, Gavoty told them in the piece he wrote when he returned: "the indiscreet and disastrous truth would be made clear
as daylight . . . that the sun makes the planets dark! . . . Time

acts on Casals as on a great vineyard: it makes him more mighty by pruning the surplus. . . ." Gavoty had an appointment with *le Maître;* as he arrived at the little house with a brood of nightingales haunting a laurel copse alongside, "there on purpose to afford crowns for the gods," Casals appeared on the threshold "surrounded by his court like a reigning monarch. . . . Two English[-speaking] ladies, discreet and intense, mounted guard for amusement's sake: they were clearly the great man's familiars and spared him the strain of interviews by conducting them themselves." And, waiting to rehearse Brahms' B-minor trio with Casals were Yehudi Menuhin wearing a loose sport shirt over saffron shorts and Eugene Istomin, gathered with the others around "the legendary figure of the patriarch."

Upstairs Gavoty and his photographer waited in Casals' bedroom while the three players rehearsed. The Brahms proceeded as delicately as the winding of a skein at a spinning wheel, Casals' voice only once or twice heard making a gentle suggestion. "I love this place; you can work here in silence," he had explained on the way upstairs. During the rehearsal Bernard Gavoty noted a bulldozer assaulting the road outside, the sound of a machine saw at steady intervals, masons chiseling a piece of stone, an artisan attaching ironwork to a door, and Follet, "the indispensable dog," chained to his kennel, barking ineffectively but with style.

In the Church of St. Peter, packed to the doors that night, there was a vastly different ambience:

> Suddenly the spotlights are switched on: the concert is about to begin. Casals enters from the sacristy which serves as his dressing-room, his 'cello in his hand. He bows low to the Queen [of the Belgians], inclines his head to the crowd and climbs on to the white wood stage set up at the level of the step on which the communion table stands: he thus has his back to the high altar. Behind him a great figure of St. Peter, wearing a red mitre, is seated under a canopy borne by angels, in the centre of the wonderful retable made of gilded wood in the Spanish style. With his fore and mid fingers the first pontiff of Christendom is blessing the pope of the 'cello . . . Casals raises his bow as if he were imitating Peter's gesture. In fact the two are essentially alike, for they both proclaim kindred dogmas: it is indeed a gospel of universal love which Casals is preaching from the high hermitage to which he has retired to rule the world.

The Bach suite in G for solo cello formed the prelude to this evening's concert. The French critic, admiring but far too independent a mind to be simply a propagandist, found the same simplicity and seriousness he had found in the morning. "Casals makes of it something other than a page of music: a message of truth. It is better than beautiful, it is true."

The remainder of the program was two Brahms trios, which Casals played with Menuhin and Istomin. The combined ages of the violinist and pianist was eleven years less than the number Casals had lived, and a certain paternal authority showed through his invariable courtesy—an impatient shake of his head or gesture with bow tip to correct a lagging tempo, a finger to his lips to assure a sudden pianissimo. Gavoty observed Menuhin sweating and Istomin compressing his full lips violently in the dangerous places while Casals remained unperturbed: "With him nothing seems difficult . . . very great artists make technique and circumstances dovetail exactly. . . . When others seem to be translating a foreign language, they are speaking the idiom native to them."

The concert finished, audience and musicians rose and exchanged bows, and a few friends moved into the sacristy where Casals smiled and answered questions as he carefully put his instrument away in its case in a dark corner. There was no exchange of compliments and hypocritical thanks but what seemed to the Parisian a surge of homage and gratitude.

"Are we on earth, or in heaven?" Queen Elisabeth was heard to ask. Bowing to kiss her hand, Casals murmured "On an earth that is . . . harmonized."

The Dowager Queen of the Belgians, more birdlike than ever at nearly eighty, was now one of the Prades summer regulars. She was often to be seen at rehearsals, sitting engrossed in the music in an armchair near the participants. Her presence invariably caused some disruption, although she certainly did not intend it to do so and often did not realize that it did. She sat beside Casals whenever possible when he was not performing, and in so doing contributed to at least one soloist's chief memory of Prades. When the German baritone Dietrich Fischer-Dieskau sang Schubert's song cycle *Die Winterreise,* accompanied by Gerald Moore, there was an electrical failure (Moore continued playing while an aide found and brought a candelabrum to the piano). But what Fischer-Dieskau remembered most clearly was the voice of Casals murmuring "Lovely! Lovely!" after each segment and Her Majesty's audible agreement.

Elisabeth of the Belgians was the most prominent of a small group of women who came devotedly to Prades and later elsewhere to be near Casals during festivals and at his birthday celebrations. She was also, except for Frasquita Capdevila, the oldest survivor of the inner coterie of Casals admirers from the early period of his career. Outsiders, including wives of orchestra members and soloists at Prades, tended both to make private sport of the possessive female "palace guard" around Casals and to fault him for allowing it. But there was a quality about Pablo Casals that drew from other people an eagerness to offer gifts, help, friendliness, many times without thought of benefit to themselves.

In January 1955 Frasquita Capdevila died. The last months were specially trying for Casals. Although Señora Capdevila, a victim of Parkinson's disease, had not been really well for many years, during the last period her condition made walking and other movement very difficult. Close friends saw Casals gently put his arm through hers to steady her and walk back and forth with her across a small downstairs room in the house for long stretches, sometimes singing a children's tune in an attempt to raise her spirits. Toward the end she called for him day and night and could scarcely bear to have him out of her sight—to the extent that her doctor threatened to move Casals to another house. Casals himself seemed to sag in spirit and physique, looking as old as his seventy-nine years; the doctor confided to several people that he had begun to fear Casals would die before Señora Capdevila.

During the last hours of Frasquita Capdevila's life the priest of Prades read a service *in articulo mortis* by which she was married to Pablo Casals, a rite the priest felt free to perform since Casals' secular wedding to Susan Metcalfe was not valid in the eyes of the Catholic church. It was a gesture of near-medieval chivalry and grateful affection for the devoted woman who had "for so many years and so constantly shared my vicissitudes." Casals had never felt romantic interest for her although for more than a quarter-century he was faithful to his promise to be her protector; her adoration for him had been an open secret for nearly sixty years.

Frasquita Vidal Puig de Capdevila's last expressed wishes were

*Casals makes a point to a local clergyman at
St. Michel de Cuxa, 1953. To the right,
Frasquita Vidal de Capdevila*

that she be buried beside Doña Pilar in the Vendrell cemetery and
that Casals play "The Song of the Birds" at the grave. At her inter-
ment, for which Casals set foot in Spain for the first time since
1939, he was too overcome to play, but Luis Casals' wife Teresina
had located a portable phonograph and a recording of *"El Cant
dels Ocells"* was played.

Casals went to San Salvador, where he moved emotionally
through his house looking once more at the souvenirs and remembering. Friends streamed into the villa, drawn by word that Casals
had returned; their joy swept away the sadness of a funeral. Some
few thought at first that he had come home permanently, others
had an idea he could be persuaded to stay. Juan Alavedra, onetime
secretary to a Republican head of the Catalan government, had
gone back to Barcelona in 1949. Enrique Casals moved back and
forth between his enterprises in Barcelona and administrative direc-

tion of the Prades festivals without difficulty from 1950 on. Businessmen who had been obliged to take themselves and their families out of Spain during the war had returned to work in their homeland. Even Joan Miró, the painter—a "special person," as Catalans are likely to term people of distinctly independent personality—no friend of the Madrid regime, had found it possible to live in Catalonia again. This was not so for Casals. He had made the private vow that he would not return to Spain while Francisco Franco was in power well before his decision was a matter of public knowledge. Only the most extraordinary pressure of another sacred promise had drawn him back, and he returned to France the day following the funeral.

It was the youngest of Pablo Casals' cello students in Prades who sensed and began spontaneously, naturally to heal the desolation in Casals after his return from Spain at the beginning of 1955. Marta Angélica Montañez y Martínez, then less than three months past her eighteenth birthday, had come to Prades in the late summer of 1954 to study cello with Casals. They had met during the 1951 Perpignan Festival, when Marta came from Puerto Rico with her uncle Rafael Montañez, a poet and flutist as well as a newspaperman, bringing greetings from Casals' Defilló relatives in his mother's native island. Marta—called Martita almost universally by family, friends, and later by a great many strangers—arrived with her cello, her teacher, and her uncle at Casals' little house in Prades for a visit that began after siesta and extended at Casals' insistence through dinner and well into the evening. She was a very pretty child with long black hair, fine coloration, a lovely, slightly shy smile. Deep in a wave of nostalgia for Doña Pilar and the homeland she had spoken about from her son's earliest recollection, Casals felt himself greeting distant family members rather than strangers and, he said many times in later years, the first time he saw Martita he had the fleeting thought that his mother must have looked like her at the same age. He acknowledged that she had genuine talent, but since she was not yet fifteen suggested that she work with her current teacher a while longer and continue her general education in New York, which could offer considerably more than Prades. That teacher, Lieff Rosanoff, had himself studied with Casals in Paris; Casals told him that when Rosanoff judged she was ready, he would accept her as a student.

Marta had begun to study violin and solfeggio with her uncle at the age of six. It was his suggestion that she begin cello, and before she was eight she had classes with Rafael Figueroa Sanabia in Puerto Rico, remaining his student until she went to the mainland United States for advanced study. She obtained her elementary schooling in the Colegio Puertorriqueño de Niñas in Santurce, graduating at thirteen from the eighth grade at the top of her class. In New York she had an enviable academic record during four years at the Marymount School of the Convent of the Sacred Heart of Mary, working at the same time toward a baccalaureate degree at the Mannes School of Music, where she continued violoncello study with Rosanoff. During her last two summers on the mainland, Marta attended summer sessions of music in Blue Hill, Maine, held for talented students selected from the entire country.

In the spring of 1954, Marta Montañez graduated from Marymount *maxima cum laude* (the school's single highest academic honor), with an award for being a top Latin student in New York State. She had also received from a competition in Puerto Rico a thousand-dollar prize to apply to further cello study. In September she and her mother, Angélica Martínez de Montañez, arrived in Prades, tired and dusty following thirteen hours en route from Paris. They stretched out for a few minutes' rest in their room in the Grand Hotel and woke to discover they had slept around the clock, missing the first appointment with Casals. Señora Montañez remained in Prades for a month, having established her daughter before she left in the house of a local widow, Mme Hebrard, about ten minutes' bicycle ride away from Casals' cottage.

From the first lessons Casals decided that the young *puertorriqueña* was one of the best students he had ever had. Not only did she have talent, she also had strong musical aptitude and a quick mind. During her first months of work in Prades, however, Marta Montañez was simply one of several students. She was at the Casals house no more frequently than the others; Casals, increasingly concerned with Señora Capdevila's illness, brightened noticeably when Marta was present, as did everyone else, and he praised her progress but did not show favoritism.

In the period that followed Casals' return from Spain at the beginning of 1955, when he seemed to everyone daily more dispirited and withdrawn into his composing, he asked if Marta might bicycle over to join him for part of his early-morning walks, and before long she was invited to join the household for coffee before teacher and student went their separate ways to practice. The never-ending stream of correspondence was always there to be answered. At eighteen Marta spoke and wrote flawless Spanish and English and very good French, which she continued to improve after she came to Prades; she began to learn Catalan; she could also type. With such qualifications, part of her time was soon taken up with the Maître's correspondence. A skillful driver, she began to chauffeur Casals on trips to settlements of Spanish refugees and elsewhere.

Between 1951 and her return to Prades as Casals' student, Marta Montañez had developed from an attractive child into a lovely young woman talented both as a cellist and as a singer. She was well-organized, fast and efficient, energetic and generous; it is not surprising that Casals very soon found her indispensable.

She was a healthy, outgoing girl who had both friends and suitors among those her own age. Himself a product of the nineteenth century and of Spain, Casals was more impressed—and startled—than he would admit at the time by young Mlle Montañez' strength and self-sufficiency. She was quite unlike any other woman he had known.

Serious though she continued to be about her cello study, and it was a general consensus that she was nearly ready for an important career, Marta brought to everything she did an irrepressible brightness of spirit and contagious gaiety. When she was in the small, rather dark house there was also present the saving grace of a sense of humor; and Casals, like Marta's fellow students, discovered that she had a magnificent gift for mimicry from which nobody was safe. Not even Harold Bauer, who had been incomparable at caricaturing the great and the famous, or Emanuel Moór, whose mime had been telling and seldom kind, could match her flair. There was about her also a less immediately identifiable quality of security and spiritual tranquility that was completely unassuming, intensely personal, and something most people who knew her well thought about only later. Part seemed to be the result of a natively generous personality, textured by a profound undemonstrative religious faith. Her parents' form of religious practice was Protestant; they allowed their children to make their own

*Marta Montañez in Marymount school uniform
in the early 1950s*

*Martita and Casals during a cello lesson in
Prades, about 1954*

devotional choices. Martita chose to enter the Roman Catholic
communion, and during her school years at Marymount had considered seriously devoting her life to work in a religious order.

Months of increased time together—walking, working at correspondence or music, visiting refugees, talking—passed without
Casals' being fully aware of the development of his feeling for
Martita. He recognized a sense of responsibility for the girl from
the Caribbean living alone in Prades. Some eighty-three years before, Pilar Defilló had been a young *puertorriqueña* alone in Vendrell, and when Martita lapsed into Puerto Rican Spanish Casals
heard echoes of his mother's speech. One of the first photographs
Casals inscribed to Martita he signed "Tío Pablo" ("Uncle
Pablo"). By the time of the 1955 Prades Festival Marta Montañez

Minigolf at Zermatt, 1955

was identified as Pablo Casals' favorite student; soon her photograph was captioned in the French press as that of Casals' adopted daughter; some thought she was a niece.

As the time approached for Casals to go to Zermatt for his annual master classes in late summer he admitted to himself that he had no interest in traveling to Switzerland unless Mártita accompanied him, and he realized his feeling for her was neither altogether paternal nor avuncular. Martita did travel to Zermatt with him; she took notes for him during classes, and outsiders began more and more to turn to her when there were questions to transmit to Casals or arrangements to be made.

Zermatt's crystalline air and alpine vistas were a salutary change for Casals after the 1955 festival concerts in provincial, dusty Prades, although he had told Alexander Schneider he considered it the best festival to date. The Zermatt Summer Academy of Music drew a number of good cellists and the great attraction was the master classes in the interpretation of cello literature given by Casals, although there were notable chamber-music sessions with Sándor Végh, Carl Engel, Willy Hauslein, and Emil Hauser. Fewer people saw and heard Casals at Zermatt than at Prades during the 1950s, but in the master classes—first at Zermatt, then in Siena, later in a 1960 series that was filmed in Berkeley, California, and in several sessions each summer through the sixties and into the seventies at Marlboro, Vermont—a considerable public had its best opportunity truly to see Pablo Casals at work. There is a long-lived debate among professional musicians about the usefulness and even the desirability of virtuoso classes: some contend that they are merely displays for a quasi-retired great name while others say that if the teacher is indeed a master they can be stimulating and important learning situations for participants and observers as well. Whatever the case, Casals' classes were the best-known events of their kind for twenty years, and their existence gave hundreds and, through repeated television broadcasts of the Berkeley series, thousands of people the opportunity to observe Casals in action, since as always he taught and lectured with cello in hand. In the performances at Prades he was playing, not teaching. Even at Zermatt, as part of the entire learning atmosphere, Casals did some playing, one year performing Beethoven's chief cello works with Horszowski.

Zermatt gave Casals a perspective and a widened vision after his years of restriction in Prades. In the summer of 1955 Casals also felt a new concern for living. He had rejoiced in the majesty of the Swiss mountains since his first youthful visit to the country; the sight of the Matterhorn beyond Zermatt, particularly, never failed to lift his thought.

And in Zermatt there had come to him an honorary membership that pleased him enormously. During his first summer teaching visit to Zermatt Casals had been enchanted to meet some of the Zermatt alpine guides. More than three dozen of the major Swiss climbing routes start from Zermatt, including those to Monte Rosa and the Matterhorn faces, and the local guides are not reticent in admitting they are the best in the world. Casals, with his open admiration for anyone who did his job superlatively well, spent hours talking about climbing and about the mountains with these men, who were as delighted by his company as he with theirs. Before the visit was over Casals had been invested with the first honorary membership of the guild of Zermatt alpine guides. He played a recital for the guides and their families in thanks, but protested he was too old to make a climb with them even after they proposed to carry him up the slopes. Casals was joined afterward in the status of honorary Zermatt guide by Tensing, the Sherpa who had just conquered Mount Everest with Edmund Hillary, and by Mieczyslaw Horszowski, who had only just turned sixty and was still an active climber. Horszowski admitted having transferred his passion for sports cars onto mountaineering about 1910 and had made his own most satisfying climbs out of Zermatt in 1911.

From Zermatt, Martita and Casals traveled on to visit Albert Schweitzer in Günsbach, had luncheon with Charlie Chaplin at his home in Vevey, visited Wagner's house in Lucerne, the Beethoven birthplace in Bonn, and were guests of Queen Elisabeth in Laeken, Belgium. Two months after the end of the Zermatt classes Pablo Casals left for his first trip to Puerto Rico, accompanied by Marta, who had been planning to visit her home. Casals had been as close to his mother's homeland as the neighboring island of Cuba, and while Doña Pilar was alive had a number of times suggested that she join him for a visit to see her childhood home and her relatives, but she had always declined. More recently several of the island's important citizens had urged him to come for a visit or make his home in Puerto Rico; one of the letters had been from Jaime Benítez, the energetic chancellor of the University of Puerto Rico, couched in such terms as to explain that Casals would be welcomed simply for himself: he should come, if he wished, without his cello. The Defilló family had prospered on Puerto Rico and other Caribbean islands in the eighty-five years since Pilar Defilló y Amiguet had traveled to Catalonia with her mother and brother; the day the *Flandre* touched dock with Casals and Martita aboard, December 11, 1955, one of the San Juan papers printed a cartoon that showed the famous arrival looking down from the ship onto a large crowd each member of which was labeled DEFILLÓ.

Three days before, the House of Representatives of the Puerto Rican legislature had named a committee to draw up a joint resolution of welcome after a brilliant hour-long eulogy by Representative Marcos Ramírez Irizarry that described the high personal and artistic virtues of Pablo Casals and called him, with Albert Einstein and Albert Schweitzer, one of the three towering figures of the contemporary world. Governor Luis Muñoz Marín issued an elegant proclamation of welcome; the newspapers carried editorials and long columns about Casals the man and the musician.

Casals and Martita, accompanied by the Governor's wife and a number of others who had participated in the official greeting, came gingerly down the steep *Flandre* gangplank. They moved through a welcoming crowd, slowed by many handshakes and tearful embraces, to an official limousine that was led by a motorcycle police escort through Old San Juan to the Plaza Colón. There Casals was serenaded by a student chorus and presented a basket of tropical fruit and then was driven to the Condado section, where he was to stay in an apartment to the door of which relatives had affixed a sign that read *El Cant dels Ocells*.

The following afternoon Martita and Casals and their relatives went to the Governor's palace, the sixteenth-century La Fortaleza, where Governor Muñoz and his wife, Doña Inés María Mendoza de Muñoz Marín, received them in the Hall of Mirrors. The Governor and Casals retired to the music room for a fifteen-minute private conversation, and afterward the party listened from a balcony to Christmas songs and typical Puerto Rican music performed in the patio below. But for Casals the most moving of the many fiestas and ceremonies was a homage in Mayagüez on December 17, a tribute to him and to the memory of his mother at her birthplace, number 21 in the calle Méndez Vigo (the house in which, it had turned out, Martita's mother Angélica had also been born, and on the same day of the year). Casals, pale with emotion, arrived at ten in the morning accompanied by Martita and Doña Inés Muñoz Marín, to the greeting of a large crowd. Casals had hoped to walk alone through the house in which Pilar Ursula Defilló y Amiguet had been born and to play his cello there for her, but a portion of the crowd pressed inside with him, and he moved to the balcony overlooking the street. There he played a lullaby he remembered his mother singing, and a Bach pastorale. Then he went to the piano to accompany Martita's singing of some songs he had written sixty years earlier. Finally, accompanied by Narciso Figueroa, he played "The Song of the Birds" before going down into the street to watch Doña Inés unveil the plaque identifying the house as Doña Pilar's birthplace "in the name of the people of Puerto Rico and of the mothers. . . ." Pablo Casals was then officially named an adopted son of Mayagüez by the mayor.

Casals began the celebration of his seventy-ninth birthday in San Juan—the serenades began at eleven o'clock on the night of the twenty-eighth of December; at midnight the chorus of the University of Puerto Rico sang "*Feliz Cumpleaños*," the Governor's wife delivered greetings, and Casals cut a large cello-shaped cake; afterward the University chorus sang sixteenth-century songs, Christmas *villancicos*, and a Puerto Rican *danzo*. Among the friends who had traveled from New York for the festivities were Martita's former teacher Lieff Rosanoff and his wife and Mieczyslaw Horszowski. On the birthday itself, there was a party with gifts from friends and an improvised musical program at a country house in the beautiful mountainous interior, near Aguas Buenas. New Year was spent with Martita and her parents and uncle at Humacao, her birthplace.

A reception at La Fortaleza given by Governor Muñoz and his wife on the night of January 19, 1956, for more than four hundred guests was the first opportunity the artistic, social, and political leaders of the island had to hear Marta Montañez play publicly since she had begun to study with Casals. Pianist Jesús María Sanromá joined her and Casals in a formal program in the spacious onetime Throne Room of the Fortaleza. Sanromá opened the program with Bach's "Italian" concerto, then accompanied Casals and his student playing sonatas by Handel and Beethoven for two violoncellos. Martita played a suite of pieces by Couperin, accompanied by Sanromá. Afterward artists and guests descended to the tropically lush Fortaleza gardens to talk and listen to native songs by a group from the inland.

Marta Montañez was considered a highly promising young talent before she went to study in Prades. After the Fortaleza concert, a Puerto Rican writer for the journal *Semana* found extraordinary the transformation that had taken place "during the time passed in the artistic and spiritual shadow" of Casals. Notable particularly was "the serenity, the aplomb, the personal dominion with which Martita confronted the crucial test of playing solo under the gaze of the premier violoncellist of the world." Certainly, Martita possessed positive natural gifts before studying with Casals.

*Marta Montañez and Pablo Casals playing
cello together in San Juan in January 1956,
during Casals' first trip to Puerto Rico and
exchanging bows during their concert in
La Fortaleza, the governor's palace, San Juan,
the same month*

She had in her interpretations a serene vigor, a delicate force that characterized and distinguished the expression of her artistic temperament. "These qualities have been refined. . . . The bow now has great precision in the hand of Martita Montañez." Added Alfredo Matilla, writing in *El Mundo*, "Marta Montañez is today an interpreter of the first rank. . . . Puerto Rico already has, among the names to be noticed, a violoncellist who will make her mark in the world of art."

On the twenty-third of January Casals left for a trip to Mexico, spending a day in Havana on the way. He spent much of his time in Veracruz, the first two days resting and talking with friends—of whom there were many in the country, since Mexico had welcomed Spanish expatriates from the beginning of the Civil War and had remained constant in its refusal of diplomatic recognition of the Franco government. Casals was greeted with flowers, songs and dances, speeches and parchments of tribute, receptions, a declaration that Casals was a guest of honor of Veracruz, an honorary doctorate from the University of Jalapa. The enormous flood of affection that greeted Casals every time he stepped from an airplane or left his car was impressive; the Veracruz telegraph office reported he received more than two thousand telegrams within the week he was there. Although the constant repetition of heartfelt but monotonous ceremonies in village squares, town halls, and private houses would have been fatiguing for some, for Casals they were both deeply moving and nourishing, and if some lacked imagination or effective stage-management, he appeared not to notice. While in Mexico, he also had the opportunity to talk with a great many important Catalan and other Spanish Republican expatriates. On January 29, the Spanish Republican Center honored Casals at a noon banquet attended by more than nine hundred, including surviving cabinet members of the prewar Republican government. On the thirtieth Casals began his return journey to Puerto Rico, with stops in Havana and Miami.

Casals had been scheduled to receive an honorary degree from the University of Puerto Rico, but soon after his return from Mexico he discovered that both Chief Justice Earl Warren of the United States and President Castan Tobenas of the Supreme Court of Spain were to be honored at the same ceremony. A convocation of international jurists was being held in San Juan at the time; inescapable political courtesy required that Governor Muñoz and Chancellor Benítez, both liberals, recognize the Spanish judge. Dismayed and disappointed, Casals sent Benítez a firm letter declining his degree. Anti-Franco demonstrators and sympathizers with Casals' position protested Tobenas' presence at both the University and the Bar Association meetings, some carrying placards with such slogans as WARREN—Sí, CASTAN TOBENAS—NO and DIGNITY AGAINST FASCISM. (Muñoz Marín and Benítez regretted the situation; there were subsequent conversations with Casals, and both men became and remained valued personal friends.)

By the beginning of February 1956 Casals had decided to make his home in Puerto Rico, although he had not yet said so publicly. Soon after his arrival Governor Muñoz and Doña Inés had broached the idea of a major music festival, to bear Casals' name, in Puerto Rico, and they had discussed the possibility of a music conservatory and a symphony orchestra for the island. Muñoz thought these all possible if Casals would settle in Puerto Rico and lend both his prestige and his active direction to the projects.

Casals had taken an immediate liking to tall, gifted, charismatic Muñoz, who had been a poet in his earlier years and whose father had been a leader in the struggle for Puerto Rican self-government in the generation before the 1898 war, and to his sensitive, brilliant, and dynamic wife. He was impressed with the cultural aspects of the program for economic development of the island, which for a third of a century had suffered under U.S. protection exploitation nearly as crippling as that of the last years of Spanish control.

Before he made up his mind, Casals had found out what he could about the musical life of the island. Puerto Rico was far from the cultural wasteland many outsiders thought it, but modern economic conditions and centuries of colonial status had stifled development of a rich potential. There was, of course, a valid folk tradition, particularly toward the center of the island, away from the few coastal cities; this delighted him. He discovered that proposals had been made to the legislature for the establishment of a conservatory of music as early as 1915 (when fifteen thousand dollars would have been adequate capitalization); subsequent attempts had been short-lived. Casals' uncle José Defilló and a composer named José Quintón had been reputable composers late in the nineteenth century, writing music that had a distinctly French flavor. By the middle 1950s there were a number of serious Puerto Rican composers, most of whom of necessity studied abroad— among them Monsita Ferrer, Héctor Campos Parsi, José Enrique Pedreira, Jack Delano, Narciso Figueroa, and Amaury Veray. Some were already known abroad, although others were still recognized chiefly in their homeland. Most composed to some degree in a contemporary idiom; Casals and some of them developed cordial friendships of mutual regard but disagreed on the course of development of the mainstream of music. Puerto Rico had at the time several well-known and accomplished pianists—including Narciso Figueroa, a student of Cortot who had trained in Madrid, and Elisa Tavárez—but the best-known Puerto Rican performing artist was Jesús María Sanromá, who had graduated from the New England Conservatory, studied with Cortot and Artur

Schnabel in Europe, and been official pianist of the Boston Symphony Orchestra as well as a concert artist for nearly twenty years. After World War II Sanromá channeled a great deal of his considerable energy into trying to develop adequate musical education in his homeland. Among a number of talented singers of serious music were María Esther Robles, who had appeared successfully on the stage in England and the United States, and the young soprano Olga Iglesias. Garciela Rivera, another Puerto Rican soprano, had sung with the San Carlo opera company, made a successful career in Italy, and sang *Lucia di Lammermoor* one season at the Metropolitan Opera in New York. The island contained a single large musical family—the Figueroa—that had developed composers and performers. Casals was told that only in the Figueroa house and at the home of Marta Montañez' parents before she left Puerto Rico to study was it possible to find evening gatherings at which chamber music was played competently.

By late February 1956 invitations from Casals and Governor Muñoz had gone to Alexander Schneider to undertake the organization of a Festival Casals in Puerto Rico. By late March the general form had been established. Casals was named musical director of the Festival Casals, Inc., chartered the next month under Fomento; Schneider was assistant musical director. The only members of the board of directors not resident in Puerto Rico were Schneider and Washington lawyer Abe Fortas. The Legislative Assembly of Puerto Rico voted seventy-five thousand dollars toward the costs of the first festival. There had been suggestions that the first festival be held on Casals' eightieth birthday, at the end of December, but Schneider pointed out that the beginning of the following May would be the best time for the soloists and orchestra, the majority of whom would come from an excellent thirty-three-member group with which Schneider and Rudolf Serkin had been recording Mozart concertos for Columbia Records. Schneider was delighted both by the prospect of an important international music festival in the Caribbean and the fact that Casals was leaving Prades to expand his life. Marta had been present for the discussions, but at no time did she try to influence Casals' decision, although he realized how happy she was to be back among her family and friends on the island that he also found most agreeable and very beautiful.

With Martita, Casals left Puerto Rico for Prades at the end

of March by plane. From Paris they flew as close to Prades as possible in a series of progressively smaller aircraft, and finished the trip by auto. Preparations for the seventh Prades Festival were made. Before leaving for another master-class series at Zermatt, Casals prepared to move from the gatekeeper's house of the Château Valroc, in which so much of the evolution of the Prades festivals had come about. At the table in the first-floor workroom music had been written and thousands of letters answered, and through the windows the sight of the Canigou had represented to Casals the existence of an immutable hope. Through the windows, too, Pablo Casals had over the years heard the sound of various musicians who had come to surprise him: the orchestra members and soloists from one of the early festivals who had slipped quietly into the garden to play the *Siegfried Idyl*, small groups called *coblas* that came to play sardanas and other Catalan music. Musical offerings continued to come wherever Casals lived; once an orchestra of players who had been members of one of those organized by the Workingmen's Concert Association arrived to play *Eine Kleine Nachtmusik* for *El Mestre;* after Casals' last participation in a Prades festival, three truckloads of Vendrelleños came to form human pyramids in honor of his ninetieth birthday, along with the choir of the Church of Santa Ana to sing for him. And while Casals was still living in the Troy estate gardener's house, the American folk singer Burl Ives came with friends to sing for Casals, saying he would barter ballads for Bach.

After Zermatt, Casals and Martita again visited Queen Elisabeth in Belgium, and then there was a grand homage to Casals at the Sorbonne on October 10, 1956, in anticipation of the fifty-seventh anniversary of his Paris début and his eightieth birthday. Following a brief, radiant eulogy by Casals' old friend Albert Sarrailh, who had left Montpellier to become Rector of the Sorbonne, Casals conducted the second half of the concert before an audience of three thousand, leading the Lamoureux orchestra and eleven cellists in Gabriel Fauré's *Élégie*, the "Three Kings" section from Casals' oratorio *El Pessebre*, and an ensemble of a hundred cellists playing his *Sardana*. Three days later Casals returned to Prades, followed by Bernard Gavoty's salute in *Le Figaro*: "Casals has returned to his mountains. *C'est vrai, c'est simple et c'est grand.*" Most of the books and papers and many of the souvenirs were packed, but some were left in the little house made available to Casals by the Spa in nearby Molitg-les-Bains to await his return in the spring for the next year's festival. Casals left Prades in late November, expecting to make his home in Puerto Rico at least seven months of the year; accompanying him were Marta Montañez and Enrique and María Casals.

An apartment for Casals and his brother and sister-in-law overlooking the sea had been found in the calle Bucaré in the Santurce section of San Juan; outside the door, rather like a doctor's shingle, was a sign with the name *Cant dels Ocells.*

The first Festival Casals de Puerto Rico had been announced for the end of April and the beginning of May 1957, and by the end of December tickets for the twelve concerts were almost all sold. Responsible officials of the Puerto Rico Industrial Development administration and Schneider, with his assistant, Dinorah Press, had wasted no time in making detailed plans after Casals' agreement in March and April 1956. Within a month most of the arrangements had been submitted for Casals' approval and all the artists invited to participate had accepted. Casals was asked if he would reconsider the Schubert C major symphony, which entailed the outlay of some twelve hundred dollars to bring over from the mainland three trombonists for a single concert (suitably proficient people were not to be found on the island).

The eightieth birthday proved to be very much of a fiesta in San Juan, with private parties, a municipal reception given by the mayor of San Juan, Felisa Rincón de Gautier, and a dinner in Casals' honor at La Fortaleza followed by a concert in the patio of the building and a reception in the gardens—a tradition that continued for Casals' birthdays throughout the years Luis Muñoz Marín was in office, and with some differences during the terms of his successors. Casals thoroughly enjoyed the celebration of his birthdays, the greetings and the music, and by the end of the festivities at the beginning of each new year was generally excessively tired.

At the time of his eightieth birthday Casals was still determined not to visit the United States so long as it continued to give vital support to the Falangist regime in Spain. He rejected an invitation to the annual dinner of the Bohemians, the New York musicians' club that had first honored him with a stupendous smoker forty-two years earlier: "So long as Franco remains, I must criticize America, and it is improper for me to accept hospitality from a country I must criticize." There was no conflict at all in changing his residence to Puerto Rico, he explained. Rather than term it United States territory, "I prefer to consider it an autonomous commonwealth. It is unrepresented in the Congress, has no voice in foreign affairs, and is therefore blameless."

The eightieth birthday greetings included cards, letters, and cables from every part of the world and ranged in content from personal felicitations and intelligence that the London Bach Society would give an important concert in honor of his birthday to a letter from a high Israeli official justifying his country's position toward Egypt and inviting Casals to visit as a guest of the government. There was also a three-page cable from Norman Thomas and others asking Casals to add his name to a protest to be sent to Marshal Tito of Yugoslavia about the three-year imprisonment of Milovan Djilas for having published an article critical of the Tito regime.

Casals recalled having told Schweitzer that one must protest as well as create; his acts and statements of protest at eighty were something he felt a man must do if he were truly alive. There was, however, a full schedule of creating—the festivals, teaching, and composing. Over the years he had written a considerable body of work—symphonies, string quartets, works for violin and for cello, songs and choral compositions—but still allowed few people to see most of it. Some of his religious compositions had just been published by the Abbey of Montserrat, for which he had written most of them; he had agreed to the publication in New York of a few of his songs; and friends saw a violin sonata he was completing and the manuscript of his oratorio. And his eighty-first year already had an extraordinarily full agenda: the first San Juan Festival would end on May 8; on the eleventh he would sail for Europe, going first to Bonn to play with Horszowski five private concerts of Beethoven cello works in the Beethovenhaus. Then he would travel to Paris to participate in the first *Concours International Pablo Casals,* a cello competition to be held in the Salle Gaveau. Other judges were Gaspar Cassadó from Spain, Rostropovich from the USSR, and Maurice Eisenberg from the United States. Next, at Prades, he would give twelve public concerts and one for students. Finally, he would take a brief holiday as houseguest of Queen Elisabeth, and then conduct a four-week master-class series at Zermatt, after which he would return to San Juan by ship in October, to spend the winter and spring in Puerto Rico.

The first months of 1957, as the first Festival Casals approached, were ones of great contentment for Casals. The move to the Caribbean and the welcome he had experienced wherever he went on his mother's island had given him the feeling of a new lease of life. He had Martita's company and help, and in Puerto Rico he could take his long morning walks throughout the winter—in Prades in recent years the cold had kept him prisoner within his house for as much as four months. Personally, he was happier than he had ever been. The world seemed to have opened for him again notwithstanding the restrictions he still maintained for himself. The new festival, from the outset much more ambitious than Prades, was both challenge and opportunity. The first concert was scheduled for the night of April 22, 1957, in the theater on the palm-studded campus of the University of Puerto Rico in Rio Piedras; members of the orchestra arrived for rehearsals a week earlier, and Casals went to the airport to meet their plane.

23

—————·•·—————

Pablo Casals arrived at the University Theater ahead of schedule for the first rehearsal of the initial Festival Casals de Puerto Rico, not long after nine in the morning of April 16, 1957. He was in good spirits and vigorous—during his visit to Mexico the year before he had allowed doctors to examine him thoroughly and they had delivered a serious but mystified opinion that his constitution and reflexes were those of a man of thirty-five. The orchestra was already in place, and several hundred spectators had gained admission to sit quietly in the large hall. The decoration of the auditorium was subdued by comparison to the exuberant interior of the Palau de la Música, but Casals felt for an instant that he was preparing once more to step before his own Barcelona orchestra.

Casals walked to the podium and greeted the members of the orchestra, who had risen, scanning the faces with eyes that were bright behind his round metal-rimmed glasses. He was glad that they were here—and that he was—he said; they should not really rehearse, but just play "as to get to know each other." First they went through a Mozart symphony (number 29). A high stool had been placed on the podium so that Casals could rehearse with less expenditure of effort, but he kept jumping up from it to urge

[493]

the orchestra on. (Among his last cautions to Enrique, who had sailed a few days earlier to begin preparations for the eighth Prades festival, had been that the sixteen-year-younger brother not over-extend himself—"rehearsing is tremendously tiring.")

The stage of the University Theater was hot even under mini-mal stage lighting, but the air-conditioning was not on out of con-sideration for Casals (who denounced it as "unnatural") and he was perspiring heavily. After a rest break, he started a run-through of Schubert's "Unfinished" symphony. Moments later he suddenly put down his baton, mumbled "Thank you, gentlemen," and stag-gered from the podium. He was helped into a bare dressing room off the backstage area. By this time an intense pain that had struck his lower chest had radiated into the left arm; he was drenched with sweat and nauseated.

Dr. José Passalacqua, Casals' physician, reached the University within half an hour and administered a sedative and medication to lessen the pain. Dr. Ramón Suarez, a heart specialist, arrived and confirmed that Casals had suffered a heart attack. Casals, who insisted on going home rather than to a hospital, remained at the theater, conscious the entire time, while a hospital bed and oxygen equipment were set up in the calle Bucaré apartment. Repeatedly he said to Martita, Schneider, and the doctors "What a shame—it is such a wonderful orchestra!"

In the long night meeting of festival and Commonwealth offi-cials, Martita, and others, the decision was made to continue with the festival in Casals' honor, whatever happened in the next hours and days. The musicians agreed, and Alexander Schneider took over rehearsals. Governor Luis Muñoz Marín faced a dilemma. The skill of Puerto Rican doctors matched that of their colleagues any-where and some of them were internationally known and re-spected. But Muñoz realized, and Casals' doctors agreed, that if the famous patient died there would be unjustified comment against Puerto Rico unless their actions included calling in the best-known medical name of the period. The Governor telephoned Paul Dudley White, the distinguished cardiologist who had treated President Dwight D. Eisenhower after his heart attack.

Within fifteen minutes of his arrival at the San Juan airport, some sixty-five hours after the seizure, Dr. White was at Casals' bedside. He found the patient sleeping, breathing normally, with good color. After examining the electrocardiograms, consultation with the local doctors, and a late-morning examination after Casals woke, White reported that Pablo Casals had suffered an acute anterior myocardial infarction, a serious heart attack. Casals had survived seventy-two crisis hours; White agreed with the medication being given. The patient must, of course, remain in bed and bring his weight down from its about-170-pound level, but White gave a "fair but guarded" prognosis. Through everything Casals continued to communicate in four languages, speaking Catalan to Martita and his sister-in-law María, French with Schneider, Spanish with the Puerto Ricans, and English with Dr. White.

Casals was confined to bed for a month, although he began brief periods sitting up in an armchair ten days after the attack. He had constant attention. Enrique's wife María was on hand, but the person Casals most wanted near him was Martita. She was nearby at all times in spite of María's repeated plaint to the doctors: "Do you think it is *safe* for a man in his condition to have a pretty young girl with him so much of the time?" Alexander Schneider, busy with rehearsals during the period of the festival, came by as often as three times a day. He was able to report the orchestra and soloists, who included Horszowski, Rudolf Serkin, and Isaac Stern, playing "like gods" to full, enthusiastic houses. Schneider conducted from the concertmaster's seat throughout; there was an empty chair on the podium. In the first days of Casals' convalescence there were often five or six friends and musicians in the apartment through the night, wanting to be nearby and ready to help.

As the first Festival Casals de Puerto Rico closed, the members of the orchestra stood in place around the empty podium, instruments in hand, as a recording of Casals' performance of "The Song of the Birds" was played. A large photograph of this moment, signed by each participant, was presented a few days later to the convalescing Maestro.

Among the medical professionals most faithfully in attendance during the first five weeks of Casals' recuperation was a young Puerto Rican doctor, Heber Amaury Rosa Silva, a close friend of Muñoz Marín and his wife and an acquaintance of the Montañez family since Martita's schooldays. He had been invited to the Governor's country house outside San Juan the day of Casals' seizure and arrived to find a state of crisis. He offered his services and a few hours later was asked to come to Casals' apartment. He spent the night with the patient, and his presence and medical knowledge seemed to reassure Casals. He came back every night for five weeks, sitting in the sickroom when Casals was wakeful and getting what sleep he could at other times. A warm rapport developed between the musician and the young physician, whom Casals would later call "the most European man in Puerto Rico." Dr. Rosa Silva's interest in music and art helped engage Casals' mind when he felt like talking—which he invariably did when he was awake, from the beginning of his recovery.

One of Dr. Rosa Silva's most lasting memories of Pablo Casals came from the first days of the convalescence. Casals, still under fairly heavy sedation for considerable pain, knew that a godchild of his was seriously ill in an apartment on the ground floor of the house. One morning about seven Casals turned to Dr. Rosa Silva and said "He has died." Rosa shook his head. "No; he is gone," Casals insisted. "I cannot hear the crying any more. I know. I remember. So many of my brothers and sisters stopped crying. . . ." Moments later the screams of the child's mother were heard. To Martita, Casals said "My mother used to sound like that."

Within two months after his heart attack Casals was walking six blocks every morning at a normal pace. His weight was down twenty pounds and, without consulting his doctors, he had begun to practice again, playing the piano intermittently for about three hours a day. Progress on the cello (at first only five minutes at a time) was much slower and frustrated Casals; he could not summon the necessary strength to the fingers of the left hand, and the doubt haunted him that he might ever recover well enough to play again. Still, he said in a letter to Paul Dudley White on the twenty-fourth of June, he was recovering "really wonderfully" and felt very well: "I am beginning to play the cello again. This will take more time because my left hand is not strong enough and is stiff and painful. It is also lack of practice. Yet, I notice that I make progress every day."

Alexander Schneider, who more than any other person had held the first Festival Casals together by force of personality, devotion, and musicianship, at the end of the festival returned to New York. From there he wrote Martita before leaving for Europe, enclosing a purposely undated letter to be given to Casals whenever she judged best, since most of it dealt with programs and soloists for the 1958 festival, including the suggestion that Casals consider inviting a young musician named Leonard Bernstein to perform and conduct. Schneider assured Casals that his strength would certainly return in a few weeks. One does not unlearn or forget perfectly natural physical movements, he said, "and since we are musicians, the movement of playing an instrument has certainly become a part of our daily physical movements."

The most important thing is the mind, and Schneider told Casals he had never seen him so clear in that area as he now was, which should give everyone—most of all Casals—confidence he would be able to do anything he wished within a short time. "God bless Martita, who is so good to you! Yes, you both have every reason to be very happy!"

While he was recovering, Casals had time to muse on the marvel of the intricate mechanism of the human heart and the miracle of its functioning and its capacity to heal, but then and later he unhesitatingly gave most of the credit for his recovery to Martita. From the moment of the heart attack she had been near him day and night, grasping immediately the full course of the medication, sensing every fluctuation of mood, offering unwavering reassurance, and according to Casals' wishes taking over decisions that could not be postponed.

Martita had brought a sense of renewed life into Casals' daily existence when she went to study with him in Prades. At the beginning of 1955, as their association grew closer, she added another considerable blessing: the energetic practicality and organizational ability of a twentieth-century Western woman. All his adult life Casals remained innocent of a great many operational details of daily living other mortals have to know something about, and his life had never gone so smoothly or comfortably as after Martita entered it. Old friends seeing Casals again after early 1955 found that he was not only in better spirits generally but also that his everyday clothing had a new flair. Impeccable when he appeared for a concert performance, Casals elsewhere tended not to be specially conscious of the sometimes venerable state of his suits and the cardigans he wore. After the move to Puerto Rico and the heart attack, Marta's presence made life daily more precious to him. It was she alone who could—and did—raise his spirits when they began to sink; no one else could cause him to laugh when self-pity and the unspoken fear of not being able to play well again set in. Never for a moment did Casals doubt her belief in his full recovery, nor did even her closest friends ever gain from her words or behavior any indication of discouragement or flagging hope.

Martita and Casals had fallen mutually and profoundly in love, and Casals felt he had discovered happiness for the first time in his life. If love should have neither limit nor boundary, wide differences in age or the opinion of others need not affect a great love between two people. Both were determined as well as courageous and were undeterred by shock and early opposition on the part of both families. There had been an obstacle to their marriage until the spring of 1957. Casals and Susan Metcalfe had not seen each other for nearly thirty years, although there had been no divorce; she had been living since 1929 in Paris, where she gave her last known recital in 1951 at the École Normale de Musique. In the early 1950s Casals had learned that she was ill and unattended, and from Prades he helped with arrangements for her care until she returned to New Jersey to live with her sisters. By 1956 he did not know with certainty that she was alive, so legal steps for a divorce were initiated. The decree became final about the time of Casals' heart attack.

Marta and Casals were married in San Juan on August 3, 1957, a Saturday, in a civil ceremony in the calle Bucaré apartment, attended by Alfredo Matilla and Dr. José Passalacqua as witnesses. A subsequent religious ceremony was performed by a Passionist father who was a friend of the couple, in the presence of a few close friends in the Capilla de la Piedad in Isla Verde in San Juan. "I was aware at the time that some people noted a certain discrepancy in our ages," Casals said for publication some years later, "—a bridegroom of course is not usually thirty years older than his father-in-law. But Martita and I were not too concerned about what others thought; it was, after all, we who were getting married—not they. If some had misgivings, I can only say with joy that our love has deepened in the intervening years. . . ." Word reached the press on the fifth of August, the day after the couple sailed for Europe aboard the *Antilles*. Very few people had been informed; Casals' brother Luis and his family in the San Salvador villa first heard the news in a radio broadcast.

The heart attack kept Casals away from Prades for the eighth

*Marta and Pablo Casals after their wedding in
Puerto Rico, August 1957*

festival there and although the newlyweds went to Zermatt in late
summer, he did not teach in the 1957 classes. At Zermatt he and
Martita were married a third time, in a Protestant ceremony, when
Ernest Cristen, a Swiss clergyman-artist-writer and longtime friend
and admirer of Casals, came to see the newlyweds and insisted
he give them his blessing ritually.

Some old friends of Casals who did not know Martita remained distant for a time. Others responded quickly. One of the
warmest congratulations came from Queen Elisabeth, who wrote
from the Château de Stuyvenberg in October: "How happy I am,
knowing dear little Martita, to learn that you are both united. My
thoughts were with you while you were sick; what happiness that

*Pablo Casals conducts the Puerto Rico
Symphony with Marta Casals as cello soloist,
in 1959*

you have been able, with your spendid constitution and your well-known vitality, to overcome the illness! I wish you the happiness you deserve, since you have dispensed it with open hands—and bow—to others, to humanity, which has such need of goodness and beauty! . . . I hope that I shall be able to see you again, dear Maître, *dear* Pau Casals, next year at Prades. . . ."

In the winter of 1957–1958 Casals conducted the first public concerts of the new Puerto Rico Symphony Orchestra, in San Juan, Ponce, and Mayagüez, and accepted presidency of the Conservatory of Music of Puerto Rico, of which Argentinian conductor-composer Juan José Castro was appointed director. Casals' residence in Puerto Rico and his active participation in these ventures had given impetus to passage of a special appropriation for them by the Commonwealth legislature. Both the symphony and the conservatory were founded under the aegis of the Festival Casals; from the first Casals had said that they, in addition to an annual music festival, were necessary for the permanent cultural benefit of the island. Casals also tried to interest labor leaders in establishment of cultural and musical societies comparable to the Workingmen's Concert Association in Catalonia—either in cooperation with the Institute of Culture of Puerto Rico or independently. The first efforts were not successful, a result more of almost total lack of understanding and organization than of direct opposition.

Casals and Martita could have bought a house in the well-built-up Santurce section of San Juan, but Casals preferred to be farther from the center, where he could live and work in quiet. They therefore built a pleasant seaside house at kilometer marker K2 H3 on the old Isla Verde highway, near one waterside limit of the city. By the time they had moved in, final preparations for the second Festival Casals de Puerto Rico were under way, with Casals very much in the middle of things. He was scheduled to play in some of the programs but was frustrated when the doctors continued to forbid him to conduct. He was also experiencing angina pectoris pains during his brisk half- to three-quarter-hour morning walks; the discomfort subsided when he slowed down and was not felt after the doctors prescribed a nitroglycerin tablet before he set out. He had the same pains in moments of emotional stress, of which there were many, despite Martita's generally successful efforts to maintain a calm environment around him.

It was one thing to suggest to Casals that he remain tranquil, another for him to stay calm. His mind was unimpaired by either the passage of time or illness; there were many disturbing things in the world; and, as he wrote Paul Dudley White in April 1958, he felt emotion more strongly than ever. "My life is made up of emotion, and I can't help it[;] but I feel stronger every day. . . . After a strong emotion in music, playing it or listening to it, I feel an oppression in my chest which passes quickly after, but it leaves me with weak feeling . . . the only after-effect that I have noticed after my illness. I continue my usual activities. I am even astonished myself at the fact that I still can play as before; I have my long walks every morning along the beach without feeling tired; eat well, sleep well. I am really so thankful. . . ."

The seventeen-day festival went well, and Casals' "usual activities" in the course of it included playing in concert four Beethoven sonatas and as part of the ensemble two Brahms sextets. He also played chamber music at home with some of the

The Casals' Isla Verde house, San Juan

musicians who came to visit. He left with Martita soon afterward for the festival in Prades, in good health and spirits. He was not yet aware of some local voices complaining because the San Juan concerts did not include modern music, especially the work of Puerto Rican composers, and because so few island musicians were members of the orchestra. There was plenty of time; he would hear these arguments in the years ahead.

At Prades the Casals stayed in a small house adjoining the spa of the Grand Thermal Hotel in Molitg-les-Bains, which was their home during the three-week 1958 Prades season and for the eight succeeding summers. It was a pleasant place in a pleasant region of the world, a constant in their lives until Casals' ninetieth year. Here, as everywhere, some of those Casals called the "unbelievers" came to know and respect and adore the new bride. In Prades as in Puerto Rico, Marta Casals saw to the details of running the house with very little help, and was almost miracu-

Casals continues to rehearse the Schubert
"Trout" quintet for a San Juan festival concert,
oblivious of a vigorous discussion going on
around him.

lously on call whenever her husband summoned to help with a precise translation, supply a missing fact or name, or participate in a decision. To her duties at Prades were added the necessity of coping with a stream of international journalists, musicians, the "amiable nymphs" who continued to gather (and felt scarcely less proprietary about Casals after his marriage), the festival organization, and the people of Prades. Schedules were met, people were received and charmed. Marta Casals never seemed ruffled. People began to marvel, and those able to look at the couple without preconceptions were warmed by an aura of deep and secure happiness between two highly gifted people.

Following the 1958 Zermatt classes Casals joined Mieczyslaw Horszowski and Sándor Végh in two private recitals in homage to Beethoven in the composer's restored birthplace in Bonn, an event originally scheduled for 1957. This appearance, Casals' first in Germany since the early 1930s, made certain of Casals' close musical colleagues thoroughly unhappy, especially those who had sought his blessing on the campaign to bar Furtwängler, Cassadó, and others from engagements in the United States after World War II. Casals thought of his visit to Bonn both as a private homage to one of the supreme masters of music and as a gesture that expressed his feeling of affection for those Germans who believed in personal liberty and in peace.

The Beethovenhaus was a dismal spot for a recital; the acoustics were far from satisfactory, disconcerting both the artists and the recording engineers, and the piano was so placed that the musicians could not always see each other. But, for Casals especially, the event was shot through with tremendous emotion and sentimental association: he played some of the works on a cello that had belonged to Beethoven. During one of the concerts the director of the Beethovenhaus Association presented Casals with an impressive diploma that proclaimed him a member. Casals duly thanked the gentleman, then told the invited audience that he actually had been a member since before the war—the one that began in 1914.

As the years succeeded one another, Casals' activity and drive did not lessen appreciably as his focus shifted and broadened. When he returned to Prades in 1958, his physician friend René Puig greeted him and urged him to slacken the pace for a little while, to rest, to take a holiday before proceeding. "No," Casals told Puig. "To stop, to retire even for a short time, is to begin to die."

Casals had definitely not retired, and by 1958 he had further defined his role in the world. In 1947 he stilled the public voice of his cello for three years, an anguished protest to rouse an insensitive world's conscience about political repression in his homeland. He vowed that he would not give public violoncello concerts in any country that recognized or aided the authoritarian government in Spain. Many individuals had been touched and impressed, but not their governments.

When he agreed to the Bach Festival at Prades in 1950, it was chiefly as conductor, the *primus inter pares* who would lead the procession that honored the greatest of composers. He performed a Bach solo suite to begin six orchestral evenings and one chamber-music evening of Bach cello sonatas with piano during the first Prades summer, but he felt that in the local church he was playing as if he had been in his own house, for audiences he considered his friends. The joy that Casals could be heard again by more than a handful of guests was so great that few questioned his rationale. (After he made his home in Puerto Rico, it was natural and acceptable to him to join fellow musicians occasionally both as player and as leader in programs during the festivals that bore his name.) As the crowds flocked to Prades and the unique spirit of the Bach homage spread, Casals realized that the public still cared about him very much, and he could not escape an awareness that if he was to convince the world of the things that were most important to him he must be heard in some fashion. He would not and could not rescind his vow not to perform elsewhere, but in certain circumstances he could allow himself to conduct.

The distinction between playing cello and conducting, always clear in Casals' mind, began to become clear in his actions within a year, when he conducted works that included his own compositions in a benefit in Zürich. Even so, in the succeeding years he had conducted relatively little outside Prades—the outstanding occasions included the second half of an evening in his honor at the Sorbonne in October 1957 and the first concerts of the new Puerto Rico Symphony in the winter of 1957–1958.

In 1958 Casals was not the same man he had been at Prades in 1947. He had continued to grow, and there was now more than the fate of Spain on his mind. Like many others, Pablo Casals was certain that the politicians and the scientists had brought the world to the brink of catastrophe by the competitive testing of nuclear weapons. Bertrand Russell, the British mathematician and philosopher Casals had met many years before in England, had been protesting the arms race publicly since the mid-1950s and had been persistent in his appeals that Casals join the effort. Only a few days after Casals' heart attack the Nobel Prize committee issued a "Statement of Conscience" by Albert Schweitzer (who had been awarded the Peace Prize in 1953), and on the last three days of April 1958 three radio appeals Schweitzer broadcast from Oslo, "Peace or Atomic War?" impressed Casals greatly. In Zürich in 1951 Casals had urged Schweitzer to protest as well as create. Casals realized that he too must speak out, in every forum he could accept, against an overwhelming danger to all people.

He was therefore interested in a request that he play in the General Assembly Hall of United Nations headquarters in October 1958, during the concert celebrating the thirteenth anniversary of the world organization. The invitation from Secretary-General Dag Hammarskjöld was brought personally by Franco Passigli, son of Casals' friend Alberto Passigli, who had succeeded his father as director of the *Amici della Musica* in Florence and joined the United Nations staff late in 1957. Hammarskjöld knew of Passigli's musical interests, and during their first conference the two discussed ways of improving the artistic level of the annual concert on United Nations Day and the one in December to mark Human Rights Day. When he learned of the Passigli family's close friendship with Casals, Hammarskjöld instructed Franco Passigli to do everything he could to bring Casals to the United Nations. In February 1958, Passigli made an unpublicized trip to Puerto Rico and spent three days with Casals trying to persuade him to accept.

The suggestion appealed to Casals, but at first he rejected it. His vow not to play publicly in any country that had diplomatic relations with Franco Spain had not changed. Eventually he understood that the United Nations headquarters is an extraterritorial enclave, although situated physically along the East River on Manhattan Island. He granted that the organization was an important forum, despite its admission of Spain. He could both speak and play there, addressing the entire world without breaking the letter or the spirit of his vow.

Casals had hoped to be able to deliver his message to the representatives of the United Nations in the General Assembly hall itself, but the organization's rules permitted addresses there only by members of delegations or officials of member governments. He therefore recorded his personal statement in Geneva several days before the October 24 concert, speaking successively in English, French, Spanish, and Italian.

> If at my age I have come here today [he said clearly and slowly], it is not because anything has changed in my moral attitude or in the restrictions that I have imposed upon myself and my career as an artist for all these years, but because today all else becomes secondary in comparison to the great and perhaps mortal danger threatening all humanity. . . . The extraordinary scientific discoveries of our century which

some great intellects, in their thirst for knowledge, have achieved, are now being exploited for the construction of instruments of monstrous destructiveness. Confusion and fear have invaded the whole world; misunderstood nationalism, fanaticism, political dogmas and lack of liberty and justice are feeding mistrust and hostility that make the collective danger greater every day, yet, the desire for peace is felt by every human being. . . . This desire has been manifested again and again in the face of the peril menacing all of us, by many distinguished personalities, in scientific writings, in the world Press, and above all by that great citizen of the world, Dr. Albert Schweitzer.

The anguish of the world caused by the continuation of nuclear danger is increasing every day. . . . How I wish that there could be a tremendous movement of protest in all countries, and especially from the mothers, that would impress those who have the power to prevent this catastrophe.

All nuclear experiments ought to be stopped altogether and I profoundly hope that the negotiations in the near future will end in an agreement that will make this possible; only later, when calm and confidence have been reestablished, then the work of the scientists could be taken up again, but only under such conditions as would benefit humanity.

In order to resolve their problems, the conflicting forces must regard as the basis for their discussions the inhumanity and uselessness of war. . . . The biggest and most powerful nations have the greater duty and responsibility for keeping peace . . . the great masses in these countries, as in every other country, want the understanding and mutual co-operation of their fellow men. It is for the Governments and those in power to see to it that the achievement of this desire will not become impossible and thus cause the terrible frustration felt by all those who are not living in unconsciousness.

It seems to me that all those who believe in the dignity of man should act . . . to bring about a deeper understanding among peoples and a sincere "rapprochement" between conflicting forces. The United Nations today represents the most important hope for peace. Let us give it all power to act for our benefit. . . .

Music, this marvelous universal language understood by everyone everywhere ought to be a source of better communication among men. This is why I make a special appeal to my fellow musicians everywhere, asking each one to put the purity of his art at the service of mankind in bringing about fraternal and enlightened relationships between men the world over.

The "Hymn to Joy" of Beethoven's Ninth Symphony has become a symbol of love. And I propose that every town which has an orchestra and chorus should perform it on the same day, and have it transmitted by radio to the smallest communities and to all corners of the world; and to perform it as another prayer through music for the Peace that we all desire and wait for.

The UN thirteenth-anniversary concert was a two-hour program broadcast to forty-eight countries with segments performed in New York, Paris, and Geneva. Casals had first thought to play three cello sonatas—Bach, Beethoven, and Brahms—accompanied by Horszowski, Serkin, and Istomin, but the other music scheduled (in Paris Yehudi Menuhin and David Oistrakh playing a Bach double violin concerto, the Indian artist Ravi Shankar, and from Geneva the last movement of Beethoven's ninth symphony conducted by Ernest Ansermet) permitted only one. In New York, Charles Munch conducted the Boston Symphony Orchestra playing Arthur Honneger's fifth symphony, Secretary-General Hammarskjöld spoke briefly, then Casals and Horszowski played Bach's Sonata No. 2 in D Major, followed by "The Song of the Birds." The concert was carried widely on television as well as on radio with Casals' statement included in the transmission during intermis-

sion; it was the first time many thousands, not concertgoers, many quite young, had ever seen or heard Casals—and it was his first appearance as an elder of the human race in the cause of peace on the earth.

At a party during the week of the UN concert Casals and Fritz Kreisler met for the first time in more than thirty years. Eighty-three-year-old Kreisler was very frail and nearly blind but radiant with reminiscence and friendship. It was Kreisler who, at the height of his own fame, had announced to the New York press on Casals' return to the United States from Europe in 1914 "The monarch of the bow has arrived!" Now he reminded Casals with laughter that the last time they had performed together, in London in 1927, Casals had played the opening cello solo of the Brahms double concerto with such overwhelming beauty that Kreisler had forgotten to come in on cue. They remembered the Granados memorial concert at the Metropolitan Opera House, and Kreisler recalled their first tour together, with Harold Bauer, through the English hinterland in 1911. That night in October 1958, even Harriet Kreisler, whom Casals had found earlier the most difficult musician's wife he ever met—including Pauline Strauss—was thoroughly agreeable. Later, at a small party in Casals' honor given by Franco Passigli and his wife Pia, Casals had a long, animated conversation with Eleanor Roosevelt. Mrs. Roosevelt, at that time no longer a member of the United States delegation to the United Nations and not a close friend of the host and hostess, had accepted immediately when she learned she would have a chance to meet Casals.

Following the United Nations concert, Casals and Martita returned to Puerto Rico for rehearsals and concerts of the Puerto Rico Symphony and an unprecedented deluge of mail, more than five thousand letters and telegrams in direct response to Casals' United Nations appearance. Casals' mail had always included surprises that ranged from the touching to the bizarre. There were requests for autographed photographs, only a small number with return postage. Letters asking for money or help came frequently; even the most deranged was of concern to Casals. The occasional completely incoherent document could only be read in disbelief and put into the file.

Casals saw all the correspondence that arrived; Martita handled answers and acknowledgments without secretarial help until the first months of 1972. Messages and tributes from strangers touched Casals and reassured him that his plea for brotherhood and peace was being heard, but the letters from fellow musicians remained most vividly in his mind—from Clara Haskil, Myra Hess, Nadia Boulanger, from Horszowski, Rudolf Serkin, Rostropovich and the Oistrakhs, Isaac Stern, Alexander Schneider, Eugene Istomin, among others. The festival orchestra sent a hand-lettered message on parchment at the end of the 1961 concerts:

> To Maître Pablo Casals
> Musicians seldom have the opportunity or the inclination to express their innermost feelings. We have been so fortunate in sharing so many memorable musical moments with you that we want in some way to say thank you for the privilege of understanding your broad and powerful scope of musical interpretation.
> We are proud of being part of Festival Casals and grateful for your musical inspiration. Under your guidance, these concerts in Puerto Rico have produced musical results on a higher plane than most of us have ever experienced before and we know that your musical influences . . . produce the same wonderful results wherever you go.
> Thank you again. We are looking forward with anticipation to many more Festivals with you.

The orchestra was right. Musicians, so eloquent through their instruments, are sometimes sparing of words on paper. Even Casals, instinctively poetic, precisely articulate and almost always eager to talk, through the years never seemed really to enjoy writing letters—his messages were almost always short and restricted to essentials. Casals treasured such letters as one that came to him from a violinist who had played under his direction in the 1971 San Juan festival:

> In the hectic rush of our rehearsals and concerts we rarely get the opportunity to express to you how deeply we appreciate the privilege and pleasure of having been able to work so closely with you all these many years.
> I was especially moved this morning at our rehearsal of "El Pessebre" when I heard again this wonderful music, so full of love and beauty. . . . Each time I play it I love it more and more because I know it is your gift to us, a

gift that will remain with us always, who have had the privilege to play and hear it and let its message of love fill our hearts.

Thank you for what I have learned here. As I have felt liberated by following your way, so have and will those to whom I shall pass on the heritage you have given us, the heritage of an age of greatness not yet gone so long as you are with us. . . .

Following luncheon on an ordinary day in San Juan, Casals went to bed for a siesta of an hour or so; afterward he returned to composition or restudying scores for forthcoming concerts if there were not visitors, which was unusual. From time to time, the Casals went to friends' homes for dinner, a party, or an evening of domino-playing; Casals much preferred to remain at home, although once he reached someone else's house he enjoyed himself. When the couple entertained at home Casals was an alert and gracious host, even in his early nineties rising quickly from his own seat to move a chair into place for a woman guest. When they were alone in the evening, Martita often turned on a television set to distract Casals from preoccupation, which usually centered on music. His concentration remained such at ninety-five that it would be unbroken even when visitors arrived until Martita announced them with a virtual fanfare—when he then turned his attention instantly and fully to them. He followed television news reports with close interest (he also generally read at least two local newspapers a day and received a packet of European journals about once a week and an envelope of Spanish clippings at least that often). His responses to certain events or developments were sometimes startling: He sat until two in the morning in a friend's Vermont home watching the television transmission of the first steps by men on the moon. "It will soon be forgotten," he said, holding to the opinion in the face of a certain excitement among his companions, including Mieczyslaw Horszowski. Another friend, although disagreeing, suddenly realized that behind that opinion was the experience of an interested mind whose curiosity had spanned the development of transportation from horseback to interplanetary space vehicle.

Since, as part of the purposeful diversion and relaxation for her husband, Martita frequently turned to television, reports soon began to circulate that Casals was a passionate devotee of Westerns.

Actually, he admitted, they were all alike. The sound and the story line did not much concern him; what intrigued him was the faces, and that the good guys always won. Further, the locale and, most of all, the railway trains were reminders of his first tour in the United States. In fact, Casals spent much less time before the television screen than reports in the 1960s suggested, and after he and Martita moved in 1971 to a spacious house overlooking San Juan he spent a great deal of nonworking time on a small terrace that looked out over trees, flowers and the buildings of the growing city toward the distant sea. Here, more often than not, he read or studied scores.

In the spring of 1960 Casals returned to California after thirty-five years, to conduct a series of master classes under the auspices of the Music Extension Division of the University of California at Berkeley. These classes, photographed with concealed cameras under the direction of Nathan Kroll, became Casals' most famous teaching sessions, still visible on educational television more than a decade afterward. They give a sense of Casals' mature public teaching method—evocative, coaxing, suggestive, subtly humorous, poetic—which one British observer found Socratic, nervous students found terrifying but revealing, and many auditors found romantic and magical.

In July 1960, Casals went for the first time to Marlboro, Vermont, site of the summer music school and festival of which the guiding spirit was Rudolf Serkin. The two had developed a close and affectionate relationship during the Prades Bach Festival and played together frequently thereafter. Casals had heard about Serkin as a prodigiously talented Czech youngster in Vienna at the end of World War I; Serkin's piano teacher, Richard Robert, and Arnold Schönberg, one of Serkin's composition professors, were acquaintances of Casals. But their paths seldom crossed after Serkin played for Casals in the house of Francesco von Mendelssohn in the 1920s. Serkin played many concerts and joint recitals in Europe with violinist Adolf Busch, whose daughter Irene he married. In 1936 he came to the United States at Toscanini's invitation to give distinguished performances of two Mozart concertos with the New York Philharmonic, after which he was recognized in North America, as he already was abroad, as one of the most poetic and sensitive pianists of his time. In the late

1940s, Serkin formed the Marlboro School of Music with Adolf Busch (who had made his home on a large farm in nearby Guilford, Vermont, at the beginning of World War II), Martial Singher—also associated with the Busch family by marriage—Marcel Moyse, and others. A summer music festival, with weekend concerts open to the public, began officially in 1950 on the campus of the small, experimental Marlboro College. By the time of Pablo Casals' first visit ten years later, the Marlboro Festival had begun to draw audiences willing to travel long distances to hear superlative performances of chamber music.

Enchanted by the rolling farmland, the hills and forests, the villages and ponds and stands of birches in the opulent summer green of southern Vermont, Casals said repeatedly from the time of his first visit to Marlboro that nowhere else was he constantly so conscious of the affinity between nature and music.

He was equally delighted by the concept and mystique of the Marlboro music colony, epitomized by the sign alongside the road at the entrance to the campus: CAUTION—MUSICIANS AT PLAY. Marlboro was not a school in a formal sense. As many as a hundred musicians—ranging from such seasoned artists as Horszowski, violist Boris Kroyt and violinist Felix Galimir, Alexander Schneider and his brother Mischa, Serkin himself, and first-chair musicians from major American orchestras to younger professional-caliber musicians with less experience selected among applicants from the Americas, Europe, and the Orient—assembled from late June through mid-August to make music together, first of all for their own pleasure and edification. Groups of almost all conceivable combinations of instruments worked together—morning, afternoon, late into the night—polishing a repertoire of

FACING PAGE
Characteristic sights at Marlboro. (Top left)
Casals greets Indian musician Ravi Shankar
and family after a master class and (top right)
talks with Rudolf Serkin during a rehearsal
break; (center) rehearsing the festival orchestra;
(bottom left) visiting at home with pianist
Eugene Istomin and Hungarian cellist Miklós
Perényi; (bottom right) leaving rehearsal

*Marta Casals backstage at Marlboro, with
Boris Kroyt beside her, is aware only of the
music and her husband as he conducts.*

compositions from Bach to twentieth-century composers' work
still in manuscript, learning by rehearsing together and performing
for the other participants in informal evening concerts. The weekend public concerts were incidental during Marlboro's early years
for most of the musicians.

Casals never felt an urge to take a holiday from music and
could never really understand those of his colleagues who, if they
could, spent a summer away from it. For him, almost incessant
music-making in the informal environment, with good musicians
drawn together by a common devotion to music, was absolutely
ideal.

The Russian musical commune Casals remembered from early
in the century may have been even more rustic than the Vermont

A master class at Marlboro

surroundings, but in some respects it could not have been more informal. The custom that startled Casals most was the tossing of paper napkins (and occasionally food) during mealtimes, a practice he supposed was an expression of exuberance and good will, with the first shot sometimes fired by Rudolf Serkin himself. A photograph of Casals and Queen Élisabeth of the Belgians, taken in 1964 at Marlboro, shows the two venerable guests sitting at table under an open umbrella presumably as protection from the danger of flying breadcrusts and spaghetti. Such folkways Casals took with good grace, and he welcomed young people backstage or at the comfortable, attractively renovated farmhouse he and Martita occupied. Often two or three of the musicians came to talk, sitting in good weather outdoors under the great sugar maple in front of the house or on the back rough-stone terrace. Here, too, Casals sat when the entire music school came for a summer outing in the rolling meadow behind the house, listening to the music of informal student ensembles that furnished the entertainment.

It was the aura of music-making that gave Casals a special joy and fulfillment at Marlboro. For the participants, for a remarkably self-contained six weeks in the summer, making music together was the center of existence. Being a part of Marlboro, according to the American composer Leon Kirchner who was composer-in-residence there for years, was living on the Magic Mountain. Pablo Casals was absolutely at home.

Casals' first Marlboro visits lasted only two weeks at most because of his participation in the Prades Festival and other summer commitments abroad; he missed 1961 completely. Later he remained the entire Malboro season, conducting portions of concerts and holding a series of master classes each year. In 1960 he conducted an orchestra of music-school participants in performances of Mozart and of Beethoven's fourth symphony. In succeeding summers he conducted in public concerts more Beethoven (six of the nine symphonies, two concertos and the Choral Fantasy with Serkin as piano soloist), Mozart, Haydn, Handel, Brahms, Wagner, Mendelssohn, Schumann, Schubert, Bach. Through the 1960s Columbia Masterworks made a number of notable records of works conducted by Casals at Marlboro, in addition to a series of highly respected records of chamber music performed by others.

Marlboro had established its own stature and identity by the cooperative excellence of the musicians who participated every summer, but the presence of Casals added a special luster for almost everyone who saw him conduct or teach or came into contact with him there. There were a few irreconcilable private dissents: For some, Casals' free, "impure" approach to Bach was heresy, and a few blamed Casals for what they considered the cult of personality that centered on him. For the others it was the extraordinary experience of being in the presence of a great musician still able to practice his art.

The 1960 presidential election in the United States was of particular interest to Casals. A letter over his signature was published in *The New York Times* on March 18; it urged that the American people vote the Democratic ticket, saying that the hope of a world subjected to dictatorship and the forces of evil depended on the victory of that party. After the election Casals wrote President-elect John F. Kennedy, congratulating him and wishing him well in the fulfillment of his mission. "Dictators," he also wrote,

> are . . . an inconceivable anachronism in the road to freedom . . . being paved for the world by the United States of America. Dictators are inconceivable in Spain, a people

with deep spiritual reserves accustomed to the role of leadership in civilization and to the cultural and philosophic dynamism of great men. Neither is dictatorship conceivable over the Russian people who are endowed with surging and meaningful potentialities, or for that matter over Latin American, Asian or Far East countries. This is the gigantic issue before the people who have elected you as their President. May God help you in discharging this tremendous responsibility.

The President-elect replied in what Casals found a most gracious letter thanking him for his confidence.

In 1961 President Kennedy proposed to honor Casals at a state dinner in the White House, asking if afterward he would play for the President and the First Lady and their guests. Casals declined the dinner, explaining that like many artists he preferred not to eat a full meal before performing or conducting. The real reason was his fear that acceptance of such an honor could suggest that he had relaxed his stand on the moral indefensibility of the American government's support of the Franco regime. (Six years later, after Casals had become profoundly disturbed by the warfare in Indochina and the morality of the United States role in it, Vice President Hubert Humphrey urged him once more to accept an invitation to a White House dinner. This time his conscience would not let him accept, but the decision preoccupied Casals for days and made him physically so ill that he curtailed his stay in Vermont, canceled scheduled engagements abroad, and returned to Puerto Rico.)

An alternative plan was presented by Abe Fortas, the attorney and amateur violinist who had originally suggested the dinner for Casals. The state dinner, which Casals would not attend, would be in honor of Governor Luis Muñoz Marín of the Commonwealth of Puerto Rico; a hundred fifty guests would be invited afterward to hear Casals, Horszowski, and Schneider play. It was understood that, if possible, there would be an opportunity for Casals to have a private conversation with the President. After much thought Casals accepted. He would go to Washington because of his admiration for Kennedy, which had grown since the inauguration, and because it would allow him personally to encourage the American President in his efforts for peace. He considered the evening a private entertainment and his participation would, therefore, not be a violation of his vow. He wrote Kennedy: "I know that your aim is to work for peace based on justice, understanding and freedom for all mankind. These ideals have always been my ideals, and have determined the most important decisions—and the most important renunciations—in my life."

The day of the concert, November 13, 1961, Pablo Casals had an hour alone with the President of the United States. They talked first about personal things, Casals' career and his encounters with Theodore Roosevelt, Kennedy's earlier life. Casals, whose assessment of other people was instant, felt tremendously drawn to the younger man who seemed to him so natural and unaffected, at once young and perceptive. They spoke of the threats to the hopes for world peace, Casals remembered, and about the prospects for a disarmament agreement. Casals naturally brought up the subject of the unabated American support of Spain and the maintenance of American military bases there. Kennedy listened gravely and sympathetically, explaining that an American chief of state is often faced with inherited situations and alignments and that there are many circumstances in which he cannot follow a course of action he might personally like. He did repeat that his goal was peace and liberty everywhere in the world and that he would do everything in his power to obtain them.

The concert itself was one of the luminous cultural events of the Kennedy administration. There was an unusual sense of excitement beforehand. Casals, Horszowski, and Schneider rehearsed in the Diplomatic Reception Room for three hours the preceding day. Letitia Baldridge, one of Mrs. Kennedy's secretaries, looked in on the Signal Corps personnel who were taping the session. These sergeants, who generally showed nothing but boredom at such times, were obviously transfixed by what they heard through their earphones, totally involved in the music Casals and his colleagues were making. After the dinner for Muñoz, the President and his party joined the guests gathered in the East Room for the music. The formally attired audience included many of the successful American composers, conductors Eugene Ormandy, Leopold Stokowski, and Leonard Bernstein, Cabinet officers, journalists and music critics, diplomats, patrons of the arts, and Washington social leaders.

Before the music, President Kennedy introduced Governor Muñoz and the three musicians and spoke briefly of the arts as integral to a free society. "The work of all artists," he said, "stands

*After the concert in the East Room of the
White House, November 13, 1961*

as a symbol of human freedom and no one has enriched that freedom more signally than Pablo Casals."

The serious program ran over an hour, in contrast to the more
usual fare of short and preferably light pieces not longer than five
minutes that had been requested of performers since the time of
Mrs. Theodore Roosevelt's musicales. It was also the first recital
Casals had given in a very long time. The opening number, a
Mendelssohn trio in D minor, lasted slightly more than half an
hour. "The moment Señor Casals drew his bow across the strings,
it was with the power and authority he always has had. Despite
his age, he has retained complete muscular control, and even in
a long, slow bow there was not the least waver at the tip," reported
Paul Henry Lang in the New York *Herald Tribune*. A set of
five short pieces by Couperin and an allegro and adagio for cello
and piano by Schumann followed; the program concluded with
Casals playing "The Song of the Birds," accompanied by

Horszowksi. The musicians rose, as had the audience; Casals walked over to embrace the President, and the formal portion of a notable evening ended. The audience dispersed gradually, "leaving," Lang said, "with a lingering affection that played on the vanished scene."

The evening had been straight out of the eighteenth century, reported *Time* magazine; "it might almost have been a concert led by Haydn at the court of the Esterhazys or a command performance by C. P. E. Bach for Frederick the Great." The advantage the common folk two centuries later had was also being able to hear the music—Columbia taped the live performance and issued a record album.

A small supper upstairs in the White House gave Casals and his colleagues an opportunity to talk with the Kennedys and a handful of guests, including Alice Roosevelt Longworth, who recalled momentarily with Casals the evening Casals had played and she had listened in the same house nearly fifty-eight years before. The exuberant comments about the music continued through the supper party; even Casals permitted himself an "It went well."

Later in the evening the President excused himself; Mrs. Kennedy remained with the guests. When Casals and Marta left, Jacqueline Kennedy went with them to their car. The autumn night seemed very chilly to Casals, and he was worried that Mrs. Kennedy would catch cold, but she stood smiling and waving until the limousine had driven away.

24

────•──••──•────

To be more than casually in contact with Pablo Casals from the outset of the 1960s was to participate in life rather than to celebrate increasing age, and the succeeding ten years were for him as productive and very nearly as active as the decade before World War II. Even in 1950, before the first Prades Festival, when he was willing to come to some terms with a distressing world, he told *Life* magazine's Lael Wertenbaker of his deepest inner life: "Every day I am reborn and every day I must begin again." Sixteen years later, on the eve of his widely publicized ninetieth birthday, he told another *Life* writer he had never enjoyed nature more than he then did and had never had a stronger feeling of belonging to nature.

About the same time, looking toward the sea sparkling in early sunlight far below the terrace of his country retreat on a steep hillside above the eastern shore of Puerto Rico, he turned to a friend disposed to speak of philosophical questions and broke off a discussion of religion with "I never felt so young!" Five years later, Casals came out from an afternoon session of work at his cello to tell a guest from the United States that, although he seldom performed in public any longer, he was actually playing better

*(Left) During the trip to Japan in the spring
of 1961; (right) Caesarea, Israel, September 1961*

than ever. The constant cello work—"I practice as if I am going
to live a thousand years"—like the restudying of scores, went on:
the steady, unrelenting steps to further refinement, toward the perfection that is always just a step beyond. The marvel of the Bach
solo-cello suites, at which he worked for more than eighty years,
is the fact that after that length of time it was still possible to
discover new meanings, fresh nuances, with every new playing.
And in the hot, muggy July of 1972 Casals was vigorously instilling
fresh understanding and beauty into the Marlboro orchestra's readings of Beethoven, Mozart, Haydn, and Mendelssohn. As in 1973
with the seldom-performed Haydn symphony number 96 and early
Beethoven symphonies, while conducting each weekend in July,
he was realizing with a superlative orchestra in each performance a
notable, coherent beauty that exhibited a perception that was still
widening. He left before the end of the Marlboro season to travel
to Israel, where conducting appearances and master classes were
scheduled for him through August.

Because Casals had reached an advanced age, it was both easy and understandable for press and public as well as Casals' friends to stress the geriatric marvel and ignore the subtler miracle of the steady continuing operation of genius. Casals himself unintentionally contributed to the picture by complaining of assorted pains and infirmities to many visitors (people who had known him well in the 1920s remembered similar plaints). What frustrated him most in his nineties was his inability to walk as easily as he had in earlier years, both a side effect of medication prescribed in the years after his heart attack for various transient problems and the result of hours of sitting. Strangers hearing a great and venerated man proclaim convincingly that he could scarcely walk anymore tended to assess his condition as more serious than was the case, and reports of Casals' feebleness spread, to be dispelled whenever he was on the podium or when the weather was fine and he was feeling particularly well.

Casals continued his international travels. He had long wanted to see the Far East and in April 1961 he and Marta traveled to Japan. Japan had become the best market for Casals' records, as it had for those of many other Western classical musicians. His presence was treated as a great event, and a reception was given for him by the Crown Prince. During two weeks in Tokyo and one in Kyoto he conducted, went sightseeing with much gusto, gave master classes, and listened to several hundred youngsters between the ages of four and twelve play Bach and Haydn works they had learned by the Suzuki method. (He was greatly impressed by this feat but disconcerted that all the children wanted to kiss him afterward.)

He felt that his trips to Israel were very important, and he admired the country and its people almost without qualification. He first traveled there in September 1961, visiting Tel Aviv, Jerusalem, and Caesarea, where he conducted and performed during the concert that inaugurated a recently excavated Roman amphitheater. He also judged a cello contest, conducted master classes, played Beethoven with Rudolf Serkin, Isaac Stern, and Eugene Istomin, and talked with Premier David Ben-Gurion. (During a 1969 visit that included a performance of *El Pessebre* he had a long morning conversation with Premier Golda Meir in the course of which he spoke of his growing belief in the crucial importance of leading children to the early realization of their own uniqueness and identity; he was overjoyed when she returned in the afternoon to continue the discussion.)

In June 1963 Casals fulfilled a lifetime desire when he conducted an uncut version of Bach's *St. Matthew Passion* in Carnegie Hall, scene of many of his solo recitals between 1914 and 1928. For him it was one of the great days of his existence. His first hearing of the work, in the Church of St. Eustache in Paris at the turn of the century, had been shattering. He had felt ill for two months afterward: the grandeur had overwhelmed him, the sublimity was too much for him. He presented it on a single day, beginning just after five in the afternoon and ending at eleven, with a two-hour dinner interval.

The Foyer Pablo Casals, a center for old and indigent Spanish refugees, was opened in Montauban in the south of France in October 1961, and the center's operation continued to receive his close attention. A remodeled garage on the rue de la Banque in the old provincial town, the Foyer was one of the most attractive and comfortable centers for the aged anywhere in France; it was run by Spanish Refugee Aid, of which Casals was honorary chairman. Many Spanish families were sent to Montauban when the French borders were finally opened to Republican refugees at the beginning of 1939; more than eleven hundred Spanish refugees were still living in the vicinity at the beginning of the 1960s. The Foyer was a place for gathering in a large living room furnished with chairs and tables, books and newspapers, and with a television set as well as a radio-phonograph and records. Perhaps the greatest luxuries for these poor in rural France were the modern toilet facilities for both men and women. Monthly food packages were given to some one hundred fifty individuals over sixty (many of whom lived on public assistance totaling about twelve dollars a month); some clothing to those who most needed it; and double-size food packets at Christmas. Copies of accounts and case histories were forwarded regularly through the years to Casals, who read them carefully.

Prades and Zermatt remained constants in Casals' life until 1966, along with the spring festivals in San Juan and, from 1962, the regular summer periods in Marlboro. In between, travel to special events continued. In the spring of 1972, for example, Casals went to Caracas, Venezuela, to participate in five concerts and to Phoenix, Arizona, where he conducted his *Sardana* for cellos and Hymn of the United Nations as part of the establishment of the Pablo Casals International Cello Library at the Arizona State University. For the latter Casals stipulated a conducting fee of five thousand dollars, and turned the check over to the Arizona Cello Society for its work and that of the library. He also accepted a cowboy hat from the Governor of Arizona and an honorary doctorate from the University. (He was eager to visit the Grand Canyon for the first time in seventy-one years, traveling by helicopter this time, but uncertain weather conditions forced him to settle for a long automobile ride to a closer natural marvel.)

"The last eighteen years have been the most important years for me," Casals said early in 1973, "or at least equally as important as the previous years. They were full of great events which summarize my life. These years were full of activities, constant trips and much work." The flexibility that is supposed to be a mark of youth continued to exist in Casals in many areas in his tenth decade, even if he felt no need to reassess his standards in relation to contemporary musical trends. Commitment and alertness to the things that interested him remained the texture of his life.

The other fact of Pablo Casals' existence was his personal happiness after 1955, the year he met Marta Montañez. Thereafter they were inseparable. Outsiders continued to question and analyze. Those who came to know the couple best accepted, and in time knew they were in the presence of, a great love between two extraordinary people that enriched and enhanced both. Casals said unequivocally that Martita had given him life; every evidence suggests that he spoke the truth. The Casals began as collaborators; their partnership ripened with the passing of time, in spirit and understanding, in music, and in everyday matters. When Casals came to complete the formalities of his gift of the Villa Casals at San Salvador to Catalonia as a music center and as a museum of his life, he specified that Marta's designation be changed from president of the governing board for her lifetime to co-founder.

The loveliest of Pablo Casals' songs was his setting—written for Martita in 1956—of three love verses by the Puerto Rican poet Tomás Blanco, strophes that use the waves of the sea, the peaceful night, the flowering sugar cane to express "how I love you. . . . I love you from the depths of my sleeplessness . . . from the heights

The notes of the closing measures of Casals'
oratorio El Pessebre *dominate the head table*
of a San Juan banquet celebrating his
eighty-fifth birthday, December 29, 1961. At
the microphone, Puerto Rican concert pianist
Jesús María Sanromá. Seated between Casals
and his wife are Governor Luis Muñoz Marín
and Doña Ines Muñoz Marín.

of my dreams . . . from the calm of my contentment. . . . I love
you beyond space and time. I love you on this earth. . . . I love
you." Many years later, concerned that a friend had not understood the intensity of his emotion and echoing another of Tomás
Blanco's lines—"love is the perfume of present happiness"—Casals
wrote:

> Marta is the great love in my whole life, the only true love.
> She fills everything in me and has made up for all the empti-

ness of my life. Nothing can be compared to our perfect
love and our ideal life together. It is a feeling I had never
experienced before. I had never been happy. I found real
happiness only with Marta.

At the time of Casals' eighty-fifth birthday, six weeks after the
1961 White House performance, a great banquet was given in his
honor in San Juan. Suspended behind the head table was a large
panel on which appeared the final six measures of Casals' oratorio
El Pessebre and its last words: "Peace to men of good will . . .
Peace!!" Pablo Casals had decided to begin another crusade, his
greatest and strongest; the climax of this choral work begun in
wartime Prades was part of the announcement that he was prepared to go anywhere in the world "to take music which has peace
as a theme to all the people in the world who want it."

"I am so unhappy when I see people who have the duty of
pronouncing themselves on injustice, on ugly things, and they stay
still and satisfied in their houses. I can't understand that," he said.
"The participation of good in the world must be general. And
everybody has the way of pronouncing himself." Now Pablo Casals was going to devote himself "to the most important mission
any man or woman can have—to do my small part toward bringing
lasting, unthreatened peace to the world."

Casals had been "pronouncing" himself in actions he considered inescapable, in words, by charitable deeds done privately, and
by playing and conducting music written by others for many
years. Except for the cello *Sardana* and some devotional music
printed by the monks of Montserrat he had so far remained reticent
about the publication of any of his own compositions. Now he
was willing to take his most ambitious work into a harsh, impatient,
divided world and conduct it as a personal message "in the cause
of international understanding and world peace."

He had completed most of the work in Prades, using for
text a long Nativity poem written in Catalan by Juan Alavedra
for his daughter. The imagery, the chorusing shepherds, angels,
and fishermen, the Magi and the articulate adoring livestock, the
intimation of suffering and triumph, the shepherd boy who offers
to play the flute for the Christ Child and invites everyone to join
hands to dance a sardana around the manger—all the elements of
Alavedra's verse moved Casals deeply and evoked themes to which
he had written music since his collaboration with Carlos Casals

on a Christmas tableau in the late 1880s. Casals wrote and orchestrated the work in a traditional musical idiom of great variety and opulent sound, with echoes of Catalan music, moments of intense lyricism and poignant harmony, for five soloists, chorus, and full orchestra.

In the difficult months of 1944 in Prades, while he was writing *El Pessebre*, Casals began to think of the work as one that could be produced to celebrate the coming of peace when the war ended. "All my feelings of sorrow, of hope, of the need for Peace were put into that work—also the purity with which I feel people should act, to enjoy fraternity." He hoped and expected to be able to conduct the first performance in a Spain to which the victorious Allies would have restored freedom and peace, "to celebrate the Peace, and condemn the horrors of War. The triumph of the Allies came . . . but my country was not freed . . . and also, the Peace was only relative. The work remained silenced."

It was silenced for years, "almost forgotten," Casals said. As the world situation grew worse and more complicated, and the possibility emerged of Casals making an appeal for peace at the United Nations in 1958, he began to think of the oratorio in wider terms, how it might be used as a plea for world peace instead of the "celebration" that had not been possible. Casals asked Alavedra to write a final "Adoration" section that would culminate with stronger emphasis on peace and fraternity. When this was done, in 1960, Casals wrote the music for the six portions of the "Adoration," ending with a final Hosanna and Gloria for chorus, soprano, and orchestra. The first hearing of the complete *El Pessebre* was in Acapulco in December 1960, in an amphitheater facing the sea, with Marta Casals singing a solo soprano role. Casals had chosen that city for the première as a tribute to Mexico for its free acceptance of Spanish exiles during and following the Civil War.

Pablo Casals' concern had grown to embrace "Peace for all men," but his longing for the freedom of his homeland had in no way lessened. "My convictions in the ideals of freedom and democracy are unchangeable," he said early in 1962. "And therefore my feelings for my country are still the same—or perhaps stronger—as years go by and I gradually lose hope of ever returning. I have dedicated many years of my life to the cause of a free Spain, and still wish to silence my instrument for that cause. But, as I thought that it was my duty to silence my instrument for that cause, I also feel that now I have the duty to do something (through music) for the cause of peace—an essential for a human being. This is why I have decided to do this crusade."

That he was willing at the age of eighty-five to work in a larger area than he had moved in since 1939 and that he proposed to do so with a work of his own composition, which would attract criticism of various kinds, is an indication of the development of Casals as an artist but even more a sign of his preoccupation with the betterment of an imperfect world. He established the Pablo Casals Foundation, to which all fees accruing to himself in connection with *El Pessebre* would be paid; all income was to be used for charitable purposes and peace efforts. Casals stipulated that he would conduct only *El Pessebre* and that his personal written plea for peace must be printed in the program. The composition that had begun at least in part as an outpouring of Casals' loneliness for Catalonia took on a broader and more noble mission. (Casals' nostalgia for his native land did not abate; it remained so strong that in his late eighties he seriously considered making a trip from the south of France to conduct *El Pessebre* in Barcelona for the benefit of victims of devastating floods in Catalonia. There were discussions with Spanish consular officials, during which Casals required various assurances. One of the chief points was a promise that there would be no retaliation against anyone in the event there were antigovernment demonstrations as a result of his presence or of the concerts. No one at a lower bureaucratic level could make a commitment on such a matter, and the inquiry was routed up through the hierarchy to Madrid. It was reported back that the subject had been taken up directly with Franco and that he had said "Pablo Casals can come back whenever he wishes—but without conditions." Some time before, a Spanish diplomat had asked Casals why he did not give up his Spanish passport, since he did not use it to go back and forth to his country. "Let Franco give up his," snapped Casals.)

The beginning of the Casals musical crusade for peace was announced publicly, and the first presentations scheduled for San Francisco in April 1962. "I am a man first, an artist second," Casals said. "As a man, my first obligation is to the welfare of my fellow men. I will endeavor to meet this obligation through music—the means which God has given me—since it transcends language, politics and national boundaries. My contribution to world peace may be small. But at least I will have given all I can to an ideal I hold sacred." The news had scarcely come from the press wires when an American official of an anti-Falangist organization published a letter condemning Casals for breaking his vow and preparing to play in the United States. There were some other reactions of unhappiness and misunderstanding, but most who paid any attention to what Casals intended doing were impressed by such an effort by a man of his years.

The first peace-crusade performances of *El Pessebre* were given in the War Memorial Opera House in San Francisco, where the United Nations charter was signed in June 1945. Enrique Jordá, Spanish-born conductor of the San Francisco Symphony, led the orchestra, a university chorus, and the soloists in the first performance; Casals directed the two subsequent ones. There were nearly seventy performances of the work throughout the world in the first decade of Casals' peace crusade. Until 1969 Casals conducted the two-hour-plus performances himself, and he missed very few of the presentations except those given in Spain beginning in the late 1960s. The audiences were large and the standing ovations and the cheers convinced Casals that the audiences had responded with understanding to the music and its message, indicating a longing as fervent as his own for a peaceful world. (Following a 1964 performance in Budapest, after many recalls of conductor and soloists, the audience continued to stand applauding until the lights were turned out in the auditorium; in Caracas in 1972, a large house was still cheering the soloists back onstage after the orchestra had boarded a bus for the airport.) But for Casals what confirmed the effective impact of the crusade from its start was the visible emotion: there was no performance of *El Pessebre* at which he did not see members of the audience and even musicians weeping openly.

The professional critics published assorted reactions. One, named Frankenstein, wrote in the San Francisco *Chronicle* in April 1962 that the oratorio was "warm, friendly, genial, and human to the highest degree." New York observers were divided. To some it was sentimental music, naïvely of the nineteenth century; others were considerably moved, sensing real inspiration in the traditional idiom and greatness in its unpretentiousness and simplicity. The reaction Casals remembered most vividly a decade later was from *New Yorker* critic Winthrop Sargeant, who said the work seemed like a cool, refreshing drink of pure spring water in the midst of a desert . . . not a moment of coyness, mannerism, self-conscious artifice, or technical display for its own sake. . . . Doubtless, people who are obsessed with the latest thing in musical fashion will point to the derivative nature of Mr. Casals' writing, which owes a little to Bach and Wagner, perhaps a little to Dvořák, and something to the clear and ingenuous tradition of the zarzuela. . . . A composer who writes in such a universally understood idiom assumes certain risks, the main one being that his personality (in more creative and less sophisticated times "soul" or "heart" would have been the word to use) is laid bare for all to hear, so if his personality is in any way cheap, dishonest, or vulgar, the result is found to be banal. Mr. Casals has assumed this risk, and the nobility of his nature . . . shines in every measure of the music. "El Pessebre" has the innocence and sincerity of true greatness.

And, beyond any debate about the music, said one reporter who had watched the responses of the San Francisco audiences, perhaps this venerable musician knew something about peace the diplomats did not.

Casals received more inquiries than could be considered. One invitation of interest was waiting when Casals and his wife returned from the first San Francisco performances; it came from Professor Lev Ginsburg of the Moscow Conservatory, offering the finest hall and the best orchestra in the city for a presentation of *El Pessebre* in Moscow. Casals sent his thanks for the invitation, and asked Marta to acquaint Ginsburg with the same details that went into every presentation of the work in the course of his crusade for peace in any country:

> Maestro Casals would give either one or two concerts solely in directing his work *El Pessebre* [*La Crèche; The Manger*]. The work, based on the Nativity of Jesus Christ, carries a message of Peace, and the finale is a great chorale of peace and fraternity.
>
> The concert was to be announced in both the programs and press announcements as an oratorio and a message of Peace in the personal crusade of Maestro Casals in the cause of Peace.
>
> A Russian translation of the text, approved by Casals, was to appear in the program. Program notes were also to have

Casals' approval, and he would furnish background material about the work. The chorus would sing in the language of the country of performance.

An orchestra, chorus of at least two hundred voices, and soloists would be available, all of first quality.

The Maestro could lead a second concert, if necessary, two days after the first, but his doctors had forbidden him to direct two days in succession.

A peace message written by Maestro Casals—which accompanies all hearings of *El Pessebre*—was to appear, with its Russian translation, in the program.

Rehearsals were to include: at least three three-hour sessions with the soloists before the commencement of orchestra rehearsals; at least two rehearsals with the chorus alone; at least two three-hour rehearsals with orchestra only and two with orchestra, chorus, and soloists.

It did not matter to Maestro Casals whether his concert was sponsored by a local organization working for the cause of peace or was part of an international congress; his message was completely personal, that of an artist, of a man of music.

Because of the strain of the presentation of *El Pessebre* the Maestro could not accept any engagements in Russia other than those concerned with the oratorio.

Maestro Casals would accept the usual conductor's fee, but for a fund destined for charity, not for himself.

A projected trip to Russia to conduct *El Pessebre* was out of the question for 1962 because the schedule was already filled (including the festival in San Juan, three weeks in Marlboro, the Prades Festival, and the Zermatt classes). The following summer was a possibility—in any event, some point when the weather would not be cold.

In the end nothing came of the plan, and by his ninety-sixth birthday Pablo Casals had still not conducted *El Pessebre* in the Soviet Union. The reason was never clear, although various speculations were offered: the overtly religious theme of the poem, the strict terms concerning dissemination of Casals' written peace plea, the probability that Casals would speak his mind openly on the subject of state control of individual activity. Casals had made no secret of his feeling when Boris Pasternak, the Russian poet and novelist who had been awarded the Nobel Prize for Literature in October 1958, was not permitted to leave the USSR to accept it. Casals was openly appalled by this treatment of an important artist, whose painter father and pianist mother he had known in Berlin in the 1920s.

During and after 1962 the oratorio was given in many North American cities, including New Orleans, Pittsburgh, Buffalo, Chicago, Washington, Phoenix, Tallahassee, Philadelphia, Omaha, and Memphis. It was also heard in England, France, Italy, Central and South America, Israel, Switzerland, Germany (West Berlin), and Hungary. The performances in Italy, in September and October 1962, were at Assisi and in the basilica of Santa Croce in Florence (while he was in Florence, Casals became one of the few non-Italians made an honorary citizen of that city). *El Pessebre* began to be heard in Spain with four performances during the Christmas season of 1967 in Barcelona. There were later impressive performances in the cathedrals of Burgos and Toledo, at the abbey of Montserrat, and, in the spring of 1972, three hearings at the Teatro Real in Madrid. The government took no official notice of the Spanish performances, but there were overflow audiences for each presentation. The work was finally recorded, mostly under Casals' direction, in San Juan in the spring of 1972.

When Casals took *El Pessebre* to London in 1963 he was given a dinner, engineered by the wife of violinist Isaac Stern, who was in town with Leonard Rose and Eugene Istomin. The great feature of the evening was a reunion with Pierre Monteux, then eighty-eight, currently conducting the London Symphony Orchestra. Monteux and his wife were escorted in after Casals arrived and he did not know they were there until Monteux tapped him sharply on the shoulder. Great embraces, tears, and pithy nonstop conversation followed. ("You cannot imagine . . . the spell the very presence of this tiny man of eighty-seven casts over all who have the privilege of knowing him—it is extraordinary!" Mme Monteux wrote.) The wives and the other musicians listened to recollections of the world of music, especially in Paris, fifty years and more before. Both Monteux and Casals dismissed Gabriel Pierné with eloquent shrugs, and Casals once more told the story of the famous lawsuit that had followed Pierné's insulting description of the Dvořák cello concerto and Casals' refusal to play. ("You were quite right, *cher ami*," said Monteux.) Monteux talked about Debussy, how "the great Claude" had stood behind him when he rehearsed and shouted "Monteux, that's a *forte*, and when I write a *forte*, I want a *forte!*" Casals said with vehemence that the modern composers' music could not last, because it has neither soul nor melody. Monteux, at that moment working on compositions by Hindemith, Benjamin Britten, and Arthur Bliss, observed that modern man is a product of his scientific and mechanical century; since scientific and mechanical production becomes obsolete soon after it appears, no doubt much modern music would have the same destiny.

Mme Monteux fondly thought that her husband, nearly two years older than his Spanish colleague although not much taller, was much the more dapper of the two: "very up-to-date in his dark serge suit, blue tie with red and white stripes, pearl tie pin, his red rosette of a Commander of the Legion of Honor; Casals, dressed much more sedately, all blacks and grays, a lovable, quaint figure and old friend." (Casals wore the rosette of Grand Officer of the Legion of Honor, which—like his Grand Cross of the Order of Isabel la Católica, awarded before the fall of the Spanish monarchy—entitled him to be addressed as "Excellency.")

Later in the week the Monteux heard *El Pessebre*. Mme Monteux, perhaps echoing an opinion of her husband, thought it composed with "profound, fervent sincerity . . . as an incentive toward peace in this world." But, she said, "I realized while listening to the rather old-fashioned and at times curiously naïve music, played beautifully by the London Philharmonic Orchestra and conducted by Don Pablo himself, the natural antipathy he must feel for modern harmonic construction."

The *Pessebre* performances that moved Casals the most took place at the ruined abbey of St. Michel de Cuxa near Prades in the autumn of 1966 and in the hall of the General Assembly of the United Nations in October 1963. The presentation in Provence, which was given as Casals approached his ninetieth birthday and just after his last participation in a Prades Festival, was suffused for him with memories of the nearly thirty years he had passed in the Prades region. Much more important, however, was its marking of the thousandth anniversary of the Catalan Assembly of Tologes, which had set up a parliamentary structure and subscribed to the medieval Truce of God that was the first widespread effort to control the feudal anarchy of Europe and to reduce warfare. The presentation at the United Nations, Casals' second appearance there, was the New York concert for United Nations Day

(Left) Pablo and Marta Casals with Pierre Monteux in London, 1963; (right) Casals conducts El Pessebre *at the United Nations, October 1963.*

on the UN's eighteenth anniversary, October 24, 1963. Casals conducted the Festival Casals Orchestra, the Cleveland Orchestra Chorus, and soloists in the most widely broadcast single performance the oratorio had received—it was carried on the United Nations shortwave service to Europe, the Middle East, Africa, and Latin America, and was carried live on television by the educational network in the United States. In his peace message included with the program Casals recapitulated most of his 1958 address, ending in an even stronger plea:

> I repeat, music, that wonderful universal language which is understood by everyone should be a source of communication among men. I once again exhort my fellow musicians throughout the world to put the purity of their art at the service of mankind in order to unite all people in fraternal ties.

With this objective in mind, I consider it my duty to offer my humble contribution in the form of a personal crusade. Let each one of us contribute as he is able until this ideal is attained in all its glory; and let us unify our fervent prayers that in the near future all humanity may be joined in a spiritual embrace.

By the time Casals was ninety, a small portable oxygen tank was part of the equipment that accompanied him wherever he traveled, along with a black bag that contained a muffler as protection against sudden chill, tobacco, an extra pipe, and usually a musical score. Casals never had to use the oxygen himself in emergency at a concert although it was utilized more than once for elderly ladies overcome by emotion, and Marta once or twice gave him the mask for a moment to restore his energy quickly during intermission. At one presentation of *El Pessebre* in a Central American republic, the orchestra was not very good; the chorus, mostly local singers, was willing but dreadful. Alexander Schneider had done his best to prepare both in rehearsals, and at the concert Casals conducted demonically to try to pull real music from the assemblage. Marta Casals, standing in the wings next to Schneider, saw her husband on the podium begin to change color but realized his complexion was growing red with fury, not pale with physical difficulty. When Casals, then nearly ninety-two, paused at the end of a section and looked down, Marta gave a startled Schneider a shove, telling him to go out and conduct the rest of the performance. Backstage she did offer Casals oxygen for two minutes. He listened to the music, which went so sour at several points that Casals groaned and clamped the oxygen mask once more over his nose and mouth.

In Budapest, where Casals conducted *El Pessebre* in the fall of 1964—its first hearing in Eastern Europe—the concert was in the great Vigidó auditorium, where he had last performed as a cellist in 1937. Casals had obvious pleasure in showing his wife parts of the beautiful city that had been one of the important musical centers of the world early in his career, but he was haunted afterward by the changes he sensed there and kept saying sadly that nowhere in the streets had he seen people smiling.

A CBS television crew followed Casals and his wife during the Budapest visit, taping part of the concert with Casals conducting Hungarian artists, and covering the reunion of Casals and the composer Zoltán Kodály. The two men had been friends since the early 1900s but had not seen each other since 1937. In the course of the visit to Kodály's home, the sound cameras recorded an exchange about fellow composer Igor Stravinsky that, broadcast out of full context, distressed Casals greatly; his sense of delicacy concerning a proper courtesy to others extended even to those with whom he disagreed strongly. Stravinsky and Casals had first met in St. Petersburg on one of Casals' first Russian tours; they had met again in Paris when Diaghilev first brought Russian ballet to Western Europe; and Stravinsky had been guest conductor for a week of concerts with the Orquestra Pau Casals in Barcelona in the early 1920s. But from the time of *The Rite of Spring*'s controversial first hearing in Paris in 1913, the musical paths of the two men went in different directions, and their ideas did not coincide when Stravinsky's composition became generally neoclassical in the 1920s. During the war years in Prades, hungry for orchestral music, Casals would nevertheless turn off the receiver quickly when the BBC transmitted Stravinsky; and to watch Casals listening in circumstances from which he could not flee, to a concert performance of *Les Noces* many years later was to see a sensitive man in pain. Nevertheless, Casals was acutely embarrassed to be publicly a part of the audience for Kodály's filmed witticism that Stravinsky could be a great musician if he weren't "like a dressmaker. . . . Only the newest fashion." (Three years later Stravinsky's wife, expressing herself in an ASCAP publication about the "autograph racket," speculated that her husband had managed to keep "the public-institution attitude" at bay better than any other eminent octogenarian. She singled out Schweitzer and Casals by name in speaking of "this age of false-hero industry," adding that Stravinsky did not like the role of patriarch.)

The summer of his ninetieth year, Casals rehearsed and conducted *El Pessebre* in the outdoor theater of Herodes Atticus in Athens, where by turning his view a bit from the orchestra he could see the lighted front of the Parthenon high on the Acropolis and where Camille Saint-Saëns had conducted his *Jeunesse d'Hercule* nearly half a century before. The weather was so hot that rehearsals were held from midnight until three in the morning. The chorus for the two performances sang in Catalan rather than in the language of the country, and the event was under the patronage of the young pianist Princess Irene, sister of King Constantine.

The Greek royal family came to call on Casals and Marta at their hotel just before they were to leave Greece, a reversal of protocol that touched Casals greatly. Included in the royal party was Juan Carlos of Spain, the grandson of Alfonso XIII, with his wife (the former Princess Sophia of Greece) and their young daughter; thus Casals met a sixth generation of Spanish Borbóns.

By the end of the trip to Greece, Casals was not well but he returned to the south of France to conduct the two performances of *El Pessebre* at St. Michel de Cuxa. On the flight back to Puerto Rico the fates interfered with Casals' vow not to set foot in Spain while Franco was head of state; his plane was forced by mechanical trouble to put down at the Madrid airport. He and his companions left the next morning in a replacement aircraft.

(Casals' physical discomfort continued after his return to Puerto Rico, and a relatively minor operation was scheduled not long after his ninetieth-birthday celebration. The day of the procedure Casals started to get out of bed, fully intending to walk to the operating room, until one of his doctors said sharply "You're not going to a picnic! Get onto that stretcher.")

The texture of Casals' personal peace crusade in the late 1960s was seldom more evident than in the presentation of *El Pessebre* at Constitution Hall in Washington on October 24, 1967, under the auspices of the United Nations Association of the United States. The same day thousands of people had converged on the city to march on the Pentagon in protest of the war in Indochina.

Casals was insulated personally from the movement in the city, but followed the developments closely through television news reports. There was, in fact, a Secret Service agent assigned during his stay who accompanied the party every time Casals left his hotel suite. (This amiable and efficient gentleman, who had made security arrangements for President Franklin Roosevelt during wartime conferences with Winston Churchill, Charles de Gaulle, and others, was puzzled at first by the air of discipleship among the friends who came to see Casals, and somewhat skeptical; by the time the Maestro left Washington about a week later, he had purchased a handsome pipe to present to Casals as a farewell gift, and his good-bye was as warm and devoted as any.)

Arrangements that immediately affected Casals and his party were made by Gerald Wagner, a Washington executive experienced in organizing special events for the White House and its occupants, with the assistance of Frederick Blatchly, a State Department officer and amateur cellist who asserted that having heard Casals in the Midwest at the age of three had made him want to become a musician. The Secret Service walkie-talkies were in evidence; the period was tense, and there were clear and specific plans for Casals' protection if there were disruptions in Constitution Hall the night of the concert. The motorcade to and from rehearsals moved smoothly but rapidly between hotel and auditorium, although without motorcycle escort. It was during one such trip after a rehearsal that the Maestro was first shown a copy of the handsome program for the concert, which had just come from the press. He demonstrated that neither his grasp of a situation nor his instant authority had flagged noticeably in his ninety-first year. How did Maestro like the program, went the question from the walkie-talkie in the end car of the motorcade to the walkie-talkie in Casals' limousine at the head. After a short pause the answer crackled back that Maestro was less than happy and wanted to see the person responsible for the program in his suite within fifteen minutes of his arrival. A biographical note concerning Juan Alavedra, author of the poem of *El Pessebre*, had inadvertently been omitted, and Casals was very angry about this slight to his collaborator and old friend. (It was too late to remedy the situation in the concert program, but a tribute to Alavedra paralleling that to Casals was soon written and appeared in the booklet for the banquet that followed the performance. Señor Alavedra, who had come from Barcelona to be present at the concert, was presented for bows with the soloists in Constitution Hall and introduced at the subsequent dinner.)

The Constitution Hall performance of *El Pessebre* was impressive and concluded without incident before a well-dressed audience that included the Vice President of the United States, Cabinet officers, members of the diplomatic corps (among them the Spanish ambassador), and leaders of Washington social and artistic circles. Not far away, although not in sight of the concert hall, a much larger and less fashionable group prepared to protest against war, some quietly and some with violence. (Casals' next trip to Washington, three and a half years later, when he traveled there to be proclaimed a citizen of all the Americas and to conduct Schubert's fifth symphony at the Pan-American Union, coincided with another giant gathering of protesters in the country's capital

Once again Casals followed closely the press reports and the television coverage of demonstrations and mass arrests. He was no stranger to such things, but he was no less horrified by the sight of armed police and soldiers, even in the face of some provocation.)

At the time of the October 1967 Washington performance of *Pessebre* Casals had a brief talk with President Lyndon Johnson in the President's office at Johnson's invitation. Casals had listened carefully to the President's televised speeches, and months before had drafted a letter to Johnson expressing his personal anguish about the continuation of the Vietnam war, but had been persuaded not to send it. The President greeted Casals courteously, but their conversation was superficial. Five years later Casals retained two vivid memories of the encounter: to Casals, Johnson's face was that of a man who had lost his direction, and he had maneuvered the discussion in such a way that it was not possible to bring up the subject of the war.

The banquet following the Washington *Pessebre* performance included speeches by Vice President Hubert Humphrey and Secretary of State Dean Rusk, music by a New York dance band so persistently loud that Casals wanted to leave immediately, and a thicket of Chamber-of-Commerce-style addresses in which Casals' short, quiet extempore response stood like a tiny unexpected flower. Much more concerned about the massive anti-war demonstrations in the city than most people realized, he began haltingly in a voice so low the microphone barely picked it up: "I was not supposed to say anything tonight. . . . But I have heard some wonderful words . . . about America, the country I love. The country I love so much and that I have known long before most of you. I have known America since 1901 [and my many returns were] not, I assure you, just for the money but for love of this country. So I can offer with all sincerity my admiration and love.

"You are the richest nation, but you are the most generous of any nation. You have helped advance every noble thing. Allow me to say . . . I have faith in you Americans. . . ."

The frequency of trips abroad was phenomenal for a man in his eighties and nineties, yet more often than not Casals arrived at the end of a long flight fresh-faced and eager for the next activity. Even so, stimulated as he was by participation in musical events, he found great contentment in his San Juan home. The low, long house, built on one level, had a feeling of spaciousness; it was comfortable but unexpectedly modest for a man of Casals' fame and station. A long hall extended most of the length of the house, with glass-front cabinets and shelves filled with mementos of the Maestro's career and many pictures on the walls. Visitors entered from a garden pathway into the center of this hall and, turning right, proceeded to a living room in which there were also pictures, busts, and more souvenirs. Satin-upholstered chairs and the small settee on which Casals usually sat, a grand piano covered with a handsomely embroidered fringed Spanish throw, and an antique Spanish crystal chandelier hanging from the peaked ceiling gave the impression of a salon of an earlier day, arranged with taste and avoiding clutter despite the bibelots and the mementos (which included a duplicate of the complete set of miniature United Nations flags Casals had admired on Secretary-General U Thant's desk). The front wall of this room was glass, giving onto the ocean that could be reached by crossing a small yard beyond the window. At night it was covered by a white curtain that, drawn, revealed a *trompe-l'oeil* Venetian scene. Off the salon was a small protected terrace with a view out toward the sea through wrought-iron grillwork, a tranquil place to sit, to read or merely to watch the changing nuances of sky and water. Casals spent many daytime hours there, sitting in a deep leather chair near a plaster replica of the Venus de Milo, reading or studying a score but seldom simply contemplating the sea.

When the house was first built, on a narrow lot between the old Isla Verde highway and the ocean, the area was quiet and pleasant, and the Casals could walk directly from the sea side of the house to the water. Within a few years, after two robberies, it became necessary to surround the entire plot with a high wire fence and later to install an electronic burglar alarm across each window and all the doors (the house was nevertheless robbed twice more during the years they lived there). Soon the daytime hours were shattered by the sound of pneumatic hammers and machinery at work in the construction of large apartment buildings nearby, and well before his ninetieth birthday a tall luxury condominium was built that overlooked the Casals house and yards. A supermarket was built a short distance down the street, with a parking lot "as big and depressing as a bomb crater"; the nearby intersection and its several approach streets became a permanent traffic bottle-

neck. The San Juan International Airport lay barely a mile down-wind, and the enormous aircraft approaching to land or taking off made a roar so overwhelming one sometimes could not hear anything else until they had passed. Casals was aware of the external intrusions, but they seemed to bother him less than they did many other people, even when he had to cup his hand around one ear to try to hear what someone sitting next to him was saying through the whine of a departing jet aircraft.

When airport noise and encroaching construction made life in the Casals' seaside Isla Verde house almost intolerable at the end of the 1960s, Marta Casals found and enlarged a gracious house on the side of a hill in the Rio Piedras section of San Juan only a few minutes' drive from the University campus. Here, for the first time in nearly thirty-five years, Casals had a home with a spaciousness approaching that of San Salvador. Martita planned and supervised construction of a large music salon above a terrace that accommodated as many as two hundred guests for private concerts and for parties at the time of Casals' birthday every year. Through both the ceiling-to-floor windows in the formal music room and the wrought-iron grillwork necessary for security on the extensive tiled terrace beneath there were spectacular views of the

---

FACING PAGE

When, by the end of the 1960s airport noise and
encroaching construction made life in the
Casals' seaside Isla Verde house almost
intolerable, Marta Casals found and enlarged
a gracious house overlooking San Juan. Here,
for the first time in nearly thirty-five years,
Casals had a home with a spaciousness
approaching that of his San Salvador villa.
After saying farewell to afternoon guests
in May 1972, Casals took a moment to rest and
look toward the sea on a small terrace (top)
where usually he would be seen studying a
score, reading, or talking with visitors. (Bottom)
Music stands in place await the making of
chamber music in the center of the large music
salon on New Year's Eve 1971.

distant center of San Juan and the curving seashore. Reconstruction had been completed, as a surprise, before Casals saw the house late in 1970. His reaction was a delighted "When can we move in?"

Usually the Casals played dominos in the evening at least once a week, most often at home with close friends but at other times with their habitual domino group of about a dozen in another couple's home. Casals sometimes said that he did not begin to play dominos until he moved to Puerto Rico, although there were those who remembered being involved not altogether willingly in games with him thirty years earlier. He was a fast player (he stopped playing chess years before because he found it too slow), and a skillful one in a game that demands a retentive memory of which player has played which combinations and a cheerful readiness to cripple one's opponents as effectively as possible. In his eighties and nineties Casals was still playing to win, expecting no quarter and giving none in the course of a game.

Neither watching television nor playing dominos is conducive to conversation, but Casals found relaxation in both during his Puerto Rican years. At the same time, he thrived on attentive company, loved to talk, and talked well. Casals received almost every afternoon after siesta the great, the humble, the interested, the curious, friends who came with friends, friends-of-friends-of-friends, and Catalans in droves. In later years his wife and close friends tried to protect him from the merely curious, not always successfully. Except for a very few family members and intimate friends who knew the household schedule and could drop in unannounced, most people made an appointment. Many, however, soon found they were not to be alone long with Casals; in the middle of a discussion or an anecdote, other people arrived, and when one rose courteously he was likely to find himself supplanted by a newcomer taking the host's full attention.

Casals was almost invariably completely polite to his guests, even those he had not expected, those whose frame of reference was considerably different from his own, or whom he did not particularly enjoy for one reason or another. Many of the important or celebrated who visited Puerto Rico paid a courtesy call on Casals: musicians, diplomats, critics of the arts, university professors, politicians, Latin American heads of state, royalty, such crusaders for human causes as Martin Luther King, Jr. The expression of ideas, responsiveness, enthusiasm, and sometimes humor stimulated him. And, while age as such did not really matter to him, he warmed noticeably to the young and was once heard to comment to his wife on learning of the impending visit of one persistent couple in their late sixties: "But they're so *old* and dull, and they keep repeating themselves!"

Perhaps the most traumatic visit to the Isla Verde house was from an American popular singer who was starring in the floor show at one of the major San Juan tourist hotels. The hotel's public relations representative, an acquaintance of the Casals, had telephoned and asked if she might bring the singer to call. In the course of an especially busy day Marta Casals had uncharacteristically forgotten the appointment and therefore had not briefed her husband about either the potential visit or the visitor. Casals had moved to his reclining chair in the dining room and begun to watch the early-evening television news when the doorbell rang. Marta Casals ushered the guests into the salon. The publicity woman apologized for arriving later than scheduled; they had been swimming and had lost track of the time. Marta went to draw her husband away from the news.

Hotel representative, when Casals entered the room: "Maestro, I want you to know our great singing star!"

Casals: "Lovely, lovely. How nice! What are you singing? Lieder? Brahms, Schubert . . . ?"

The night-club star slumped deep into his chair while the woman rattled on. "Maestro! His records make *millions*! He's the great *pop* singer. . . ."

Casals: "Oh."

It was a short visit—and the visitors had indeed just come from a swim. There were wet impressions on the satin upholstery when they left.

While Casals enjoyed long and sometimes rambling conversation on many subjects, faced with an interview he sat waiting for questions, one writer thought, "like a timid passenger in an airplane bracing himself before take-off." He had, of course, been talking to journalists for well over half a century but—although a working newspaperman did have a challenge in getting fresh quotes—as his ninety-fifth birthday came and passed he found that many who interviewed him, sometimes having traveled thousands of miles, still asked how it had come about that he had chosen the cello for his instrument. Or, they asked once again about contemporary music, his opinion about rock'n'roll ("Poison put to sound," a brutalization of both life and art), or about the other Spanish Pablo ("Do not tell me that anyone can understand Picasso when he paints a woman with five noses protruding from different parts of her body. How can anyone get anything out of such nonsense? It is not human!"). Once in a while someone would ask him about the young woman who garnered some passing publicity by playing a cello recital in a topless gown and the remark of the judge who fined her: "I don't think Casals would play better without his pants" ("I don't know since I don't play the cello with my trousers off"). As the birthdays progressed, more and more asked the secret of his longevity. (When Casals was in New York in October 1971 to conduct at the United Nations, he posed for a well-known and highly balletic sculptor who was making still another Casals bust. There was conversation, with television cameras running. At last came the inevitable "What is the secret?" Casals looked up toward his questioner, scarcely pausing, looking fit and like a man in his sixties. "I live," he said. "Very few people live.")

In spite of tiresome questions, Casals was courteous, although not long after his ninetieth birthday he finally decided he had been taken advantage of too often and began to avoid even the most unobtrusive tape recorders whenever he could. The closest he came to a public explosion in such circumstances was during the descent of a well-known New York writer for yet another interview. This gentleman had written about Casals before; he had also published a devastating review of one of Casals' latest concerto recordings, although neither Casals nor his wife remembered it at the time. He began to ask questions so supremely banal that Casals finally turned to Marta and asked fiercely in Catalan "Who is this man? Why is he asking these stupid questions?"

What Pablo Casals began to speak about to the journalists and his other visitors by the middle 1960s was something of such profound simplicity that few of the interviews included much about it. He began to speak quietly and insistently about the unique miracle of individual existence. Friends who had not seen him for some months after the ninetieth-birthday celebration in San Juan at the end of December 1966—a jubilant time of public ceremonies and private parties, messages from chiefs of state and celebrated musicians as well as from friends and strangers—were awed by

Public celebrations of Casals' ninetieth birthday in 1966 included a gala homenaje *at the Tapía Theater in San Juan and a concert in the patio of La Fortaleza attended by Vice President and Mrs. Hubert Humphrey and an international audience.*

*Delight in playing chamber music purely for
pleasure remained as great for Casals in his
nineties as when he had played with Ysaÿe,
Kreisler, and others in Europe early in the
century. In the 1960s and 1970s he played for
hours with visiting colleagues (including
Alexander Schneider as seen here).*

his energy, alertness, and aura of what some called timelessness,
others youth.

In the mid-1960s the Casals built a small but comfortable
country house for a weekend retreat on high land between mountains and ocean about forty miles from San Juan. Casals named
the property *El Pessebre*. Here the couple could relax with Rosa
and Luis Cueto Coll, the intimate friends who generally accompanied them, joined for a few hours at a time by a handful of
other friends and relatives. Whenever Casals' closest musical associates—especially Mieczyslaw Horszowski and Alexander Schneider—flew down from the mainland United States to visit, there
was music much of the day: string trios most of the morning and

two or three more after Casals' siesta. While Casals was resting, Schneider, an exuberant and expert chef, would be likely to dash off to a nearby fishing village to select freshly caught seafood for a variety of bouillabaisse, returning to find Marta Casals and the women guests preparing other food amid animated general conversation occasionally interrupted by one of Martita's spontaneous impersonations of a relative, a famous musician, or even of her husband.

Walking among the flowers near the hillside house on a radiant weekend morning, Casals could say to a friend that he had never felt so young as at that moment and—in the early 1970s—"never have I had so much hope." Yet the tranquil house overlooked a naval installation, and one of the offshore islands Casals could see more clearly than some of his companions was a practice bombing range for the U.S. Navy.

The daily news was full of violence and death. "We continue to act like barbarians. Like savages, we fear our neighbors on this earth—we arm against them, and they arm against us. I deplore to have had to live at a time when man's law is to kill." We ought to think, he said, "that we are one of the leaves of a tree and the tree is all humanity. We can't live . . . without the others, without the tree . . . we are only a leaf. Now we must think of the whole, the whole . . . by intelligence, and naturally when there is intelligence there is love." Casals would direct attention to a flower or to a tree, stressing the infinite variety of leaves and petals on a single organism.

Casals was concerned more and more about children, in whom, he had begun to feel, lay the only hope for future peace in the world. When human beings of any age know *who* they are and *where* they are, he believed, then they find God. The youngest children must be told "Do you know what you are? You are a marvel. You are unique. In all of the world there is no other child exactly like you. In the millions of years that have passed there has never been another child precisely like you. And look at your body—what a wonder it is! your legs, your arms, your cunning fingers, the way you move! You may become a Shakespeare, a Michelangelo, a Beethoven. You have the capacity for anything!" And, once each child has come to cherish his own value, it will not be possible for him to kill or not to love.

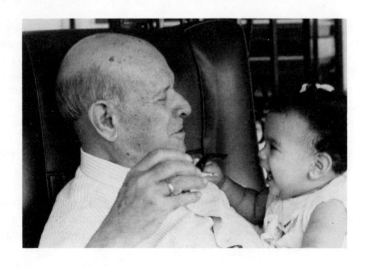

Pablo Casals and a godchild, May 1970

Love, freedom, lyric fantasy—all within order—Casals had preached to his students and demonstrated in his own music-making; now he was certain they were the only solutions to violence. He began to speak of these things, over and over—to political leaders, to musicians, to everyone who came near enough to hear him. "We teach the children in school that two and two make four, that Paris is the capital of France. They must also be led to know what they are!"

Casals completed and orchestrated his "Hymn of the United Nations" with little more than time for proper copying before rehearsals began for the United Nations Day concert in October 1971. It had remained a challenge to the finish, when the poet requested changes in accentuation for special word stress. But Casals rose to challenge, and produced a moving, deceptively simple three-minute work for orchestra and mixed chorus to W. H. Auden's forty-two-line poem of which the core is "Let music for peace/Be the paradigm./For peace means to change/At the right time/As the World-Clock/Goes Tick and Tock."

*In late 1971 Casals, Marta, and Mexican architect
Enrique Lazáro inspect a model of perhaps the
most lavish gift ever offered Casals—the house
and adjoining amphitheater (rear of model) then
being built for him in a luxury development
near Guadalajara, Mexico.*

The Hymn was given its first hearing at the beginning of the
United Nations Day concert on October 24 in the General Assembly Hall, which forty-eight hours earlier had been echoing with
acrimonious debate on the admission of mainland China and on
conflict in the Middle East. The orchestra was that of the Festival
Casals, the chorus was that of the Manhattan School of Music and
the United Nations Singers, supplemented by Marta Casals and
Olga Iglesias, who had flown up from Puerto Rico to add her
voice to a chorus that lacked body in the dry acoustics of the
auditorium. Casals came out to the podium on the arm of a UN
usher slowly, almost haltingly, a result of being nearly blinded

(Top) Casals conducting a Bach triple-keyboard concerto with Rudolf Serkin, Mieczyslaw Horszowski, and Eugene Istomin as soloists; (bottom left) Casals conducting the first performance of his "Hymn of the United Nations" in the General Assembly hall on October 24, 1971; (bottom right) accepting the greeting of Secretary-General U Thant

by the television lights rather than fragility, and seemed almost to have to be lifted to the awkwardly high podium. But once he picked up the baton and raised it to cue the Hymn's four opening diatonic *tutti* chords, Marta Casals, standing in the third row of the chorus, knew everything would go well.

After the first hearing of the Hymn, Secretary-General U Thant spoke briefly and then presented the newly established United Nations Peace Medal to Casals and, in absentia, to Auden, who was in Europe at the time. Casals conducted Bach's D minor concerto for two violins, with Isaac Stern and Alexander Schneider as soloists, then retired while Schneider led the "Dumbarton Oaks Concerto" for chamber group that Igor Stravinsky had written for the United Nations in 1938. Casals returned to direct a Bach triple-keyboard concerto with Miecyzslaw Horszowski, Rudolf Serkin, and Eugene Istomin as soloists, and another performance of the Hymn.

Casals gestured to the international audience that was on its feet; his cello was brought out. As Schneider held the Bergonzi-Goffriller, Casals began to speak, rather softly at first, saying he had not played in public for forty years, but today he *had* to play. "I will play a short piece of the Catalonian folklore," he said, the voice strengthening. "This piece is called 'The Song of the Birds.' The birds in the sky, in the space, cry out when they fly: 'Peace! Peace! Peace!' "—gesturing upward and outward with his arms, the last "Peace!" half a sob. "And the music is music that Bach and Beethoven and all the great would have loved, and it is the soul of my country, Catalonia."

Casals sat to play, with the great room in absolute silence. Eyes closed, half hunched over the instrument, he played the familiar cradle song through to the fading of a last upward pianissimo note that for an instant made it seem possible the human spirit could achieve peace.

Casals led, perhaps, an ideal life, one he characterized as always doing what he most enjoyed—a life of extraordinary accomplishment in the art of music within the "narrow and laborious world of the virtuoso." He remained involved in the world of his fellow creatures to an extent no other virtuoso of music had ever done. A man who was unable not to love, who believed that the greatest human experience is "the love of all humanity, the love that goes

*Playing "The Song of the Birds" at the end of
the October 1971 United Nations Day concert*

out to the entire world . . . more important than the love of a
man for a woman. To understand that is to know the meaning
of life. For then you understand suffering. Everything is more
important than music when it is a question of human pain. Everything that is human, whatever we must be to others in time of
need, that is more important than one's feeling of love for something beautiful, for music, for paintings. How can there be any
question? Humanity is far more important than music. You can

do much for humanity with music, with anything noble. But greater than all is love, love for all the living."

Pablo Casals, by his ready admission, began the first period of sustained personal happiness in his life when he was eighty years old, at the side of a talented and adoring woman who grew radiantly more beautiful as the days and the years passed. If he seemed aloof to many who knew and liked him at various stages of his life, it was less from unconsciousness of and lack of regard for others than from his enormously full and self-sufficient life within himself and from the authoritative humility of a tremendous security. In what flowed outward from the inner fountain of spirit many of his fellow creatures found a benediction and an inspiration.

Many celebrated names wrote tributes to the art and personality of Pablo Casals. They were often couched elegantly or poetically, but none is more profound than a letter written by Thomas Mann about a year before his death in answer to a query by José María Corredor. Mann had spent a lifetime crafting novels and stories full of the ironies of the lives of artists, and he had stopped writing testimonials about other people, but he replied:

> You ask my opinion of Pablo Casals? I cannot call it an opinion. It is deepest veneration, and an admiration that has an element of rejoicing in it. For here is a phenomenal human being in whom captivating artistry is combined with resolute refusal to make any concessions to evil. He will not tolerate moral debasement or injustice. His very existence purifies and elevates our conception of the artist. Here is an artist whom, for once, irony cannot touch. In a brutalized age, Pablo Casals provides an example of proud, utterly incorruptible integrity.
>
> In him there is no trace of escapism, nor any of that esthetic neutralism in questions of humanity, that readiness for prostitution, so often characteristic of our dear tribe of artists. None of that: "I play for anyone who pays me." A fantastic talent that the world is mad about, that can be certain of tempestuous triumphs everywhere. People offer fortunes to do business with him—but he sets up conditions that have nothing to do with money and success. . . . The world is up to its neck in guilt for what has happened to the land of his birth, Spain; but that same world wants to

revel in his genius. He will have none of it. . . . [Prades]
has become the symbol of an artistry that respects itself and
will not be seduced; the symbol of the indissoluble unity
of art and morality.

A victorious unity—for the hermit's mountain has become the goal of pilgrims from all over the world. Yes, the
world streams toward him who has refused to come to it.
The Prades Festivals testify to the magnetic force of great
character as much as they do to musical enthusiasm. In-
evitably, they have become a protest against the domination
of evil.

What a triumph! How heartening it is! Time and again
the fragile human race has needed men who will save its
honor. This artist is one such—a savior of the honor of humanity. Gladly I say that his existence is a comfort to me,
as it is to thousands.

———•◄►•———

Compositions by
Pablo Casals

This list, although incomplete, reflects substantially the body and variety of Casals' surviving compositions from the summer of 1892, when he was fifteen, until 1972. Casals did not keep an orderly catalog of his early work, and it is possible other youthful compositions will be found when all the papers at the San Salvador villa are put into proper order. For a quarter-century following 1902, the demands of his career as instrumentalist and then conductor as well diverted Casals from composing, and (except for his *Sardana* for cello orchestra) his production actually began again with devotional choral works written for and dedicated to the Abbey of Montserrat. He maintained strongly that most of his composition should await posthumous publication, to stand or fall on its own merits and not be affected by his reputation as a musician, although as the years passed he permitted the monks of Montserrat to publish the religious music he had written for their choir; some of his songs have been published in Spain, Puerto Rico, and the United States; the score and orchestral parts of his oratorio *El Pessebre* were in press in August 1973. Photocopies of a few unpublished works are to be found in libraries in Europe and North America, and there is a considerable number of sketches for symphonic works in the composer's archives.

Despite Casals' reluctance to offer much of his own composition to the public, enough of it was known as early as 1941 for Gilbert Chase to make an initial assessment in his *The Music of Spain:* "In the course of his busy life Casals has found time to compose works that entitle him to serious consideration as a creative artist."

The help of Marta Montañez de Casals in preparing and checking this material is gratefully acknowledged.

Title	Date and place of composition	Dedication
A tú—desde Santas Creus —Queixa Song to a text by Juan Ramón	August 18, 1892 Santas Creus	Fernando Ramón Soler
Misa de Gloria Chorus and organ	1892 Barcelona	
Minuetto for string instruments	1892 Barcelona	
Concerto for violoncello and piano	1892 Barcelona	
String quartet	1893 Barcelona	
Preludio for piano	1893 Madrid	
Festívola (sardana llarga) [published 1908, Barcelona]	1893(?)	
Balada for piano	1893 Madrid	Countess of Morphy
Romanza Song to a text by Heinrich Heine	1893 Madrid	

Compositions

Title	Date and place of composition	Dedication
Pastoral for violoncello and piano	1893 Madrid	
Cançó Catalana for piano	1893 Sardanyola	
Cuatro Romanzas sin Palabras for piano	1894 Madrid	Señora Dolores de Alsina
Romanza for voice and piano	1894 Madrid	Countess of Morphy
Preludio Organico No. 1	1895 Madrid	
Preludio Organico No. 2, for piano	1895 Paris	
Cançó Catalana No. 1 Song for soprano and piano to a text by Jacinto Verdaguer [published 1968, New York]	1895 Sans	
Cançó Catalana No. 2 Song to a text by Apeles Mestres [published 1967, New York]	1895	
Mazurka for piano	1895 Madrid	Señorita María Luisa Ritter
En Sourdine Song to a poem by Paul Verlaine	1895(?)	
Cançó Catalana No. 3 Song to a text by Apeles Mestres	1896 Barcelona	
Cançó Catalana No. 4 Song to a text by Apeles Mestres	1896 Barcelona	
Reverie for violoncello and piano	1896 Barcelona	
Andante for violoncello and piano	1896(?)	
Cançó Catalana No. 5 Song to a text by Apeles Mestres	1897 Barcelona	

Title	Date and place of composition	Dedication
Clar de Lluna Song for chorus to a text by Jaime Ramón	1897 Barcelona	*La Lira* chorus, Vendrell
Els Mesos Twelve songs for male chorus to poems by Apeles Mestres; first eleven *a cappella*, twelfth scored for string orchestra plus two harps. [*Cançó de Març* (5-part male chorus *a cappella*) and *Cançó de Novembre* (4-part male chorus *a cappella*) scheduled for publication 1973, New York]	1897	
Adios Song to a text by Ramón Soler	1897 Barcelona	
Romanza for violoncello and piano	1897 Barcelona	
Fulla d'Album for violoncello and piano	1897 Barcelona	
La Vision de Fray Martín Symphonic poem, inspired by a poem of Nuñez de Arce	1898 Barcelona	Queen María Cristina
Preludio Organico No. 3	1898 Barcelona	
Son Image, romance for voice and piano	1898 Barcelona	Crista Morphy
Au Cimitière au Jour des Morts Song to a text by François Coppée	1899 Paris	
La Fiancée du Nil for soprano and orchestra. Text by Mignon Palmer	1899 Paris	

Compositions

Title	Date and place of composition	Dedication
Absence Song to a text by Matthew Arnold	1902 San Francisco	
Sardana for violoncello orchestra [score and parts published 1967, New York]	1927	London Cello Club
Salve Montserratina For male chorus and organ [published 1953, Barcelona; for 4-part mixed chorus, 1966, New York]	1932 San Salvador	Montserrat
Rosarium beatae Virgini Mariae (*Rosario de la Verge de Montserrat*) For chorus and organ or piano [published 1952, Barcelona]	1932 Montserrat	Montserrat
O vos omnes For male chorus [published 1953, Barcelona; in *Musique et liturgie* (Paris), 1954, for mixed chorus *a cappella;* for mixed chorus and for 4-part male choir *a cappella* 1965, New York. Orchestration for brass ensemble (4 horns, 3 trumpets, 3 trombones, tuba) by Leopold Stokowski, published 1970, New York]	1932(?)	Montserrat
Ave Maria de l'Abat Mercet For chorus and organ	1933 San Salvador	Montserrat
Eucaristica For chorus and organ or piano [published 1950s,	1934 San Salvador	Montserrat

Title	Date and place of composition	Dedication
Barcelona; for treble chorus and organ or piano, 1967, New York]		
Poème for violoncello and piano	1935 San Salvador	
Canción de Cuna Song to a text by Juan Llongueras	1935	María Elena Terrats
De Cara al Mar Song for soprano and piano to a text by Juan Llongueras [published 1967, New York]	1935	Juan Llongueras
Balada de la Nova Solveig Song for soprano and piano to a text by Ventura Gassol Rovira [published 1967, New York]	1936–1937	Ventura Gassol and Conchita Badia
Cançó dels Elefants for voice and piano. Text by P. Jaquetti	1938 Prades	
Roda de Nadal for piano	1939 Prades	
Silenci Song for contralto and piano to a text by Juan Alavedra	1940 Prades	
Set Paraules de Jesus en Creu for contralto and piano	1942 Prades	
Nigra sum (decepta ex Canticis) For 3-part treble choir and organ or piano [published 1953, Barcelona; for 3-part treble chorus, 1966, New York; for 3-part male chorus, 1968, New York]	1942 Prades	Montserrat

Compositions

Title	Date and place of composition	Dedication
Recordare Virgo Mater For mixed chorus and organ [published Barcelona, 1952; for 4-part mixed chorus with organ, 1966, New York]	1942 Prades	Montserrat
Tota pulchra For mixed chorus [published 1955, Barcelona; for 4-part mixed chorus *a cappella* with tenor solo *ad lib*, 1966, New York]	1942 Prades	Montserrat
Cançó a la Verge For 2-part treble chorus [published 1950s, Barcelona; for 2-part chorus and organ or piano with new material, 1968, New York]	1942 Prades	Montserrat
Poema del Breçol	1943 Prades	Señora Rita Gual on the birth of her daughter Ana María
Sant Marti del Canigo: Sardana del l'Exili For orchestra or *cobla* [score and parts published 1967, New York]	1943 Prades	Danielle Puig
Prelude for piano	1943 Prades	Alexander Seiler
El Pessebre, oratorio Text by Juan Alavedra [choral score published 1962, New York; orchestral score and parts, 1974, New York]	1944–1946 Prades 1959–1960 Puerto Rico	Marta Casals
Misteri del Sant, oratorio Text by José S. Pons	1949(?) Prades	

Title	Date and place of composition	Dedication
Alla Minuetto for piano	1955 Prades	M. Horszowski
Tres Estrofas de Amor Song for soprano and piano to a text by Tomás Blanco [published 1959, San Juan; 1968, New York]	1957 Puerto Rico	Marta Casals
Ven a Mí Song for contralto and piano to a text by María García Lema	1958 Puerto Rico	Ruth Fernandez
Oracio a la Verge de Montserrat Text by Carles Gubern	1959 Puerto Rico	
Himno Escuela Villa Prades Text by E. Rentas Lugo	1959 Puerto Rico	
El Angél Travieso Song for soprano and piano to a text by Rafael Montañez [published 1967, New York (text translated by Robert Hess)]	1959 Puerto Rico	Olga Iglesias
Canço de l'Avi Text by Carles Gubern	1965	Mariana García Gubern
Coral de Navidad Text by José R. Passalacqua	1966 Puerto Rico	
Plegaria a la Virgen de la Providencia Text by Rafael Montañez	November 1968 Puerto Rico	
Cuando Vuela a Nacer Text by Alfredo Matilla	1971 Puerto Rico	Marta Casals

Compositions

Title	Date and place of composition	Dedication
Himno a las Naciones Unidas Text by W. H. Auden [published 1971, New York]	1971 Puerto Rico	Marta Casals
Sonata for violin and piano	1945(?) Prades (first 2 mvts) 1964 Puerto Rico (3d mvt) 1972 Puerto Rico (4th mvt)	

TRANSCRIPTIONS

El Cant dels Ocells, medieval Catalan folk song. First transcription for cello and piano, then for string chamber orchestra, then for solo cello with accompaniment by orchestra of celli [score and parts published 1972, New York].

Fauré, *Après un Rêve* (Songs, Op. 7), transcription for violoncello and piano [published 1942, New York].

Casals made a great many other transcriptions and adaptations for cello, including one of the Spanish dance No. 5, *"Andaluza,"* by his close friend Enrique Granados.

———
——•—•—•——
———

Discography

Compiled by Teri Noel Towe

Thomas Edison developed his first tin-foil phonograph only a few months after Pablo Casals was born but, although the recording industry had become a substantial business by the early years of the twentieth century, Casals did not make commercial recordings until early in 1915, at the age of thirty-eight. He has never particularly enjoyed the process, even though it no longer entails playing into a large horn, but his concerto recordings and his performances of the unaccompanied Bach suites for cello remain high points of recorded music.

This list is confined to recordings made for commercial release. Unreleased recordings exist of many rehearsals and most concerts of the Prades, San Juan, and Marlboro festivals. There are rumors of missing transcribed performances of the Casals–Cortot–Thibaud trio. Casals' appearances at the United Nations were taped, as were fifty master classes at Berkeley, California, in the early

1960s, and there are many private tapes of music made by Casals and friends in Casals' homes in Puerto Rico.

Assistance in collection of the data was given by Thomas Frost, Mary Alice Wotring, and Pierre Bourdain of Columbia Records; M. Scott Mampe of Philips; Peter Munves and John Pfeiffer of RCA; Julian Rice of Angel Records; Walter Legge of EMI; James Banthos of Peters International; Gregor Benko of the International Piano Library; Charles Haynes of Pearl Records; Jack Meltzer of the Merit Music Shop, New York; Brent Williams, secretary-treasurer of the Musicians Foundation; David Hall, curator of the Rodgers and Hammerstein Sound Archives, Library and Museum of the Performing Arts at Lincoln Center, New York; Mrs. Barbara Seltzer; and Maestro and Señora Casals.

NOTE: Record numbers indicate a 33⅓ monophonic recording (including LP transfers of 78-rpm disks) unless otherwise noted.

• indicates beginning of data concerning recordings of a different arrangement, version, or portion of the listed work.

ABBREVIATIONS

*	Available in August 1973	S	Stereophonic recording
A	Acoustic recording	R	Monophonic recording elec-
E	Electrical recording		tronically reprocessed for
Q	Quadraphonic recording		stereo

LABELS

HMV—All European companies using the His Master's Voice label
CBS—European issues by American Columbia
RCA—European issues from RCA Victor
Angel, Da Capo, EMI Columbia, HMV, and *Electrola*—subsidiaries of Electric Music Industries, Ltd.
Columbia, Odyssey and *Epic*—subsidiaries of Columbia
RCA and *Victor*—subsidiaries of RCA Red Seal
Philips-Réalités—a special product of Philips
All others—independent labels

Sources checked include: list prepared by Columbia Records at author's request; private discography prepared by Gerald A. Pollack, Washington, D.C. (Casals archives); discography by Richard Freed, *Saturday Review* (Dec. 29, 1966) and New York Concert Hall Programs (April 1970); record lists in Moeschlin/Seiler and Müller-Blattau (see bibliography); *World Encyclopedia of Recorded Music*, including both supplements; Sackville-West and Shawe-Taylor, *The Record Guide* (London, 1950); all three editions of Darrell's *The Gramophone Shop Encyclopedia;* the *Schwann* and *Long Player* catalogues; a list of Japanese numbers from ANZ, Inc., Tokyo; July 1968 British CBS catalogue; 1939–1940 RCA Victor catalogue; 1971–1973 Peters International catalogues; 1972 *Diapason, Catalogue Classique et Diction,* Paris.

I. Recordings by Pablo Casals as Cellist or Conductor and Recordings Made under Casals' Supervision

ANONYMOUS

El Cant dels Ocells ("The Song of the Birds"). Medieval Catalan folk song. Arranged for cello and piano by Pablo Casals

Pablo Casals, cello
Mieczyslaw Horszowski, piano
> Recorded in 1958 for the sound track of the motion picture *Windjammer*
> *Columbia* CL 1158, CS 8651[S]* (USA).

Pablo Casals, cello
Mieczyslaw Horszowski, piano
> Recorded in concert at the White House, Washington, D.C., November 13, 1961
> *Columbia* KL 5726, SGM 1 (USA). *CBS* BRG 72035 (Europe).

• Arranged for cello and orchestra by Enrique Casals from Pablo Casals' arrangement for cello and piano

Pablo Casals, cello and conductor
Prades Festival Orchestra
> Recorded in Prades, France, June 1950
> *Columbia* 73249-D[78], A 1937[45], ML 4926, ML 5226 (USA). *CBS* 8.601[45], EP 8.527[45]* (France). *Philips* 409.008[45] (Europe).

BACH, JOHANN SEBASTIAN (1685–1750)

Brandenburg Concerto No. 1 in F Major, BWV 1046

Alexander Schneider, violin
Lucien Thevet, Gilbert Coursier, French horns
Marcel Tabuteau, Laila Storch, John Mack, oboes
Maurice Allard, bassoon
Fernando Valenti, harpsichord *continuo*
Pablo Casals, conductor
Prades Festival Orchestra
> Recorded in Prades, France, June 1950
>> *Columbia* ML 4345, SL 161 (USA). *EMI*
>> *Columbia* FCX 115 (England). *Philips* L 1.309 (Europe).

Alexander Schneider, violin
John Mack, Ronald Richards, Peter Christ, oboes
Myron Bloom, Robert Johnson, French horns
Donald MacCourt, bassoon
Rudolf Serkin, piano *continuo*
Pablo Casals, conductor
Marlboro Festival Orchestra
> Recorded in Marlboro, Vermont, July 1964
>> *Columbia* M2L 331, M2S 731[S]*, D3S 816[S]* (USA). *CBS* MET
>> 3001, SET 3001[S]* (England).

Brandenburg Concerto No. 2 in F Major, BWV 1047

Alexander Schneider, violin
Marcel Mûle, soprano saxophone
John Wummer, flute
Marcel Tabuteau, oboe
Paul Tortelier, cello *continuo*
Fernando Valenti, harpsichord *continuo*
Pablo Casals, conductor
Prades Festival Orchestra
> Recorded in Prades, France, June 1950
>> *Columbia* ML 4345, SL 161 (USA). *EMI Columbia* FCX 115 (England). *Philips* L 1.309 (Europe).

Alexander Schneider, violin
Robert Nagel, trumpet
Ornulf Gulbransen, flute
John Mack, oboe

Leslie Parnas, cello *continuo*
Peter Serkin, harpsichord *continuo*
Pablo Casals, conductor
Marlboro Festival Orchestra
>   Recorded in Marlboro, Vermont, July 1965
>   *Columbia* M2L 331, M2S 731[S]*, D3S 816[S]*, MS 7514[S]*, MG 31261[S]* (USA). *CBS* MET 3001, SET 3001[S]* (England).

Brandenburg Concerto No. 3 in G Major, BWV 1048

Fernando Valenti, harpsichord *continuo*
Pablo Casals, conductor
Prades Festival Orchestra
>   Recorded in Prades, France, June 1950
>   *Columbia* ML 4345, SL 161 (USA). *EMI Columbia* FCX 115 (England). *Philips* L 1.309 (Europe).

Peter Serkin, harpsichord *continuo*
Pablo Casals, conductor
Marlboro Festival Orchestra
>   Recorded in Marlboro, Vermont, July 1964
>   *Columbia* M2L 331, M2S 731[S]*, D3S 816[S]* (USA). *CBS* MET 3001, SET 3001[S]* (England).

Brandenburg Concerto No. 4 in G Major, BWV 1049

Alexander Schneider, violin
John Wummer, Bernard Goldberg, flutes
Fernando Valenti, harpsichord *continuo*
Pablo Casals, conductor
Prades Festival Orchestra
>   Recorded in Prades, France, June 1950
>   *Columbia* ML 4346, SL 161 (USA). *EMI Columbia* FCX 116 (England). *Philips* L 1.310 (Europe).

Alexander Schneider, violin
Ornulf Gulbransen, Nancy Dalley, flutes
Rudolf Serkin, piano *continuo*
Pablo Casals, conductor
Marlboro Festival Orchestra
>   Recorded in Marlboro, Vermont, July 1964
>   *Columbia* M2L 331, M2S 731[S]*, D3S 816[S]* (USA). *CBS* MET 3001, SET 3001[S]* (England).

• Mvt. 3, *Presto* (extracted from the Marlboro recording of
the full concerto)
>   *Columbia* S 31333[S]* (USA).

Brandenburg Concerto No. 5 in D Major, BWV 1050

Eugene Istomin, piano
Joseph Szigeti, violin
John Wummer, flute
Pablo Casals, conductor
Prades Festival Orchestra
>   Recorded in Prades, France, June 1950
>   *Columbia* ML 4346, SL 161 (USA). *EMI Columbia* FCX 116 (England). *Philips* L 1.310 (Europe).

Rudolf Serkin, piano
Alexander Schneider, violin
Ornulf Gulbransen, flute
Pablo Casals, conductor
Marlboro Festival Orchestra
>   Recorded in Marlboro, Vermont, July 1964
>   *Columbia* M2L 331, M2S 731[S]*, D3S 816[S]* (USA). *CBS* MET 3001, SET 3001[S]* (England).

Brandenburg Concerto No. 6 in B Flat Major, BWV 1051

Fernando Valenti, harpsichord *continuo*
Pablo Casals, conductor
Prades Festival Orchestra
>   Recorded in Prades, France, June 1950
>   *Columbia* ML 4347, SL 161 (USA). *EMI Columbia* FCX 116 (England). *Philips* L 1.310 (Europe).

Peter Serkin, harpsichord *continuo*
Pablo Casals, conductor
Marlboro Festival Orchestra
>   Recorded in Marlboro, Vermont, July 1964
>   *Columbia* M2L 331, M2S 731[S]*, D3S 816[S]* (USA). *CBS* MET 3001, SET 3001[S]* (England).

Cantata No. 147, *Herz und Mund und That und Leben*, BWV
147: Mvt. 10, *"Jesu bleibet meine freude"* ("Jesu, joy of man's
desiring"). Arranged for chorus and orchestra by Thomas Frost

Pablo Casals, conductor
Columbia Symphony Orchestra and Chorus
> Recorded at Columbia's 30th Street studio, New York, March 5,
> 1966
>> *Columbia* CSM 388, CSS 388[S] (USA). This recording was part
>> of *Great Songs of Christmas, Volume Six*, a promotional album issued
>> by Goodyear in conjunction with Columbia Masterworks.

Cantata No. 170, *Vergnügte Ruh', Beliebte Seelenlust,* BWV 170

Jennie Tourel, mezzo-soprano
Pablo Casals, conductor
Prades Festival Orchestra
> Recorded in Prades, France, June 1952
>> *Columbia:* not released.

Cantata No. 208, *Was mir behagt,* BWV 208: Mvt. 9, *"Schafen können sicher weiden"* ("Sheep may safely graze"). Arranged for chorus and orchestra by Thomas Frost

Pablo Casals, conductor
Columbia Symphony Orchestra and Chorus
> Recorded at Columbia's 30th Street studio, New York, March 5,
> 1966
>> *Columbia* MS 7322[S]*, MS 7514[S]*, MG 31261[S]* (USA).

Concerto No. 5 in F Minor for Harpsichord and String Orchestra, BWV 1056

Clara Haskil, piano
Pablo Casals, conductor
Prades Festival Orchestra
> Recorded in Prades, France, June 1950
>> *Columbia* ML 4353, SL 161 (USA). *EMI Columbia* CX 1109, FCX
>> 325 (England). *Philips* L 1.511 (Europe).

Concerto in A Minor for Harpsichord, Flute, Violin, and String Orchestra, BWV 1044

Mieczyslaw Horszowski, piano
John Wummer, flute
Alexander Schneider, violin

Pablo Casals, conductor
Prades Festival Orchestra
> Recorded in Prades, France, June 1950
>
> *Columbia* ML 4352, SL 161 (USA). *EMI Columbia* CX 1113, FCX 326 (England). *Philips* L 1.511 (Europe).

Concerto No. 3 in C Major for Organ after Vivaldi, BWV 594: Mvt. 2, *Recitativo*. Arranged for cello and piano by Marie Rosanoff

Pablo Casals, cello
Eugene Istomin, piano
> Recorded in Prades, France, May or June 1953
>
> *Columbia* ML 4926 (USA). Note: The other movements of the concerto from which this excerpt was taken were transcribed by Bach from Antonio Vivaldi's *Concerto for Violin, String Orchestra, and Continuo*, Opus 7, No. 5, but the *Recitativo* is an original composition by Bach, inserted in place of the original Vivaldi slow movement. (Some scholars question Bach's authorship of this transcription.)

Concerto No. 1 in A Minor for Violin, String Orchestra, and Continuo, BWV 1041

Isaac Stern, violin
Fernando Valenti, harpsichord *continuo*
Pablo Casals, conductor
Prades Festival Orchestra
> Recorded in Prades, France, June 1950
>
> *Columbia* ML 4353, SL 161 (USA). *EMI Columbia* CX 1109, FCX 325 (England). *Musicians Foundation* TF 1001* (USA).

Concerto in D Minor for Violin, String Orchestra, and Continuo, BWV 1052. Arranged by Joseph Szigeti from the Concerto No. 1 in D Minor for Harpsichord and String Orchestra, BWV 1052

Joseph Szigeti, violin
Leopold Mannes, piano *continuo*
Pablo Casals, conductor
Prades Festival Orchestra
> Recorded in Prades, France, June 1950
>
> *Columbia* ML 4353, SL 161 (USA). *EMI Columbia* CX 1109, FCX 326 (England).

Concerto in D Minor for Two Violins, String Orchestra, and Continuo, BWV 1043

Isaac Stern, Alexander Schneider, violins
Fernando Valenti, harpsichord *continuo*
Pablo Casals, conductor
Prades Festival Orchestra
    Recorded in Prades, France, June 1950
        Columbia ML 4351, SL 161 (USA). *EMI Columbia* FCX 155, QCX 155 (England). *Musicians Foundation* TF 1001* (USA).

Concerto in C Minor for Violin, Oboe, String Orchestra, and Continuo, BWV 1060. Arranged from the Concerto No. 1 in C Minor for Two Harpsichords and String Orchestra, BWV 1060

Isaac Stern, violin
Marcel Tabuteau, oboe
Fernando Valenti, harpsichord *continuo*
Pablo Casals, conductor
Prades Festival Orchestra
    Recorded in Prades, France, June 1950
        Columbia ML 4351, SL 161 (USA). *EMI Columbia* FCX 155, QCX 155 (England). *Philips* L 1.511 (USA).

English Suite No. 6 in D Major, BWV 811: Mvt 5, Gavottes 1 and 2. Arranged for cello and piano by Polain

Pablo Casals, cello
Nikolai Mednikoff, piano
    Recorded in 1931
        Victor 1349[E,78] (USA). *HMV* DA 1030[E,78] (Europe). Note: This disk is labeled simply "Musette." The order of the gavottes is reversed, Gavotte No. 1 being played as the trio for No. 2.

"Komm, Süsser Tod" ("Come, Sweet Death"), BWV 478, from the collection of *Geistliche Lieder* known as the *Schemelli Gesangbuch*. Arranged for cello and piano by Alexander Siloti

Pablo Casals, cello
Blas Net, piano
    Recorded in 1931
        Victor 7501[E,78], LCT 1002, WCT 3[45] (USA). *HMV* DB 1400 [E,78] (Europe).

Pastorale in F Major for Organ, BWV 590: Mvt. 3, *Aria.* Arranged for cello and orchestra.

Pablo Casals, cello and conductor
Perpignan Festival Orchestra
    Recorded in Perpignan, France, summer 1951

    Columbia SL 168 bonus disk, SL 170 bonus disk, ML 4926, A 1922[45] (USA).

Saint Matthew Passion, BWV 244: No. 47, *"Erbarme dich, mein Gott"*

Jennie Tourel, mezzo-soprano
Pablo Casals, conductor
Perpignan Festival Orchestra
    Recorded in Perpignan, France, summer 1951

    Columbia ML 4640 (USA).

Sonata No. 1 in G Major for Viola da Gamba and Harpsichord, BWV 1027

Pablo Casals, cello
Paul Baumgartner, piano
    Recorded in Prades, France, June 1950

    Columbia ML 4349, SL 161 (USA). *Philips* AL 01.407L (Europe).

Sonata No. 2 in D Major for Viola da Gamba and Harpsichord, BWV 1028

Pablo Casals, cello
Paul Baumgartner, piano
    Recorded in Prades, France, June 1950

    Columbia ML 4349, SL 161 (USA). *Philips* AL 01.407L (Europe).

Pablo Casals, cello
Mieczyslaw Horszowski, piano
    Recorded in rehearsal and in concert at the United Nations, October 24, 1958

    Columbia: not released.

Sonata No. 3 in G Minor for Viola da Gamba and Harpsichord, BWV 1029

Pablo Casals, cello
Paul Baumgartner, piano
Recorded in Prades, France, June 1950
Columbia ML 4350, SL 161 (USA). *EMI Columbia* CX 1110 (England). *Philips* AL 01.407L (Europe).

Pablo Casals, cello
Eugene Istomin[?], piano
Recorded in Prades, France, in May or June, 1953
Columbia: not released.

Sonata No. 2 in A Minor for Violin Unaccompanied, BWV 1003: Mvt. 3, *Andante*. Arranged for cello and piano by Alexander Siloti

Pablo Casals, cello
Blas Net, piano
Recorded in 1931
Victor 7368[E,78] (USA). *HMV* DB 1404[E,78] (Europe).

Suite No. 1 in G Major for Cello Unaccompanied, BWV 1007

Pablo Casals, cello
Recorded in Paris, June 2, 1938
Victor M 742[E,78], 17658/64[E,78], AM 742[E,78], 17665/71[E,78], DM 742[E,78], 17672/78[E,78] (USA). *HMV* DB 3671/3[E,78], COLH 16, (Europe); C 061-00.892M* (France). *Angel* COLH 16, CB 3786* (USA); GR 71, GR 2016*, GP 2071C* (Japan). *Electrola* E 80496 (Germany). *Da Capo* 1 C 147-00892/94M* (Germany).

Suite No. 2 in D Minor for Cello Unaccompanied, BWV 1008

Pablo Casals, cello
Recorded in London, November 23, 1936
Victor M 611[E,78], 15671/76[E,78], AM 611[E,78], 15677/82[E,78], DM 611[E,78], 16015/20[E,78], LCT 1104, WCT 1104[45] (USA). *HMV* DB 3399/3401[E,78], COLH 16 (Europe); C 061-00.892M* (France). *Angel* COLH 16, CB 3786* (USA); GR 71, GR 2016*, GR 2071C* (Japan). *Electrola* E 80496 (Germany). *Da Capo* 1 C 147-00892/94M* (Germany).

Discography

Suite No. 3 in C Major for Cello Unaccompanied, BWV 1009

Pablo Casals, cello
Recorded in London, November 23, 1936

Victor M 611[E,78], 15671/76[E,78], AM 611[E,78], 15677/82[E,78], DM 611[E,78], 16015/20[E,78], LCT 1104, WCT 1104[45] (USA). *HMV* DB 3402/04[E,78], COLH 17 (Europe); C 061-00.893M* (France). *Angel* COLH 17, CB 3786* (USA); GR 72, GR 2017*, GR 2071C* (Japan). *Electrola* E 80497 (Germany). *Da Capo* 1 C 147-00892/94M* (Germany).

• *Prelude* and *Sarabande*

Pablo Casals, cello
Recorded in New York, April 23, 1915
Columbia A 5782[A,78], SL 185 bonus disk (USA). *Musicians Foundation* TF 1001* (USA).

• *Bourrée*

Pablo Casals, cello
Recorded in New York, April 23, 1915
Columbia A 5697[A,78] (USA).

• *Gigue*

Pablo Casals, cello
Recorded in New York, April 15, 1916
Columbia A 5875[A,78] (USA).

Suite No. 4 in E Flat Major for Cello Unaccompanied, BWV 1010

Pablo Casals, cello
Recorded in Paris, June 13, 1939

Victor DM 1302[E,78], 12-0890/96[E,78] (USA). *HMV* W1528/30[E,78]; DB 6538/40[E,78], COLH 17 (Europe); C 061-00.893M* (France). *Angel* COLH 17, CB 3786* (USA); GR 72, GR 2017*, GR 2071C* (Japan). *Electrola* E 80497 (Germany). *Da Capo* 1 C 147-00892/94M* (Germany).

Pablo Casals, cello
Recorded in Prades, France, May or June 1953
Columbia: not released.

Suite No. 5 in C Minor for Cello Unaccompanied, BWV 1011

Pablo Casals, cello
> Recorded in Paris, June 13, 1939
>
> *Victor* DM 1302[E,78], 10/96[E,78], 12-0890/96[E,78] (USA). *HMV* DB 6541/44[E,78] (Europe); COLH 18 (USA); C 061-00.894M* (France). *Angel* COLH 18, CB 3786* (USA); GR 73, GR 2018*, GR 2071C* (Japan). *Electrola* E 80498 (Germany). *Da Capo* 1 C 147-00892/94M* (Germany).

Pablo Casals, cello
> Recorded in Prades, France, May or June 1953
> *Columbia:* not released.

• Sarabande

Pablo Casals, cello
> Recorded at the Grand Amphithéâtre of the Sorbonne, Paris, October 10, 1956, at a concert in honor of Casals' eightieth birthday
> *Philips* AL 77.408L, 6521 012[R]* (Europe). *Philips-Réalités* C-2 (Europe).

Suite No. 6 in D Major for Cello Unaccompanied, BWV 1012

Pablo Casals, cello
> Recorded in Paris, June 3, 1938
>
> *Victor* M 742[E,78], 17658/64[E,78], AM 742[E,78], 17665/71[E,78], DM 742[E,78] 17672/78[E,78] (USA). *HMV* DB 3674/77[E,78], COLH 18 (Europe); C 601-00.894M* (France). *Angel* COLH 18, CB 3786* (USA); GR 73, GR 2018*, GR 2071C* (Japan). *Electrola* E 80498 (Germany). *Da Capo* 1 C 147-00892/94M* (Germany).

Suite (Ouverture) No. 1 in C Major, for Two Oboes, String Orchestra, and Continuo, BWV 1066

Marcel Tabuteau, Laila Storch, oboes
Maurice Allard, bassoon
Fernando Valenti, harpsichord *continuo*
Pablo Casals, conductor
Prades Festival Orchestra
> Recorded in Prades, France, June 1950
>
> *Columbia* ML 4348, SL 161 (USA). *EMI Columbia* FCX 323, CX 1108 (England). Note: In this recording, Casals omits the *Menuets*, which are marked *alternativement* and are therefore optional.

John Mack, Joseph Turner, oboes
Joyce Kelley, bassoon
Ruth Laredo, piano *continuo*
Pablo Casals, conductor
Marlboro Festival Orchestra
> Recorded in Marlboro, Vermont, July 1966

> *Columbia* M2L 355, M2S 755[S]* (USA). *CBS* 72517/8]S]* (England).
> Included in Columbia's *Casals at 90* package.

Suite (*Ouverture*) No. 2 in B Minor, for Flute, String Orchestra, and Continuo, BWV 1067

John Wummer, flute
Fernando Valenti, harpsichord *continuo*
Pablo Casals, conductor
Prades Festival Orchestra
> Recorded in Prades, France, June 1950

> *Columbia* ML 4348, SL 161 (USA). *EMI Columbia* FCX 323, CX
> 1108 (England).

Ornulf Gulbransen, flute
Ruth Laredo, piano *continuo*
Pablo Casals, conductor
Marlboro Festival Orchestra
> Recorded in Marlboro, Vermont, July 1966

> *Columbia* M2L 355, M2S 755[S]*, D3S 816[S]* (USA). *CBS*
> 72517/8[S]* (England). Included in Columbia's *Casals at 90* package.

Suite (*Ouverture*) No. 3 in D Major, for Three Trumpets, Two Oboes, Tympani, String Orchestra, and Continuo, BWV 1068

Henry Nowak, Wilmer Wise, Louis Opalesky, trumpets
John Mack, Patricia Grignet, oboes
John Wyre, tympani
Ruth Laredo, piano *continuo*
Pablo Casals, conductor
Marlboro Festival Orchestra
> Recorded in Marlboro, Vermont, July 1966

> *Columbia* M2L 355, M2S 755[S]*, D3S 816[S]* (USA). *CBS* 72517/8
> [S]* (England). Included in Columbia's *Casals at 90* package.

• Mvt. 2, *Air* (extracted from the Marlboro recording of the full suite)

> *Columbia* MS 7501[S]*, MS 7519[S]*, MGP 13[S]*, MG 31261[S]*, MQ 32054[Q]* (USA).

• Arranged for cello and orchestra

Pablo Casals, cello
Unidentified orchestra
> Recorded in New York, May 5, 1916
> *Columbia* A 5756[A,78] (USA).

> Recorded in New York, April 29, 1920
> *Columbia* 49814[A,78], 28026-D[A,78] (USA); 7357[A,78] (England). *Pearl* GEM 105* (England). *Everest* 3323[R]* (USA).

• Arranged for cello and piano

Pablo Casals, cello
Otto Schulhof, piano
> Recorded in 1931
> *Victor* 7368[E,78] (USA). *HMV* DB 1404[E,78] (Europe).

Suite (Ouverture) No. 4 in D Major, for Three Trumpets, Three Oboes, Bassoon, Tympani, String Orchestra, and Continuo, BWV 1069

Henry Nowak, Wilmer Wise, Louis Opalesky, trumpets
John Mack, Patricia Grignet, Joseph Turner, oboes
Joyce Kelley, bassoon
John Wyre, tympani
Ruth Laredo, piano *continuo*
Pablo Casals, conductor
Marlboro Festival Orchestra
> Recorded in Marlboro, Vermont, July 1966
> *Columbia* M2L 355, M2S 755[S]* (USA). *CBS* 72517/8[S]* (England). Included in Columbia's *Casals at 90* package.

Toccata, Adagio, and Fugue in C Major, BWV 564: Mvt. 2, *Adagio.* Arranged for cello and piano by Pablo Casals from the arrangement for piano by Alexander Siloti.

Pablo Casals, cello
Edouard Gendron, piano
> Recorded February 21, 1925
> *Victor* 6501[A,78] (USA).

Pablo Casals, cello
Nikolai Mednikoff, piano
   Recorded in Europe, February 28, 1927

> *Victor* 6501[E,78], 6635[E,78], DM 1302[E,78], 12-0890[E,78], LCT 1002, WCT 3[45], LCT 1050, WCT 72[45], LM 2699* (USA); LM 2699 (Europe). *RCA* 430.296* (Europe); 644.520* (France); RED 2019* (Japan). *HMV* DB 1067[E,78] (Europe). Note: Both the acoustic and the electrical versions were issued as Victor 6501. The listing in the 1936 edition of *The Gramophone Shop Encyclopedia of Recorded Music* indicating Blas Net as the pianist in Victor 6635 and HMV DB 1067 is in error.

BEETHOVEN, LUDWIG VAN (1770–1827)

Six Minuets for Piano, Grove's No. 167: No. 2 in G Major. Arranged for cello and piano

Pablo Casals, cello
Otto Schulhof, piano
   Recorded in 1931

> *Victor* M 134[E,78], 7570[E,78], AM 134[E,78], 7571[E,78], DM 134[E,78], 17192[E,78] (USA). *HMV* DB 1419[E,78] (Europe). *WRC* SH 121* (England). *Angel* GR 2207* (Japan).

Overture to von Collin's drama *Coriolan*, Opus 62

Pablo Casals, conductor
London Symphony Orchestra
   Recorded in London, 1930

> *Victor* 9279[E,78], 36291[E,78] (USA). *HMV* DB 1409[E,78], AB 371[E,78] (Europe).

Overture to the incidental music for *Die Ruinen von Athen* (*The Ruins of Athens*), Opus 113

Pablo Casals, conductor
Orquestra Pau Casals
   Recorded in Barcelona, 1932

> *HMV* M 96[E,78], D 1728[E,78], AB 567[E,78], ES 639[E,78] (Europe).

Sonata in F Major for Horn and Piano, Opus 17. Arranged for cello and piano by the composer

Pablo Casals, cello
Mieczyslaw Horszowski, piano
    Recorded in concert in the Beethovenhaus, Bonn, September 1958
    Philips PHM 500120, PHS 900120[S] (USA); ABL 3270, L 505L,
    A 00 505L, 835 019 AY[S] (Europe). *Turnabout* 34490[S]* (USA).
    Murray Hill S 4759[S]* (USA).

Sonata No. 1 in F Major for Cello and Piano, Opus 5, No. 1

Pablo Casals, cello
Mieczyslaw Horszowski, piano
    Recorded in Europe, 1939
    HMV DB 3908/3910[E,78] (Europe); J 153 50136/40* (Spain). *Victor*
    M 843[E,78], 18285/87[E,78], DM 843[E,78], 18288/90[E,78] (USA).

Pablo Casals, cello
Rudolf Serkin, piano
    Recorded in Prades, France, May or June 1953
    Columbia ML 4876, SL 201 (USA). *Odyssey* 32 360016[R]* (USA).
    Philips AL 01.285L* (Europe).

Pablo Casals, cello
Wilhelm Kempff, piano
    Recorded in concert in Prades, France, 1961
    Philips A 02210L, 835.101 AY[S]* (Europe).

Sonata No. 2 in G Minor for Cello and Piano, Opus 5, No. 2

Pablo Casals, cello
Mieczyslaw Horszowski, piano
    Recorded in Europe, 1939
    HMV DB 3911/3913[E,78] (Europe); J 153 50136/40* (Spain). *Club
    Venezoliano del Disco* M 33 No 1.079 (Venezuela).

Pablo Casals, cello
Rudolf Serkin, piano
    Recorded in Perpignan, France, summer, 1951
    Columbia ML 4560, SL 170, ML 4572, SL 169, SL 201 (USA). *Odyssey*
    32 36 0016[R] (USA). *Philips* AL 01.285L, A 01384L (Europe). *EMI
    Columbia* CX 1093, QCX 10068 (England). *CBS* 72217* (Germany).

Pablo Casals, cello
Mieczyslaw Horszowski, piano
> Recorded in concert in the Beethovenhaus, Bonn, September 1958
> *Philips* AL 00507L, ABL 3272 (Europe); PHC 9099[S] (USA).

Sonata No. 3 in A Major for Cello and Piano, Opus 69

Pablo Casals, cello
Otto Schulhof, piano
> Recorded in Europe, 1931

> *HMV* DB 1417/1419[E,78] (Europe); J 153 50136/40* (Spain).
> *Victor* M 134[E,78]; 7568/70[E,78], AM 134 [E,78], 7571/73[E,78],
> DM 134[E,78] 17192/94[E,78] (USA). *Columbia* M5 30069* (USA).

Pablo Casals, cello
Rudolf Serkin, piano
> Recorded in Prades, France, May or June 1953
> *Columbia* ML 4878, SL 201 (USA). *Odyssey* 32 36 0016[R]* (USA).
> *Philips* AL 01.286L, A 01359L (Europe).

Sonata No. 4 in C Major for Cello and Piano, Opus 102, No. 1

Pablo Casals, cello
Mieczyslaw Horszowski, piano
> Recorded at the Abbey Road Studios of the Gramophone Company, Ltd., London, 1937
> *HMV* DB 3065/3066[E,78] (Europe); J 153 50136/40* (Spain). *Victor*
> 14366/14367[E,78] (USA).

Pablo Casals, cello
Rudolf Serkin, piano
> Recorded in Prades, France, May or June 1953
> *Columbia* ML 4878, SL 201 (USA). *Odyssey* 32 36 0016[R]* (USA).
> *Philips* AL 01.286L, A 01359L (Europe).

Sonata No. 5 in D Major for Cello and Piano, Opus 102, No. 2

Pablo Casals, cello
Mieczyslaw Horszowski, piano
> Recorded at the Abbey Road Studios of the Gramophone Company, Ltd., London, 1937
> *HMV* DB 3914/3916[E,78] (Europe); J 153 50136/40* (Spain). *Club
> Venezoliano del Disco* M 33 No 1.079 (Venezuela).

Pablo Casals, cello
Rudolf Serkin, piano
 Recorded in Prades, France, May or June 1953
 Columbia ML 4878, SL 201 (USA). *Odyssey* 32 36 0016[R]* (USA).
 Philips AL 01.286L (Europe).

Pablo Casals, cello
Mieczyslaw Horszowski, piano
 Recorded in concert in the Beethovenhaus, Bonn, September 1958
 Philips AL 00507L, ABL 3272 (Europe); PHC 9009[S] (USA).

Symphony No. 1 in C Major, Opus 21

Pablo Casals, conductor
Orquestra Pau Casals
 Recorded in Barcelona, 1932
 HMV DB 1729/1731[E,78], AB 556/558[E,78] (Europe). *Victor* M
 159[E,78], 11418/20[E,78] (announced as "in preparation" but apparently never issued in USA).

Symphony No. 4 in B Flat Major, Opus 60

Pablo Casals, conductor
Orquestra Pau Casals
 Recorded in Barcelona, 1932
 HMV M 96[E,78], D 1725/8, AB 564/567[E,78] (Europe). *Victor*
 L 11600[E; an experimental "coarse groove" LP] (USA).

Symphony No. 8 in F Major, Opus 93

Pablo Casals, conductor
Marlboro Festival Orchestra
 Recorded in concert at the Marlboro Festival, Vermont, July 14,
 1963
 Columbia ML 6331, MS 6931[S]* (USA). *CBS* 72523, 72523[S]*
 (England). Included in Columbia's *Casals at 90* package.

Trio No. 1 in E Flat Major for Piano, Violin, and Cello, Opus 1, No. 1

Eugene Istomin, piano
Joseph Fuchs, violin
Pablo Casals, cello
 Recorded in Prades, France, May or June 1953
 Columbia ML 5291 (USA). *CBS* 75475 (France). *Odyssey* 32 46 0001
 (USA) [announced but not released].

Trio No. 2 in G Major for Piano, Violin, and Cello, Opus 1, No. 2

Eugene Istomin, piano
Alexander Schneider, violin
Pablo Casals, cello
   Recorded in Perpignan, France, summer 1951
   Columbia SL 170, SL 169, ML 4561, ML 4573 (USA). *Odyssey* 32
   46 0001 (USA) [announced but not released].

Trio No. 3 in C Minor for Piano, Violin, and Cello, Opus 1, No. 3

Mieczyslaw Horszowski, piano
Sándor Végh, violin
Pablo Casals, cello
   Recorded in concert in the Beethovenhaus, Bonn, September 1958
   Philips G 05 364L, A 00 505L, L 505L, ABL 3270, 835019[S] (Europe);
   PHM 500120, PHS 900120[S] (USA). *Odyssey* 32 46 0001[S] (USA)
   [announced but not released]. *Turnabout* 34490[S]* (USA). *Murray
   Hill* S 4759[S]* (USA).

Trio No. 4 in B Flat Major for Piano, Clarinet or Violin, and Cello, Opus 11

Eugene Istomin, piano
Alexander Schneider, violin
Pablo Casals, cello
   Recorded in Perpignan, France, summer, 1951
   Columbia SL 170, SL 169, ML 4559, ML 4571* (USA). *Odyssey*
   32 46 0001 (USA) [announced but not released]. *Philips* L 1.458
   (Europe).

Trio No. 5 in D Major for Piano, Violin, and Cello, Opus 70, No. 1, "Geister"

Eugene Istomin, piano
Joseph Fuchs, violin
Pablo Casals, cello
   Recorded in Prades, France, May or June 1953
   Columbia ML 5291 (USA). *CBS* 75475 (France). *Odyssey* 32 46 0001
   (USA) [announced but not released].

Mieczyslaw Horszowski, piano
Sándor Végh, violin
Pablo Casals, cello
    Recorded in concert in the Beethovenhaus, Bonn, September 1958
    Philips G 05 365 R, ABL 3271 (Europe).

Karl Engel, piano
Sándor Végh, violin
Pablo Casals, cello
    Recorded in concert in Prades, France, in 1961
    Philips A 02210L, 835 101 AY[S]* (Europe).

Trio No. 6 in E Flat Major for Piano, Violin, and Cello, Opus 70, No. 2

Eugene Istomin, piano
Alexander Schneider, violin
Pablo Casals, cello
    Recorded in Perpignan, France, summer, 1951
    Columbia SL 170, SL 169, ML 4559, ML 4571 (USA). *Odyssey* 32 46 0001 (USA) [announced but not released]. *Philips* L 1.458 (Europe).

Trio No. 7 in B Flat Major for Piano, Violin, and Cello, Opus 97, *"Archduke"*

Alfred Cortot, piano
Jacques Thibaud, violin
Pablo Casals, cello
    Recorded in Kingsway Hall, London, November 1928
    HMV M 78 [E,78], DB 1223/6[E,78]; COLH 29 (Europe); C 161 50089/91M* (Italy); J 153 50136/40* (Spain). *Victor* M 92[E,78], 8196/200[E,78], AM 92[E,78], 8201/205[E,78], DM 92[E,78], 17224/28 [E,78] (USA). *Angel* COLH 29 (USA); GR 77, GR 2010*, GR 2074D* (Japan).

Eugene Istomin, piano
Alexander Schneider, violin
Pablo Casals, cello
    Recorded in Perpignan, France, summer 1951
    Columbia SL 170, SL 169, ML 4562, ML 4574 (USA). *Odyssey* 32 46 0001 (USA) [announced but not released].

Mieczyslaw Horszowski, piano
Sándor Végh, violin
Pablo Casals, cello
Recorded in concert in the Beethovenhaus, Bonn, September 1958
Philips A 00 506 L, ABL 3273, 835 020 AY[S] (Europe); PHM 500 016, PHS 900 016[S] (USA). *Turnabout* TVS 3441[S]* (USA). *Murray Hill* S 4759[S]* (USA). *SQN* 112X[S]* (USA).

Twelve Variations in G Major on "See, the Conquering Hero Comes!" from Handel's *Judas Maccabaeus* for Cello and Piano, Grove's No. 157

Pablo Casals, cello
Rudolf Serkin, piano
Recorded in Perpignan, France, summer, 1951
Columbia ML 4640 (USA). *Odyssey* 32 36 0016[R] (USA).

Seven Variations in E Flat Major on *"Bei Männern, welche Liebe fühlen"* from Mozart's *Die Zauberflöte*, Grove's No. 158

Pablo Casals, cello
Alfred Cortot, piano
Recorded in Kingsway Hall, London, June 1927
HMV DA 915/916[E,78], COLH 92 (Europe); J 153 50136/40* (Spain); C 161 50089/91* (Italy). *Angel* GR 2051*, GR 2074D*, GR 77 (Japan). *Victor* 1749/1750[E,78] (USA).

Pablo Casals, cello
Rudolf Serkin, piano
Recorded in Perpignan, France, summer, 1951
Columbia SL 170, SL 169, ML 4560, ML 4572, ML 4877, SL 201, K3L 233 (USA). *Odyssey* 32 36 0016[R]* (USA). *Philips* A 01352L, A 01384L (Europe). *EMI Columbia* CX 1093, QCX 10068 (England). *CBS* 72217* (Germany).

Twelve Variations in F Major on *"Ein Mädchen oder Weibchen"* from Mozart's *Die Zauberflöte*, Opus 66

Pablo Casals, cello
Rudolf Serkin, piano
Recorded in Perpignan, France, summer 1951
Columbia SL 170, SL 169, ML 4560, ML 4572, ML 4877, SL 201 (USA). *Odyssey* 32 36 0016[R]* (USA). *Philips* A 01352L, A 01348L (Europe). *EMI Columbia* CX 1093, QCX 10068 (England). *CBS* 72217* (Germany).

BOCCHERINI, LUIGI (1743–1805)

Concerto in B Flat Major for Cello and Orchestra. "Original" version, edited by Maurice Gendron

Maurice Gendron, cello
Pablo Casals, conductor
L'Orchestre des Concerts Lamoureux
Recorded in Paris, 1958

> *Epic* LC 3817, BC 1152[S] (USA). *Philips* A02067L, 835069[S]* (Europe); PHS 900-172[S] (USA).

• Arranged by Friedrich Grützmacher

Pablo Casals, cello
Sir Landon Ronald, conductor
London Symphony Orchestra
Recorded in London, 1937

> *HMV* DB 3056/3058[E,78] (Europe); J 153 50141/3* (Spain). *Victor* M 381[E,78], 14500/02[E,78], AM 381[E,78], 14503/05[E,78], DM 381[E,78], 16786/88[E,78], LCT 1028, WCT 41[45] (USA). *Columbia* M5 30069* (USA).

Sonata No. 6 in A Major for Cello and Piano

Pablo Casals, cello
Blas Net, piano
Recorded in Europe, 1931

> *HMV* DB 1392[E,78] (Europe). *Victor* 7258[E,78] (USA). *Columbia* M5 30069* (USA).

• Mvt. 2, *Allegro*

Pablo Casals, cello
Charles A. Baker[?], piano
Recorded in the USA, April 19, 1916

> *Columbia* 48710[A,78], 68025-D[A,78], SL 185 (USA); 7359[A,78] (England). *Pearl* GEM 105* (England). *Everest* 3323[R]* (USA). Note: The pianist in this recording is not identified on any of the labels, but Baker accompanied Casals in a number of disks recorded on April 14, 1916, and it is a reasonable assumption that he was also the pianist for this recording made five days later.

BRAHMS, JOHANNES (1833–1897)

Concerto in A Minor for Violin, Cello, and Orchestra, Opus 102

Jacques Thibaud, violin
Pablo Casals, cello
Alfred Cortot, conductor
Orquestra Pau Casals
    Recorded in Barcelona, June 1929

> *HMV* M 85[E,78], DB 1311/14[E,78], DB 7004/07[E,78], COLH 75 (Europe); J 153 50141/3* (Spain). *Angel* COLH 75 (USA); GR 75, GR 2044*, GR 2074D* (Japan). *Seraphim* IC 6043* (USA). *Victor* M 99[E,78], 8208/11[E,78], AM 99[E,78], 8212/15[E,78] (USA).

Sapphische Ode for voice and piano, Opus 94, No. 4. Arranged for cello and piano

Pablo Casals, cello
Walter Golde, piano
    Recorded in the USA, February 2, 1924
    Columbia 68088-D[A,78], 7075-M[A,78] (USA).

Serenade No. 2 in A Major, Opus 16

Pablo Casals, conductor
Marlboro Festival Orchestra
    Recorded in concert at the Marlboro Festival, Vermont, August 10, 1968
    Marlboro Recording Society MRS 1[S]* (USA).

Sextet No. 1 in B Flat Major for Strings, Opus 18

Isaac Stern, Alexander Schneider, violins
Milton Katims, Milton Thomas, violas
Pablo Casals, Madeline Foley, cellos
    Recorded in Prades, France, June 1952
    Columbia SL 185, SL 182, ML 4703, ML 4713 (USA). *CBS* BRG 72.324 (Europe); ABL 3085 (England). *Philips* AL 01.170L (Europe).

• Mvt. 2, *Andante*

> *Philips* AE 409.118[45] (Europe).

Sonata No. 1 in E Minor for Cello and Piano, Opus 38

Pablo Casals, cello
Eugene Istomin, piano
    Recorded in concert at the Festival Casals in Prades, France, 1953
    Columbia: not released.

Sonata No. 2 in F Major for Cello and Piano, Opus 99

Pablo Casals, cello
Mieczyslaw Horszowski, piano
    Recorded in Europe, 1937
        HMV DB 3059/3062[E,78] (Europe); J 153 50136/40* (Spain). *Victor*
        M 410[E,78], 14699/702[E,78], AM 410[E,78], 14703/06[E,78], DM
        410[E,78], 16504/07[E,78] (USA). *Columbia* M5 30069* (USA).

Pablo Casals, cello
Mieczyslaw Horszowski, piano
    Recorded in Prades, France, May or June 1953
    Columbia: not released.

Trio No. 1 in B Major for Piano, Violin, and Cello, Opus 8

Dame Myra Hess, piano
Isaac Stern, violin
Pablo Casals, cello
    Recorded in Prades, France, June 1952
    Columbia SL 185, SL 184, ML 4709, ML 4719 (USA). *Philips* AL
    01.207L (USA).

Trio No. 2 in C Major for Piano, Violin, and Cello, Opus 87

Dame Myra Hess, piano
Joseph Szigeti, violin
Pablo Casals, cello
    Recorded in Prades, France, June 1952
    Columbia SL 185, SL 184, ML 4720, ML 4710 (USA). *Philips* AL
    01.294L (Europe). Bruno Walter Society WSA-714* (USA).

Trio No. 3 in C Minor for Piano, Violin, and Cello, Opus 101

Eugene Istomin, piano
Isaac Stern, violin
Pablo Casals, cello
    Recorded in Prades, France, June 1952
    Columbia: not released.

Variations on a Theme by Haydn, Opus 56a

Pablo Casals, conductor
London Symphony Orchestra
    Recorded in London, 1930
      Victor G 16[E,78], 9287/9289[E,78] (USA). *HMV* D
      1376/1378[E,78], AB 331/333[E,78] (Europe).

Pablo Casals, conductor
Marlboro Festival Orchestra
    Recorded in Marlboro, Vermont, summer 1969
    Columbia M5 30069[S]* (USA).

BRUCH, MAX (1838–1920)

Kol Nidrei for cello and orchestra, Opus 47

Pablo Casals, cello
Unidentified orchestra
    Recorded January 18, 1915
    Columbia A 5722[A,78] (USA).

Pablo Casals, cello
Sir Landon Ronald, conductor
London Symphony Orchestra
    Recorded in England, 1937
      HMV DB 3063/3064[E,78] (Europe). *Victor* M 680[E,78],
      14842/43[E,78], LCT 1028, WCT 42[45] (USA). *World Record Club*
      SH 121* (England). *Angel* GR 2207* (Japan).

• Arranged for cello and piano

Pablo Casals, cello
Edouard Gendron, piano
    Recorded April 3, 1923
    Columbia 68019-D [A,78] (USA).

CAMPAGNOLI, BARTOLOMEO (1751–1827)

Romanza

Pablo Casals, cello
Charles A. Baker, piano
    Recorded January 27, 1915
      Columbia A5654[A,78], SL 185 bonus disk (USA). *Pearl* GEM 105*
      (England). *Everest* 3323[R]* (USA).

CASALS, ENRIQUE (1892–   )

Lluny

Cobla of Gerona
    Recorded in Prades, France, 1955, "under the supervision of Pablo Casals"
    Angel 35475 (USA). *HMV* FELP 117 (France).

Tarragona

Cobla of Gerona
    Recorded in Prades, France, 1955, "under the supervision of Pablo Casals"
    Angel 35475 (USA). *HMV* FELP 117 (France).

CASALS, PABLO (1876–1973)

El Pessebre, oratorio in five parts on a text by Juan Alavedra. "Complete" recording (abridgement by the composer)

Olga Iglesias, soprano
Maureen Forrester, mezzo-soprano
Paulino Saharrea, tenor
Carlos Serrano, baritone
Pablo Elvira, baritone
Chorus of the Conservatory of Music of Puerto Rico, Sergije Rainis, director
Festival Casals de Puerto Rico Orchestra
Pablo Casals, conductor
    Recorded in Puerto Rico, June 1972
    Recorded by Columbia for Festival Casals. Data concerning label not firm at press time.

• From Part Three, *Los Tres Reyes Magos* (*Les Trois Mages*)

Ensemble of 102 cellos
Pablo Casals, conductor
    Recorded in concert at the Grand Amphithéâtre of the Sorbonne, Paris, October 20, 1956
    Philips L77.408L, 6521 012[R]* (Europe). *Philips-Réalités* C 2 (Europe).

Festivola (sardana)

Cobla of Gerona
> Recorded in Prades, France, 1955, "under the supervision of Pablo Casals"
>
> *Angel* 35475 (USA). *HMV* FELP 117 (France).

Sant Marti del Canigo: Sardana de l'Exili

Pablo Casals, conductor
Prades Festival Orchestra
> Recorded in Prades, France, June 1950
>
> *Columbia* 73249-D[78], 3-73249-D[78], 4-73249-D[78], ML 4926 (USA). *CBS* 8.601[45], EP 8.527[45]* (France). *Philips* 409.008[45] (Europe).

Cobla of Gerona
> Recorded in Prades, France, 1955, "under the supervision of Pablo Casals"
>
> *Angel* 34575 (USA). *HMV* FELP 117 (France).

Sardana for cello orchestra

Pablo Casals, conductor
Ensemble of 102 cellos
> Recorded in concert at the Grand Amphithéâtre of the Sorbonne, Paris, October 20, 1956
>
> *Philips* L77.408L, 6521 012[R]* (Europe). *Philips-Réalités* C 2 (Europe).

Six Songs:
Cançó Catalana No. 1 (text by Jacinto Verdaguer)
Cançó Catalana No. 2 (text by Apeles Mestres)
De cara al mar (text by Juan Llongueras)
Tres estrofas de amor (text by Tomás Blanco)
Balada de la nova Solveig (text by Ventura Gassol)
El Angél Travieso (text by Rafael Montañez)

Olga Iglesias, soprano
Mieczyslaw Horszowski, piano
> Recorded in Marlboro, Vermont, summer 1966, in the presence of the composer
>
> *Columbia* ML 6336, MS 6936[S] (USA); included in Columbia's *Casals at 90* package.
>
> Note: For other recordings of Casals' compositions, see Section II.

CASSADÓ, GASPAR (1897–1966)

Requiebros

Pablo Casals, cello
Blas Net, piano
 Recorded in Europe, 1930
  HMV DB 1391[E,78] (Europe). *Victor* 7660[E,78] (USA). *Columbia*
  M5 30069 (USA).

CHOPIN, FRÉDÉRIC FRANÇOIS (1810–1849)

Nocturne in E Flat Major for Piano, Opus 9, No. 2. Arranged
for cello and piano by David Popper

Pablo Casals, cello
Walter Golde, piano
 Recorded April 30, 1920
  Columbia 49820[A,78], 8901M[A,78], 68024D[A,78] (USA); 7357
  [A,78] (England). *Pearl* GEM 106* (England). *Everest* 3323[R]*
  (USA). Note: The pianist is not identified on any of the labels, but
  Walter Golde had made a recording with Casals the preceding day.

Pablo Casals, cello
Nikolai Mednikoff, piano
 Recorded in Europe, January 20, 1926
  HMV DB 966[E,78] (Europe). *Victor* 6589[E,78], LM 2699* (USA).
  RCA LM 2699*, 430.296* (Europe); 644.520* (France); RED 2019*
  (Japan).

Prelude in D Flat Major for Piano, Opus 28, No. 15. Arranged
for cello and piano by Sieveking

Pablo Casals, cello
Nikolai Mednikoff, piano
 Recorded in Europe, January 19, 1926
  HMV DB 966[E,78] (Europe). *Victor* 6589[E,78], LM 2699* (USA).
  RCA LM 2699*, 430.296* (Europe); 644.520* (France); RED 2019*
  (Japan).

COUPERIN, FRANÇOIS, "Le Grand" (1668–1733)

Pièces de Concert. Arranged for cello and piano by Paul Bazelaire

Pablo Casals, cello
Mieczyslaw Horszowski, piano
    Recorded in concert at the White House, Washington, D.C., November 13, 1961
    Columbia KL 5726* (USA). *CBS* BRG 72035* (Europe).

CROUCH, FREDERICK NICHOLLS (1808–1896)

Kathleen Mavourneen. Arranged for cello and orchestra

Pablo Casals, cello
Unidentified orchestra
    Recorded May 1 or 4, 1920
    Columbia 79154[A,78], 33008-D[A,78] (USA).

CUI, CÉSAR ANTONOVITCH (1835–1918)

Berceuse, Opus 20, No. 18

Pablo Casals, cello
Walter Golde, piano
    Recorded February 18, 1924
    Columbia 2037-M[A,78] (USA).

DEBUSSY, CLAUDE ACHILLE (1862–1918)

Petite Suite for piano four hands: *"Menuet."* Arranged for cello and piano by Gürt

Pablo Casals, cello
Nikolai Mednikoff, piano
    Recorded in Europe, 1927
    Victor 1191[E,78] (USA). *HMV* DA 862[E,78] (Europe).

DEL RIEGO, TERESA (MRS. TERESA LEDBETTER) (1876–1968)

"Oh, Dry Those Tears." Arranged for cello and piano

Pablo Casals, cello
Walter Golde, piano
>   Recorded March 30 or 31, 1923
>   *Columbia* 2037-M[A,78] (USA).

DVOŘÁK, ANTONÍN (1841–1904)

Concerto in B Minor for Cello and Orchestra, Opus 104

Pablo Casals, cello
George Szell, conductor
The Czech Philharmonic Orchestra
>   Recorded in Prague, April 1937
>   *HMV* M 306[E,78], DB 3288/3292[E,78], DB 8420/24[E,78], COLH
>   30 (Europe); HQM 7013* (England); J 153 50141/3* (Spain). *Angel*
>   COLH 30 (USA); GR 74, GR 2012*, GR 2074D* (Japan). *Electrola*
>   E 80614 (Germany). *Victor* M 458[E,78], 14936/40[E,78], AM
>   458[E,78], 14941/45[E,78], DM 458[E,78], 16365/69[E,78], WCT
>   39[45], LCT 1026 (USA).

Pablo Casals, cello
Alexander Schneider, conductor
Festival Casals de Puerto Rico Orchestra
>   Recorded in concert in the theater of the University of Puerto
>   Rico during the 1960 Festival Casals
>   *Everest* LPBR 6083, SDBR 3083[S] (USA).

Seven Gypsy Songs, Opus 55: No. 4, "*Kdyžmne stará matka*" ("Songs My Mother Taught Me"). Arranged for cello and piano by Heinrich Grünfeld

Pablo Casals, cello
Blas Net, piano
>   Recorded in Europe, 1930
>   *HMV* DB 1399[E,78] (Europe). *Victor* 7193[E,78], LCT 1050, WCT
>   72[45] (USA).

Discography

ELGAR, SIR EDWARD (1857–1934)

Concerto for Cello and Orchestra in E Minor, Opus 85

Pablo Casals, cello
Sir Adrian Boult, conductor
BBC Symphony Orchestra
   Recorded at the Abbey Road Studios of EMI, London, 1945
   HMV M 394[E,78], DB 6338/6341S[E,78], DBS 9043, DB
   9044/46[E,78] (Europe); J 153 50141/3* (Spain). *World Record Club*
   SH 121* (Europe). *Angel* GR 2207* (Japan).

Salut d'Amour: Morceau Mignon for Small Orchestra, Opus
12. Arranged for cello and orchestra

Pablo Casals, cello
Unidentified orchestra
   Recorded January 15, 1915
   Columbia A 5679[A,78] (USA).

• Arranged for cello and piano

Pablo Casals, cello
Romano Romani, piano
   Recorded January 24 and March 15, 1922
   Columbia 80158[A,78], 33031-D[A,78] (USA).

FALLA, MANUEL DE (1876–1946)

Canciones Populares Españoles: No. 5, *"Nana"* (berceuse).
Arranged for cello and piano

Pablo Casals, cello
Eugene Istomin, piano
   Recorded in concert at the Festival Casals in Prades, France, 1953
   Columbia ML 4926, A 1937[45] (USA). *CBS* 8.601[45], EP 8.527[45]*
   (France). *Philips* 409.008[45] (Europe).

FAURÉ, GABRIEL (1845–1924)

"Après un rêve." Arranged for cello and piano by Pablo Casals

Pablo Casals, cello
Charles A. Baker, piano
   Recorded March 1915
   Columbia A 6020[A,78] (USA).

Pablo Casals, cello
Nikolai Mednikoff, piano
    Recorded January 5, 1926
        HMV DA 731[E,78] (Europe). *Victor* 1083[E,78], LM 2699* (USA).
        RCA LM 2699*, 430.296 (Europe); 644.520* (France); RED 2019*
        (Japan).

Élégie for cello and orchestra, Opus 24

Paul Bazelaire, Maurice Maréchal, Gaspar Cassadó, Rudolf von Tobel,
    Étienne Pasquier, André Lévy, Gaston Marchesini, Guy Fallot,
    Charles Bartsch, Jean Vaugeois, cellos
Pablo Casals, conductor
L'Orchestre des Concerts Lamoureux
    Recorded in concert in the Grand Amphithéâtre of the Sorbonne,
    Paris, October 10, 1956
        Philips L 77.408L, 6521 012[R]* (Europe). *Philips-Réalités* C 2 (Europe).

GARRETA, JULI (1875–1925)

Innominada

Cobla of Gerona
    Recorded in Prades, France, 1955, "under the supervision of Pablo
    Casals"
        Angel 35475 (USA). *HMV* FELP 117 (France).

La Rosada

Cobla of Gerona
    Recorded in Prades, France, 1955, "under the supervision of Pablo
    Casals"
        Angel 35475 (USA). *HMV* FELP 117 (France).

GLAZUNOV, ALEXANDER (1865–1936)

Melodie Arabe for cello and piano, Opus 20, No. 1

Pablo Casals, cello
Edouard Gendron, piano
    Recorded April 3 or 4, 1923
        Columbia 80923[A,78], 33030-D[A,78], 2010-M[A,78], 184-M[A,78]
        (USA).

GODARD, BENJAMIN (1849–1895)

Jocelyn: Berceuse, *"Cachés dans cet asile."* Arranged for cello and piano

Pablo Casals, cello
Nikolai Mednikoff, piano
    Recorded January 20, 1926
        HMV DB 1039[E,78] (Europe). *Victor* 6630[E,78], LM 2699* (USA). *RCA* LM 2699*, 430.296* (Europe); 644.520* (France); RED 2019* (Japan).

GOLTERMANN, GEORG EDUARD (1824–1898)

Cantilena from *Concerto in A minor for Cello and Orchestra,* Opus 14

Pablo Casals, cello
Unidentified orchestra
    Recorded April 15, 1916
        Columbia A 5847[A,78] (USA); 7359[A,78] (England). *Pearl* GEM 106* (England). *Everest* 3323[R]* (USA).

GRANADOS, ENRIQUE (1867–1916)

Danzas Españolas: No. 5, *"Andaluza"* (*"Playera"*). Arranged for cello and piano by Pablo Casals

Pablo Casals, cello
Charles A. Baker, piano
    Recorded April 14, 1916
    Columbia A 5847[A,78] (USA).

Pablo Casals, cello
Nikolai Mednikoff, piano
    Recorded in Europe, 1929
        Victor 1311[E,78] (USA). *HMV* DA 1015[E,78] (Europe). Both disks mislabeled *"Rondella Aragonesa."*

Goyescas: "Intermezzo." Arranged for cello and piano by Gaspar Cassadó

Pablo Casals, cello
Edouard Gendron, piano
> Recorded February 21, 1925
> *Victor* 6501[E,78] (USA).

Pablo Casals, cello
Nikolai Mednikoff, piano
> Recorded in Europe, February 28, 1927
> *HMV* DB 1067[E,78] (Europe). *Victor* 6501[E,78], 6635[E,78], LCT 1050, WCT 72[45], LM 2699* (USA). *RCA* LM 2699*, 430.296* (Europe); 644.520* (France); RED 2019* (Japan). Note: Both the acoustic and electrical versions were issued by Victor as 6501.

HANDEL, GEORGE FRIDERIC (1685–1759)

Overture to *Berenice: Minuet.* Arranged for cello and piano

Pablo Casals, cello
Walter Golde, piano
> Recorded February 16, 1924
> *Columbia* 2036-D[A,78] (USA).

Serse: "*Ombra mai fù*" ("*Largo*"). Arranged for cello and orchestra

Pablo Casals, cello
Unidentified orchestra
> Recorded January 15, 1915
> *Columbia* A 5649[A,78], SL 185 bonus disk (USA). *Musicians Foundation* TF 1001* (USA).

• Arranged for cello and piano

Pablo Casals, cello
Walter Golde [?], piano
> Recorded April 23, 1920
> *Columbia* 49802[A,78], 68061-D[A,78], 7053-M[A,78] (USA). Note: The pianist is not identified on the labels, but Walter Golde accompanied Casals in a recording made two days earlier.

Discography

HAYDN, FRANZ JOSEPH (1732–1809)

Concerto for Cello and Orchestra in D Major, Opus 101. "Original" version, edited by Maurice Gendron

Maurice Gendron, cello
Pablo Casals, conductor
L'Orchestre des Concerts Lamoureux
    Recorded in Europe, 1958
        Philips A 02067L, 835.069 AY[S]* (Europe); PHS 900172[S] (USA).
        Epic LC 3817, BC 1152[S] (USA).

• Mvts. 1 and 2. Arranged by François Gevaërt

Pablo Casals, cello
Sir Adrian Boult, conductor
BBC Symphony Orchestra
    Recorded in the Abbey Road Studios, London, 1945. (A complete recording was planned, but the sessions were broken off when Casals began his postwar withdrawal from public performance.)
    HMV: not released

• Mvt. 2

Pablo Casals, cello
Unidentified orchestra
    Recorded April 15, 1916
    Columbia A 5875[A,78] (USA).

• Mvt. 2. Arranged for cello and piano

Pablo Casals, cello
Walter Golde, piano
    Recorded February 2, 1924
    Columbia 68061-D[A,78], 7053-M[A,78] (USA).

Sonata No. 9 in D Major for Keyboard: Adagio. Arranged for cello and piano

Pablo Casals, cello
Eugene Istomin, piano
    Recorded in concert in Perpignan, France, summer 1951

    Columbia SL 167 bonus disk, SL 170 bonus disk, ML 4926, A 1922[45] (USA).

Minuet No. 11 in G Major

Pablo Casals, cello
Charles A. Baker [?], piano
Recorded April 22, 1916

Columbia [?]A 5821[A,78] (USA). Note: Columbia's recording data indicate this recording was released as A 5821, but that disk also includes another Haydn Minuet (see next item) and the Saint-Saëns *Allegro Appassionato*, both of which have matrix numbers different from this minuet. That Charles A. Baker accompanied Casals in this recording can be supposed from the fact that he made another record with Casals on the same day.

Sonata for Violin and Viola in C Major: Minuet with Variations. Arranged for cello and piano by Alfredo Piatti

Pablo Casals, cello
Charles A. Baker, piano
Recorded April 14, 1916
Columbia A 5821[A,78] (USA).

Pablo Casals, cello
Blas Net, piano
Recorded in Europe, 1930

HMV DB 1391[E,78], DB 3064[E,78] (Europe); J 153 50136/40* (Spain). *Angel* GR 2207* (Japan). *Victor* 7501[E,78], M 680[E,78], 14843[E,78] (USA). *World Record Club* SH 121* (Europe). *Columbia* M5 30069* (USA).

Symphony No. 45 in F Sharp Minor, "Farewell"

Pablo Casals, conductor
Festival Casals de Puerto Rico Orchestra
Recorded in concert in the theater of the University of Puerto Rico on May 9, 1959
Columbia ML 5449, MS 6122 (USA).

Symphony No. 94 in G Major, "Surprise"

Pablo Casals, conductor
Marlboro Festival Orchestra
Recorded in concert at the Marlboro Festival, Vermont, July 9, 1967
Columbia MGP 32[S]*, M 31130[S]* (USA).

Symphony No. 95 in C Minor

Pablo Casals, conductor
Marlboro Festival Orchestra
    Recorded in concert at the Marlboro Festival, Vermont, July 8, 1967
    Columbia M 31130[S]* (USA).

Trio No. 1 in G Major for Piano, Violin, and Cello, Opus 73, No. 2

Alfred Cortot, piano
Jacques Thibaud, violin
Pablo Casals, cello
    Recorded in Europe July 7, 1926
    HMV DA 895/896[E,78], COLH 12, HLM 7017* (Europe); J 153 50136/40* (Spain); C 161 50089/91M* (Italy). *Angel* GR 2009*, GR 2074D*, GR 76 (Japan); COLH 12 (USA). *Victor* 3045/3046X[E,78] (USA). *Da Capo* 1 C 047-01 148M* (Europe).

HILLEMACHER, PAUL JOSEPH [pen name for Paul Joseph William Hillemacher (1852–1933) and Lucien Joseph Edward Hillemacher (1860–1909)]

Gavotte Tendre for cello and piano

Pablo Casals, cello
Nikolai Mednikoff, piano
    Recorded January 4, 1926
    HMV DA 862[E,78] (Europe). *Victor* 1191[E,78], LM 2699* (USA). *RCA* LM 2699*, 430.296* (Europe); 644.520* (France); RED 2019* (Japan).

HINKSON

"Would God I Were the Tender Apple Blossom" ("Londonderry Air"). Arranged for cello and piano

Pablo Casals, cello
Romano Romani, piano
    Recorded January 24 and March 15, 1922
    Columbia 80159[A,78], 33032-D[A,78], 2009-M[A,78] (USA).

KREISLER, FRITZ (1875–1962)

Chanson Louis XIII et Pavane (in the style of François Couperin) for violin and piano. Arranged for cello and piano

Pablo Casals, cello
Charles A. Baker [?], piano
    Recorded April 22, 1916
        Columbia A 5907[A,78] (USA). Note: The pianist is not identified
        on the disk label, but Casals and Baker made another recording to-
        gether on the same date.

LASERNA, BLAS DE (1751–1816)

Tonadilla. Arranged for cello and piano by Gaspar Cassadó

Pablo Casals, cello
Blas Net, piano
    Recorded in Europe, 1931
        HMV DA 1118[E,78] (Europe). *Victor* 1542[E,78] (USA).

LASSEN, EDUARD (1830–1904)

"Thine Eyes So Blue and Tender." Arranged for cello and piano

Pablo Casals, cello
Walter Golde, piano
    Recorded April 29, 1920
        Columbia 79147[A,78], 33032D[A,78], 2009M[A,78] (USA).

LISZT, FRANZ (1811–1886)

Liebestraum No. 3 in A Flat Major for piano. Arranged for cello and orchestra

Pablo Casals, cello
Unidentified orchestra
    Recorded March 5, 1915
        Columbia A 5756[A,78] (USA).

• Arranged for cello and piano

Pablo Casals, cello
Walter Golde, piano
    Recorded April 28, 1920
    Columbia 49812[A,78], 68023-D[A,78] (USA).

MACDOWELL, EDWARD (1861–1908)

Woodland Sketches, Opus 51, for piano: No. 1, "To a Wild Rose." Arranged for cello and piano

Pablo Casals, cello
Walter Golde, piano
    Recorded January 31, 1923
    Columbia 80817[A,78], 33030-D[A,78], 2010-M[A,78], 184-M[A,78] (USA).

MENDELSSOHN-BARTHOLDY, FELIX (1809–1847)

Lieder ohne Wörte: No. 30 in A Major, Opus 62, No. 6, *"Frühlingslied"* ("Spring Song"). Arranged for cello and piano

Pablo Casals, cello
Charles A. Baker [?], piano
    Recorded April 19, 1916
    Columbia A 6020[A,78] (USA). Note: The pianist in this recording is not identified on the labels, but Baker accompanied Casals in several recordings made on April 14, 1916, and it is a reasonable assumption that he was also the pianist for this one, made five days later.

• No. 36 in E Major, Opus 67, No. 6, "Serenade." Arranged for cello and piano

Pablo Casals, cello
Walter Golde, piano
    Recorded February 2, 1924
    Columbia 33048-D[A,78], 2011-M[A,78], X 317[A,78] (USA).

[607]

• No. 49 in D Major, Opus 109, for cello and piano

Pablo Casals, cello
Blas Net, piano
> Recorded in Europe, 1930
> > *HMV* DB 1399[E,78] (Europe). *Victor* 7193[E,78], LCT 1050, WCT 72[45] (USA).

Symphony No. 4 in A Major, Opus 90, "Italian"

Pablo Casals, conductor
Marlboro Festival Orchestra
> Recorded in concert at the Marlboro Festival, Vermont, July 13, 1963
> > *Columbia* ML 6331, MS 6931[S]*, MGP 32[S]* (USA); *CBS* 72523, 72523[S]* (England). Included in Columbia's *Casals at 90* package.

Trio No. 1 in D Minor for Piano, Violin, and Cello, Opus 49

Alfred Cortot, piano
Jacques Thibaud, violin
Pablo Casals, cello
> Recorded in Kingsway Hall, London, June 1927
> > *Victor* M 126[E,78], 8223/26[E,78] (USA). *HMV* M 50[E,78], DB 1072/75[E,78] (USA); COLH 75 (Europe). *Angel* COLH 75 (USA); COLH 75, GR 2044*, GR 2074-D* (Japan). *Seraphim* IC 6044* (USA).

Mieczyslaw Horszowski, piano
Alexander Schneider, violin
Pablo Casals, cello
> Recorded in concert in the East Room of the White House, Washington, D.C., November 13, 1961
> > *Columbia* KL 5726 (USA). *CBS* BRG 72035* (Europe).

MOORE, THOMAS (1779–1852)

"Believe Me If All Those Endearing Young Charms." Arranged for cello and orchestra by Stevenson [?]

Pablo Casals, cello
Unidentified orchestra
> Recorded May 1 or 4, 1920
> > *Columbia* 79155[A,78], 33008[A,78], 2021-M[A,78] (USA).

MORERA, ENRIQUE (1863–1942)

La Nit de l'Amor (sardana)

Cobla of Gerona
Chorus of GE y EG of Gerona
    Recorded in Prades, France, 1955, "under the supervision of Pablo Casals"
    Angel 35475 (USA). *HMV* FELP 117 (France).

MOZART, WOLFGANG AMADEUS (1756–1791)

Ch'io mi scordi di te (Recitativo andantino), Non temer amato bene (Rondo andante), KV 505, concert aria for mezzo-soprano and orchestra with keyboard obbligato

Jennie Tourel, mezzo-soprano
Mieczyslaw Horszowski, piano
Pablo Casals, conductor
Perpignan Festival Orchestra
    Recorded in Perpignan, France, summer 1951
    Columbia ML 4640 (USA).

Concerto No. 1 in G Major for Flute and Orchestra, KV 313

John Wummer, flute
Pablo Casals, conductor
Perpignan Festival Orchestra
    Recorded in Perpignan, France, summer 1951
    Columbia SL 168, SL 170, ML 4567, ML 4555 (USA).

Concerto No. 9 in E Flat Major for Piano and Orchestra, KV 271, "Jeune homme"

Dame Myra Hess, piano
Pablo Casals, conductor
Perpignan Festival Orchestra
    Recorded in Perpignan, France, summer 1951
    Columbia SL 168, SL 170, ML 4556, ML 4568 (USA). *EMI Columbia* CX 1091, FCX 225 (England). *Philips* A 01351 L (Europe).

Concerto No. 14 in E Flat Major for Piano and Orchestra, KV 449

Eugene Istomin, piano
Pablo Casals, conductor
Perpignan Festival Orchestra
    Recorded in Perpignan, France, summer 1951
    Columbia SL 168, SL 170, ML 4567, ML 4555 (USA).

Concerto No. 22 in E Flat Major for Piano and Orchestra, KV 482

Rudolf Serkin, piano
Pablo Casals, conductor
Perpignan Festival Orchestra
    Recorded in Perpignan, France, summer 1951

    Columbia SL 168, SL 170, ML 4557, ML 4569 (USA). *EMI Columbia* CX 1092, FCX 226 (England). *Philips* A 01352 L (Europe).

Concerto No. 27 in B Flat Major for Piano and Orchestra, KV 595

Mieczyslaw Horszowski, piano
Pablo Casals, conductor
Perpignan Festival Orchestra
    Recorded in Perpignan, France, summer 1951

    Columbia SL 168, SL 170, ML 4570, ML 4558 (USA).

Divertimento No. 11 in D Major for Oboe, Horns, and Strings, KV 251

Marcel Tabuteau, oboe
Alexander Schneider, violin
Pablo Casals, conductor
Perpignan Festival Orchestra
    Recorded in Perpignan, France, summer 1951

    Columbia SL 167, SL 170, ML 4554, ML 4566 (USA). *EMI Columbia* CX 1090, FCX 227 (England).

Concerto No. 5 in A Major for Violin and Orchestra, KV 219, "Turkish"

Erica Morini, violin
Pablo Casals, conductor
Perpignan Festival Orchestra
    Recorded in Perpignan, France, summer 1951
    Columbia SL 167, SL 170, ML 4565, ML 4553 (USA).

Idomeneo, Re di Creta, KV 366: No. 19, *"Zeffiretti lusinghieri"*

Jennie Tourel, mezzo-soprano
Pablo Casals, conductor
Perpignan Festival Orchestra
    Recorded in Perpignan, France, summer 1951
    Columbia ML 4640 (USA).

Quintet for Strings in D Major, KV 593: Mvt. 2, *Larghetto.* Arranged for cello, clarinet, and string quartet

Pablo Casals, cello
Unidentified clarinetist and string quartet
    Recorded April 21, 1916
    Columbia A 5953[A,78] (USA); 7153[A,78] (England). *Pearl* GEM
    105* (England). *Everest* 3323[R]* (USA).

Serenade No. 12 in G Major for Strings, "Eine kleine Nacht-musik," KV 525

Pablo Casals, conductor
Perpignan Festival Orchestra
    Recorded in Perpignan, France, summer 1951
    Columbia SL 167, SL 170, ML 4551, ML 4563 (USA). *EMI Columbia*
    CX 1088, FCX 223 (England).

Pablo Casals, conductor
Marlboro Festival Orchestra
    Recorded in concert at the Marlboro Festival, Vermont, July 16, 1967
    Columbia MS 7446[S]* (USA).

Sinfonia Concertante for Violin, Viola, and Orchestra in E Flat Major, KV 364

Isaac Stern, violin
William Primrose, viola
Pablo Casals, conductor
Perpignan Festival Orchestra
    Recorded in Perpignan, France, summer 1951
        Columbia SL 167, SL 170, ML 4552, ML 4564 (USA). *EMI Columbia* CX 1089, FCX 224 (England).

Symphony No. 29 in A Major, KV 201

Pablo Casals, conductor
Perpignan Festival Orchestra
    Recorded in Perpignan, France, summer 1951
        Columbia SL 167, SL 170, ML 4551, ML 4563 (USA). *EMI Columbia* CX 1088, FCX 223 (England).

Symphony No. 35 in D Major, KV 385, "Haffner"

Pablo Casals, conductor
Marlboro Festival Orchestra
    Recorded in concert at the Marlboro Festival, Vermont, July 30, 1967
        Columbia ML 6466, MS 7066[S]*, D3S 817[S]* (USA).

Symphony No. 36 in C Major, KV 425, "Linz"

Pablo Casals, conductor
Festival Casals de Puerto Rico Orchestra
    Recorded in concert in the theater of the University of Puerto Rico during the 1959 Festival Casals de Puerto Rico
        Columbia ML 5449, MS 6122[S], D3S 817[S]* (USA).

Symphony No. 38 in D Major, KV 504, "Prague"

Pablo Casals, conductor
Marlboro Festival Orchestra
    Recorded in concert at the Marlboro Festival, Vermont, July 7, 1968
        Columbia D3S 817[S]* (USA).

Symphony No. 39 in E Flat Major, KV 543

Pablo Casals, conductor
Marlboro Festival Orchestra
    Recorded in Marlboro, Vermont, July 12, 1963
      Columbia D3S 817[S]* (USA).

Symphony No. 40 in G Minor, KV 550

Pablo Casals, conductor
Marlboro Festival Orchestra
    Recorded in concert at the Marlboro Festival, Vermont, July 6, 1968
      Columbia MS 7262[S]*, D3S 817[S]* (USA).

Symphony No. 41 in C Major, KV 551, "Jupiter"

Pablo Casals, conductor
Marlboro Festival Orchestra
    Recorded in concert at the Marlboro Festival, Vermont, July 15, 1967
      Columbia ML 6466, MS 7066[S]*, D3S 817[S]*, MGP 32[S]* (USA).

POPPER, DAVID (1843–1913)

Chanson Villageoise, Opus 62, No. 2

Pablo Casals, cello
Edouard Gendron, piano
    Recorded 1925
Victor 1083[E,78] (USA). *HMV* DA 731[E,78] (Europe).

Gavotte No. 2 in D Major, Opus 23

Pablo Casals, cello
Romano Romani, piano
    Recorded January 23 and March 15, 1922
      Columbia 98012[A,78], 68025-D[A,78] (USA); 7358[A,78] (England).

Mazurka in G Minor, Opus 11, No. 3

Pablo Casals, cello
Charles A. Baker, piano
    Recorded April 23, 1915
      Columbia A 5697[A,78] (USA); 7358[A,78] (England). *Pearl* GEM 106* (England). *Everest* 3323[S]* (USA).

[613]

Pablo Casals, cello
Nikolai Mednikoff, piano
 Recorded in 1930
 HMV DA 1030[E,78] (Europe).

Danses Espagnoles, Opus 54

• No. 2, "Serenade"

Pablo Casals, cello
Charles A. Baker, piano
 Recorded January 24, 1915
 Columbia A 5650[A,78], SL 185 bonus disk (USA).

• No. 5, "Vito"

Pablo Casals, cello
Nikolai Mednikoff, piano
 Recorded in 1929
 HMV DA 1015[E,78] (Europe). *Victor* 1311[E,78] (USA).

RIMSKY-KORSAKOV, NIKOLAI (1844–1908)

The Tale of the Tsar Saltana, Act III: "The Flight of the Bumblebee." Arranged for cello and piano

Pablo Casals, cello
Blas Net, piano
 Recorded in Europe, 1930
 HMV DB 1399[E,78] (USA). *Victor* 7193[E,78], LCT 1050, WCT 72[45] (USA).

RUBINSTEIN, ANTON (1830–1894)

Melody in F Major for Piano, Opus 3, No. 1. Arranged for cello and orchestra

Pablo Casals, cello
Unidentified orchestra
 Recorded January 15, 1915
 Columbia A 5649[A,78] (USA).

[614]

• Arranged for cello and piano by David Popper

Pablo Casals, cello
Walter Golde, piano
    Recorded April 24, 1920
      Columbia 49804[A,78], 68026-D[A,78] (USA).

Pablo Casals, cello
Nikolai Mednikoff, piano
    Recorded January 20, 1926
      Victor 1178[E,78], LCT 1050, WCT 72[45], LM 2699* (USA). *RCA* LM 2699*, 644.520* (Europe); 430.296* (Germany); RED 2019* (Japan); *HMV* DA-833[E,78] (Europe).

Soirées de Saint Petersbourg, Opus 44: No. 1, Romance in E Flat Major

Pablo Casals, cello
Walter Golde, piano
    Recorded January 30, 1923
      Columbia 80815[A,78], 33031-D[A,78], 2021-M[A,78] (USA).

SAINT-SAËNS, CAMILLE (1835–1921)

Allegro Appassionato for cello and piano, Opus 43

Pablo Casals, cello
Charles A. Baker, piano
    Recorded April 22, 1916
      Columbia A 5821[A,78] (USA).

Le Carnaval des Animaux (*The Carnival of the Animals*) for orchestra and two pianos: No. 13, "*Le Cygne*" ("The Swan"). Arranged for cello and piano

Pablo Casals, cello
Charles A. Baker, piano
    Recorded January 24, 1915
      Columbia A 5650[A,78], SL 185 bonus disk (USA). *Musicians Foundation* TF 1001* (USA).

Pablo Casals, cello
Walter Golde, piano
  Recorded April 22, 1920
  Columbia 49796[A,78], 68027-D[A,78], 7021-M[A,78], 5092-M[A,78]
  (USA).

Pablo Casals, cello
Nikolai Mednikoff, piano
  Recorded January 31, 1928
  Victor 1143[E,78], LCT 1002, LCT 1050, WCT 3[45], WCT 72[45],
  LM 2699* (USA). *RCA* LM 2699* (Europe); 430.296* (Germany);
  644.520* (France); RED 2019* (Japan); *HMV* DA 776[E,78]
  (Europe).

SCHUBERT, FRANZ PETER (1797–1828)

Moments Musicals, Opus 94, D. 780: No. 3 in F Minor. Arranged for cello and piano by Hugo Becker

Pablo Casals, cello
Nikolai Mednikoff, piano
  Recorded January 4, 1926
  Victor 1143[E,78], LCT 1050, WCT 72[45], LM 2699* (USA). *RCA*
  LM 2699* (Europe); 430.296* (Germany); 644.520* (France); RED
  2019* (Japan). *HMV* DA 776[E,78] (Europe).

Quintet in C Major for Two Violins, Viola, and Two Cellos, Opus 163, D. 956

Isaac Stern, Alexander Schneider, violins
Milton Katims, viola
Pablo Casals, Paul Tortelier, cellos
  Recorded in Prades, France, June 1952
  Columbia SL 183, SL 185, ML 4704, ML 4714, M5 30069* (USA).
  Philips AL 01.188L (Europe); ABL 3100 (England). *CBS* 61.043*
  (France).

Sándor Végh, Sándor Zöldy, violins
Gyorgy Janzer, viola
Pablo Casals, Paul Szabo, cellos
  Recorded in concert at the Prades Festival, France, summer 1961
  Philips A 02209L, 835 100 AY[S]* (Europe). *Turnabout* 34407[S]*
  (USA). *Murray Hill* S 4759[S]* (USA).

Symphony No. 5 in B Flat Major, D. 485

Pablo Casals, conductor
Prades Festival Orchestra
Recorded in Prades, France, May or June 1953
Columbia: not released.

Symphony No. 8 in B Minor, D. 759, "Unfinished"

Pablo Casals, conductor
Marlboro Festival Orchestra
Recorded in concert at the Marlboro Festival, Vermont, July 13, 1968
Columbia MS 7262[S]*, MGP 32[S]* (USA).

Trio No. 1 in B Flat Major for Piano, Violin, and Cello, Opus 99, D. 898

Alfred Cortot, piano
Jacques Thibaud, violin
Pablo Casals, cello
Recorded in Kingsway Hall, London, July 6, 1926
HMV M 20[E,78], DB 947/50[E,78], DB 7419/22[E,78], COLH 12, HLM 7017* (Europe); J 153 50136/40* (Spain); C 161 50089/91* (Italy). *Angel* COLH 12 (USA); GR 76, GR 2005*, GR 2074D* (Japan). *Victor* M 11[E,78], 8070/73[E,78], AM 11[E,78], 8074/77 [E,78], LCT 1141 (USA). *Electrola* E 80487 (Germany). *Da Capo* 1 C 047-01 148M* (Europe).

Eugene Istomin, piano
Alexander Schneider, violin
Pablo Casals, cello
Recorded in Perpignan, France, summer 1951
Columbia SL 185, SL 183, ML 4705, ML 4715 (USA). *Philips* AL 01.435 L (Europe).

Trio No. 2 in E Flat Major for Piano, Violin, and Cello, Opus 100, D. 929

Mieczyslaw Horszowski, piano
Alexander Schneider, violin
Pablo Casals, cello
Recorded in concert at the Prades Festival, France, June 1952
Columbia SL 185, SL 183, ML 4706, ML 4716 (USA). *Philips* AL 01.107 L (Europe); ABL 3009 (England).

SCHUMANN, ROBERT (1810–1856)

Abendlied for piano, four hands, Opus 85, No. 12. Arranged for cello and piano

Pablo Casals, cello
Charles A. Baker [?], piano
    Recorded April 21, 1916
        Columbia A 5907[A,78] (USA); 7210[A,78] (England). *Pearl* GEM 106* (England). *Everest* 3323[R]* (USA). Note: Although the Columbia label does not name the pianist for this recording, Baker made a recording with Casals the following day during the same series of recording sessions.

Pablo Casals, cello
Nikolai Mednikoff, piano
    Recorded 1930
        Victor 6630[E,78] (USA). *HMV* DB 1039[E,78] (Europe).

• Arranged for cello and orchestra

Pablo Casals, cello
Unidentified orchestra
    Recorded April 23, 1920
        Columbia 49801[A,78], 68024-D[A,78], 7020-M[A,78], 5090-M[A,78], 7360[A,78] (USA).

Adagio and Allegro in A Flat Major for French horn and piano, Opus 70. Arranged for cello and piano

Pablo Casals, cello
Mieczyslaw Horszowski, piano
    Recorded in concert in the East Room of the White House, Washington, D.C., November 13, 1961
    Columbia KL 5726 (USA); *CBS* BRG 72035 (Europe).

Concerto in A Minor for Violoncello and Orchestra, Opus 129

Pablo Casals, cello
Eugene Ormandy, conductor
Prades Festival Orchestra
    Recorded in Prades, France, May or June 1953
        Columbia ML 4926, M5 30069* (USA). *Odyssey* 32 16 0027* (USA). *Philips* A 01617R (England); AL 01.369L, G 05621R (Europe).

Fünf Stücke im Volkston for violoncello and piano, Opus 102

Pablo Casals, cello
Leopold Mannes, piano
    Recorded in Prades, France, June 1952
        Columbia SL 185, SL 184, ML 4708, ML 4718 (USA). *Odyssey* 32
        16 0027* (USA).

Kinderscenen for piano, Opus 15: No. 7, *"Traümerei."*
Arranged for cello and orchestra

Pablo Casals, cello
Unidentified orchestra
    Recorded April 14, 1915
        Columbia A 5679[A,78], SL 185 bonus disk (USA).

• Arranged for cello and piano

Pablo Casals, cello
Walter Golde, piano
    Recorded April 21, 1920
        Columbia 49795[A,78], 68023-D[A,78], 7020-M[A,78], 5091-M[A,78]
        (USA).

Pablo Casals, cello
Otto Schulhof, piano
    Recorded in 1927
        Victor 1178[E,78], LCT 1050, WCT 72[45] (USA). *HMV* DA
        833[E,78] (Europe). *Angel* GR 2207* (Japan). *World Record Club*
        SH 121* (England).

Trio No. 1 in D Minor for Piano, Violin, and Violoncello,
Opus 63

Alfred Cortot, piano
Jacques Thibaud, violin
Pablo Casals, cello
    Recorded in Europe, 1928
        Victor M 52[E,78], 8130/33[E,78], AM 52[E,78], 8134/37[E,78], LCT
        1141 (USA). *HMV* M 95[E,78], DB 1209/12[E,78] (Europe); COLH
        301* (France).

Mieczyslaw Horszowski, piano
Alexander Schneider, violin
Pablo Casals, cello
  Recorded in Prades, France, June 1952
    Columbia SL 185, SL 184, ML 4708, ML 4718 (USA). *Philips* AL
    01.369 L (USA).

SGAMBATI, GIOVANNI (1841–1914)

Serenata Napoletana for violin and piano, Opus 24, No. 2.
Arranged for cello and piano

Pablo Casals, cello
Walter Golde, piano
  Recorded January 31, 1923
    Columbia 2036-D[A,78] (USA).

TARTINI, GIUSEPPE (1692–1770)

Concerto in D Major for Violoncello and Orchestra: Mvt. 3,
Grave ed espressivo. Arranged for cello and piano

Pablo Casals, cello
Blas Net, piano
  Recorded 1930
    HMV DB 1400[E,78] (USA). *Victor* 7760[E,78] (USA). *Columbia*
    M5 30069* (USA).

Concerto in D Minor for Violoncello and Orchestra: Mvt. 2,
Adagio

Pablo Casals, cello
Unidentified orchestra
  Recorded January 15, 1915
    Columbia A 5654[A,78] (USA). *Pearl* GEM 105* (England). *Everest*
    3323[R]* (USA).

TCHAIKOWSKY, PËTR ILICH (1840–1893)

Melody in E Flat Major for Violin and Piano, Opus 42, No. 3. Arranged for cello and piano

Pablo Casals, cello
Walter Golde, piano
> Recorded February 16, 1924
> *Columbia* 33048-D[A,78] 2011-M[A,78] (USA).

The Months for piano, Opus 37a: No. 10, "Autumn Song" ("October"). Arranged for cello and piano

Pablo Casals, cello
Walter Golde, piano
> Recorded February 16, 1924
> *Columbia* 68088-D[A,78], 7075M[A,78] (USA).

VALENTINI, GIUSEPPE (1681–1740)

Sonata No. 10 in E Major for Violin and Basso Continuo: Mvt. 3, *Allegro—tempo di gavotta.* Arranged for cello and piano by Alfredo Piatti (the famous Valentini *Gavotte*)

Pablo Casals, cello
Blas Net, piano
> Recorded in 1934
> *HMV* DA 1118[E,78] (Europe). *Victor* 1542[E,78] (USA). *Columbia* M5 30069* (USA).

VIVALDI, ANTONIO (1678–1741)

Concerto Grosso No. 11 in D Minor, Opus 3, No. 11, from *L'Estro Armonico:* Mvt. 4, *Largo.* Arranged for cello and piano by Stutschewsky

Pablo Casals, cello
Blas Net, piano
> Recorded in 1934
> *HMV* DA 1118[E,78] (Europe). *Victor* 1542[E,78] (USA). *Columbia* M5 30069* (USA). Note: The Victor disk identifies the piece as "Vivaldi: Intermezzo."

WAGNER, RICHARD (1813–1883)

Die Meistersinger von Nürnberg, Act III: *"Morgenlich leuchtend im rosigen Schein"* (*"Preislied"*). Arranged for cello and piano from the arrangement for violin and piano by August Wilhelmj

Pablo Casals, cello
Nikolai Mednikoff, piano
 Recorded January 19, 1926

  Victor 6620[E,78], LCT 1050, WCT 72[45], LM 2699* (USA). *RCA*
  LM 2699* (Europe); 430.296* (Germany); 644.520* (France); RED
  2019* (Japan). *HMV* DB 1012[E,78] (Europe).

Tannhäuser, Act III, scene 2: *"O du mein holder Abendstern"* (*"Song to the Evening Star"*). Arranged for cello and piano

Pablo Casals, cello
Charles A. Baker [?], piano
 Recorded April 21, 1916

  Columbia A 5953[A,78] (USA); 7360[A,78] (England). *Pearl* GEM
  106* (England). *Everest* 3323[R]* (USA). Note: The pianist in this
  recording is not identified on the label, but Baker made recordings
  with Casals during the same series of recording sessions.

Pablo Casals, cello
Romano Romani or Walter Golde, piano
 Recorded April 29, 1920, or January 27, 1922

  Columbia 49813[A,78] 68027-D[A,78], 7021-M[A,78], 5092-M[A,78]
  (USA). Note: It is not clear which of the two takes was actually
  issued, or whether both takes were. Romani was probably the accompanist in April 1920 and Golde in January 1922, since they worked
  with Casals in other recording sessions around those dates.

Pablo Casals, cello
Nikolai Mednikoff, piano
 Recorded in 1926

  Victor 6620[E,78], LCT 1050, WCT 72[45], LM 2699* (USA). *RCA*
  LM 2699* (Europe); 430.296* (Germany); 644.520* (France); RED
  2019* (Japan). *HMV* DB 1012 [E,78] (Europe).

II. Rehearsal, Documentary, and Inscription Records

REHEARSAL RECORDS

1. *June 1950.* A rehearsal of the first movement, *Allegro,* from Johann Sebastian Bach's Concerto No. 1 in A Minor for Violin, String Orchestra, and Continuo, BWV 1041. Recorded in the dining room of the College Moderne des Jeunes Filles in Prades, France.

Isaac Stern, violin
Fernando Valenti, harpsichord *continuo*
Pablo Casals, conductor
Prades Festival Orchestra
> *Columbia* SL 169 bonus disk, SL 170 bonus disk (USA).

2. *October 9, 1956.* A rehearsal of the *Élégie* for cello and orchestra, Opus 24, by Gabriel Fauré. Recorded in the Grand Amphithéâtre of the Sorbonne in Paris.

Paul Bazelaire, Maurice Maréchal, Gaspar Cassadó, Rudolf von Tobel, Étienne Pasquier, André Lévy, Gaston Marchesini, Guy Fallot, Charles Bartsch, Jean Vaugeois, cellos
Pablo Casals, conductor
L'Orchestre des Concerts Lamoureux
> *Philips* L 77.408, 6521.012[R]* (Europe). *Philips-Réalités* C 2 (Europe).

3. *April 16, 1957.* A rehearsal of the first movement, *Allegro moderato,* from Schubert's Symphony No. 8 in B Minor, D. 759 ("Unfinished"). A portion of the rehearsal during which Casals, then eighty years old, was stricken with the heart attack that prevented him from participating in the first Festival Casals de Puerto Rico. Recorded in the theater of the University of Puerto Rico in Rio Piedras, Puerto Rico.

Pablo Casals, conductor
Festival Casals de Puerto Rico Orchestra
> *Columbia* ML 5236 (USA).

4. *October 24, 1958.* A rehearsal of the Sonata No. 2 in D Major for Viola da Gamba and Harpsichord, BWV 1028, by

Johann Sebastian Bach. Recorded in the General Assembly auditorium of the United Nations.

Pablo Casals, cello
Mieczyslaw Horszowski, piano
Columbia: not released.

5. *July 1964 and July 1965.* Excerpts of rehearsals of the six Brandenburg Concertos by Johann Sebastian Bach. Recorded in Marlboro, Vermont, during the Marlboro Music Festival. Columbia titled the disk "An Historic Document—Casals Rehearses Bach."

> *Columbia* BM 10 in M2L 331, BS 10 in M2S 731[S]* (USA).

DOCUMENTARY RECORD

Casals: A Living Portrait

A portrait of Pablo Casals in his own words and music performed or conducted by him. Edited from existing voice tapes and conversations with Casals in November 1966 by H. L. Kirk. Transitional narration by Kirk spoken by Isaac Stern. The recording touches on Casals' life, philosophy, and attitudes toward Bach, liberty, war, and peace. Issued for Casals' ninetieth birthday.

> *Columbia* PC 1* (USA). Included as a bonus disk in M2L 355, M2S 755, ML 6361, MS 6961, M5 30069, and in Columbia's *Casals at 90* package.

THE CASALS INSCRIPTION

> *The core of any important enterprise or activity must be character and knidness*
>
> PABLO CASALS

in Casals' handwriting, marked with a stylus into a soft wax or vinyl disk appears on Columbia bonus disks included in sets SL 167, SL 168, and SL 169 (USA).

A few of the early records Casals made for Columbia in the United States carry Casals' signature similarly inscribed by stylus on a master disk.

SPOKEN INTRODUCTION

> The special album issued by the Musicians Foundation in New York contains a short message taped by Casals in October 1971. (*Musicians Foundation* TF 1001* [USA])

Discography

III. Recordings of Compositions by Pablo Casals

In addition to recordings by Casals of his own music, found in Section I, these recordings existed in early 1973:

El Pessebre: From Part Three, *Los Tres Reyes Magos* (*Les Trois Mages*)

Jerome Kessler, conductor
I Cellisti
> *Orion* ORS 7037[S]* (USA).

Opera sacra

> *Nigra sum*
> *Rosarium beatae virgini Mariae*
> *Salve Montserratina*
> *O vos omnes*
> *Canço a la Verge*
> *Tota pulchra*
> *Eucaristica*
> *Recordare Virgo Mater*

Dom Ireneu M. Segarra, OSB, conductor
Dom Gergori Estrada, organist
Capella and Escolanía of the Benedictine Abbey at Montserrat, Spain
> *Harmonia Mundi* HM 30632* (Europe). *Vergara* 11.0.001 L* (Spain). *Everest* SDBR 3196[R]* (USA).

Sant Marti del Canigo: Sardana de l'Exili

Andre Kostelanetz, conductor
Kostelanetz Orchestra
> *Columbia* MS 7319[S]* (USA).

Sardana for cello orchestra

John Barbirolli, conductor
London Cello School
> Recorded in London, March 28, 1928
> *HMV* AF 207[E,78] (Spain); SLS 796/1-2 (England). Note: In the LP version the *Sardana* is on the monophonic disk of a two-record set; the other disk is stereophonic.

Jerome Kessler, conductor
I Cellisti
> *Orion* ORS 7037[S]* (USA).

Notes

Direct quotations not otherwise attributed in text or notes are from Casals. While he seldom said anything twice in precisely the same way any more than he played or conducted with exactly the same nuance, he told favorite anecdotes to many people in similar terms over the years. Everyone who writes about Pablo Casals is the debtor both of those who have already written about him and of the overlapping oral tradition that begins to accrue around the life and endeavors of any legendary figure. In the case of Casals, the strata began to build early in his career. Where there are conflicting reports, an effort was made to ascertain the facts, although in some instances a choice had to be governed by the most logical probability.

Source data concerning material from newspapers appear in text or notes as fully as possible. Some of the clippings in the press book that Pilar Casals kept during her son's childhood and adolescence are not fully identified; neither are some later ones in Casals' own archive, nor are all those in the files of the great libraries. Reviews and critiques in periodicals are often unsigned; name or initials of the reviewer have been indicated when they are known.

These notes include both citation of sources and material of interest in clarifying specific areas. Full titles and publication data appear in the bibliography. If cited material comes from a single book or article by an author, only the author's last name and the appropriate page reference appear in the notes after the first mention; otherwise a shortened title will also be found. *See, see also,* and *compare* indicate that additional material, fuller treatment, and sometimes contradictory presentation will be found in the source.

1876–1899

CHAPTER 1

Page

7   "Bergonzi–Goffriller" cello: The fine eighteenth-century instrument was made by Matteo Goffriller while he was working in Cremona in the house of Antonio Stradivari's notable student Carlo Bergonzi. Casals liked to refer to this particular cello by the names of both great luthiers. See note to pages 455–56 on Casals' chief instruments.

8   Kenney article: Boston *Globe* (morning edition), August 7, 1970.

11   Péguy in 1913, "The world has changed less since Jesus Christ than it has in the last thirty years": quoted Shattuck, *Banquet Years,* 1.

12   The United States of America: see Brown's *Year of the Century* for a wide view of the United States at the time of Casals' birth.

17   son of an impoverished nobleman: Kaufmann and Hansl, *Artists in Music of Today,* 19; this is a volume of drawings of prominent musicians by Louis Lupas, each accompanied by a page of biography that is longer on romance than fact and often very funny.

21–22   Defilló family: Raimunda Defilló appears to have been of German descent, although Casals asserted with increasing conviction that his lineage was undilutedly Catalan after the sixteenth century. Elisa Vives de Fabrigas' biography in Catalan includes material about Casals' family heritage and about the early years of his parents.

24   weddings: recorded in municipal and church archives in Vendrell and cited by Señora Vives, who also includes some of the long-told stories of the courtship.

24–25   Carlist wars: see particularly Theo Aronson's *Royal Vendetta* for an engrossing treatment of the background, course, and consequences of this dynastic struggle for control of the Spanish throne. Edmondo de Amicis' *Spain and the Spaniards* gives many glimpses of life in Spain during Casals' childhood.

25   birth of first son: Birth and death dates of the Casals children follow Vives de Fabrigas and were verified where possible in municipal records in Spain. Señora Vives also includes the *remeiera* story.

Notes

CHAPTER 2

35   gourd "cello": quotations from "The Story of My Youth," Casals' 1930 piece for *Windsor Magazine,* London.

35–36   Vendrell church organ: Frederic Martí Albanell, *Notes Historiques de L'Orgue del Vendrell* (Vendrell: Impremta Ranon, 1929), published at the time Casals had the instrument restored in memory of his father.

37   Santa Ana bell tower: The wild olive tree was transplanted during a renovation of the church in the 1920s (see p. 376). The mutilated angel was repaired at the same time and still stands, as it has for two centuries, referred to both by natives and the guidebooks as *el ángel negre* (the black angel).

37   *The Shadow of the Cathedral:* This speech appears in an almost-verbatim translation in Dutton's 1919 American edition, pp. 130–31.

41   "Everything is accomplished by . . . twelve years old": quoted Corredor, *Conversations with Casals,* 23.

CHAPTER 3

45   García: for a fuller treatment of this remarkable musical family see Chase, *Music of Spain,* 210–16.

46   bow-arm position: compare Bauer's remarks about the restricted playing fashion of the period, Bauer, *His Book,* 15–16.

46   Casals did not invent the idea of extension. An important cello method published by Michel Corrette in the 1740s has a fingering system essentially the same as Casals', but he knew nothing of the book's existence when he began to study in Barcelona.

47–48   Benet Boixados is still remembered in Vendrell and Barcelona. His personality and zeal are the subject of strongly differing opinions, but he made an indelible early impression on Casals.

50–51   Café Tost: It still stands, greatly changed, as the Café Monumental at 25 calle Mayor de Gracia.

57   concert in Barcelona: A musical event at ten in the morning on Sunday, November 30, sponsored by the municipality of Barcelona and held on the first floor of the Restorant del Parque. Both parents were present for the performance. The *Ilustración Musical* notice appeared at the beginning of the week.

CHAPTER 4

58   *patria chica*: see Crow, *Spain,* 2.

60   "I forgot entirely . . .": Casals, "The Story of My Youth."

61   "How could anyone think . . . my artistic life": *ibid.*

61 Professor Sánchez had been pianist of the trio in which José García played cello at the Vendrell Catholic Center in 1888.

61–63 Albéniz: see Chase, 150–59.

64 Granados: *ibid.*, 160–65.

66 *María del Carmen:* official première was at the end of June 1898 in Madrid. Casals nevertheless insisted it was this work for which he prepared an orchestra in Barcelona at fifteen, and Granados' daughter Natalia states that the opera was in existence by 1891 or 1892.

67 "epoch of distress . . . terrible": Casals to Louis Biancolli in an interview published in *McCall's*, May 1966.

67 "I was religious . . . eyes to see": *ibid.*

68 "If we truly have the awareness . . . find God": *ibid.* In maturity Casals was deeply reverent in his conception of a power higher than man, but he resisted the conventional religious labels.

68 "Marxist ideology . . . 'brothers' ": quoted Corredor, *Conversations*, 29.

70 "My greatest wish . . . fatal crisis": *ibid.*, 28.

70 "She was an exceptional woman . . . she saved me": Biancolli interview.

70–71 municipal scholarship: The loss was not merely a personal disappointment. In the Barcelona *La Vanguardia* for May 26, 1893, Juan Puiggarí reviewed a concert given the day before by the winner, a young cellist named Pujal, and the Catalan Concert Society. The praise for Señor Pujal is distinctly qualified, and Puiggarí devotes the final third of his piece to lamenting "once more" the short-sightedness of the Municipal Corporation in giving the award to someone of the caliber of Pujal while forcing an artist of the "recognized nobility" of the young Casals to go elsewhere in search of patronage and means of sustenance.

CHAPTER 5

74 the Infanta Isabel: see also Aronson, *Royal Vendetta*, 134–35; Espinós Moltó, *Arbós*, 19; and Ortega-Morejon, *Isabel de Borbón*.

76 Bretón: see Chase, 143–44.

77 The Count of Morphy: see also the Espasa *Enciclopedia Universal*, 36:1158; Julio de Atienaz, *Nobiliario Español* (Madrid: Aguilar, 1948), 1557; and Cortés Cavanillas' biography of Alfonso XII.

79 Morphy's library eventually went to a member of the Count's family, not to Casals.

83 Palacio de Oriente staff and horses, Queen's allowance: see Harding, *Imperial Twilight*, 285.

83   María Cristina: See Aronson's interesting fuller treatment in *Royal Vendetta* and the books by Cortés Cavanillas, the Infanta Eulalia, Antón del Olmet, Carraffa, and Loyarte.

85   "charming face and manner": Duff, *Victoria Travels*, 286–88. The two queens met at San Sebastián in 1888, when Victoria visited María Cristina, becoming the first reigning British sovereign to enter Spain.

85   antidote for nausea: Aronson, *Royal Vendetta*, 132.

87   "violoncellist of such extraordinary merit. . . .": *El Pensamiento Galaico*, Santiago de Compostela, September 24, 1894.

88   Corvino anecdote: see the magazine *Tremontana* (Perpignan), July–August 1951.

89   resounding success, "a real occasion": "*. . . fué una verdadera solemnidad, un éxito.*"

90–91   The Morphy–Monasterio exchange appears, in Spanish, in *Academia* (Bulletin of the Real Academia de Bellas Artes de San Fernando, Madrid), triennium 1955–1957, pp. 133–35.

91   "constant longing . . . dream": from Tomás Bretón's eulogy of Morphy to the Academia de Bellas Artes, September 25, 1899.

91–92   Spanish opera: compare Chase, chap. ix, and Carl Van Vechten's 1918 volume also called *The Music of Spain*.

92   "Spanish opera does not exist . . .": quoted Chase, 138.

CHAPTER 6

99   Quotation from "The Story of My Life."

103   *Diario del Comercio* report: March 20, 1896.

105   Jeanbernet party for Saint-Saëns: By the nineties it was fashionable among Continental society to adopt English phrases; the *Diario Mercantil's* report of the midnight supper read "A media noche se sirvió un espléndido 'lunch.' . . ."

105   "Do *I* send you *my* works . . . ?": quoted Harding, *Saint-Saëns*, xiii.

106   San Sebastián engagement: It was during this visit that Casals, not wishing to be antisocial, accompanied his colleagues to his first—and last—bullfight.

106–7   Sarasate embodied all the superficial flamboyance of musical romanticism with spectacular virtuosity. Albert Spalding remembered him as a bewitching violinist of prodigious facility and stylistic elegance, with a tone of "silvery sheen and piercing sweetness." Saint-Saëns, like Casals, used the imagery of ballet about Sarasate's bravura playing—passages that fly out into space the way a dancer defies gravity. Unlike his great rival Joachim, Sarasate also embodied most of the romantic musical faults, which resulted in Casals' relatively low valuation of his fellow Spaniard. For Sarasate the instrument came first, not the music, and in his musical approach "you had the paradox of a player who made trivial music sound important, and deep music sound trivial" (Spalding, *Rise to Follow*, 36).

CHAPTER 7

114 "like a bird!": from an undated American press clipping that claims to quote a Madrid review of the début. Another clipping reports the Queen's having said "Madame Nevada is a songbird, pure and simple!"

114–15 hissing incident: *The New York Times* reported the story on April 17, 1899, based on London *Daily Mail* dispatches. The *World* printed first-person accounts from Nevada and her husband, cabled from London on April 22, and on November 20 the *Evening Journal* printed "a graphic description of Spain and the Spanish, as seen by [Mme Nevada]" that concludes with reference to the Seville experience.

115 London début: see the notice in *The Musical News*, London, May 27, 1899. Some Spanish and Catalan publications maintain that Casals' first public performance in London was a performance of the Saint-Saëns cello concerto at the Crystal Palace. Documentation of this has not been found, although it appears that Casals did play the Saint-Saëns work during his first trip to London in a benefit for the Prince of Wales's Hospital Fund, and therefore possibly in the presence of the future Edward VII.

116 "background for conversation": see Bauer (49–50) for a withering assessment of the big London parties from a musician's viewpoint, and compare Henry Wood, *My Life of Music*, 55.

116 Tosti, born in the Abruzzi in 1846 and educated in Naples, settled in London about 1880, the year he was named singing teacher to the British royal family. He wrote facilely, producing sentimental songs in Italian, French, and English such as "Amore," "At Vespers," and "Mother," although his later "Serenata" and "Mattinata" reached a higher artistic level. He sang pleasantly, accompanied well-known singers at parties, and for £50 arranged musical evenings for fashionable hostesses. Many of the divas of the period remember him affectionately in their memoirs; he is also mentioned by hostesses usually less pleasantly, since the singers' fees were often very high; from serious musicians of the time he drew almost unanimous scorn. He was knighted in 1908.

116–17   Constance Eliot, Lady Enid Layard, and Blanche Ponsonby: For a fuller treatment of Lady Layard see, particularly, Waterfield's *Layard of Nineveh* and Lina Duff-Gordon's *Castle in Italy;* she also figures briefly but bizarrely in the last years in Venice of Frederick Rolfe, author of *Hadrian VII* (see Weeks' *Corvo*). At the turn of the century the interest of such women as the Guest sisters in London, Emma Nevada, and Mathilde Marchesi and Betina Ram among others in Paris, helped immeasurably in assuring that Casals was heard. Enid Layard's diary in the British Museum reveals that she gave the first dinner party in the five years since she had been widowed essentially to introduce Casals to people who would be useful to him in London.

119–21   Command performance at Osborne: based on Casals' recollections and on Margaret Deneke's *Ernest Walker*, 56–59; Robert Mackworth-Young, Librarian of Windsor Castle, supplied clarification of several points. Although in ensuing years Casals went to some pains to make clear that his birthday was December 29 despite the later entry in Vendrell municipal records, in 1899 he entered his name in the British royal birthday book on the page for December 30.

119   Victoria sang Gluck "quite charmingly": Mendelssohn, July 19, 1852, quoted Lee, *Queen Victoria*, 193.

120   "two six-foot Indians . . .": Deneke, 58.

121   Casals' delivery of the Count of Morphy's introduction and Lamoureux's reactions were witnessed by Charles Chevillard, the conductor's son-in-law and successor. Chevillard described the incident to *his* son-in-law, Charles Kiesgen, Casals' longtime Paris manager, who recounted it to the author and also supplied helpful information on other points.

121   bull neck and cannonball head: Harding, *Saint-Saëns*, 135. Schonberg sketches both the abrasive ways and the musical importance of Lamoureux in *Pianists* and *Conductors*.

122   "I could see . . .": "The Story of My Youth."

123   "the entire absence of that murmur . . .": Runciman, *Old Scores*, 273.

124   disruptions of Wagner: Skinner, *Elegant Wits*, 20–21.

124   "the six old gentlemen . . . in Paris": in *The World* (London), July 2, 1890.

125   slight edge . . . romantic overtones: Skinner, *Elegant Wits*, 63.

125   reviews: the *Ménestral* review appeared on November 19, the others within the intervening week.

126–27   letter to Monasterio, December 18, 1899: full text, in Spanish, is in *Academia*, 99.

1900–1919

CHAPTER 8

131 Montmartre was still the artists' quarter; "Montparnasse was a dingy suburb enlivened by English and American painters" (Bell, *Old Friends*, 144).

133 Café Suez, Café Rouge: Paris at turn of the century was full of little music-halls and *cafés-chantants*, some rather sweaty. A few of the *cafés-concerts*, notable among them the Rouge and the Suez, boasted ensembles that played classical music exclusively, although there as elsewhere waiters circulated during the performances taking orders for drinks (see, for example, Bell, 159–60).

134 Paris transportation: Bell, 144, 159; Pinkney, *Napoleon III and the Rebuilding of Paris*, 17; Skinner, *Elegant Wits*, 2–3.

135 street illumination: Pinkney, 73–74.

135 theatrical personalities: Knapp and Chipman, *Yvette*, 188.

135 society women at lectures: Skinner, *Elegant Wits*, 63.

137 Pauline Viardot-García survived "with her kohl-shaded eyes" until 1910, her ninetieth year. Her voice had been powerful and of a prodigious range but (according to Camille Saint-Saëns in his *Musical Memories*) a little harsh, with a quality that could be likened to "the taste of a bitter orange." She had a statuesque beauty; both her voice and her face were irregular "but full of contrast and expression." She cut a wide swath through the world with personality, consummate artistry despite the flawed equipment, and a stunning intelligence. Schumann dedicated his beautiful *Liederkreis* (opus 24) to her and Saint-Saëns his *Samson et Dalila*. She was the first to sing the solo part of Brahms' *Alto Rhapsody*. Felix Mendelssohn's godson Felix Moscheles told Szigeti of her reading *Tristan* at sight, Wagner standing by the piano to turn pages, breaking in when he could no longer contain his enthusiasm: "N'est-ce pas, Matame, n'est-ce pas, Matame, que c'est suplime?" Her compositions, which Saint-Saëns said she "concealed as though they were indiscretions," were "rediscovered" and some presented to considerable acclaim in the United States in the 1960s.

137–38 Casals at Marchesi fete, December 12, 1899: called to the author's attention by Ernest de Popper, Mme Marchesi's grandson, who also permitted him to read a still-unpublished biography of Mathilde Marchesi. The celebration was a major social event as well as a musical occasion and was attended by considerable publicity in Paris; the American *Musical Courier* carried reports about the impending concert throughout December and a lengthy report of the evening in the issue for January 17, 1900, noting that the instrumental solos had been played by "the reigning favorite, M. Pablo Casals" and that the composer had taken over the piano for Mme Kleeberg to accompany when Casals played Saint-Saëns' *Le Cygne* and *Allegro Appassionato*.

139 Mme Ephrussi's salon: Mieczyslaw Horszowski kindly supplied eyewitness recollections of the salons of Mme Ephrussi and Paul Clemenceau as well as the gatherings at Casals' Villa Molitor house. Mme Lacroix, Mrs. Ram, even Mme Ephrussi have received little mention by memoirists and social historians writing about the intellectual and artistic life of Paris from the end of the nine-teenth century to the beginning of the First World War. The salon of Paul Clemenceau (brother of "the Tiger of France," with whom he disagreed violently about both music and politics) and his Viennese wife was a brilliant one for a number of years before and after the 1914 war. Another notable, more exclusively artistic group gathered regularly in the rue d'Athènes studio of Ida and Cipa Godebski, who received every Sunday evening. Writers, musicians, painters, politicians, and interested members of the *haute bourgeoisie* frequented the gatherings. Casals' friends and colleagues in Paris attended; long afterward Casals spoke about only a few salons he remembered visiting. Casals' career involved travel almost from the beginning, and after he had his own estab-lishment in Paris he preferred to entertain at home.

140 Madame Ménard-Dorian: George D. Painter generously gave information from his own research. Brief biographical data about the Ménard-Dorians appear in volume twenty-two of *Journal: mémoires de la vie littéraire* by Edmond and Jules de Goncourt (Monaco: Les Editions de l'Imprimerie nationale de Monaco, 1956–58), and there are a number of references to them in the journals themselves. Letters from both Ménard-Dorians appear in the published volume of Eugène Carrière's correspondence from 1898 on.

140 leading hostess of the political Left: Fraser and Natanson, *Léon Blum*, 90.

140 Dreyfusard headquarters: Vishniac, *Léon Blum*, 37.

140 salon was political: Painter, *Proust*, I, 281; biographical notes in Goncourt, *Journal*, vol. 22.

141 Cortot and Proust as Ménard guests: That Cortot (and Rodin) were Ménard guests was pointed out by George Painter. For Marcel Proust at the rue de la Faisanderie, see Vishniac, 37. Casals did not recall having seen Proust, although he was well acquainted with such friends of the writer as Saint-Saëns and Édouard Risler, and Reynaldo Hahn dedicated a composition of him. The artistic-

intellectual coterie in Paris early in the century was intercon-
nected, often by family (Cortot's wife Clothilde was a cousin
of Léon Blum, Henri Bergson a cousin by marriage of Proust),
and by interests. Casals moved in these circles from the beginning
of his international career.

141 Edmond de Goncourt on "socialism . . . silk sheets": journal
entry for October 3, 1895. Mme Ménard as still a powerful political hostess in the 1920s: see Kessler, *In the Twenties*, 144.

141 wretchedness: compare Skinner, *Elegant Wits*, 7–8.

141–42 anarchism: *ibid.*, 15.

142–45 Dreyfus affair and musicians: see Bauer, 87–88, and Schonberg, *Pianists*, 334.

145 Péguy: see Shirer, *Collapse of the Third Republic*, 57.

145 Bauer–Casals meeting: Casals often said they met at Mrs. Ram's;
Bauer said a note from Emma Nevada first brought them together.
Bauer's autobiography chronicles their early association with great
good spirits and also conveys what it was like to be a musician
in the 1890s and early 1900s.

146 Bauer's theory: Bauer, 92–93.

147 letter to Monasterio, September 1, 1900: full text, in Spanish,
Academia, 98.

CHAPTER 9

149–52 1884–1885 American tour: see Rosenthal, *Mapleson Memoirs*.

150–51 Nevada's San Francisco performance: *ibid.*, 227–28.

152 Raymond Duncan's toga: Casals' memory combined two periods
of time on this detail. At the time of the Nevada tour Duncan
dressed conventionally and impeccably and enjoyed such worldly
pleasures as fine sherry and good cigars. Not until the 1920s,
after going to Greece with his sister Isadora to build a never-
finished temple to the dance, did he become an ascetic given to
wearing toga, tunic, and sandals, his hair in braids, who established
a colony in Neuilly from which milk goats were driven through
the streets of Paris. (See, for instance, the descriptions in Ishbel
Ross' *The Expatriates*.)

153 opening performances: The tour had been announced to begin
ten days earlier than it did; in October Mme Nevada's manager
reported a postponement to allow a week's rest after the voyage
and also to enable Casals to appear in Paris before sailing.

154 Nevada occasionally forgot: Wechsberg, *Red Plush and Black
Velvet*, 15.

154 "a sort of trick songstress": Mallet, *Life with Queen Victoria*,
174.

155 Prize fight: Sixty-seven years later Casals remembered hating

the whole thing. It was possible to reconstruct the general route of the tour between mid-December 1901 and the first of March 1902 from occasional reports that appeared in the *Musical Courier*.

157 Bernhardt's coal-mine descent: Skinner, *Madame Sarah*, xvii.

157–58 The stories about exploring the mine at Wilkes-Barre, gambling in Texas, and the walk out into the desert were favorite Casals anecdotes from his first American tour, told and published many times thereafter.

160–62 Details of arrival and stay in San Francisco in early March 1902 are based on reportage in the San Francisco *Chronicle* for February and March. The first publicity appeared on February 23. Quoted reviews are from the *Chronicle*.

163 Dr. Mayer told the press: San Francisco *Chronicle*, March 18, 1902.

164 Nevada's triumphal return: mentioned in the San Francisco press at the time of concerts in the Bay area; the New York *Morning Telegram* carried an exclusive dispatch describing the event on April 8; and the *Musical Courier* reported in detail later in the month. Emma Nevada continued her career as a singer until 1910, after which time she devoted herself to teaching and to fostering the career of her daughter, Mignon. By the beginning of World War II she was living in a convent in England. She died in June 1940 in Liverpool.

164 Gertrude Stein and El Greco: This story appears in Juan Alavedra's biography and was repeated in Kahn, *Joys and Sorrows*. Gertrude Stein, however, appears not to have traveled west before going to Europe in 1902; in any event, Casals' injury did not require a cast.

CHAPTER 10

165 Moreira de Sá: The picture of a remarkable man emerges from the recollections of Casals and Harold Bauer and from *In Memoriam Bernardo V. Moreira de Sá*. Helena Moreira de Sá e Costa was helpful in supplying information about her grandfather and her countrywoman Guilhermina Suggia.

166 Bach–Verdi: Bauer, 93.

166–67 Recital for María Cristina: see Bauer, 104–5.

167–68 "I had a bad habit . . . Pagliacci": Stein, *Journal into the Self*, 202–3.

168 Queen Elisabeth of Rumania (1843–1916) collected and published Rumanian legends. Using the name Carmen Sylva (she was given this bardic name in a ceremony in Wales), she also composed many prose and verse works of her own, writing fluently in English, French, German, and Rumanian. Considered no-

table in her output are *Pensées d'une reine* (1882) and *The Bard of the Dimbovitza*, an English version of Elena Vacarescu's folksong collection.

170 "comrades . . . never a dull moment": Bauer, 106. Dates of the 1903 South American tour appear in *Moreira de Sá*. For Bauer's recollections of the 1903 tour, see pages 98–99 of his book.

171–72 Casals-Bauer ensemble: see Bauer, 107–9.

172 Like Martin Luther: *ibid.*, 108.

172–75 White House performance: portions based with permission on Mrs. L. Lohmeyer Soules' unpublished Catholic University dissertation "Music at the White House during the Administration of Theodore Roosevelt." John H. Steinway furnished information about the White House pianos and Steinway's long advisory relationship with the presidential staff.

173 glare from the "gold" White House piano: see Adella Prentiss Hughes, *Music Is My Life*, 90.

176 Franko concert: Casals appeared in a program that included a Bach concerto grosso, the first Brandenburg concerto, and a Mozart symphony—one movement of which opened the concert, the other two being played at the end.

178 Bauer's description of the 1904 South American tour: Bauer, 99–101.

180 "one of the greatest shows": *ibid.*, 100.

183 "the lovely Amelia of Portugal": *ibid.*, 102–3.

183 an Erard "covered with paintings . . .": *ibid.*, 103.

183 Portuguese medal: Casals had been decorated by the Portuguese court during one of his earliest performances for Amelia and Carlos. In addition to the Spanish cross of Isabel la Católica, by 1901 he also wore the medals of caballero of the orders of Carlos III and of Santiago. The French Legion of Honor came to him while he was still in his early thirties, and by the outbreak of World War I he had been awarded orders by Italy, Rumania, and Austria as well.

CHAPTER 11

185 "bubbled with conversations . . . secular convent": Alavedra, *Casals*, 174.

186–88 The Bergson–Casals conversations are sketched in Corredor, *Conversations*, 46–47. The translation "weight of gold" for Casals' phrase *peso de oro* does not carry the overtones of the containment of a personal, secret treasure that many performing artists say they feel in this context.

188–89 private chamber-music sessions: a good description from the point of view of Fritz Kreisler, who began to take part regularly about 1910, appears in Lochner, *Kreisler*, 134–35.

189 Casals–Cortot–Thibaud trio: Cortot recalled the formation of the trio as a public entity as a chance result of the three artists staying in the same house near Fontainebleau about 1905. Casals added that "there was no sense of permanency in it as a chamber music ensemble. We were simply three friends who were all very busy but felt nevertheless an urgent need to be together, and above all to make music together. We decided to form a Trio and devote to it a few weeks every year." "Each one of us," Cortot noted, "retained the privileges of his individual conception of any given work," which resulted in what some later listeners to the trio's records winced at as unspecified rubato at moments and similar currently unfashionable approaches. But, "that . . . atmosphere of imaginative independence and companionship resulted in a unique unity of spirit. The artists were in love with the music . . . ." (See Joan Chissell's review of a reissue of Schubert and Haydn trios recorded in 1926, in *The Times* of London, July 7, 1973.)

190 authority, aristocracy, masculinity of Cortot's art: see Schonberg, *Pianists*, 383.

191 compelling presence: Spalding, 216.

192 criticism: It is difficult to find negative criticism of Casals' artistry as a cellist in contemporary journalistic reviews throughout his long public performing career, even from writers who excoriated other musicians. There are occasional reports that he had difficulty with a new string during a recital, and Diran Alexanian told pupils of small memory lapses during concerts. Some critics, particularly early in Casals' career, noted that his tone was relatively small, and many remarked that his manner onstage was almost as far as possible from the flamboyant virtuoso stereotype as could be; both are recounted as facts, not necessarily as shortcomings. Even his closest musical colleagues occasionally disagreed with a Casals chamber-music tempo but, more often than not, suffered it in silence. By the early 1970s certain musicians—like Pierre Fournier in a New York broadcast—dismissed Casals' playing as outdated and too romantic, but only Casals' "poetic" approach to the music of Bach, as a performer early in the century and later as a conductor, stirred a lasting tempest among the purists and traditionalists.

193–95 *personality* and a student: Spalding, 261–63.

195 "to discern the second reality": Mauclair, *Idées vivantes*.

195 Carrière to Mme Ménard: full letter, in French, Carrière, *Écrits et lettres*, 255.

196 "We all sat there . . .": Mauclair, *Trois crises;* the incident is also mentioned by Jean-René Carrière.
197 "the old deaf one": Bauer, 82.
197–98 Ravel: see Bauer, 82–83; Casella, *Music in My Time,* 60–61; Stuckenschmidt, *Ravel.*
200 disruptive presence: Alavedra, *Casals,* 174.
201–2 Röntgen letters: translated extracts of letters written by Julius Röntgen, published in *Brieven van Julius Röntgen.*

CHAPTER 12

Research on Moór begins with and must often return to Max Pirani's *Emanuel Moór.*
206 first New York appearance: Odell records nine New York appearances between 1885 and 1888 at times and in circumstances that would have been uninspiring even for an artist much more patient than Emanuel Moór.
208 "I will truly rejoice . . .": quoted Pirani, 46.
208 "My dear friend . . .": full letter, in French, *ibid.,* 47.
210 Moór at Bayreuth: "Bitte, mein Herr, können Sie mir sagen wer diese langweilige Oper geschrieben hat?" Pirani, 49.
212–13 "the most important concerts of the year": *Musical America,* March 7, 1908. The succeeding extract quotation is from the same dispatch.
213 "storms of intelligent applause . . . correct in form": *ibid.*
214 *L'Éclair* notice is from an undated clipping following the concert.
215–17 agreement on Bach: see Pirani, 49–50.
216 Bach had become for Casals everything in music: By his early eighties Casals would say in a broadcast interview simply "Bach is my best friend."
217 "his idiom . . . austerity": quoted Pirani, 89.
218 "a musician who has written . . . very earnestly": Felix Borowski, Chicago *Record Herald,* January 19, 1914; entire Borowski review should be read in conjunction with a long, somewhat puzzled piece on Moór by Edward Burlingame Hill in the Boston *Transcript* for April 15, 1908.

CHAPTER 13

Casals' experiences in Russia and his early impressions of country and people are evoked in Alavedra's *Pablo Casals* and touched on in Corredor, *Conversations,* but the soundest help in tracing facts about the 1905–1913 tours came from Ginsburg, *Pablo Casals,* particularly chap. 3, which deals with Casals' Russian concerts and musical associations. Prof. Ginsburg, who teaches cello at the Moscow Conservatory, also supplied answers to a number of detailed questions on the subject.

219 "Lose your pocketbook . . . never your passport": see Cowles, *1913*, 107–8, for some of the hazards of traveling to Russia before World War I.

220 forced him to strip: Word spread quickly and caused anxiety for more than one musician booked in Russia; see, for instance, Spalding, 198.

221 The Kaiser liked Bach: Cowles, *1913*, 58.

221 Frau Wolff: Walter, *Theme and Variations*, 37–38, 298; Piatigorsky, *Cellist*, 117. Many clients remembered her with real affection, but all agreed she was formidable.

222 Father George Gapon and Bloody Sunday: see Cowles, *Russian Dagger*, 254–55.

222 telephone call to Siloti: see "M" in *La Suisse*.

222 impresario's nightmare . . . Ysaÿe: Some Spanish reports, published long afterward, say the scheduled artist was Marya Freund, a singer enormously popular with Russian audiences at the time.

223 "shone undiminished . . .": *Rachmaninoff's Recollections Told to Oskar von Riesemann* (New York: Macmillan, 1934), 36.

224 Mme Siloti was the daughter of Tretiakov, who presented the Tretiakov Gallery (the Museum of Modern Art) in Moscow to the state.

224 Siloti: Miss Kyriena Siloti supplied information about her father and shared her recollections of Casals' first trip to Russia.

225 Saint-Saëns concerto: Casals appeared in the fourth segment of a full program. Beforehand Siloti had conducted Taniev's first symphony, two Borodin romances (sun by E. Petzenko), and the Overture and Serenade from Lalo's ballet *Namouna*. After the concerto came Liadov's Russian Songs for Orchestra as well as first performances of Rimsky's *Dubinushka* symphony and a new Glazunov setting of "The Song of the Volga Boatmen."

225 Borisiak reaction: Portions of Borisiak's 1929 publication are quoted by Ginsburg.

226 music of "elegiac grace . . . passion": *Grove's Dictionary*.

228 Liadov: Descriptions of Russian musicians in this chapter are based in part on Malko's *A Certain Art* and Seroff's *The Mighty Five*. Casals enjoyed recalling the personalities he encountered during his Russian tours, and pianist Wiktor Labunski (who was a young student in St. Petersburg at the time) reminisced engagingly about the people and the period and also permitted the author to read his unpublished memoirs.

229 "the ability to read and see": Malko gives a wryly sympathetic

picture of Glazunov that was strengthened by interviews with others who had known him in Russia and, later, in France.

231 Russian destiny to dominate the world: Casals felt this strongly from the time of his first tour in imperial Russia. It was, however, not new: see Cowles' *Russian Dagger*, which deals with Russia's attempts to expand in Europe in the sixty years before World War I.

231 gloomy bigotry: *Rachmaninoff's Recollections Told to Oskar von Riesemann*, 96. It is not clear whether this is a verbatim reflection of Rachmaninoff or to some extent an interpolation of Riesemann.

231–32 Cui: Wiktor Labunski's recollection.

237 symphonic orchestra—wedding present: Casella, 96.

238–39 "The smell of burning logs . . .": Gollancz, *Journey Towards Music*, 169.

239 "Everything spawns fear . . .": quoted Alavedra, *Casals*, 145.

CHAPTER 14

241 Casals' letters to Julius Röntgen: A collection of forty-one communications from Casals to Röntgen, plus programs and some photographs, is in the collection of the Haags Gemeentemuseum in The Hague, where Dr. Clemens von Gleich was of assistance in supplying copies and supplementary information. Other programs, chiefly of Casals' Dutch appearances, are in the Openbare Muziekbibliotheek, Amsterdam.

241 "could raise a piano quintet . . . a small orchestra": Smyth, *Impressions That Remained*, 142.

242 "composer, viola-player . . .": *ibid.*

242 "There was one more . . .": *ibid.*, 144.

245 Ludwig Wüllner: a well-known performer of the period. Elena Gerhardt noted that he was called "the singer without a voice."

247 Grieg to his publisher: quoted Corredor, *Conversations*, 107.

247 wooden figures from a Noah's Ark: Smyth, 401.

248 Grieg visit to Liszt: see Schonberg, *Pianists*, 165.

248 Carreño's octaves: *ibid.*, 131–32.

248 Grieg as conductor: Smyth, 401–2.

249 Grieg's refusal to visit France: see Bauer, 143–44. The *Musical Courier* for October 11, 1899, printed a translation of Grieg's message: "Like every foreigner, I am so indignant at the contempt with which justice is treated in your country that I do not feel disposed to come in relation with a French public."

250 Madame Tieventhal: She and her husband were close friends of the Röntgens, very much interested in music, and frequently

entertained local and visiting musicians in their Amsterdam home.

254 Tertis on Ysaÿe: Tertis, *Cinderella No More*, 40–41.

254 "aristocratic gourmet": M. Montagu-Nathan, "Eugène Ysaÿe," *Musical Times*, 1 (July 1931), 595.

254 Ysaÿe fishing: Lochner, 62.

254 poker and music: see Antoine Ysaÿe, 104–5.

CHAPTER 15

262 Joachim: His bow arm had weakened by the end of the century and rheumatism had contracted the fingers of his left hand, but "the structure of a cathedral remained, even if the stained-glass windows had been shattered . . . a great musical line was suggested, even if a trembling bow marred . . . realization" (Spalding, 36). Casals was much more in sympathy with Joachim's disciplined musicianship than with Sarasate's lack of it, although he reacted strongly against anything that seemed to him to get in the way of the inner meaning of the music, even if it was a striving for "classical purity."

263 Lady Speyer: Draper, *Music at Midnight*, 147.

263 tennis, then Brahms: Speyer, *My Life and Friends*, 198.

264 "Casals . . . took up the challenge . . .": *ibid.*, 199.

264 "From the moment when Casals started . . . right way to play Bach": *ibid.*, 197–98.

264 Donald Francis Tovey: Mary Grierson's biography is a chief source of information about this remarkable man and a book in which Casals figures prominently.

267 "after an hour . . .": Speyer, 167.

267 "he knew the whole of music": Busch, *Pages from a Musician's Life*, 96.

268 "Did the old bear growl . . . ?": Spalding, 78.

268 "blond, stolid giant"; Brahms and Beecham; Shaw quoted: see Schonberg, *Conductors*, 180–81.

269 "behind his gold spectacles . . .": *ibid.*, 181.

272 Borwick–Moór incident: compare Pirani, 70–71.

272 Paderewski: *ibid.*, 73.

272–73 *Times* review: January 27, 1911.

273 Sir Henry Wood observations: *My Life of Music*, 321.

276 Tovey tribute: London *Times*, September 1932.

CHAPTER 16

277–78 *Zeneközlöny* review: 1912, p. 242. Translation furnished by Imre Kun, concert manager who represented Casals in Budapest for many years, author of a radio play based on Casals' life and of *Thirty Years among Artists*, who supplied much information about Casals' visits to Hungary.

280 Beethoven Gold Medal: see Elkin, *Royal Philharmonic*, 70–71.

281–84 "Mrs. Draper's cellar": Muriel Draper came to London with her singer husband in the summer of 1911 after two years in Italy, and took a house in Holland street, Kensington, for the 1911–1912 season, then moved to Edith Grove, where she remained until the early war years. Her *Music at Midnight* recalls in adoring detail her life in those years, endless evenings of music, and the people who were her guests. Arthur Rubinstein, who admired her, describes her (she was then in her twenties) as a woman with a fine, graceful figure, excellent pale complexion, and remarkably beautiful hands. Her narrow, high-cheekboned face, with a slightly flat nose and "exuberantly large mouth with thick red lips," Rubinstein recalls as disquieting. She had both exceptional intelligence and an aggressive personality. (See Rubinstein's *My Young Years*, 388–89, and passages elsewhere in that book for glimpses of Muriel Draper and the evenings of music in her studio.)

For Casals later, the London chamber-music sessions lacked the magic of those of a few years earlier in Paris and at Ysaÿe's houses in Belgium. For sidelights not otherwise available on the Edith Grove music and the relationship between Casals and Rubinstein, see *My Young Years*, *passim*; for important insights into both Casals' generosity and his occasional inflexibility, see especially 140–41, 376, 382–83, 390–91, 425–26.

Quotations in this section are from Mrs. Draper unless otherwise indicated.

282–83 "Prodigious . . . experience": Tertis, 63–64.

285–87 Pierné confrontation: One of the celebrated episodes of Casals' career. Many people appear to have heard about it, but efforts to establish the date and verify details through court records or newspaper accounts were unproductive.

289 Tovey's unorthodox technique of dressing; Einstein's theory: see Busch, 96–98.

289–90 "In spite of the heat . . ."; "Donald is calmer . . .": quoted Grierson, 161. Tovey's two surviving letters from the early part of his visit reflect joyous good spirits and unaccustomed energy; he reports "conditions are [later adding "or seem"] so simple in this climate . . ." and that "This place & house & people are most simple & straight & touching." ". . . Madame Mère Casals is a very quiet little old lady with Pablo's nose projecting from the blue goggles which conceal the rest of her . . . ." Only the host and hostess know much French, so most of the conversation goes on in Catalan. "We are *in* the Mediterranean," he begins the second letter; "if it had any tides we should undoubtedly be drowned. The waves make a continuous accompaniment which drowns all other sounds not in the same room of the house, except the grasshoppers." In the water Horszowski, who had happily scaled the Matterhorn, displayed complete terror of "lifting his feet off the bottom even when supported by two people!"

During the holiday Tovey continued working at top speed on his opera *The Bride of Dionysus*, and Robert Trevelyan, the librettist, had traveled to San Salvador with him. Quite possibly he overextended himself in the unfamiliar climate. And, despite his comments about the simplicity of life at San Salvador, he was in a milieu the customs and traditions of which were almost totally alien to him. A friend later described Tovey privately as "innocent as only a well-brought-up Englishman could be in those days," and added that he had remained very much sheltered and very British despite his frequent visits abroad.

291 Tovey's biographer suggests: *ibid.*
291 "quite a new interpretation": Wood, 361.
291 Tovey dashed to Liverpool: Grierson, 162–63.

CHAPTER 17

293 Susan Metcalfe: Primary sources of information about her career until 1914, and to a considerable extent afterward, are reports in newspapers and musical journals and surviving recital programs. Louis Metcalfe Kobbé, her nephew, and European relatives clarified the family's history.

295 Reviews: It is difficult to assess fairly Susan Metcalfe's qualities as a young artist. The New York reviewers in the early 1900s tended to cancel one another out, to the extent that the *Musical Courier* occasionally ran parallel extracts of the conflicting opinions of competing critics about a single concert. From the turn of the century until early 1908, most of the metropolitan reviewers agreed that she had good points but were unanimous in noting shortcomings. Richard Aldrich, music critic of *The New York Times*, who could be irascible in print, covered the March 1904 Mendelssohn Hall recital in which both Metcalfe and Casals were featured. He found that she had a true feeling for many of the songs, a still-limited range of expression, but thought her singing intelligent, sincere, and possessed of "some of the subtler elements of beauty." (That afternoon Casals showed, Aldrich said, "much

taste and a highly polished style . . . playing [that] is musical in the best sense," beautiful phrasing, accurate intonation, and "fine and delicate perception in all he does.") Three years later Aldrich characterized the Metcalfe voice as "slender and delicately beautiful" and said that the singer reflected "fastidious taste and wide knowledge of song literature." An anonymous reviewer reported that only Marcella Sembrich at the time constructed song programs so well.

295 "quaintly garbed and Hepnered": William Hepner's fashionable hairdressing establishment was located on Broadway near 42d Street.

296 decision to marry: compare Alavedra, *Casals*, 289.

296 Muriel Draper found him glowing: in her *Music at Midnight*, 143.

296 attempt to counsel Casals: Alavedra, *Casals*, 289.

296–97 newspaper report of the wedding: *The New York Times* published a much more restrained and more nearly accurate notice on Sunday, April 5, 1914. (The American publicity at the time of the wedding stated that Casals had been cellist of the Paris Opéra for many years, a report that subsequently made its way into standard biographical reference works.)

299 Casals to Granados: translated extract from a copy furnished by the Granados family.

300 "his skill with the racquet . . .": *Musical America*, September 1914.

300 "We are here in safety . . ."; "I hope that . . .": quoted Pirani, 82.

302 "offers of contracts . . . did not even trickle": Imre Kun to author.

303–4 letter to Granados: translated from a copy furnished by the Granados family.

308 recordings: Between January 15, and April 23, 1915, Casals recorded sixteen pieces that were released on phonograph disks; the following spring he made eleven in six sessions, also in New York. He made no more records until April 1920, but except for 1921 he did every year through 1932, when he recorded for the first time as a symphonic conductor, with the Orquestra Pau Casals in Barcelona.

310 scoring problems: Kolodin, *Metropolitan Opera*, 260, notes that the orchestration for *Goyescas* was improved by "unknown hands."

310 press coverage: the Granados' arrival in mid-December was noted by the New York papers, but full coverage began to build about

a month later, with long advance stories about the opera, production, composer, and librettist in the editions for the Sunday before opening night; all major New York newspapers covered the première as a major cultural event. See also Fernandez Cid, *Granados;* Longland in *Hispanic Notes; Opera Magazine* 3 (1916), 10–13; *Musical Observer* 13 (1916), no. 3; and *Opera News* 7 (1916), no. 12, p. 4 and no. 13, pp. 2–3, 5; and Chase, 162–63.

310 Gatti-Casazza's reactions: see his *Memories of the Opera*, 283–84.

313 payment in gold: Briggs, *Requiem*, xv.

313 memorial concert: see *The New York Times*, May 8, 1916.

313 Paderewski: He and Casals did not meet again, but Casals was very much conscious of his actions as a Polish patriot, including refusals at times to play while his country was not free.

313 "Psalms against war": quoted Grierson, 181.

314 Casals to Moór: quoted Pirani, 86–87 (in French).

315 joint recitals: One such concert, in New York in January 1916, included two Brahms songs with cello obbligato; Casals accompanied Metcalfe on piano for the other songs on the program and played a Bach solo cello suite. *The New York Times'* Richard Aldrich said "Mrs. Casals sings with riper and more finished art" as well as surer control and better intonation than before; "pity [that] her diction [is] not a little more clear-cut and polished." For the unaccompanied Bach Aldrich had nothing but praise. These recitals were a very small element in Casals' career at the time, and he soon approached them with little joy. He reacted impatiently in later years to the widely repeated story that he had considered giving up his career in order to apply himself to furthering his wife's. Once, weary of travel and the demands of the public, he had merely said to American impresario Loudon Charlton that he was tempted to stop giving concerts and devote himself to composing. There is nevertheless one pleasant glimpse of the couple performing together fairly early in the marriage. On the free evening between two Casals appearances in Cleveland, Adella Prentiss Hughes gave a small dinner party for the Casals, Cleveland Orchestra conductor Nikolai Sokoloff and his wife, and three other couples: "After cordials had been served and good talk had been enjoyed, Casals got up, went to the piano, and said, 'I feel like making music. Susan, come and sing with me.' The impromptu recital was an exquisite experience" (Hughes, *Music Is My Life*, p. 166).

315 Casals' note to Ratan Devi: original is in the possession of Mrs. Walter Abel, New York.

318 Pavlova season: see report in *Musical America*, April 15, 1919.

1919–1945

CHAPTER 18

323 "a beautiful woman": quoted by Lael Wertenbaker in *Life*, May 15, 1950.

333 Adrian Boult: Sir Adrian supplied further reactions during a brief conversation in London in October 1970. The quotations that follow are from his 1923 report, "Casals as Conductor," published in *Music and Letters*.

337 heavy stick: After 1950, Casals generally used a fairly light, relatively short baton that he sometimes put down on the music stand, conducting with his hands alone. His hands were mobile and often very graceful when he directed, and during lyric passages the left hand frequently was held vibrating over his heart—a characteristic of many conductors who have been string players.

340–41 Clavé: see also Chase, 170.

344 "The Holy Trinity": in a glowing report Ysaÿe wrote for *Action Musicale* (Brussels), July 15, 1927.

344–46 Casals–Cortot–Thibaud evening with Ysaÿe in Brussels: see Antoine Ysaÿe, 141–42.

347 justified a new claim: *The New York Times*, April 8, 1922.

CHAPTER 19

350 "I think of you . . . compose!": quoted Pirani, 99 (in French).

352 "a sense of style . . .": see Milly Stanfield's tribute in *The Strad*. Gerald Moore, the fine pianist who worked with many of the ranking cellists of his time, accompanied Guilhermina Suggia in England in the 1920s. He found her both modest and shy, a woman of striking appearance rather than beauty, of compelling personality, but far from the fiery prima donna she appeared. The tone she produced from her superb Montagnana and Stradivarius cellos was somewhat small, but her playing was secure and her style persuaded one that her performances were passionate and intense, when they were in fact "calculated, correct, and classical and, like her nature, equable." Suggia contributed two interesting pieces to *Music and Letters* soon after Fox-Strangways began it—"The Violoncello," in which she pays warm tribute to Casals' art, in March 1920, and "Violoncello Playing" in April 1921.

353 railway encounter: Reid, *Sargent*, 112–13.

354–56 Chicago recital: compare Spalding, 263–65, from which quoted material comes.

356 growing estrangement: Whatever conflicts and tensions existed

privately, they were apparent to few outside the intimate circle. Willem Valkenier, a member of the Orquestra Pau Casals, remembered being invited a few times in the early 1920s to Casals' house on the Diagonal in Barcelona, where "there was music and Mme Susan Metcalfe sang some songs accompanied very sensitively on the piano by Don Pablo. She had a lovely voice, albeit not big, and she sang beautifully." She attended most rehearsals of the orchestra and all the concerts. "She was a lovely lady . . . *une grande dame*, a worthy wife of a prince of musicians."

356 Landowska: She disagreed with Casals' taste in music as well, at least once. During a vigorous discussion of whether or not a mordent was indicated in a musical passage Landowska turned to Casals to deliver her famous "You play Bach your way; I'll play him his way."

357 Alexanian: Casals declined to attempt to set down his approach to cello technique and interpretation, but Alexanian's book is based on it; portions are quoted in Littlehales, *Pablo Casals*. See also Alvin, "The Logic of Casals's Technique."

357 master-class approach: Of special interest is a transcript of notes taken during Casals' 1921 public classes at the École Normale, published in October of that year in *Music and Letters* under the title "A Violoncello Lesson."

358 Piatigorsky: 127–29.

359 "an emanation of Casals . . .": Gollancz, 214.

361 Röntgen on the Schubert contest: quoted Grierson, 234. For the contest itself, see Gelatt, *Fabulous Phonograph*, 239–40. See also Clara Clemens, *My Husband Gabrilowitsch* (New York: Harper, 1938), 200–3.

361 Langford on Casals' Schumann: Manchester *Guardian*, November 17, 1921, recalling a 1910 performance with the Hallé.

361–62 Schumann with Bruno Walter: Walter, 292–93.

362 Weingartner announcement: Gollancz, 211.

362–65 Barbirolli: based on a long conversation in San Juan, June 1969; quotations are from that session unless otherwise noted. See also the Reid and Kennedy biographies.

363 Post-mortems in the *Musical Times* and *The Times* of London are quoted in Reid, *Barbirolli*, 92–93.

365 Vaughan Williams' fantasia: There are references to the work in Ursula Vaughan Williams' biography of her husband; in Reid, *Barbirolli*; in Michael Kennedy's *Barbirolli* and *Works of Vaughan Williams*; and in Day, *Vaughan Williams*.

366 Casals did not return to the United States on tour: Fred Gaisberg, the English HMV executive who knew Casals well, nevertheless felt that he could easily have recouped his subsidy of the Orquestra Pau Casals by further American tours but, "typical of him,"

refused to do so "for purely domestic reasons." Gaisberg, *The Music Goes Round*, 214.

366 Elisabeth of the Belgians: See the treatment of this longtime friend of Casals in Aronson, *Defiant Dynasty*, and Owen, *Elisabeth;* there are references of interest also in Lochner and Antoine Ysaÿe, and contemporary glimpses up to the time of the U.S. entry in World War I in Brand Whitlock's *Belgium.* For a sense of her eccentric Wittelsbach heritage, including artistic interests, see Channon, *The Ludwigs of Bavaria.*

367 "busy trivialities": Aronson, *Defiant Dynasty*, 139.

367 "if she insists on playing": *ibid.*, 140.

370 "She knew exactly what to do": *ibid.*, 192.

371 Loti visit: *ibid.*, 190–91. Tertis visit: Tertis, *Cinderella No More*, 43.

371 "flowers and caviar": Antoine Ysaÿe, 148.

372 "Viva la Republica!": Aronson, *Royal Vendetta*, 154.

CHAPTER 20

384 Pahissa to Kessler: Kessler, *In the Twenties*, 293.

384–85 death of Ysaÿe: see Antoine Ysaÿe, 152–53; Tertis, 41–42.

386–88 For background of the period of the Republic in Spain and the Spanish Civil War, primary reliance has been on Hugh Thomas' book, but valuable information also came from people who knew Casals during those years.

391 letter to Furtwängler: see Geissmar, *Two Worlds of Music*, 82–83. Dr. Geissmar, in 1933 Furtwängler's assistant in Berlin, did not note the portion of the letter that expressed Casals' surprise that the conductor should remain in Germany under Nazi administration.

392 1933 Brahms Festival: *ibid.*, 63, 78.

392–93 Correspondence about Tovey concerto: quoted Grierson, 276–77, 279.

396 "enemy of . . . his own music": for an orchestra member's memory of Tovey as conductor see Russell (34–35) and, for one view of him as performer, Wood, 246–47.

396 Busch and Suggia responses: Grierson, 313n.

400 arrest legend: see Thomas, 178. The author is grateful to Prof. Thomas for aid in tracing the source of the report.

404 climate of terror: see Thomas; Orwell, *Homage;* and Morgulas, *The Siege.* The Morgulas volume, although fiction, suggests vividly the irrationality and terror of the first months of revolution and war in Spain.

405 the six weeks preceding his sixty-first birthday: A sheaf of Casals'

notes and information supplied by his manager suggest the pace of his life in November and December 1937. He left Barcelona on November 7, arriving in Paris the following day, and left Paris on the ninth for an overnight trip to London.

Nov. 11 Manchester (Elgar, Bach suite; £183.15.0)

12 Cambridge 8:30 University (with Horszowski)

13 Hastings rehearsal 12 noon, concert 3 P.M. (Elgar concerto, Bach suite)

15 Rehearsal 10 A.M. Maida Vale (Tovey concerto)

16 Rehearsal 10 A.M. Queen's Hall

17 BBC rehearsal 11:30 A.M.; concert Queen's Hall 8:15 P.M.

20 Rehearsal BBC orchestra 10–1, 2:30–5:30

21 Rehearsal BBC orchestra 10–1; BBC Sunday Studio Concert 6:30 P.M. (Handel Concerto Grosso in F, Schubert "Tragic" Symphony, Wagner *Siegfried Idyll* and *Meistersinger* Prelude, conducted by Casals)

25 Amsterdam Concertgebouw closed rehearsal 11 A.M.; concert 8:15 P.M. (Haydn concerto, Willem Mengelberg conducting; fee 1500 florins, to be paid at end of concert)

27 The Hague Concertgebouw concert 8 P.M. (Haydn concerto; Mengelberg; same terms)

Dec. 3 Prague Philharmonic rehearsal 11 A.M., concert 8 P.M. (Schumann concerto. Fee £300 for one concerto, £400 if program contains two)

5 Vienna Gesellschaft der Musikfreunde (Haydn concerto)

7 Budapest rehearsal 10 A.M., concert 8 P.M. (Boccherini and Dvořák concertos, conductor Dohnányi; £275, to be paid part in rail tickets, balance in pounds sterling) Depart immediately after the concert, 12:25 A.M., arrive Bucharest 9:15 P.M.

9–11 Bucharest Royal Cultural Foundation (Schumann concerto, Brahms double concerto with Enesco; £500 for two concerts, to be sent before the concerts to Midland Bank, London) Leave Bucharest 12th at 1:45 P.M., arrive Zürich 1:38 A.M. 14th

14 Zürich Tonhalle orchestra (Schumann concerto, Bach suite in D minor; conductor Dr. Volkmar Andreae; Swiss francs 3000)

21 Paris morning rehearsal, evening concert: Boccherini, Schumann, and Haydn concertos

23   Amsterdam solo recital (accompanist Johannes Röntgen; 2000 florins, payable at end of concert)

412   Newman visit and Ysaÿe photograph: an anecdote Casals told
often and with obvious pleasure.

412   "If it was practical . . .": Crow, 195.

415   Alavedra's report about Cortot: Alavedra, *Casals*, 358.

1945–1973

CHAPTER 21

426   "Have you played for the soldiers?": Tertis, 63.

428–30   Gerald Moore: from *Am I Too Loud?* and to author.

435   Churchill passes by: Described to the author by Milly Stanfield,
who was a member of Casals' party.

439   Alavedra recorded the visit to Mistral's tomb in his *Casals*
(374–75), and Casals recalled it in conversations with the author.

444   the gospel according to Casals: Moore, 138.

445–47   description of Casals' living quarters: based on Arthur Conte,
La légende de Pablo Casals, from which the quoted portions also
come.

452   American and English accounts: Some of Casals' royalty accounts
were unavailable to him in the late 1940s as a result of agreements
among the Allied governments at the end of World War II in
Europe. Casals' rage was monumental when he learned, in the
summer of 1948, that his British funds not only were still blocked
but were being administered by the Custodian of Enemy Property.

452   "with the fervor of a youngster . . .": Lael Wertenbaker in *Life*,
May 15, 1950.

CHAPTER 22

453–54   "agreeable . . . village";   "professionals . . . exist":   Paul
Moor, "Casals at Prades," *Theatre Arts*.

455   "commercialized rat-race": *ibid.*

455–56   Casals' "Bergonzi-Goffriller" cello: This eighteenth-century
instrument, made by a Tyrolean craftsman named Matteo Goffriller, who settled in Cremona and was associated with the great
luthier Carlo Bergonzi, had been Casals' primary performance instrument for nearly fifty years and in a very real sense his closest
companion. As a child in Vendrell he had a half-size cello, which
was replaced by a three-quarter cello constructed by a Barcelona

instrument-maker when he entered school. His father bought him his first full-size cello the same day he discovered the Bach cello suites in a Barcelona music-shop, when he was thirteen. Queen María Cristina made possible the purchase of his first important violoncello, a fine Gagliano. Casals bought the Goffriller soon after his first Paris appearances, and it remained with him until after he made his home in Puerto Rico. (There the pervasive humidity so endangered the wood that the cello had to be stored in a vault in New York and Casals could use it only when he traveled to Europe or to Vermont in the summers. When it was brought to Puerto Rico in the early 1970s and stored in an air-conditioned room of Casals' house, the damp heat caused a body seam to open, and it had to be returned to the New York vault.) Casals said that, except once, he had never been tempted to own a Stradivarius; for him, they had too much personality—when he played on one he could never forget he had a Stradivarius in his hand—and they were also too large for him to handle comfortably. The single Strad cello that had tempted him, said to be the finest one in existence, belonged to Francesco von Mendelssohn in Berlin; Casals made an offer for it that Mendelssohn did not accept. A luthier named Laberte in Mirecourt, France, made an exact copy of the Goffriller cello for Casals in the early 1920s, an instrument he found excellent until climate changes during an American tour destroyed some of its tone. Isabella Stewart Gardner willed Casals a cello, which he gave to one of his students. For his daily cello work in Puerto Rico in the 1960s and 1970s Casals used a cello from a modern French instrument-maker.

457 "all ivy and colonels . . .": Moor.

457 "something of the air of the stage-manager": *ibid.*

457–58 "many hands ached"; "with housekeeper and dog"; "certainly he played . . . standing-room": *ibid.*

459 recordings of the Bach suites: Casals recorded suites 2 and 3 in London November 23, 1936, suites 1 and 6 in Paris on June 2 and 3, 1938, and the remaining two on June 13, 1939, in Paris. "The life which these works have," said Bernard Haggin, who heard Casals first in 1913, "is the life created by the coloring, the movement, the tensions of Casals's phrasing. . . . This is something you would almost not believe you had heard in a performance, after it was over; but you can put the needle back at the beginning of the Sarabande of No. 2 and find that it did happen, and there it is on the record for all time" (Haggin, *Music Observed* [New York: Oxford University Press, 1964], p. 167).

460 Istomin: quoted by Paul Moor.

461 Casals' farewell: *ibid.*

462 St. Michel de Cuxa: described in her *New Yorker* "Letter from Prades" by Janet Flanner (Genêt).

465 admission of Spain to UN: Casals immediately resigned from the UNESCO Musical Fund Committee, as did two others.

466 "My hands exist . . .": Emil Ludwig, "Pablo Casals," *Galeria de retratos*, 226. Casals confirmed to the author that, very rarely, there had been blood around the fingernails, but the stories of hours of practicing and performing so passionate that the fingertips were bloody are romantic and untrue: Casals' technical control was far too great for such a thing to happen, no matter how long he played. Even in his mid-nineties, his fingertips were smooth. As Maurice Eisenberg points out, only bad cellists have calluses.

469 "It is good for one's soul . . .": Gerald Moore, 138.

470–72 Quotations are from Gavoty, *Pablo Casals*.

472 Queen Elisabeth: She had the means and retained the impulse to be a free spirit, moving in a changed world with what Theo Aronson calls "all the authority, the internationalism, the blithe disregard of public opinion that had characterized royalty in a time long past." She scandalized the Belgian government by traveling to Peking and Moscow during a cold-war period but rejected wedding invitations as too fatiguing. In her seventies and eighties she continued to sunbathe, swim, take cold baths and long walks, and do yoga exercises. She would be up long after midnight or well before dawn, tiptoeing among the trees holding a tape-recorder microphone to record birdsong, once approaching within three feet of a nightingale by whistling its call. And she practiced tirelessly at the violin, always bringing at least one with her when she came to Prades. Somebody found her at six one morning in the bottom of an old bomb crater in Belgium playing away as if her life depended on it. "It's such a lovely morning," she said, "and the acoustics are perfect." (On a visit to the Château of Laeken in the late 1950s Casals agreed to play trios with Her Majesty after dinner, and the best available pianist was pressed into service—a good concert artist who had little experience playing chamber music. After a bit, perspiring heavily, he whispered desperately to Marta Casals, who was turning pages for him: "Whom should I follow, Her Majesty or the Maestro?") Casals always remembered Elisabeth's well-directed philanthropies and her answer before World War I to someone who asked her why she put energy into yet another program of social betterment for the poor: "Since I could, I must."

483 eulogy by Marcos Ramírez Irizarry: see Puerto Rico Dept. of Education, *Pablo Casals en Puerto Rico*, 21–25.

484 *Semana* review: Rafael Torres Mazzoranna in the January 25, 1956, issue.

489 by plane: Casals made his first transatlantic flight because all the available French passenger ships put in at a Spanish port before docking at Le Havre.

489 preparation to move from the Troy family's Château Valroc: Casals was moving from his fourth home in Prades. He lived in the Grand Hotel from the beginning of 1937 until 1940, in a house on the Route Nationale for about a year, 1940–1941, in the Villa Colette from 1941 until 1949, and in the gardener's house of the Troy estate 1949–1957.

490–91 "So long as Franco remains . . ."; "[Puerto Rico] autonomous commonwealth . . . blameless": F. C. Schang, "At Eighty Pablo Casals Is at Summit of Powers," *Musical America*, January 1957.

CHAPTER 23

493 constitution and reflexes: Pablo Casals, although a compact man, was built like a Japanese wrestler. The impression of fragility he sometimes gave in public in his eighties and nineties was to a considerable extent misleading. His grip was of uncompromising strength. He possessed a disciplined nervous concentration, particularly when he played cello; the analogy more than one fine fellow cellist used was that of a first-rate tennis player.

494 Paul Dudley White: Dr. White spent a long lunchtime in Boston talking with the author and also permitted him to examine notes and correspondence dealing with the case.

498 "I was aware . . .": Kahn, *Joys and Sorrows*, 277.

513 master classes: Casals' observations during his public classes, even in transcript and therefore without the sight and sound of the point he was illustrating or commenting on, remain useful and interesting to musicians; they also reveal facets of his approach to music and life. See those printed, for example, as "A Violoncello Lesson" in *Music and Letters*, October 1921. Their content ranged from "*Naturalité et simplicité, c'est très difficile*" to precise suggestions of bowing, fingering, or attack required in a given phrase. Casals' sense of delicacy in handling human situations showed often in these classes. Much of the spontaneous humor that existed in them arose through Casals' illustration on the cello of the traditional "purist" method of playing Bach, but the wit that could be sharp when he allowed it to be sometimes could be heard, as when he said to a student who had played almost inaudibly and not too well in a Marlboro session in the early 1970s "Either you have a *very* acute ear or I am going deaf!"

521 Paul Henry Lang: New York *Herald Tribune*, November 14, 1961.

522 *Time:* November 24, 1961.

CHAPTER 24

523 "Every day I am reborn . . .": *Life*, May 15, 1950.

529 "I am so unhappy . . .": extracted from television track of *Casals at 88* (CBS-TV) in the documentary record *Casals: A Living Portrait* (Columbia Records, 1966).

530 "All my feelings of sorrow, of hope . . .": explanation in a letter Casals wrote in 1962.

531 Franco's reaction: The story was still being told in Madrid in the early 1970s that when an agitated bureaucrat came to the dictator with news that Pablo Casals was thinking of returning to Spain, Franco said "Who?"

533 Sargent review: *The New Yorker*, June 30, 1962.

535 "You cannot imagine . . .": Doris Monteux, *It's All in the Music*, 120.

536 "very up-to-date . . .": *ibid.*, 124. "profound, fervent sincerity . . .": *ibid.*, 126.

547 "like a timid passenger in an airplane . . .": *Life*, December 11, 1966.

548 "Poison put to sound"; "Do not tell me that anyone can understand Picasso . . .": Schang interview in *Musical America*.

551 "we are one of the leaves of a tree . . .": from *Casals: A Living Portrait*.

556 "narrow and laborious world . . .": Jullian, *Prince of Aesthetes*, 164.

556 "the love of all humanity . . .": Biancolli interview in *McCall's*.

557–58 Mann letter: translated by Richard Winston for this book.

Bibliography

UNPUBLISHED SOURCES

Maestro and Señora Casals permitted the author to examine their archives in Puerto Rico, including correspondence (some of which extends back to Casals' student years in Madrid), music manuscripts, photographs, press clippings, programs, photographic copies of material still stored in France and at the Villa Casals in San Salvador, recordings, and souvenirs of Casals' career. Some correspondence between Casals and Enrique Granados was made available by Señora Natalia Granados de Carreras, through the courtesy of Mercèdes Guarro Tapis of Barcelona, who also assisted in locating other unpublished material in Barcelona and Vendrell. Señor Joan Maragall of Barcelona made available the complete file of programs of the Orquestra Pau Casals and other materials from the archives of the Orfeo Català and assisted greatly in the search for information in Madrid. Also studied were the collection of letters from Casals to Julius Röntgen in the Music Department of the Haags Gemeentemuseum in The Hague; letters from Casals to Mrs. Robert Trevelyan in the Trinity College Library, Cambridge; and the Tovey correspondence in the Reid Music Library at the University of Edinburgh. The diaries of Lady Enid Layard are in the British Museum. Queen Victoria's journal, which includes an entry concerning Casals, is in the Windsor Palace library.

SELECTED PUBLISHED SOURCES

Principal books, pamphlets, and articles consulted include:

Aguilar, Paco. *A Orillas de la Música*. Buenos Aires: Losoda, 1946. Section titled "Un día de P. Casals."

Alavedra, Juan. "Casals and Kennedy," *Bulletin* of the Instituto de Estudios Norteamericanos, Barcelona, 13 (spring-summer 1967).

———. *La extraordinaria vida de Pablo Casals*. Barcelona: Aymá, 1969. 121 pp., illustrated. For children; versions in Catalan and Spanish.

———. *Pablo Casals*. Barcelona: Plaza & Janes, 1963. 416 pp., illustrated. In Spanish, translated from the 1962 Catalan edition (Barcelona: Aldos) by Fernando Gutiérrez. Preface by Casals.

———. *El poema del pessebre*, 3d. ed. Barcelona: Editorial Selecta, 1966. 256 pp., illustrated. In Catalan. Poem of the oratorio, anecdotes, list of performances.

Aldrich, Richard. *Concert Life in New York 1902–1923* (ed. Harold Johnson). Freeport, N.Y.: Books for Libraries Press, 1971.

Alexanian, Diran. "La Technique et l'esthétique de Pablo Casals," *Le Monde Musical*, July 1921, 230–34.

———. *Traité théorétique et pratique du violoncelle*. Paris: Salabert, 1922. In French and English.

Alvarez Acosta, Miguel. *A la Luz de Casals: Tres discursos*. Mexico, 1959.

Alvin, Juliette. "The logic of Casals's technique," *Musical Times* (London), 71 (1930), 1078–79.

Amicis, Edmondo de. *Spain and the Spaniards*. Philadelphia: Henry T. Coates, 1895. 2 vols.

Antón del Olmet, Luis, and A. García Carraffa. *Alfonso XIII*. Madrid: Aldrededor, 1913–1914.

Aronson, Theo. *Defiant Dynasty: The Coburgs of Belgium*. Indianapolis: Bobbs-Merrill, 1968.

———. *Royal Vendetta: The Crown of Spain 1829–1965*. Indianapolis: Bobbs-Merrill, 1966.

Balsan, Consuelo Vanderbilt. *The Glitter and the Gold*. London: Heinemann, 1953.

Batcheller, Tryphosa Bates. *Royal Spain of Today*. New York: Longmans, Green, 1913.

Bauer, Harold. *His Book*. New York: Norton, 1948.

Bell, Clive. *Old Friends: Personal Recollections*. New York: Harcourt, 1957.

Biancolli, Louis. Interview with Casals, *McCall's*, May 1966.

Borisiak, A. A. *Essays on the Cello School of Pablo Casals*. Moscow, 1929. In Russian.

Boult, Adrian C. "Casals as Conductor," *Music and Letters,* 4 (April 1923), 149–52.

Briggs, John. *Requiem for a Yellow Brick Brewery.* Boston: Little, Brown, 1969.

Brown, Dee. *The Year of the Century: 1876.* New York: Scribner's, 1966.

Busch, Fritz. *Pages from a Musician's Life.* Translated by Marjorie Strachey. London: The Hogarth Press, 1953.

Carrière, Eugène. *Écrits et lettres choisies.* Paris: Mercure de France, 1909.

Carrière, Jean-René. *De la vie d'Eugène Carrière.* Toulouse: Édouard Privat, 1966.

Casals, Pablo. "The Story of My Youth," *Windsor Magazine* (London), November 1930, 717–23.

Casella, Alfredo. *Music in My Time.* Translated and edited by Spencer Norton. Norman: University of Oklahoma Press, 1955.

Channon, Henry. *The Ludwigs of Bavaria.* London: John Lehmann, 1952.

Chase, Gilbert. *The Music of Spain,* 2d. ed. New York: Dover, 1959.

Cherniavsky, David. "Casals's teaching of the cello," *Musical Times,* 93 (September 1952), 398–400. Also in Italian and English in *Rivista Musicale Italiana,* April–June 1953.

Christen, Ernest. *Instantanés: Allégories du temps présent.* Neuchâtel: Editions H. Messeiller, n.d. Pp. 33–42, "L'Ode à la joie torpillée: Casals pacificateur."

———. *Pablo Casals: l'homme, l'artiste.* Geneva: Labor et Fides, 1956; Paris: Librairie protestante, 1956. 174 pp., illustrated.

Conte, Arthur. *La légende de Pablo Casals.* Perpignan: Éditions Proa, 1950. 154 pp., 6 photographs by Gjon Mili.

Cooke, Charles. "All about 'That Gold Piano in the White House,'" Washington *Star,* August 21, 1966.

Cooke, James Francis. *Musical Travelogues.* Philadelphia: Presser, 1934. Casals, "Musical History of Barcelona," pp. 108–15.

Corredor, José María. *Casals: biografía ilustrada.* Barcelona: Ediciones Destino, 1967. 149 pp., highly illustrated. Text is extracted from *Conversations.*

———. *Converses amb Casals.* Barcelona: Editorial Selecta, 1967. Updated edition in Catalan of 1954 volume. English version, translated by André Mangeot from 1954 French edition, *Conversations with Casals* (New York: Dutton, 1956). 240 pp. Introduction by Casals. Citations in notes are of Dutton paperback edition.

Cortés Cavanillas, J. *Alfonso XII: el rey romántico.* Madrid: Aspas, 1943.

Costa-Amic, B. (ed.). *Pau Casals: un hombre solitario contra Franco*. Mexico: Ediciones Biblioteca Catalana, 1955. 94 pp.

Cowles, Virginia. *1913: An End and a Beginning*. New York: Harper, 1967.

———. *The Russian Dagger: Cold War in the Days of the Czars*. New York: Harper, 1969.

Cron, Theodore O., and Burt Goldblatt. *Portrait of Carnegie Hall*. New York: Macmillan, 1966.

Crow, John A. *Spain: The Root and the Flower*. New York: Harper, 1963.

Day, James. *Vaughan Williams*. London: Dent, 1961.

Deneke, Margaret. *Ernest Walker*. London: Oxford University Press, 1949.

Downes, Olin. *Olin Downes on Music* (ed. Irene Downes). New York: Simon and Schuster, 1957.

Dozier, Thomas. "Las Memorias de Pablo Casals," *Life en Español*, May 4, May 18, and June 1, 1959.

Draper, Muriel. *Music at Midnight*. New York: Harper, 1929.

Duff, David. *Victoria Travels*. New York: Taplinger, 1970.

Duff-Gordon, Lina. *A Castle in Italy*. New York: Thomas Y. Crowell, 1961.

Eastman, Max. *Great Companions*. New York: Farrar, Straus, 1949.

Einstein, Alfred. *Essays on Music*. New York: Norton, 1956.

Eisenberg, Maurice. "Hommage à Pablo Casals," *Le Monde Musical*, September 1934.

———. "Pablo Casals at 80: a tribute," *Violins and Violinists*, 18 (January–February 1957), 4–6.

Elkin, Robert. *Royal Philharmonic*. New York: Rider, 1946. Foreword by Casals.

Espinós Moltó, Víctor. *El Maestro Arbós*. Madrid: Espasa-Calpe, 1942.

Eulalia, HRH The Infanta. *Court Life from Within*. London: Cassell, 1915.

———. *Memoirs of a Spanish Princess*. New York: Norton, 1937.

Fernández Cid, Antonio. *Granados*. Madrid: Samarán, 1956.

FitzLyon, April. *The Price of Genius: A Life of Pauline Viardot*. New York: Appleton-Century, 1964.

Flanner, Janet [Genêt]. "Letter from Prades," *The New Yorker*, June 17, 1950.

Forsee, Alysea. *Cellist for Freedom*. New York: Thomas Y. Crowell, 1965. 229 pp., illustrated. For children.

Foster, Myles Birket. *History of the Philharmonic Society of London*. London: John Lane, 1912.

Fraser, Geoffrey, and Thadée Natanson. *Léon Blum*. London: Gollancz, 1937.

Gaisberg, Fred. *The Music Goes Round*. New York: Macmillan, 1942. (Also published as *Music on Record.*)

García Borrás, José. *Pablo Casals, peregrino en América: tres semanas con el maestro*. Mexico, 1957. 349 pp., illustrated.

Gatti-Casazza, Giulio. *Memories of the Opera*. New York: Scribner's, 1941.

Gavoty, Bernard. *Pablo Casals*. Photographs by Roger Hauert. Geneva: R. Kister, 1956. 30 pp., highly illustrated. Translated from the 1955 French edition by F. E. Richardson.

Geissmar, Berta. *Two Worlds of Music*. New York: Creative Age, 1946. Published in England as *The Baton and the Jackboot*.

Gelatt, Roland. *The Fabulous Phonograph*, rev. ed. New York: Appleton, 1965.

———. *Music Makers*. New York: Knopf, 1953.

Gerhardt, Elena. *Recital*. London: Methuen, 1953.

Ginsburg, Lev S. *Pablo Casals*. Moscow, 1966. 244 pp., illustrated; includes score of Casals' sardana for cellos. In Russian.

Gollancz, Victor. *Journey Towards Music*. New York: Dutton, 1965.

Grierson, Mary. *Donald Francis Tovey: A Biography Based on Letters*. London: Oxford University Press, 1952.

Grindea, Miron. "Pablo Casals at the Academy." London: The Royal Academy of Music, 1945.

Grove's Dictionary of Music and Musicians. New York: St. Martin's Press, 1955.

Harding, Bertita. *Imperial Twilight: The Story of Karl and Zita of Hungary*. Indianapolis: Bobbs-Merrill, 1939.

Harding, James. *Saint-Saëns and His Circle*. London: Chapman & Hall, 1965.

Hind, Pamela. "Casals as Teacher," *The RCM Magazine*, 66 (1950), 96.

Hughes, Adella Prentiss. *Music Is My Life*. New York: World, 1947.

In Memoriam Bernardo V. Moreira de Sá. Porto: Livraria Tavares Martins, 1947.

Jullian, Philippe. *Prince of Aesthetes: Count Robert de Montesquiou 1855–1921*. New York: Viking, 1965.

Kahn, Albert E. *Joys and Sorrows: Reflections by Pablo Casals*. New York: Simon and Schuster, 1970. 314 pp., illustrated.

Katchen, Julius. "The Miracle of Pablo Casals," *Music and Musicians*, January 1961, 14.

Kaufmann, Helen L., and E. von B. Hansl. *Artists in Music of Today*. Drawings by Louis Lupas. New York: Grosset & Dunlap, 1933.

Kennedy, Michael. *Barbirolli*. London: MacGibbon & Kee, 1971.

———. *The Hallé Tradition*. Manchester: University of Manchester Press, 1960.

————. *The Works of Ralph Vaughan Williams*. London: Oxford University Press, 1964.

Kessler, Count Harry. *In the Twenties*. New York: Holt, 1971.

Knapp, Bettina, and Myra Chipman. *That Was Yvette*. London: Frederick Muller, 1966.

Kolodin, Irving. *The Metropolitan Opera*. New York: Knopf, 1967.

Krehbiel, Henry Edward. *"The Bohemians" (New York Musicians' Club): A Historical Narrative and Record*. New York, 1921.

Lee, Sir Sidney. *Queen Victoria*. London: John Murray, 1904.

Littlehales, Lillian. *Pablo Casals: A Life*. New York: Norton, 1948; Spanish edition, Mexico, 1951. 232 pp., illustrated. The pioneer biography, written in 1929 and updated in 1948, by a cellist friend of Casals and Susan Metcalfe Casals.

Llongueras, Juan, Juan Ramon, and María Carratelà. *Pau Casals*. Barcelona: Edicions de "La Nova Revista," 1927. 63 pp., illustrated.

Lochner, Louis P. *Fritz Kreisler*. New York: Macmillan, 1950.

London Bach Group. "Homage to Pablo Casals on His 80th Birthday." London, 1956.

Longland, Jean. "Granados and the Opera *Goyesca[s]*," *Notes Hispanic* (Hispanic Society of America), 5 (1945), 95–112.

Loyarte, Adrián de. *Biografía de SM la Reina María Cristina. . . .* San Sebastián: Libreria Internacional, 1936, 1938.

Ludwig, Emil. "Pablo Casals," in *Galeria de retratos*. Madrid: Aguilar, 1960.

Lugo Romero, Américo. "Casals el incomparable," *Música* (Bogotá), 6 (1941), 201–6.

[M] on Casals' first Russian visit, *La Suisse* (Geneva), May 25, 1958.

Maldonado, Teófilo. *Hombres de Primera Plana*. Barcelona: Ediciones Rumbos, 1958. Pp. 412–13.

Malko, Nicolai. *A Certain Art*. New York: Morrow, 1966.

Mallet, Victor (ed.). *Life with Queen Victoria*. Boston: Houghton Mifflin, 1968.

Mannes, David. *Music Is My Faith*. New York: Norton, 1938.

Mauclair, Camille. *Idées vivantes*. Paris: Librairie Georges Baranger, 1904. Pp. 61–92, "Eugène Carrière et la Psychologie du Mystère."

————. *Trois crises de l'art actuel*. Paris: Fasquelle, 1906.

Mauron, Marie. "La cloche aux étoiles de Pablo Casals." Avignon: Palais du Roure, l'Isle sonante, 1956.

Monteux, Doris. *It's All in the Music*. New York: Farrar, Straus, 1965.

Moor, Paul. "Casals at Prades," *Theatre Arts*, October 1950.

Moore, Gerald. *Am I Too Loud?* New York: Macmillan, 1962.

Morgulas, Jerrold. *The Siege*. New York: Holt, 1972.

Müller-Blattau, Joseph Maria. *Casals*. Berlin: Rembrandt Verlag, 1964. 64 pp., highly illustrated. In German.

Navarro Costabella, J. *Pablo Casals: la vida del gran musico.* [Barcelona], 1947. 32 pp. A Spanish interview.

Nelson, James (ed.). *Wisdom: Conversations with the Elder Wise Men of Our Day.* New York: Norton, 1958.

O'Connell, Charles. *The Other Side of the Record.* New York: Knopf, 1947.

Odell, George C. D. *Annals of the New York Stage,* Vol. 13. New York: Columbia University Press, 1942.

Ortega-Morejon, José Maria. *Doña Isabel de Borbón.* Madrid: Aspas [1943].

Orwell, George. *Homage to Catalonia.* New York: Harcourt (Harvest Books), 1952.

Owen, Sidney Cunliffe. *Elisabeth, Queen of the Belgians.* London: Herbert Jenkins, 1954.

"Pablo Casals, Compositeur," *Musique Latine,* No. 1 (January 1951).

"Pablo Casals and his violoncello by Matteo Goffriller," *Violins,* 10 (October 1949), 262.

Painter, George D. *Proust.* Boston: Little, Brown, 1959. 2 vols.

Parker, H. T. *Eighth Notes: Voices and Figures of Music and the Dance.* New York: Dodd, Mead, 1922.

Piatigorsky, Gregor. *Cellist.* Garden City, N.Y.: Doubleday, 1965.

Pinkney, David H. *Napoleon III and the Rebuilding of Paris.* Princeton: Princeton University Press, 1958.

Pirani, Max. *Emanuel Moór.* London: P. R. Macmillan, 1959. Preface by Casals.

Puerto Rico Department of Education. *Pablo Casals en Puerto Rico, 1955–1956* (Publicaciones ser. 3, no. 106). San Juan, 1957. 86 pp., illustrations.

Quitin, José. *Eugène Ysaÿe.* Brussels: Bosworth, 1938.

Read, Oliver, and Walter L. Welch. *From Tin Foil to Stereo: Evolution of the Phonograph.* Indianapolis: H. W. Sams, 1959.

Reid, Charles. *John Barbirolli.* New York: Taplinger, 1971.

———. *Malcolm Sargent.* London: Hamish Hamilton, 1968.

Riesemann, Oskar von. *Rachmaninoff's Recollections as told to Oskar von Riesemann.* New York: Macmillan, 1934.

Röntgen, Julius. *Brieven van Julius Röntgen.* Amsterdam: H. J. Paris, 1934. Chiefly in German.

Rosenthal, Harold (ed.). *The Mapleson Memoirs.* New York: Appleton-Century, 1966.

Ross, Ishbel. *The Expatriates.* New York: Crowell, 1970.

Rubinstein, Arthur. *My Young Years.* New York: Knopf, 1973.

Runciman, John F. *Old Scores and New Readings*. London: At the Sign of the Unicorn, 1899.

Russell, Thomas. *Philharmonic Decade*. London: Hutchinson, 1945.

Schang, F. C. "At Eighty Pablo Casals Is at Summit of Powers," *Musical America*, January 15, 1957.

Schonberg, Harold C. *The Great Conductors*. New York: Simon and Schuster, 1967.

———. *The Great Pianists*. New York: Simon and Schuster, 1963.

Schweitzer, Albert. *Out of My Life and Thought*. New York: Holt, 1949.

Schwerké, Irving. *Views and Interviews*, 4th ed. Foreword by Leonard Liebling. Paris: printed by Les Orphelins-Apprentis d'Auteuil, 1936.

Seiler, Alexander J. P. *Casals*. Photographs by P. Moeschlin. Olten: Walter, 1956. 115 pp., highly illustrated.

Seltsam, William H. *Metropolitan Opera Annals*. New York: Wilson, 1947.

Seroff, Victor I. *The Mighty Five*. Freeport, N.Y.: Books for Libraries Press, 1948.

Shattuck, Roger. *The Banquet Years: The Origins of the Avant-Garde in France*, rev. ed. New York: Random House (Vintage Books), 1968.

Shirer, William L. *The Collapse of the Third Republic*. New York: Simon and Schuster, 1969.

Skinner, Cornelia Otis. *Elegant Wits and Grand Horizontals*. Boston: Houghton Mifflin, 1962.

———. *Madame Sarah*. Boston: Houghton Mifflin, 1966.

Smyth, Ethel. *Impressions That Remained*. New York: Knopf, 1946.

Spalding, Albert. *Rise to Follow*. New York: Holt, 1943.

Speyer, Edward. *My Life and Friends*. London: Cobden-Sanderson, 1937.

Spinoza, Margarita. "Pablo Casals—an Artist's Life," *Musical Courier*, May 28, 1918.

Stanfield, Milly B. "Casals—and Us," *The Strad* (1945), 177–78, 228–30.

———. Tribute to Guilhermina Suggia, *The Strad* (September 1950), 154–55.

Stein, Leo. *Journey into the Self*. New York: Crown, 1950.

Stricker, Noemi. *Peregrinos del Mundo / Pilgrims of the World: Pau Casals—Albert Schweitzer*. San Juan: Festival Casals, 1957. 41 pp. Poems, originally in French. Spanish version by Tomás Blanco, English by Harriet de Onis.

Stuckenschmidt, H. H. *Maurice Ravel: Variations on His Life and Work*. Philadelphia: Chilton, 1968.

Bibliography

Stutschewsky, Joachim. "Pablo Casals," *Musik* (Berlin) (August 1931), 813–16.
Suggia, Guilhermina. "The Violoncello," *Music and Letters*, 1 (March 1920), 104–11.
———. "Violoncello Playing," *Music and Letters*, 2 (April 1921), 130–34.
Szigeti, Joseph. *With Strings Attached*. London: Cassell, 1949.
Taper, Bernard. "Casals at Ninety-Two," *New Yorker* (April 19, 1969), 123–34.
———. *Cellist in Exile: a portrait of Pablo Casals*. New York: McGraw-Hill, 1962. 120 pp., illustrated. Handsomely produced expanded version of 1961 *New Yorker* profile.
Tertis, Lionel. *Cinderella No More*. New York: British Book Centre, 1953.
Thomas, Hugh. *The Spanish Civil War*. New York: Harper (Colophon Books), 1963.
Thomson, Virgil. *Music Reviewed, 1940–1954*. New York: Random House (Vintage Books), 1967.
Trueta, Joseph. *The Spirit of Catalonia*. New York: Oxford University Press, 1946.
Tudor, Andrei. *Enescu*. Bucharest: Verlag für Fremdsprachige Literatur, 1957. In German.
Valaitis, Vytas. *Casals*. New York: Grossman (Paragraphic Books), 1966. Unpaged. Text selected by Theodore Strongin. Photographs by *Newsweek* photographer Valaitis.
Van Vechten, Carl. *The Music of Spain*. New York: Knopf, 1918.
Vandervelde, Lalla. *Monarchs and Millionaires*. New York: Adelphi, 1925.
Vaughan Williams, Ursula. *R. V. W.: A Biography of Ralph Vaughan Williams*. London: Oxford University Press, 1964.
Vishniak, Mark. *Léon Blum*. Paris: Flammarion, 1937.
Vives de Fabrigas, Elisa. *Pau Casals*. Barcelona: Rafael Dalmau, 1966. 453 pp., illustrated. In Catalan.
von Tobel, Rudolf. *Pablo Casals*. Zürich: Rotapfel-Verlag, 1941, 1945. 140 pp., illustrated. In German.
Walter, Bruno. *Theme and Variations*. New York: Knopf, 1946.
Waterfield, Gordon. *Layard of Nineveh*. New York: Praeger, 1968.
Wechsberg, Joseph. *Red Plush and Black Velvet: The Story of Melba and Her Times*. Little, Brown, 1961.
Weeks, Donald. *Corvo*. London: Michael Joseph, 1971.
Whitlock, Brand. *Belgium*. New York: Appleton, 1919. 2 vols.
Williams, Roger L. *The World of Napoleon III*. New York: Macmillan (Collier Books), 1962. Chap. 4, "Jacques Offenbach and Parisian Gaiety."

Wood, Henry J. *My Life of Music*. London: Gollancz, 1938.
Ysaÿe, Antoine, and Bertram Ratcliffe. *Ysaÿe: His Life, Work and Influence*. London: Heinemann, 1947. Preface by Yehudi Menuhin.

Journals and newspapers consulted include:

Étude, Life, McCall's, Le Monde Musical, Monthly Musical Record, Music and Letters, Music and Musicians, Music Review, Musical America, Musical Courier, The Musical Quarterly, The Musical Times, The Musician, New Republic, The New Yorker, La Revue Musicale, Saturday Review, Theatre Arts, Time.

Baltimore: *Sun*. Barcelona: various newspapers from the 1890s to 1973. Boston: *Christian Science Monitor, Globe, Herald Traveler, Transcript*. Chicago: *Record Herald*. London: *Daily Express, News Chronicle, Observer, The Times*. Madrid: chief newspapers 1927–1935, 1946–1973. Manchester: *Guardian*. New York: *Herald Tribune, Telegraph, Times, World*. Paris: *L'Express, Le Figaro, L'Humanité*. Providence: *Journal*. San Francisco: *Chronicle*. San Juan: *El Mundo, Star*. Washington, D.C.: *Post, Star*.

Acknowledgments

Marta Montañez de Casals was sympathetically helpful throughout this book's evolution. She never failed to answer requests for information or to find documents, programs, and photographs that were needed, and once was at the typewriter long after midnight before departing with her husband on an early-morning flight abroad, answering queries so that a portion of the manuscript would not be delayed. Her charm, consistent good humor, and hospitality are, like her practical assistance, gratefully acknowledged.

Establishment of many facts as well as much understanding of Casals' life in Catalonia and elsewhere in Spain would have been impossible without the energy, imagination, and unselfishness of Mercèdes Guarro Tapis and Don Juan Maragall of Barcelona. Mariona Guarro de Martinez Girona and her family offered friendliness, research assistance, and unforgettable hospitality to strangers in their land. Elizabeth Martinez y Guarro translated with skill, patience, and notable cheerfulness. Others in Barcelona who were helpful include Natalia Granados de Carreras and Dr. Antonio Carreras; José Garrut of the Archivo de Historia de la Ciudad; Antonio Aragó Cabañas, vice-director of the Archivo de la Corona de Aragón; Francisco Herrada Martinez; Conchita Badía de Augustin; and Pau Dini, the youngest alumnus of the Orquestra Pau Casals. Luis and Teresina Casals showed us the Villa Casals at San Salvador in warm October twilight. At Montserrat,

Father Antoni Ramón y Arrufat recalled Casals' visits there; Father Gregori Estrada, the organist, located music manuscripts; and Brother Oliva Torras was an urbane guide.

In Madrid, I am indebted to the Marqués de Mondejar, Jefe de Casa to Prince Juan Carlos de Borbón, who received us at the Palacio de la Zarzuela; Juan de Contreras, Marqués de Lozoya; Federico Javier Lema Martinez; Hortensia Lo Cascio Loureiro de Rodriguez de Alba of the Conservatory library; Evelyn Clancy de Fernandez de Mesa of the U.S. Embassy; Carlos Fernandez Shaw of the Spanish Ministry of Foreign Affairs; and Dr. Jaime Varela, who assisted in my search of Madrid newspapers.

Joachim Röntgen of The Hague is due particular thanks, as are his brother Franz, Mrs. Nellie Spruijt, and Dr. Clemens von Gleich of the Haags Gemeentemuseum. In Amsterdam assistance came from Mrs. F. Kuin-Roovers of the Openbare Muziekbibliotheek and from Dr. Marius Flothuis of the Concertgebouworkest.

I gladly acknowledge the friendship and aid of Signor and Signora Franco Passigli in Florence and of Miklós Perényi in Budapest. Thanks are due Helena Moreira de Sá e Costa of Portugal; Mlle Nadia Boulanger, Mme Antoinette Risler, Charles Kiesgen, and Paul Tortelier in France; Walter Legge in Switzerland; M. Barthélemy of the Conservatoire Royal de Musique in Liège; Antoine Ysaÿe, Brussels; Imre Kun, Budapest; Dietrich Fischer-Dieskau, Berlin; Christian Hoch, Vienna; Prof. Lev Ginsburg of the Moscow Conservatory; and Christina Mohede of the editorial department of the *Dagens Nyheter*, Stockholm.

Special help in England came from Sir John Barbirolli; Sir Adrian Boult; Mrs. Patricia Bradford of Trinity College Library; Mrs. Ursula Vaughan Williams; Humphrey Burton of the BBC; R. Fleury of the Central Music Library, London; Mark Hamilton; Michael Kennedy; Robert Mackworth-Young, Librarian of Windsor Castle; Michael S. Anderson, Reid Music Library, Edinburgh; Alec Hyatt King, Music Room, British Museum; Mrs. Yehudi Menuhin; Gerald Moore; George D. Painter; Lionel Tertis; Hugh Thomas; Gordon Waterfield; Oliver Davies, Librarian of the Royal College of Music; and Lisa Van Gruisen.

Continuing appreciation is acknowledged to Dr. Heber Amaury Rosa Silva and Prof. Jorge Ivan Rosa Silva of San Juan. Amaury Rosa Silva introduced me to Casals in 1960, read the manuscript of this book twelve years later, gave useful guidance on medical and other matters, and in the years between proved himself a friend both to my wife and myself and of the Casals. Jorge Rosa Silva also went carefully through the long manuscript, searched records in Puerto Rico, clarified points of history, and offered reactions that were invariably stimulat-

Acknowledgments

ing. Rosa San Miguel de Cueto and Luis Cueto Coll were kind, helpful and generously hospitable through many years. I am grateful for the friendship and help of Aquiles and Angélica Montañez, Olga Iglesias, and Mr. and Mrs. Horace Gill and the assistance of Jesús María Sanromá, Señora Pilar Defilló de Acevedo, Alfredo Matilla, and Abelardo Ambrosiani of Telemundo.

Thanks are due Thomas Frost, Director of Masterworks, Columbia Records, and to engineer Raymond Moore of the same organization. Assistance from the United Nations came through Mrs. Murray Fuhrman, María Carmen Poblador Valls, Thomas Prendergast, and Mr. R. Sarma. Aid in checking translated material came from Lea Blumenfeld, Lux Elsner, Elsa Christensen Granade, Charity Randall, Laureano Medina, and Louise Bushnell.

I am grateful to Mieczyslaw Horszowski for friendship and encouragement and remain in awe of his knowledge, civilization, and spirit. I must also express special appreciation for the help of Siso Gandará and the interest and assistance of Maurice and Paula Eisenberg and of Milly Stanfield; and gratitude to Mr. and Mrs. Rudolf Serkin.

Acknowledgment with appreciation is also made to Philip D. Beam, Bowdoin College; Frederick J. R. Blachly; Mr. and Mrs. Isidore Cohen; Anthony Checchia; Marcia Davenport; Mr. and Mrs. Ernest de Popper; Alfred C. Edwards; Margaret Petherbridge Farrar and John Chipman Farrar; Fritz Friedler; Janet Flanner; Mr. and Mrs. Felix Galimir; J. A. Gibernau; Bernard Greenhouse; Zora Cheever Gross; Jesse Glasgow, Baltimore *Sun;* David Hall, New York Public Library; James R. Ketchum, former Curator of the White House; Louis Metcalfe Kobbé; Boris and Sonya Kroyt; Mrs. Anka Landau; Wiktor Labunski; Ruth and Jaime Laredo; Alfred W. Lees; Alice Roosevelt Longworth; William Koshland; Maureen McManus; Ann Mitchell, Boston Symphony Orchestra; Dr. Bernard Myers, New York Public Library; Doris Madden; Ronald Nelson; Mrs. John DeWitt Peltz of the Metropolitan Opera Association; Olga Kobbé Pitkin and John G. Pitkin; Christine Reed of the Festival Casals' New York office; Jay Rosenfeld, *Berkshire Eagle;* Francis Roudebush; Klaus G. Roy, Cleveland Orchestra; Frank Salomon; Berenice Myers Shotwell; Steven L. Solomon, Boston Symphony Orchestra; Kyriena Siloti; Janos Starker; Barbara Seltzer; Alexander Schneider; John H. Steinway; Kurt Stone; Caroline Thomas; Virgil Thomson; Walter Toscanini; Willem Valkenier; Mgr. Béla Varga; Gerald Wagner; Dr. Paul Dudley White; personnel of The New York Public Library, particularly in the music library at Lincoln Center; and librarians of The Brooks Memorial Library, Brattleboro.

Acknowledgment of permission to publish previously unpublished documentary material is made to H. M. Queen Elizabeth II, for gra-

[669]

cious permission to reproduce an entry from Queen Victoria's diary, preserved at Winsdor Castle; Marietta Bitter (Mrs. Walter Abel); Ursula Vaughan Williams; Joachim Röntgen; Gerald Moore; Isidore Saslav; the Haags Gemeentemuseum; Richard Winston; Frau Thomas Mann; and Mrs. L. Lohmeyer Soules.

Sydney Beck, director of libraries at the New England Conservatory, formerly head of special collections in the music division of the New York Public Library and curator of the Toscanini Memorial Archives, generously read galley proof and gave me and the book the benefit of his wide and penetrating knowledge of music and musicians. My wife took days from her own demanding schedule as an editor also most helpfully to read the proof.

And to Carl D. Brandt there continues a debt of appreciation that can be satisfied only in small measure by acknowledgment here—not least for major editorial help and guidance.

Illustration Credits

Many prints made available for use in this book carried no indication of the original photographer, but a careful effort has been made to supply identification whenever it could be found.

SOURCES

Archivo Mas, Barcelona: 50, 62, 65, 194, 297 right
Author's Collection: 334, 408
Tryphosa Bates Batcheller, *Royal Spain of Today* (New York: Longmans, Green, 1913): 75, 92
Luis and Teresina Casals y Defilló: 386
Casals Collection: ii, 1, 18, 20, 23, 69, 94 left, 108 left, 143, 201, 244, 288 top, 294, 321, 352, 378 bottom and top right, 379, 382, 413, 423, 470, 480, 485, 499, 500, 524, 537 left
Culver Pictures: 298 bottom right
Escuela Municipal de Música, Barcelona: 55 top left
Antonio Fernández-Cid, *Granados* (Madrid: Samarán, 1956), 288 bottom
Haags Gemeentemuseum, The Hague: 210, 214, 220, 261, 298 top
Francisco Herrada Martínez, Barcelona: 26, 36, 55 bottom left and right, 78, 108 bottom, 125, 127, 129, 181, 190, 223, 259, 330, 345, 378 left center, 401 left, 403, 479

Illustrated London News, 1894: 111 right
Louis M. Kobbé: 177, 297 left
Angélica Montañez: 478
El Mundo, San Juan: 553
Musical Courier (January 15, 1902): 156
New York Public Library: 111, 156, 368
Radio Times Hulton Picture Library, London: 118 bottom right
Helena de Sá e Costa: 169, 198
Tate Gallery, London: 352
United Nations: 537 right, 554, 556
Ursula Vaughan Williams: 274
José María Vilar y de Orovio: 290
Elisa Vives de Fábrigas, *Pau Casals* (Barcelona: Dalmau, 1966): 94 right
Gordon Waterfield: 118 left

PHOTOGRAPHERS

Erica Anderson: 468
Isaac Berez: 524 right
David Cain: 503, 514 center and bottom right
Jean Dieuzaide, Photo YAN, Toulouse: 474
Antonio and Emilio Fedits, Barcelona: 108 right
Frank Gehbauer: 470 right
Gerschel, Paris: 127
Horace Gill, San Juan: 499, 528
Don Hunstein for Columbia Records: 502 right, 509 left and bottom, 549; from Casals Collection: 447, 502 left
H. L. Kirk: 4, 6, 10, 12, 30, 38, 52, 84, 514 bottom left, 544, 550, 552; from Casals Collection: 108 right, 118 top right, 159
George Kossuth: 354
Marceau, New York: 156, 159
Gjon Mili: 509 right
Yutaka Nagata, UN: 556
Enrique Puigdengolas, Barcelona: 378 top left
Margaret B. Rodriguez, La Fortaleza: 485 right
François René Roland: 470 left
Paul Senn: 401 right, 417, 448
Mark Shaw: 521 (Reprinted with the permission of Farrar, Straus & Giroux, Inc. from *The John F. Kennedys: A Family Album* by Mark Shaw, copyright © 1959, 1960, 1961, 1962, 1963, 1964 by Mark Shaw.)
John M. Snyder: 514 top, 516, 517
Rubén Valentín, *El Mundo:* 553

Illustration Credits

Eugène Carrière: 143 bottom right, 201 left
Ramón Casas: 297 right
Augustus John: 352
Ricardo Opissa: 194
John Singer Sargent: 297 left
Luisa Vidal Puig: 102

Index

Index

Index

Bizet, Georges, 63, 64
Carmen, 63–64, 309
Blanco, Tomás, 527–528, 566, 595
Blasco-Ibáñez, Vicente, 37, 39, 303, 373
Blatchly, Frederick J. R., 541
Blériot, Louis, 184
Bliss, Arthur, 537
Bloch, Ernest, 339, 450
Bloody Sunday, 221–222, 226
Blum, Léon, 140
Blumenfeld, Felix, 224
Boccherini, Luigi
Concerto in B-flat Major for cello and orchestra, op. 34, 351, 590
Böellmann, Léon, 236
Variations Symphoniques, 161
Bohemians, The (New York), 490
Boïto, Arrigo, 314
Boixados, Benet, 44, 47–48
Boixados, Fidèlia Felip de (PC's godmother). *See* Felip, Fidèlia
Boixados, María, 44, 47–48
Bonaparte, Princess Mathilde, 139
Borbón dynasty, 11–13, 24, 25, 375, 540
Bordeaux, 414–415
Bori, Lucrezia, 302, 311
Borisiak, A. A., 225–226, 227
Borodin, Alexander, 16, 229, 231
Borwick, Leonard, 264, 272
Bösendorfersaal (Vienna), 271
Boston *Globe*, 7, 8, 306–307
Boston *Herald*, 217
Boston *Post*, 306
Boston Symphony Orchestra, 154, 185, 304–307, 488, 508
Boston *Transcript*, 155, 305–307
Boucherit, Jules, 126, 132, 145
Boulanger, Nadia, 377, 511
Boult, Adrian C., 274, 333–339, 396, 425, 427, 428
Brahms, Johannes, 15, 51, 53, 124, 136, 197, 242, 262, 263, 267, 268, 280, 284, 285, 286, 348, 393, 446
"Academic Festival" Overture, 269
Concerto in A minor for violin, cello, and orchestra, op. 102, 238, 263, 271, 279, 359, 508
Quartet in C minor, op. 60, 282–283
Quartet in G minor, op. 25, 172

recordings, 591–593
Sonata in F Major for cello and piano, op. 99, 264
Variations on a Theme by Haydn, op. 56a, 348
Brandoukov, Anatol, 204
Brema, Marie, 272
Brenoteau (clarinetist), 123
Bretón y Hernandez, Tomás, 76–77, 91, 93, 104, 107, 397
Britt, Horace, 340
Britten, Benjamin, 536
Bruch, Max
Kol Nidrei, 302, 308, 366, 593
Brussels, 96–100
Brussels Conservatory, 63, 77, 81, 95, 96–100
Budapest, 273, 274, 276, 277, 293, 319, 383, 531, 538–539
Budapest String Quartet, 449
Buenos Aires, 178–179
Burke, Anita. *See* Moór, Anita
Burke, Laurence, 300, 314
Burmester, Willy, 277–278
Busch, Adolf, 186, 284, 304, 314, 513
Busch, Fritz, 267, 289, 313–314, 339, 342, 391, 396
Busoni, Ferruccio, 188, 254, 280–281
Byron, SS, 178

Café del Centro (Vendrell), 18, 54
Café-concerts, 190
Cafés, musical, 51, 133, 190
Café Rouge (Paris), 133, 190
Café Suez (Paris), 133
Café Tost (Barcelona), 50–54, 56–59, 61, 63, 64, 105, 133, 326
Cajatta, Ida, 311
Calle de San Quintín, No. 8 (Madrid), 82–83, *84*
Calvé, Emma, 136, 149
Cambridge University, 433, 441
Campos Parsi, Héctor, 487
Cancan, 13, 101
Canigou, Mount, 418, 432, 436, *448*, 449, 489
Cant dels Ocells, El ("The Song of the Birds"), 421, 432, 439, 460, 474, 483, 495, 508, 521, 556, 567, 570
Capdevila, Frasquita Vidal de (neé Frasquita Vidal Puig), 405, 411, 414, 417, 452, 473–474, *474*, 476

Index

Index

Index

Index

Index

Index

Index

Index

Schubert, Franz (*continued*)
"Serenade," 35
Symphony No. 5 in B flat
Major, 541
Symphony No. 7 in C Major,
336–338, 490
Symphony No. 8 in B minor,
"Unfinished," 347, 361, 494
Trio No. 1 in B flat Major, 359,
364
Schulhof, Otto, 383
Schumann, Clara, 242, 263, 267
Schumann, Elizabeth, 339
Schumann, Robert, 60, 262, 267
Concerto in A minor for violon-
cello and orchestra, op. 129,
235, 245, 246, 285, 358, 361,
364, 375, 425, 427, 442, 618
Fünf Stücke im Volkston, 280,
619
Schweitzer, Albert, 5, 11, 394, 396,
445, 451, 467, *468*, 482, 483,
491, 505, 507, 539
Scriabin, Alexander, 16, 236–237
Selva, Blanche, 342, 357
Sembrich, Marcella, 136
Serkin, Irene Busch, 515
Serkin, Rudolf, 5, 358, 450, 455,
488, 495, 508, 511, 513, *514*,
515, 517, 518, 525, *554*, *555*
Servais, Adrien François, 98, 99,
344
Setti, Giulio, 310
Seurrat, Albert, 414, 437
Shadow Song (*Dinorah*), 103, 155
Shankar, Ravi, 508, *514*
Shaw, George Bernard, 116, 124,
268–269
Siloti, Alexander, 168, 220, 222–225,
223, 231, 232, 235–239, 248, 319,
404
Siloti Concerts, 222
Siloti, Kyriena, 224
Singher, Martial, 515
Slovo (Moscow), 227–228
Smallens, Alexander, 318
Smyth, Ethel, 242, 247
Socías, Bienvenido, 214, 252, 300
Sociedad de Cuartetos (Madrid),
88–91
Società del Quartetto di Milano,
246, 247
Société des apaches, 197
Soldat, Marie, 264

Soldevila, Josep, 327
"Song of the Birds." *See* "*Cant dels
Ocells*"
Songs, PC's, 34, 315, 527–528, 595
"*Souvenir de Spa*" (Servais), 98,
99, 103
Spalding, Albert, 268, 354–356
Spanish-American War, 109–110,
114–115
Spanish Civil War, 398–409
Spanish language, 28, 80
Spanish Refugee Aid, 441, 526, 532;
see also Refugees
Speyer, Edward, 260–264, 267, 291,
301, 468
Speyer family, 136–137
Speyer, Lady, 263, 351
Spinoza, Margarita, 316
Spirit of Catalonia, The (Trueta),
433
Stage fright, 61, 163, 279
Stein, Gertrude, 164, 195
Stein, Leo, 164, 167, 195
Stein, Michael, 163, 164, 167
Stein, Sarah Solomans, 163, 164
Steinbach, Fritz, 209, 210
Steinway piano, 144, 172–173, 206
Steinway & Sons, 172–174
Stern, Isaac, 455, 495, 511, 525, 535,
555
Stick technique, PC's, 8, 337
Stokowski, Leopold, 304, 350, 450,
520
Strauss, Johann, 64, 92
Strauss, Richard, 16, 53–54, 104,
176–177, 221, 233, 235, 250, 331,
339
Don Juan, 54
Don Quixote, 176, 291
Strauss-De Ahna, Pauline, 176–177,
510
Stravinsky, Igor, 285, 339, 449, 539
Dumbarton Oaks concerto, 555
Les Noces, 539
Rite of Spring, 539
Stumpff (concert manager), 243
Suarez, Dr. Ramón, 494
Suggia, Guilhermina, 189, 192, *198*,
199–202, 212–214, 236, 252–254,
259, 260, 283, *288*, 291, 351–353,
352, 362, 396, 428, 467
Sullivan, Arthur, 119
Sussex, SS, 312, 313
Suzuki method, 525

Index

Index